Lecture Notes in Artificial Intelligence 10142

Subseries of Lecture Notes in Computer Science

More information about this series at http://www.springer.com/series/1244

Markus Wagner · Xiaodong Li
Tim Hendtlass (Eds.)

Artificial Life and Computational Intelligence

Third Australasian Conference, ACALCI 2017
Geelong, VIC, Australia, January 31 – February 2, 2017
Proceedings

 Springer

Editors
Markus Wagner
The University of Adelaide
Adelaide, SA
Australia

Tim Hendtlass
Swinburne University
Melbourne, VIC
Australia

Xiaodong Li
RMIT University
Melbourne, VIC
Australia

ISSN 0302-9743   ISSN 1611-3349   (electronic)
Lecture Notes in Artificial Intelligence
ISBN 978-3-319-51690-5   ISBN 978-3-319-51691-2   (eBook)
DOI 10.1007/978-3-319-51691-2

Library of Congress Control Number: 2016961325

LNCS Sublibrary: SL7 – Artificial Intelligence

Printed on acid-free paper

This Springer imprint is published by Springer Nature
The registered company is Springer International Publishing AG
The registered company address is: Gewerbestrasse 11, 6330 Cham, Switzerland

Preface

This volume contains the papers presented at the Australasian Conference on Artificial Life and Computational Intelligence (ACALCI 2017) held from January 31 to February 2, 2017, in Geelong, Australia.

The research areas of artificial life and computational intelligence have grown significantly over recent years. The breadth is reflected in the papers addressing diverse aspects in the domain, from theoretical developments to learning, optimization, and applications of such methods to real-world problems.

This volume presents 32 papers, many of them authored by leading researchers in the field. After a rigorous evaluation of all 47 submissions by the international Program Committee, 32 manuscripts were selected for single-track oral presentation at ACALCI 2017. All papers underwent a full peer-review with three to four reviewers per paper.

The ACALCI 2017 international Program Committee consisted of over 63 members from six countries, based on their affiliation. We would like to thank the members of the international Program Committee, the ACALCI Steering Committee, the local Organizing Committee, and other members of the organization team for their commendable efforts and contributions to the conference.

We would like to acknowledge the support from RMIT University, Melbourne, and the organizers of the Australian Computer Science Week (ACSW), who kindly allowed ACALCI 2017 to be co-located with ACSW 2017 at Deakin University, Geelong.

The support and assistance from Springer and EasyChair are gratefully acknowledged.

November 2016

Markus Wagner
Xiaodong Li
Tim Hendtlass

Organization

Conference Chairs

General Chair
Xiaodong Li — RMIT University, Australia

Program Co-chairs
Markus Wagner — University of Adelaide, Australia
Tim Hendtlass — Swinburne University, Australia

Paper and Poster Award Committee Chair

Vic Ciesielski — RMIT University, Australia

Special Session Chair

Aldeida Aleti — Monash University, Australia

Treasurer and Registration Chair

Andy Song — RMIT University, Australia

Publicity Chairs

Fabio Zambetta — RMIT University, Australia
Kai Qin — RMIT University, Australia
Bing Xue — Victoria University of Wellington, New Zealand

Webmaster

Wanru Gao — University of Adelaide, Australia

Program Committee

Alan Blair — University of New South Wales, Australia
Alan Dorin — Monash University, Australia
Aldeida Aleti — Monash University, Australia
Andrea Soltoggio — Loughborough University, UK
Andreas Ernst — Monash University, Australia
Andrew Lewis — Griffith University, Australia

Andy Song	RMIT University, Australia
Aneta Neumann	University of Adelaide, Australia
Arindam Dey	University of South Australia, Australia
Bing Xue	Victoria University of Wellington, New Zealand
Brad Alexander	University of Adelaide, Australia
Brijesh Verma	Central Queensland University, Australia
Daniel Le Berre	CNRS - Université d'Artois, France
Dianhui Wang	La Trobe University, Australia
Fabio Zambetta	RMIT University, Australia
Frank Neumann	University of Adelaide, Australia
Frederic Maire	Queensland University of Technology, Australia
Hussein Abbass	University of New South Wales, Australia
Ickjai Lee	James Cook University, Australia
Inaki Rano	Intelligent Systems Research Centre, UK
Irene Moser	Swinburne University of Technology, Australia
Jeff Chan	University of Melbourne, Australia
Jianhua Yang	Western Sydney University, Australia
Junbin Gao	University of Sydney, Australia
Junhua Wu	University of Adelaide, Australia
Kai Qin	RMIT University, Australia
Kevin Korb	Monash University, Australia
Lee Altenberg	Konrad Lorenz Institute for Evolution and Cognition Research, Austria
Marc Adam	University of Newcastle, Australia
Marcus Gallagher	University of Queensland, Australia
Marcus Randall	Bond University, New Zealand
Markus Wagner	University of Adelaide, Australia
Michael Mayo	University of Waikato, New Zealand
Mohamed Abdelrazek	Swinburne University of Technology, Australia
Mohammad Reza Bonyadi	University of Adelaide, Australia
Muhammad Iqbal	Victoria University of Wellington, New Zealand
Nasser Sabar	RMIT University, Australia
Ning Gu	University of South Australia
Oliver Obst	Western Sydney University, Australia
Pablo Moscato	University of Newcastle, UK
Paul Kwan	University of New England, Australia
Peter Whigham	University of Otago, New Zealand
Ran Cheng	University of Surrey, UK
Regina Berretta	University of Newcastle, UK
Robert Burdett	Queensland University of Technology, Australia
Stephan Chalup	University of Newcastle, UK
Stephen Chen	York University, UK
Tim Hendtlass	Swinburne University, Australia
Tom Cai	University of Sydney, Australia
Tommaso Urli	CSIRO Data61/NICTA, Australia
Vicky Mak	Deakin University, Australia

Wanru Gao	University of Adelaide, Australia
William Raffe	RMIT University, Australia
Winyu Chinthammit	University of Tasmania, Australia
Xiaodong Li	RMIT University, Australia
Yi Mei	Victoria University of Wellington, New Zealand

Contents

Optimisation Algorithms and Applications

Artificial Life and Computational Intelligence

Extending the Delaunay Triangulation Based Density Measurement to Many-Objective Optimization

Yutao Qi[1(✉)], Haodong Guo[1], and Xiaodong Li[2]

[1] School of Computer Science and Technology, Xidian University, Xi'an, China
ytqi@xidian.edu.cn
[2] School of Science, RMIT University, Melbourne, Australia

Abstract. This paper investigates the scalability of the Delaunay triangulation (DT) based diversity preservation technique for solving many-objective optimization problems (MaOPs). Following the NSGA-II algorithm, the proposed optimizer with DT based density measurement (NSGAII-DT) determines the density of individuals according to the DT mesh built on the population in the objective space. To reduce the computing time, the population is projected onto a plane before building the DT mesh. Experimental results show that NSGA-II-DT outperforms NSGA-II on WFG problems with 4, 5 and 6 objectives. Two projection strategies using a unit plane and a least-squares plane in the objective space are investigated and compared. Our results also show that the former is more effective than the latter.

Keywords: Evolutionary multi-objective optimization · Diversity preservation · Delaunay triangulation · Density measurement

1 Introduction

Pareto-dominance based multi-objective evolutionary algorithms (MOEAs) are shown to be effective for solving multi-objective optimization problems (MOPs) involving two or three conflicting objectives [1]. Many representative MOEAs, like NSGA-II [2] and SPEA2 [3], are in this category. In Pareto-dominance based MOEAs, solutions are compared according to the first order criterion of dominance relation and the second order criterion of density measurement. However, when dealing with many-objective optimization problems (MaOPs), which considers four or more objectives [4], the second order criterion starts to play an increasingly more important role. The reason is that the proportion of non-dominated solutions in the evolving population becomes exceedingly large as the number of objectives is increased. In such a case, the density measurement may be the only effective criterion determining which individual in the evolving population will survive.

The crowding method, including niching [5, 6] and crowding distance based sorting [2, 7], is an important kind of diversity preservation technique in MOEAs. In this kind of methods, the density measurement of an individual in the evolving population is determined by the distances between a specific individual and its neighbors [2, 8]. For example, the crowding distance of an individual is defined as the average distance of its

M. Wagner et al. (Eds.): ACALCI 2017, LNAI 10142, pp. 3–11, 2017.
DOI: 10.1007/978-3-319-51691-2_1

two neighboring individuals on each objective [2]. It works well on bi-objective problems, but loses its effectiveness on MOPs with three or more objectives. The vicinity distance of a particular individual is determined by its k-nearest neighbors in the objective space [8], where k is usually equal to the number of objectives. It has been proved that the NSGA-II algorithm with the vicinity distance based diversity preservation method can provide a better population diversity than the original NSGA-II using the crowding distance measure, especially in the case of tri-objective problems [8].

However, according to the observations in our previous work [9], the density measurement based on the vicinity distance is only reasonably accurate when the k-nearest neighbors of a specific individual are scattered around it in the objective space. When this is not the case, this density measurement will become inaccurate [9]. Such inaccuracy comes from the ignorance of the relative position between individuals. In addition, the parameter k should be assigned to an appropriate value which is not necessarily equal to the number of objectives. Deb suggested to maintain population diversity by using an Voronoi diagram of the population for 3-objective optimization problems [10], however, it is unclear if this can be applied to MaOPs. In our previous work, we developed a new density measurement based on Delaunay Triangulation (DT) which corresponds to the dual graph of the Voronoi diagram. We have verified its effectiveness on tri-objective problems [9]. Before calculating the DT distance of a specific individual, a DT mesh is first built on the evolving population in the objective space. Based on the DT mesh, the DT distance of a specific individual can be computed by using its neighboring individuals in the DT mesh. In the neighborhood relationship . based on the DT mesh, which was proposed in our previous work [9], both the Euclidean distance and the relative position between individuals are considered. In addition, the number of neighbors is adaptively determined by the DT mesh.

In this paper, the DT based density measurement is extended to the scenario of MaOPs to investigate its performance on problems with 4, 5 and 6 objectives. Considering the high time complexity of DT mesh construction, this paper proposes that the individuals in the evolving population are first projected onto a plane in the objective space before building the DT mesh to reduce the dimensionality. The contributions of this paper are as follows:

- The DT based density measurement is extended to solve MaOPs, and its effectiveness is validated.
- Two projection strategies using a unit plane and least-squares plane in the objective space are investigated and compared.

The remainder of this paper is organized as follows. Section 2 describes the DT based density measurement. Section 3 presents the workflow of the proposed method. Section 4 provides the experimental studies. Section 5 concludes this paper.

2   The Delaunay Triangulation Based Density Measurement

A Delaunay triangulation on a point set nicely partitions the convex hull polygon of the point set into regular triangles, as shown in Fig. 1. It was originally defined on point sets in a plane [11], but can be easily extended to high dimensional scenario [12].

Given a point set P in the d-dimensional Euclidean space E^d, a k-simplex ($k \leq d$) is defined as the convex combination of $k + 1$ affinely independent points in P, called vertices of simplex. For example, a triangle is a 2-simplex and a tetrahedron is a 3- simplex. An s-face of a simplex is the convex combination of a subset of $s + 1$ vertices of a simplex. For example, a 2-face is a triangular facet, 1-face is an edge, 0-face is a vertex. A triangulation $T(P)$ defined on P is a set of d simplexes such that:

(1) A point p in E^d is a vertex of a simplex in $T(P)$ if and only if $p \in P$.
(2) The intersection of two simplexes in $T(P)$ is either empty or a common face.
(3) The set $T(P)$ is maximal, i.e., there does not exist any simplex that can be added to $T(P)$ without violating the previous rules.

A Delaunay triangulation on point set P, denoted as $DT(P)$, is a particular triangulation, such that the hypersphere circumscribing of each simplex does not contain any point from P. The $DT(P)$ is unique if there are no $d + 2$ points in P lying on the same hypersphere [11].

In this work, the point set P is an evolving population of individuals in the d-dimensional objective space. Given the Delaunay triangulation mesh $DT(P)$ on population P, the DT distance of a specific individual x_i in P, denoted as $D(x_i)$, can be determined by its connected neighbors $\{x_j | x_j \in N(x_i)\}$ in $DT(P)$, where $N(x_i)$ denotes the neighboring set of individual x_i with size k_i. The DT distance of individual x_i is defined in the following:

$$D(x_i) = \left(\coprod_{x_j \in N(x_i)} |x_i x_j| \right)^{1/k_i} \quad x_i \in DT(P) \tag{1}$$

In which, $|x_i x_j|$ denotes the Euclidean distance between individual x_i and x_j in the objective space. The DT distance can be easily incorporated in to the NSGA-II algorithm by replacing the crowding distance in the non-dominated sorting procedure [2]. We discard the boundary determination process which is used in our previous work [9], in other words we use Eq. (1) to determine the density of all the points.

Figure 1 illustrates the DT mesh built on a population of individuals in the objective space and shows how to calculate DT distance for each individual. As shown

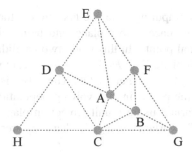

Fig. 1. An example of the density measurement based on the DT mesh.

in this figure, the individual A has 5 connected neighbors {B, C, D, E, F} in the DT mesh. The DT distance of this individual can be calculated by $(|AB| \times |AC| \times |AD| \times |AE| \times |AF|)^{1/5}$. The DT distance of A is a rough and quick estimation of the area surrounded by the points {B, C, D, E, F}.

3   The NSGA-II-DT Algorithm and Its Variations

The NSGA-II-DT algorithm follows the main framework of NSGA-II. It replaces the crowding distance measurement in NSGA-II with the Delaunay triangulation based measurement. The details of NSGA-II-DT are summarized in the Algorithm 1.

Algorithm 1: NSGA-II-DT	
1. $t=0$, $P_t =$*Initialization*(N);	Initialize a population of N individuals at random.
2. *While* stop criteria not met *do*	Main loop
3. $Q_t =$ *Evolve* (P_t);	Evolve and create offspring set Q_t.
4. $R_t = P_t \cup Q_t$;	Combine parent and offspring population.
5. $P_{t+1} = \emptyset$ *and* $i=1$;	
6. *Normalization*(R_t);	Objective normalization of population members
7. $F =$ *FastNondominatedSort*(R_t);	$F = (F_1, F_2, ...)$ all nondominated fronts of R_t.
8. *While* $|P_{t+1}|+|F_i| \leq N$	Until the parent population is filled.
9. *DT-distance-assignment*(F_i);	Calculate DT distance of each individual in F_i.
10. $P_{t+1} = P_{t+1} \cup F_i$;	Include i-th non-dominated front
11. $i = i+1$;	Check the next front for inclusion.
12. *End while*	
13. *Sort* $(F_i, \prec_n)$;	Sort using crowded-comparison-operator $\prec_n$.
14. $P_{t+1} = P_{t+1} \cup F_i[1:(N-|P_{t+1}|)]$;	Choose the first $N - |P_{t+1}|$ elements of F_i.
15. $t = t+1$;	Go to the next iteration
16. *End while*	

It is known that the time complexity of building DT mesh on a set of N points is $O(N^{\lceil d/2 \rceil} + N \log N)$ [12], and the size of Delaunay faces is $O(N^{\lfloor (d+1)/2 \rfloor})$ [16], we need to traverse the faces to get the neighborhood list of each individual, in which d is the dimensionality of the points in the DT mesh. To be specific, the time complexity is $O(N^2)$ for 3 or 4 objective problems which is the time complexity of the original selection operator in NSGA-II, $O(N^3)$ for 5 or 6 objective problems. It can be seen that the time complexity of DT mesh construction grows rapidly as the objective number increases.

In order to reduce the computing time, we first project the evolving population in the d-dimensional objective space onto a plane, and then build the DT mesh on the resulting $(d-1)$-dimensional points. In this work, two candidate projection planes are investigated. One is the unit plane $F_1 + F_2 + \cdots + F_d = 1$, in which $F_i (i = 1, \ldots, d)$ is the i-th objective function of the target MaOP. The other is the least-squares plane which is a linear fitting of the points in the evolving population [13]. In this work, we denote the NSGA-II-DT variant using a unit projection plane as NSGA-II-DT-1, and another of NSGA-II-DT variant using a least-squares projection plane as NSGAII-DT-2.

An objective normalization technique (line 6 in Algorithm 1) is incorporated into NSGA-II-DT and its variations for dealing with disparately scaled objectives. Given a population of individuals R_t, we first identify the maximum and minimum value for each objective function, denoted as z_i^{max} and z_i^{min} $(i = 1, \ldots, d)$. Then, the objective value of each individual in R_t can be normalized as:

$$F_i'(\mathrm{x}) = \frac{F_i(\mathrm{x})}{z_i^{max} - z_i^{min}} \quad \text{for } i = 1, \ldots, d \qquad (2)$$

4 Experimental Studies

In this section, NSGA-II-DT and its variants are compared with NSGA-II using the crowding distance [2] and the vicinity distance [8] based non-dominated sorting, denoted as NSGA-II and NSGA-II-VD respectively. Experimental studies are conducted on WFG problems with 4, 5 and 6 objectives [14].

The inverted generational distance (IGD) metric [15] is employed to evaluate the performances of the compared algorithms. Given a set of uniformly scattered points P^* over the PF of the target MaOPs and the solution set P obtained by the compared algorithms, the IGD value of P can be calculated as follows.

$$IGD(P, P^*) = \frac{\sum_{v \in P^*} d(v, P)}{|P^*|} \qquad (3)$$

where $d(v, P)$ is the minimum Euclidean distance between a particular point v in P^* and the solutions in P. $|P^*|$ denotes the size of P^*. IGD is a comprehensive metric that considers both convergence and diversity of the obtained solution set. IGD has a nonnegative value and the lower the better.

In our experiments, the compared algorithms have the same population size of 200 for 4-objective problems, 400 for 5-objective problems and 600 for 6-objective problems. The simulated binary crossover (SBX) and polynomial mutation operators [8] are employed. In the SBX operator, the crossover probability is set to 1.0 and the distribution index is set to 20. In the polynomial mutation operator, the mutation probability is set to 1/n where n is the number of decision variables. All runs of the compared algorithms are terminated when the number of function evaluations reaches the upper limit of 250,000 for 4-objective problems, 300,000 for 5-objective problems and 350,000 for 6-objective problems.

Tables 1, 2 and 3 compare the performances of NSGA-II-DT and its variants with NSGA-II and NSGA-II-VD on WFG problems with 4, 5 and 6 objectives. The mean and standard deviation (in parentheses) of IGD values are presented, where the best results among the compared algorithms are highlighted in bold. The Wilcoxon Rank-Sum test [17] with confidence level 0.95 has been applied to assess the statistical significance of the experimental results. The symbols "+", "=" and "−" in the following tables respectively indicate that the proposed algorithm performs statistically better than, equivalent to and not as good as the compared algorithms. In these tables, for each compared algorithm on each benchmark problem, a performance ranking between 1 and 5 is assigned based on the relative performances of compared algorithms in term of the average IGD value. The last line of each table illustrates the average ranking of the compared algorithms.

As shown in Tables 1, 2 and 3, NSGA-II-DT has average rankings of 1.375, 1.000 and 1.125 on MaOPs with 4, 5 and 6 objectives respectively, which indicate that NSGA-II-DT outperforms NSGA-II, NSGA-II-VD and its two simplified variations. NSGA-II-DT-1 using unit projection plane performs better than NSGA-II-DT-2 using the least-squares projection plane. However, the comparative advantage decreases as the number of objectives goes up. NSGA-II-DT-2 performs not as well as NSGA-II-VD on MaOPs with 4 and 5 objectives. But NSGA-II-DT-2 outperforms NSGA-II-VD on 6 objective problems. NSGA-II performs the worst on the investigated MaOPs.

When looking at the comparisons on average running time in Table 4, NSGA-II runs the fastest, NSGA-II-DT costs the most of the CPU time. NSGA-II-DT-1 and NSGA-II-DT-2 reduce the run time of NSGA-II-DT down to less than one-third of its original computing time on 4 objective problems, less than one-fourth on 5 objective problems and less than one-ninth on 6 objective problems. When comparing NSGA-II-DT-1 and NSGA-II-DT-2 with NSGA-II-VD, they cost a similar amount of the run time on 4 objective problems. However, due to the complexity of building the DT mesh, NSGA-II-DT-1 and NSGA-II-DT-2 cost more than two times of the CPU time than NSGA-II-VD on 5-objective problems and more than9 times of the CPU time than NSGA-II-VD on 6-objective problems.

Table 1. Performance comparisons on 4-objective WFG problems.

Problems	NSGA-II-DT	NSGA-II-DT-1	NSGA-II-DT-2	NSGA-II-VD	NSGA-II
WFG1	4.500E-01 (4.007E-02)	3.801E-01 (1.965E-02)−	**3.394E-01** **(1.289E-02)−**	4.457E-01= (1.882E-02)	4.444E-01= (2.537E-02)
WFG2	**2.829E-01** **(1.321E-02)**	4.280E-01+ (1.985E-02)	3.436E-01+ (1.436E-02)	4.745E-01+ (2.381E-02)	5.516E-01+ (2.719E-02)
WFG4	**5.727E-01** **(9.105E-03)**	6.575E-01+ (1.179E-02)	7.679E-01+ (2.855E-02)	6.865E-01+ (1.816E-02)	7.591E-01 (1.733E-02) +
WFG5	6.184E-01 (3.617E-02)	**5.994E-01-** **(1.498E-02)**	7.334E-01+ (3.684E-02)	6.378E-01+ (3.890E-02)	6.774E-01+ (4.638E-02)
WFG6	**5.780E-01** **(2.243E-02)**	6.394E-01+ (4.077E-02)	7.560E-01+ (5.591E-02)	7.013E-01+ (5.812E-02)	7.125E-01+ (6.141E-02)
WFG7	**5.484E-01** **(7.136E-03)**	7.092E-01+ (2.063E-02)	7.505E-01+ (2.252E-02)	7.585E-01+ (1.602E-02)	8.261E-01+ (2.552E-02)
WFG8	**6.498E-01** **(9.839E-03)**	8.640E-01+ (1.818E-02)	9.185E-01+ (3.084E-02)	9.126E-01+ (2.572E-02)	9.366E-01+ (1.871E-02)
WFG9	**5.521E-01** **(2.7410E-02)**	6.300E-01+ (1.499E-02)	7.303E-01+ (2.107E-02)	6.395E-01+ (1.231E-02)	7.437E-01+ (2.393E-02)
Average Rank	**1.375**	2.000	3.625	3.500	4.500

Table 2. Performance comparisons on 5-objective WFG problems.

Problems	NSGA-II-DT	NSGA-II-DT-1	NSGA-II-DT-2	NSGA-II-VD	NSGA-II
WFG1	**3.506E-01**	4.949E-01+	3.985E-01+	5.545E-01+	5.166E-01+
	(1.072E-02)	(2.080E-02)	(1.638E-02)	(2.263E-02)	(2.625E-02)
WFG2	**3.826E-01**	7.042E-01+	4.503E-01+	6.445E-01+	6.710E-01+
	(1.069E-02)	(3.275E-02)	(2.217E-02)	(3.023E-02)	(3.595E-02)
WFG4	**8.803E-01**	9.962E-01+	1.094E+00+	1.036E+00+	1.148E+00+
	(7.635E-03)	(1.544E-02)	(1.631E-02)	(1.299E-02)	(2.630E-02)
WFG5	9.303E-01	**9.097E-01−**	1.051E+00+	9.810E-01+	1.098E+00+
	(3.966E-02)	**(1.5218E-02)**	(2.669E-02)	(3.626E-02)	(6.658E-02)
WFG6	**8.909E-01**	9.569E-01+	1.069E+00+	1.011E+00+	1.069E+00+
	(2.0127E-02)	(2.0400E-02)	(2.844E-02)	(1.511E-01)	(3.390E-02)
WFG7	**8.645-01**	1.061+00+	1.093+00+	1.165E+00+	1.228E+00+
	(6.542E-03)	(1.584E-02)	(2.820E-02)	(1.371E-02)	(2.136-02)
WFG8	**9.903-01**	1.183E+00+	1.301E+00+	1.374E+00+	1.441E+00+
	(8.190E-03)	(7.277-02)	(2.862E-02)	(2.459E-02)	(2.496E-02)
WFG9	**8.636E-01**	9.814E-01+	1.090E+00+	9.952E-01+	1.307E+00+
	(3.690E-02)	(1.334E-02)	(2.451E-02)	(2.016E-02)	(2.822E-02)
Average Rank	**1.000**	2.000	3.000	2.875	4.250

Table 3. Performance comparisons on 6-objective WFG problems.

Problems	NSGA-II-DT	NSGA-II-DT-1	NSGA-II-DT-2	NSGA-II VD	NSGA-II
WFG1	**4.570E-01**	6.385E-01+	5.300E-01+	6.700E-01+	7.222E-01+
	(9.509E-03)	(2.544E-02)	(1.691E-02)	(1.811E-02)	(2.236E-02)
WFG2	**5.560E-01**	1.080E+00 +	7.863E-01+	8.274E-01+	9.239E-01 +
	(2.450E-02)	(4.537E-02)	(7.094E-02)	(2.570E-02)	(3.763E-02)
WFG4	**1.271E+00**	1.403E+00+	1.474E+00+	1.441E+00+	1.653E+00+
	(7.510E-03)	(1.477E-02)	(2.001E-02)	(2.046E-02)	(7.632E-02)
WFG5	1.342E+00	**1.324E+00−**	1.437E+00+	1.348E+00+	1.671E+00+
	(5.245E-02)	**(1.881E-02)**	(2.364E-02)	(5.013E-02)	(2.244E-02)
WFG6	**1.319E+00**	1.372E+00+	1.442E+00+	1.847E+00+	1.737E+00+
	(7.468E-02)	(1.612E-02)	(2.621E-02)	(1.473E-02)	(5.265E-02)
WFG7	**1.265E+00**	1.489E+00+	1.452E+00+	1.596E+00+	1.685E+00+
	(1.031E-02)	(1.852E-02)	(2.039E-02)	(1.497E-02)	(1.812E-02)
WFG8	**1.323E+00**	1.547E+00+	1.535E+00+	1.726E+00+	1.951E+00+
	(9.708E-03)	(2.224E-02)	(2.253E-02)	(2.832E-02)	(3.359E-02)
WFG9	**1.250E+00**	1.407E+00+	1.492E+00+	1.445E+00+	1.908E+00+
	(1.246E-02)	(1.783E-02)	(2.115E-02)	(2.397E-02)	(3.788E-02)
Average Rank	**1.125**	2.625	2.875	3.625	4.750

Table 4. Comparisons on average CPU times in seconds per run.

Problems	Obj. Num.	NSGA-II-DT	NSGA-II-DT-1	NSGA-II-DT-2	NSGA-II-VD	NSGA-II
WFG1	4	114.250	32.407	32.413	32.621	28.909
	5	109.690	212.960	190.380	75.550	73.469
	6	12410.000	1212.700	1227.500	138.540	132.630
WFG2	4	90.561	31.880	31.715	33.173	31.994
	5	828.920	199.790	171.240	86.007	73.703
	6	10625.000	1109.900	935.360	154.590	136.690
WFG4	4	105.020	35.569	36.006	35.746	28.892
	5	847.700	214.920	202.190	83.388	76.790
	6	12423.000	1376.100	1247.700	143.190	140.860
WFG5	4	147.130	37.312	37.576	33.603	32.631
	5	1157.700	242.070	216.840	82.187	74.764
	6	18139.000	1493.900	1365.600	130.170	134.850
WFG6	4	151.190	35.429	35.527	32.800	30.891
	5	1524.400	226.050	201.350	81.661	73.314
	6	17850.000	1703.800	1496.700	110.600	131.750
WFG7	4	131.830	37.733	37.807	35.644	33.795
	5	1130.800	258.920	206.440	85.062	74.520
	6	9708.500	1671.500	1463.200	130.730	107.400
WFG8	4	85.475	38.661	39.501	36.810	33.159
	5	1096.000	179.750	202.880	101.500	80.891
	6	6384.300	918.980	809.180	132.630	120.76
WFG9	4	84.212	38.690	39.060	39.066	32.982
	5	609.790	213.600	195.610	85.674	77.495
	6	7288.100	829.010	776.710	111.510	131.530
Average	4	113.71	35.96	36.20	34.93	31.66
	5	913.13	218.51	198.37	85.13	75.62
	6	11853.49	1289.49	1165.24	131.50	129.56

5　Conclusions

In this paper, we have studied the performance of the NSGA-II algorithm with Delaunay triangulation based density measurement (NSGA-II-DT) on many-objective optimization problems (MaOPs). To reduce the computing time, NSGA-II-DT is simplified by projecting the objective vectors of the individuals in the population onto a plane before building the DT mesh. Two projection strategies using a unit plane and a least-squares plane in the objective space are investigated and compared. Experimental results have demonstrated that NSGA-II-DT outperforms the compared algorithms on WFG problems of 4, 5 and 6 objectives. Our results also show that the projection strategy using the unit plane is more effective than using the least-squares plane.

References

1. Zhou, A., Qu, B.-Y., Li, H., Zhao, S.-Z., Suganthan, P.N., Zhang, Q.: Multiobjective evolutionary algorithms: a survey of the state of the art. Swarm Evol. Comput. **1**, 32–49 (2011)
2. Deb, K., Pratap, A., Agarwal, S., Meyarivan, T.: A fast and elitist multiobjective genetic algorithm: NSGA-II. IEEE Trans. Evol. Comput. **6**, 182–197 (2002)
3. Zitzler, E., Laumanns, M., Thiele, L.: SPEA2: improving the strength Pareto evolutionary algorithm for multiobjective optimization. In: Evolutionary Methods for Design, Optimisation, and Control, pp. 95–100. CIMNE, Barcelona (2002)
4. Purshouse, R.C., Fleming, P.J.: On the evolutionary optimization of many conflicting objectives. IEEE Trans. Evol. Comput. **11**(6), 770–784 (2007)
5. Li, X.: Niching without niching parameters: particle swarm optimization using a ring topology. IEEE Trans. Evol. Comput. **14**, 150–169 (2010)
6. Kim, H., Liou, M.-S.: New fitness sharing approach for multi-objective genetic algorithms. J. Glob. Optim. **55**, 579–595 (2013)
7. Luo, B., Zheng, J., Xie, J., Wu, J.: Dynamic crowding distance - a new diversity maintenance strategy for MOEAs. In: 4th International Conference on Natural Computation, ICNC 2008. pp. 580–585 (2008)
8. Kukkonen, S., Deb, K.: A fast and effective method for pruning of non-dominated solutions in many-objective problems. In: Runarsson, T.P., Beyer, H.-G., Burke, E., Merelo-Guervós, Juan, J., Whitley, L.,Darrell, Yao, X. (eds.) PPSN 2006. LNCS, vol. 4193, pp. 553–562. Springer, Heidelberg (2006). doi:10.1007/11844297_56
9. Qi, Y., Yin, M., Li, X.: A Delaunay triangulation based density measurement for evolutionary multi-objective optimization. In: Ray, T., Sarker, R., Li, X. (eds.) ACALCI 2016. LNCS (LNAI), vol. 9592, pp. 183–192. Springer, Heidelberg (2016). doi:10.1007/978-3-319-28270-1_16
10. Deb, K.: Multi-Objective Optimization using Evolutionary Algorithms. Wiley, Chichester (2001)
11. Dwyer, R.A.: A faster divide-and-conquer algorithm for constructing Delaunay triangulations. Algorithmica **2**, 137–151 (1987)
12. Cignoni, P., Montani, C., Scopigno, R.: DeWall: a fast divide and conquer Delaunay triangulation algorithm in E^d. Comput. Aided Des. **30**(5), 333–341 (1998)
13. Chernov, N.: Circular and Linear Regression: Fitting Circles and Lines by Least Squares. Monographs on Statistics & Applied Probability. Chapman & Hall/CRC, Boca Raton (2010)
14. Huband, Simon, Barone, Luigi, While, Lyndon, Hingston, Phil: A scalable multi-objective test problem toolkit. In: Coello Coello, Carlos, A., Hernández Aguirre, Arturo, Zitzler, Eckart (eds.) EMO 2005. LNCS, vol. 3410, pp. 280–295. Springer, Heidelberg (2005). doi:10.1007/978-3-540-31880-4_20
15. Zitzler, E., Thiele, L., Laumanns, M., Fonseca, C.M., Da Fonseca, V.G.: Performance assessment of multiobjective optimizers: an analysis and review. IEEE Trans. Evol. Comput. **7**, 117–132 (2003)
16. Seidel, R.: Exact upper bounds for the number of faces in d-dimensional Voronoi diagram. In: Applied Geometry and Discrete Mathematics – The Victor Klee Festschrift, DIMACS Series in Discrete Mathematics and Theoretical Computer Science, pp. 517–529 (1991)
17. Wilcoxon, F.: Individual comparisons by ranking methods. Biom. Bull. **1**(6), 80–83 (1945)

Emotion, Trustworthiness and Altruistic Punishment in a Tragedy of the Commons Social Dilemma

Garrison Greenwood[1], Hussein A. Abbass[2(✉)], and Eleni Petraki[3]

[1] Electrical and Computer Engineering Department,
Portland State University, Portland, OR, USA
greenwd@pdx.edu
[2] School of Engineering and Information Technology, University of New South Wales,
Canberra, ACT 2600, Australia
h.abbass@adfa.edu.au
[3] Faculty of Education, Science, Technology and Mathematics,
University of Canberra, Canberra, Australia
Eleni.Petraki@canberra.edu.au

Abstract. Social dilemmas require individuals to tradeoff self interests against group interests. Considerable research effort has attempted to identify conditions that promote cooperation in these social dilemmas. It has previously been shown altruistic punishment can help promote cooperation but the mechanisms that make it work are not well understood. We have designed a multi-agent system to investigate altruistic punishment in tragedy of the commons social dilemmas. Players develop emotional responses as they interact with others. A zero order Seguno fuzzy system is used to model the player emotional responses. Players change strategies when their emotional level exceeds a personal emotional threshold. Trustworthiness of how other players will act in the future helps choose the new strategy. Our results show how strategies evolve in a finite population match predictions made using discrete replicator equations.

1 Introduction

Social dilemmas are situations where individuals must choose between self interests and group interests. Typically individuals must decide whether to "cooperate" for the benefit of the group or to "defect" for their own benefit. Many challenging problems such as public land usage, pollution control, and overpopulation are examples of social dilemmas. Such dilemmas have two conflicting properties: (1) individuals benefit the most by defecting, regardless of what others do, and (2) everyone does better with mutual cooperation than with mutual defection. Unfortunately, most social dilemmas end with everyone defecting.

Mathematical games are well-suited for studying social dilemmas. In each round of these N-player games ($N > 2$), a population of individuals chooses whether to cooperate or defect. Players receive a payoff based on their own

© Springer International Publishing AG 2017
M. Wagner et al. (Eds.): ACALCI 2017, LNAI 10142, pp. 12–24, 2017.
DOI: 10.1007/978-3-319-51691-2_2

choices and the choices others make. The goal is to gain insight into the human decision making process by observing how cooperation levels evolve over time. The most extensively investigated social dilemma game is the *public goods game*. Recently investigators have started to look at the *tragedy of the commons* (ToC) game [1] which some argue is a better model of real-world problems.

In a ToC game individuals consume a finite resource which is called public good. Cooperators limit their consumption rate to help preserve the public good while defectors consume at a higher rate. Some percentage of the public good is periodically renewed but overconsumption will eventually deplete it. Cooperators act in the best interests of the group; defectors act in their own self-interest. The social dilemma is "resolved" if all individuals cooperate—i.e., the defectors all become cooperators. The inevitable outcome, regrettably, is everyone defects and the public good is depleted.

Researchers have proposed several methods of preventing the inevitable outcome. One of the most promising is introducing a third strategy: altruistic punishment [2]. Defectors are free riders who exploit the actions of cooperators. Punishers impose a penalty on defectors to coerce them to switch strategies. This punishment is altruistic in the sense that the punisher pays a cost for penalizing those defectors.

In some of our previous work [3] we used discrete replicator equations to see how altruistic punishment can help resolve a ToC in a finite population. These coupled, first order differential equations predict how the frequency of cooperation (C), defection (D) and altruistic punishment (P) evolve. Our results showed the ToC can be resolved if the penalty imposed by the punishers is high enough. Unfortunately, despite the power of these replicator equations, they do have one limitation. The strategy frequencies evolve via Darwinian evolution. This means the evolution is determined strictly by fitness. (The amount consumed is a measure of fitness.) Strategies that have fitness greater than the average population fitness grow, while strategies with fitness less than the population average decrease. Consequently, there is no way of determining how individuals respond to other player's choices so there is no way of gaining insight into the decision making process.

That previous work showed two ways of increasing the punishment: keep the penalty β fixed and increase the number of punishers or keep the frequency of punishers x_2 fixed and increase β. (The punishment equals $x_2\beta$.) Altruistic punishment can effectively help resolve a ToC so long as the punishment level is high enough.

In our current work we take a different approach. We formulated a multi-agent system where each player (agent) makes their strategy choice independently. Each player has an emotional response to the actions of others. A strategy change is made if the emotional level breaches some threshold. The new strategy picked is based on trustworthiness—i.e., the expectation of how other players will choose in future rounds. These emotional levels grow according to a set of fuzzy rules. Specifically, each player's emotional state is modelled by a zero order Seguno fuzzy system. Our results are remarkably similar to the results predicted by the discrete replication equations. The difference now is, since player's actions are independently decided, our new approach provides a much more effective framework for studying how emotions and trustworthiness affect the human decision making process in social dilemmas.

2   Background

Humans naturally develop emotions as they interact with others. These emotions could be satisfaction, joy, annoyance, anger, sadness, or guilt. If these emotions grow strong enough they can cause individuals to change how they act in the future. In part this choice depends on trustworthiness—i.e., it depends on how they expect others to act in the future based on their prior actions.

The interplay of emotion, trust and judgement has been investigated in many studies in the literature. Research on the field of social neuroeconomics discusses the connection between emotion and decision making. Sanfey [4] suggests decisions of trust are dependent on altruism and reciprocation for the trust game to work. A link has been identified between affective states, such as positive and negative feelings on unrelated judgements [5,6]. Emotions affect a variety of decision making processes, including decisions such as whether to trust a stranger, a politician, or a potential competitor [6]. Moreover, emotion has been shown to affect related concepts like altruism, risk preferences, and the perceived likelihood of future events [7–9].

An extensive literature on Emotion exists in the field of social psychology. The majority of this literature explain how emotions get produced and how emotional states may impact decisions, including trusting decisions.

For example, Dunn and Sweitzer [10] point out that moods influence judgement in that people engage in specific behaviours because they are motivated to maintain or repair a current mood state. The authors however suggest that positive and negative feelings-valence, as observed in mood models are not the only determinants of trust judgments. They distinguish between emotion and mood and claim that emotion is a much more complex state than mood. Emotional states are shorter in duration, more intense and incorporate varied cognitive appraisals, which include individual perceptions of certainty, control over the outcome, appraisal of the situation and attribution of the cause of the emotion. Emotions with the same valence but different control appraisals (self or other) have been found to have differential impact on trust and decision making.

Mood and emotion are complex concepts and have been discussed here to provide a general context for this research. The causes for emotional change or emotional production per se are beyond the scope of this paper. Instead, we chose a level of abstraction to enable us to focus on the impact of emotion on game dynamics.

3   System Description

A ToC is an N player game ($N > 2$). Each round players will consume a fixed portion of a fixed resource. The amount consumed depends on the strategy.

C players are interested in preserving the resource so they voluntarily limit the amount consumed. On the other hand, D players are self-interested so they consume a higher amount of the resource. Periodically a fraction of the resource is renewed. However, if the overall consumption rate is too high the renewal amount is insufficient and the resource is ultimately depleted. Too many D players will eventually deplete the resource. Hence, the only way to "resolve" the ToC game is to have the player population contain only C players because then the consumption rate is less than the renewal rate so the resource is always available.

D players are free riders because they exploit cooperators. The best individual outcome is to defect, regardless of what other players do. Unfortunately this leads to the inevitable outcome of everyone defecting and the fixed resource being depleted. One way of convincing D players to change strategy is to introduce a third type of player who is an altruistic punisher.

Definition 1. *Altruistic punishment is punishment inflicted on free riders even if costly to the punisher and even if the punisher receives no material benefits from it.*

P players consume the same amount as a C player but they also penalize D players. This reduces the D player's return hopefully making defection less desirable. The punishment is altruistic in the sense the P player pays a small cost to inflict this punishment. Thus the payoff to a P player is less than a C player.

But there is another problem. C players exploit P players because they benefit from punishing D players but they don't pay any cost for punishing them. This is referred to as the *2nd order free riding problem*. (D players are 1st order free riders.) To address the 2nd order free riding problem punishers will also penalize C players who won't punish. The P player pays an additional cost for this punishment as well. Previous work has shown altruistic punishment, properly applied, can help resolve social dilemmas [11,12].

The proposed method is summarized in Algorithm 1 and is explained in more details below.

Let N be the population size and let k_1, k_2, k_3 be the number of C, P and D players respectively where $\sum_i k_i = N$. Then the frequency of a strategy i in the population is $x_i = k_i/N$. Let CR_1 be the consumption rate for a D player and CR_2 the consumption rate for C or P players where $CR_1 > CR_2$. Then the payoff to a player ℓ is

$$\pi(\ell) = \begin{cases} CR_1 - k_2\beta & \text{defectors} \\ CR_2 - ck_2\gamma & \text{cooperators} \\ CR_2 - c[(k_3\alpha) + (k_1\eta)] & \text{punishers} \end{cases} \tag{1}$$

Input : Players_List(Emotion_threshold,Emotion_level,Strategy,Payoff)
Output: Players_List(Emotion_threshold,Emotion_level,Strategy,Payoff)
if *First Generation* **then**
| Emotion_level ← 0
| Emotion_threshold ← rand(5,10)
end
for *Each Player* **do**
| Play Strategy
end
for *Each Player* **do**
| Update Payoff
| Observe Actions of Other Players
| Calculate Delta_change in Emotion Using the Fuzzy Rules
| Emotion_level ← Emotion_level + Delta_change
| **if** *Emotion_level ≥ Emotion_threshold* **then**
| | Update strategy
| | Emotion_level ← 0
| **end**
end

Algorithm 1. The logic for updating agents' emotion levels and strategies.

The punishments and costs are summarized as follows:

1. $\beta > 1$ is the punishment each punisher inflicts on a defector
2. $\gamma > 1$ is the punishment each punisher inflicts on a cooperator
3. punishers pay a cost $\alpha > 1$ for each defector punished
4. punishers pay a cost $\eta > 1$ for each cooperator punished.
5. $c = 0$ if there are no D players to remove all costs and punishments. Otherwise $c = 1$

In the simulations we used $N = 20, CR_1 = 82, CR_2 = 39, \alpha = 1.0, \gamma = 0.2$ and $\eta = 0.1$. β varied depending on the investigation. The initial public goods capacity was 5000 units and decreased each round (82 units for each D player and 39 units for each C or P player). After each round, the remaining capacity was increased by 25%.

Each player has an emotional level (initialized to 0) and an emotional threshold randomly assigned between 5.0 and 10.0. During each round the emotional levels can change in response to actions taken by the other players. Players change to a new strategy when their emotional level exceeds their personal emotional threshold. The thresholds were different for each player because individuals react differently to situations. For instance, the actions of other players may anger some players while others may be merely irritated.

We designed a zero order Seguno fuzzy system to model the emotional state of the players. The emotional levels of each player changes based on the fuzzy rules (see Table 1). Players know the strategies of other players by observing their consumption rates. The antecedents for most rules use strategy frequencies but two rules use assessed penalties. For instance, a C player is "satisfied" if the frequency of cooperators is high so there is little or no change in the emotional level. On the other hand they are "annoyed" if they are paying a high penalty for free riding (moderate change) and "angry" if the frequency of defectors is high and the frequency of punishers is low (large change). The rationale for these rules is given in the table.

Trapezoidal membership functions were used for all of the antecedents based on strategy frequencies. These are shown in Fig. 1. A Heavyside function was used for the antecedents using penalties. Specifically, the membership function for Rule # 2 is

$$\mu(k_2\gamma) = \begin{cases} 0 & k_2\gamma \leq CR_2/2 \\ 1 & \text{otherwise} \end{cases} \tag{2}$$

and the membership function for Rule # 5 is

$$\mu(k_2\beta) = \begin{cases} 0 & k_2\beta \leq CR_1/2 \\ 1 & \text{otherwise} \end{cases} \tag{3}$$

The reasoning behind this type of membership function is penalties are tolerable so long as they are not too heavy. A penalty is considered intolerable if it reduces the payoff by more than 50%.

Output membership functions in a zero order Seguno fuzzy system are constants. The function will output the values 0, 1 and 5 corresponding to the three emotional states, satisfied, annoyed and angry, respectively. The constants were chosen to produce no emotional change (satisfaction), a moderate change (annoyed) or a large change (angry). A weighted average defuzzification method was used. Defuzzification determines the change in a player's emotional state by adding the crisp output value to the current emotional level of a player. A strategy is changed when a player's emotional state exceeds their personal threshold. The underlying idea is that if a threshold has been breached, then

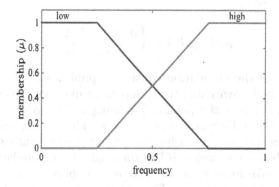

Fig. 1. Membership functions used to determine emotional state. The domain of discourse is the strategy frequency for all rules except for one C and one D rule (see text).

staying with the current strategy is no longer acceptable—i.e., a strategy change is necessary. Even though all players with a given strategy have their emotional levels increased by the same crisp output value, they do not necessarily change strategies at the same time. That's because each player has a different emotional threshold. The emotional level of a player is reset to zero when a strategy change occurs.

Table 1. Fuzzy rulebase

No	Player	Rule	Rationale
1	C	**IF** x_1 is high **THEN** y is satisfied	Public good being maintained
2	C	**IF** $k_2\gamma$ is high **THEN** y is annoyed	Paying high penalty for free riding
3	C	**IF** x_3 is high **AND** x_2 is low **THEN** y is angry	Little effort to stop defection
4	D	**IF** x_1 is high **THEN** y is satisfied	Small penalty paid for defecting
5	D	**IF** $k_2\beta$ is high **THEN** y is angry	Paying high penalty for free riding
6	P	**IF** x_3 is low **AND** x_1 is low **THEN** y is satisfied	Few free riders
7	P	**IF** x_3 is low **AND** x_1 is high **THEN** y is annoyed	Many 2nd order free riders
8	P	**IF** x_3 is high **THEN** y is angry	Many 1st order free riders

NOTE: All antecedents use strategy frequencies except Rules 2 and 5. $x_i^t = k_i/N$ is the frequency of strategy i at time t, where N is the population size and $\sum_i k_i = N$.

Figure 2 summarizes the conditions used by players to switch strategies. The rationale for these conditions is provided below.

D players switch to either a cooperator or a punisher depending on the number of P players in the population. The probability a defector will switch to a punisher is given by

$$\text{prob}_{\text{DP}}(k_2) = \begin{cases} 0 & k_2 < N/2 \\ 1 & \text{otherwise} \end{cases} \quad (4)$$

If more than half the population consists of punishers, then the penalty for defecting is quite high. Switching to a cooperator may not make sense because with that many punishers the penalty for being a 2nd order free rider is also likely to be high. These high penalties can be avoided by becoming a punisher. Moreover, by switching to a punisher, the defector can retaliate against those other defectors who didn't switch. If less than half of the population are punishers, then it may make more sense to become a cooperator since the 2nd order free riding penalty is relatively low. This strategy change is modelled as a probability to reflect the uncertainty in how individual defectors will choose a new strategy.

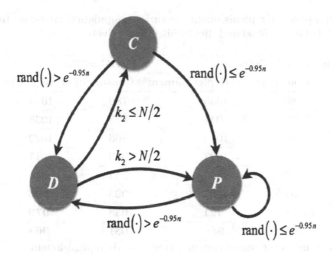

Fig. 2. Conditions to switch strategies. See text for variable definitions.

C and P players also choose their next strategy probabilistically. However, this probability is interpreted as a level of trustworthiness and other players will change their strategies as well to help resolve the ToC. This gives rise to a much more subtle and complex reasoning process.

There is little point in switching from C to P, since doing so, would do little to prevent the public good from becoming depleted. On the other hand, it would be beneficial to become a punisher if the increased penalty might induce defector strategy changes. Thus, the decision whether a cooperator switches to a punisher or a defector depends on the current status of the public good.

An example will help to clarify the idea. Suppose the public good capacity is 5000 units and player consumption rates are the same as their payoffs (minus any costs or penalties). Then by Eq. (1) each defector consumes 82 units and each cooperator or defector consumes 39 units. Table 2 shows the public good status for various population mixtures after one round with a 25% replenishment of the public good. The public good is preserved only if $k_3 \leq 5$ because the 25% replenishment restores at least the amount that was consumed. When $k_3 > 5$ the replenishment cannot compensate for the consumption so eventually the public good will be depleted.

To further illustrate the problem consider the specific case where $k_3 = 6$ and $k_1 + k_2 = 14$ with an initial public goods capacity of 5000 units. That mixture consumes 1038 units per round reducing the public good capacity to 3962 units after the first round. A 25% replenishment only raises the capacity to 4953 units, short of the 5000 unit initial capacity. The consumption rate exceeds the replenishment rate with this population mixture. One D player must switch to maintain the public good. Suppose no D player switched and one more round is played. Table 2 shows that the replenishment exceeds the consumption only if $k_3 \leq 4$. In other words, to grow the public good now requires at least two D

Table 2. consumption vs replenishment for various population mixtures. Initial public good capacity (IPGC) = 5000 and 4953 units, respectively.

k_3	$k_1 + k_2$	IPGC = 5000		IPGC = 4953	
		Consumption	Replenishment[a]	Consumption	Replenishment*
0	20	780	1055	780	1043
1	19	823	1044	823	1033
2	18	866	1034	866	1022
3	17	909	1023	909	1011
4	16	952	1012	952	1000
5	15	995	1001	995	**990**
6	14	1038	**991**	1038	**979**
7	13	1081	**980**	1081	**968**

[a]Bold indicates mixtures where consumption exceeds replenishment

players to switch strategy. Thus the status of the public goods determines how many D players must switch.

Cooperators can breach their emotional threshold if they are annoyed for a sufficiently long enough period or quickly if they are angry. C switches to P with probability

$$\text{prob}_{\text{CP}}(n) = e^{-0.95n} \tag{5}$$

where n is the number of defectors that must switch to preserve the public good. This probability, shown in Fig. 3, is actually a measure of trustworthiness that the required number of D players will switch. If the consumption rate is less than the replenishment rate then $n = 0$ because even with the D players present the public good remains viable. The C player then switches to a punisher with probability 1.0 believing the additional penalty on the defectors will cause some of them to switch. *However, if the C player does not trust a sufficient number will switch, then the C player defects.* It is important to note each C player independently decides whether to switch to P or D. P players also switch strategies if they are annoyed or angry. They use the same trustworthiness function Eq. (5) to make decisions. If the P player trusts that a sufficient number of D players can be coerced to switch with a higher penalty, then β increases by 20%. *Conversely, if a P player does not trust a sufficient number of D players will switch, then the P player defects instead.* In both instances the switch to defector is because the player does not trust a sufficient number of defectors will switch and so the public good cannot be saved. The players thus decide to act in their own self interest and consume as much as they can while some public good still remains.

The ToC game was run for 500 iterations but could be terminated early for three reasons: (1) the public good is completely depleted, (2) some public good remains but the population consists entirely of defectors—i.e., $k_3 = N$, or

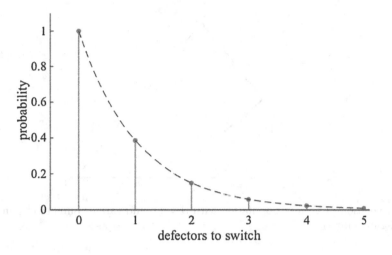

Fig. 3. Probability mass function interpreted as a level of trustworthiness the number of defectors will switch $D \rightarrow C, P$ if $C \rightarrow P$ or if $\beta \uparrow$ for punishers. Dashed line is the equation $\exp(-0.95n)$.

(3) the ToC is resolved—i.e., $k_3 = 0$. This latter condition is a fixed point in the 2-D simplex as shown by the following theorem:

Theorem. Every point on the $x_1 - x_2$ boundary is a fixed point.

Proof. $k_3 = 0$ on every point of the $x_1 - x_2$ boundary. Consequently, all players get the same payoff because no costs or penalties are imposed. There is therefore no incentive to change strategies in the future.

4   Results

The first investigation was designed to see how β affects the evolution of strategies within the population. Recall there are two ways of increasing defector punishment: fix k_2 and increase β or fix β and increase k_2. The first way is intuitively obvious; let β grow without bound and eventually defectors see no payoff whatsoever; at that point there is no reason to continue defecting. But practically speaking β is bounded—punishers are limited in how much punishment they can impose—so the only realistic way of increasing punishment is to increase the number of punishers. To test this idea we conducted a series of simulations fixing β at 4.0 and k_3 at 6 ($x_3 = 0.3$). We then increased the number of k_2 players and decreased the number of k_1 players accordingly to keep $\sum_i k_i = N$. Figure 4 shows that, if less than half the population are punishers, there simply isn't enough punishment to cause defector strategy changes. In other words, $k_2 \beta$ is not a high price to pay for defecting. However, once more than half of the population contains punishers, the ToC is resolved (red trajectory). More importantly, the slope of the trajectory shows both cooperators and defectors

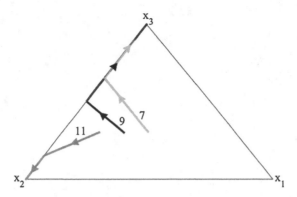

Fig. 4. Evolution of a finite population with $\beta = 4.0$ and various number of punishers. (Color figure online)

are switching to punishers. Eventually punishers completely take over the population. These results match well with the replicator equation predictions despite that in this study β was considerably lower.

The second investigation was designed to see how different player mixtures affected the population evolution. β was initialized at 7.0 in all runs. First consider the red trajectory in Fig. 5. The population was initialized at $k_i = [7\ 7\ 6]$ (equivalently $x_i = [0.35\ 0.35\ 0.3]$). The population quickly reaches a fixed point with some cooperators but mostly punishers which resolved the ToC. The brown trajectory was initialized at $k_i = [3\ 3\ 14]$ (equivalently $x_i = [0.15\ 0.15\ 0.7]$). There were not enough punishers present. All of the cooperators switched to defectors and shortly thereafter the punishers switched to defectors as well. Eventually defectors take over the population.

The black trajectory is more interesting. The population started with $k_i = [14\ 3\ 3]$ (equivalently $x_i = [0.70\ 0.15\ 0.15]$). Initially, the vast majority of players

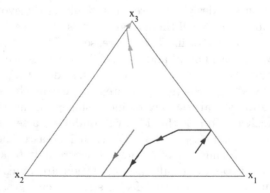

Fig. 5. Evolution of a finite populations for various β values. red: initial [7 7 6] $\beta = 7$; brown: initial [3 3 14] $\beta = 7$; black: initial [14 3 3] $\beta = 7$. (Color figure online)

are cooperators. Following the trajectory, all of the punishers quickly decided to become defectors leaving only defectors and cooperators in the population. Cooperators don't punish defectors; thus, under normal circumstances one would expect defectors to prevail. But surprisingly some cooperators decided to become punishers. It is noticeable that the slope of the trajectory at this time is parallel to the $x_1 - x_2$ boundary which means the number of defectors isn't changing. However, the increased punishment from the growing number of P players starts to take effect. Eventually all defectors switch and the ToC is resolved.

5 Conclusion

Despite the widespread usage of replicator equations, they do suffer from one limitation: a lack of ability to provide insight into the human decision making process. Under replicator dynamics, strategies evolve strictly via Neo-Darwinistic principles. There is neither reproduction nor mutation. Strategies that produce payoffs higher than the population average grow while those less than the population average decline. Replicator equations can predict *what* strategy changes might occur, but they cannot explain is *why* they occur. Replicator equations only suggest proximate causes.

In this investigation, we considered a more realistic model that reflects human behavior. It takes into account that humans have emotions and rely on their experience to evaluate the trustworthiness of opponents. We have demonstrated a more practical and realistic approach to the modelling of strategies and strategy-change.

However, we only considered three emotions. Most notably guilt was not included. Guilt has been shown to be a motivating force in social dilemmas especially when inter-group competition is involved [13]. In the current model defectors change strategies only when the penalty for defecting is excessive. An obvious extension is to see how guilt might convince a player to switch from defection to cooperation.

References

1. Hardin, G.: The tragedy of the commons. Science **162**(3859), 1243–1248 (1968)
2. Barclay, P.: Trustworthiness and competitive altruism can also solve the tragedy of the commons. Evol. Hum. Behav. **25**(4), 209–220 (2004)
3. Greenwood, G.: Altruistic punishment can help resolve tragedy of the commons social dilemmas. In: Proceedings of IEEE Conference on Computational Intelligence and Games (2016, accepted, to appear)
4. Sanfey, A.G.: Social decision-making: insights from game theory and neuroscience. Science **318**(5850), 598–602 (2007)
5. Forgas, J.P.: On feeling good and getting your way: mood effects on negotiator cognition and bargaining strategies. J. Personal. Soc. Psychol. **74**(3), 565 (1998)
6. Forgas, J.P.: Affective influences on attitudes and judgments. Oxford University Press (2003)

7. Capra, C.M.: Mood-driven behavior in strategic interactions. Am. Econ. Rev. **94**(2), 367–372 (2004)
8. Lerner, J.S., Keltner, D.: Fear, anger, and risk. J. Personal. Soc. Psychol. **81**(1), 146 (2001)
9. DeSteno, D., Petty, R.E., Wegener, D.T., Rucker, D.D.: Beyond valence in the perception of likelihood: the role of emotion specificity. J. Personal. Soc. Psychol. **78**(3), 397 (2000)
10. Dunn, J.R., Schweitzer, M.E.: Feeling and believing: the influence of emotion on trust. J. Personal. Soc. Psychol. **88**(5), 736 (2005)
11. Bravo, G., Squazzoni, F.: Exit, punishment and rewards in commons dilemmas: an experimental study. PLOS ONE **8**(8), e69871 (2013)
12. Bailiet, D., Mulder, L., Lange, P.V.: Reward, punishment and cooperation: a meta-analysis. Psychol. Bull. **137**(4), 594–615 (2011)
13. Puurtinen, M., Mappes, T.: Between-group competition and human cooperation. Proc. Roy. Soc. Lond. B: Biol. Sci. **276**(1655), 355–360 (2009)

Equity Option Strategy Discovery and Optimization Using a Memetic Algorithm

Richard Tymerski$^{(\boxtimes)}$, Garrison Greenwood, and Devin Sills

Department of Electrical and Computer Engineering, Portland State University,
Portland, OR 97201, USA
tymerski@ee.pdx.edu, {greenwd,dsills}@pdx.edu

Abstract. Options in finance are becoming an increasingly popular investment instrument. Good returns, however, do depend on finding the right strategy for trading and risk management. In this paper we describe a memetic algorithm designed to discover and optimize multi-leg option strategies for the S&P500 index. Strategies comprising from one up to six option legs are examined. The fitness function is specifically designed to maximize profitability while seeking a certain trade success percentage and equity drawdown limit. Using historical option data from 2005 to 2016, our memetic algorithm discovered a four-leg option strategy that offers optimum performance.

Keywords: Memetic algorithms · Financial options

1 Introduction

The use of options in finance is gaining popularity as an investment/trading vehicle as evidenced by the vastly increasing yearly volume of these contracts traded on options exchanges, such as the CBOE (Chicago Board of Options Exchange). This is a testament to the great flexibility these investment vehicles offer. They may be used to profit from an opinion on market direction and/or volatility or used for hedging.

In this paper, we are seeking to find the answer to the following question: if we employ a systematic approach to option's trading where at the start of each month an option's strategy is entered into the market and left untouched until expiration in the following month, what would be the most profitable strategy as seen over the full set of available historical data? This question is examined for option strategies consisting of one to six option transactions (or "legs") and are not restricted to just currently used strategies. A further question that is answered is the relative profitability of each of these strategies and consequently which might be considered the optimum strategy overall?

Apart from using single-leg option's strategies, such as the short put, there are also a wide number of other standard multi-leg option's trading strategies available such as vertical spreads, strangles and iron condors. Multi-decade backtests of the short put and vertical spread strategies on the S&P500 index were

© Springer International Publishing AG 2017
M. Wagner et al. (Eds.): ACALCI 2017, LNAI 10142, pp. 25–38, 2017.
DOI: 10.1007/978-3-319-51691-2_3

reported in [1,2] highlighting their efficacy. In contrast to choosing a specific strategy to backtest, in this paper, we utilize an evolutionary algorithm to search from amongst the vast array of combinations of options.

Option strategies are based on a variety of decision factors such as whether the option should be a "call" or "put" and whether it should be "short" or "long". In addition a desired "strike price" must be given. The present study uses a *memetic algorithm* to search for a suitable set of these decision factors. The goal is to find strategies that can maximize profitability while at the same time achieve a minimum trade success rate threshold. In some cases a trader may want to combine two or more option transactions (legs) to implement an investment strategy. Our memetic algorithm is specifically designed to accommodate such strategy searches. We evaluated from one to six leg option strategies using historical data. The results indicate four-leg options tend to perform the best in terms of profitability.

To the best of our knowledge, this is the first time that a systematic approach to the generation and search of multi-leg option strategies guided by predefined performance metrics has been undertaken and reported.

2   Equity Option Overview

A stock option is a contract between two parties (the buyer and seller) that is traded on a public exchange. These contracts exist for only a limited time span and cease to exist at a specified expiration date. Since transactions involving the stock directly will not be involved here, there is no need to go through the definition of what the contract allows one to do and/or what obligations are involved. Nevertheless, the option price is derived from the underlying stock price. (Consequently options are considered a derivative). So, for example, if you have an option on IBM, its price would be greatly determined at what price IBM stock is currently trading. This is referred to as the price of the underlying.

There are just two types of option contracts

1. *call* option
2. *put* option

For each of these we can initially buy or sell them to enter into a position. Thus, as an initiating trade we have four possibilities:

1. buy a call option, hereafter referred to as a long call option
2. sell a call option, hereafter referred to as a short call option
3. buy a put option, hereafter referred to as a long put option
4. sell a put option, hereafter referred to as a short put option

Note that for the short call and short put cases one does not need to have first bought the option to be able to sell it.

A most important aspect of these option types is the unique profit/loss (P/L) profiles they feature. To place these in some context, let's first consider the P/L

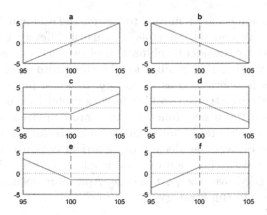

Fig. 1. Profit/loss (P/L) profiles: (a) long stock, (b) short stock, (c) long call, (d) short call, (e) long put, (f) short put. Option profiles are at expiration. The horizontal axis represents the price of the underlying and the vertical axis is the P/L.

profile of stocks. Generally when one enters into a stock position it is with the idea of making a profit when the stock increases in price. This is what is referred to as a long stock position and its P/L profile is shown in Fig. 1a. The horizontal axis zero crossing point represents the price at which the stock was initially purchased. This is shown arbitrarily as 100 in Fig. 1a. Consequently, for stock prices above 100 a profit is made and conversely prices below this represent a loss.

One may also enter into a short stock position in which profit is made when the stock price decreases in value. The associated P/L profile is shown in Fig. 1b.

Let us now consider option P/L profiles shown in Figs. 1c–f. These represent the P/L at option expiration. The price at which the P/L profiles change slope is referred to as the *strike* price. This appears as 100 in the figures. There are usually many options with different strikes available for a stock. These are shown in a table referred to as the *option chain*. An example of an option chain is shown later. As we can see in these profiles the value of the option is highly dependent on where the underlying stock price is in relation to the option strike price. This is referred to as *moneyness*, and leads to the following three situations:

1. At the money (ATM) – the underlying price is at the option strike price.
2. Out of the money (OTM) – the underlying price is on the horizontal segment of the P/L profile.
3. In the money (ITM) – the underlying price is on the sloping segment of the P/L profile.

One can enter into an option trade anywhere in the moneyness continuum. The degree of moneyness can be quantified by using the *delta* parameter of the option which is generally available on trading platforms. ATM, OTM and ITM options have absolute delta values equal to 0.5, less than 0.5 and greater than 0.5, respectively, with values ranging in a continuum from 0 to 1. We will examine delta values in a later option chain table.

So far the discussion has been limited to buying and selling individual options. However, one can buy and sell multiple options of different types at different strikes. In this paper we consider combinations of two to six options. This results in interesting and varying P/L profiles for the composite structure. Each combination of options is referred to as a *strategy*. It is the purpose of this paper to discover and optimize strategies which feature useful P/L profiles. The optimization is based on the fitness functions that are employed. We will use two different functions which are discussed in the next section. These will be evaluated with the use of over one decade of historical option's data. In the end we will have answered the question of what would have been the best option's strategy to have traded over the past decade. And more specifically, what were to best strikes to use in this strategy?

3   Memetic Algorithm Based Search

In genetics the instructions for building proteins are given by *genes*. In memetics, *memes* are building blocks of cultural know-how that can be replicated and transmitted. These memes carry instructions for carrying out behavior that can be passed on via mutation [3]. Moscato coined the term *memetic algorithm* (MA) which combined population based search with a refinement method [4]. MAs have been successfully used in a variety of real-world problem domains such as flowshop scheduling [5], bioinformatics [6] and molecular structure problems [7].

In MAs each individual in a population represents a potential solution. New solutions are found using some nature-inspired process such as recombination in a genetic algorithm or via swarm intelligence operations. These transitional dynamics are stochastic which therefore lacks any domain specific information that could improve the search results. In simple MAs, which are used in this work, local search operations are added as a refinement. This refinement can be interpreted as a meme that contains domain specific information. The augmentation of a population-based search with a local refinement—resulting in a MA—produces a more effective result than could be obtained with a population-based search alone.

In this work the *genome* is an N-bit binary string that encodes a trading strategy. This binary string is partitioned into four equal size segments (see Fig. 2). Each segment represents one of four trading options: a long call option; a short call option; a long put option; or a short put option. Suppose $N=160$. Then there are 40 strike prices within each option type. Each bit within a segment corresponds to a unique strike price. A bit set to logic 1 thus chooses a particular option type at a specific strike price. A *strategy* consists of a combination of options—i.e., with multiple bits in the binary string set to logic 1.

In determining the fitness of a potential solution the following restrictions were employed in order to achieve desired results:

1. The slopes of all non-zero slope segments of the P/L profile were restricted to be that of a single option type. The majority of option strategies are of this type and so, for this study, this restriction was put in place.

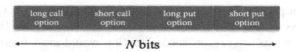

N bits

Fig. 2. The MA genome

2. Strategies containing a long call and short call at the same strike were discarded. Similarly for long put and short put combinations.
3. Due to margin considerations only slightly in the money options were permitted. The term *margin* refers to the amount of money required in the trading account in order to put on a strategy. Deep in the money options require a lot more funding. A somewhat arbitrary decision of allowing just the first three ITM strikes was made.

For any particular candidate solution, violating any of the above conditions resulted in a zero fitness value being returned.

The feasibility of a candidate solution was determined on one option chain. If it failed a zero fitness was returned. However, if it passed then the profitability of this particular trade was recorded as was the option configuration and associated delta values of the strike prices. The delta values and option types were then used to map the discovered strategy to other historical option chains for which other trade P/L's can now be determined. At the end of this procedure an array of trade P/L values for the total historical data period is now available.

We examined the use of two different fitness functions. For the first, the average P/L per trade and percentage of profitable trades were determined. If the percentage of profitable trades exceeded a threshold value (we used a threshold of 80%) the average P/L value was returned as the fitness value, otherwise it was set to zero. The MA found solutions which maximized the average P/L value. The second fitness function extends the first. A cumulative sum of the array of trade P/L values produces the historical equity curve. Now the extra threshold of requiring the equity drawdown to be with certain limits (we used a quite restrictive 10% drawdown figure) was imposed on top of the percentage profitability requirement before setting the fitness value to the average P/L value determined.

The MA is run for 100 generations with a population size of 100. Each individual encodes a trading strategy with K options; thus each individual has exactly K bits set to logic 1 and the $N - K$ remaining bits are logic 0. These K bits can be in just one segment or, more generally, distributed among the 4 segments. A preliminary analysis indicated the vast majority of solutions in the search space are infeasible—i.e., they have zero fitness. The initial population is randomly generated but only feasible individuals are kept. We did this initialization with a simple (albeit, effective) brute force method. Specifically, a large number of N-bit strings were randomly generated but only feasible solutions were put into the initial population.

In traditional population-based searches individuals undergo stochastic operations such as recombination to create new potential solutions. However, given that feasible solutions are sparse, recombination would most likely not be effective. (In early trials we found the overwhelming majority of offspring produced via recombination were infeasible.) Consequently, we simply cloned each parent and then let local refinement improve the offspring.

The local refinement used follows the *Lamarkian Learning* paradigm [8]. Lamarkian inheritance assumes traits acquired during an individual's lifetime are directly passed on to its offspring. Implementing Lamarkian learning is straightforward. A parent is cloned and then mutated. The resultant offspring replaces its cloned parent in the population if and only if it has higher fitness. Each mutation resets one randomly chosen logic 1 bit and sets a different bit to logic 1. In the spirit of Lamarkian learning, which conducts only a local search, the newly set bit will be in the same segment as the bit that was reset. For example, if a logic 1 bit in the short put option segment was reset, then the randomly chosen bit to set would also be in the short put option segment. Thus a refinement keeps the same option type but chooses a different strike price. In this work each cloned parent was subjected to 4 mutations.

We also used elitism to help improve the search result—i.e., the best fit individual from the previous generation was cloned and replaced the worst fit individual in the current generation.

4   Evolutionary Algorithm Search Results

In this section we will examine the results of a number of evolutionary algorithm optimization runs used to determine optimal option configurations as determined by the chosen fitness functions. We consider two different fitness functions with the aim of maximizing

1. Total profit achieved with the probability of a profitable trade being obtained of greater that 80%.
2. As in (1) but with the further requirement that the maximum drawdown in equity is limited to less than 10%. This objective mitigates the risk in the option trading strategy.

The data used in the following studies is the full set of option data available from IVolatility.com for the S&P500 ETF (Exchange Traded Fund) which has ticker symbol SPY. This ETF reflects the price of a composite of 500 large capitalization stocks traded on US stock exchanges. As such, it is considered a proxy for the overall US market. The option data available spans the time period from 2005 to 2016. More specifically the first trade is placed on January 10, 2005 and the last trade is completed on July 15, 2016.

A description of the trading strategy follows. The initiation of a trade occurs on the first trading day of each month. Of the various option expiry periods available, the options which expire on the 3rd Friday of the following month are chosen. This is the usual monthly option expiration cycle. Recently weekly expiration cycle options have become available but are not used in this study. This results in an option holding time of about 45 days, on average which is our desired holding period. In our study once a trade is initiated it is held until expiration. This results in being able to use the option pricing on entry from the data and expiration profit/loss graph to determine option prices at exit (expiry). With the data available, there are a total of 138 trades.

The option data used provides EOD (end of day) pricing of calls and puts at various strike prices. This price data is presented as bid and ask prices at each of the strikes. The bid and ask values represents the prices at which options may be sold and bought, respectively, and were used as such in our work. Also provided is the option delta for calls and puts at each strike price. Table 1 shows representative data for options on October 1, 2010 which expire on November 19, 2010. (The data in this table will also be used in determining the expiration profit/loss graphs that will be shown in the sequel.) Columns 2 to 4 and 6 to 8 show the bid, ask and delta values for calls and puts, respectively, for the strike prices shown. Note that the delta values for puts are negative, as per the definition of delta, however, we are mainly interested in the absolute value. The strike values are shown in the 5th column in Table 1. For the SPY ETF, strikes are available at 1 point increments. This is generally not the case for other securities where strike values may be in 5 or 10 point increments. The strikes used in our study have been restricted to a range of strikes where call and put options both have an absolute delta value greater than 0.025. This resulted in 41 different strike values which are shown in Table 1.

The evolutionary algorithm uses the data to determine which option strategies maximize the fitness functions. Six different strategies are found for the two different fitness functions. These are categorized dependent on the number of options used by the strategy. These may vary from one to six. Note that the strategies discovered are not restricted to previously known option strategies. Furthermore, with the results obtained for strategies comprising a different number of options, it will be possible to assess an optimal number of options in a strategy.

4.1   Maximizing Profit for a 80% Profitable Strategy

In this subsection we examine the results of using the first fitness function with the evolutionary algorithm. As mentioned above this aims to find strategies which maximize the profit where over 80% of trades were profitable over the period of the historical data.

Table 2 shows the results for the strategies discovered. In particular, the average profit per trade, total profit for the whole period examined, percentage of trades that are profitable and the subsequent maximum equity drawdown experienced are shown. This last metric assumes an initial cash equity of $10,000.

One-Leg Option's Strategy: With just one option there are only four possible choices for the strategy: long call, short call, long put or short put. The best strategy discovered under the first fitness requirement was the short put. In

Table 1. End of day SPY option chain data on October 1, 2010 for options with expiry on November 19, 2010. The price of the underlying was 114.61. This data is used to produce Figs. 3 and 5.

Row no.	Call - bid	Call - ask	Call - delta	Strike price	Put - bid	Put - ask	Put - delta
1	25.69	25.97	0.9709	89	0.14	0.17	−0.02538
2	24.71	24.99	0.96767	90	0.16	0.19	−0.02868
3	23.73	24.02	0.96376	91	0.18	0.21	−0.03211
4	22.76	23.04	0.95969	92	0.20	0.23	−0.03568
5	21.79	22.07	0.95492	93	0.23	0.26	−0.04056
6	20.80	21.14	0.94891	94	0.26	0.29	−0.04561
7	19.85	20.13	0.94476	95	0.29	0.32	−0.05088
8	18.89	19.17	0.93825	96	0.33	0.36	−0.05751
9	18.02	18.17	0.92893	97	0.37	0.41	−0.06493
10	17.07	17.22	0.92083	98	0.42	0.46	−0.07321
11	16.13	16.28	0.91137	99	0.48	0.51	−0.08236
12	15.20	15.35	0.90054	100	0.56	0.57	−0.09308
13	14.28	14.42	0.88878	101	0.62	0.65	−0.10495
14	13.36	13.50	0.87600	102	0.70	0.74	−0.11843
15	12.44	12.59	0.86211	103	0.79	0.83	−0.13263
16	11.56	11.70	0.84499	104	0.90	0.93	−0.14958
17	10.67	10.82	0.82705	105	1.03	1.06	−0.16900
18	9.81	9.96	0.80629	106	1.16	1.19	−0.18901
19	8.99	9.10	0.78312	107	1.31	1.35	−0.21226
20	8.17	8.27	0.75779	108	1.51	1.53	−0.23896
21	7.37	7.47	0.72966	109	1.69	1.73	−0.26698
22	6.61	6.69	0.69850	110	1.92	1.96	−0.29869
23	5.87	5.95	0.66440	111	2.18	2.22	−0.33340
24	5.17	5.23	0.62741	112	2.49	2.51	−0.37132
25	4.50	4.56	0.58739	113	2.81	2.84	−0.41191
26	3.87	3.93	0.54459	114	3.17	3.21	−0.45546
27	3.28	3.33	0.49921	115	3.58	3.63	−0.50167
28	2.74	2.79	0.45171	116	4.03	4.07	−0.55041
29	2.25	2.29	0.40253	117	4.54	4.59	−0.60043
30	1.81	1.85	0.35261	118	5.10	5.15	−0.65152
31	1.43	1.47	0.30331	119	5.71	5.80	−0.70137
32	1.11	1.15	0.25603	120	6.37	6.49	−0.75037
33	0.84	0.87	0.21069	121	7.10	7.22	−0.79662
34	0.62	0.66	0.17032	122	7.86	8.00	−0.84080
35	0.45	0.49	0.13473	123	8.67	8.94	−0.87056
36	0.32	0.36	0.10453	124	9.53	9.80	−0.90383
37	0.23	0.26	0.08014	125	10.42	10.70	−0.93211
38	0.16	0.19	0.06061	126	11.34	11.63	−0.95526
39	0.11	0.14	0.04552	127	12.28	12.57	−0.97723
40	0.08	0.10	0.03419	128	13.25	13.53	−0.96887
41	0.06	0.08	0.02708	129	14.22	14.51	−0.97616

particular, in option parlance, the 30 delta put (i.e. delta = 0.30) was found to be optimal. From row 22 in Table 1 we see that the resulting option to be used when placing the trade on October 1, 2010 would have been the 110 strike option which is noted in Table 2. The average profit per trade achieved in the historical period examined was approximately $41. Whilst the percentage of profitable trades was 81.9%, the equity suffered a maximum 60% drawdown. Note that large drawdowns are suffered by all strategies under the current fitness optimization rubric. The P/L profile is shown in Fig. 3a.

Two-Leg Option's Strategy: With two options (with identical expirations) the possibilities are expanded to include well known strategies such as vertical (credit or debit) spreads, strangles and risk reversals. The optimum strategy discovered was a strangle using a put delta of 21 and call delta of 13.5. Since two options are sold the overall profitability is increased by the receipt of two options' premiums. This is reflected in the P/L values shown in Table 2. The maximum drawdown is reduced in comparison with the previous short put strategy as the put strike in this new strategy is further away at a 21 delta thus mitigating losses for SPY downside price movements. The P/L profile using data from Table 1 is shown in Fig. 3b.

Three-Leg Option's Strategy: The P/L profile for this strategy is shown in Fig. 3c. In relation to known strategies this strategy may best be described as a risk reversal with an OTM (out of the money) short call which caps the upside profitability. Note that even though profitability is seemingly restricted, the short call brings in extra premium.

Four-Leg Option's Strategy: The P/L profile for this strategy is shown in Fig. 3d. This profile is similar to that of the three options' strategy but now there is an even higher strike call being sold which brings in further premium. Table 2 shows that this strategy has an average P/L of $68 per trade which results in it being the most profitable strategy of the six.

Five and Six Leg Option's Strategies: The P/L profiles for these strategies are shown in Fig. 3e and f, respectively. These profiles are similar to the four options' strategy but in the present cases it appears that cheap far OTM options are chosen to satisfy the required option tally and don't provide any further benefit.

Conclusion from the Results Presented in Table 2: The results of the four options' strategy show it to be the best from those shown in Table 2. The resulting equity curve for this strategy is shown in Fig. 4 where the starting capital is assumed to be $10,000. The equity curve simply represents the ongoing cumulative sum of all trade profits and losses. The large equity drawdown of 48.3% occurred during the global financial crisis of 2008 and is due to just two extreme losing trades. These two trades were the ones initiated in October and November, 2008. This extreme equity drawdown characteristic is true of all the strategies presented in Table 2 as no effort was made to mitigate this risk. In the next section we will examine results of a reformulated fitness metric which aims to restrict the maximum drawdown to an acceptable level.

Table 2. Option strategies obtained for maximizing profit where over 80% of trades are profitable in historical data period.

Number of options	Option type (P/C)	Long/short (L/S)	Delta (absolute) value)	Example (Table 1 data)	Average profit per trade ($)	Total profit ($)	Percent profitable (%)	Maximum drawdown (%)
1	P	S	0.300	110	41	5677	81.9	60.0
2	P	S	0.212	107	55	7528	81.1	34.5
	C	S	0.135	123				
3	P	S	0.267	109	52	7145	80.4	60.4
	C	L	0.403	117				
	C	S	0.256	120				
4	P	S	0.212	107	68	9437	81.2	48.3
	C	L	0.403	117				
	C	S	0.211	121				
	C	S	0.135	123				
5	P	S	0.267	109	56	7723	81.2	58.4
	C	L	0.303	119				
	C	S	0.135	123				
	C	S	0.105	124				
	C	L	0.027	129				
6	P	S	0.032	91	65	8940	80.4	48.9
	P	L	0.036	92				
	P	S	0.212	107				
	C	L	0.403	117				
	C	S	0.211	121				
	C	S	0.135	123				

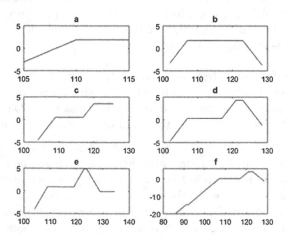

Fig. 3. Profit and loss (P/L) profiles for the set of 6 strategies presented in Table 2. The price of the underlying (SPY) is 114.61. (a) One option: short put, (b) two options: strangle, (c) three options: risk reversal with an OTM call, (d) four options, (e) five options, and (f) six options.

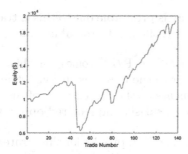

Fig. 4. Equity curve for the four leg option strategy over the period of January 10, 2005 to July 19, 2016. The large drawdown is the result of two losing trades during the 2008 financial crisis.

4.2 Maximizing Profit for a 80% Profitable Strategy While Limiting the Maximum Equity Drawdown to Less Than 10%

In this subsection we consider an enhancement to the fitness function from the previous subsection in that a maximum equity drawdown is specified. The results are shown in Table 3 where a targeted limit of maximum drawdown was specified as 10%. We will examine each of the six strategies next.

One Leg Option's Strategy: Here we find that no strategy was able to meet the dual requirements of 80% of trades being successful whilst limiting the maximum drawdown to 10%. However the strategy closest to achieving this was the short put placed at one extreme of the considered range of strikes. This resulted in a maximum drawdown of 13.5% which at the same time improving the percentage of profitable trades to 94.9%. However, at this extreme strike value insufficient premium is garnered so that the average profit per trade is an unacceptable $3. The P/L profile for this strategy is shown in Fig. 5a.

Two-Legs Option's Strategy: The strategy chosen is known as a put vertical credit spread. Basically it comprises of a short put, placed at a 13 delta, hedged by a long put, placed at a 7 delta. The difference between the strike values determines the maximum loss that this strategy can suffer. However, the average profit per trade is also low at just $13. The P/L profile for this strategy is shown in Fig. 5b.

Three-Legs Option's Strategy: The P/L profile for this strategy is shown in Fig. 5c. Here we see that the profile has components of a previously discussed strategy called a strangle, along with a lower strike long put. The strangle short call is placed at a 17 delta with short put placed at a 13.5 delta. The lower strike put appearing at a 5.8 delta limits the downside losses.

Four-Legs Option's Strategy: The P/L profile for this strategy is shown in Fig. 5d. This profile resembles the three option leg strategy profile but with an extra lower strike long put which further mitigates downside losses. In fact, in extreme downside moves this strategy is profitable due to this extra long added put. With an average profit of $36, this is the most profitable strategy appearing in Table 3.

Five-Legs Option's Strategy: The P/L profiles for this strategy are shown in Fig. 5e. This profile is similar to the four-legs options' strategy but in the present case a short put option appears at the low extreme of the available strikes which appears to be placed there to satisfy the required option tally.

Six-Legs Option's Strategy: The P/L profiles for this strategy are shown in Fig. 5f. This profile resembles the four-legs option's strategy along with an imbedded put credit spread where greater gains are achieved for moderate underlying upside moves. This strategy with an average profit per trade of $33 is the second most profitable strategy shown in Table 3.

Conclusion from the Results Presented in Table 3: Again we find that the four-legs option's strategy appears to be the best of all considered. The equity curve for this strategy is shown in Fig. 6, where we see that we have avoided the large equity drawdown previously seen during the global financial crisis of 2008. However, this comes at the price of slightly reduced profitability over the full time period.

Table 3. Option strategies obtained by maximizing profit where over 80% of trades are profitable while restricting the maximum drawdown to less than 10% (when possible) in the historical data period.

Number of options	Option type (P/C)	Long/short (L/S)	Delta (absolute) value)	Example (Table 1 data)	Average profit per trade ($)	Total profit ($)	Percent profitable (%)	Maximum drawdown (%)
1	P	S	0.025	89	3	408	94.9	13.5
2	P	L	0.073	98	13	1735	93.5	9.2
	P	S	0.133	103				
3	P	L	0.058	96	30	4113	80.4	9.9
	P	S	0.135	103				
	C	S	0.170	122				
4	P	L	0.036	92	36	4967	82.6	8.6
	P	L	0.041	93				
	P	S	0.212	107				
	C	S	0.105	124				
5	P	S	0.025	89	30	4190	81.2	9.9
	P	L	0.041	93				
	P	L	0.046	94				
	P	S	0.150	104				
	C	S	0.135	123				
6	P	L	0.036	92	33	4527	80.4	8.7
	P	L	0.046	94				
	P	S	0.212	107				
	P	L	0.371	112				
	P	S	0.412	113				
	C	S	0.105	124				

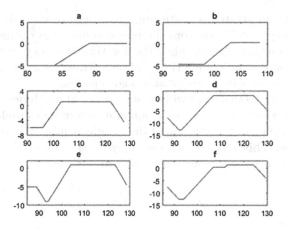

Fig. 5. Profit and loss (P/L) profiles for the set of 6 strategies presented in Table 3. The price of the underlying is 114.61. (a) One option (short put), (b) two options (vertical put credit spread), (c) three options, (d) four options, (e) five options, and (f) six options.

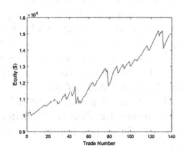

Fig. 6. Equity curve for the four-legs option's strategy over the period from January 10, 2005 to July 19, 2016. The maximum drawdown has now been limited to under 10% with the appropriate choice of option strategy.

5   Conclusions

In this paper a memetic algorithm has been used in the search of option strategies which feature optimum performance based on a backtest using SPY option data from January 2005 to July, 2016. Performance was first quantified in terms of profitability and percentage of profitable trades. From a search of option strategies ranging from 1 to 6 option legs, an optimum 4 legs strategy was found which featured the highest profitability for a greater than 80% winning trade percentage. However the equity drawdown during the 2008 global financial crisis was found to be unacceptably large, as with all the other strategies found which did not consider this risk metric. Subsequently, the performance criteria was reformulated to include equity drawdown by limiting it to be less than 10%. Further searching over option strategies featuring 1 to 6 legs resulted in again finding that a 4-legs strategy (different from the previous one) was optimum.

To the best of our knowledge, this is the first time that a systematic approach to the generation and search of multi-leg option's strategies guided by predefined performance metrics has been undertaken and reported.

Future extensions to this work will consider other fitness functions. For example, in order to maximize the *return on capital* it becomes desirable to include in the fitness evaluation a determination of the margin requirements of all potential solution strategies. This will also tend to mitigate the risk of the strategy since the margin requirement is a reflection of inherent risk.

References

1. Del Chicca, L., Larcher, G., Szoelgenyi, M.: Modeling and performance of certain put-write strategies. J. Altern. Invest. **15**(4), 74–86 (2013). Spring
2. Del Chicca, L., Larcher, G.: A comparison of different families of put-write option strategies. ACRN J. Finan. Risk Perspect. **1**(1), 1–14 (2012)
3. Blackmore, S.: The Meme Machine. Oxford University Press, New York (1999)
4. Moscato, P.: On evolution, search, optimization, genetic algorithms and martial arts: toward memetic algorithms. Technical report 826, Caltech Concurrent Computation Program, California Institute of Technology, Pasadena, CA (1989)
5. Ishibuchi, H., Yoshida, T., Murata, T.: Balance between genetic search and local search in memetic algorithms for multiobjective permutation flowshop scheduling. IEEE Trans. Evol. Comput. **7**(2), 204–223 (2003)
6. Richer, J.-M., Goëffon, A., Hao, J.-K.: A memetic algorithm for phylogenetic reconstruction with maximum parsimony. In: Pizzuti, C., Ritchie, M.D., Giacobini, M. (eds.) EvoBIO 2009. LNCS, vol. 5483, pp. 164–175. Springer, Heidelberg (2009). doi:10.1007/978-3-642-01184-9_15
7. Nguyen, Q.C., Ong, Y.S., Kuo, J.L.: A hierarchical approach to study the thermal behavior of protonated water clusters $H^+(H_2O)_n$. J. Chem. Theory Comput. **5**(10), 2629–2639 (2009)
8. Chen, X., Ong, Y., Lim, M., Tan, K.C.: A multi-facet survey on memetic computation. IEEE Trans. Evol. Comput. **15**(5), 591–607 (2011)

Co-Evolving Line Drawings
with Hierarchical Evolution

Darwin Vickers[1,2], Jacob Soderlund[1], and Alan Blair[1(✉)]

[1] School of Computer Science and Engineering,
University of New South Wales, Sydney, Australia
d.vickers@unsw.edu.au, j.soderlund@student.unsw.edu.au,
blair@cse.unsw.edu.au
[2] Data61, CSIRO, Sydney, Australia

Abstract. We use an adversarial approach inspired by biological coevolution to generate complex line drawings without human guidance. Artificial artists and critics work against each other in an iterative competitive framework, forcing each to become increasingly sophisticated to outplay the other. Both the artists and critics are implemented in HERCL, a framework combining linear and stack-based Genetic Programming, which is well suited to coevolution because the number of competing agents is kept small while still preserving diversity. The aesthetic quality of the resulting images arises from the ability of the evolved HERCL programs, making judicious use of register adjustments and loops, to produce repeated substructures with subtle variations, in the spirit of low-complexity art.

Keywords: Artist-critic coevolution · Artificial creativity · Adversarial training

1 Introduction

Several recent papers have explored the development of aesthetically pleasing images using an evolutionary approach [6,8–11,13]. In most cases, human interaction is required to guide evolution towards pleasing images. However, Machado et al. [10] use an experimental approach inspired by coevolution in nature, which allows novel imagery to be generated without human interaction (see also [11]). The core of the coevolution process is the adversarial relationship between an *artist* and a *critic*. The aim of the critic is to distinguish *real* art from artificial art (produced by the coevolving artist). The aim of the artist is to produce images that the critic will believe to be real.

At the beginning of the process, a set of critics are trained on a predetermined set of *real* and *fake* images. Then, a set of artists are evolved to produce art which *fools* the previously-evolved critics. The images produced by the artists are then added to the fake dataset that is used to train critics in the next generation, and the process is iterated indefinitely. Both the artist and the critic must

© Springer International Publishing AG 2017
M. Wagner et al. (Eds.): ACALCI 2017, LNAI 10142, pp. 39–49, 2017.
DOI: 10.1007/978-3-319-51691-2_4

increase in sophistication at each generation in order to surpass the adversary. The hope is that the continual increase in sophistication will produce imagery that is appealing, or at least interesting, from a human perspective.

In previous approaches, images were typically generated by artists using pixel-based methods, where a shade or colour is assigned to each pixel in the image [8], often based on its x and y co-ordinates, using either a tree-based Genetic Program [9,10] or a neural network [13]. The critic used either a tree-based GP [9] or a neural network [10] for classification, with input based on certain statistical features of the image.

In the present work, we adapt this coevolution approach to the framework of hierarchical evolutionary re-combination (HERCL) as introduced in [2], which combines features from linear GP and stack-based GP. Each agent (artist or critic) is a program written in a simple imperative language with instructions for manipulating a stack, registers and memory. The full list of HERCL commands is given in Table 1.

Table 1. HERCL commands

Input and Output	Stack Manipulation and Arithmetic
i fetch INPUT to input buffer	# PUSH new item to stack $\quad ...... \quad \mapsto ......x$
s SCAN item from input buffer to stack	! POP top item from stack $\quad ...... x \mapsto ......$
w WRITE item from stack to output buffer	c COPY top item on stack $\quad ...... x \mapsto ......x,x$
o flush OUTPUT buffer	x SWAP top two items $\quad ...y,x \mapsto ...x,y$
	y ROTATE top three items $\quad z,y,x \mapsto x,z,y$
Registers and Memory	− NEGATE top item $\quad ...... x \mapsto .....(-x)$
< GET value from register	+ ADD top two items $\quad ...y,x \mapsto ...(y+x)$
> PUT value into register	* MULTIPLY top two items $\quad ...y,x \mapsto ...(y*x)$
^ INCREMENT register	**Mathematical Functions**
v DECREMENT register	
{ LOAD from memory location	r RECIPROCAL $\quad ..x \to ..1/x$
} STORE to memory location	q SQUARE ROOT $\quad ..x \to ..\sqrt{x}$
	e EXPONENTIAL $\quad ..x \mapsto ..e^x$
Jump, Test, Branch and Logic	n (natural) LOGARITHM $\quad ..x \mapsto ..\log_e(x)$
j JUMP to specified cell (subroutine)	a ARCSINE $\quad ..x \mapsto ..\sin^{-1}(x)$
	BAR line (RETURN on . | HALT on 8 |)	h TANH $\quad ..x \mapsto ..\tanh(x)$
= register is EQUAL to top of stack	z ROUND to nearest integer
g register is GREATER than top of stack	? push RANDOM value to stack
: if TRUE, branch FORWARD	**Double-Item Functions**
; if TRUE, branch BACK	
& logical AND	% DIVIDE/MODULO $..y,x \mapsto ..(y/x),(y \bmod x)$
/ logical OR	t TRIG functions $..\theta,r \mapsto ..r\sin\theta,r\cos\theta$
~ logical NOT	p POLAR coords $..y,x \mapsto ..\mathrm{atan2}(y,x),\sqrt{x^2+y^2}$

HERCL does not use a population as such, but instead maintains a stack or *ladder* of candidate solutions (agents), and a *codebank* of potential mates (see Fig. 1). At each step of the algorithm, the agent at the top rung of the ladder is

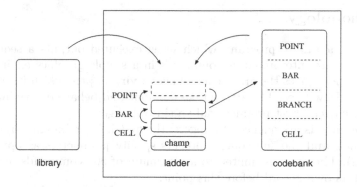

Fig. 1. Hierarchical evolutionary re-combination. If the top agent on the ladder becomes fitter than the one below it, the top agent will move down to replace the lower agent (which is transferred to the codebank). If the top agent exceeds its maximum number of allowable offspring without ever becoming fitter than the one below it, the top agent is removed from the ladder (and transferred to the codebank).

either mutated or crossed over with a randomly chosen agent from the codebank, or from an external library. Crossovers and mutations are classified into different levels according to what portion of code is modified. A large crossover at the lowest rung of the ladder is followed up by a series of progressively smaller crossovers and mutations at higher rungs, concentrated in the vicinity of the large crossover (see [2] for further details).

In the present work, both the artists and the critics are HERCL programs. The artist's output is interpreted as a sequence of commands in a simple drawing environment. The critic takes as input a set of features computed from the image, and returns a number between 0 and 1 representing its confidence that the image is real.

The advantages of using the HERCL framework in this context are as follows:

(a) It enables the artist to work at the level of line drawing rather than per-pixel manipulation, thus allowing the exploration of a different artistic modality which is arguably closer to the way humans draw with pen and paper.
(b) The functionality of the artist is extended with programming constructs such as loops, stack manipulation and incrementing or decrementing of registers, as well as various basic math functions.
(c) The ladder and codebank arrangement of the HERCL framework keeps the number of competing artists and critics relatively small, thus allowing computationally efficient coevolution.

The use of a stroke-based model for drawing is similar to Simon Colton's system The Painting Fool [4], whose output is more visually complex. Colton's software aims to produce a painterly rendering of a single image, whereas we are more interested in creating a system capable of generating novel, non-representational imagery based on a collection of images.

2 Methodology

Each artist is a HERCL program, which when executed outputs a sequence of messages that are interpreted as commands in a simple graphics environment. This environment gives the artist control over a virtual pen, which it can rotate and move to draw lines. The artists take no input and behave deterministically, and therefore each artist produces only a single image.

Each message is a sequence of integers; the first integer (modulo 5) specifies the command, and the subsequent integers specify parameters as appropriate (see Table 2). The artist is limited to a maximum of 900 commands, but it can also halt of its own accord before this point.

Table 2. Line drawing commands

0	TOGGLE		lift pen on/off page
1	MOVE	x	move pen forward by x pixels ($0 \leq x \leq 15$)
2	TURN	x	turn x degrees clockwise
3	SIZE	p	set pen radius to p pixels ($1 \leq p \leq 4$)
4	COLOUR	v	set greyscale value [in greyscale mode]
	COLOUR	$l\,h\,s$	set colour in HSV colour space [in full-colour mode]

Typically the artist is allowed to use any instruction in the HERCL syntax, but in some experiments we disallowed the use of the branch-back instruction, preventing the artist from implementing loops.

The critics are also HERCL programs, which take as input a set of features computed from an image, and are required to output a single number between 0 and 1, similar to the classification tasks of [3]. The set of features extracted from the image is primarily based on those used by Datta et al. [5] in their work on computationally assessing photograph quality, as well as some from [10]. We also add some features based on corner detection as this pertains specifically to the line-based drawing method used by our system.

The full list of features is shown in Table 3. For colour images, certain properties are calculated independently across the Hue, Saturation and Value channels, resulting in three features. In greyscale mode, the image effectively consists only of a Value channel, and so the features with superscript H or S are not provided to the critic. All features except N_P and N_C are scaled to within [0,1]. Corner weight and number are computed using the Harris & Stephens corner detection algorithm, as implemented in OpenCV 2.4. In total, there are 19 features in greyscale mode and 33 in full-colour mode.

When evolving an artist, its fitness is determined by how well it fools the set of critics. The image produced by an artist is first converted into a feature vector, and the critics each give a score based on this vector. The cost function for the artist is a weighted sum of critics from all previous generations, with older critics contributing less. For an artist in generation n,

Table 3. Image features

Feature	Abbreviation	Source
Mean	M^H, M^S, M^V	[5, 10]
Standard deviation	S^H, S^S, S^V	[5, 10]
Greyscale entropy	H	[10]
Mean edge weight	M_E	[10]
Standard deviation of edge weight	S_E	[10]
Number of homogenous patches	N_P	[5]
Mean of largest patch	P_1^H, P_1^S, P_1^V	[5]
Mean of 2nd-largest patch	P_2^H, P_2^S, P_2^V	[5]
Mean of 3rd-largest patch	P_3^H, P_3^S, P_3^V	[5]
Mean of 4th-largest patch	P_4^H, P_4^S, P_4^V	[5]
Mean of 5th-largest patch	P_5^H, P_5^S, P_5^V	[5]
Size of largest patch	A_1	[5]
Size of 2nd-largest patch	A_2	[5]
Size of 3rd-largest patch	A_3	[5]
Size of 4th-largest patch	A_4	[5]
Size of 5th-largest patch	A_5	[5]
Convexity factor	C	[5]
Mean corner weight	M_C	-
Number of corners	N_C	

$$\text{cost} = 1 - \sum_{i=1}^{n} \left(\frac{1}{2}\right)^{n-i-1} c_i$$

where c_i is the average score across all critics in generation i. Artists are considered successful when they have achieved a cost below 0.1. The main reason for using critics from all previous generations is that sometimes the most recent critics will be good enough that the artist is initially unable to produce an image which gets a non-zero score. This leaves the artist with a flat fitness landscape and prevents it from evolving successfully. Including critics from previous generations helps the artists to improve, particularly in the early generations, and could perhaps also help prevent suboptimal cycles of forgetting and re-learning in the coevolutionary dynamics [1].

A library is maintained of the successful artist code from all previous generations. Code from this library is made available for crossovers and mutations when evolving the next generation of artists. This enables the artists to evolve by adapting and re-using code from earlier artists, and encourages them to build on the artistic "style" developed in previous generations (see Figs. 3, 4 and 5). However, this may also limit diversity by encouraging similar code throughout the run.

Fig. 2. One example image from each dataset: Chinese characters and Colour. (Color figure online)

Critics are evolved against a labeled dataset consisting of feature vectors computed from the real and fake image datasets. The target value is 1 for real images and 0 for fake images. The cost for the critic is the cross-entropy function:

$$\text{cost} = -t\log(z) - (1 - t)\log(1 - z)$$

where t is the target label (0 or 1) and z is the value produced by the critic. Any critic producing a value ≤ 0 for a real image or ≥ 1 for a fake image receives a *penalty* and is excluded from both the ladder and the codebank. This, combined with the logarithmic divergence in the cost function, strongly encourages critics to produce values inside the interval $(0, 1)$ rather than at the extremes. This makes it easier for the artists to evolve because the fitness landscape has a continuous gradient.

As in [10], the real and fake datasets are given equal weight, so that the relative sizes of the two sets do not affect the critic's evolution. Critics are accepted when they achieve a cost below 0.1.

3   Experiments

We focus primarily on the results of two runs of the coevolution process, using a starting set of images of Chinese characters. We call the two runs **Loops** and **No Loops**. The difference between them is that for the latter, we disabled the branch-back instruction, preventing loop structures from appearing in the artist code. Both these runs operate in greyscale mode.

The starting dataset consists of 290 greyscale images of Chinese characters from Wiktionary, each 80×80. There is no particular reason for using this dataset other than that it contains images that could be feasibly generated within our drawing framework.

We also conducted one additional run, **Colour**, to demonstrate the colour-mode capability. This run used a dataset of 67 colour images taken from a Google Images search for "circle", with search settings restricting size to 128×128 and specifying 'Full colour'. The resulting images all contain circles or round objects, but generally in combination with other elements or symbols.

For each run, there were three critics and ten artists evolved independently in each generation (each with its own ladder and codebank).

4   Results and Discussion

A selection of generated images from each run is shown in Figs. 3, 4 and 5. Aesthetic qualities of the images are difficult to quantitatively assess, but it is clear that the system is capable of generating quite a diverse range of complex imagery with no human guidance.

It is clear from the results, and Fig. 3 in particular, that the complexity of the images is increasing across phases. This demonstrates that the adversarial artist-critic relationship is successful in driving the development of complexity.

The difference between the images in Figs. 3 and 4 is notable. We see that allowing loops results in highly structured patterns in the images, whereas disallowing loops results in images with a more freehand appearance.

The code for the No Loops run tends to be longer, because each stroke has to be coded individually. In the Loops run, there are many cases where the evolved code is quite short but manages to generate surprisingly elaborate images. For example, the left image in the 2nd bottom row of Fig. 4 was generated by this code:

```
[<wx<*23.#-!cw8v{.v<wwcv<wwow.v<*vwo;:]
```

The possibility of creating complex images from short programs draws parallels with Schmidhuber's theory of low-complexity art [12]. What makes these images particularly interesting (and perhaps aesthetically pleasing) is that they often contain repeated structures which are similar but not quite identical. The evolved HERCL programs make use of loops and register adjustments to introduce subtle differences in these substructures, thus mimicking certain developmental processes in the natural world. This phenomenon can be compared with the pixel-based approach of [8], where local agents following evolved rules were used to create an overall "natural-looking" image.

Greyscale entropy is the feature most commonly used by the critics (see Figs. 6, 7 and 8). Other important features include the mean and standard deviation of the overall image (M^V, S^V) and the edge weight (M_E, S_E), the convexity (C) and the size and mean value of the 2nd largest patch (A_2, P_2^V). For the Colour task, which was trained on "circle" images, the mean corner weight and mean of the largest and 3rd largest patch in the H and S channels are also used.

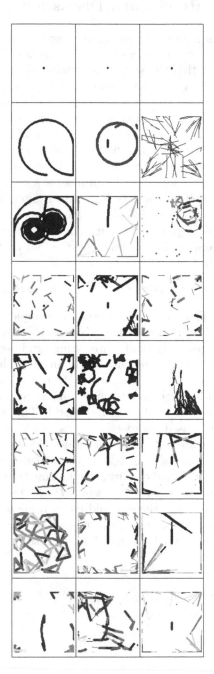

Fig. 3. Three images each from generations 1 to 8 of No Loops run.

Fig. 4. Three images each from generations 1 to 8 of the Loops run.

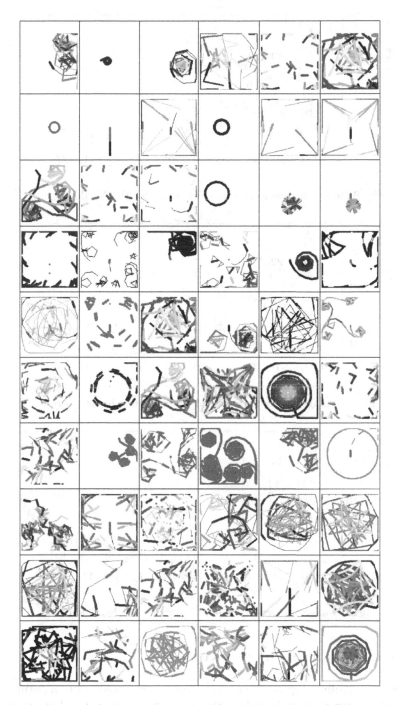

Fig. 5. Six images each from generations 3,5,7,8,9,11,13,15,17,18 of Colour run. (Color figure online)

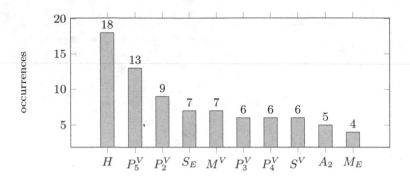

Fig. 6. Image features most used by critics for the No Loops run.

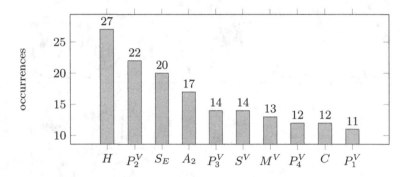

Fig. 7. Image features most used by critics for the Loops run.

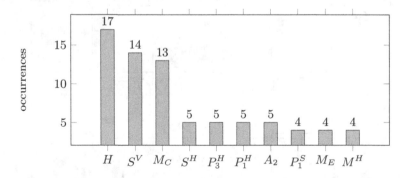

Fig. 8. Image features most used by critics for the Colour run.

5   Conclusion and Future Work

We have successfully adapted the coevolutionary art paradigm to a natural line-drawing environment. The fact that HERCL programs can act as both artist and critic is testament to the versatility of the HERCL framework. Discrimination based on statistical features of the image, combined with the inherent preference for shorter programs, are enough to drive complexity and produce aesthetically pleasing images.

However, there are clearly certain local and global properties of the images which are not being captured by these statistical features. In future work, we plan to explore the use of deep convolutional neural networks in the role of the critic, similar to the generative adversarial networks recently introduced for image generation [7]. Another avenue of investigation would be the use of multi-cell HERCL programs (which allow jumping to subroutines), or additional line drawing commands for moving to a specified (or previously stored) location on the canvas, to see whether the paradigm can be scaled up to larger and more sophisticated images.

References

1. Axelrod, R.: The Evolution of Cooperation. Basic Books, New York (1984)
2. Blair, A.: Learning the Caesar and Vigenere Cipher by hierarchical evolutionary re-combination. In: Congress on Evolutionary Computation, pp. 605–612 (2013)
3. Blair, A.D.: Transgenic evolution for classification tasks with HERCL. In: Chalup, S.K., Blair, A.D., Randall, M. (eds.) ACALCI 2015. LNCS (LNAI), vol. 8955, pp. 185–195. Springer, Heidelberg (2015). doi:10.1007/978-3-319-14803-8_15
4. Colton, C.: Stroke matching for paint dances. In: International Symposium on Computational Aesthetics in Graphics, Visualization and Imaging (2010)
5. Datta, R., Joshi, D., Li, J., Wang, J.Z.: Studying aesthetics in photographics images using a computational approach. In: Proceedings of European Conference on Computer Vision, pp. 288–301 (2006)
6. Galanter, P.: Computational aesthetic evaluation: past and future. In: McCormack, J., d'Inverno, M. (eds.) Computers and Creativity, pp. 255–293. Springer, Berlin (2012)
7. Goodfellow, I., Pouget-Abadie, J., Mirza, M., Xu, B., Warde-Farley, D., Ozair, S., Courville, A., Bengio, Y.: Generative adversarial nets. In: Advances in Neural Information Processing Systems, pp. 2672–2680 (2014)
8. Kowaliw, T., Dorin, A., McCormack, J.: Promoting creative design in interactive evolutionary computation. IEEE Trans. Evol. Comput. 16(4), 523 (2012)
9. Li, Y., Hu, C.-J.: Aesthetic learning in an interactive evolutionary art system. In: Chio, C., et al. (eds.) EvoApplications 2010. LNCS, vol. 6025, pp. 301–310. Springer, Heidelberg (2010). doi:10.1007/978-3-642-12242-2_31
10. Machado, P., Romero, J., Manaris, B.: Experiments in computational aesthetics: an iterative approach to stylistic change in evolutionary art. In: Romero, J., Machado, P. (eds.) The Art of Artificial Evolution, pp. 381–415. Springer, Berlin (2008)
11. Saunders, R., Gero, J.S.: Artificial creativity: a synthetic approach to the study of creative behaviour. Comput. Cogn. Models Creat. Des. V, 113–139 (2001). Key Centre of Design Computing and Cognition. University of Sydney, Sydney
12. Schmidhuber, J.: Low-complexity art. Leonardo, J. Int. Soc. Arts Sci. Technol. 30(2), 97–103 (1997)
13. Secretan, J., Beato, N., D'Ambrosio, D.B., Rodriguez, A., Campbell, A., Folsom-Kovarik, J.T., Stanley, K.O.: Picbreeder: a case study in collaborative evolutionary exploration of design space. Evol. Comput. 19(3), 373–403 (2011)

Reliability Estimation of Individual Multi-target Regression Predictions

Martin Jakomin$^{(\boxtimes)}$ and Zoran Bosnić

Faculty of Computer and Information Science, University of Ljubljana,
Večna pot 113, Ljubljana, Slovenia
{martin.jakomin,zoran.bosnic}@fri.uni-lj.si

Abstract. To estimate the quality of the induced predictive model we generally use measures of averaged prediction accuracy, such as the relative mean squared error on test data. Such evaluation fails to provide local information about reliability of individual predictions, which can be important in risk-sensitive fields (medicine, finance, industry etc.). Related work presented several ways for computing individual prediction reliability estimates for single-target regression models, but has not considered their use with multi-target regression models that predict a vector of independent target variables. In this paper we adapt the existing single-target reliability estimates to multi-target models. In this way we try to design reliability estimates, which can estimate the prediction errors without knowing true prediction errors, for multi-target regression algorithms, as well. We approach this in two ways: by aggregating reliability estimates for individual target components, and by generalizing the existing reliability estimates to higher number of dimensions. The results revealed favorable performance of the reliability estimates that are based on *bagging variance* and *local cross-validation* approaches. The results are consistent with the related work in single-target reliability estimates and provide a support for multi-target decision making.

Keywords: Multi-target regression · Reliability estimate · Supervised learning · Prediction error

1 Introduction

The aim of supervised learning is to generalize knowledge contained in learning data and minimize prediction error on yet unseen examples. To estimate the quality of the induced predictive model we generally use measures of averaged prediction accuracy, such as the relative mean squared error on test data. Although such evaluation does provide information about the general model performance, it fails to provide local information about reliability of individual predictions. Note that in this paper we use term *reliability* to denote *estimated accuracy*, as the true predictive accuracy for unseen (and therefore unlabeled) examples is not known.

© Springer International Publishing AG 2017
M. Wagner et al. (Eds.): ACALCI 2017, LNAI 10142, pp. 50–60, 2017.
DOI: 10.1007/978-3-319-51691-2_5

Having the individual prediction reliability estimates at disposal can represent a strategic advantage of a decision support system, especially in risk-sensitive fields, such as medicine, finance or industry. Since a professional's decisions that are made by consulting a decision support system can have severe consequences, reliability estimates for individual predictions can provide grounds for making more informed decisions.

Related work in this field already presented several ways for computing reliability estimates for individual predictions. These can be divided to model-specific, which are tied to particular model formalizations (e.g. confidence intervals in linear regression, variance of target labels in decision tree leaves etc.), or model-independent, which are designed as wrappers around the learning algorithm and therefore treat it as a black box. Since the latter family is more general, we chose it as a focus of our work. Although several model-independent reliability estimates have already been proposed for classification [1,2] as well as for regression [3,4], they are intended for use only with single-target predictive models.

Opposed to single-target models, multi-target models aim at predicting a vector of independent target variables, which can also be of different variable types. In this paper we extend the existing reliability estimates for individual regression predictions [3,4] (described in Sect. 2.2) to such multi-target models with the aim to estimate reliability of the entire vector of target variables as a whole. In this way we try to design reliability estimates, which can estimate the prediction errors without knowing true prediction errors, for multi-target regression algorithms, as well. We propose two main approaches to achieve this goal, the first one being the aggregation of reliability estimates for individual target components, and the second one being the generalization of the existing reliability estimates to higher dimensions. We compare the proposed approaches by correlating them to the actual prediction error of test examples and rank them by their performance.

The paper is structured as follows. Section 2 describes the related work in multi-target modeling and existing single-target reliability estimates for regression. Section 3 describes the adaptation of reliability estimation to multi-target predictors. In Sect. 4 we provide evaluation and experimental results and in Sect. 5 we conclude the paper.

2 Related Work

2.1 Multi-target Modeling

The task of multi-target regression (also called multivariate or multi-response regression) is simultaneously predicting multiple continuous target variables. The learning examples take form of $(\vec{x}_i, \vec{y}_i)$ where $\vec{x}_i = (x_{i1}, x_{i2}, \ldots, x_{ik})$ is a vector of k attributes and $\vec{y}_i = (y_{i1}, y_{i2}, \ldots, y_{id})$ is a vector of d target attributes. As one could build a separate model for each of the target attributes and then combine the results, the better way is to predict all of the target attributes $\vec{y}_i$ at once. In this way, the dependencies of the target attributes are implicitly modeled as well, producing better predictive performance. The other advantage of described multi-target model is that the size and complexity of the produced model is smaller than the combined size of the single-target models [5,6].

Multi-target regression trees are an example of multi-target regression models. They represent a generalization of single-target regression trees that model dependency between several input attributes and a single target continuous variable. In contrast to the latter, multi-target regression trees predict a vector of prediction values that is represented by each leaf of the tree. To induce such a tree, the adapted impurity measures for each inner nodes are used to determine the appropriate split. While many tree induction algorithms exist, most of them are based on the CART model [7] – such are the Segal's [8] and De'Ath's [9] multivariate regression trees. Some others, such as multi-objective regression trees (MORTs) [10], perform multi-target modeling by extending the predictive clustering trees [11]. Multi-target trees have also been extended into multivariate random forests model [12] or combined via stacking [13] to achieve better predictive accuracy.

In contrast to multivariate trees, linear regression has a trivial extension to the multi-target regression. Instead of solving one system of linear equations, we need to solve d of them:

$$Y_{n\times d} = X_{n\times (k+1)}\beta_{(k+1)\times d} + E_{n\times d}.$$

Here, Y is a matrix of n, d-dimensional vectors of target attributes, X is a matrix of n attribute vectors (with k attributes and values of $x_{i0} = 1$ for all i), β is a coefficient matrix and E is the residual matrix. After all coefficients are calculated by minimizing the squared error on training examples [14], we can use the system of d linear equations to predict each target variable separately.

Similar straightforward extension to multi-target regression is also the k-nearest neighbor method (kNN). Firstly, the k nearest examples are retrieved from the learning set and then the label sets of those neighbors are aggregated in some manner [15].

In our experimental work we evaluate the proposed reliability estimates with these three models, i.e. multi.target regression trees, multi-target linear regression and k-nearest neighbors.

2.2 Reliability Estimation of Single-Target Predictions

Several reliability estimates for single-target regression models have already been proposed in the related work [3,4]. All of the following reliability estimates are designed as model-independent wrappers and work by manipulating the dataset. We focus on estimates that use sensitivity analysis approach (i.e., estimates $SAvar$ and $SAbias$), bagging (estimate $BAGV$) and local cross-validation (estimate LCV). They are defined as follows:

1. The principle of **sensitivity analysis** is to build multiple regression models based on small variations in input dataset and observe the magnitude

of changes in outputs. The algorithm for computation of estimates $SAvar$ and $SAbias$ takes a learning dataset $L = \{(\vec{x}_i, y_i)\}, i = 1 \ldots n$, learning algorithm M and a query example $\vec{q} = (\vec{x}', \_)$ as input. It returns the prediction for $\vec{q}$ and a reliability estimate for that particular example. The algorithm starts by computing the initial prediction K for $\vec{q}$ using model M on the initial dataset L. Afterwards, it builds multiple *sensitivity* models $M_{\varepsilon_i}, i = 1, \ldots, e$ by augmenting L with artificially labeled query example into $L_{\varepsilon_i} = L \cup (\vec{x}', K + f(\varepsilon_i)), i = 1, \ldots, e$, where $f(\varepsilon_i)$ represents a magnitude of change that was introduced into the learning data. As an outcome, several *sensitivity predictions* $K_{\varepsilon_i}, i = 1, \ldots, e$ are obtained for the query example $\vec{q}$. The assumption of the process is that big differences between initial prediction K and sensitivity predictions K_{ε_i} indicate low reliability of prediction K, as small changes of the learning dataset should not cause big deviations in the output. The prediction bias and variance are further modeled as reliability estimates $SAvar$ and $SAbias$ as follows:

$$SAvar = \frac{\sum_i (K_{\varepsilon_i} - K_{-\varepsilon_i})}{e}$$

$$SAbias = \frac{\sum_i (K_{\varepsilon_i} - K) + (K_{-\varepsilon_i} - K)}{2e}$$

where e represents a number of sensitivity models, as described above.

2. Traditional **bagging** (i.e., ensemble of predictors that are induced on several samplings of the original dataset with replacement and have the same cardinality) can be generalized to yield reliability estimate as follows. Assuming that the ensemble contains m regression models, each of them giving prediction $K^{(i)}, i = 1, \ldots, m$, the final prediction $K^{(*)}$ can be defined as an average $K^{(*)} = \frac{\sum_m K^{(i)}}{m}$ and the reliability estimate as a variance (higher value indicating greater instability – lower reliability):

$$BAGV = \frac{1}{m} \sum_{i=1}^{m} \left(K^{(i)} - K^{(*)} \right)^2$$

3. **Local cross-validation** approach analyses local characteristics of the input space. The algorithm first finds N nearest examples $NEAR = \{(\vec{x}_j, y_j)\}, j = 1, \ldots, N$ of the query example $\vec{q} = (\vec{x}', \_)$ and performs the leave-one-out procedure. For each nearest neighbor $(\vec{x}_j, y_j), j = 1, \ldots, N$, a local model using all the remaining nearest neighbors $(NEAR \setminus (\vec{x}_j, y_j))$ is induced, and a prediction K_j for the $(\vec{x}_j, y_j)$ is computed. In this way, a local error $E_j = y_j - K_j$ is computed for all nearest neighbors and the reliability estimate LCV is expressed as their weighted sum:

$$LCV = \frac{\sum_{(\vec{x}_i, y_i) \in NEAR} d(\vec{x}_i, \vec{x}') \cdot (y_j - K_j)}{\sum_{(\vec{x}_i, y_i) \in NEAR} d(\vec{x}_i, \vec{x}')}$$

where $d()$ is a distance function between learning examples.

In the following section we focus at applying these single-target reliability estimates with multi-target regression models.

3   Reliability Estimation of Multi-target Predictions

Multi-target regression predictions try to model true values $\vec{y} = (y_1, y_2, \ldots, y_d)$,
$y_i \in \mathbb{R}$ and therefore also take the form of a vector $\vec{K} = (K_1, K_2, \ldots, K_d)$,
$K_i \in \mathbb{R}$. Here we propose three different approaches for estimating reliabilities of
multi-target regression predictions. Each of them is described in the subsequent
sections.

3.1   Independent Estimation for Each Target Variable

We start by estimating reliability of each target variable independently and construct a vector of corresponding estimates. We compute reliability estimates from
Sect. 2.2 for every component of the prediction vector $\vec{K} = (K_1, K_2, \ldots, K_d)$ to
produce the corresponding vector of reliability estimates $\vec{r} = (r_1, r_2, \ldots, r_d)$.
Every target variable y_i is treated independently as the only target variable,
ignoring others within the target vector.

3.2   Aggregation of Independent Reliability Estimates

Since a single overall estimate for entire target vector enables simpler comparison
with other predictions and interpretability, we aggregate the individual reliability
estimates into a joint reliability estimate for entire prediction vector. For this we
use two approaches: (1) computation of the arithmetic mean (denoted as AM in
the following) and (2) the Euclidean (or second) norm (denoted as l^2):

$$l^2 = \sqrt{\sum_{i=1}^{d} r_i^2}$$

3.3   Generalization to Multi-target Prediction

Finally, we generalize the described estimates so they can be used with a higher
number of dimensions, i.e. with the entire prediction vector $\vec{K}$. We achieve this
by modifying the existing methods to measure the distances between prediction
vectors instead by computing differences (subtractions), as shown in Sect. 2.2.
The used distances can be arbitrary distance measures; in our evaluation we
experiment with the Euclidean distance. In the following we describe adaptations
of *SAvar*, *SAbias*, *BAGV* and *LCV*.

Sensitivity Analysis. We preserve the same process of sensitivity analysis and replace the subtractions in reliability estimate definitions with distances, as follows:

$$SAvar^+ = \frac{\sum_i dist(\overrightarrow{K}_{\varepsilon_i}, \overrightarrow{K}_{-\varepsilon_i})}{e}$$

$$SAbias^+ = \frac{\sum_i dist(\overrightarrow{K}_{\varepsilon_i}, \overrightarrow{K}) - dist(\overrightarrow{K}_{-\varepsilon_i}, \overrightarrow{K})}{2e}$$

where e represents a number of sensitivity models, $dist()$ is a distance measure between vectors of target variables, $\overrightarrow{K}$ is an initial prediction vector and $\overrightarrow{K}_{\varepsilon_j}, j = 1, \ldots, e$ are the vectors of sensitivity predictions.

Variance of Bagged Model. We begin by building a bagged ensemble of m multi-target regression models, where each model contributes its own prediction vector $\overrightarrow{K}^{(i)}$ for the query example. We determine the aggregated prediction of the ensemble as a centroid $\overrightarrow{K}^{(*)} = \frac{\sum_{i=1}^m \overrightarrow{K}^{(i)}}{m}$ of the individual prediction vectors and define the reliability estimate $BAGV^+$ as the variance of distances between bagged prediction vectors and their centroid $\overrightarrow{K}^{(*)}$:

$$BAGV^+ = \frac{1}{m} \sum_{i=1}^m dist(\overrightarrow{K}^{(i)}, \overrightarrow{K}^{(*)})^2$$

where $dist()$ is a distance function between vectors of target variables.

Local Cross-Validation Reliability Estimate. The generalization of the reliability estimate LCV is straightforward as well, as we only need to redefine the definition of the local error as the distance between the local prediction vector $\overrightarrow{K}_j$ and the vector of actual values $\overrightarrow{y}_j$:

$$LCV^+ = \frac{\sum_{(\overrightarrow{x}_i, \overrightarrow{y}_i) \in NEAR} d(\overrightarrow{x}_i, \overrightarrow{x}') \cdot dist(\overrightarrow{y}_j, \overrightarrow{K}_j)}{\sum_{(\overrightarrow{x}_i, \overrightarrow{y}_i) \in NEAR} d(\overrightarrow{x}_i, \overrightarrow{x}')}$$

where $d()$ is the distance function for finding the nearest neighbors and $dist()$ is the distance function between target variable vectors.

4   Evaluation and Results

We evaluated all three proposed approaches using 10 datasets and 3 regression models. The datasets were collected from the UCI data repository of machine learning datasets [16]. Since we used Euclidean distance to measure differences in vectors of target variables, we had to normalize the continuous attributes in dataset to the interval $[0, 1]$ to avoid bias of the distance function to attributes with greater span of values. We defined the target attributes on our own to be meaningful according to the domain problem. The details about the used datasets are shown in Table 1.

Table 1. Description of the used datasets (in very large datasets, a random sample of 800 instances was only taken).

Dataset	No. of examples	No. of discrete attributes	No. of continuous attributes	No. of target attributes
wimbledon	113	8	18	3
wpbc	194	0	31	2
skillcraft	800*	4	11	4
cbm	800*	0	16	2
slump	103	0	6	3
wine	800*	0	10	2
student	395	30	0	3
housing	506	1	11	2
dow-jones	720	3	9	2
parkinsons	800*	2	22	2

Evaluation Protocol. We tested the proposed reliability estimates using the leave-one-out (LOO) cross-validation, omitting one test (i.e., query) example in every iteration. For such test example $\vec{q} = (\vec{x}, \vec{y})$, we computed the following:

1. multi-target regression prediction $\vec{K}$,
2. prediction error $\vec{y} - \vec{K}$ and its mean across target attributes $\frac{1}{d}\sum_{i=1}^{d}(K_i - y_i)^2$,
3. vector of single-target reliability estimates $\vec{r}$,
4. three variants of multi-target reliability estimates
   (a) arithmetic mean of the reliability vector AM,
   (b) second norm of the reliability vector l^2,
   (c) the generalized estimates ($SAvar^+$, $SAbias^+$, $BAGV^+$ and LCV^+).

Within all three variants of the multi-target reliability estimates we used the Euclidean distance as the distance metric $dist()$ between predictions. For computation of $SAvar$ and $SAbias$ we used the default [4] set of sensitivity parameters $E = \{0.01, 0.1, 0.5, 1.0, 2.0\}$ and $f(\varepsilon) = \varepsilon \cdot (high - low)$ where $high$ and low are interval boundaries of the target variable labels. As $SAbias$ estimate returns a signed value, its absolute value was used for evaluation. For computation of the $BAGV$, we used ensembles with $m = 50$ models. Finally, with LCV estimate we considered 5 nearest neighbors and used an Euclidean distance as a distance function $d()$ between examples.

In our experiments we evaluated if the reliability estimates truly indicate the magnitude of the prediction error. Since the prediction error is known for test examples (but was hidden for the computation of the reliability estimates), we compute the Pearson correlation coefficients between predictions and reliability estimates and evaluate them for the statistical significance using the two-tailed t-test with threshold p-value of 0.05.

Regression Models. We used the following three multi-target regression models (all implemented in the Python library "scikit-learn" [17]) with default parameters:

1. *multi-target regression trees (RT)*: with the mean squared error as a splitting criterion and maximum tree depth of 6,
2. *multi-target linear regression (LR)*: no explicit parameters,
3. *multi-target k-nearest neighbors (kNN)*: with the number of neighbors $k = 5$, uniform weights and Euclidean distance measure.

4.1 Performance with Different Predictive Models

As described earlier, we computed a vector of single target reliability estimates $\vec{r}$ and three variants of aggregated multi-target reliability estimates (AM, l^2 and $+$) for each reliability estimation approach ($SAvar$, $SAbias$, $BAGV$ and LCV) and multi-target regression model (RT, LR, kNN). We computed Pearson correlation coefficients between the reliability estimates and prediction errors and evaluated them for statistical significance. In Table 2 we report the percentage of domains with statistically significant positive and negative correlations between prediction errors and reliability estimates for every reliability estimation approach and used regression model. Since for the vector of single-target reliability estimates we computed the correlation coefficient for each component separately, the table reports the averaged percentage of domains with the significant correlation coefficient across all target variables. This result serves as a baseline (upper and lower bound) for evaluating the aggregated multi-target reliability estimates.

Table 2. Percentage of domains with statistically significant positive and negative correlations between prediction errors and reliability estimates for three multi-target models and four reliability estimation approaches. Cells are in a form: *positive/negative* correlations.

Model	$SAvar$				$SAbias$			
	$\vec{r}$	AM	l^2	$+$	$\vec{r}$	AM	l^2	$+$
RT	33/32	40/20	40/20	40/20	5/10	20/10	20/10	20/10
LR	55/5	50/0	50/0	50/0	17/0	20/0	20/0	20/0
kNN	0/41	0/50	0/50	0/50	72/0	50/0	50/0	40/0
Avg	**29/26**	**30/23**	**30/23**	**30/23**	**31/3**	**30/3**	**30/3**	**26/3**
Model	$BAGV$				LCV			
	$\vec{r}$	AM	l^2	$+$	$\vec{r}$	AM	l^2	$+$
RT	69/10	70/0	70/0	70/0	70/0	50/0	50/0	50/0
LR	65/0	60/0	60/0	60/0	60/3	50/0	60/0	60/0
kNN	82/0	70/0	70/0	70/0	79/0	60/0	60/0	60/0
Avg	**72/3**	**66/0**	**66/0**	**66/0**	**69/1**	**53/0**	**56/0**	**56/0**

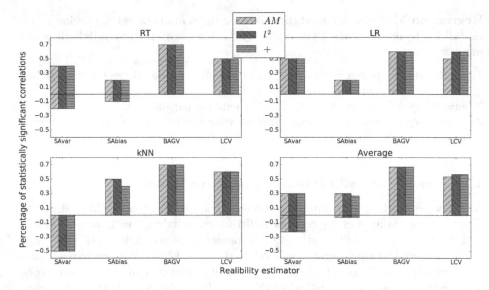

Fig. 1. Percentage of domains with statistically significant positive (above axis) and negative correlations (below axis) for proposed aggregated approaches AM, l^2 and $+$, for different regression models.

These results are also visually displayed in Fig. 1 along with their averages across regression models. The table and the figure show that the best result was achieved using all variants of the reliability estimate $BAGV$ combined with the multi-target regression trees (RT) and kNN (70% of domains with statistically significant positive correlations and 0% of domains with negative correlations). The estimate LCV follows as the second best, while the estimates $SAvar$ and $SAbias$ achieved much lower performance. The reason for bad performance of the $SAvar$ estimate with the kNN model is that the local neighborhoods of an example in the initial and sensitivity models are very similar (the only exception is the additionally inserted example); as such, the examples cancel out within the definition of $SAvar$ almost completely, effectively making the estimate independent of the query example. That explains 50% domains with negative correlations in the combination with the kNN model, so that result should be interpreted with the grain of salt.

If we disregard $SAvar$, the best average results were achieved using multi-target kNN regression model, followed by linear regression. All findings are comparable to the related work on the reliability estimation of single-target regression predictions [3], where $BAGV$ and LCV achieved the highest scores as well. By analysing our four proposed variants, we can see that all three aggregation approaches (AM, l^2 and $+$) perform comparably with each other.

4.2   Correlations with the Prediction Error

Figure 2 displays an alternative view of the results: the average correlation coefficients between reliability estimates and prediction error, averaged across all datasets.

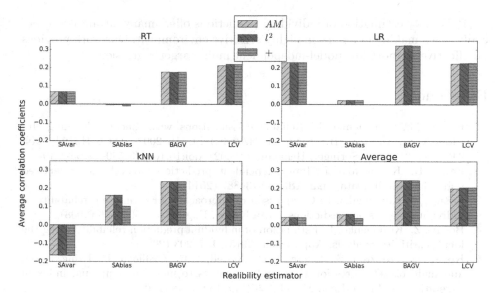

Fig. 2. Average Pearson correlation coefficients for reliability estimate variants AM, l^2 and + for different regression models.

From the results we can see that all of the proposed estimate variants achieve the highest average correlations with reliability estimates $BAGV$ (average correlation around 0.24) and LCV (average correlation around 0.20), while $SAvar$ and $SAbias$ perform worse. They both score an average correlation coefficient lower than 0.1 and did not reach the average bound for statistical significance.

5   Conclusion

In the paper we proposed several approaches for estimating the reliabilities of individual multi-target regression predictions. The aggregated variants (AM, l^2 and +) produce a single-valued estimate which is preferable for interpretation and comparison. The last variant (+) is a direct generalization of the single-target estimators from the related work.

Our evaluation showed that best results were achieved using the $BAGV$ and the LCV reliability estimates regardless the estimate variant. This complies with the related work on the single-target predictions, where these two estimates also performed well. Although all of the proposed variants achieve comparable results, our proposed generalization of existing methods (+) is still the preferred variant due to its lower computational complexity (as estimates are only calculated once for all of the target attributes) and the solid theoretical background.

In our further work we intend to additionally evaluate other reliability estimates in combination with several other regression models. We also plan to test the adaptation of the proposed methods to multi-target classification.

Reliability estimation of individual predictions offers many advantages especially when making decisions in highly sensitive environment. Our work provides an effective support for model-independent multi-target regression.

References

1. Kukar, M., Kononenko, I.: Reliable classifications with machine learning. In: Elomaa, T., Mannila, H., Toivonen, H. (eds.) ECML 2002. LNCS (LNAI), vol. 2430, pp. 219–231. Springer, Heidelberg (2002). doi:10.1007/3-540-36755-1_19
2. Pevec, D., Kononenko, I.: Input dependent prediction intervals for supervised regression. Intell. Data Anal. **18**(5), 873–887 (2014)
3. Bosnić, Z., Kononenko, I.: Comparison of approaches for estimating reliability of individual regression predictions. Data Knowl. Eng. **67**(3), 504–516 (2008)
4. Bosnić, Z., Kononenko, I.: Estimation of individual prediction reliability using the local sensitivity analysis. Appl. Intell. **29**(3), 187–203 (2008)
5. Kocev, D., Džeroski, S., White, M.D., Newell, G.R., Griffioen, P.: Using single- and multi-target regression trees and ensembles to model a compound index of vegetation condition. Ecol. Model. **220**(8), 1159–1168 (2009)
6. Kocev, D., Vens, C., Struyf, J., Džeroski, S.: Ensembles of multi-objective decision trees. In: Kok, J.N., Koronacki, J., Mantaras, R.L., Matwin, S., Mladenič, D., Skowron, A. (eds.) ECML 2007. LNCS (LNAI), vol. 4701, pp. 624–631. Springer, Heidelberg (2007). doi:10.1007/978-3-540-74958-5_61
7. Breiman, L., Friedman, J., Stone, C.J., Olshen, R.A.: Classification and Regression Trees. CRC Press, New York (1984)
8. Segal, M.R.: Tree-structured methods for longitudinal data. J. Am. Stat. Assoc. **87**(418), 407–418 (1992)
9. De'Ath, G.: Multivariate regression trees: a new technique for modeling species-environment relationships. Ecology **83**(4), 1105–1117 (2002)
10. Struyf, J., Džeroski, S.: Constraint based induction of multi-objective regression trees. In: Bonchi, F., Boulicaut, J.-F. (eds.) KDID 2005. LNCS, vol. 3933, pp. 222–233. Springer, Heidelberg (2006). doi:10.1007/11733492_13
11. Blockeel, H., De Raedt, L., Ramon, J.: Top-down induction of clustering trees (2000). arXiv preprint: arXiv:cs/0011032
12. Segal, M., Xiao, Y.: Multivariate random forests. Wiley Interdisc. Rev.: Data Min. Knowl. Discov. **1**(1), 80–87 (2011)
13. Džeroski, S., Ženko, B.: Stacking with multi-response model trees. In: Roli, F., Kittler, J. (eds.) MCS 2002. LNCS, vol. 2364, pp. 201–211. Springer, Heidelberg (2002). doi:10.1007/3-540-45428-4_20
14. Golub, G., Kahan, W.: Calculating the singular values and pseudo-inverse of a matrix. J. Soc. Ind. Appl. Math. Ser. B: Numer. Anal. **2**(2), 205–224 (1965)
15. Tsoumakas, G., Katakis, I., Vlahavas, I.: Mining multi-label data. In: Maimon, O., Rokach, L. (eds.) Data Mining and Knowledge Discovery Handbook, pp. 667–685. Springer, New York (2009)
16. Lichman, M.: UCI machine learning repository. School of Information and Computer Sciences, University of California, Irvine (2013). http://archive.ics.uci.edu/ml
17. Pedregosa, F., Varoquaux, G., Gramfort, A., Michel, V., Thirion, B., Grisel, O., Blondel, M., Prettenhofer, P., Weiss, R., Dubourg, V., Vanderplas, J., Passos, A., Cournapeau, D., Brucher, M., Perrot, M., Duchesnay, E.: Scikit-learn: machine learning in Python. J. Mach. Learn. Res. **12**, 2825–2830 (2011)

Feedback Modulated Attention Within a Predictive Framework

Benjamin Cowley$^{(\boxtimes)}$ and John Thornton

School of ICT, Institute for Integrated and Intelligent Systems,
Griffith University, Brisbane, Australia
benjamin.cowley@griffithuni.edu.au,
j.thornton@griffith.edu.au

Abstract. Attention is both ubiquitous throughout and key to our cognitive experience. It has been shown to filter out mundane stimuli, while simultaneously communicating specific stimuli from the lowest levels of perception through to the highest levels of cognition. In this paper we present a connectionist system with mechanisms that produce both exogenous (bottom-up) and endogenous (top-down) attention. The foundational algorithm of our system is the Temporal Pooler (TP), a neocortically inspired algorithm that learns and predicts temporal sequences. We make a number of modifications to the Temporal Pooler and place it in a framework which is inspired by predictive coding. We use a novel technique in which feedback connections elicit endogenous attention by disrupting the learned representations of attended sequences. Our experiments show that this approach successfully filters attended stimuli and suppresses unattended stimuli.

Keywords: Attention · Hierarchical Temporal Memory · Predictive coding

1 Introduction

Attention lies at the heart of cognitive experience. It enables our conscious perception to focus upon specific elements within the vast and dynamic sensorium. It manifests in many forms: following an object along the horizon, concentrating on a melody, or mentally solving a mathematical problem. This ubiquity suggests that attentional mechanisms must be intrinsic to any truly biological approach to artificial intelligence.

It has been proposed that attention plays a role in the earliest levels of cognition and perception, acting to *filter* out stimuli that are not selected as the target of attention [3,13]. Under this paradigm only the attended stimulus reaches the highest levels of cognition, while unattended stimuli are filtered out at the early levels of sensory perception. This filtering of stimuli is also reflected in neural recordings, where attention has been shown to enhance the responses of neurons in the neocortex that encode the attended stimulus, while simultaneously suppressing that of unattended stimuli [17,21]. The ability to filter specific stimulus

© Springer International Publishing AG 2017
M. Wagner et al. (Eds.): ACALCI 2017, LNAI 10142, pp. 61–73, 2017.
DOI: 10.1007/978-3-319-51691-2_6

has obvious advantages to artificial intelligence systems (e.g. reducing the problem space), as such there has been a renewed interest in applying attentional mechanisms to connectionist systems in recent years (we discuss some of this work in Sect. 2).

Our model fits into a broad body of work that understands the brain as a prediction machine which self-organises to form generative predictions (or hypotheses) of its current and future states. Predictive coding [4,19] has emerged as the most promising interpretation of this theory, with top-down and lateral predictions suppressing the responses of feature encoding *error-units*. This flow of information and forming of hypotheses has since been generalised as free-energy minimisation by Friston [8].

Our model attempts to reconcile attentional filtering with predictive suppression of stimuli. Lateral predictions (formed in the same neocortical region) suppress the feedforward output of that region. Surprising stimulus (not predicted) are communicated as feedforward output to the higher regions. This forms an exogenous (bottom-up) attentional mechanism based on the Bayesian surprise theory of exogenous attention, where the least predictable stimulus is the most salient [11] (note that free-energy can also be formulated as Bayesian surprise [8]). Endogenous (top-down) attention is modulated by feedback that causes a targeted disruption in the learned representations. This disruption inhibits predictions on attended stimuli, and thus the attended stimuli is output from the region using the same feedforward pathway as endogenous attention.

For simplicity, and to focus on the mechanisms of extracting information using attention, we implement our model in a single layer system. The foundational algorithm for this system is the Temporal Pooler (TP) [9]. TP is a connectionist algorithm that has been shown to perform strongly in the domain of on-line learning anomaly detection [15]. To the TP we add feedback connections, new types of neurons, and place it in a predictive framework inspired by predictive coding; we refer to this system as Temporal Pooler plus Attention (TP+A).

The TP algorithm is based on the Hierarchical Temporal Memory (HTM) model of the neocortex [10], a predictive model similar to predictive coding, and employs a number of components directly based on neocortical biology. TP neurons self-organise using a Hebbian learning inspired method to form *synapses* to a subset of other neurons, in contrast to many deep learning systems that use less biologically plausible methods, such as backpropagation on fully connected neurons [2]. To implement attentional mechanisms we use the same basic learning policies and structures as TP, thereby inheriting the biological plausibility of the HTM approach. In this way TP+A provides a model for how attention may be implemented in the neocortex, while simultaneously providing a proof-of-concept for a system that could be incorporated into future AI systems.

2   Related Work

In recent years there have been an increasing number of studies applying attentional mechanisms to connectionist systems, with much of this work focusing on visual attention. One such approach is to select only part of an image to be processed at high resolution [24]. This method has been successfully applied to a number of domains, including object tracking [5], recognition [5,24], and image caption generation [1]. Another method applied to connectionist systems is to use attentional mechanisms to modulate representational nodes in the system. Wang et al. [25] used two separate neural networks, one encoding the input and the other encoding top-down prior beliefs of the input's class; the output vectors of both networks were combined to produce a modified representation of the output. This approach was applied to classifying and de-noising handwritten digits. Attention inspired techniques have also been used to improve the classification of images using convolutional neural networks [23]. Here feature nodes of the network were modulated over successive time-steps using a reinforcement learning policy.

There have been a number of models that attempt to reconcile various attention related phenomena with predictive coding. Rao and Ballard [20] expanded their earlier work on predictive coding in the visual cortex [19] by showing how attentional visual search may work. They applied an outlier mask that suppressed stimuli which least conformed to a generative model, while making stimuli that were more likely under the generative model to be more salient. Subsequently Spratling [22] also expanded Rao and Ballard's original work by showing that their equations are mathematically identical to some models of bias competition, a theory that attention emerges through the modulation of representational nodes by bias weighting [6]. To demonstrate this model, feedback signals, which simulated endogenous attention, were fed into the system and resulted in phenomena consistent with binding. Perhaps the most prevalent theory of attention in predictive coding is that of precision weighting [4,7]. This is achieved by increasing the 'gain' on error units that are predicted to provide the most precise information vis-à-vis the current environment.

Applying TP to a framework based on predictive coding is similar to work of McCall and Franklin [16], who embedded TP in a predictive coding framework and tested it for robustness to noise on random temporal sequences. Their system uses two hierarchical layers, where the feedforward output from the bottom layer is the prediction-error. This is formed by subtracting the state of the bottom layer from feedback sent from the top layer. Feedforward and feedback use bi-directional connections, in contrast to a method introduced by Kneller and Thornton [12] which uses separate, more biologically plausible, uni-directional connections. Here, feedback connections are formed using TP's learning method, while feedforward connections use the HTM spatial pooler algorithm.

3   Temporal Pooler Plus Attention

TP+A is designed to perform five tasks: (1) form predictions on temporal sequences; (2) output prediction errors; (3) output temporal sequences that are the target of attention (attentional filtering); (4) learn temporal sequences; (5) learn relationships between attention signals and the temporal sequences. Tasks 1 and 4 are performed using the TP algorithm (described in Subsects. 3.1 and 3.4), task 2 is accomplished by embedding the TP in a framework inspired by predictive coding (described in Subsect. 3.2), and tasks 3 and 5 are achieved using our attentional feedback mechanism (described in Subsects. 3.3 and 3.4).

3.1   Predicting Temporal Sequences

TP+A forms predictions on feedforward input formatted as sparse temporal sequences; we use the TP algorithm to make these predictions. TP was initially developed as part of the Cortical Learning Algorithms package (CLA) [9], which also included the HTM spatial pooler. TP comprises a number of structures named *columns*, which are based on mini-columns found in the neocortex [18]. Columns can be set into an *active-state* by feedforward boolean input. The resulting activation and deactivation of the columns over successive time-steps forms the temporal sequences on which the system learns and predicts.

Each column contains a number of artificial neurons called *prediction-cells* [9]. Prediction-cells have a number of dendrite *segments*, and each segment contains a number of *synapses*. Synapses are uni-directional connections to prediction-cells in other columns that become active when the prediction-cell they are connected to is in an active-state. When the number of active synapses in a segment is greater than the value of parameter *actiThreshold* the segment enters an active-state. This, in turn, sets the prediction-cell into a *predictive-state*. When a column enters an active-state and one of its prediction-cells was in a predictive-state, that prediction-cell enters an active-state. If, however, a column is in an active-state and no prediction-cell was in a predictive-state then all prediction-cells in that column enter an active-state, representing that any number of temporal features could have activated the column. It is through this method that TP encodes and produces predictions on temporal sequences; for a more in-depth discussion of the algorithm see the CLA white paper [9].

3.2   Outputting the Prediction Error

TP+A applies the TP within a framework based on predictive coding. Our method differs somewhat from McCall and Franklin [16] who used bi-directional connections between levels to form and communicate errors and predictions. Because our study only concerns a single level we only rely on the lateral predictions (formed by TP) to detect errors. The errors are output by adding a new type of cell to the TP called an *error-cell*. Each column has one error-cell. When a column is active and this activity was not predicted by a prediction-cell then the error cell will be in an active-state. The state of each error-cell will

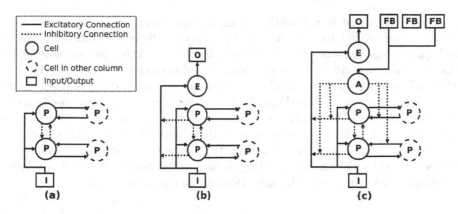

Fig. 1. Diagram of connections within columns. P: prediction-cell, I: input, O: output, E: error-cell, FB: feedback input, A: attention cell. Arrows indicate direction of information flow. (a) TP column; excitatory connections between prediction-cells can put them into a predictive-state, if placed into an active-state when in a predictive-state, they will inhibit other prediction-cells in their column. (b) TP column embedded in a predictive architecture; output is produced by an error-cell, which is set into an active-state by a connection to the input, active prediction-cells inhibit this connection. (c) TP+A column; an attention-cell is excited by feedback axons. When active, the attention-cell inhibits the inhibitory connections to the input/error-cell connection and also the dendrite segments of that synapse to prediction-cells in its column.

comprise the feedforward output of TP+A. In Fig. 1b we provide a diagram of a TP column and its connections embedded in this system.

3.3   Attentional Filtering

Our model uses top-down signals to elicit endogenous attention. In TP+A we achieve this using feedback *axons* that input sparse codes into the system. A new type of cell, the *attention-cell*, associates this sparse code with activation of its column. Each column has a single attention-cell and these have a number of segments with a number of synapses that can connect to an axon. The activity of these synapses and segments determine whether or not the attention-cell is placed into an active-state using the same method that determines the predictive-state of prediction-cells (outlined in Subsect. 3.1). The method we use for connecting to feedback is the same as Kneller and Thornton [12], however in experiments they used the Spatial Pooler algorithm and not the TP (so time-steps were not a factor); the feedback also did not elicit endogenous attention.

If an attention-cell is in an active-state, then the error-cell of its column will also be in an active-state whenever the column is active-state, even if this activity was predicted. This causes attended sequences to be output by the error-cells, where usually they would be suppressed. By using the error-cells to output attended sequences we remove any need for adding new output channels or separate data representations. A second effect elicited by an attention-cell when in an active-state is that it will *inhibit* (make inactive) segments of prediction-cells in other columns that have synapses to prediction-cells in its column. Columns which have prediction-cells that have been inhibited in this way are more likely to be in an active-state that was not predicted, due to the disruption of the prediction process caused by the inhibition. This, counter-intuitively, is of benefit as the segments that are inhibited are likely to be forming predictions based on the attended sequence. Thus, column activations caused by an attended sequence can be output by the error-cells even if that column's attention-cell has not learned the feedback pattern, preserving the associations between column activations learned by TP when outputting an attended sequence. Figure 1c provides a diagram of a column with the attention-cell and its connections.

3.4   Learning

Both prediction-cells and attention-cells use the same TP Hebbian-based learning algorithm [9]. In prediction-cells this algorithm governs the creation and destruction of synapses to prediction-cells in other columns, while in attention-cells it governs the connection of synapses to feedback axons. For improved clarity we have also included pseudo-code in Algorithm 1 which has been generalised for use with both prediction-cells and attention-cells.

Algorithm 1. Learning Under the Markov Assumption

Input: *column* //column learning is to be performed on
Input: t //current time-step
Input: $newSyns, minThreshold, connThresh, permInc, permDec$ //parameters
 1: **if** $column.isActiveAndNotPredicted(t)$ **then**
 2:    $potSyns \leftarrow getActivePotentialSynapses(t - 1)$
 3:    $segment \leftarrow findClosestSegment(column, potSyns, minThreshold)$
 4:    **if** $segment = null$ **then**
 5:       $cell \leftarrow getRandomCell(column)$
 6:       $createNewSegment(cell, potSyns, newSyns)$
 7:    **else**
 8:       $addNewSynapses(segment, potSyns, newSyns)$
 9: **else if** $column.isActiveAndPredicted(t)$ **then**
10:    **for each** $cell$ **in** $column$ **where** $cell.inPredictiveState(t - 1)$ **do**
11:       **for each** $segment$ **in** $cell$ **where** $segment.active$ **do**
12:          **for each** $synapse$ **in** $segment$ **where** $synapse.active$ **do**
13:             $incrementPermanence(synapse, permInc, connThresh)$
14: **else if** $column.isInactiveAndPredicted(t)$ **then**
15:    **for each** $cell$ **in** $column$ **where** $cell.inPredictiveState(t - 1)$ **do**
16:       **for each** $segment$ **in** $cell$ **where** $segment.active$ **do**
17:          **for each** $synapse$ **in** $segment$ **where** $synapse.active$ **do**
18:             $decrementPermanence(synapse, permDec, connThresh)$

Cells are initialised with no synapses or segments, these are first created in response to column activity. Whenever a column is in an active-state and this was not predicted by any of its prediction-cells (or, in the case of learning feedback, its attention-cell was not in an active-state), we add new synapses to a cell (lines 1–8). We search all cells for a single segment that has the greatest overlap with the set of potential synapses (other prediction-cells for prediction-cell learning, or feedback axons for attention-cell learning) that were active in the previous time-step; we then add a number of synapses up to the value of parameter *newSyns* to the chosen segment (line 8). If no segment had an overlap above parameter *minThresh* then we add a new segment to a random cell (line 6), this segment will have the value of *newSyns* of the potential synapses. Each synapse has a *permanence* value; when the permanence value is above parameter *connThresh* the synapse is *connected* and can affect their cell's state, otherwise it will be *disconnected* and cannot affect their cell's state. Synapse permanence is decremented by the value of *permDec* whenever the synapse contributes to a cell falsely predicting its column will be active (lines 14–18; disconnecting of a synapse is handled by *decrementPermanence()*). Synapses have their permanence incremented by the value of *permInc* whenever they were in an active-state and their segment correctly predicts their column will be active, even if they are disconnected (lines 9–13; connecting of a synapse is handled by *incrementPermanence()*). This is the method that the TP uses for learning under the Markov assumption (only the current time-step can predict the next), but the TP can learn to predict further in time by engaging this method to learn the cells which were active the time step prior to a successful prediction. However, for efficiency we learn under the Markov assumption in this treatment.

4   Experiments and Analysis

To test whether the TP+A can successfully attentionally filter sequence input we performed experiments using two separate input types: *burst sequences* (which allows us to easily visualise the output) and *frequent feature sequences* (to test filtering when a subset of columns in a sequence are persistently active).

We use a similar experimental design across all tests. The TP+A has 256 columns and at each time-step is fed a sparse binary input of length 256, where one element activates one column. We use a single iteration of a 150,000 time-step training set; between time-step 100,000 and 125,000 whenever a target sequence is active we apply feedback input that simulates top-down input from a higher level. The feedback is a randomly generated sparse binary pattern with 256 elements where each element has 0.025 chance of been set to one. Each element of this pattern corresponds to a single feedback axon, an element set to one sets its corresponding axon to active. After training, we switch off learning and use a 10,000 time-step test set that we apply both with attentional feedback and without. We used the prediction error on the test set to tune the values of *permInc, permDec, connPerm,* and *actiThreshold* for both prediction-cell and attention-cell synapses. The number of cells used is 15; exploratory experiments showed that this number performed robustly across both sequence types. The quantitative results given are averaged across 10 experimental runs, using different random seeds for the TP+A. To quantify output for particular sequences

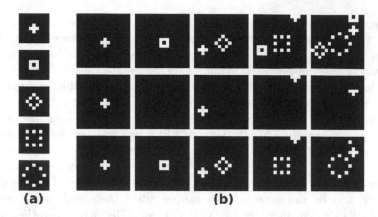

Fig. 2. (a) A sample of a sequence used during the burst sequence tests; white squares are active columns, black squares represent no column activity; the top image is the first time-step, and the bottom image is the fifth and final time-step. (b) A sample of five time-steps (running left to right) of testing; the first row is the input, second row is the system without attention active, and the third row is the system with attention on; the middle burst is the target of attention.

we use the *sequence error* metric, this is the number of activations of error-cells divided by the number of column activations for each time-step after the first (we exclude the first as a sequence begins at random in our experiments).

4.1   Burst Sequences

For the first of our experiments we use feedforward input that comprises sequences which, when formatted in two dimensions, form a distinct visual 'bursting' pattern. These type of sequences were used to allow us to better display the attentional mechanisms; an example of the sequence is shown in Fig. 2a. The sequences are five time-steps long and can occur at 64 possible starting positions. Given that a single TP/TP+A region is not translation invariant, each starting position constitutes a separate sequence. We used the following methodology for producing the input: at each time-step a sequence has a probability of 0.005 of becoming active (unless it is already active, in which case the probability is 0.0); if no sequence is currently active we randomly select one to become active (this is done to ensure there is column activity on every time-step). We select one sequence to be the target sequence for the attentional feedback mechanism.

A sample of the output from TP+A during testing is illustrated in Fig. 2b; where the sequence located in the centre is the target of endogenous attention by way of feedback. In the second row we see that when there is no active feedback TP+A suppresses the majority of input; as sequences begin at random, the first instances will be mostly unpredicted. The third row displays similar suppression as the second, except for the target burst which is output in its entirety. However, some imperfections in the system are also illustrated; in the last time-step we can see that one element of a newly beginning sequence is suppressed without attention, while during attention it is not suppressed, as is an element of the sequence beginning the previous time-step. These irregularities are caused by the interactions between simultaneous sequences and the attention mechanism. The predicted element in the newly beginning sequence would, had the sequence not started, be a false prediction. However, when attention is active the disruption caused by the attention cell incorrectly causes output not associated with the target sequence. This is reflected in a quantitative analysis: during testing when attention is not active sequence error for the unattended sequences is 0.02, rising to 0.22 when it is active. However countering this is the sequence error for the attended sequences where the mean average for this set is a perfect 1.0 (i.e. the entirety of the attended sequences is output). These results indicate that on this set TP+A's attention mechanisms have successfully learned to output attended sequences, although there is some residual output of unattended sequences.

4.2 Frequent Feature Sequences

The frequent feature sequences experiments are designed to test TP+A's attentional mechanisms when the sequences contain frequently recurring features. This is of interest as attended stimuli commonly have such features (e.g. a stationary object, or auditory frequencies). To build the target sequence we chose 15 distinct input elements at random; each of these elements we assign a probability, p, that it will be active on any give time-step (8 have $p = 0.2$, 4 have $p = 0.4$, 2 have $p = 0.6$, 1 have $p = 0.8$). We also have five background sequences with 30 elements chosen at random (these each have $p = 0.2$), these five sequences are concatenated to form a 100 time-step long background sequence that is fed into TP+A and continuously looped during training and testing. The target sequence will be fed into the system at random time-steps (with a probability of 0.01; or 0.0 if it is already active) and will overlap with the background sequences.

The results from these experiments show an improvement over the bursting sequences vis-à-vis the sequence error for non-attended sequences (the background) during attention: with an average of 0.02; compared with 0.01 with no attention. The target sequence averages 0.95 sequence error during attention, compared with 0.02 when not attended. These results indicate that features occurring frequently within a single sequence may improve the capability of TP+A in separating the target sequence. In Fig. 3a we have included a graph of error-cell activity during endogenous attention; note that while error-cells related to target sequence are very active, those for the background are much less so.

To ascertain the exogenous attention capabilities of the system, we inserted an extra sequence (constructed with the same methodology as the target sequence) during testing. There was no training on this sequence, so the system should be 'surprised' by the sequence and output it as error. We graph these results in Fig. 3b; as can be seen this sequence is highly active, while the background sequence is largely suppressed. The average sequence error for the surprising sequence is 0.97, while the background is >0.01. This shows that the TP+A outputs surprising input, while suppressing predictable input.

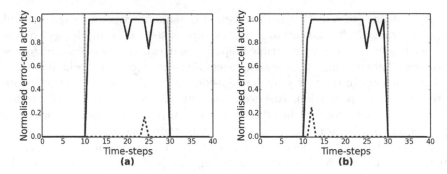

Fig. 3. Graph of error-cell activity, normalised so maximum possible activity is 1.0; solid line is target sequence, dashed line is background sequences, vertical dotted lines designate beginning and end of sequence. (a) Error-cell activity during endogenous attention. (b) Error-cell activity with a surprising sequence (exogenous attention).

5   Discussion

In this work we have presented a model implemented as a connectionist system, TP+A, which is based on two separate theories of neocortical function, HTM and predictive coding. This system is designed to attentionally filter sequences using biologically plausible methods such as feedback, inhibition, and Hebbian learning. Results from our experiments, provided in Sect. 4, show that TP+A is capable of filtering out mundane (predicted) input sequences while simultaneously outputting sequences that are attended to. This paradigm of attention is in line with results from cognitive studies that show early levels of perception filter out unattended stimulus while conveying attended stimulus [13]. The use of feedback connections to illicit this type of attention makes this mechanism akin to endogenous attention, where the higher levels of cognition (or, in our case, higher levels of the hierarchy) control the attentional mechanisms of the lower levels. As well as endogenously attended input, TP+A will also relay any input that is surprising (unpredicted). Because TP+A uses the same output channel for both surprising and attended input, higher levels of the hierarchy would treat these signals identically. This is advantageous because a surprising stimulus should, and does, attract attention; studies have shown that in free viewing exercises participants attention is directed to the most 'surprising' features of scenes [11].

TP is designed to be a general purpose algorithm, capable in operating under any temporal modality. TP+A inherits this and adds to it mechanisms for both exogenous and endogenous attention. This goal of generality sets aside TP+A from many other connectionist attention systems which are specific to visual attention [5,14]. We also use biologically inspired learning methods that exist in the original TP in contrast to systems which apply the less biologically plausbile backpropagation (such as [25]), or systems that require the combination of divergent techniques (such as backpropagation and reinforcement learning [23]).

TP+A offers two advantages over the precision weighting accounting of attention in predictive coding [7]. Firstly, TP+A has the internal resources to calculate the precision of error signals without predictive coding's need of a secondary system that learns to predict such precisions. This can be achieved by an analysis of the state of the TP (within a HTM hierarchy): here, a high precision error state is indicated by a small number of temporally extended sequences, whereas a low precision state is indicated by a larger number of shorter sequences. Secondly, the TP+A approach does not require that we only attend to those aspects of a feature that are associated with high precision error signals. So, for example, we can endogenously attend to features that are perfectly predicted (and so emit no error signals), or we can attend to aspects of a feature associated with relatively low precision and ignore aspects with high precision errors. The phenomenology of ordinary experience suggests that we can endogenously attend in this way, but existing predictive coding models have difficulty explaining this. Our model of attention matches more closely to that of Spratling [22], who also used simulated feedback to stimulate endogenous attention. However, this model was focused on binding (where disparate features are 'bound' into a singular object), whereas ours reconciles predictive suppression with filtering. Binding in our model, could be achieved in a hierarchical system where associations between different input streams are learned at higher levels of the hierarchy. However, with our use of the TP algorithm, TP+A could be said to apply binding of *locally* encoded features, which are then fed upward due to the dendrite inhibition mechanism.

Future work will focus on the incorporation of TP+A into a hierarchy, where higher layers would need mechanisms to automatically elicit endogenous attention from lower layers, instead of simulating this feature as we did in this treatment. A fully functioning HTM hierarchy that is capable of action, attention, and recognition is still only theoretical. Through the inclusion of a mechanism for attention we believe we have made a significant step towards this goal.

6 Conclusion

We have presented a model for attention in a framework where prediction errors are suppressed. We proposed that endogenously triggered attentional filtering could be achieved through the targeted disruption of predictions. To implement this model we placed the neocortically inspired TP algorithm into a framework inspired by predictive coding. We added feedback mechanisms and a new neuron, the attention-cell; we refer to this connectionist system as TP+A. Our experiments show that TP+A successfully displayed phenomena consistent with both endogenous and exogenous attention. Future work will focus on integrating TP+A into a hierarchical system.

References

1. Ba, J., Salakhutdinov, R.R., Grosse, R.B., Frey, B.J.: Learning wake-sleep recurrent attention models. In: Advances in Neural Information Processing Systems, pp. 2575–2583 (2015)
2. Bengio, Y., Lee, D.H., Bornschein, J., Lin, Z.: Towards biologically plausible deep learning (2015). arXiv preprint: arXiv:1502.04156
3. Broadbent, D.E.: Perception and Communication. Oxford University Press, Oxford (1958)
4. Clark, A.: Surfing Uncertainty: Prediction, Action, and the Embodied Mind. Oxford University Press, Oxford (2015)
5. Denil, M., Bazzani, L., Larochelle, H., de Freitas, N.: Learning where to attend with deep architectures for image tracking. Neural Comput. **24**(8), 2151–2184 (2012)
6. Desimone, R., Duncan, J.: Neural mechanisms of selective visual attention. Annu. Rev. Neurosci. **18**(1), 193–222 (1995)
7. Feldman, H., Friston, K.J.: Attention, uncertainty, and free-energy. Front. Hum. Neurosci. **4**, 215 (2010)
8. Friston, K.: The free-energy principle: a unified brain theory? Nat. Rev. Neurosci. **11**(2), 127–138 (2010)
9. Hawkins, J., Ahmad, S., Dubinsky, D.: Hierarchical temporal memory including HTM cortical learning algorithms. Technical report, Numenta, Inc., Palto Alto (2010)
10. Hawkins, J., Blakeslee, S.: On Intelligence. Macmillan, New York (2007)
11. Itti, L., Baldi, P.F.: Bayesian surprise attracts human attention. In: Advances in Neural Information Processing Systems, pp. 547–554 (2005)
12. Kneller, A., Thornton, J.: Distal dendrite feedback in hierarchical temporal memory. In: Proceedings of the 2015 International Joint Conference on Neural Networks (2015)
13. Lachter, J., Forster, K.I., Ruthruff, E.: Forty-five years after broadbent (1958): still no identification without attention. Psychol. Rev. **111**(4), 880 (2004)
14. Larochelle, H., Hinton, G.E.: Learning to combine foveal glimpses with a third-order Boltzmann machine. In: Advances in Neural Information Processing Systems, pp. 1243–1251 (2010)
15. Lavin, A., Ahmad, S.: Evaluating real-time anomaly detection algorithms - the numenta anomaly bench. In: 14th International Conference on Machine Learning and Applications (2015)
16. McCall, R., Franklin, S.: Cortical learning algorithms with predictive coding for a systems-level cognitive architecture. In: Second Annual Conference on Advances in Cognitive Systems Poster Collection, pp. 149–166 (2013)
17. Moran, J., Desimone, R.: Selective attention gates visual processing in the extrastriate cortex. Science **229**(4715), 782–784 (1985)
18. Mountcastle, V.B.: The columnar organization of the neocortex. Brain **120**(4), 701–722 (1997)
19. Rao, R.P., Ballard, D.H.: Predictive coding in the visual cortex: a functional interpretation of some extra-classical receptive-field effects. Nat. Neurosci. **2**(1), 79–87 (1999)
20. Rao, R.P., Ballard, D.H.: Probabilistic models of attention based on iconic representations and predictive coding. In: Neurobiology of Attention, pp. 553–561 (2004)

21. Reynolds, J.H., Chelazzi, L.: Attentional modulation of visual processing. Annu. Rev. Neurosci. **27**, 611–647 (2004)
22. Spratling, M.W.: Predictive coding as a model of biased competition in visual attention. Vis. Res. **48**(12), 1391–1408 (2008)
23. Stollenga, M.F., Masci, J., Gomez, F., Schmidhuber, J.: Deep networks with internal selective attention through feedback connections. In: Advances in Neural Information Processing Systems, pp. 3545–3553 (2014)
24. Tang, Y., Srivastava, N., Salakhutdinov, R.R.: Learning generative models with visual attention. In: Advances in Neural Information Processing Systems, pp. 1808–1816 (2014)
25. Wang, Q., Zhang, J., Song, S., Zhang, Z.: Attentional neural network: feature selection using cognitive feedback. In: Advances in Neural Information Processing Systems, pp. 2033–2041 (2014)

A Batch Infill Strategy for Computationally Expensive Optimization Problems

Ahsanul Habib[✉], Hemant Kumar Singh, and Tapabrata Ray

School of Engineering and Information Technology,
The University of New South Wales, Canberra, ACT, Australia
ahsanul.habib@student.adfa.edu.au, {h.singh,t.ray}@adfa.edu.au
http://www.mdolab.net, http://www.unsw.adfa.edu.au

Abstract. Efficient Global Optimization (EGO) is a well established iterative scheme for solving computationally expensive optimization problems. EGO relies on an underlying Kriging model and maximizes the expected improvement (EI) function to obtain an infill (sampling) location. The Kriging model is in turn updated with this new truly evaluated solution and the process continues until the termination condition is met. The serial nature of the process limits its efficiency for applications where a *batch* of solutions can be evaluated at the same cost as a single solution. Examples of such cases include physical experiments conducted in batches for drug design and material synthesis, and computational analyses executed on parallel infrastructure. In this paper we present a multi-objective formulation to deal with such classes of problems, wherein instead of a single solution, a batch of solutions are identified for concurrent evaluation. The strategies use different objectives depending on the archive of the evaluated solutions. The performance the proposed approach is studied on a number of unconstrained and constrained benchmarks and compared with contemporary MO formulation based approaches to demonstrate its competence.

Keywords: Expensive optimization · Efficient Global Optimization · Multiple infill sampling criterion

1 Introduction and Background

In engineering optimization problems, the performance of *designs* or *solutions* are often assessed using computationally expensive simulations or physical experiments. Since computational and/or physical resources are limited, efficient optimization methods that use minimal number of evaluations to deliver the optimum solution(s) are sought. The objective(s) and constraint(s) are often highly nonlinear or even *black-box* which makes it challenging to identify optimal/near optimal solutions within a limited budget.

To deal with the above challenges, population based stochastic optimization algorithms have been used over the years coupled with approximation models. Such approaches have been extensively studied in the literature and are collectively

© Springer International Publishing AG 2017
M. Wagner et al. (Eds.): ACALCI 2017, LNAI 10142, pp. 74–85, 2017.
DOI: 10.1007/978-3-319-51691-2_7

referred to as surrogate assisted optimization (SAO). Various forms of approximations have been used in the context of SAO, such as Kriging, Response Surface Methods, Radial Basis Functions, etc., a review of which could be found in [1].

Kriging is one of the most popular models for approximations, as in addition to the predicted value, it also estimates the uncertainty in prediction. Jones et al. [2] first exploited this uncertainty measure to propose Efficient Global Optimization (EGO) approach unconstrained optimization problems. In this approach, an infill location is identified for evaluation based on maximization of the expected improvement (EI) function. For any location in the variable space, the EI function can be calculated based on the predicted response and the uncertainty associated in the prediction. Upon evaluating the solution at this infill solution, the underlying Kriging model is updated and the process continues until a stopping condition is met. The EI function consists of two parts [2], the first part, has a high value for locations where the predicted value is likely to be better than the best function value obtained so far, whereas the second part has a high value where uncertainty of the prediction is high. In literature, many variants of EGO have been proposed to balance these two components, i.e., exploration (desirable in early stages of the search) and exploitation (desirable in later stages). In one such approach, Schonlau [3] proposed a modified version of EI function referred to as generalized expected improvement (GEI), where an additional parameter g was used to achieve the control between global exploration and local exploitation. The parameter g was assigned a high value initially to facilitate global exploration (more emphasis on part-1 of EI) and was assigned a lower value in later stages to focus on local search (more emphasis on part-2 of EI). Another strategy to control these entities was suggested by Sasena [4], where g was gradually decreased over iterations.

To deal with problems involving constraints, Schonlau et al. [5] penalized the GEI values of the candidate solutions with a term probability of feasibility (PF). PF was individually computed for each constraint using a Kriging model. Assuming all constraints are independent, the overall PF can be calculated as the product of individual values. Forrester et al. [6] also suggested a similar approach, where instead of GEI, the EI function was penalized. In another study [7], the expected violation (EV) function was used instead of PF. While PF measures the probability of a candidate solution being feasible, the EV calculates the expectation of a candidate solution being infeasible. To sample near constraint boundaries, a user-defined allowable threshold value of constraint violation was suggested by Parr et al. [8]. There has also been use of screening strategies using Support Vector Machine (SVM) classifiers [9]. Solutions that are likely to be feasible were identified using the SVM classifier and the one with the best EI was evaluated. Although the approach was novel, training a SVM with limited number of samples is an issue. While a two-class classifier was used in the study, for highly constrained optimization problems, there may be only infeasible solutions to begin with.

All the methods discussed above refer to serial variants of EGO, where, the evaluation of the solution affects the underlying model through the model update process, which in turn affects the selection of the next infill location. If the user has an option and resources to evaluate multiple solutions simultaneously, such serial approaches tend to be highly inefficient. To deal with such classes of problems, batch evaluation strategies within EGO have been proposed with limited success. In [10], local optimal solutions of the GEI function was used as infill samples. On the other hand, to deal with the requirement of prescribed batch sizes, two strategies were introduced in [11] for multi-point sampling, known as *Kriging Believer* and *Constant Liar*. Although these strategies discussed about batch evaluation, the infill solutions were identified in a serial process.

Recently, Multi-objective (MO) formulations have also been suggested to deal with batches. For unconstrained problems, Feng et al. [12] suggested to consider *EI* part-1 and *EI* part-2 as two objectives of a MO problem. On the other hand, Parr et al. [13] proposed an MO formulation for solving constrained problems, where the EI and PF of each constraint were treated as separate objectives. It is important to highlight that in the presence of three or more constraints, such a formulation would result in a *many-objective* optimization problem (4 or more objectives), which are known to be significantly more difficult to solve compared to 2- or 3-objective problems [14]. Lately, Durantin et al. [15] proposed a tri-objective method where they circumvented this challenge by multiplying the individual PFs to express the combined PF as one maximization objective. The other two objectives were the EI (maximize) and the summation of prediction variance of constraints (minimize). They have included the last objective for the cases when the global optimum lies within the region where the prediction variance of the constraints are high. They might get the benefit in case of active constraints, however, for other constraints it may introduce unnecessary increase in function evaluations inside the feasible zone. Besides, although they followed an MO formulation, their method only considered single point infill strategy which was chosen based on maximum of the product of EI and PF from the non-dominated (ND) solutions.

The inspiration of this work is based on several observations from existing literature. The paper attempts to make the following contributions:

- We present a batch infill strategy which relies on a multi-objective formulation.
- This formulation takes into consideration the existing archive of all evaluated solutions. Three states are possible: (a) all solutions evaluated are infeasible (highly constrained optimization problems), (b) all solutions are feasible (typically unconstrained optimization problem, but could also be a mildly constrained problem) or (c) when at least one feasible solution has been evaluated.
- The performance of the proposed strategy is objectively analyzed using different types of problems including ones involving very low feasibility that have been rarely investigated in EGO literature.
- The performance of the strategy is quantitatively compared with contemporary multiple infill strategy based approaches.

2   Proposed Approach

This work originates from the review of multi-point (batch) infill sampling strategies and constrained EGO literature. Having discussed the background for various components in the previous section, this section briefly outlines the proposed approach. The pseudo-code of the overarching framework is presented in Algorithm 1. The details of each components are also elaborated in consequent subsections.

Algorithm 1. MO-EGOg: Generalized MO based Efficient Global Optimization with batch evaluation of infill samples

Input: N = No. of initial samples, q = No. of constraints, k = No. of infill samples per iteration, Archive = Repository of all truly evaluated solutions

Stopping Condition: $FE_{max} = 100 \times d$; where d is the no. of variables.

```
1:  FE = 0
2:  pop_init ← initialize()
3:  evaluate(pop_init)
4:  Archive ← archive update(pop_init)
5:  (x_best, f_best) ← update best solution(Archive)
6:  Models ← construct Kriging models(Archive)
7:  while FE < FE_max do
8:      x_infills ← identify infill samples()
9:      evaluate(x_infills)
10:     Archive ← archive update(Archive, x_infills)
11:     Models ← update Kriging models(Archive)
12:     (x_best, f_best) ← update best solution(Archive)
13:     FE = FE + k
14: end while
15: Return: x_best and f_best
```

2.1   Initialization

A predefined number of solutions is generated initially within the given variable bounds. Here, we have employed Latin Hypercube Sampling (LHS) method; although, any other method such as – random generation or full-factorial design can be used.

2.2   Archive Update

Upon generating the initial solutions, their corresponding objective and constraint responses are evaluated parallely and the values are reserved in the Archive, which is updated any time a new sample is evaluated.

2.3   Constructing/Updating Kriging Models

All unique solutions from the Archive are used to construct the Kriging models separately for each objective and constraints.

2.4   Identifying Infill Samples

In this approach, an MO problem needs to be solved initially to generate a set of candidate solutions. Later, the infill samples are selected from this candidate solutions set. The whole process consist of the following steps–

Assigning Objectives in MO Optimization Problem

Our proposed approach requires solving an MO problem (bi-objective in this study) to generate the candidate solutions. However, the objectives of the MO problem depend upon the history of the archived solutions. There can be three possible scenarios in which the objectives are assigned in following manners–

- When all archived solutions are infeasible, the best solution is the one having minimum constraint violation measure, cv_{min}. The objectives are hence, $EI^{cv_{min}}$ and PF. Here, $EI^{cv_{min}}$ denotes the EI which is computed with respect to the objective response of the solution having minimum constraint violation.
- If one or more feasible solutions exist among the archived solutions, the objectives are both parts of EI (calculated with respect to the best feasible objective response) penalized by the PF, which we indicate as, $EI_1^{f_{min(feas)}} \times PF$ and $EI_2^{f_{min(feas)}} \times PF$.
- Finally, if there are all feasible solutions in the archive, the objectives are the two parts of EI. We symbolize them as EI_1 and EI_2.

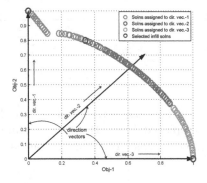

Fig. 1. Generation of direction vectors for $k = 3$ and selection of infill samples from candidate ND solutions.

Solving the MO Problem and Finding Infill Samples

Solving the above-mentioned bi-objective optimization problem results in a ND front (say, $\mathbf{P}$) with corresponding ND set of variables (say, $\mathbf{Q}$). Any MO optimization algorithm can be used to solve this problem. In our study, we have used NSGA-II algorithm [16]. Now, selecting the infill samples from the candidate ND set of solutions is done with the following steps–

- Construct $\mathbf{dir}_{1:k}$ in the objective space via normal boundary intersection (NBI) [17] (see Fig. 1 for $k = 3$) in a clockwise manner, i.e., $\mathbf{dir}_1$ is along *Obj-k* ... $\mathbf{dir}_k$ is along *Obj-1*.
- Calculate $\mathbf{p_{dist}}$, the perpendicular distances from all points in $\mathbf{P}$ to all vectors in $\mathbf{dir}$.
- Assign all $\mathbf{P}$ (and $\mathbf{Q}$) to one of $\mathbf{dir}_{1:k}$ based on minimum $\mathbf{p_{dist}}$. For equal $\mathbf{p_{dist}}$, assign them randomly.
- Group all $\mathbf{P}$s assigned along k^{th} direction into $\mathbf{G}_k$.
- Find $\mathbf{P}_1$ and $\mathbf{P}_k$, two extreme points of $\mathbf{P}$, from $\mathbf{G}_1$ and $\mathbf{G}_k$.
- Find $\mathbf{x}_1$ and $\mathbf{x}_k$ from $\mathbf{Q}$ which are the corresponding solutions of $\mathbf{P}_1$ and $\mathbf{P}_k$.
- Store $\mathbf{x}_1$ and $\mathbf{x}_k$ as $\mathbf{x}_{infills}$.
- Remove $\mathbf{dir}_1$ and $\mathbf{dir}_k$ from $\mathbf{dir}$.
- Similarly, remove $\mathbf{G}_1$ and $\mathbf{G}_k$ from $\mathbf{G}$.
- Select $\mathbf{x}_2 \ldots \mathbf{x}_{k-1}$ from $\mathbf{G}_2 \ldots \mathbf{G}_{k-1}$ having maximum shortest distance to an already evaluated solution and append with $\mathbf{x}_{infills}$.

2.5 Updating Best Solution

The best solution is updated whenever any new evaluated infill solution is better than the best in the Archive.

3 Numerical Experiments

In this section we will objectively assess the effectiveness of our approach by solving several numerical problems and compare with conventional single infill criterion based EGO (unconstrained and constrained) and MO based single and multiple infill criterion approaches within EGO framework.

For unconstrained problems, we compare our approach with EGO and EGO-MO [12], while for constrained problems, we compare with the approaches presented in [6,13,15]. As explained in [15], $EI \times PF$ infill criterion is the most robust among all single infill constrained handling approaches within EGO framework and appeared in the book by Forrester et al. [6]. For this reason, we have chosen this single infill approach for comparison and refer to it as *Forrester_EGO*. Similarly, the bi-objective formulation based multiple infill criterion described in Parr et al.'s work [13] is called Parr_Bi and tri-objective formulation based single infill criterion formulation depicted in Durantin et al. [15] is named as Durantin_Tri. Here, we will first perform an in-depth comparison and analyze the results delivered by the above-mentioned approaches for a batch size of 3. Later, the results will be statistically verified by batch sizes of 5 and 7.

3.1 Experimental Settings

The general settings while running MO-EGOg are– (a) Initial sample size was set to $3d - 1$, (b) Stopping condition was set as the maximum number of function evaluations which was, $100 \times d$ (where, d is the number of variables), (c) 20 independent runs were conducted using for each problem and the statistics across these runs was used to evaluate the performance of each approach.

For solving the MO problems, NSGA-II [16] was used with a population size 100 evolved over $50 \times d$ generations. The crossover distribution index was set to 20 and Crossover probability was 0.9 with mutation distribution index 30 and mutation probability $1/d$. These settings have been kept consistent throughout the study.

3.2 Performance Metrics

The performance metrics to quantitatively assess the performance are–

- **Absolute Error**: Absolute difference between the best objective value obtained after the termination of the search process and the true optimum of the problem under study.
- **Performance Profile** [18]: In this study, performance profile is used as a statistical tool for visually observing the performance of different approaches on *median absolute error (AE)* metric for the set of problems under study. The x-axis of a performance profile plot is the goal value, τ (which in this case represents the median AE of a particular approach relative to the best performing approach for a particular problem) while the y-axis, $\rho_s(\tau)$ denotes the cumulative distribution of the median AE (i.e., the percentage of problems an approach is able to solve within a factor τ with respect to the best approach). Based on this, it is possible to compare the approaches on a given level of goal value τ. Moreover, the overall performance of individual approaches can also be estimated by calculating the area $(\int \rho_s(\tau) d\tau)$ under the corresponding profile curve. The approach having a larger area is deemed performing better than others.
- **Error Boxplots** [19]: Error Boxplots from different runs are also plotted to visually observe the difference in the error of median runs as well as the robustness of the approaches. Generally, the smaller the inter-quartile range of a respective box-plot, the more that approach is immune to the randomness of the search process.
- **Wilcoxon Signed Rank (WSR) Test** [20]: WSR test is performed to determine the statistical difference of absolute errors obtained from all feasible runs between our proposed approach and other approaches for each problem under study. The " $-$ ", " $+$ " and " $\approx$ " signs mean that the distribution of the feasible results set of the respective approach has a statistically lower, higher or equivalent median values compared to our proposed approach.

3.3 Experimental Results

Unconstrained Problems: Table 1 presents the comparison based on absolute error metric for our proposed approach, EGO [2] and EGO-MO [12] for $k = 3$ based on 20 independent runs. The problems under study are Six-hump Camelback [21], Branin [21], Goldstein-price [21], Hartman-3 [22] and Hartman-6 [22].

As mentioned above, for unconstrained problems, our approach considers the same objectives in the MO formulation as EGO-MO. However, the main difference is the direction vector aided grouping and infill selection process instead of Fuzzy C-means clustering employed by the authors in [12]. The advantage of our approach is evident from the following table.

Table 1. Comparative error statistics among EGO, EGO-MO and MO-EGOg for k = 3. WSR test results are indicated as (–), (+) or (≈) for statistically lower, higher or equivalent median values compared to MO-EGOg.

Prob.	Approaches	Min	Mean	Median	Max	Std.
Camel	EGO	2.0689E-02	1.8123E-01	1.5064E-01 (+)	4.0728E-01	1.1284E-01
	EGO-MO	4.1064E-06	8.8395E-02	**2.0727E-05** (+)	6.7955E-01	1.7358E-01
	MO-EGOg	2.3948E-07	1.9205E-05	2.2112E-05	2.8330E-05	9.4472E-06
Branin	EGO	5.3518E-06	9.1751E-04	5.9051E-04 (+)	6.0869E-03	1.2871E-03
	EGO-MO	3.5815E-07	6.1213E-05	3.0239E-06 (+)	2.6986E-04	9.2453E-05
	MO-EGOg	3.6020E-07	2.0356E-05	**1.2696E-06**	1.9685E-04	4.8438E-05
Goldstein-Price	EGO	2.2613E-01	2.7668E+00	1.3932E+00 (+)	1.0946E+01	2.7215E+00
	EGO-MO	1.1155E-01	8.4426E+00	6.2782E+00 (+)	2.6493E+01	7.8166E+00
	MO-EGOg	5.1938E-06	1.4322E-04	**8.5192E-05**	7.3313E-04	1.7482E-04
Hartman-3	EGO	3.0681E-05	5.1800E-04	4.2918E-04 (+)	1.4356E-03	3.6457E-04
	EGO-MO	2.0868E-05	7.8117E-05	**3.3400E-05** (–)	3.7225E-04	9.3924E-05
	MO-EGOg	2.6571E-05	9.0364E-05	7.1093E-05	4.6946E-04	9.5815E-05
Hartman-6	EGO	1.9565E-04	3.8222E-02	1.6790E-03 (+)	1.3777E-01	5.8002E-02
	EGO-MO	2.1367E-04	3.5981E-02	1.5906E-03 (≈)	1.3914E-01	5.7833E-02
	MO-EGOg	2.3419E-04	3.9309E-02	**8.0838E-04**	1.4895E-01	6.0519E-02

From the table, one can observe that EGO-MO offers better median absolute error for 2 out of 5 problems (for Camel and Hartman-3) while our proposed approach delivers better median absolute errors in rest of the problems. However, according to the WSR test considering all 20 runs, EGO-MO has statistically significantly better median error value for Hartman-3 problem, while EGO has statistically equivalent median error value for Hartman-6 problem. For rest of the problems, our proposed approach offers statistically significantly better absolute error values. A close look at the error Boxplots in Fig. 2 obtained from all runs for all unconstrained problems will help understand the quality of each approach considering all independent runs. Moreover, the above statement can be further verified from the normalized median error performance profile plots. Here, the performance profile plots are illustrated for $k = 3, 5,$ and 7 in Fig. 4. In all cases, the plots show that, 100% (all 5 problems) are solved by all approaches for all batch sizes. However, from these plots it can be observed that the performance profile plot of our approach always lies to the left of all other performance profile plots which is the indication of having a larger area under the profile curve, hence, visually exhibiting a better performance compared to other approaches.

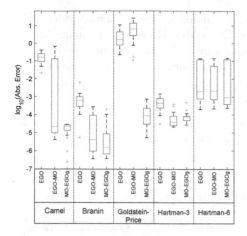

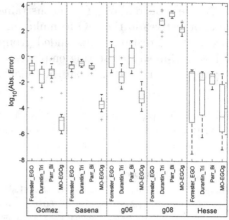

Fig. 2. Unconstrained problems error Boxplots for $k = 3$ for 20 independent runs.

Fig. 3. Constrained problems error Boxplots for $k = 3$ for 20 independent runs.

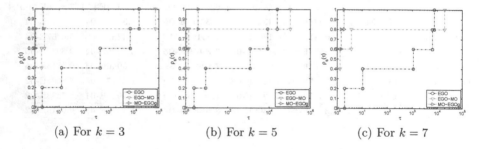

(a) For $k = 3$ (b) For $k = 5$ (c) For $k = 7$

Fig. 4. Unconstrained problems error performance profile plot for $k = 3, 5$ and 7.

Constrained Problems: Table 2 presents the comparison based on absolute error metric for our proposed approach, Forrester_EGO [6], Durantin_Tri [15] and Parr_Bi [13] for $k = 3$ based on 20 independent runs. The problems under study are Gomez [21], Sasena [4], g06 [23], g08 [23] and Hesse [24]. One notable point here is that, although the problems g06 and g08 are only 2 variable problems, the feasibility their ratios are 0.0066% and 0.8560% [23], which are extremely low. Hence, none of the initial samples were feasible in any of the 20 runs. These problems are introduced to show the effectiveness of our approach in the scenario when all initial samples are infeasible and how fast it can converge towards feasible region.

From Table 2, it can be observed that, for all constrained problems our proposed approach deliver the best median error while also being statistically significantly superior according to WSR test. Here, it is also important to take note that for g06 problem, Forrester_EGO was able to obtain feasible solution in only 1 out of 20 runs, while Parr_EGO delivered feasible solutions in 16 out of 20

Table 2. Comparative error statistics and number of feasible runs among Forrester_EGO, Parr_Bi, Durantin_Tri and MO-EGOg for $k = 3$. WSR test results are indicated as $(-)$, $(+)$ or $(\approx)$ for statistically lower, higher or equivalent median values compared to MO-EGOg.

Prob.	Approaches	Min	Mean	Median	Max	Std.	Feas. runs
Gomez	Forrester_EGO	3.7113E-03	2.1022E-01	1.5681E-01 (+)	9.1121E-01	2.0279E-01	20
	Parr_Bi	1.9731E-02	1.2911E-01	8.6955E-02 (+)	6.5044E-01	1.4653E-01	20
	Durantin_Tri	5.9248E-04	7.7087E-02	3.6043E-02 (+)	3.2955E-01	9.6259E-02	20
	MO-EGOg	9.9100E-07	7.8641E-05	**1.0369E-05**	1.3546E-03	3.0048E-04	20
Sasena	Forrester_EGO	2.2509E-02	1.7648E-01	1.9041E-01 (+)	3.7514E-01	8.9856E-02	20
	Parr_Bi	6.0158E-02	2.0950E-01	1.8361E-01 (+)	4.9128E-01	1.1660E-01	20
	Durantin_Tri	5.0094E-02	3.0362E-01	2.8992E-01 (+)	5.7788E-01	1.4944E-01	20
	MO-EGOg	1.2478E-05	2.5913E-04	**1.7095E-04**	1.0911E-03	2.6191E-04	20
g06	Forrester_EGO	3.5789E+03	3.5789E+03	$-^{\dagger}$	3.5789E+03	0.0000E+00	1
	Parr_Bi	9.9355E+02	2.3396E+03	2.6372E+03 (+)	3.8705E+03	9.3881E+02	16
	Durantin_Tri	3.8273E+01	1.0634E+03	5.4453E+02 (+)	4.5561E+03	1.3717E+03	20
	MO-EGOg	6.2791E+00	4.0821E+01	**3.6567E+01**	8.6013E+01	2.1650E+01	20
g08	Forrester_EGO	3.0330E-08	4.2849E-02	5.3965E-02 (+)	9.5357E-02	3.4623E-02	20
	Parr_Bi	2.9322E-03	3.0940E-02	3.1444E-02 (+)	7.2739E-02	2.1964E-02	20
	Durantin_Tri	5.7283E-07	2.6086E-02	1.5429E-02 (+)	6.9550E-02	2.8145E-02	20
	MO-EGOg	8.0649E-09	2.3911E-03	**6.5015E-08** (+)	3.3819E-02	7.9490E-03	20
Hesse	Forrester_EGO	5.3152E-02	3.7184E+00	5.4762E-01 (+)	1.4264E+01	4.9449E+00	20
	Parr_Bi	4.6977E-02	2.6992E+00	6.7779E-01 (+)	1.6734E+01	3.9976E+00	20
	Durantin_Tri	2.8711E-03	9.0891E-02	2.5463E-02 (+)	7.8023E-01	1.7898E-01	20
	MO-EGOg	5.5925E-05	2.6625E-01	**5.2117E-04**	5.2390E+00	1.1705E+00	20

†Median run not feasible

runs. On the other hand, our proposed approach MO-EGOg and Durantin_Tri obtained feasible solutions in all 20 runs. The error Boxplots will visually confirm this statements which are depicted in Fig. 3. Moreover, the similar median error performance profile plots in Fig. 5 for $k = 3, 5$ and 7 also indicate that our proposed approach is able to solve all constrained problems under study with minimum absolute error and is invariant to the infill batch size.

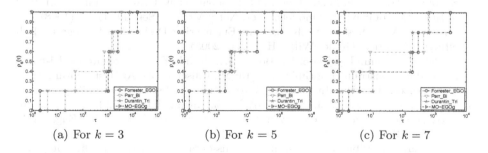

(a) For $k = 3$ (b) For $k = 5$ (c) For $k = 7$

Fig. 5. Constrained problems error performance profile plot for $k = 3, 5$ and 7.

4 Summary and Future Work

Efficient global optimization (EGO) in its conventional form is designed for serial operation, i.e., one infill solution is evaluated in each iteration. The serial nature of the original EGO process limits its efficiency for applications where a *batch* of solutions can be evaluated at the same cost as a single solution. In this paper we present and analyze a multi-objective formulation based approach to deal with such classes of problems, where instead of a single solution, a batch of solutions is identified and evaluated concurrently. The strategies use different objectives depending on the archive of the evaluated solutions. The performance of our approach is analyzed using 5 unconstrained and 5 constrained test problems covering the above problem classes and compared with conventional single infill criterion based EGO and MO formulation based single and batch evaluation strategies. A quantitative analysis of performance of the strategies across the complete problem space is achieved using performance profiles and statistical analysis across multiple independent runs. The results demonstrate that the proposed approach offers the best performance across the range of problems. As an extension, we are currently developing an approach to incorporate EGO based batch infill methods to solve multi-/many-objective optimization problems as well as to find the knee solutions of to several classes of problems. In the future work, we intend to solve some engineering design problems to observe the effectiveness and limitations of our proposed approach for real-world applications.

References

1. Jin, Y.: Surrogate-assisted evolutionary computation: recent advances and future challenges. Swarm Evol. Comput. **1**(2), 61–70 (2011)
2. Jones, D.R., Schonlau, M., Welch, W.J.: Efficient global optimization of expensive black-box functions. J. Global Optim. **13**(4), 455–492 (1998)
3. Schonlau, M.: Computer experiments and global optimization. Ph.D. thesis, University of Waterloo (1997)
4. Sasena, M.J.: Flexibility and efficiency enhancements for constrained global design optimization with kriging approximations. Ph.D. thesis, University of Michigan (2002)
5. Schonlau, M., Welch, W.J., Jones, D.R.: Global versus local search in constrained optimization of computer models. Lect. Notes-Monogr. Ser. **34**, 11–25 (1998)
6. Forrester, A., Sobester, A., Keane, A.: Engineering Design Via Surrogate Modelling: A Practical Guide. Wiley, Hoboken (2008)
7. Audet, C., Denni, J., Moore, D., Booker, A., Frank, P.: A surrogate-model-based method for constrained optimization. In: Multidisciplinary Analysis Optimization Conferences, American Institute of Aeronautics and Astronautics (2000)
8. Parr, J., Forrester, A.I.J., Keane, A.J.: Enhancing infill sampling criteria for surrogate-based constrained optimization. J. Comput. Methods Sci. Eng. **12**(1–2), 25–45 (2012)
9. Basudhar, A., Dribusch, C., Lacaze, S., Missoum, S.: Constrained efficient global optimization with support vector machines. Struct. Multi. Optim. **46**(2), 201–221 (2012)

10. Ponweiser, W., Wagner, T., Vincze, M.: Clustered multiple generalized expected improvement: a novel infill sampling criterion for surrogate models. In: Proceedings of IEEE Congress on Evolutionary Computation (CEC), pp. 3515–3522. IEEE (2008)

11. Ginsbourger, D., Le Riche, R., Carraro, L., et al.: A multi-points criterion for deterministic parallel global optimization based on gaussian processes, HAL: hal-00260579

12. Feng, Z., Zhang, Q., Zhang, Q., Tang, Q., Yang, T., Ma, Y.: A multiobjective optimization based framework to balance the global exploration and local exploitation in expensive optimization. J. Global Optim. **61**(4), 677–694 (2015)

13. Parr, J.M., Keane, A.J., Forrester, A.I.J., Holden, C.M.E.: Infill sampling criteria for surrogate-based optimization with constraint handling. Eng. Optim. **44**(10), 1147–1166 (2012)

14. Ishibuchi, H., Tsukamoto, N., Nojima, Y.: Evolutionary many-objective optimization: a short review. In: Proceedings of IEEE Congress on Evolutionary Computation (CEC), pp. 2419–2426. IEEE (2008)

15. Durantin, C., Marzat, J., Balesdent, M.: Analysis of multi-objective Kriging-based methods for constrained global optimization. Comput. Optim. Appl. **63**(3), 903–926 (2016)

16. Deb, K., Pratap, A., Agarwal, S., Meyarivan, T.: A fast and elitist multiobjective genetic algorithm: NSGA-II. IEEE Trans. Evol. Comput. **6**(2), 182–197 (2002)

17. Das, I., Dennis, J.E.: Normal-boundary intersection: a new method for generating the pareto surface in nonlinear multicriteria optimization problems. SIAM J. Optim. **8**(3), 631–657 (1998)

18. Dolan, E.D., Moré, J.J.: Benchmarking optimization software with performance profiles. Math. Program. **91**(2), 201–213 (2002)

19. Gibbons, J.D., Chakraborti, S.: Nonparametric Statistical Inference. Springer, Heidelberg (2011)

20. Nelson, L.S.: Evaluating overlapping confidence intervals. J. Qual. Technol. **21**(2), 140–141 (1989)

21. Dixon, L.C.W., Szegö, G.P.: The global optimization problem: an introduction. Towards Global Optim. **2**, 1–15 (1978)

22. Goldstein, A.A., Price, J.F.: On descent from local minima. Math. Comput. **25**(115), 569–574 (1971)

23. Liang, J.J., Runarsson, T.P., Mezura-Montes, E., Clerc, M., Suganthan, P.N., Coello, C.C., Deb, K.: Problem definitions and evaluation criteria for the CEC 2006 special session on constrained real-parameter optimization. J. Appl. Mech. **41**, 8 (2006)

24. Hesse, R.: A heuristic search procedure for estimating a global solution of nonconvex programming problems. Oper. Res. **21**(6), 1267–1280 (1973)

Automatic Clustering and Summarisation of Microblogs: A Multi-subtopic Phrase Reinforcement Algorithm

Mahfouth Alghamdi and Haifeng Shen[✉]

School of Computer Science, Engineering and Mathematics,
Flinders University, Adelaide, Australia
{algh0227,haifeng.shen}@flinders.edu.au

Abstract. There is a phenomenal growth of microblogging-based social communication services and subscriptions in recent years. Through these services, users publish a large number of posts within a short period time, making it extremely hard for readers to keep track of a trending topic. A solution to this issue is text summarisation, which can generate a short summary of a trending topic from multiple posts. Most of the existing summarisation algorithms were proposed for long documents and do not work well for short microblogging posts. The PR (Phrase Reinforcement) algorithm was particularly designed to summarise microblogs, however it is merely able to generate a single-post summary that conveys a single topic, potentially overlooking other important information from the posts. In this paper, we contribute the PRICE (Phrase Reinforcement: Iteration, Clustering and Extraction) algorithm by extending the original PR algorithm with the ability to generate both multi-post and single-post summaries that span over multiple subtopics. Experimental evaluation results show that the PRICE algorithm outperforms the original PR algorithm in terms of both ROUGE-1 and Content metrics.

Keywords: Microblogging · Text summarisation · Phrase Reinforcement

1   Introduction

Microblogging is one of the latest Web 2.0 technologies that have been successfully used in various social communication services [6]. It is a simplified type of blogging in which its content is limited in length, normally 200 characters or fewer. One key objective of a microblogging service is to allow users to exchange succinct information such as news, status updates, and pictures with each other in a real-time or quasi-real-time fashion [11]. Ever since the inception of Twitter in 2006, the application of microblogging has skyrocketed, extending from unstructured personal status updates to more structured services such as entertainment [22], e-Business [4], e-Government [19], and e-Learning [8]. With these services, people post millions of messages every day, for example, over 500 million tweets were posted per day in 2013 [14]. A significant challenge that emerges

© Springer International Publishing AG 2017
M. Wagner et al. (Eds.): ACALCI 2017, LNAI 10142, pp. 86–98, 2017.
DOI: 10.1007/978-3-319-51691-2_8

in these services is that the returned posts, when looking for a topic phrase, are simply sorted according to recency not relevancy. As a result, a reader is compelled to manually read through all the posts in sequence in order to keep track of a trending topic, which is extremely hard when the reader is under a tight time constraint, for example, when a TV presenter reads real-time messages from the viewers regarding the program [7], or when a lecturer reads real-time feedback from the students posted through digital backchannel streams [12].

A solution to this issue is automatic summarisation [20], which can generate a short summary of the original text. While this technique has mainly been applied to lengthy documents in order to generate a summary that is significantly shorter than yet still conveys important information in the original documents [13], the main objective of automatic summarisation of microblogs is to extract important information on a trending topic from the relevant posts rather than shortening the posts since each post is already short itself [27]. In addition, text summarisation based on well-established approaches to natural language processing does not work well for microblogging lexicon that is full of emotions, abbreviations, dialects and slangs [29]. Several text summarisation algorithms, which were developed in recent years for general purpose summarisation, work reasonably well for microblogs [18]. Nevertheless, the PR (Phrase Reinforcement) algorithm, which was particularly intended for summarising microblogs, works better when a trending topic has a dominant phrase pattern around the central topic [27]. However it is merely able to generate a single-post summary that conveys a single topic, potentially overlooking other important information from the posts.

In this paper, we contribute the PRICE (Phrase Reinforcement: Iteration, Clustering and Extraction) algorithm by extending the original PR algorithm with the ability to generate both multi-post single-post summaries that span over multiple subtopics. The algorithm first classifies the posts into clusters, each expressing a subtopic, then iteratively applies the PR algorithm to each of the clusters, generating a multi-post multi-subtopic summary, and finally applies the PR algorithm again to the posts in the summary to generate a single-post multi-subtopic summary. Experimental evaluation results show that the PRICE algorithm outperforms the original PR algorithm in terms of both ROUGE-1 and Content metrics. The rest of the paper is organised as follows. We first describe some relevant microblogging summarisation algorithms in the next section. We then present our multi-subtopic summarisation approach, including the original PR algorithm, the clustering algorithm, and the PRICE algorithm. After that, we discuss the experimental evaluation on the proposed algorithm, including data, metrics, and results. Finally, we conclude the paper with a summary of major contributions and future work.

2   Related Work

Text summarisation has a long history of nearly half a century. Early investigation on extractive summarisation was founded on plain heuristic characteristics of the sentences like their place in the document [2], the overall frequency of the words they have [17], or the importance of the sentences as indicated by some key phrases [9]. Late work incorporated more refined approaches such as machine learning [5] and natural language processing [24] and extended to new forms of documents like websites [32], discussion forums [25], blogs [1] and emails [3]. The objective of automatic text summarisation in most cases is to decrease the quantity of content that has to be read from lengthy documents. In recent years, attention has been turned to summarising short and informal microblogging posts. As such a post is already shorter than a typical document summary, the main objective is instead to extract a trending topic from the posts [27].

Among the recent summarisation solutions, some work reasonably well for microblogging posts, including SumBasic [30], the Centroid-based algorithm [26], hybrid $tf.idf$ [28], the graph-based abstractive algorithm [23], and the key-bigram extraction based algorithm [31]. Inspired by the observation that words occurring frequently in document clusters are more likely to occur in human-produced summaries than those occurring less frequently, SumBasic is able to generate generic multi-document summaries. SumBasic is an iterative greedy algorithm where in every iteration the tweet containing the words with the highest probability is selected. The probability of a word is defined as the word's frequency over the total number of words in the set of tweets, which is abridged once a tweet has been selected. The centroid-based algorithm uses a centroid tweet to compare a set of tweets [26]. The set's centroid is defined as the linear sum of the $tf.idf$ vectors of the tweets over the total number of tweets in the set. The set of tweets are then scored through cosine similarity to this centroid vector and those scored highest are chosen to be included in the summary.

Similarly, hybrid $tf.idf$ extends the standard $tf.idf$ algorithm by first assigning each sentence a weight and then choosing the top-weighted sentence as the summary. The tf component of the algorithm is calculated by uniting the entire tweets into one document, while the idf component is calculated as per standard $tf.idf$ by taking each tweet as an independent document. A normalisation method is used to prevent the algorithm from being biased towards longer sentences [28]. In the graph-based abstractive algorithm, each sentence has special words that determine its start and end. The algorithm generates a summary of tweets by extracting bigrams (nodes) that have the highest scoring path [23]. The key-bigram extraction based algorithm is a combination of three statistical methods - hybrid $tf.idf$, TextRanking and Latent Dirichlet Allocation - to extract the key-bigrams set from a collection of tweets [31]. The extracted sentences are ranked using the techniques of overlapping similarity and mutual information, while the top ranked sentences are chosen to generate the summaries.

These algorithms mostly use weighting schemes to generate summaries, however, the PR algorithm was specifically designed to extract a single-post trending topic from a set of tweets, which is founded on the observation that people often use similar words or expressions to define a specific topic [27]. More details on the PR algorithm are given in the following section.

3   Multi-subtopic Summarisation of Microblogging Posts

The original PR algorithm is only able to generate single-topic summaries. The PRICE algorithm extends it with the ability to generate multi-subtopic summaries through clustering and iterative extractive summarisation. Before presenting the PRICE algorithm, we first introduce the original PR algorithm and the K-means clustering algorithm.

3.1   The Original PR Algorithm

Beginning with an initial inquiry phrase, the PR algorithm builds a graph to represent the common sequence of words from the posts. For example, following are some posts made after the death of "Papa Wemba" on Twitter:

1. *congolese singer Papa Wemba dies after collapsing on stage in abidjan in ivory coast*
2. *RT: Papa Wemba was the 1st non south african artist in french colony*
3. *congolese music star Papa Wemba dies on stage*
4. *world music star Papa Wemba dies after collapsing on stage*

The PR algorithm is made up of two halves, where the sub-graph on the left of the root node incorporates words that come up in particular positions to the left side of the root node's phrase, while another sub-graph is situated at the right side of the root node. Initially, the root node and the current node are the same and the algorithm gradually adds each of the distinctive words into the graph as new nodes. Each duplicated word is assigned a count representing the number of times it has occurred in the set of posts. Figure 1 shows the PR graph constructed from the above posts.

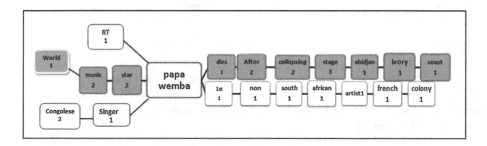

Fig. 1. The PR graph with the root node of "Papa Wemba"

Once the graph is built, the algorithm weighs the individual nodes in order to account for the disparities in the words' informational content. The root node "Papa Wemba" has zero weight and so do the stop words. The algorithm initialises the weight of each remaining word with its count value. If the word occurs away from the root node, its weight is then penalised by its distance to the root using the following equation: $\forall N_i, W(N_i) = C(N_i) - D(N_i, root) \times \log_b C(N_i)$, where N_i is a node, $W(N_i)$ is its weight, $C(N_i)$ is its count, $D(N_i, root)$ is the distance between N_i and the root node, and logarithm base b is used to customise the algorithm to generate a shorter or longer summary (a larger b tends to generate a longer summary). After that, the algorithm searches for the path with the highest total weight by comparing all paths starting from the root node to each non-root node. This path is denoted the best partial path as it only represents one half of the summary. The algorithm is repeated by initialising the root node with the partial summary and then rebuilding a new graph in order to generate the remaining half of the summary. The complete summary is the most heavily weighed path in the new graph. The highlighted nodes in Fig. 1 correspond to the full summary of those posts: *world music star Papa. Wemba dies after collapsing stage abidjan ivory coast.*

3.2   The K-means Clustering Algorithm

The original PR algorithm explained above can only generate a single-post single-topic summary. To allow for a multi-subtopic summary, we will first cluster the posts using the K-means algorithm [10]. Before the posts are clustered, they need to be converted into vectors and Algorithm 1 describes the process of converting a post into a vector.

Algorithm 1. Vectorise(P_i): V_{P_i}

Input: P_i - a post
Output: V_{P_i} - the vector value of P_i
1: $V_{P_i} \leftarrow 0$
2: $W \leftarrow tokenise(P_i)$ {W: set of words in P_i}
3: **for** ($\forall W_j \in W$) **do**
4:     $V_{W_j} \leftarrow 0$ {V_{W_j}: vector value of W_j}
5:     **for** ($\forall C_k \in W_j$) **do**
6:         $L_k \leftarrow tolower(L_k)$ {L_k: letter in W_j}
7:         $V_{L_k} \leftarrow (int)L_k$ {V_{L_k}: vector value of L_k}
8:         $V_{W_j} \leftarrow V_{W_j} + V_{L_k}$
9:     **end for**
10:    $V_{P_i} \leftarrow V_{P_i} + V_{W_j}$
11: **end for**
12:
13: **return** V_{P_i}

Algorithm 2. PRICE(P): S_P

Input: P - set of posts
Output: S_P - single-post multi-subtopic summary of P
1: $CK \leftarrow Kmeans(P)$ {CK: set of k clusters}
2: $S_{CK} \leftarrow \phi$ {S_{CK}: multi-post multi-subtopic summary for the set of clusters CK}
3: **for** ($\forall C_i \in CK$) **do**
4:     $S_{C_i} \leftarrow PR(C_i)$ {S_{C_i}: single-post single-topic summary for cluster C_i}
5:     $S_{CK} \leftarrow S_{CK} + S_{C_i}$
6: **end for**
7: $S_P \leftarrow PR(S_{CK})$
8:
9: **return** S_P

Initially, the algorithm randomly selects k posts as the cluster centroid from all the computed feature vectors and then assigns each post to their closest cluster centroid according to Jaccard Distance that measures dissimilarity between two posts of P_i and P_j:

$$D(P_i, P_j) = 1 - \frac{|P_i \cap P_j|}{|P_i \cup P_j|} = \frac{|P_i \cup P_j| - |P_i \cap P_j|}{|P_i \cup P_j|}.$$

It is clear that the distance is small if the two posts are similar and that the distance is $0/1$ if the two posts are identical or completely different. The centroid of each cluster is calculated by first summing up all the post vectors and then dividing the sum by the total number of posts within the cluster:

$$c_i = \frac{\sum v \in V_i}{n_i},$$

where c_i is the centroid of the i-th cluster, n_i is the total number of posts in the i-th cluster, and V_i is the set of post vectors in the i-th cluster. When a new post is added to a cluster, the centroid of that cluster is updated by choosing the post closest to previously calculated centroid. The algorithm is repeated until all posts are assigned to the corresponding clusters.

3.3 The PRICE Algorithm

Algorithm 2 illustrates the PRICE algorithm in detail. It first classifies the posts into k clusters each of which has a subtopic surrounding the original trending topic using the K-means algorithm. After that, it iteratively applies the PR algorithm to all clusters to generate a multi-post multi-subtopic summary (each post in the summary corresponds to a subtopic). Finally, it applies the PR algorithm again to the posts in the summary to generate a single-post multi-subtopic summary.

4 Experimental Evaluation

To evaluate the performance of the PRICE algorithm, we collect posts from Twitter and use the ROUGE-1 and the Content metrics [15] to compare the summary generated by PRICE with those automatically generated by a random algorithm and the original PR algorithm as well as those manually produced by human experts.

4.1 Data Collection and Pre-processing

We used Twitter API to collect the top 30 trending topics from different geographical locations using *Yahoo! WOEID Lookup*[1]. We downloaded approximately 1500 tweets for each trending topic and selected the top 50 tweets for summarisation. Pre-processing tweets is an essential step so as to remove noisy data that will affect the performance of both the clustering and the summarisation algorithms, considering that microblogging posts are generally characterised as an unstructured and informal means of communication. Algorithm 3 describes our data cleansing process adopted from [27].

4.2 Automatic and Manual Summarisation

To estimate lower and upper performance bounds for the purpose of positioning the PRICE algorithm and comparing it with the PR algorithm, we adopt manual summarisation by human experts and automatic summarisation by a random algorithm. Random summarisation is a naive approach used to derive a lower bound for performance comparison of automatic summarisation algorithms. It was implemented by randomly choosing one out of the 50 posts as the summary

---

[1] http://zourbuth.com/tools/woeid/.

Algorithm 3. Cleansing(P): C_P

Input: P - set of posts
Output: C_P - cleansed P
 1: Convert any HTML-encoded or Unicode character into its ASCII equivalent or remove it if no equivalent exists
 2: Filter out embedded URLs
 3: Discard the post if it is spam
 4: Discard the post if it is not in English
 5: Discard the post if another post by the same user has already been acquired in order to prevent a single user from dominating a topic
 6: Break each post into sentences and then each sentence into unigrams with sentence detector tools of *nl-sent.bin* and *ark-tweet-nlp*
 7: Detect the sentence that contains the topic phrase for the purpose of evaluation
 8:
 9: **return** C_P

---

of each trending topic. Manual summarisation was used to get a performance upper bound and for that purpose two volunteers were asked to produce a manual summary of no more than 140 characters (as ROUGE-1 is highly sensitive to summary length) based on its 50 tweets for each trending topic. The volunteers were given instructions so as to produce the best possible summaries using only information contained within the posts.

To evaluate the PRICE algorithm, each of the 30 trending topics was clustered into $k = 2, 3, 4, 5$ subtopics. For each subtopic, the algorithm iterated 1000 times to avoid the sensitivity of random seeding.

4.3   Evaluation Metrics

We use ROUGE-N [15] to evaluate the performance of the PRICE algorithm. It comprises measures to automatically decide the quality of a summary by comparing it to summaries produced by human experts. These measures count the number of overlapping units such as n-grams, word sequences, and word pairs between an automatic summary and a model summary (also known as a gold standard) [16] produced by human experts, which are described as follows.

$$ROUGE\text{-}N = \frac{\sum_{S \in MS} \sum_{gram_n \in S} Count_{match}(gram_n)}{\sum_{S \in MS} \sum_{gram_n \in S} Count(gram_n)},$$

where MS is the set of manual summaries, n is the length of the n-gram $gram_n$, and $Count_{match}(gram_n)$ is the maximum number of n-grams co-occurring in an automatic summary and the set of manual summaries. ROUGE-N is a recall-based metric since it compares the number of matching n-grams with the total number of n-grams within the manual summaries. However, it can be converted into precision-based metric by redefining $Count(gram_n)$ to be the number of n-grams within the automatic summaries. In order to consider both recall and precision for the ROUGE-N metric, we introduce F-Measure, a composite measure combining both precision and recall, which was not used by the original ROUGE-N:

$$F\text{-}Measure = 2 \times \frac{Precision \times Recall}{Precision + Recall}.$$

We particularly chose ROUGE-1 (n = 1 for unigrams) for our evaluation as it performs particularly well for short summaries [15], ideal for evaluating microblogging summarisation algorithms.

We also use Content metric to measure the completeness of an automatically generated summary by comparing how much information of a manually produced summary is captured by the automatic summary. To achieve this, we asked the third volunteer to rate how well an automatically generated summary expresses the meaning of a manual summary based on a 5-Likert scale: none (1), hardly any (2), some (3), most (4) and all (5) [15].

4.4 Results

We first evaluate the two manual summaries in order to get an upper bound. We then evaluate the summaries generated by the random algorithm in order to get a lower bound. Table 1 shows their ROUGE-1 and Content results.

Table 1. Performance lower and upper bounds

Summarisation method	ROUGE-1			Content
	Precision	Recall	F-Measure	
Manual 1	0.249	0.166	0.208	4.1
Manual 2	0.166	0.249	0.208	3.7
Manual avg.	0.208	0.208	0.208	3.9
Random	0.127	0.141	0.132	2.25

We can observe that the random algorithm's average F-Measure of 0.132 is not bad as compared to the manual's upper bound of 0.208 possibly due to two reasons. First, overlapping of unigrams within all posts appears high as many posts use similar words and ROUGE-1 only compares common words between manual and automatic summaries. Second, overlapping of unigrams in manual summaries is generally low as different people tend to extract different words in their summaries. However, when we compare random and manual based on the Content metric, random's score of 2.25 (hardly any) is significantly lower than that of the manual, 3.9 (some to most), implying the random method captures significantly less meaning of the manual summaries.

Table 2. Summaries generated by PRICE, PR, and human experts

Trending topic	Method	Multi-post summary	Single-post summary
#Papa Wemba	Manual 1	-	Congolese singer Papa Wemba dies after collapsing on stage in abidjan in ivory coast. He was a great musician, who will be mourned
	Manual 2	-	Papa Wemba collapsed and died after being take off stage in Africa, people were very sad and shocked (he was an amazing musician)
	PR ($b = e$)	-	A truly great loss to african music had interviewed him years back in addis Congo music legend Papa Wemba dies after collapsing on stage by the associated press via nyt
	PRICE ($b = e$, $k = 2$)	A truly great loss to african music had interviewed him years back in addis Congo music legend Papa Wemba dies after collapsing on stage by the associated press via yt	A truly great loss to african music had interviewed him years back in addis Congo music legend Papa Wemba, a congolese rumba musician, one of Africa's most popular musicians, has died he was 66
		Rock it till you die for it unforgettable loss epic singer rip Papa Wemba a congolese rumba musician one of Africa most popular musicians has died he was 66	

Table 2 contains the manual summaries produced by the two volunteers and the automatic summaries generated the PR ($b = e$) and the PRICE ($b = e, k = 2$) algorithms. It is clear that only the PRICE algorithm can generate a multi-post summary spanning over two subtopics: (a) Papa Wemba dies, and (b) Papa Wemba is one of Africa's most popular musicians. PRICE's single-post summary also covers the same two subtopics, while PR only contains a single topic: Papa Wemba dies.

Figure 2(a) depicts PRICE's ROUGE-1 performance in relation to the parameters of $b \in \{e, 10, 50, 100, 1000\}$ when $k = 2$. It is clear that increasing b in the order of e, 10, and 50 improves its F-Measure from 0.137, to 0.149, and to 0.150. After that, further increasing b to 100 and 1000 actually decreases its performance (F-Measure drops to 0.149 and further to 0.144). Figure 2(c) shows PRICE's ROUGE-1 performance in relation to different k values. It reveals a pattern similar to that in Fig. 2(a) for $k = 3, 4$, but its performance starts to drop slightly when $k = 5$ (consult Table 3 for details). Figures 2(b) and (d) illustrate the Content metric in relation to b and k. The results are similar to those for the ROUGE-1 metric, where the performance peaks at $b = 50$ and $k = 2, 3, 4$.

Figure 3 shows PR's ROUGE-1 and Content performance in relation to b. Its ROUGE-1 performance peaks at $b = 100$ with the F-Measure of 0.150 (0.147 when $b = 50$), while its Content performance peaks at $b = 50$ with the value of 3.2. Results from the PRICE and the PR algorithms confirm that they are both sensitive to the length of a summary, which is relatively long as compared to the posts. Therefore a large b (50/100) would yield good results. For the PRICE algorithm, the number of subtopics is another important factor. Thanks to the nature of microblogging posts, a summary is only expected to contain a small set of subtopics and consequently a small k (2/3/4) would yield good results.

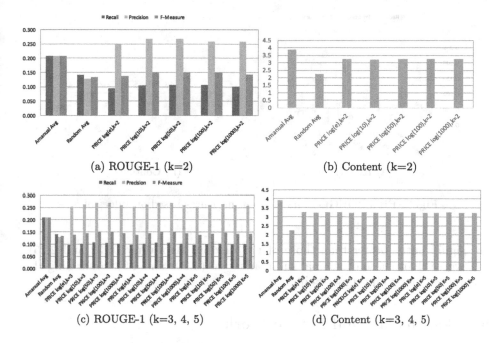

(a) ROUGE-1 (k=2)

(b) Content (k=2)

(c) ROUGE-1 (k=3, 4, 5)

(d) Content (k=3, 4, 5)

Fig. 2. PRICE's ROUGE-1 and Content measures based on values of b and k

Table 3. Performance comparison of manual, random, PR and PRICE

Summarisation method	ROUGE-1			Content
	Precision	Recall	F-Measure	
Manual avg.	0.208	0.208	0.208	3.9
Random	0.127	0.141	0.132	2.25
PR ($b = 50$)	0.251	0.105	0.147	3.2
PRICE ($b = 50$, $k = 2$)	0.268	0.105	0.150	3.26
PRICE ($b = 50$, $k = 3$)	0.269	0.105	0.150	3.26
PRICE ($b = 50$, $k = 4$)	0.270	0.105	0.150	3.26
PRICE ($b = 50$, $k = 5$)	0.265	0.102	0.146	3.26

A summary of the best performance of the PRICE algorithm as compared to that of the best of the original PR algorithm and those of the manual summarisation and the random algorithm is elaborated in Table 3. It can be seen that PRICE's performance peaks at $b = 50$ with the F-Measure of 0.150 and with the Content measure of 3.26, and is seemingly independent of k as long as it is small. In contrast, PR's performance at $b = 50$ is 0.147 and 3.2 respectively, both lower than those of the PRICE algorithm, confirming that the PRICE algorithm makes a clear improvement over the original PR algorithm. In addition, both the ROUGE-1 and the Content measures of the PRICE algorithm (0.150 and 3.26)

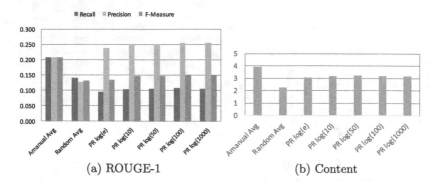

Fig. 3. PR's ROUGE-1 and Content measures based on values of b

are significantly better than those of the random algorithm (0.132 and 2.25), but worse than those of manual summarisation (0.208 and 3.9), confirming the theoretical lower and upper bounds.

5   Conclusions and Future Work

While the PR algorithm is a good choice for summarising microblogging posts, it is only effective when the trending topic does not contain subtopics. Our main contribution is the PRICE algorithm for summarising posts that contain multiple subtopics revolving around a trending topic. The PRICE algorithm first harnesses a clustering algorithm to group posts expressing the same subtopics into clusters, then iteratively applies the PR algorithm to each of the clusters generating a multi-post multi-subtopic summary, and finally applies the PR algorithm again to the posts in the summary generating a single-post multi-subtopic summary. Experimental evaluation results confirm that the PRICE algorithm outperforms the original PR algorithm in terms of both the ROUGE-1 and the Content metrics.

We are conscious of the limitations in this work. First of all, we only included the top 50 posts of each trending topic in our experimental evaluation. We plan to investigate whether and how the inclusion of a large set of posts, e.g., 500 posts per topic, will influence PRICE's performance as compared that of PR and whether the performance improvement is statistically significant. We also plan to apply the PRICE algorithm to more standard datasets in addition to the microblog data in order to test whether the proposed algorithm is general enough to reproduce similar results. Second, the K-means clustering algorithm was used as a touch stone and we want to systematically study the impact of different clustering algorithms on PRICE's performance. Last but not least, evaluation using the ROUGE-1 and Content metrics relies on human-authored model summaries and human judges. Given the small number of human experts involved in our experiments, subjectiveness and bias are likely an issue. We plan to adopt the Pyramid method [21] that combines multiple human models to yield a more reliable gold-standard as well as an automatic assessment method [16] that does not rely on a gold-standard.

References

1. Balahur, A., Lloret, E., Boldrini, E., Montoyo, A., Palomar, M., Martínez-Barco, P.: Summarizing threads in blogs using opinion polarity. In: Proceedings of the Workshop on Events in Emerging Text Types, pp. 23–31 (2009)
2. Baxendale, P.B.: Machine-made index for technical literature: an experiment. IBM J. Res. Dev. 2(4), 354–361 (1958)
3. Carenini, G., Ng, R.T., Zhou, X.: Summarizing email conversations with clue words. In: Proceedings of the 16th International Conference on World Wide Web, pp. 91–100 (2007)
4. Chua, A.Y., Banerjee, S.: Customer knowledge management via social media: the case of Starbucks. J. Knowl. Manag. 17(2), 237–249 (2013)
5. Chuang, W.T., Yang, J.: Extracting sentence segments for text summarization: a machine learning approach. In: Proceedings of the 23rd Annual International ACM SIGIR Conference on Research and Development in Information Retrieval, pp. 152–159 (2000)
6. DeVoe, K.M.: Bursts of information: microblogging. Ref. Libr. 50(2), 212–214 (2009)
7. Doughty, M., Rowland, D., Lawson, S.: Co-viewing live TV with digital backchannel streams. In: Proceedings of the 9th International Interactive Conference on Interactive Television, pp. 141–144 (2011)
8. Ebner, M., Lienhardt, C., Rohs, M., Meyer, I.: Microblogs in higher education - a chance to facilitate informal and process-oriented learning? Comput. Educ. 55(1), 92–100 (2010)
9. Edmundson, H.P.: New methods in automatic extracting. J. ACM 16(2), 264–285 (1969)
10. Hartigan, J.A., Wong, M.A.: Algorithm as 136: a k-means clustering algorithm. J. R. Stat. Soc. Ser. C (Appl. Stat.) 28(1), 100–108 (1979)
11. Java, A., Song, X., Finin, T., Tseng, B.: Why we Twitter: understanding microblogging usage and communities. In: Proceedings of the 9th WebKDD and 1st SNA-KDD 2007 Workshop on Web Mining and Social Network Analysis, pp. 56–65 (2007)
12. Jiranantanagorn, P., Shen, H., Goodwin, R., Teoh, K.K.: Classense: a mobile digital backchannel system for monitoring class morale. Int. J. Learn. Teach. 1(2), 161–167 (2015)
13. Jones, K.S.: Automatic summarising: the state of the art. Inf. Process. Manag. 43(6), 1449–1481 (2007)
14. Krikorian, R.: New tweets per second record, and how! (2013). https://blog.twitter.com/2013/new-tweets-per-second-record-and-how. 16 August 2013
15. Lin, C.Y., Hovy, E.: Automatic evaluation of summaries using n-gram co-occurrence statistics. In: Proceedings of the 2003 Conference of the North American Chapter of the Association for Computational Linguistics on Human Language Technology, vol. 1, pp. 71–78 (2003)
16. Louis, A., Nenkova, A.: Automatically assessing machine summary content without a gold standard. Comput. Linguist. 39(2), 267–300 (2013)

17. Luhn, H.P.: The automatic creation of literature abstracts. IBM J. Res. Dev. **2**(2), 159–165 (1958)
18. Mackie, S., McCreadie, R., Macdonald, C., Ounis, I.: Comparing algorithms for microblog summarisation. In: Kanoulas, E., Lupu, M., Clough, P., Sanderson, M., Hall, M., Hanbury, A., Toms, E. (eds.) CLEF 2014. LNCS, vol. 8685, pp. 153–159. Springer, Heidelberg (2014). doi:10.1007/978-3-319-11382-1_15
19. Nam, T.: Suggesting frameworks of citizen-sourcing via government 2.0. Gov. Inf. Q. **29**(1), 12–20 (2012)
20. Nenkova, A., McKeown, K.: A survey of text summarization techniques. In: Aggarwal, C.C., Zhai, C. (eds.) Mining Text Data, pp. 43–76. Springer, New York (2012)
21. Nenkova, A., Passonneau, R., Mckeown, K.: The pyramid method: incorporating human content selection variation in summarization evaluation. ACM Trans. Speech Lang. Process. **4**(2), Article 4 (2007)
22. Nichols, J., Mahmud, J., Drews, C.: Summarizing sporting events using Twitter. In: Proceedings of ACM International Conference on Intelligent User Interfaces, pp. 189–198 (2012)
23. Olariu, A.: Efficient online summarization of microblogging streams. In: Proceedings of the 14th Conference of the European Chapter of the Association for Computational Linguistics, pp. 236–240 (2014)
24. Regina, B., Elhadad, M.: Using lexical chains for text summarization. In: Advances in Automatic Text Summarization, pp. 111–121 (1999)
25. Ren, Z., Ma, J., Wang, S., Liu, Y.: Summarizing web forum threads based on a latent topic propagation process. In: Proceedings of the 20th ACM International Conference on Information and Knowledge Management, pp. 879–884 (2011)
26. Rosa, K.D., Shah, R., Lin, B., Gershman, A., Frederking, R.: Topical clustering of tweets. In: Proceedings of the ACM SIGIR 3rd Workshop on Social Web Search and Mining (2011)
27. Sharifi, B., Hutton, M.A., Kalita, J.: Summarizing microblogs automatically. In: Human Language Technologies: The 2010 Annual Conference of the North American Chapter of the ACL, pp. 685–688 (2010)
28. Sharifi, B., Hutton, M.A., Kalita, J.K.: Experiments in microblog summarization. In: Proceedings of the IEEE Second International Conference on Social Computing, pp. 49–56 (2010)
29. Uvarova, N.: Abstractive microblogs summarization. Master's thesis, Gjøvik University College (2015)
30. Vanderwende, L., Suzuki, H., Brockett, C., Nenkova, A.: Beyond sumbasic: task-focused summarization with sentence simplification and lexical expansion. Inf. Process. Manag. **43**(6), 1606–1618 (2007)
31. Wu, Y., Zhang, H., Xu, B., Hao, H., Liu, C.: Automatic microblog summarization based on unsupervised key-bigram extraction. Int. J. Comput. Commun. Eng. **4**(5), 363–370 (2015)
32. Zhang, Y.Z., Zincir-Heywood, N., Milios, E.: Summarizing web sites automatically. In: Xiang, Y., Chaib-draa, B. (eds.) AI 2003. LNCS, vol. 2671, pp. 283–296. Springer, Heidelberg (2003). doi:10.1007/3-540-44886-1_22

Generation and Exploration of Architectural Form Using a Composite Cellular Automata

Camilo Cruz[1(✉)], Michael Kirley[2], and Justyna Karakiewicz[1]

[1] Melbourne School of Design, University of Melbourne, Melbourne, Australia
ccruz@student.unimelb.edu.au, justynak@unimelb.edu.au
[2] Department of Computing and Information Systems, University of Melbourne,
Melbourne, Australia
mkirley@unimelb.edu.au

Abstract. In this paper, we introduce a composite Cellular Automata (CA) to explore digital morphogenesis in architecture. Consisting of multiple interleaved one dimensional CA, our model evolves the boundaries of spatial units in cross sectional diagrams. We investigate the efficacy of this approach by systematically varying initial conditions and transition rules. Simulation experiments show that the composite CA can generate aggregate spatial units to match the characteristics of specific spatial configurations, using a well-known architectural landmark as a benchmark. Significantly, spatial patterns emerge as a consequence of the evolution of the system, rather than from prescriptive design decisions.

1 Introduction

The production of high density housing in many large cities has typically focused on optimizing the use of space, disregarding the quality of the inhabitable spaces being built. Attributes such as access to sunlight, ventilation, and storage space, which are generally regarded as essential for 'better living' [23], have often been overlooked. In response to the increased development of living spaces that are commonly perceived to be sub-standard [11], new urban design rules and regulations have recently been proposed in Melbourne, Australia. From a design perspective, the introduction of revised planning rules provides the impetus to investigate new methods for the creative exploration of design space in search of novel ways to produce liveable spaces.

In this paper, we introduce a 'digital morphogenesis' method to tackle this design challenge. Here, a composite cellular automata (CA) consisting of multiple, regularly spaced interleaved 1D CA provides the structure for a designer to interactively 'generate and explore' the design search space. The composite CA includes a combination of 'self-assembly,' 'pattern formation' and 'best variant' selection to produce, in this case, cross sectional diagrams of spatial configurations. Metrics for the evaluation of emergent attributes of the spatial configurations are introduced in order to allow the designer to interactively select instances that satisfy the requirements of the task in unexpected ways, potentially leading towards a novel manner of representing and understanding the design.

© Springer International Publishing AG 2017
M. Wagner et al. (Eds.): ACALCI 2017, LNAI 10142, pp. 99–110, 2017.
DOI: 10.1007/978-3-319-51691-2_9

Our approach represents a departure from the oversimplification that the 'form–follows–function' paradigm, strongly enforced on the design practice during the modern movement [6]. The rationale behind our 'bottom-up' design methodology is to define a way in which low-level design elements [20] interact in, and with space, in order to enable the exploration of design solution space, rather than focusing on optimizing a solution based on a fixed set of requirements. Detailed simulation experiments demonstrate a proof-of-concept that our composite CA model can automatically synthesize shape and topology, *in silico*, producing abstract diagrams of spatial configurations that, given the characteristics of the constituent elements (building blocks), can be easily translated into architectural cross sections.

The remainder of this paper is organised as follows. In Sect. 2, we introduce work related to computational morphogenesis and generative design. This is followed by a formal description of CA and a brief review of CA in architectural design. Our model is introduced in Sect. 3. In Sect. 4, the simulation experiments are described and results presented. We summarise the results and discuss the implications of our findings, before briefly outlining avenues for future work in Sect. 5.

2   Background

2.1   Computational Morphogenesis

Generative systems have been used to investigate novelty in architecture and urban design since Aristotle [22, p. 30]. Beyond classic examples of generative systems (Greek orders, Da Vinci's central plan churches, Durand's elements, etc.) there are examples of form generation techniques often used in architecture and urban design in the twentieth century, e.g. Alexander's work with 'patterns' [1] and Stiny's 'shape grammars' [28].

Computational (or digital) morphogenesis techniques, use digital media as a generative tool for the derivation of and manipulation of 'form' [12,13], where abstract computer simulations are used to foster the gradual development and adaptation of shapes [29]. Using bottom-up generative methods, they combine a number of concepts including self organization, pattern formation, self-assembly and 'form-finding.' Self-organization is a process that increases the order and statistical complexity of a system as a result of local interactions between lower-level, simple components [4,26]. Emergence represents the concept of the patterns, often unpredictable ones, which form in large scale systems [16,21]. Emergent properties arise when a complex system reaches a combined threshold of diversity, organization and connectivity. For example, the self-assembly of geometric primary elements (or 'building blocks') may, in some systems, be an emergent form-finding property guided by strict rules dictating 'bonding' patterns [8,17].

2.2   Cellular Automata

CA are discrete dynamical systems comprising a number of typically identical simple components (or cells), with local connectivity over a regular lattice whose global configuration changes over time, according to a local state transition rule. CA implementations and functions, regardless of their complexity, regularity and constraints, require the definition of characteristics (cells, cell-states and neighbourhood) that can be directly interpreted as spatial configurations. Formally, a CA is defined by:

- an array of cells of length L^D (where D is the number of dimensions)
- a neighbourhood size n for each cell $c \in L$
- an alphabet of cell states $\Sigma = \{s_i, \dots, s_{|\Sigma|}\}$
- a discrete time step $t = 0, 1, \dots$
- a state $s(c, t) \in \Sigma$ for each cell $c \in L$ at time t
- a transition function $\psi : \Sigma^{|n|} \to \Sigma$

At time $t + 1$, the state of each cell c is updated in parallel using the transition function and the defined local neighbourhood n. For an elementary 2 state 1D CA with $n = 3$ neighbours, there are $2^8 = 256$ possible transition rules. For a 2 state 2D CA with $n = 4$ neighbour (von Neumann neighbouhood) there are $2^{32} = 4 \times 10^9$ possible transition rules. The number of rules can be reduced if different symmetries are adopted. However, as the number of states and neighbourhood size increase, the state space significantly increases.

CA can be seen as a space for exploratory creativity. Von Neumann [30] showed that CA may produce very sophisticated self-organized structures, given a finite number of cells states and short range interactions.

CA have been used effectively to help explain natural phenomena involving strong and explicit spatial constraints [32,33]. They have been used to model morphogenesis processes [25], and as a model to generate simple shapes [7], or specific 2D or 3D target patterns [5]. CA have also been used as part of a more general 'meta-design' design process in engineering [9,18].

2.3   Cellular Automata and Design

In architecture, 3D implementations of CA have been typically used to produce diagrams of abstract spatial configurations that can serve as starting points for the further development of architectural or urban form. The cells of the CA represent 3D spatial units with programmatic characteristics (e.g., housing units, rooms, public spaces, circulation spaces, etc.), which results in functionally deterministic outputs.

Coates *et al.* [6] present a 3D model using cubic cells with binary states ('occupied'/'empty') in search for emergent patterns, emulating the work of Conway and his 'Game of Life' [10]. For this purpose, he explores a series of rule combinations and neighbourhoods. The aim of these experiments was to find mechanisms for the generation of spatial structures with potential to be used in architectural design. Krawczyk [19] uses a similar implementation of 3D CA to evolve spatial configurations, focusing on how can the abstract outputs of the model be translated into architectural form. The translation is performed by manipulating the characteristics of the cells once the model has stopped running, which brings this approach closer to a more traditional design process. Here, the CA time evolution is presented as an exploration, where desired outcomes or other parameters that allow for the evaluation of the system's performance are not defined.

Herr and Kvan [14] present a different approach, where the constraint of a fixed, regular lattice for the CA is removed and the designer may interact with the time evolution of the system, steering the evolution of the CA according to design goals. This approach integrates the shaping of a design solution with the reformulation of the design problem, thus reducing the post-processing of outcomes to detailing. Araghi *et al.* [2] describe the use of CA in the development of high density housing where the generation of variety based on additional design objectives (accessibility and lighting) is the goal. The design requirements are mapped to cell states within the local neighbourhood, and the transition rules inform the development of the system. The definition of 3D cells implies a design operation that binds the form of the cell to a particular function, which renders the results of the development of said models functionally static.

3   Model

Our composite CA is a digital morphogenesis tool that can be used at the early stages of an architectural design process. The composite CA is built as an array of evenly spaced interleaved 1D CA (Fig. 1a), arranged on a grid (Fig. 1b). With this arrangement it is possible to produce spatial configurations where the 'cells' of the CA have a 'form-making' role, rather than being functionally predefined. Our approach focuses on how space can be physically reshaped and characterised as the system evolves, which represents a departure from the typical use of CA

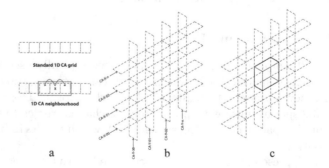

a   b   c

Fig. 1. (a) A standard 1D CA. (b) The configuration for our composite 1D CA consisting of interleaved horizontal and vertical 1D CA. (c) A representative example of one spatial unit, defined by the activation of its boundaries.

in architecture and urban design, where the characteristics of the space are prescribed by design.

What differentiates our composite CA from a standard 2D CA is the fact that the multiple 1D CA act as the edges of encapsulated 'spatial units' (Fig. 1c). That is, each edge of a spatial unit is actually a discrete cell in a 1D CA and is governed by a state transition rule. Here, each cell has a binary state – it can be either active (on) of inactive (off). If a cell in a 1D CA is off, the spatial units on either side of it are connected. System dynamics generate 'complex' patterns consisting of concatenated spatial units, defined by active/inactive edges. The emergent structures are highly sensitive to individual cell states and transition rules, a system with some similarities to bond percolation models and abstract genetic regulator systems [31].

In our composite CA, there are two possible states for each cell. Given the configuration of the interleaved 1D CA, this results in 16 different possible configurations for each of the encapsulated spatial units, illustrated in Fig. 2.

In Fig. 3, we show representative examples of the complex spatial topologies that emerge as a result of the concatenation or combination of multiple edges being active/inactive at the same time, which illustrates the exploratory power of the model. In Fig. 3b, we label the centre of each individual spatial unit and

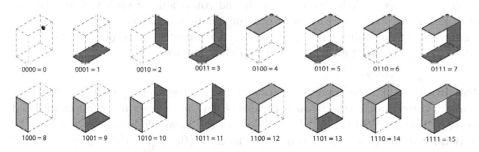

Fig. 2. 3D representation of the 16 spatial configurations the model is capable of producing for a single 2D spatial unit. Binary counting is used to number the active edges.

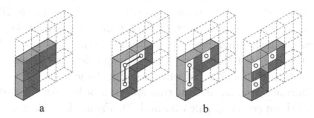

Fig. 3. (a) A standard 2D CA, where each cell is a spatial unit in itself (3 cell configuration). (b) 3D representation of three possible spatial unit configurations of size 3 units that can be produced with the proposed composite CA model. The centre of each spatial unit is labelled with a red circle (node). Connecting spatial units are also shown (edges). (Color figure online)

include connecting edges between adjacent spatial units where appropriate. It is this formation of aggregates or clusters of connected 2D 'encapsulated spatial units' that subsequently generates a volumetric matrix for spatial organisation to be used by the designer.

Unlike a traditional 2D CA, where the characteristics of the cells are defined by their state, in the composite 1D CA, spatial units are neutral, and acquire their characteristics depending on the configuration of their boundaries.

4   Experiments

A series of simulation experiments were carried out to evaluate the efficacy of the proposed composite CA model, focussing specifically on the configuration and characterization of space. The key question guiding the experimental design: *Can the composite CA be used to effectively generate diagrammatic cross-sections of architectural form?*

4.1   Methodology

We start by systematically examining the dynamics of instantiated instances of the composite CA by varying the initial conditions of each CA and transition rules. We then examine whether the composite CA can generate (evolve) aggregate spatial units, with specific spatial attributes, corresponding to configurations representing a mix of open and closed spaces.

Parameters. The composite CA consists of $x \times y$ regularly spaced 1D CA, where x and y correspond to the number of cells (L) in the corresponding horizontal and vertical 1D CA. We examine $L = 10$. We set the local neighbourhood size $n = 3$, and limited the alphabet of cell states to $\Sigma = \{0, 1\}$ (i.e. the cell representing the boundaries of the spatial units are either active or inactive).

The state transition rules are drawn from Wolfram's [32] elementary 1D CA rules – representative rules from classes III and IV are used, where Class III (random) contains rules that generate outcomes with no discernible patterns and Class IV (complexity) contains rules that generate discernible patterns that repeat at unpredictable frequencies and locations, as the system develops. Classes I (uniformity) and II (repetition) have been disregarded at this stage, since they tend to yield configurations that become static in time.

We use a different state transition rule for each of horizontal and vertical 1D CA. From class III we selected rules 30 and 60. From class IV we selected rules 54 and 110 (other rules were tested but are not reported in this paper).

In order to allow the experiments to generate a variety of spatial configurations, each simulation trial was run for a maximum of 200 time steps, starting from uniformly randomly drawn initial cell states. The entire system is updated simultaneously in discrete time steps.

Analysis. We introduce a phenotypic diversity measure on the space of the composite CA to analyse emergent behaviour. Specifically, we examine the embedded 'connectivity graph' where nodes within the graph correspond to the centre of active adjacent spatial units in the model (see Fig. 3b). The structure of connected nodes define a 'local cluster' or clusters of adjacent spatial units, possibly corresponding to arbitrarily shaped geometric forms, defined by active/inactive cells of the composite CA. This graph-based analysis provides a concise way to examine the spontaneous formation of 'motifs' that represent a wide variety of spatial attributes. Clusters act as a conduit for circulation through different interconnecting spatial units and provide a balance between the open and closed space. It is worth noting that some of the nodes are located outside the boundaries of the $x \times y$ 'lattice'. When a cluster has one of its nodes with that condition, it is considered an open cluster.

We use three graph theoretic metrics to characterize the emergent dynamics for specific rules and time-evolution of the composite CA: **M1** the degree distribution of nodes – the regularity of the aggregation of spatial units (where a low degree distribution represents a more irregular spatial configuration); **M2** the mean and standard deviation of cluster size – quantifies the level of fragmentation of space; and **M3** the ratio of the number of open and closed clusters (where a cluster is considered open when it has one or more nodes outside of the lattice) – quantifies porosity or the connectivity of the spatial configurations to the exterior.

4.2   Results

Time Evolution of the Composite CA. Snap-shots of the evolving connectivity graphs, corresponding to the emergent spatial forms for two different rule combinations at time steps $t = (50, 100, 150, 200)$, are shown in Fig. 4. It is inter-

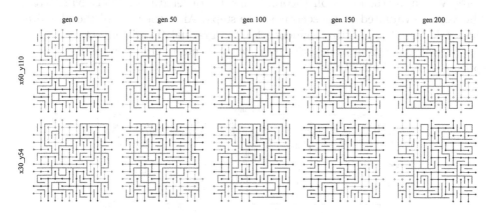

Fig. 4. Snap shots of the evolving composite CA. The top and bottom rows show the connectivity graphs at times t = 0, t = 50, t = 100, t = 150 and t = 200 for rule x60_y110 and x30_y54 respectively. Note that some of the nodes are outside of the lattice (Color figure online)

esting to note the variety of cluster sizes and shapes that are being generated, which provides a wide search space for exploring spatial attributes.

The emergent spatial unit structure – represented by clusters – change shape significantly over the course of the simulated evolutionary time, to a point where there is no apparent relationship between generations evolved using a particular set of rules. For instance, looking at rule combination $x60\_y110$ (Fig. 4, top row), after 50 generations it is possible to observe an aggregation of similarly sized shapeless clusters, where the most recognisable elements are the $size = 2$ closed clusters. However, looking at generation 100 of the same rule combination, it is possible to note the re-appearance of closed $size = 4$ formations, also found at time step $t = 0$, which exist either as closed clusters or as part of larger ones. These formations can be interpreted as large, regular empty spaces, which differentiates them from other formations by their attributes – they can be thought of as motifs. Similarly, looking at time step $t = 50$, in the snapshots corresponding to rule combination $x30\_y54$ (Fig. 4, bottom row), close to the top right corner, it is possible to observe a series of formations cycling around a single boundary, which could be interpreted as a large subdivided regular area, providing a different set of spatial attributes. It is important to note that all these new instances are generated by the same structural constraints, or transition rules.

To conclude the preliminary analysis, we plot time series values of the cosine similarity metric (Eq. 1) between the evolving spatial configurations at each time step of the simulation in Fig. 5.

$$\text{similarity} = cos(\theta) = \frac{\sum\limits_{i=1}^{m} \mathbf{V}_{i,(t)} \times \mathbf{V}_{i,(t+1)}}{\sqrt{\sum\limits_{i=1}^{m} \mathbf{V}_{i,(t)}^2} \times \sqrt{\sum\limits_{i=1}^{m} \mathbf{V}_{i,(t+1)}^2}} \tag{1}$$

Here, $\mathbf{V}$ is a vector of graph theoretic metrics of length m, {**M1, M2, M3**}. The vector evaluated at consecutive time steps. An inspection of the plot provides additional supporting evidence for the gradual transition between alternative spatial configurations. However, what is most interesting is the sudden spikes/drops in similarity values (e.g., at $t = 100$ for $x30\_y60$) over the course of

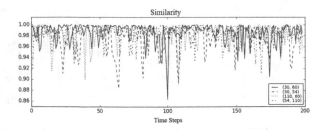

Fig. 5. Cosine similarity *vs* time, where the vector of feature at each time corresponds to average cluster size, std. dev for average cluster size, open clusters/closed clusters ratio.

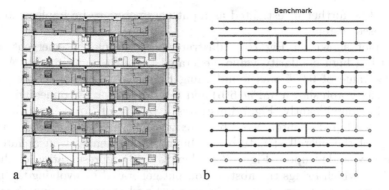

Fig. 6. Typical section of 'Unitéd'habitation' by Le Corbusier (a) and its representation as connectivity graph (b), generated using the alphabet of 16 possible spatial units illustrated in Fig. 2. (Color figure online)

the time evolution of the model – reminiscent of 'punctuated equilibria,' consistent with innovative/adaptive behaviour [24].

Attribute Matching. In the second phase of our analysis, the goal was not to match any given spatial pattern exactly, but rather to investigate whether 'interesting' smaller building blocks (correspond to local cluster or motifs) could be evolved. The emergent abstract spatial configurations would then be translated into architectural cross sections as part of the early stage of design. As a benchmark, the typical section of the interlocking dwelling units of the 'Unitéd'habitation' by Le Corbusier is used (see Fig. 6). This choice of benchmark was motivated by its formal characteristics that allow for a series of potentially desirable attributes in terms of lighting, ventilation and circulation performance

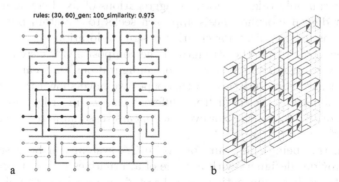

Fig. 7. (a) Connectivity graph for evolved spatial configuration with cosine similarity value = 0.975 corresponding to the typical section of Fig. 6. (b) 3D representation of the evolved connectivity graph, which brings the abstract output of the model to a language that can be easily interpreted from an architectural perspective. (Color figure online)

that could be further investigated as input parameters to be implemented into the proposed system.

The plot shown in Fig. 7(a) illustrates an example of emergent spatial form, with a high similarity value, generated by our composite CA. A cosine similarity value of 0.975 was found using Eq. 1 where A was the benchmark connectivity graph shown in Fig. 6(b) and B was the evolved connectivity graph in the plot. Significantly, Fig. 7 illustrates a variety of 'forms', which can be detailed, developed or interpreted by a designer at a later stage, where implicit meanings of the overall structure and boundary elements of an architectural space are expanded upon. Figure 7(a) depicts a 3D representation of the plot in Fig. 7(b), which brings the abstract output generated by evolving the model, into a language that can easily be interpreted and recognised by architectural designers as a spatial configuration to be further developed and detailed.

5   Discussion and Conclusion

In this paper, we have described a composite CA that can be used to generate a variety of spatial configurations by defining the boundaries of 'encapsulated spatial units,' as well as their interconnections. The characteristics of the generated space emerge as a consequence of the evolution of the CA, rather than being prescribed by design, as properties of the cells, as it happens with more common implementations of CA in architecture and design. Our goal was to explore the formation of aggregates or clusters of encapsulated spatial units, in search for 'interesting' spatial organizations with potential to be detailed, developed and/or interpreted by a designer at a later stage. Our model was able to produce clusters of a wide variety of sizes, shapes and with different 'spatial attributes' (regularity, openness, fragmentation, among others). We have described metrics that can be used to evaluate the emergent patterns against design criteria, which for the moment can only take the form of aggregations of fixed configurations (see Fig. 2). Our digital morphogenesis approach seeks to maintain both flexibility and fluidity, as it is required for creative design exploration.

It can be argued that the strength of the composite CA system is based on its capability to produce a vast array of configurations that can be evaluated in terms of their characteristics. In this paper we have shown the analysis of a few rule combinations, selected from different classes, in order to demonstrate the efficacy of the approach. However, it appears reasonable to expect different results if different rules are used.

With all this being said, our composite CA system can be described as a tool that provides designers with a range of alternatives to satisfy given design requirements, rather than acting as a direct design tool for completed design solutions. In its current state, the ability of the model to generate/search the state space is defined by transition rules and the time evolution of the model. In our experiments, the benchmark target was a pre-defined spatial configuration. However, we found that searching for a fixed, static configuration limited the possibilities by constraining the desired output to what has already been imagined by other designer, defeating the ultimate purpose of the model – generating a design space, and searching through it using design criteria, looking for emergent spatial configurations. Therefore, introducing protocols to search for characteristics of the space (e.g., open *vs.* closed space, or mean cluster size), rather than specific fixed patterns, is seen as a strategy that suits the purpose of enabling the emergence of unexpected spatial configurations. In this regard, the development of more accurate metrics to represent 'spatial attributes', the development of mechanisms to incorporate modifications to the rules as the system evolves, as well as the introduction of external influences, are seen as plausible paths to pursue in order to extend the system's capabilities.

The graph theoretic analysis of the composite CA time evolution has some similarities with concepts from 'space syntax' [15,27]. In space syntax, graphs are used to represent the sub-divided space in order to identify specific configurations, which are then analyzed via social relations and properties. In contrast, in our approach we search for configured space in terms of physical attributes, which may be understood as a connected set of discrete units, rather than a continuum [3]. This configure space then acts as input into subsequent evolutionary cycles in a search for new, emergent, spatial configurations.

There are many opportunities to extend this work. One interesting direction would be to 'fine tune' the metrics to better reflect design requirements. Another avenue is to explore the use of evolutionary algorithms to search for design 'motifs' encapsulated by specific metrics and to examine design trade-offs.

References

1. Alexander, C., Ishikawa, S., Silverstein, M.: A Pattern Language: Towns, Buildings. Construction. Oxford University Press, Oxford (1977)
2. Araghi, S.K., Stouffs, R.: Exploring cellular automata for high density residential building form generation. Autom. Constr. **49**, 152–162 (2015)
3. Bafna, S.: Space syntax a brief introduction to its logic and analytical techniques. Environ. Behav. **35**(1), 17–29 (2003)
4. Camazine, S.: Self-Organization in Biological Systems. Princeton University Press, Princeton (2003)
5. Chavoya, A., Duthen, Y.: A cell pattern generation model based on an extended artificial regulatory network. Biosystems **94**(1), 95–101 (2008)
6. Coates, P., Healy, N., Lamb, C., Voon, W.: The use of cellular automata to explore bottom up architectonic rules. Eurographics Association UK (1996)
7. De Garis, H.: Genetic programming artificial nervous systems artificial embryos and embryological electronics. In: Schwefel, H.-P., Männer, R. (eds.) PPSN 1990. LNCS, vol. 496, pp. 117–123. Springer, Heidelberg (1991). doi:10.1007/BFb0029741
8. Dorin, A., McCormack, J.: Self-assembling dynamical hierarchies. Artif. Life **8**, 423–428 (2003)
9. Doursat, R.: The growing canvas of biological development: multiscale pattern generation on an expanding lattice of gene regulatory nets. In: Minai, A., Braha, D., Bar-Yam, Y. (eds.) Unifying Themes in Complex Systems, pp. 205–210. Springer, Heidelberg (2008)
10. Gardner, M.: The fantastic combinations of john conways new solitaire games. Mathematical Games (1970)

11. Government, V.S.: Better Apartments Draft Design Standards. Environment, Land, Water and Planning (2016). Draft version
12. Hensel, M., Menges, A.: Differentiation and performance: multi-performance architectures and modulated environments. Architect. Des. **76**(2), 60–69 (2006)
13. Hensel, M., Menges, A., Weinstock, M.: Emergence: Morphogenetic Design Strategies. Wiley-Academy, Chichester (2004)
14. Herr, C.M., Kvan, T.: Adapting cellular automata to support the architectural design process. Autom. Constr. **16**(1), 61–69 (2007)
15. Hillier, B., Hanson, J.: The Social Logic of Space. Cambridge University Press, Cambridge (1984)
16. Holland, J.H.: Adaptation in Natural, Artificial Systems: An Introductory Analysis with Applications to Biology, Control, and Artificial Intelligence. MIT Press, Cambridge (1992)
17. Kondacs, A.: Biologically-inspired self-assembly of two-dimensional shapes using global-to-local compilation. In: Proceedings of the 18th International Joint Conference on Artificial Intelligence, pp. 633–638. Morgan Kaufmann Publishers Inc. (2003)
18. Kowaliw, T., Grogono, P., Kharma, N.: Bluenome: a novel developmental model of artificial morphogenesis. In: Deb, K. (ed.) GECCO 2004. LNCS, vol. 3102, pp. 93–104. Springer, Heidelberg (2004). doi:10.1007/978-3-540-24854-5_9
19. Krawczyk, R.J.: Architectural interpretation of cellular automata. In: Generative Art Conference, Milano (2002)
20. Lynch, K.: Good City Form. MIT Press, Cambridge (1981)
21. Man, G.M.: The Quark, the Jaguar: Adventures in the Simple and the Complex (1994)
22. Mitchell, W.J.: Computer-Aided Architectural Design. Wiley, New York (1977)
23. The Office of the Victorian Government Architect. Better apartments - a discussion paper. Technical report, Department of Environment, Land, Water and Planning (2015)
24. Paperin, G., Green, D., Sadedin, S.: Dual-phase evolution in complex adaptive systems. J. R. Soc. Interface **8**(58), 609–629 (2011)
25. Sayama, H.: Self-protection and diversity in self-replicating cellular automata. Artif. Life **10**(1), 83–98 (2004)
26. Shalizi, C.R.: Methods, techniques of complex systems science: an overview. In: Deisboeck, T.S., Yasha Kresh, J. (eds.) Complex Systems Science in Biomedicine, pp. 33–114. Springer, Heidelberg (2006)
27. Steadman, P.: Architectural Morphology: An Introduction to the Geometry of Building Plans. Taylor & Francis, Milton Park (1983)
28. Stiny, G.: Introduction to shape and shape grammars. Environ. Plann. B **7**(3), 343–351 (1980)
29. Thompson, D.W., et al.: On Growth and Form. Cambridge University Press, Cambridge (1942)
30. Von Neumann, J., Burks, A.W., et al.: Theory of self-reproducing automata. IEEE Trans. Neural Netw. **5**(1), 3–14 (1966)
31. Watson, J.D., et al.: Molecular biology of the gene. Molecular biology of the gene, 2nd edn. (1970)
32. Wolfram, S.: Universality and complexity in cellular automata. Phys. D: Nonlinear Phenom. **10**(1), 1–35 (1984)
33. Wolfram, S.: A New Kind of Science, vol. 5. Wolfram Media, Champaign (2002)

Wrapper Feature Construction for Figure-Ground Image Segmentation Using Genetic Programming

Yuyu Liang$^{(\boxtimes)}$, Mengjie Zhang, and Will N. Browne

School of Engineering and Computer Science,
Victoria University of Wellington, P.O. Box 600, Wellington 6140, New Zealand
{yuyu.liang,mengjie.zhang,will.browne}@ecs.vuw.ac.nz

Abstract. Figure-ground segmentation is a process of separating regions of interest from unimportant backgrounds. It is challenging to separate objects from target images with high variations (e.g. cluttered backgrounds), which requires effective feature sets to capture the discriminative information between object and background regions. Feature construction is a process of transforming a given set of features to a new set of high-level features, which considers the interactions between the previous features, thus the constructed features can be more meaningful and effective. As Genetic programming (GP) is a well-suited algorithm for feature construction (FC), it is employed to conduct both multiple FC (MFC) and single FC (SFC), which aims to improve the segmentation performance for the first time in this paper. The cooperative coevolution technique is introduced in GP to construct multiple features from different types of image features separately while conducting feature combination simultaneously, called as CoevoGPMFC. One wrapper method (wrapperGPSFC) is also designed, and one well-performing embedded method (embeddedGPSFC) is introduced as a reference method. Compared with the original features extracted by existing feature descriptors, the constructed features from the proposed methods are more robust and performance better on the test set. Moreover, the features constructed by the three methods achieve similar performance for the given segmentation tasks.

Keywords: Figure-ground segmentation · Genetic programming · Feature construction · Coevolution

1 Introduction

Figure-ground segmentation is a process of separating regions of interest from unimportant backgrounds, which is regarded as a crucial middle-level task in the fields of image processing and computer vision [14]. The goal of figure-ground segmentation is to capture the target regions to facilitate the subsequent higher-level tasks, e.g. scene understanding [6], object recognition [7]; therefore, the results of figure-ground segmentation can affect the performance of the subsequent tasks.

© Springer International Publishing AG 2017
M. Wagner et al. (Eds.): ACALCI 2017, LNAI 10142, pp. 111–123, 2017.
DOI: 10.1007/978-3-319-51691-2_10

To achieve accurate segmentation performance on images with high variations (e.g. cluttered backgrounds and/or varying objects), a good feature space
that can capture difference between object pixels and background ones is a prerequisite. As there are many existing image descriptors, they often provide high
dimensional features with irrelevant information, and often can not match the
patterns in various image domains [13]. In addition, for a given test dataset, it
is often not clear of the optimal feature representation beforehand [13]. As it is
infeasible to try all possible features, conducting feature construction on the features extracted by existing descriptors is necessary, which can produce high-level
features with more distinctive information between objects and backgrounds.

Genetic programming (GP) is an evolutionary computation technique, which
can evolve a population of solutions (computer programs) by transforming populations of solutions into new and normally better populations to solve given
problems [4]. GP has been regarded as a well-suited technique for feature construction due to the following reasons. Firstly, GP can use tree-like representation, in which various kinds of functions can be used to combine input features to
linear or non-linear forms without pre-defining the structure. The input features
can be low/middle-level primitive features extracted by existing feature descriptors. GP is flexible and does not require any assumptions or constraints on the
input features [9]. Secondly, GP has high search ability and has the potential to
find global optima, so it is more likely for GP to handle large search space (often
faced by feature construction tasks).

There are different categorization criteria for FC methods. Based on whether
a single feature or multiple features is/are constructed, there are SFC [2] and
MFC methods [10]. In addition, FC methods can fall into three branches based
on how to evaluate the constructed new features in the FC process, i.e. wrapper,
filter and embedded approaches [11]. Wrapper and embedded methods evaluate
the constructed features based on the feedback of a learning algorithm; while
filter methods depend on general characteristics of features. Embedded methods
conduct feature construction and build a learning model in one step; while filter
and wrapper methods treat them as two separate steps. Based on the feedback
of a learning algorithm, it is likely for wrapper methods to construct more effective features than filter methods, yet they are more computationally intensive;
while filter methods are more efficient [11]. Since modifications to the learning algorithm may cause poor performance [12], embedded methods are more
conceptually complex.

1.1   Goal

Feature construction has not been commonly studied to solve image segmentation problems, which deserves more exploration. Our previous work [8] works on
filter and embedded SFC using GP for figure-ground segmentation. Better results
have been achieved by the combined feature set (adding the single constructed
feature into the original feature set) than the original features. However, wrapper
SFC/MFC has not been exploited for complex segmentation problems; therefore,
this paper aims to design wrapper methods to construct both a single feature and

multiple features using GP. Specifically, the cooperative coevolution technique is introduced in GP to construct multiple features separately from different types of image features; while combining the constructed features simultaneously. This method is called as CoevoGPMFC. A wrapper SFC method, WrapperGPSFC, is also designed. In addition, the embedded SFC method, EmbeddedGPSFC [8], is used as a reference method due to its good performance. Specifically, we investigate the following objectives:

1. whether the constructed feature set can outperform the original features on complex segmentation tasks;
2. which one of the proposed methods can construct more effective features;
3. how to reveal the effectiveness of the constructed features in distinguishing object and background pixels.

The rest of this paper is organized as follows. Section 2 introduces the proposed methods. Section 3 describes experiment preparations, i.e. datasets and evaluation measures. In Sect. 4, results are provided and analyzed. Conclusions are drawn in Sect. 5.

2 The Proposed Methods

2.1 CoevoGPMFC

Algorithm 1 shows the pseudo code of the proposed method, CoevoGPMFC. Compared with the standard GP, the major difference lies in the initialisation stage and the fitness evaluation stage (highlighted in blue color). Specifically, the target problem is formulated into multiple subproblems. In the initialisation stage, multiple subpopulations are set up, each of which represents one subproblem. Then the coevolutionary search proceeds in each sub-population independently, except for the fitness evaluation of each individual [5], which relies on other individuals.

Figure 1 shows the fitness evaluation of an individual, which is individual j in the sub-population i. Firstly, one representative individual from each of the remaining subpopulations are selected to form the context of the target individual. The fittest individuals in other subpopulations from the previous generation are selected as the representative individuals in this work. Secondly, the selected individuals are combined with the target individual, which are actually three feature construction functions. With the input of primitive features, the internal train/test datasets are transformed based on the feature construction functions (three high-level features are constructed for each internal train/test sample). Thirdly, a classifier (e.g. decision tree) is trained and evaluated based on the transformed internal train/test sets to produce the classification accuracy, which is assigned to the target individual as its fitness value.

input : M: the number of subpopulations;
         G: the maximum number of generations;
         The terminal set, function set and GP parameters (Sect. 3.1).
output: Solutions (feature construction functions).

```
1  for m = 0 to M-1 do
2  │   For subpopulation Pm, determine the subpopulation size Nm;
3  │   Create an initial population of Nm GP trees at iteration zero (Pm0) using the
   │   Ramped half-and-half method;
4  end
5  g ← 1
6  while g < G − 1 and the ideal individual (the individual with fitness value == 1.0 )
   is not found do
7  │   for m = 0 to M-1 do
8  │   │   Fitness assignment: Individuals from subpopulation Pm are tested by grouping
   │   │   them with the fittest individuals in the other subpopulations from the previous
   │   │   generation and assessing their joint fitness (Fig. 1);
9  │   │   Create Pm(g+1) from Pmg:
10 │   │   begin
11 │   │   │   Set Pm(g+1) empty;
12 │   │   │   for i = 0 to Nm − 1 do
13 │   │   │   │   Conduct crossover, mutation or reproduction operations based on the
   │   │   │   │   individuals from Pmg;
14 │   │   │   │   Add the child/children to Pm(g+1);
15 │   │   │   end
16 │   │   end
17 │   end
18 │   g ← g + 1;
19 end
20 Return the M best individuals from M subpopulations.
```

Algorithm 1. Pseudo-code of Coevolutionary method (GP procedure is in red and coevolution procedure is in blue).

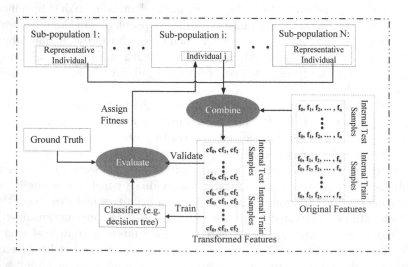

Fig. 1. The fitness evaluation of one individual in cooperative coevolution (N is the number of subpopulations; f_0 and cf_0 means a feature and a constructed feature with the index 0 respectively; internal train/test sets means the train and test set used in the internal GP evolution process for fitness evaluation).

2.2   WrapperGPSFC

The proposed WrapperGPSFC uses the classification accuracy for the fitness evaluation, which is the same as CoevoGPMFC. The fitness evaluation of an individual is shown in Fig. 2. The whole tree rooted on the root node is employed as a feature construction function, based on which the internal train/test samples are transformed to new samples. The new internal train/test sets are then employed to train and evaluate a classifier (e.g. decision tree), and the classification accuracy is generated as the fitness value of this individual.

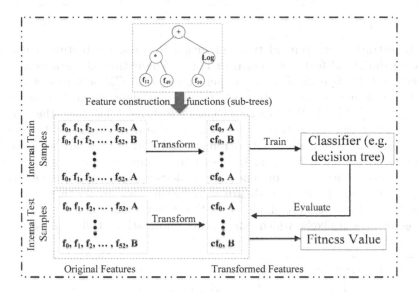

Fig. 2. The fitness evaluation of an individual in WrapperGPSFC method.

3   Experiment Preparations

3.1   GP Settings

Table 1 describes the function set, including five mathematical operators and two conditional operators. Major GP parameter settings are shown in Table 2, except for the population size. For CoevoGPMFC, the sizes of three subpopulations are 1024, 32 and 256 respectively; while for SFC methods (i.e. WrapperG-PSFC and EmbeddedGPSFC), as there is only one single subpopulation, the size is 1312. Figure 3 shows the terminal set. As there are three subpopulation in CoevoGPMFC, each subpopulation takes one type of image features as its terminal set (texture features for subpopulation 0; color features for subpopulation (1) grayscale statistical features for subpopulation (2). For other methods, as there is only one subpopulation, the terminal set is the same, which contains all the three types of features. Several feature descriptors are employed in this

Table 1. Function set.

Function name	Definition	Function name	Definition
$+(a_1, a_2)$	$a_1 + a_2$	$-(a_1, a_2)$	$a_1 - a_2$
$*(a_1, a_2)$	$a_1 * a_2$	$\%(a_1, a_2)$	$\begin{cases} a_1/a_2 & \text{if } a_2! = 0 \\ 0 & \text{if } a_2 == 0 \end{cases}$
$L(a_1)$	$Log\|a_1\|$		
$>(a_1, a_2)$	$\begin{cases} a_1 \text{ if } a_1 > a_2 \\ a_2 \text{ if otherwise} \end{cases}$	$<(a_1, a_2)$	$\begin{cases} a_1 \text{ if } a_1 < a_2 \\ a_2 \text{ if otherwise} \end{cases}$

work to extract three general types of image features, i.e. texture, color and grayscale statistical features, shown in Fig. 3. The extracted features are normalized to [0,1]. Specifically, this paper employs 40 Gabor filters, generated from five common scales $(4, 4\sqrt{2}, 8, 8\sqrt{2}, 16)$ and eight common orientations $(0, \frac{\pi}{8}, \frac{2\pi}{8}, \frac{3\pi}{8}, \frac{4\pi}{8}, \frac{5\pi}{8}, \frac{6\pi}{8}, \frac{7\pi}{8})$ to extract Gabor features. Therefore, there are 40 Gabor features in each feature vector (Fig. 3). The mean filter and the median filter, which are commonly used to remove noise in images, are employed to extract local statistical features. LBP can transform an image to an array of integer labels, which can represent the small-scale image appearance. As the mean, median and LBP methods are local feature descriptors that operate in blocks, three block sizes are employed in this paper, including 3×3 pixels, 5×5 pixels and 9×9 pixels, which can capture information at different scales.

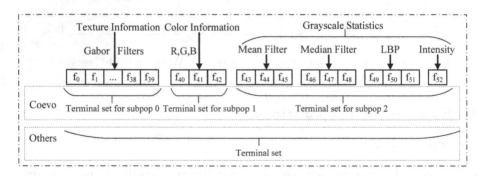

Fig. 3. Low/middle-level features (Coevo means the CoevoGPMFC method; Others refer to WrapperGPSFC and EmbeddedGPSFC; f_0 is a feature with 0 as its index and so forth; subpop represents subpopulation).

3.2   Datasets

Two standard datasets, the Weizmann horse dataset [1] and Pascal VOC2012 (VOC, Visual Object Classes) [3], are employed in this paper. Both datasets consist of images with high variations, which are considered as difficult segmentation tasks. Figure 4 displays several examples along with the ground truth images

Table 2. GP parameter settings.

Parameter	Setting	Parameter	Setting
Generation	51	Initialisation	HalfBuilder
Crossover rate	0.80	Mutation rate	0.19
Reproduction rate	0.01	Maximum depth	8

(object in white and background in black color). Specifically, the Weizmann dataset has 328 horse images with varying horse positions. Moreover, certain images have cluttered backgrounds (e.g. horse227 and horse306), and there are images with low quality (e.g. horse264). The average size of the Weizmann images is around 250 × 200 pixels. There are 178 aeroplane images in the Pascal dataset, which are considered more complex than the Weizmann images, due to the high variations in object sizes and object shapes (e.g. airliners, fighters and biplanes), and the cluttered backgrounds. Moreover, some images contain multiple objects (e.g. 2010_003127), and there are noisy/blurred images, e.g. image 2007_001761 (blurred by motion) and image 2010_002939 (containing noise). Their average size is around 500 × 350 pixels.

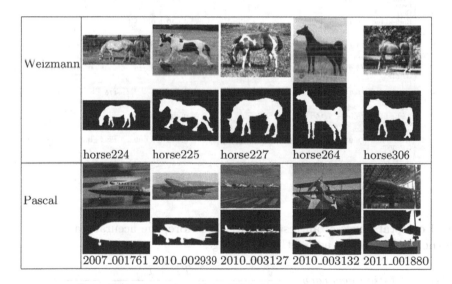

Fig. 4. Example images.

3.3 Evaluation Measures

The segmentation accuracy (Eq. 1) and F_1 score (Eq. 2) are utilised to evaluate the segmentation results, which are simple and commonly used. Both measures reach the worst at 0 and the best at 1. Specifically, TP, TN, FP and FN stand for true positives, true negatives, false positives and false negatives respectively

Table 3. Training performance (#F means the number of features; ↑, ↓ or = mean significantly better, worse or similar, compared with original features).

Dataset	Method (#F)	Training accuracy (%)		
		J48	NB	PART
Weizmann	Original features (53)	97.13	70.78	84.52
	EmbeddedGPSFC (1)	78.73 ± 0.90		
	WrapperGPSFC (1)	76.95 ± 1.12 ↓	75.55 ± 1.38 ↑	76.70 ± 1.57 ↓
	CoevoGPMFC (3)	78.14 ± 0.66 ↓	75.68 ± 0.94 ↑	77.20 ± 0.58 ↓
Pasccal	Original features (53)	94.92	79.48	89.52
	EmbeddedGPSFC (1)	84.51 ± 0.30		
	WrapperGPSFC (1)	84.07 ± 0.29 ↓	83.40 ± 0.37 ↑	84.14 ± 0.33 ↓
	CoevoGPMFC (3)	85.18 ± 0.71 ↓	83.17 ± 0.34 ↑	84.32 ± 0.65 ↓

Table 4. Test performance (#F means the number of features; ↑, ↓ or = mean significantly better, worse or similar, compared with original features).

Dataset	Method (#F)	Segmentation accuracy (%)			Test F_1 score		
		J48	NB	PART	J48	NB	PART
Weizmann	Original features (53)	69.84	72.38	76.98	0.544	0.565	0.566
	Embedded GPSFC (1)	77.18 ± 1.49 ↑			0.630 ± 0.013 ↑		
	Wrapper GPSFC (1)	74.74↑ ±1.21	74.02↑ ±2.10	74.16↓ ±1.75	0.605↑ ±0.011	0.598↑ ±0.013	0.603↑ ±0.015
	Coevo GPMFC (3)	74.97↑±1.39	74.38↑±1.53	75.26↓±1.88	0.603↑±0.013	0.596↑±0.010	0.600↑±0.012
Pasccal	Original features (53)	75.44	83.56	79.60	0.442	0.475	0.475
	Embedded GPSFC (1)	78.06 ± 1.15			0.484 ± 0.008 ↑		
	Wrapper GPSFC (1)	78.27↑±1.28	79.83↓±1.15	78.09↓±1.16	0.482↑±0.009	0.489↑±0.009	0.480↑±0.009
	Coevo GPMFC (3)	78.46↑±1.62	80.07↓±0.94	77.82↓±1.63	0.486↑±0.014	0.496↑±0.007	0.477↑±0.013

based on total pixels of all test images. Therefore, the accuracy and F_1 scores are the average values across the test images.

$$segmentation\ accuracy = \frac{TP + TN}{Total.Pixel.Number.of.All.Test.Images} \quad (1)$$

$$
\begin{aligned}
F_1 &= 2 * Precision * Recall/(Precision + Recall) \\
Precision &= TP/(TP + FP) \\
Recall &= TP/(TP + FN)
\end{aligned}
\quad (2)
$$

3.4 Experiment Design

The Weizmann dataset has 328 horse images, two thirds of which are used as training images (218 images), and the remaining of which (110 images) are for testing. Twenty samples are extracted from each training image (10 from object/background pixels respectively) to form the training samples. The Pascal dataset contains 178 aeroplane images for segmentation, 88 images of which are for training and 90 images are for testing (suggested by Everingham [3]). Since Pascal images are larger than Weizmann images, 50 samples (25 from object/background pixels respectively) are extracted from each training image. For wrapper FC methods, i.e. CoevoGPMFC and WrapperGPSFC, the training set is split to internal train/test sets for fitness evaluation (two thirds of total samples as the internal train set; the remaining as the internal test set). Three standard classifiers, i.e. J48, Naïve Bayes (NB) and PART, from the Weka package are selected to evaluate the constructed features. All GP related experiments run 30 independent times, and the results are the average of 30 best solutions (one single best solution from each run).

4 Results

4.1 Training and Test Performance

According to Table 3, the training performance of the constructed multiple features produced by CoevoGPMFC and the constructed single features by EmbeddedGPSFC and WrapperGPSFC are generally worse than that of the original features on both datasets, except for NB based experiments. However, on the test dataset (shown in Table 4), the constructed features from all the three methods achieve better segmentation performance than that of original features in F1 score. It reflects that the constructed features are more robust and have higher generalization ability than the original features for the given complex segmentation tasks. Note that compared with the original features based on the test accuracy, the constructed features from WrapperGPSFC and CoevoGPMFC are worse using PART on Weizmann dataset and features from all three methods are worse using NB and PART on Pascal dataset, while all the constructed features achieve higher F1 scores on both datasets. As the majority part of most test images is background, the test samples of each image are unbalanced; therefore, F1 score is more reliable than the test accuracy.

When comparing CoevoGPMFC with the wrapper SFC method – Wrapper GPSFC, CoevoGPMFC achieves generally better training accuracies on both datasets; and a little better or similar results for testing performance. In addition, compared with another embedded SFC method – EmbeddedGPSFC, CoevoGPMFC produces features with varying segmentation performance. Specifically, on the test sets, CoevoGPMFC achieves lower scores on Weizmann dataset based on both evaluation measures (segmentation accuracy and F1 score) than EmbeddedGPSFC; while it achieves higher scores on Pascal dataset. Even though there occurs varying results on different datasets based on

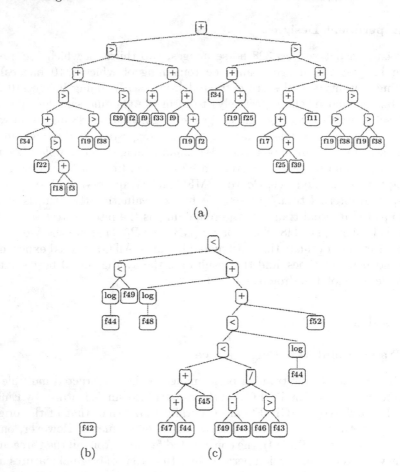

(a)

(b)   (c)

Fig. 5. Example FC functions evolved by the CoevoGPMFC method based on J48 ((a), (b) and (c) are the best solutions of subpopulation 0, 1 and 2 respectively).

different classifiers, statistical results in Tables 3 and 4 indicate that features constructed by all the three proposed methods, i.e. CoevoGPMFC, WrapperGPSFC and EmbeddedGPSFC, achieve similar segmentation performance.

4.2   Further Analyses

Figure 5 displays one best group of feature construction functions evolved by the CoevoGPMFC method. Figure 5b shows that the FC function is to select the feature f_{42}, and no further operation is implemented. Based on these functions, test samples of a Pascal test image (Fig. 6a) are transformed into the constructed feature spaces respectively. Figure 6b, c and d show the object/background histogram in the spaces. It can be seen that the majority of object pixels and background pixels can be separated in all the constructed feature spaces. Moreover, Fig. 6c shows that feature f_{42} itself is distinctive, which explains that the

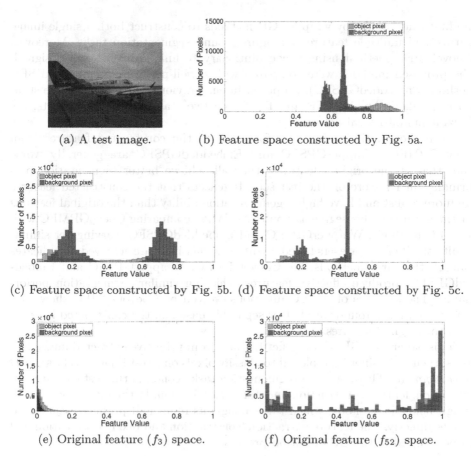

(a) A test image.   (b) Feature space constructed by Fig. 5a.

(c) Feature space constructed by Fig. 5b. (d) Feature space constructed by Fig. 5c.

(e) Original feature (f_3) space.   (f) Original feature (f_{52}) space.

Fig. 6. Distribution of class *object/background* pixels in different feature spaces.

solution in Fig. 6c only selects f_{42} without operations. In contrast, Fig. 6e and f display the object/background histogram based on two original features, e.g. f_3 and f_{52}, which are used in the solutions in Fig. 5. Both figures show that the majority of background and object pixels are overlapping, and are not as separable as in the constructed feature spaces, which reflects that the constructed features contain more distinguishing information than the original ones. Therefore, the proposed CoevoGPMFC method can evolve useful functions to build effective high-level features.

5   Conclusions and Future Work

This paper developed two wrapper FC methods: one is a MFC method (CoevoGPMFC) and the other is a SFC method (WrapperGPSFC), which aim to produce more effective features from primitive image features to improve the segmentation performance on complex figure-ground segmentation tasks. This is the first time to employ wrapper GP methods to construct both a single image feature and multiple features for figure-ground segmentation tasks. Moreover, a novel MFC method using a coevolutionary technique in GP was designed. The proposed methods were compared with a well-performing embedded SFC method (EmbeddedGPSFC), proposed in our previous work [8], by three standard classifiers, i.e. J48, NB and PART, on two standard image datasets, i.e. Weizmann and Pascal datasets.

Even though the training performance of the constructed features from CoevoGPMFC, WrapperGPSFC and EmbeddedGPSFC are generally worse than that of the original features, they all achieve better segmentation performance in F1 score on the test sets. It reflects that the constructed features are more robust and have higher generalization ability than the original features for the given complex segmentation tasks. When comparing CoevoGPMFC with the SFC methods, WrapperGPSFC and EmbeddedGPSFC, varying yet similar results on different datasets based on different classifiers are achieved. It indicates that all the three methods, i.e. CoevoGPMFC, WrapperGPSFC and EmbeddedGPSFC, produce effective features achieving similar segmentation performance. The analyses of the FC functions evolved by CoevoGPMFC show that objects and backgrounds are better separable based on the constructed features than the original features.

This paper uses GP to construct features from primitive extracted image features, then a classifier is employed to classify pixels on a test image as class *object* or *background*. Therefore, the segmentation tasks contains three stages: feature extraction, feature construction and pixel classification. In the future, we plan to design new GP methods, which takes images as input and produces segmented images directly. The feature extraction/construction and pixel classification will all be realized in the GP evolution process.

References

1. Borenstein, E., Ullman, S.: Combined top-down/bottom-up segmentation. IEEE Trans. Pattern Anal. Mach. Intell. **30**(12), 2109–2125 (2008)
2. Cano, A., Ventura, S., Cios, K.J.: Multi-objective genetic programming for feature extraction and data visualization. Soft Comput. 1–21 (2015). doi:10.1007/s00500-015-1907-y
3. Everingham, M., Eslami, S.A., Van Gool, L., Williams, C.K., Winn, J., Zisserman, A.: The Pascal visual object classes challenge: a retrospective. Int. J. Comput. Vis. **111**(1), 98–136 (2014)
4. Koza, J.R.: Genetic Programming: on the Programming of Computers by Means of Natural Selection, vol. 1. MIT Press, Cambridge (1992)
5. Krawiec, K., Bhanu, B.: Coevolution and linear genetic programming for visual learning. In: Cantú-Paz, E., et al. (eds.) GECCO 2003. LNCS, vol. 2723, pp. 332–343. Springer, Heidelberg (2003). doi:10.1007/3-540-45105-6_39
6. Kumar, M.P., Koller, D.: Efficiently selecting regions for scene understanding. In: 2010 IEEE Conference on Computer Vision and Pattern Recognition (CVPR), pp. 3217–3224. IEEE (2010)

7. Lee, Y.J., Grauman, K.: Object-graphs for context-aware visual category discovery. IEEE Trans. Pattern Anal. Mach. Intell. **34**(2), 346–358 (2012)
8. Liang, Y., Zhang, M., Browne, W.N.: Feature construction using genetic programming for figure-ground image segmentation. In: Leu, G., Singh, H.K., Elsayed, S. (eds.) Intelligent and Evolutionary Systems. PALO, vol. 8, pp. 237–250. Springer, Heidelberg (2017). doi:10.1007/978-3-319-49049-6_17
9. Neshatian, K.: Feature manipulation with genetic programming (2010)
10. Neshatian, K., Zhang, M., Andreae, P.: A filter approach to multiple feature construction for symbolic learning classifiers using genetic programming. IEEE Trans. Evol. Comput. **16**(5), 645–661 (2012)
11. Poli, R.: Genetic programming for image analysis. In: Proceedings of the 1st Annual Conference on Genetic Programming, pp. 363–368. MIT Press (1996)
12. Roth, V., Lange, T.: Adaptive feature selection in image segmentation. In: Rasmussen, C.E., Bülthoff, H.H., Schölkopf, B., Giese, M.A. (eds.) DAGM 2004. LNCS, vol. 3175, pp. 9–17. Springer, Heidelberg (2004). doi:10.1007/978-3-540-28649-3_2
13. Sondhi, P.: Feature construction methods: a survey. sifaka. cs. uiuc. edu, **69**, 70–71 (2009)
14. Zou, W., Bai, C., Kpalma, K., Ronsin, J.: Online glocal transfer for automatic figure-ground segmentation. IEEE Trans. Image Process. **23**(5), 2109–2121 (2014)

Surrogate-Assisted Multi-swarm Particle Swarm Optimization of Morphing Airfoils

Francesco Fico[1], Francesco Urbino[1], Robert Carrese[1,2,3], Pier Marzocca[2],
and Xiaodong Li[3(✉)]

[1] Politecnico di Torino, Turin, Italy
[2] School of Aerospace Mechanical and Manufacturing,
RMIT University, Melbourne, VIC, Australia
[3] School of Science (Computer Science and Software Engineering),
RMIT University, Melbourne, VIC, Australia
xiaodong.li@rmit.edu.au

Abstract. This paper presents a study to design, analyze and optimize an airfoil trailing edge, i.e., shape morphing of the airfoil trailing-edge topology. The primary idea behind morphing is to improve the wing performance for different flight conditions. Modern aircrafts are designed for unique operating conditions. In order to obtain the best configuration, a dynamic optimization algorithm has been developed based on a Multi-swarm Particle Swarm Optimization algorithm (MPSO), a population-based stochastic optimization algorithm inspired by the social interaction among insects or animals. However, with respect to aircraft design and in the context of computational fluid dynamics (CFD), function evaluations are computationally expensive; typically requiring large computational grids to obtain a reasonable representation of the flow-field. In this paper, the developed MPSO algorithm is combined with a Kriging surrogate representation of the objective space, to alleviate the computational effort. The topology of the trailing edge is defined and characterized by four control points. Two different hypothetical mission profiles are analyzed. The results exhibit an improvement of around 2% with respect to the original airfoil for every flight condition treated.

1   Introduction

One of the major challenges in aerospace design is to improve aircraft efficiency during operation, a requirement borne from the need to accommodate for rising fuel prices and the mitigation of emissions. The research effort in aircraft design is primarily driven by this incentive. One of most widely-used strategies by modern aircraft is using movable control surfaces to improve flight performance. For example, flaps and slats, whilst traditionally used during take-off and landing manoeuvres, can also be used to introduce a variable camber to the wing, thus providing scope for determining the optimum configuration for a given flight condition. However, when constrained by limited freedom of movement, it is unlikely that optimal solutions for every possible cruise condition are attainable. Furthermore, control surface devices result in geometrical discontinuities, which can often reduce the aerodynamic efficiency. In contrast, a morphing

© Springer International Publishing AG 2017
M. Wagner et al. (Eds.): ACALCI 2017, LNAI 10142, pp. 124–133, 2017.
DOI: 10.1007/978-3-319-51691-2_11

wing can potentially conform to provide optimal performance at any desired flight condition. Morphing wing technology can be used for flow-control, aerodynamic tailoring, improved flight dynamics during manueveres, and improve the aeroelastic performance and dynamic load response of military aircraft [1,4,5,7].

In this paper a conceptual two-dimensional study is considered. The upper section of the trailing edge is deformable, since it is possible to achieve similar results to a fully morphing airfoil [2] without the drastic increase in complexity and weight. A multi-swarm heuristic, combining surrogate models for the alleviation of the computational effort are considered. Surrogates are used in lieu of the computationally expensive computational fluid dynamic (CFD) model, whereby the swarm directly navigates the surrogate landscape in order to find the region in the design space where the optimal solutions are likely located [3].

The dynamic optimization framework is developed to characterize the entire flight envelope, providing the best aerodynamic design, including morphing parameters as well, for that configuration. The framework allows for the identification of different optimal solutions, where the transition between different flight configurations (and therefore different shape topologies) is ultimately dependent on minimum energy expenditure during morphing. This ensures that during transition of flight configurations, the algorithm places a priority to solutions which avoid drastic changes between successive configurations, with minimal structural and logistic problems.

2   Geometrical Parametrization

The original (i.e. base) airfoil selected is the NACA 23012, which is a mildly-cambered low-speed airfoil. The topology of the morphing trailing edge is controlled using four control points, situated along the upper trailing edge section, as shown in Fig. 1. We choose as original airfoil a *NACA 23012*. The morphing

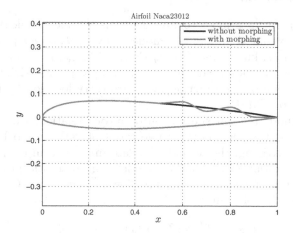

Fig. 1. An example of a morphed airfoil, compared with the original one, the design variables in input are: inputs = [1,0,1,0].

is theoretically achieved by manipulating the vertical (i.e. y) coordinate of the control points. Since the exact configuration is not known in advance, a random population of design candidates is first generated, and the optimization framework hones in on the optimal deviation of the vertical (i.e. y) coordinates from the original position. The boundaries of the design space are restricted to $\mathbf{y} \in [-0.015, 0.015]$, to ensure a robust topology the and manufacturable shape is guaranteed. To facilitate the optimization process, the boundaries are normalized to unity, where a value of 0 corresponds to the lowest position for the y coordinate and 1 to the highest position. The four control points provide the basis for shape morphing, where a piecewise cubic Hermite polynomial interpolation scheme is used.

3   Surrogate Model

A major obstacle in using population-based optimization frameworks is the often prohibitive computational expense of the numerical model. To this end, the pursuit of higher-order shape parameterization techniques, able to define arbitrarily complex shapes with minimal design variables, is highly desirable. Nevertheless, for true multi-disciplinary aircraft design, the numerical model is the most prohibitive element of the framework. The use of surrogate models are very popular for aerospace design applications since they can be used in lieu of the original and more costly computational model of the problem [3]. In this context, the surrogate model can play a very valuable role in increasing the feasibility of using population-based algorithms in conceptual aircraft design. The surrogates are constructed using data obtained from the high-fidelity numerical model, and provide cheap approximations of the original objective functions and constraints at new locations.

3.1   Kriging Method

Of particular significance in surrogate models is the methodology used. In this study, the approximated values are modeled by a *Gaussian process* governed by prior covariances, known as *Kriging* (Krige, 1951), which is an interpolating method featuring the observed data at all sample points. Kriging provides a statistical prediction of the function at an arbitrary location by minimizing its mean squared error (MSE).

Kriging methods rely on the notion of autocorrelation. Correlation is usually thought of as the tendency for two types of variables to be related. For the derivation of Kriging, the output of a deterministic computer experiment is treated as a realization of a random function (or stochastic process), which is defined as the sum of a global trend function $f^T(\mathbf{x})\beta$ and a Gaussian random function $Y(x)$ as the following:

$$y(\mathbf{x}) = f^T(\mathbf{x})\beta + Y(x), \qquad \mathbf{x} \in \Re^m, \tag{1}$$

where $f(\mathbf{x})$ is defined by a set of regression basis functions and β denotes the vector of the corresponding coefficients, m is the number of dimensions, and $\mathbf{x}$ is the vector of design variables. Now we can obtain the correlation function of our variables which is only dependent on the Euclidean distance between any two points $\mathbf{x}^{(i)}$ and $\mathbf{x}^{(l)}$ in the design space. The random variables are correlated with each other using the basis expression:

$$Corr[Y(\mathbf{x})^{(i)}, Y(\mathbf{x})^{(l)}] = exp\left(-\sum_{j=1}^{k} \theta_j |x_j^{(i)} - x_j^{(l)}|^{p_j}\right). \tag{2}$$

The correlation depends on the Euclidean distance and two undefined parameters θ and p that have to be obtained by means of a numerical optimization technique. At this point it is possible to formulate the prediction expression:

$$\hat{y}(\mathbf{x}) = (\hat{\mu}) + \psi^T \Psi^{-1}(\mathbf{y} - \mathbf{1}\hat{\mu}), \tag{3}$$

where ψ is the vector of the basis function, Ψ is the correlation matrix, $\mathbf{1}$ is a vector of one, centered around the n sample points and are added to a mean base term $\hat{\mu}$.

4 Particle Swarm Optimization

Particle Swarm Optimization (PSO) is a population-based stochastic optimization technique, inspired by social behavior of bird flocking or fish schooling, and belongs to the family of swarm intelligence techniques [13]. The potential candidates, called particles, navigate the objective landscape, with their movements guided by the best known position of each particle as well as the entire swarm's best known position. The process is iterated until a satisfactory (or converged) solution is found. Each particle keeps track of its coordinates in the problem space, which are associated with the best solution (in terms of fitness) it has achieved so far. This position is called *pbest*. Another position that is tracked by the standard version of the particle swarm optimizer is the overall best position, and its fitness value, obtained so far by any particle in the population. This location is called *gbest*.

The particle swarm optimization (PSO) search process consists of, at each time step, changing the velocity (accelerating) of each particle towards its *pbest* and *gbest* locations (standard version of PSO). Acceleration is weighted by a random term, with separate random numbers being generated for acceleration towards the *pbest* and *gbest* locations.

The original process for implementing the standard version of PSO is provided in Algorithm 1. In the algorithm, a, b and c are constants that separately control the importance of the three directions which determine the next velocity and position of the particle. The three components are usually referred to as inertia (v_{ti}), cognitive influence ($p_{bti} - x_{ti}$), and social influence ($g_{bt} - x_{ti}$).

Algorithm 1. Standard PSO Algorithm

1: Initialise all particles i with random positions x_i^0 as well as random velocities v_i^0
2: Initialise the particle's best known position (pb_i^0) to its initial position.
3: Calculate the initial swarm's best known position gb^0.
4: **repeat**
5: **for all** Particle i in the swarm **do**
6: Pick random numbers:
7: Update the particle's velocity: $v_i^{t+1} = a \cdot v_i^t + b \cdot r_p \cdot (pb_i^t - x_i^t) + x \cdot r_g \cdot (gb^t - x_i^t)$
8: Compute the particle's new position: $x_i^{t+1} = x_i^t + v_i^{t+1}$
9: **if** fitness (x_i^{t+1}) ¡ fitness (pb_i^t) **then**
10:    Update the particle's best known position: $pb_i^{t+1} = x_i^{t+1}$
11: **end if**
12: **if** fitness (pb_i^{t+1}) ¡ fitness $(gb^t))$ **then**
13:    Update the swarm's best known position: $gb^{t+1} = pb_i^{t+1}$
14: **end if**
15: **end for**
16: **until** termination criterion is met
17: **return** The best known position: gb.

4.1 Optimization in a Dynamic Environment

Many real-world problems are dynamic in the sense that the global optimum location and value may change with time. The task for the optimization algorithm is to track this shifting optimum. In this context it is possible to adapt the particle swarm to work in a dynamic environment and in presence of multiple peaks. The choice of using PSO is obvious, since it shows very useful characteristics for a dynamic environment: simple implementation, very few algorithm parameters, very efficient global search algorithm, and insensitive to the scaling of design variables. However the standard PSO is affected by two problems: outdated memory; and diversity loss [16]. The first one happens as the environment changes when the optima may shift in location and/or value. Particle memory (namely the best location visited in the past, and its corresponding fitness) may no longer be consistent after the change, with potentially sub-optimal effects on the search. The problem of outdated memory is typically solved by either assuming that the algorithm knows just when the environment change occurs, or that it can detect changes. In either case, the algorithm must act with an appropriate response. Equally troubling as outdated memory is an insufficient diversity after change. The population takes time to re-diversify and re-converge, resulting in being unable to track a moving optimum. Loss of diversity arises when a swarm converges onto a peak. There are two possibilities: when a change occurs, the new optimum location may either be within or outside the collapsing swarm. In the former case, there is a good chance that a particle will find itself close to the new optimum within a few iterations and the swarm will successfully track the moving target, assuming that the swarm as a whole has sufficient diversity. However, if the optimum shift is significantly far from the swarm, the low velocities of the particles will inhibit re-diversification and tracking, and the swarm can even oscillate about a false attractor and along a line perpendicular to the true optimum, in a phenomenon known as linear collapse [14].

In this study we resolve this issue by combining two techniques to treat the dynamic problems: Charged Particle Swarm Optimization (CPSO) [14] and Multi-swarm Particle Swarm Optimization (MPSO) [14]. CPSO introduces a repulsive mechanism that can either be between particles, or from an already detected optimum. In this model, a swarm is comprised of a charged and a neutral sub-swarm. Charge enhances diversity in the vicinity of the converging PSO sub-swarm, so that optimum shifts within this cloud should be trackable. Implementing the charged PSO is simple, since its structure is similar to the canonical one, with the addition of an acceleration term in the swarm equations of motion, which is called electrostatic acceleration a_i [15]. The main idea behind MPSO is to split the population of particles into several interacting swarms. The aim of these swarms is to position each on different promising peaks of the fitness landscape. Splitting the main swarm into independent sub-swarms is unlikely to be effective, since the swarms will not interact. The idea is to use some parameters to control the interaction between swarms, including two mechanisms known as exclusion and anti-convergence [17].

Exclusion controls the local interaction between swarms, preventing swarms from staying on the same peak. Anti-convergence deals with the issue as each swarm converges onto a peak, i.e., the particles of the swarms are in close proximity to the attractor. The problem is that if there are more peaks than the number of swarms, it is necessary to ensure that at least one swarm is kept free for detecting any possible change in the environment.

5   Implementation of the Surrogate Model

Given that the operating principles of optimization and surrogates are defined; their synergy and integration into the framework must be considered. The surrogate is treated as a partially-online black-box emulating function, with inputs as the normalized control points, and the airfoil lift coefficient (C_L), which defines the flight condition. A *local* surrogate is referred to cases where C_L is fixed (and so the flight condition). Alternatively, the *global* surrogate refers to cases where C_L is an additional participating input variable.

The difference between the two objective landscapes is that the local model ensures more accuracy for a defined flight condition, whereas the global provides a better prediction for the whole objective landscape. For this reason, it is possible to discern at least three different approaches:

1. Local surrogates (four variables, i.e. the four control points):
   (a) Apply optimization directly to the surrogate model.
   (b) Optimize the surrogate with CFD and compute the optimization.
2. Global surrogates (five variables, i.e. the four control points and the lift C_L):
   (a) Apply optimization directly to the surrogate model.
   (b) Optimize the surrogate with CFD and execute the optimization.

3. Mixed approach: using a global surrogate with local surrogates optimized with CFD.

A direct application of an optimization method without using the surrogate is rare, since the computational cost is very high. Each above approach can be evaluated in terms of: flexibility to the designer, computational intensity and accuracy. The mixed approach proved to be most efficient. In this case the global surrogate provides the general information of the space design and the local surrogates are used as swarms to locate the optima.

6   Application

The practical application of the framework is based on a generic modular, long endurance unmanned aerial system which intends to fulfil the primary roles of unarmed reconnaissance, data collection, and surveillance. The morphing optimization will be performed for a hypothetical flight path. This is composed of three mission objectives which correspond to three different configurations. We want to find the three optimal configurations to minimize the objective of the specific phase as restricting the energy spent when performing the morphing. The three mission objectives considered are:

- Maximum range
- Maneuvering at a defined angle of attack
- Maximum endurance

Both the range and endurance depend on the rate of fuel consumption of the propulsion system, and therefore, on the type of engine. The range is considered to be the maximum distance the aircraft can fly and the endurance as the maximum possible flight duration (irrespective of distance covered, i.e. loitering). As one might expect, there is a flight condition (attitude and velocity) that will provide the best range for a given aircraft, and a different flight condition that will give us maximum endurance. It is clear that if we want to maximize flight endurance for a defined configuration, we have to minimize the function $f^* = \frac{C_D}{C_L}$, where C_D is the aerodynamic drag coefficient. Alternatively, to maximize the range, the cost function to be minimized is $f^* = \frac{C_D}{C_L^{1/2}}$. The maneuvering has been performed for a fixed angle of attack trying to minimize $f^* = (\frac{1}{CL^2})$. There are six design parameters to define both range and endurance, which are four morphing control points, as well as the wing angle of attack (α) and airspeed (V). For simplicity, the altitude is fixed.

7   Results

The optimal framework approach in terms of accuracy, flexibility and computational cost is the mixed approach. Different combinations of parameters were considered, to determine the optimal swarm population size, number of swarms, and size of the initial training dataset (i.e. number of samples), and are consolidated in Table 1. It is important to note the time of change: such that after every 40 iterations the optimization framework dynamically changes its objective.

The velocities are obtained after having optimized the airfoil without morphing and found out which are the best to accomplish each objective. The results obtained for each case are shown in Table 2. Each optimization routine provides four ideal shapes for each objective, with each solution ranked according to the percentage of improvement and energy expenditure. The improvement, except for the maneuvering phase, is quite small. Indeed, for range and endurance, the average improvement is of the order of 1%. Minimum energy expenditure is determined based on the minimum amount of structural deformation required to transition between successive states. After this trade-off was performed, the best three profiles for completing the mission are obtained, which can be seen in Fig. 2. It is interesting to note the effects of the morphing on the aerodynamic performance coefficients. For the range the result does not change much, as compared to the original, instead for the maneuvering we have some interesting improvements. After the first input point there is a regain in pressure and

Table 1. Input parameters for MPSO

Inputs	
Number of swarms	12
Particles of each swarm	20
Density (kg/m3)	1,225
Velocity (m/s)	25, 30, 29
Maximum iterations	120
Change interval	40
Number of samples	30

Table 2. Results for range, maneuvering and endurance.

	Morphed airfoils				Original airfoil				Improvement (%)
	C_L (-)	C_D (-)	f* (-)	α (deg)	C_L (-)	C_D (-)	f* (-)	α (deg)	
Range $f^* = \frac{C_D}{\sqrt{C_L}}$ $V = 29.2 \frac{m}{s}$	0.76	0.0109	0.0125	6.6	0.78	0.0112	0.0127	6.6	1.3
	0.79	0.0112	0.0126	6.9					0.5
	0.82	0.0114	0.0126	6.9					0.5
	0.76	0.0109	0.0125	6.6					1.1
Maneuvering $f^* = 1/C_L^2$ $V = 30 \frac{m}{s}$	0.74	0.0122	1.8211	6.0	0.71	0.0116	1.9802	6.0	5.0
	0.74	0.0127	1.8126						5.3
	0.74	0.0122	1.8093						5.5
	0.73	0.0123	1.8723						3.9
Endurance $f^* = C_D/C_L$ $V = 24.9 \frac{m}{s}$	0.98	0.0132	0.0134	8.6	1.09	0.0147	0.0135	9.8	0.7
	0.97	0.0129	0.0134	8.5					0.8
	0.96	0.0127	0.0132	8.4					1.9
	0.97	0.0130	0.0133	8.6					1.2

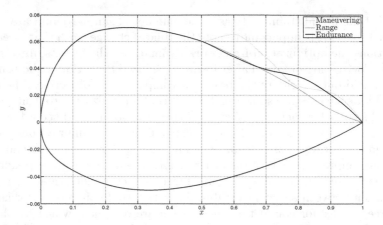

Fig. 2. Best airfoils shape for range, maneuvering and endurance.

consequently an increase of lift, this is exactly what we want to achieve during this phase. Furthermore, the pitching moment C_M is affected by the morphing.

8   Conclusion

This paper has presented a dynamic optimization of a morphing trailing edge. A population-based dynamic optimization framework is developed, utilizing the Multi-swarm Particle Swarm Optimization algorithm, in combination with Kriging surrogate models, used to alleviate the computational effort of the high-fidelity numerical solver. The conceptual study illustrated significant improvement in the flight performance is attainable, with the major improvement experienced during the phase of maneuvering. In this context an improvement in aerodynamic performance of approximately 5% is observed, as compared to the original profile. Cruise aerodynamic performance was improved by 1% to 3%, which is still significant since minimal energy expenditure in morphing the trailing edge topology of the original profile is considered. Starting from this and passing from an experimental validation of the numerical analysis, morphing could, in future, replace the current use of multiple aerodynamic devices (such as flaps and slats). The framework developed provides a clear scope for future research direction. The conceptual application simply considers a static two-dimensional analysis, the real benefits of adopting a dynamic swarm framework would be to consider the optimal execution of time-accurate aircraft maneuvers.

References

1. Siclari, M.J., Nostrand, W., Austin, F.: The design of transonic airfoil sections for an adaptive wing concept using a stochastic optimization method. In: 34th Aerospace Sciences Meeting and Exhibit, pp. 15–18 (1996)

2. Lyu, Z., Martins, J.: Aerodynamic shape optimization of an adaptive morphing trailing-edge wing. J. Aircr. **52**, 1951–1970 (2015). 15th AIAA/ISSMO Multidisciplinary Analysis and Optimization Conference, Atlanta, July

3. Parno, M.D., Fowler, K.R., Hemker, T.: Framework for particle swarm optimization with surrogate functions. Technical report TUD-CS-2009-0139, August 2009

4. Gamboa, P., Lau, F.J.P., Vale, J., Suleman, A.: Optimization of a morphing wing based on coupled aerodynamic and structural constrains. Am. Inst. Aeronaut. Astronaut. (AIAA) J. **47**, 2087–2104 (2009)

5. Yurkovich, R.N.: Analysis of the integration of active aeroelastic wing into a morphing wing. In: 50th AIAA Structures Structural Dynamics and Materials Conference (2009)

6. Forrester, J., Sbester, A., Keane, A.J.: Engineering Design via Surrogate Modelling. Wiley and Sons Inc., United Kingdom (2008)

7. Stanewsky, E.: Adaptive wing and flow control technology. Aerosp. Sci. **37**(7), 583–667 (2001)

8. Blum, C., Merkle, D.: Swarm Intelligence: Introductions and Applications. Springer, Heidelberg (2007)

9. Jin, Y., Branke, J.: Evolutionary optimization in uncertain environment a survey. IEEE Trans. Evol. Comput. **9**(3), 303–3170 (2005)

10. Yang, S., Ong, Y.S., Jin, Y.: Evolutionary Computation in Dynamic and Uncertain Environments. Springer, Heidelberg (2007)

11. Wickramasinghe, U.K., Carrese, R., Li, X.: Designing airfoils using a reference point based evolutionary many-objective particle swarm optimization algorithm. In: WCCI IEEE World Congress on Computational Intelligence (2010)

12. Watts, M., Winarto, H., Carrese, R.: Multi-objective design exploration and its application to formula one airfoils. In: AIAC14: Fourteenth Australian Aeronautical Conference Melbourne: Royal Aeronautical Society, Australian Division; Engineers Australia, pp. 195–204 (2011)

13. Kennedy, J., Eberhart, R.: Particle swarm optimization. In: IEEE (1995)

14. Blackwell, T.M., Bentley, P.J.: Dynamic search with charged swarms. In: Langdon, W.B., et al. (ed.) Genetic and Evolutionary Computation Conference, pp. 19–26. Morgan Kaufmann (2002)

15. Blackwell, T.M.: Swarms in dynamic environments. In: Cantú-Paz, E., et al. (eds.) GECCO 2003. LNCS, vol. 2723, pp. 1–12. Springer, Heidelberg (2003). doi:10.1007/3-540-45105-6_1

16. Blackwell, T., Branke, J., Li, X.: Particle swarms for dynamic optimization problems. In: Blum, C., Merkle, D. (eds.) Swarm Intelligence, pp. 193–217. Springer, Heidelberg (2007)

17. Blackwell, T.M., Branke, J.: Multi swarms, exclusion and anti-convergence in dynamic environments. IEEE Trans. Evol. Comput. **10**, 459–472 (2005)

18. Li, X., Branke, J., Blackwell, T.: Particle swarm with speciation and adaptation in a dynamic environment. In: Keijzer, M., et al. (eds.) Proceedings of Genetic and Evolutionary Computation Conference, GECCO 2006, pp. 51–58. ACM Press (2006)

19. Queipo, N.V., Haftka, R.T., Shyy, W., Goel, T., Vaidyanathan, R., Tucker, P.K.: Surrogate based analysis and optimization. Prog. Aerosp. Sci. **41**, 1–28 (2005)

20. Han, Z., Zhang, K.: Surrogate-based optimization. In: Roeva, O. (ed.) Real-World Applications of Genetic Algorithms. InTech (2012). ISBN: 978-953-51-0146-8

21. Hassan, R., Cohanim, B., De Weck, O.: A comparison of particle swarm optimization and the genetic algorithm. In: American Institute of Aeronautics and Astronautics (2004)

Applying Dependency Patterns in Causal Discovery of Latent Variable Models

Xuhui Zhang[1(✉)], Kevin B. Korb[1], Ann E. Nicholson[1], and Steven Mascaro[2]

[1] Faculty of Information Technology, Monash University,
Melbourne, VIC 3800, Australia
{Xuhui.Zhang,Kevin.Korb,Ann.Nicholson}@monash.edu
[2] Bayesian Intelligence Pty Ltd., Clarinda, VIC 3169, Australia
Steven.Mascaro@bayesian-intelligence.com

Abstract. Latent variables represent unmeasured causal factors. Some, such as intelligence, cannot be directly measured; others may be, but we do not know about them or know how to measure them when making our observations. Regardless, in many cases, the influence of latent variables is real and important, and optimal modeling cannot be done without them. However, in many of those cases the influence of latent variables reveals itself in patterns of measured dependency that cannot be reproduced using the observed variables alone, under the assumptions of the causal Markov property and faithfulness. In such cases, latent variables may be posited to the advantage of the causal discovery process. All latent variable discovery takes advantage of this; we make the process explicit.

Keywords: Bayesian networks · Causal discovery · Latent variables

1 Introduction

Bayesian networks (BNs) are powerful tools for reasoning about uncertainty and using complex probability distributions. Judea Pearl helped popularize them [11], bringing together various algorithms enabling their relatively efficient updating in his seminal 1988 text. While sparse networks are tractable, generating them from human expert opinion in their application reintroduced the so-called knowledge bottleneck for constructing expert systems, so it was natural that attention quickly turned to their automated generation from sample data [15]. While there has been a great deal of work on the machine learning of Bayesian networks since then, relatively little of it has treated the learning of BNs with latent (or hidden) variables, despite latent variable models being one of the most widely used modeling approaches, for example, in the social sciences. Here we present a new approach to BN learning in the presence of latents.

1.1 Causal Bayesian Networks

A *Bayesian network* is a directed acyclic graph (DAG) where each node represents a random variable, and the structure encodes the independence relations

© Springer International Publishing AG 2017
M. Wagner et al. (Eds.): ACALCI 2017, LNAI 10142, pp. 134–143, 2017.
DOI: 10.1007/978-3-319-51691-2_12

among the variables in the d-separation relation [11]. The *Markov property*, which is a precondition of BN models being valid, records this relation: variables d-separated in a BN are (conditionally) independent in the system being modeled. Given these independencies, the joint distribution for a Bayesian network with variables $X_1, \ldots, X_k$ factorizes as:

$$p(x_1, \ldots, x_k) = \prod_{i=1}^{k} p_i(x_i | \pi(x_i)), \tag{1}$$

where $\pi(x_i)$ denotes the joint values of the parents of variable X_i in the network.

A *casual Bayesian network* (CBN) is just a Bayesian network under a causal interpretation of its arcs. That is, in addition to representing probabilistic dependencies and independencies, its arcs represent causal influences, so that, for example, interventions on a parent variable in the real system will result in changes in the distributions of its children variables (see [6]). Under such an interpretation, the Markov property is called the *causal Markov property*.

Causal discovery algorithms roughly come in two varieties, constraint-based learners and metric learners. Constraint-based learners, such as PC [15], apply direct statistical tests for conditional dependencies and independencies between subsets of variables, constructing networks with corresponding d-separation properties. Metric learners, such as K2 and CaMML [4,7], score whole networks at once, searching the model space for an optimal score. Another well-known metric discovery approach, "Structural Expectation Maximization (SEM)", developed by Nir Friedman [5], optimizes BIC or MDL scores using Expectation Maximization.[1]

All varieties of causal discovery algorithms assume the causal Markov property; that is, where the data show (conditional) independencies, the models discovered will (generally) likewise show independencies, in the form of d-separation. Similarly, they assume *faithfulness*, meaning the models discovered will (generally) not include arc structures (d-connected relationships) which carry no conditional dependencies. Faithfulness implies that a CBN is a proper encoding of pattern of dependencies between measured variables. While there is some dispute in the philosophy of science about the proper boundaries of these assumptions [1], causal discovery algorithms operate non-problematically under them across a wide range of problems, and we assume them in our work here.

Under these assumptions, certain dependency patterns, we call them "triggers", can reliably indicate the presence of unmeasured causes. In this paper, we first explain these triggers, and then consider how they might be applied in constraint-based causal discovery, comparing these techniques with some popular alternatives. We conclude with ideas for their future application in metric causal discovery.

---

[1] Indeed, Friedman applied SEM to the problem of latent variable discovery as well. Our empirical results here don't include SEM due to time constraints after some initial difficulty in obtaining SEM code.

1.2   Latent Variable Discovery

Latency is both ubiquitous and important. For example, while Galileo developed accurate mathematical laws of motion, they remained unexplained until Newton came up with the previously unmeasured concept of gravity. Gravitational waves have recently been successfully measured, but for several centuries the variable played a key role in physical theory without any direct measurement. Latent variable modelling has a long history in statistics, starting with Spearman's (1904) work on intelligence testing. Although factor analysis and related methods are used to posit latent variables and measure their hypothetical effects, they do not provide clear means for deciding on adding latent variables when the dependency pattern implied by a given BN doesn't match the observed dependencies.

One solution is to always use a fully connected structure, since they can be parameterized to represent *any* dependency pattern in the observed variables. However, updating fully connected networks is computationally exponential, and the parameterization process for them is likewise exponential. Incorporating latent variables can often greatly simplify a model relative to any fully observed model with the same probability distribution, as Friedman [5] pointed out using the example in Fig. 1.

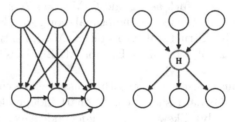

Fig. 1. An illustration of how introducing a latent variable H can simplify a model [5].

But another substantial advantage of latent variable models is that they can often better encode the conditional dependencies and independencies in the data. As shown in Fig. 2, if we assume the data show the independencies $W \perp\!\!\!\perp \{Y, Z\}$ and $Z \perp\!\!\!\perp \{X, W\}$, it is impossible to construct a network in the observed variables alone that reflects both of these independencies while also reflecting the dependencies implied by the d-connections in the latent variable model (i.e., with the model being faithful). We call dependency patterns with this property—not being capable of encoding in the observed variables alone assuming both the causal Markov property and faithfulness—*triggers*,[2] since they can act as triggers to extend a search of the causal model space to incorporate latent variables.

---

[2] Note that we will indifferently refer to the causal models that generate these dependency patterns triggers as well.

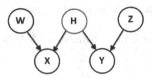

Fig. 2. The Big W: a causal structure with four observed variables and one latent variable H.

2 Triggers in Latent Variable Discovery

Here we report a systematic search for triggers in models with five or fewer observed variables and with one latent variable. Latent variables are typically considered only in scenarios where they are common causes [15], i.e., having two or more children. As Friedman [5] points out, a latent variable as a leaf or as a root with only one child would marginalize out without affecting the distribution over the remaining variables. So too would a latent variable that mediates only one parent and one child. Therefore, our trigger algorithm restricts itself to looking for latent common causes. For simplicity, we also restrict it to looking for triggers with single latent variables rather than multiple latent variables; however, it will be clear from the algorithm that it could readily be extended to look for two or three latent variables at a time.[3]

First, we generated all possible fully observed DAGs for a given number of observed variables. For each model we produced all possible d-separating evidence sets. For n observed variables, there are $1 + \Sigma_{i=1}^{n-1} C_n^i$ evidence sets, including the empty set. For example, for the three variables A, B and C, there are seven evidence sets: $\phi, \{A\}, \{B\}, \{C\}, \{AB\}, \{AC\}, \{BC\}$. We then generated all the conditional dependencies and independencies based on such evidence sets. We then examined all possible (single) latent variable models for each DAG by replacing every pair of connected observed variables by a hidden common cause. Finally, if the exact set of dependencies implied by a latent variable model could not be matched by any observed DAG, the dependency pattern of the latent variable model was identified as a trigger.

The number of distinct triggers, ignoring labels and isolated nodes, is shown in Table 1. There are two triggers for four observed variables (where "H" represents the hidden variable), shown as Figs. 3, and 4 shows some example structures of the 57 possible triggers given five observed variables.

The triggers potentially provide us with better explanations of the dependencies within the data than any model with only observed variables. As we noted above, a fully connected model can always be parameterized to fit those dependency patterns, but the price in complexity may well be too high. Smaller

---

[3] Note that these restrictions imply, for example, that we would not be finding any such latent variable model as that in Fig. 1. However, these restrictions apply only to our search for useful triggers and their models; subsequent search through the latent variable model space can find these models, as Friedman's work [5] demonstrates.

Table 1. Number of triggers found

Number of observed variables	Number of DAGs	Number of triggers
3	6	0
4	31	2
5	302	57

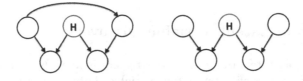

Fig. 3. Triggers of four observed variables.

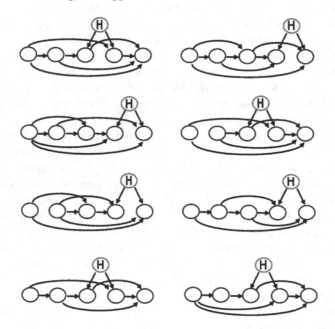

Fig. 4. Some examples of triggers of five observed variables.

fully observed models will not fit the data exactly, and, whereas that may not matter if the sample size is small, given a larger number of observations, the more exactly fitting latent model must eventually become the better explanatory model. Ideally, we should like to modify causal discovery algorithms to be able to identify such cases and return the best explanatory models, rather than only the best observational model.

3   Generating Simulated Datasets of Triggers

Among the most popular and widely used causal discovery algorithms are FCI
and PC, developed by Clark Glymour's group and implemented in TETRAD V
[16], PC in particular having been reimplemented in numerous Bayesian network
platforms. Both algorithms can identify latent variables, which are reported as
bi-directed arcs, instead of the normal causal arc, oriented in a single direction.
However, no previous latent variable discovery algorithm has attempted to use
triggers in the discovery process, as we propose to do here.

As an initial exploration of the potential for using triggers we implemented a
trigger filter for PC, yielding "Trigger-PC", and compared the results with the
unaltered FCI and PC algorithms. Trigger-PC simply returns any latent variable
model corresponding to an identified trigger patterns (identified using χ-square)
and otherwise invokes PC.

The datasets[4] we used were generated from all fully observed as well as all
(single) latent variable models with four or five observed variables, and both
the observed and latent variable have either two or three states. We wanted to
test learning performance given a range of dependency strengths, from weak to
medium to strong, so we used a GA algorithm to find parameters reflecting such
ranges, as determined by mutual information between neighboring nodes. For
each of the three varieties of network, we simulated artificial datasets of three
sizes using Netica [8,9]: 100, 1000 and 10000. As Table 2 shows, we produced
datasets for every trigger structure of four and five observed variables. We did
the same thing for all possible DAG structures (ignoring isolated nodes) without
latent variables (Table 3), in order to check for false positives. The result was a
set of about 6000 data sets for comparing our algorithms. This large number of
datasets was due to the different number of states (either 2 or 3), arc strengths
(low, medium and high) and sample sizes (100, 1000 and 10000). For example,
there are 57 trigger structures for 5 observed variables, so there are $57*2*3*3 =$
1026 simulated datasets.

Table 2. Number of simulated datasets for trigger structures

Number of observed variables	Number of trigger structures	Total number of simulated datasets
4	2	36
5	57	1026

---

[4] The datasets are available at: https://sourceforge.net/projects/triggers-of-bn-latent-
variable/.

Table 3. Number of simulated datasets for DAG structures (no latent variable)

Number of observed variables	Number of DAG structures	Total number of simulated datasets
4	24	432
5	268	4824

4   Learning Triggers by FCI and PC Algorithms

We tested FCI, PC and Trigger-PC using the datasets described above, producing confusion matrices. Triggers were used to determine True Positive (TP) and False Negative (FN) results, while fully observed networks (DAGs with no latents) were used for False Positive (FP) as well as True Negative (TN) results. If the latent node in every trigger structure is the common cause of two variables X and Y, then TP, FN, FP and TN are defined as in Table 4.

Table 4. Definitions of TP, FN, TN and FP (in the syntax of FCI and PC)

	Definitions
TP	The learned model has a bi-directional arc between X and Y
FN	The learned model lacks a bi-directional arc between X and Y
TN	The learned model has no bi-directional arcs
FP	The learned model has one or more bi-directional arcs

For the results reported here, we used the default value (0.05) as the significance level (alpha) for all algorithms; we do not report the results for optimized alphas, as those were not interestingly different. We did not repeat tests on individual networks in order to compute confidence intervals, as the cumulative results of 6318 tests tell the story sufficiently well. Table 5 shows the confusion matrix we use, and all the results are shown in Table 6.

FCI and PC perform quite similarly. They can both find latent variables when they are there, but with a weak recall rate (TP/Positives) of around 20%. They also mostly avoid misidentifying ordinary models as latent variable models, but still have false positive rate of around 13%. Trigger-PC, on the other hand, is *much* more reluctant to claim the existence of latent variables, with a recall rate of only 3%. However, its false positive rate is also very dramatically lower, at only 0.08%.

The ideal test would be to use a cost/reward matrix to measure the expected value of these correct and incorrect identifications. However, since we are not dealing with a specific application, but a general method, we have no cost matrix. Still, it is plausible that the worst outcome is a false positive. If latent discovery is meant to somehow supplement or extend existing causal discovery methods (as we intend), then perhaps the worst outcome is to positively mislead causal

Table 5. Definition of confusion matrices for identifying latent variables

	Algorithm	
	Latent	No latent
Positive	TP	FP
Negative	FN	TN

Table 6. Result of confusion matrices for identifying latent variables

	FCI		PC		Trigger-PC	
	Latent	No latent	Latent	No latent	Latent	No latent
Positive	211	767	205	615	35	4
Negative	851	4489	857	4641	1027	5252

discovery to search in areas of a model space that introduce non-existent structure. By contrast, failing to prompt such a search when it is warranted (false negatives) will not degrade existing discovery methods. In any case, we consider these preliminary results for trigger-discovery to be quite promising. We now consider (briefly and speculatively) how we can incorporate trigger discovery in metric learning.

5   Causal MML (CaMML)

Minimum Message Length (MML) was invented by Chris Wallace (1968), combining Bayes' rule [2] with Shannon information [13]. The relationship between message length, the model (M) and the data (D) given the model is:

$$msglen = -\ln(P(M)) - \ln(P(D|M)) \qquad (2)$$

This forces a trade-off between the benefits of fitting the data and avoiding model complexity. MML differs from K2 [4] and MDL [12], as it considers the relevance to a discovery metric for DAGs of multiple linear extensions and selects a parameterized mode instead of a model class [7].

Causal discovery via MML (CaMML) [3] applies an MML metric in an MCMC (Metropolis) sampling process to learn the best fully observed causal model from sample data [7]. It uses the totally ordered models (TOMs) [7] to represent their associated DAGs. All TOMs are sampled and the posterior distributions are estimated by applying the MML score:

$$P_{MML}(M) = e^{-I_{MML}(M)} \qquad (3)$$

where I_{MML} is the MML score (message length) of the given TOM (M).

6   Applying Triggers in CaMML

We propose to add a pre-processing phase to CaMML which will perform a heuristic search for triggers in the data by testing subsets of variables for the corresponding dependency structures (with either our existing χ-square test or a new MML test). The subsets will be found using Markov blanket (MB) discovery, which is a related research program we are pursuing. The MBs will either be sufficiently small for our existing (or modestly extended) trigger pattern discovery tools, or we will need to develop heuristics to select proper subsets of the MBs.

When triggers are found, a latent variable will be created for the subsequent sampling process. Since CaMML supports prior probabilities for arcs (O'Donnell et al. [10]), we will also add arc priors for connecting the latent variable to its children, as required by the trigger, so that the latent variable submodel corresponding to the trigger is favored in the sampling.

The sampled model space will be enhanced by adding latent variables while extending the search method appropriately. For example, if we add a latent variable H as a common cause to variable A and B, their total ordering will have two linear extensions, namely, $\langle H, A, B \rangle$ and $\langle H, B, A \rangle$. So, the Metropolis search will incorporate both possibilities. Additionally, certain soft constraints on model mutations will need to be added; for example, a latent variable common cause should not become a child of its children (although it may become a child of other variables). Similarly, arc deletions which leave a latent variable a parent of a single child are pointless, and so will be avoided.

Introducing latents also introduces new issues with parameterization. The arity of each latent variable will need to be determined, and each of those possible values will introduce new distributions in the latent variable's children. All of these parameters will have to be estimated from data that includes no observations of the latent variables, a kind of task which can be done by likelihood optimization, such as EM.

Given that there are $2^{k(k-1)/2}$ potential combinations of arcs and $k!$ possible orderings, there are exactly $2^{k(k-1)/2} \times k!$ TOMs, where k is the number of variables. CaMML samples over this space. Furthermore, adding latent variables will potentially greatly expand this space. In order to achieve reasonable results in reasonable time, as we said above, we will use priors over the model space to bias the search in favor of latent models for which we have found direct evidence. Also, the new parameterization processes will be, at least in the first instance, conducted locally (e.g., within Markov blankets) rather than optimizing likelihoods across the entire set of variables. Whether such methods suffice for good sized models or whether additional heuristics will be needed is a matter for future research.

7   Conclusion

We have here presented triggers as potentially strong aids to causal discovery in the presence of unmeasured variables. Applying them in a simple extension of

PC, we have compared this Trigger-PC with the existing PC and FCI for latent discovery, finding a quite different performance and one which augurs well for the use of triggers in a more robust causal discovery program. We have sketched out a method for incorporating trigger identification in such a program and are proceeding with its implementation.

References

1. Arntzenius, F.: Reichenbach's Common Cause Principle, The Stanford Encyclopedia of Philosophy (Fall 2010 Edition). Zalta, E.N. (ed.). http://plato.stanford.edu/archives/fall2010/entries/physics-Rpcc/
2. Bayes, T., Price, Mr.: An essay towards solving a problem in the doctrine of chances. Philos. Trans. Roy. Soc. Lond. (1763). Reprinted in Biometrika **45**(3/4), 293–315 (1958)
3. CaMML. https://github.com/rodneyodonnell/CaMML
4. Cooper, G.F., Herskovits, E.: A Bayesian method for the induction of probabilistic networks from data. Mach. Learn. **9**(4), 309–347 (1992)
5. Friedman, N.: Learning belief networks in the presence of missing values and hidden variables. In: Fisher, D. (ed.) Proceedings of the Fourteenth International Conference on Machine Learning, pp. 125–133. Morgan Kaufmann, San Francisco (1997)
6. Korb, K.B., Hope, L.R., Nicholson, A.E., Axnick, K.: Varieties of causal intervention. In: Zhang, C., Guesgen, H.W., Yeap, W.-K. (eds.) PRICAI 2004. LNCS (LNAI), vol. 3157, pp. 322–331. Springer, Heidelberg (2004). doi:10.1007/978-3-540-28633-2_35
7. Korb, K.B., Nicholson, A.E.: Bayesian Artificial Intelligence, 2nd edn. CRC Press, Boca Raton (2010)
8. Netica API. https://www.norsys.com/netica_api.html
9. Netica API. https://www.norsys.com/netica-j/docs/javadocs/norsys/netica/Net.html#FORWARD_SAMPLING
10. O'Donnell, R.T., Nicholson, A.E., Han, B., Korb, K.B., Alam, M.J., Hope, L.R.: Causal discovery with prior information. In: Sattar, A., Kang, B. (eds.) AI 2006. LNCS (LNAI), vol. 4304, pp. 1162–1167. Springer, Heidelberg (2006). doi:10.1007/11941439_141
11. Pearl, J.: Probabilistic Reasoning in Intelligent Systems. Morgan Kaufmann, San Mateo (1988)
12. Rissanen, J.: Modeling by shortest data description. Automatica **14**(5), 465–471 (1978)
13. Shannon, C.E.: A mathematical theory of communication. Bell Syst. Tech. J. **27**(3), 379–423 (1948)
14. Spearman, C.: General intelligence, objectively determined and measured. Am. J. Psychol. **15**(2), 201–292 (1904)
15. Spirtes, P., Glymour, C.N., Scheines, R.: Causation, Prediction, and Search, 2nd edn. MIT press, Cambridge (2000)
16. TETRAD V. http://www.phil.cmu.edu/projects/tetrad/current.html
17. Wallace, C.S., Boulton, D.M.: An information measure for classification. Comput. J. **11**(2), 185–194 (1968)

An Evolutionary Multi-criteria Journey Planning Algorithm for Multimodal Transportation Networks

Mohammad Haqqani[(✉)], Xiaodong Li, and Xinghuo Yu

School of Science (Computer Science and Software Engineering),
RMIT University, Melbourne, Australia
mohammad.haqqani@rmit.edu.au

Abstract. This paper considers the problem of personalized journey planning in complex and large urban areas. Journey planners are considered as one of the promising solutions for enhancing the transportation quality in urban cities, hence reducing the congestion and pollution. Popular journey planning systems, like Google Maps or Yahoo! Maps, usually ignore users preferences. In this context, however, passengers are active components of the system having their own preferences towards traveling and willing to take different routes based on their own preferences, e.g., the fastest, least transfer, or cheapest journey. A potential remedy to this problem is to incorporate passengers' preferences into the optimization phase of the journey planning system. In this work, an adapted multi-criteria evolutionary algorithm, which incorporates passengers' preferences into the journey planner, is proposed to solve this problem. The proposed solution was tested over the dataset of city of Melbourne and the experimental results demonstrates that the proposed approach, is able to recommend more relevant journeys to the passengers.

Keywords: Multi-modal journey planning · Personalized journeying · Genetic algorithm · Evolutionary algorithm

1 Introduction

Journey planning is becoming increasingly important in metropolitan transportation networks. In general, a journey planning problem can be considered as a multi-criteria scheduling problem, aiming to provide a traveler with various alternative plans for a specific journey query. In this context, travelers are usually faced with many alternatives, and selecting a plan that *'best'* meet their needs (particularly for the passengers who are unfamiliar with the transportation network) becomes a tedious task [20].

Most existing *'intelligent'* commercial planners only have a small set of predefined preferences (e.g., preferred/prohibited highways or public transit modes) available to the passengers to choose from and sometimes to rank them (e.g. Yahoo! trip planner, Google Map, PTV journey planner, OpenTripPlanner) [4].

© Springer International Publishing AG 2017
M. Wagner et al. (Eds.): ACALCI 2017, LNAI 10142, pp. 144–156, 2017.
DOI: 10.1007/978-3-319-51691-2_13

Although these planners are becoming increasingly reliable and provide an reasonable level of assistance to passengers, most of them have very limited capabilities when it comes to taking into account sophisticated user preferences: the ability to dynamically tailor information to the individual needs of each passenger [20]. In designing such a system, passengers play an active role and their preferences should be considered to provide a high quality service [3]. One possibility to resolve this issue is integration of the passengers' preferences into optimization process of the journey planning. This way, more relevant journey plans can be identified and recommended to passengers.

As one would expect, this is not a straightforward task. In fact, multi-criteria journey planning is considered as NP-complete problems [11]. As a more general-purpose optimization method, evolutionary algorithm (EA) demonstrates promising performance on solving the multi-criteria combinatorial optimization problems [10]. EA does not require gradient information, and can evolve a set of solutions in parallel over successive iterations, and ultimately obtain a set of alternative solutions. With these considerations, in this paper we employ EA for multi-modal journey planning considering multiple criteria in order to provide optimal alternative journeys to the travelers.

We investigate how passengers' preferences can be incorporated into an EA aiming to produce a set of alternative journeys to recommend to the passengers. To achieve this goal, we express passenger preference via a weight vector associated with the journey criteria. The objective of the proposed model is to guide the search into the regions of the solution space that are more appealing to the passengers. The proposed algorithm has been evaluated on the data set of the real-life Melbourne urban transportation network [1]. Our experimental results indicate that the test problems were solved within a reasonable amount of time while recommending more relevant itineraries to the travelers. In short, our contributions are the design of an EA-based multi-criteria journey planner, a weight assignment strategy to utilize the user preferences, and our empirical evaluation of the journey planner.

The paper is organized as follows. In the next section, some preliminaries for the rest of the paper are first provided. Section 3 reviews the related works, and Sect. 4 describes the modeling of the transportation network. Section 5 gives a detailed description and formulation of the proposed algorithm. In Sect. 6, the experimental results are evaluated to show the proficiency of the proposed method. Finally Sect. 7 concludes this study.

2 Preliminaries

In this section, we will define some basic concepts first. We assume that the network has a set of nodes $S = \{s_1, s_2, ..., s_m\}$ and a set of edges $R = \{r_1, r_2, ..., r_k\}$ connecting these nodes and a user query. Each query consists of an origin s_1, a destination s_2, a departure time t_1 and a subset of allowed transportation modes.

Definition 1. *Journey Plan: A journey plan p can be represented as a sequence of stations $(s_1, s_2, ..., s_d)$ where s_1 and s_d is the origin and the destination* *respectively. The cost function, $\{C : p \to R^{k+}\}$ assigns the k dimensional cost vector $(c_p^1, c_p^2, ..., c_p^k)$ for journey plan p.*

Definition 2. *Pareto-dominance: For two journey plans $p_1, p_2 \in P$, we say that p_1 dominates p_2, i.e. $p_1 \succ p_2$ iff $\forall c_1^j \wedge c_2^j : c_1^j \leq c_2^j$ and $\exists c_1^j < c_2^j, j \in \{1, 2, ..., k\}$.*

Definition 3. *Pareto-optimal: If $\forall x \in P : \nexists x \succ p$, the journey plan p is called Pareto-optimal.*

Definition 4. *Pareto-optimal Set: It is the set of all Pareto-optimal journey plans. Formally, Pareto-optimal set of journey plans $= \{p: \forall x \in P : \nexists x \succ p\}$.*

Definition 5. *Multi-criteria Journey Planning: It is the process of finding the Pareto-optimal set of plans with respect to query q and transportation network N.*

3   Prior Work

In the past decades, an increasing number of multi-modal journey planning systems are becoming available which provide travel suggestions for travelers while supporting multiple transportation modes [4].

Genetic Algorithm (GA) has been used to solve journey planning for years. In [12] Gen et al. proposed the first approach to solve such kinds of difficult-to-solve problems by proposing a priority-based encoding method using constant chromosomes length to represent paths. Davies and Lingras presented a GA based strategy to find the shortest path in [9] which adapts the recommended journey to the changing network information by rerouting it during the execution time. They focused on the shortest walk problem, where a new Crossover operator was used to take walking condition into account (i.e. good or bad). All aforementioned research focused on single criterion problems.

Many studies using GA exist in literature for solving personalized multi-criteria route planning problems such as tourist sightseeing [7], and car navigation system [8]. In [7,8] a GA-based planner is proposed using a novel objective function for generating multiple routes in a car navigation problem. To evaluate the fitness a few attributes such as distance, number of turns, mountain or river side routes are considered as penalties for the objective function. In [13], Huang et al., applied GA to calculate a set of weights for different objectives and sum them up as the final cost. For multi-modal journey planning problem, a GA-based approach is presented in [2]. Authors showed the robustness of this approach through an experiment and concluded that proposed algorithm can more efficiently explore the search space. They considered a bi-criteria problem considering the length and waiting time of a journey. While all these researches explored different aspects of a journey planning problem, none has taken into account the passengers preferences to compute personalized journey plans. Ziliaskopoulos and Wardell proposed a multi-modal journey planner algorithm according to the principles of dynamic programming that considers the arcs travel time and switching delays [18]. Bielli et al. [5] introduced a tool for finding the shortest path in a multi-modal network using geographic information system (GIS). A similar approach was presented by Zografos and Madas, which considered the shortest path in terms of least-time shortest path, least number of mode transfers, or mode and road preferences [19].

4   Problem Formulation

4.1   Input Network

A multi-modal journey planning task is determined by a user query (i.e., a request to the planner), and the snapshot of a multi-modal transit network. In this section, we provide a formal definitions of these parameters. The transportation modes that we focus on are public transit modes (e.g., bus or train), bicycles available in the bike-sharing stations, and walking.

A multi-modal network snapshot can be represented as a structure (N, R, H, M_w, M_c) that encodes knowledge about the current status and the predicted evolution of a transport network during a time horizon $[0, T] \subset R$. The variable N represents a set of locations on the map (e.g., bus station and bike stations). In addition, given a user query, the origin and the destination locations are added to N. R defines a set of routes. A route r is an ordered sequence of $n \in N$ locations, equivalent to the stops along the route. H is a collection of trips such that, each trip, $h \in H$, is a vehicle (e.g. a bus) going along a route as a sequence of nodes $(v_1, \ldots, v_m)$. The trip k departs at node v_1 at a specific time and proceeds to nodes $(v_2, \ldots, v_m)$ in the order determined by the route. M_w and M_c provide walking and cycling times for pairs of locations in the network.

A user query is shown by a tuple (o, d, t_0, m, q), where o and d are the origin and the destination locations; t_0 is the start time; m specifies a subset of transportation modes that should be considered; and q defines parameters such as the maximum walking and cycling time, allowed by the user.

In order to model the transportation network, we represent every movement in the multi-modal network by a leg. Each leg has a start node, an end node, an expected start time, and an expected end time. Formally speaking, letting L denote the set of legs, a leg corresponding to index $i \in L$ is defined by $((v_i^k, t_i^k), (v_{(i+1)}^k, t'^k_{(i+1)}), k)$, where v_i^k is the start node, $v_{(i+1)}^k$ is the end node, t_i^k is the expected start time, $t'^k_{(i+1)}$ is the expected end time, and the mode number k is the index of the scheduled trip service that executes leg i.

Using this model, a path (i.e., journey plan) can be represented as a sequence of legs $(i_1, i_2, \ldots, i_m)$ where $i_{(h+1)}$ is among the successors of the leg i_h for all $h \in \{1, \ldots, m-1\}$. Each path is evaluated against N criteria. In this paper, the journey criteria includes travel time, monetary cost, CO_2 emission, and personal energy consumption as journey's criteria.

4.2 Weight Assignment Strategies

In the literature, weight assignment strategies are divided into two main categories [14]: (1) Assigning fixed weights (equal or unequal) to each objective, known as Fixed Weight strategy (FW) and (2) Assigning random weights to each criterion based on a set of pre-defined constraints, known as Randomly Weights Assignment strategy (RAW). In this paper, we examine both strategies with our proposed algorithm.

The Random Weights Assignment strategy (RAW) [14], randomly generates normalized weights for each objective while meeting constraints defined by the passenger. Formally, given a constraint $w_1 \geq w_2$, RAW first generates a value from 0 to 1 for w_2 followed by generating a second value for w_1 from w_2 to 1. It is worth noting that RAW dynamically changes the weights at each generation until the best solution is obtained or the termination criterion is met. The goal is to ensure that multiple search directions can be explored [14].

To estimate the fixed weight vectors for the travelers, we proposed a method using Analytical Hierarchy Process (AHP) [9]. In the AHP, a scale of numbers is required to make a pairwise comparison. For this purpose, the linguistic terms equal, moderate, strong and extreme importance are enumerated using the numbers 1, 3, 5, and 7, respectively. Formally, using definitions 6 to 9, pair-wise statements are calculated based on the passengers preferences which demonstrate the strength of their preferences. Then, the preference information is converted to weightings using an estimation procedure (Eq. 2).

Definition 6. *Objective i is 'moderately more important' than objective j (i.e. $i > j$) iff user prefers objective i over j.*

Definition 7. *Objective i is 'strongly more important' than objective j (i.e. $i \gg j$) iff $\exists k | i > j$ and $k > j$ and $i > k$.*

Definition 8. *Objective i is 'extremely more important' than objective j (i.e. $i \ggg j$) iff $\exists k | i > j$ and $k \gg j$ and $i > k$.*

Definition 9. *Objective i and j are considered 'equally important' (i.e. $i \sim j$) iff none of the above definitions apply to them.*

The preference statements specified are converted to a matrix M where, $m_{i,j}$ is the importance of objective i compared with objective j.

$$m_{i,j} = \begin{cases} 1 & \text{iff} \quad i \sim j \\ 3 & \text{iff} \quad i > j \\ 5 & \text{iff} \quad i \gg j \\ 7 & \text{iff} \quad i \ggg j \end{cases} \tag{1}$$

Finally, for each criterion, the weights can be calculated by:

$$w_i = \frac{(\prod_j m_{i,j})^{\frac{1}{5}}}{\sum_i (\prod_j m_{i,j})^{\frac{1}{5}}} \tag{2}$$

5   Proposed Method

In this section, we describe the proposed evolutionary-based solver for personalized journey planning.

5.1   Personalized Multi-criteria Genetic Algorithm (PMGA)

NSGA-II [10] is a fast and elitist multi-criteria genetic algorithm characterized by its effective non-domination sorting and diversity preservation. NSGA-II algorithm tries to approximate the whole Pareto front and to distribute the obtained non-dominated solutions evenly. However, in preference-based multi-criteria optimization, we are only interested in a particular region of the Pareto front according to a preference vector expressed by the user.

The core idea of PMGA lies in replacing the crowding distance indicator used in NSGA-II with a journey utility indicator which expresses the quality of a specific journey based on user preferences (Algorithm 1). The proposed algorithm attempts to find a set of preferred Pareto-optimal journeys for a specific traveler where the journeys' utility are higher, i.e., individual solutions are added into the next population based on the utility indicator rather than the crowding distance. In other words, using preferences' weight vector, a value of μ is calculated and assigned to each individual solution s belonging to the population. The utility function is defined as below where j refers to a journey. Note that, a higher value of μ indicates that j is a better journey hence has a higher chance to be in the next generation.

$$\mu(j, w) = \sum_{o=1}^{P} w_o \left(\frac{U_j^o - min_j(U_j^o)}{(max_j(U_j^o) - min_j(U_j^o))} \right) \tag{3}$$

where w_o is weighing of the objective o satisfying ($\sum_{o=1}^{P} w_o = 1$) and U_j^o is utility of each criterion in a journey given by:

$$U_j^o = \sum_{m=1}^{M} a_m^o X_{m,j} \tag{4}$$

where a_m^o is unit of criterion o for mode m, and $X_{m,j}$ is the distance traveled by transportation mode m in route j (km). Note that the higher utility indicates that a particular journey is closer to the user preferences and therefore is more preferable to the commuter.

In the following, we describe the basic operators of the algorithm.

5.2   Basic Operators of the Proposed Algorithm

The proposed GA-based multi-criteria journey planner engine works in five steps. Encoding of the chromosomes and initialization are the first step. Each chromosome represents a path in the multi-modal network and is defined as a set of legs.

Algorithm 1. PMGAs algorithm

1: **procedure** PMGA(N, b)
2:      $pop \leftarrow randPop(), t \leftarrow 1, P_t \leftarrow 1, Q_t \leftarrow \emptyset$ ▷ Initialization
3:      Select individuals from Q_t, apply crossover and
          mutation and add the offspring into Q_t
4:      $R_t \leftarrow Q_t + P_t$
5:      Sort R_t into non-dominated fronts $F = \{F_1, F_2, ..., F_k\}$
6:      $P_{t+1} \leftarrow \emptyset, i \leftarrow 1$
7:      Until $|P_t + 1| + |F_i| \leq N$
          $|P_t + 1| \leftarrow |P_t + 1| \cup |F_i|, i \leftarrow i + 1.$
8:      For each individual s in the F_i calculate the $\mu(s)$
9:      Sort F_i based on μ
10:     Select individuals from F_i until $|P_{t+1} = N$
11:     $t \leftarrow t + 1, Q_t \leftarrow \emptyset$
12:     go to step 3 until the termination condition is satisfied
13: **end procedure**

Since the number of legs in a path is not predefined, variable length chromosomes are used.

Initialization: The Random Walks algorithm (RW) [16] is used to initialize the population. This method enables us to explore the search space better by generating more diverse paths comparing with other approaches such as A*, depth-first, and breadth-first search algorithms [16]. Note that during population initialization; a station might be visited twice. Therefore, the repair function is applied to the chromosomes to remove possible loops in the path.

Crossover: As shown in Fig. 1, in order to apply the crossover operation, two parents should have at least one common gene (leg) except for source and destination legs. One possible crossover point (i.e., common leg) is randomly picked whenever there are many possible crossover points. If a matching leg is found, then the solutions are crossed after the matching leg as shown in Fig. 1. Finally, the repair function is applied to the generated offspring to remove possible loops.

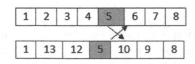

Fig. 1. Crossover: gray nodes represent crossover nodes

Mutation: Mutation is implemented by selecting a sub-path from the chromosome and replacing it with a new path. First, we randomly select two trip legs from a solution which is the candidate for mutation. Then, a new time horizon T' is defined equal to the departure time of the second leg. Then RW is utilized to find an alternative path connecting selected two service legs. Fig. 2 clarifies the proposed mutation operator. The repair function is also applied after mutation to eliminate loops along the path. Note that both crossovers and mutations are applied with predefined probabilities coming from a uniform distribution.

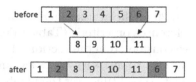

Fig. 2. Path mutation: dark gray vertices represent the local source and destination vertices, and the light gray vertices represent a different path connecting them.

Repair Function: Since each chromosome is a set of legs connecting transit stations, modifying the value of any genes during crossover and mutation may cause the chromosome to show invalid paths. To overcome this issue, a repair procedure is introduced to ensure that newly generated chromosomes show feasible path (i.e., have no loops). This procedure is done by identifying and removing the genes from a solution which are building a loop as following.

In a given path, first, all legs that have common departure station is found. Then, the sub-path between these two legs is removed excluding the second leg (i.e., the leg with a greater departure time). Figure 3 demonstrates an example of the repair function.

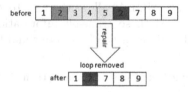

Fig. 3. An example of repair function

6 Experiment

In this Section, we evaluate the performance of the proposed scheme. We used the real GFTS data [1], from city of Melbourne, Australia, consisting of several information such as stop locations, routes, and timetable. A total of 3617 locations considered including 3559 bus stops, 44 bike stations, and 14 points of interest. For the multi-modal network, all pairs of nodes, within $0.25\,km$ radius, are connected by walking legs. Cycling legs are only available between two bike stations within the distance of one hour. The speed of walking and cycling legs is

5 km/h and *12 km/h* respectively. We implemented our algorithm in MATLAB, and performed our experiments on a 2.2-GHz Core-i5 Intel PC.

To build the synthesized dataset, on which the tests were performed, a set of 20 passengers were created and for each user, and a set of 100 random queries are assigned as follows:

Passengers: we defined 20 artificial passengers with a set of predefined constraints based on their preferences on criteria (Table 1 demonstrates 5 randomly selected passengers that we considered in this section). For example, for a particular user, the constraints are set to $w_1 > w_2$, $w_3 > w_1$, and $w_2 > w_4$ which indicates that the travelers prefers travel time over the number of transfer, monetary cost over travel time and CO_2 emission over energy expedition of the journey. We applied RAW and the proposed FW strategy [15] to generate weight vector for a particular user based on his/her preferences constraint.

Query: for each passenger, a set of 100 journey queries (instances) are created. Each service k operating within the time horizon is extracted from the timetables as described in Sect. 2. The maximum walking and cycling time is set to 15 and 60 min respectively.

Solver Settings: for each instance listed above, the experiment is repeated 25 times and the average result is recorded. Regarding to the PMGA settings, crossover, and mutation probabilities are set to 1.0 and 0.4 per iteration respectively. Population size is set to 100 and the maximum function evaluations is set to 10000 (i.e. 100 generations).

In order to evaluate the effectiveness of the proposed algorithm, it has been tested against two evolutionary algorithms namely NSGA-II [10], and G-MOEA [6]. G-MOEA is a modified version of MOEA/D [17] algorithm and utilizes decomposition methods to convert a multi-criteria optimization problem into a single-criterion problem. G-MOEA, allows the user to specify the linear trade-off between criteria and uses these trade-off information to guide the search towards the more desired regions of the Pareto-optimal front.

Table 1. 5 randomly selected passengers and their preference statements

User	Preference statements
1	$w_1 \geq w_2, w_3 \geq w_1, w_2 \geq w_1$
2	$w_2 \geq w_1, w_3 \geq w_4$
3	$w_1 \geq w_3, w_3 \geq w_2, w_1 \geq w_2$
4	$w_2 \geq w_3, w_3 \geq w_4, w_2 \geq w_1$
5	$w_1 \geq w_2$

6.1 Quality Indicators

The permanence of each algorithm is investigated in terms of both diversity and convergence. Therefore, we use two metrics, Inverted Generational Distance

(IGD) [17] and Hyper-Volume (HV) [17] for measuring diversity and convergence respectively. Each metric is calculated based on the obtained solutions of each algorithm.

Hyper-Volume: Hyper-volume Metric (HV) measures the volume between all solutions in an obtained solution set and a nadir point (i.e., a vector of the worst objective function values obtained by the solution set) defined as:

$$HV(Q) = volume \left(\bigcup_{i=1}^{Q} c_i \right) \qquad (5)$$

where Q is the solution set and c_i is a hypercube constructed by taking a solution i and the nadir point as its diagonal corners. Note that higher HV values indicate a better convergence and diversity of solutions on the Pareto-optimal front.

Inverted Generational Distance: Inverted Generational Distance (IGD) [17] is a metric that can measure both diversity and convergence of the solutions simultaneously. it calculates the average closest distance of the sample points on the Pareto-optimal front to the obtained solutions, and is defined as:

$$IGD(P^*, Q) = \frac{\sum_{v \subset P} d(v, Q)}{|P|} \qquad (6)$$

where $d(v, Q)$ is the Euclidean distance between each solution v in Pareto-optimal solution set P^* and the nearest member in the obtained solution set Q.

It is worth noting, as the true Pareto-optimal set is unknown in our study, we merged the solution sets of all algorithms and used the non-dominated solutions of the merged solution sets as the substitute to the true Pareto-optimal front. Table 2 shows the mean and the standard deviation for 25 independent runs of PMGA, NSGA-II, and G-MOEA using three different performance measures.

6.2 Experimentation Results and Discussion

Table 2 shows for each algorithm the average journey utility in the estimated Pareto-optimal front. It can be seen that PMOGA outperformed NSGA-II by a big margin, since NSGA-II did not consider user preferences and treated all the criteria with equal priority. As to G-MOEA, PMOGA found better journey solutions as PMGA used the journey utility as an indicator to guide the search. Regarding to different weight assignment strategies, we observed that in most cases, the proposed FW strategy can help PMGA to achieve a better performance. The reason why FW performed better than RAW can be explained as follow: AHP captures both subjective and objective evaluation measures, providing a more accurate direction for guiding the search towards finding optimal solutions, thus proposing more suitable journeys in terms of journey quality.

With regarding to the hyper-volume (HV) indicator, our proposed algorithm with fixed weight strategy (PMGA+FW) outperformed other algorithms in most cases. This suggests that FW assignment produced a good approximation of preference weights, i.e., more accurate direction towards the Pareto-optimal front, thereby finding a better approximation of the preferred Pareto-optimal front.

Table 2. Results on the test problems. The mean and standard deviation of 25 independent runs are reported.

User	Metric	PMGA+FW	PMGA+RAW	NSGA-II	G-MOEA
1	Utility	**7.6990e-01** **(1.9860e-02)**	6.3420e-01 (3.7020e-02)	5.6340e-01 (2.8780e-02)	7.1710e-01 (5.6020e-02)
	HV	**4.6030e-01** **(2.4710e-02)**	2.0320e-01 (4.1180e-02)	3.5990e-01 (8.6500e-02)	4.4570e-01 (4.8940e-02)
	IGD	**3.5230e-03** **(2.9190e-04)**	6.1850e-03 (8.5370e-04)	5.4080e-03 (7.2420e-05)	5.9250e-03 (2.8520e-05)
2	Utility	7.8680e-01 (4.3380e-02)	**7.8740e-01** **(1.8890e-02)**	6.9010e-01 (1.3440e-02)	7.0990e-01 (4.4870e-02)
	HV	**8.3940e-01** **(4.2310e-02)**	7.4250e-01 (7.2060e-02)	3.0390e-01 (2.3520e-02)	6.9530e-01 (3.3700e-02)
	IGD	**4.2830e-03** **(6.6900e-05)**	6.6750e-03 (2.9330e-04)	5.0350e-03 (4.9110e-05)	6.1350e-03 (6.8430e-05)
3	Utility	**7.3580e-01** **(1.7710e-02)**	7.3110e-01 (1.4780e-02)	5.0680e-01 (6.1820e-02)	7.2350e-01 (6.1930e-02)
	HV	7.0660e-01 (4.9140e-02)	**7.7210e-01** **(4.9270e-02)**	5.2010e-01 (1.6490e-02)	6.8130e-01 (1.1230e-02)
	IGD	5.4070e-03 (3.8250e-05)	**7.6040e-04** **(5.9930e-05)**	6.0110e-03 (1.2330e-05)	6.4890e-03 (5.1690e-05)
4	Utility	**7.5160e-01** **(2.0550e-02)**	7.4120e-01 (3.9540e-02)	5.8770e-01 (3.3730e-03)	6.5710e-01 (4.6070e-02)
	HV	**8.0810e-01** **(5.0680e-02)**	7.7810e-01 (1.3970e-02)	3.7260e-01 (8.5590e-02)	2.5310e-01 (3.5500e-03)
	IGD	**2.4550e-04** **(7.4080e-05)**	2.7790e-03 (8.2220e-04)	5.4860e-03 (5.6280e-05)	4.7030e-03 (4.3930e-05)
5	Utility	**6.4870e-01** **(6.4940e-02)**	5.6630e-01 (2.7740e-02)	5.4630e-01 (2.5110e-02)	6.3150e-01 (2.4680e-02)
	HV	**6.7680e-01** **(7.2420e-02)**	6.5910e-01 (5.3760e-02)	5.6430e-01 (6.0050e-02)	6.6790e-01 (3.9480e-02)
	IGD	2.3230e-03 (6.4330e-05)	**1.4130e-03** **(1.6840e-05)**	7.3830e-03 (2.8980e-05)	2.5030e-03 (5.8230e-05)

With regard to the IGD indicator, the values of IGD indicate that, in most cases, the final solution set obtained by PMGA+FW is closer to the Pareto-optimal front than the other methods, which means that proposed algorithm gave a better approximation of the Pareto-optimal front. After closely examining the results, we noticed that the solutions that have a high value of the travel time are not well approximated. This is due to the time-expansion nature of the graph and the fact that we use the random walk approach for population initialization and mutation, which gave a higher chance for solutions with a small amount of time to be found.

7   Conclusion

In this work, we have modeled the personalized multi-criteria journey planning problem in multi-modal transportation networks and provided a modified version of NSGA-II algorithm to solve the problem. The proposed approach has been tested on a transit network of Melbourne, Australia, to evaluate the algorithm. The experimental results demonstrated that the proposed approach, i.e., PMGA, is able to provide a good approximation of the desired area of Pareto-optimal front, which is more relevant to the passengers.

References

1. http://www.gtfs-data-exchange.com. Accessed 25 July 2016
2. Abbaspour, R.A., Samadzadegan, F.: Time-dependent personal tour planning and scheduling in metropolises. Expert Syst. Appl. **38**(10), 12439–12452 (2011)
3. Bast, H., Delling, D., Goldberg, A., Müller-Hannemann, M., Pajor, T., Sanders, P., Wagner, D., Werneck, R.F.: Route planning in transportation networks. arXiv preprint arXiv:1504.05140 (2015)
4. Bell, P., Knowles, N., Everson, P.: Measuring the quality of public transport journey planning. In: IET and ITS Conference on Road Transport Information and Control (RTIC 2012), pp. 1–4 (2012)
5. Bielli, M., Caramia, M., Carotenuto, P.: Genetic algorithms in bus network optimization. Transp. Res. Part C: Emerg. Technol. **10**(1), 19–34 (2002)
6. Branke, J., Kaußler, T., Schmeck, H.: Guidance in evolutionary multi-objective optimization. Adv. Eng. Softw. **32**(6), 499–507 (2001)
7. Chakraborty, B.: GA-based multiple route selection for car navigation. In: Manandhar, S., Austin, J., Desai, U., Oyanagi, Y., Talukder, A.K. (eds.) AACC 2004. LNCS, vol. 3285, pp. 76–83. Springer, Heidelberg (2004). doi:10.1007/978-3-540-30176-9_10
8. Chakraborty, B.: Simultaneous multiobjective multiple route selection using genetic algorithm for car navigation. In: Pal, S.K., Bandyopadhyay, S., Biswas, S. (eds.) PReMI 2005. LNCS, vol. 3776, pp. 696–701. Springer, Heidelberg (2005). doi:10.1007/11590316_112
9. Davies, C., Lingras, P.: Genetic algorithms for rerouting shortest paths in dynamic and stochastic networks. Eur. J. Oper. Res. **144**(1), 27–38 (2003)
10. Deb, K., Pratap, A., Agarwal, S., Meyarivan, T.A.M.T.: A fast and elitist multi-objective genetic algorithm: NSGA-II. IEEE Trans. Evol. Comput. **6**(2), 182–197 (2002)
11. Gary, M.R., Johnson, D.S.: Computers, intractability: a guide to the theory of NP-completeness (1979)
12. Gen, M., Cheng, R., Wang, D.: Genetic algorithms for solving shortest path problems. In: IEEE International Conference on Evolutionary Computation, pp. 401–406. IEEE (1997)
13. Huang, B., Cheu, R.L., Liew, Y.S.: Gis and genetic algorithms for hazmat route planning with security considerations. Int. J. Geog. Inf. Sci. **18**(8), 769–787 (2004)

14. Konak, A., Coit, D.W., Smith, A.E.: Multi-objective optimization using genetic algorithms: a tutorial. Reliab. Eng. Syst. Saf. **91**(9), 992–1007 (2006)
15. Letchner, J., Krumm, J., Horvitz, E.: Trip router with individualized preferences (trip): incorporating personalization into route planning. In: Proceedings of the National Conference on Artificial Intelligence, vol. 21, p. 1795. AAAI Press/MIT Press, Menlo Park, Cambridge (1999, 2006)
16. Wang, F., Landau, D.P.: Efficient, multiple-range random walk algorithm to calculate the density of states. Phys. Rev. Lett. **86**(10), 2050 (2001)
17. Zhang, Q., Li, H.: MOEA/D: a multiobjective evolutionary algorithm based on decomposition. IEEE Trans. Evol. Comput. **11**(6), 712–731 (2007)
18. Ziliaskopoulos, A., Wardell, W.: An intermodal optimum path algorithm for multi-modal networks with dynamic arc travel times and switching delays. Eur. J. Oper. Res. **125**(3), 486–502 (2000)
19. Zografos, K., Madas, M.: Optimizing intermodal trip planning decisions in interurban networks. Transp. Res. Rec.: J. Transp. Res. Board, (1850) 61–69 (2003)
20. Zografos, G.K., Androutsopoulos, K.N.: Algorithms for itinerary planning in multimodal transportation networks. IEEE Trans. Intell. Transp. Syst. **9**(1), 175–184 (2008)

Estimating Passenger Preferences Using Implicit Relevance Feedback for Personalized Journey Planning

Mohammad Haqqani$^{(\boxtimes)}$, Xiaodong Li, and Xinghuo Yu

School of Science (Computer Science and Software Engineering),
RMIT University, Melbourne, Australia
mohammad.haqqani@rmit.edu.au

Abstract. Personalized journey planning is becoming increasingly popular, due to strong practical interests in high-quality route solutions aligned with commuter preferences. In a journey planning system, travelers are not just mere users of the systems, instead they represent an active component willing to take different routes based on their own preferences, e.g., the fastest, least number of changes, or cheapest journey. In this work, we propose a novel preference estimation method that incorporates implicit relevance feedback methods into the journey planner, aiming to provide more relevant journeys to the commuters. Our method utilizes commuters' travel history to estimate the corresponding preference model. The model is adaptive and can be updated iteratively during the user/planner interactions. By conducting experiments on a real dataset, it can be demonstrated that the proposed method provide more relevant journeys even in absence of explicit ratings from the users.

Keywords: Personalized journey planning · Preference learning · Multi-modal journey planning

1 Introduction

In modern life, route planning is gaining more and more importance. As transportation networks become more complex and mobility in our society more important, the demand for efficient methods in route planning increases even further. Journey planning has become an important component of a transportation system, assisting commuters by providing information that reduces barriers to traveling. In its simplest form, a journey planner system finds the *'best'* route between the origin and the destination of the journey, for a given transportation network [2]. A more realistic planner combines other types of information such as real-time data about traffic jams or transit conditions to find better quality routes [18].

Currently, the majority of *'intelligent'* commercial journey planners only have a small set of predefined preferences (e.g., preferred highways or public transit

© Springer International Publishing AG 2017
M. Wagner et al. (Eds.): ACALCI 2017, LNAI 10142, pp. 157–168, 2017.
DOI: 10.1007/978-3-319-51691-2_14

modes) made available for passengers to choose from and rank [Yahoo! trip planner, PTV journey planner, Google Map, openTripPlanner) [7]. Although these planners are reliable and offer an acceptable assistance to commuters, they have limited capabilities, especially when it comes to tailoring information based on the individual needs of passengers [11]. This issue could be alleviated by incorporating users' preferences into the optimization process of the journey planning. This way, more suitable journey plans can be identified and recommended to the commuters.

Moreover, as urban transport networks continue to expand in size and complexity, so does the amount of available information to the commuters. For example, Melbourne's public transportation network has more than 700 routes with thousands of stations [1]. The preference information can also be used to reduce the complexity of the planner by reducing the search space for a particular user, i.e., searching for relevant transit information.

In this paper, we investigate the possibility of providing personalized travel information, by mining the commuters' travel history, with little or no direct feedback from the commuters. In order to reveal the individual differences in the travel patterns, we describe a probabilistic preferences learning approach, based on implicit feedback, to model the commuter's preferences. The choice of this theoretical framework is motivated by several reasons: firstly, implicit feedback is very well suited to the problem, as it is not convenient for a commuter to explicitly express her preferences; secondly, the probabilistic nature of the model makes it more tolerant towards inconsistent journeys and its performance improves as the user interacts with the system.

To achieve the aforementioned goals, we introduce a preference learning (PL) approach, whereby passenger preferences are expressed as a weight vector associated with the journey criteria. The objective of the PL model is to learn the criteria weights for a particular user (i.e. passenger's preferences over journey criteria). For this purpose, we define a multi-criteria decision making problem (MCDM) in which a decision maker (i.e. commuter) evaluates a pair of solutions (i.e. journeys) against each other. These pairwise inclinations (a $\succ$ b) form the training dataset which is used to reveal the relative preference weight vector that this commuter associates with the journey criteria. To obtain a binary comparison in the form of a $\succ$ b, for a particular query, we assume the user prefers the selected journey a to another journey b which is recommended by the system. In summary, the contributions of this work are listed as follows:

– First, we propose a preference learning algorithm to learn the travelers behavioral patterns to be used in personalized journey recommendation. This learning model, improves the quality of the journey plans, and recommend journeys that better satisfy the passenger requirements.

– Second, we demonstrate and evaluate the value of relevance feedback methods in the area on journey planning on the real-world data.

The rest of the paper is structured as follows: In the next section, we review the related works. In Sect. 3, we describe the problem formulation, and in Sect. 4

our proposed preference learning method. The experimental results are presented in Sect. 5. We conclude the paper in Sect. 6.

2   Prior Work

Journey planners often recommend multiple journeys for a user query. A variation of the time-dependent shortest path algorithm is usually applied to search into a directed graph consisting of nodes, corresponding to points of interests such as public transit stations, and edges corresponding to a possible route between them [9]. The search may be optimized on different criteria, for example, the fastest, least changes or cheapest journeys [17].

Designing a personalized journey planner is not trivial for several reasons [16]. The large size and complex transportation networks, besides different types of passengers, are just a few challenges that a personalized service has to overcome. Apart from that, the notion of *'journey quality'* is difficult to define and is likely to change from person to person, resulting in the shortest trip being rarely the best one for a given user.

In the last decade, a several studies have been conducted into the problem of personalized journey planning. Most of these methods are based on explicit feedback of the commuters [4,12,14,15]. Analysis of trip planner log files [13] can help improve transit service by providing better journeys to the commuters. Log files were useful for identifying new locations to be assessed for better understanding commuters' behaviors. In [19], the fuzzy set theory was utilized to model complex user preferences where preferences were explicitly expressed and integrated in a query language.

Journey personalisation by mining public transport data has been addressed in [18]. For this purpose, a relation between urban mobility and fare purchasing habits in London public transport is established. The authors revealed a relation between fare purchasing habits [18] and urban mobility, and proposed personalized ticket recommendations based on the estimated future travel patterns.

Liu et al. [14] combined knowledge about the transportation network with brute-force search to propose a route planning system. The authors demonstrated that how geographical knowledge can be used to reveal the useful route segments of the network to the planner. To this end, authors assumed that users prefer main roads, hence the planner combine the main roads to form the plan.

In [15] the authors proposed a journey planner which is able to learn preferences using user feedback. In this work, users' are asked to express their preferences among recommended journeys when interacting with the system. A training dataset is formed using the feedback resulting from these interactions and a perceptron-style training algorithm is applied to the training set. The authors assumed a fixed user preference model which only concern route length, driving time and turn angles.

McGinty and Smyth [16] proposed a case-based route planning approach that generates routes which reflect implicit preferences of individual users. Unlike [5], they did not assume a fixed preference model. Instead, the user preference is represented as a collection previous route sections that were considered as satisfactory by the traveler. New queries are answered by reusing and combining those relevant satisfactory sections.

Studies on context-aware journeying can be found in [2,10,18]. In these works, authors integrated the context of a journey, such as travel time, traffic condition, weather conditions, etc. to provide personalize journey plans. They exploit a weighted function f to compute the overall score of a journey. Each of these route characteristics are weighted, to express the importance of them, using predefined weights explicitly specified by the users.

The main aspect which distinguishes our approach from the works [2,10,18] is that similar to [4,12,16] we use implicit feedback to model the user preferences. Moreover, unlike [5,6], we aim to provide a robust and iterative model, as opposed to a fixed model, to learn the passenger preferences.

3 Problem Formulation

3.1 Input Network

A multi-modal journey planning task is determined by a user query (i.e., a request to the planner), and the snapshot of a multi-modal transit network. In this section, we provide a formal definitions of these parameters. The transportation modes that we focus on are public transit modes (e.g. bus, train, etc.), bicycles available in the bike-sharing stations, and walking.

A multi-modal network snapshot is represented as a structure (N, R, H, M_w, M_c) that encodes knowledge about the current status and the predicted evolution of a transport network during a time horizon $[0, T] \subset R$. The variable N represents a set of locations on the map (e.g., bus station and bike stations). In addition, given a user query, the origin and the destination locations are added to N. R defines a set of routes. A route r is an ordered sequence of $n \in N$ locations, equivalent to the stops along the route. H is a collection of trips such that, each trip, $h \in H$, is a vehicle (e.g. a bus) going along a route as a sequence of nodes $(v_1, \ldots, v_m)$. The trip h departs at node v_1 at a specific time and proceeds to nodes $(v_2, \ldots, v_m)$ in the order determined by the route. M_w and M_c provide walking and cycling times for pairs of locations in the network.

A user query is shown by a tuple (o, d, t_0, m, q), where o and d are the origin and the destination locations; t_0 is the start time; m specifies a subset of transportation modes that should be considered; and q defines parameters such as the maximum walking and cycling time, allowed by the user.

In order to model the transportation network, we represent every movement in the multi-modal network by a leg. Each leg has a start node, an end node, an expected start time, and an expected end time. Formally speaking, letting L denotes the set of legs, a leg corresponding to index $i \in L$ is defined by $((v_i^k, t_i^k), (v_{(i+1)}^k, t'^k_{(i+1)}), k)$, where v_i^k is the start node, $v_{(i+1)}^k$ is the end node, t_i^k is the expected start time, $t'^k_{(i+1)}$ is the expected end time, and the mode number k is the index of the scheduled trip service that executes leg i.

Using this model, a path (i.e. journey plan) can be represented as a sequence of legs $(i_1, i_2, \ldots, i_m)$ where $i_{(h+1)}$ is among the successors of the leg i_h for all $h \in \{1, \ldots, m - 1\}$. Each path is evaluated against N criteria. In this paper, the journey criteria includes travel time, monetary cost, CO_2 emission, and personal energy consumption.

3.2 Personalized Multi-criteria Journey Planning Paradigm (MCJP)

The MCJP models are typically focused on delivering the best solutions for a given query. We consider a MCJP paradigm as shown in Fig. 1, characterized with:

- a set of journeys $S = \{j_1, j_2, \ldots, j_M\}$. Formally, each journey can be represented as a vector $j_i = \{j_i^{(1)}, j_i^{(2)}, \ldots, j_i^{(N)}\}$ where, $j_i^{(j)}$ is the evaluation of the journey j_i against criterion c_j and N is the number of criteria.

- the set of pairwise rankings of journeys, $R = \{r_1, r_2, , r_M\}$, as given by the commuter.

Each commuter is represented by a weight vector $w = \{w_1, w_2, \ldots, w_N\}$ where each criterion $c_j, j = (1, \ldots, N)$, is associated with a weight value, w_j. The objective of the present work is to infer this weight vector w, as shown in the MCDM paradigm in Fig. 1.

From a set of journeys S, we construct a set of pairwise inclinations $(J, j) \vdash S$ satisfying $J \succ j$ (i.e. the passenger prefers Journey J over j) where $J = (J_1, J_2, \ldots, J_N)$ and $j = (j_1, j_2, , j_N)$ are journeys evaluated against N criteria. $U(j, w)$, denotes the utility of a particular journey for a particular passenger. Equation 1 calculates the utility of a journey based on its criteria value as well as the user preferences' weight vector. Note that, we assume the passengers are rational, meaning that if a passenger prefers journey a over b (i.e. $a \succ b$), the utility of journey a must be greater that b (i.e. $U(a, w) \geq U(b, w)$). The journey utility, $U(j, w)$, for a particular passenger is defined as:

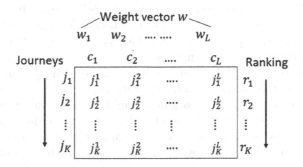

Fig. 1. Multi-criteria journey planning paradigm

$$U(j, w) = \sum_{o=1}^{P} w_o \left(\frac{U_j^o - min_j(U_j^o)}{(max_j(U_j^o) - min_j(U_j^o))} \right) \tag{1}$$

where w_o is weighing of the objective o satisfying ($\sum_{o=1}^{P} w_o = 1$) and U_j^o is utility of each criterion in a journey given by:

$$U_j^o = \sum_{m=1}^{M} a_m^o X_{m,j} \tag{2}$$

where a_m^o is unit of criterion o for transportation mode m, and $X_{m,j}$ is the distance traveled by mode m in journey j (km).

Note that the higher utility indicates that a particular journey is closer to the user preferences and therefore is more preferable to the commuter.

Formally, letting TS as the training set, consisting of pairwise inclinations, $TS = t_1, t_2, \dots, t_K$, where K is the number of pairs in the training set, the objective is to find a weight vector, i.e. $w = (w_1, w_2, \dots, w_N) \in R^N$, for a particular user such that Eq. 3 holds good for the whole training set:

$$U(J, w) \geq U(j, w),$$
$$\sum_{i=1}^{N} W_i = 1 \tag{3}$$

where, $U(j, w)$, indicates to the utility of a particular journey for a particular passenger.

4   Proposed Preference Learning Method

In this section, we construct the underlying preference model of a passenger from his/her revealed preferences, by applying preference learning (PL) methods. We provide the preference information in the form of pairwise comparisons between solutions. We aim to estimate the criteria weight vector that this passenger has in mind given the set of journeys and the pairwise preferences revealed by his/her travel history. Once the passenger's preference model is learnt, in the form of the weight vector, it is then used to predict her ranking for a new set of journeys. The comparison of this prediction with the 'true ranking' offers a means for assessing the performance of our method.

More specifically, using the training dataset, we estimate the 'most likely' weight vector that the traveler has in mind for the different criteria; i.e., maximum likelihood estimation. The obtained weight vector is subsequently applied to a new set of journeys (test dataset) and the corresponding journey utility scores are determined to rank them. We determine the performance accuracy of the preference learning process by comparing the predicted rankings with the actual ground truth rankings. In the following section, we describe the preference learning method.

4.1 Preferences Estimating

As mentioned earlier, the training dataset is used to estimate a probabilistic model which results in the 'most likely' weight vector that the traveler has in mind for the different criteria, i.e., a weight vector w^* which maximizes the probability of having $U(J, w) > U(j, w)$, when $J \succ j$ in the training set. To calculate the probability of $J \succ j$, for a pairwise inclinations, we utilized the preference model of discrete choice presented in [3], that is:

$$P(J \succ j|w) = \frac{exp(U(J, w))}{exp(U(J, w)) + exp(U(j, w))} \qquad (4)$$

Note that the probability of $J \succ j$ would increase with the increasing value of $U(J, w) - U(j, w)$ and for $U(J, w) - U(j, w) = 0$, results in the probability of 0.5 which represents a tie.

Since pairs are independent, the probability of $J \succ j$ for a complete sample of training set, TS, is given by

$$P(TS, w) = \prod_{n=1}^{K} P(J_n \succ j_n|w)$$

$$= \prod_{n=1}^{K} \frac{exp(U(J_n, w))}{exp(U(J_n, w)) + exp(U(j_n, w))} \qquad (5)$$

where, K is the total number of pairs.

Note that $P(S|w)$ is likelihood function of the weight vector w that takes the shape of a N-dimensional surface covered by it based on the maximum likelihood estimation (MLE). The preference weight vector estimator, w^*, is the maximizer of this function, i.e. $w^* = argmax_{w \in R^N} P(S|w)$.

To obtain a minimization problem we consider $-P(S|w)$, and the log-likelihood is being used since $P(S|w)$ and its log function are monotonically related to each other. It can be written as Eq. 6 as a constrained optimization problem and returns the maximum likelihood estimator w^*, given the training set, TS.

$$minimize : -\log(P(TS, w)) = -\sum_{n=1}^{K} U(J_n, w) +$$

$$+ \sum_{n=1}^{K} \log(exp((U(J_n, w))) + \log(exp(U(j_n, w)))$$

$$(6)$$

$$subject\ to :$$

$$+ \sum_{i=1}^{N} w_i = 1,$$

$$+ w_i \in [0, 1],\ for\ i = 1...N.$$

Since $P(S|w)$ is differentiable, we use the gradient descent method to obtain the updating rule for the weights $(w_i, i = (1, , N))$

$$w_i(I + 1) = w_i(I) - \beta \frac{\partial(P(TS|w))}{\partial w_i} \qquad (7)$$

which results in Eq. 8 where, $w_i(I)$ denotes the estimate of w_i after Ith iteration, and β ($0 \leq \beta \leq 1$) denotes the learning rate.

$$w_i(I + 1) = w_i(I) + \beta \left(\frac{exp(U(J_n, w))}{exp(U(J_n, w)) + exp(U(j_n, w))} (J_i - j_i) \right) \qquad (8)$$

4.2   An Illustrative Example of Our Approach

Let us consider a person with a weight vector (.4, .4, .1, .1) who wants to go from city A to city B, with a departure at 16:00. Considering the journey criteria as travel time, monetary cost, CO_2 emission and energy consumption respectively, we can infer that he/she prefers a route which is fast and not expensive. Assume that the following journeys are recommended to his/her, as shown in Table 1, in which columns 1 to 4 represent the criteria values for each journey. The obtained utility score, are calculated in accordance with his/her weight vector, is given in column 7 of Table 1. As we mentioned earlier, we assume the commuters are rational hence he/she is going to select the 3rd journey simply because it has the highest utility score. Based on her selection, the following pairwise inclinations are generated: $((j_3 \succ j_1), (j_3 \succ j_2), (j_3 \succ j_4))$.

Table 1. An example of query result

Journey	Criteria				Predicted score	Actual score
k	C_1	C_2	C_3	C_4		
1	.2	.3	.3	.2	.251	.25
2	.2	.2	.1	.5	.239	.22
3	.4	.3	.2	.1	.292	.31
4	.1	.2	.4	.2	.143	.14

In a real world scenario, however, it is rare to have the prior knowledge of the accurate preferences weight vectors. This limits the usefulness of such an approach in practice. Our PL-based approach does not require users to explicitly define their preferences. Instead, it requires only the travel history of users, pairwise inclinations, which are used to generate the preference weight vector. Let (.33, .42, .09, .16) be the learned weight vector as the result of preference learning method. The obtained utility scores, calculated in accordance with the estimated weight vector, is given in column 6 of Table 1 which result in selection of the 3rd journey again due to the highest utility score. Although our preference-based approach is simple and intuitive, it is robust, being probabilistic in nature, and it's performance improves with bigger datasets as the user/system interactions increase.

5 Experiment

In this section, we evaluate the performance of the proposed scheme. We used the real GFTS data [1], from city of Melbourne, Australia, consisting of several information such as stop locations, routes, and timetable. A total of 3617 locations considered including 3559 bus stops, 44 bike stations, and 14 points of interest. For the multi-modal network, all pairs of nodes, within 0.25 km radius, are connected by walking legs. Cycling legs are only available between two bike stations within the distance of one hour. The speed of walking and cycling legs is 5 km/h and 12 km/h respectively. We implemented our algorithm in MATLAB, and performed our experiments on a 2.2-GHz Core-i5 Intel PC.

To simulate user preferences, we synthesized 30 random queries for a set of 50 users as follows:

Passengers: we defined 50 artificial passengers with a set of predefined constraints based on their preferences on criteria. For example, for a particular user, the constraints are set to $w_1 > w_2$, $w_3 > w_1$, and $w_2 > w_4$ which indicates that he/she prefers travel time over number of transfer, monetary cost over travel time and CO_2 emission over energy expedition. We used Random Weight Assignment strategy (RWA) [7] to generate weight vector for a particular user based on his/her preference constraints.

Query: for each passenger, a set of 30 journey queries (instances) are created. Each service k operating within the time horizon is determined by a scheduled route extracted from the timetables as described in Sect. 2. The maximum walking and cycling time is set to 15 and 60 min respectively.

In order to test and compare the accuracy of the proposed techniques, we use a leave-one-out approach. A bit more concretely, we randomly select a passenger and a query, and recommend five journeys to the passenger. Then, we utilize the actual and estimated weight vector to rate the recommended journeys. Finally, in order to evaluate the accuracy of the prediction, we compare the predicted with the actual ratings. We utilized the MAE (Mean Absolute Error) metric in order to evaluate the accuracy of such predictions [8, 17]. The MAE is derived using the following equation:

$$MAE = \frac{1}{n} \sum_{i=1}^{n} |f_i - y_i| \tag{9}$$

where n is the number of predictions, f_i is the predicted rank of the journey i and y_i is the actual value. In short, MAE presents the average difference between the predicted rank and the actual rank.

In order to interpret the values of MAE, it is important to consider the scale on which the ratings are performed. Indeed, an MAE of 0.5 indicates that the predictions, on average, differed by 0.5 of the actual ranking. In order to evaluate the impact of this difference, it is important to consider the scale of the predictions. For example, a MAE of 0.5 on a scale of 5 represents 10% whereas on a scale of 20, it only represents 2.5% and consequently a lower impact on accuracy. Since, for each query, five journeys are recommended to the user, we assess the actual impact of prediction on scale of 5. Figure 3 highlights the average impact of MAE of the ten randomly selected passengers which indicates that in almost 80% of the instances the estimated weight vector ranked the journeys similar to the actual user (Table 2).

Table 2. MAE comparision

	Passengers									
	1	2	3	4	5	6	7	8	9	10
Avg MAE	0.850	0.894	0.886	1.06	1.04	1.004	0.894	1.02	1.06	1.000
Max MAE	1.600	2.000	2.000	1.800	1.800	2.000	2.000	1.800	1.600	1.800

We utilize the journey utility metric to evaluate the performance of PL-based estimator, and observed its evolution through the preference learning phase of the algorithm. Figure 2 demonstrates the average utility of the selected journey (i.e. first ranked journey) for a randomly selected passenger for each iteration. As it shown in Fig. 2, as the algorithm improves the estimated preferences (i.e. red line), the average utility of selected journeys increases and gets closer to the average utility of the actual user (i.e. blue line) which means the model is successful in terms of preferences learning.

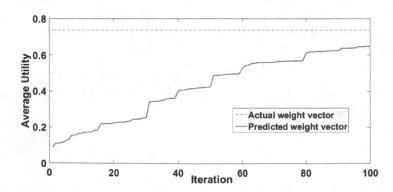

Fig. 2. Average journey utility comparision for a randomly selected passenger (Color figure online)

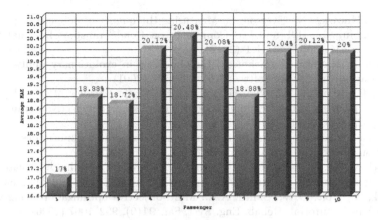

Fig. 3. Average MAE interpretation

6   Conclusion

This paper has examined the problem of personalized journey planning. Our learning algorithm seeks to estimate a commuter's preference model, based on her historical travel data in the form of pair-wise inclinations of journeys. Our proposed scheme is unique in a way that it does not require the explicit rating for journeys as a prerequisite, and is therefore quite practical in the real life scenarios. The proposed method helps to understand the priorities that a passenger has in mind and it can be applied to suggest more relevant journeys to the commuters. Besides, the probabilistic nature of the model makes it robust to inconsistent travel histories preference statements. Although the experimental results show the usefulness of the proposed approach, further investigations should be applied on real data, as opposed the synthetic data, to better prove its performance.

References

1. http://www.gtfs-data-exchange.com. Accessed 25 July 2016
2. Adomavicius, G., Tuzhilin, A.: Toward the next generation of recommender systems: a survey of the state-of-the-art and possible extensions. IEEE Trans. Knowl. Data Eng. **17**(6), 734–749 (2005)
3. Aggarwal, M.: On learning of weights through preferences. Inf. Sci. **321**, 90–102 (2015)
4. Balke, W.-T., Kiessling, W., Unbehend, C.: A situation-aware mobile traffic information system. In: Proceedings of the 36th Annual Hawaii International Conference on System Sciences, p. 10. IEEE (2003)
5. Balke, W.-T., Kießling, W., Unbehend, C.: Performance and quality evaluation of a personalized route planning system. In: SBBD, pp. 328–340. Citeseer (2003)
6. Balke, W.-T., Kießling, W., Unbehend, C.: Personalized services for mobile route planning: a demonstration. In: Proceedings of the International Conference on Data Engineering 2003, pp. 771–773. IEEE Computer Society Press (1998)

7. Bell, P., Knowles, N., Everson, P.: Measuring the quality of public transport journey planning. In: IET and ITS Conference on Road Transport Information and Control (RTIC), pp. 1–4. IET (2012)
8. Branke, J., Kaußler, T., Schmeck, H.: Guidance in evolutionary multi-objective optimization. Adv. Eng. Softw. **32**(6), 499–507 (2001)
9. Casey, B., Bhaskar, A., Guo, H., Chung, E.: Critical review of time-dependent shortest path algorithms: a multimodal trip planner perspective. Transp. Rev. **34**(4), 522–539 (2014)
10. Clarke, F., Ekeland, I.: Solutions périodiques, du période donnée, des équations hamiltoniennes. Note CRAS Paris **287**, 1013–1015 (1978)
11. Herlocker, J.L., Konstan, J.A., Terveen, L.G., Riedl, J.T.: Evaluating collaborative filtering recommender systems. ACM Trans. Inf. Syst. (TOIS) **22**(1), 5–53 (2004)
12. Konak, A., Coit, D.W., Smith, A.E.: Multi-objective optimization using genetic algorithms: a tutorial. Reliab. Eng. Syst. Saf. **91**(9), 992–1007 (2006)
13. Lathia, N., Capra, L.: Mining mobility data to minimise travellers' spending on public transport. In: Proceedings of the 17th ACM SIGKDD International Conference on Knowledge Discovery and Data Mining, pp. 1181–1189. ACM (2011)
14. Letchner, J., Krumm, J., Horvitz, E.: Trip router with individualized preferences (trip): incorporating personalization into route planning. In: Proceedings of the National Conference on Artificial Intelligence, vol. 21, pp. Menlo Park, CA; Cambridge, MA; London; AAAI Press; MIT Press; 1999, 2006 (1795)
15. Liu, B.: Intelligent route finding: combining knowledge, cases and an efficient search algorithm'. In: ECAI, vol. 96, pp. 380–384. Citeseer (1996)
16. McGinty, L., Smyth, B.: Personalised route planning: a case-based approach. In: Blanzieri, E., Portinale, L. (eds.) EWCBR 2000. LNCS, vol. 1898, pp. 431–443. Springer, Heidelberg (2000). doi:10.1007/3-540-44527-7_37
17. Pelletier, M.-P., Trépanier, M., Morency, C.: Smart card data in public transit planning: a review. CIRRELT (2009)
18. Trépanier, M., Chapleau, R., Allard, B.: Can trip planner log files analysis help in transit service planning? J. Publ. Transp. **8**(2), 5 (2005)
19. Yuan, J., Zheng, Y., Xie, X., Sun, G.: Driving with knowledge from the physical world. In: Proceedings of the 17th ACM SIGKDD International Conference on Knowledge Discovery and Data Mining, pp. 316–324. ACM (2011)

Quantitative Assessment of Heart Function: A Hybrid Mechanism for Left Ventricle Segmentation from Cine MRI Sequences

Muhammad Sohaib and Jong-Myon Kim[(✉)]

School of Electrical Engineering, University of Ulsan, Ulsan, South Korea
suhaib_durrani@yahoo.com, jongmyon.kim@gmail.com

Abstract. In this paper, we propose a hybrid approach for segmenting the left ventricle out of magnetic resonance sequences and apply results of the segmentation for heart quantification. The hybrid approach uses a thresholding-based region growing algorithm coupled with gradient vector flow (GVF). Results of the segmentation steps were used for the quantification process and yielded values of 175.4 ± 51.52 (ml), 66 ± 38.97 (ml), and 61.60 ± 12.79 (%) for end diastolic volume (EDV), end systolic volume (ESV), and ejection fraction (EF), respectively.

Keywords: Gradient vector flow · Left ventricle · Segmentation · Cine MRI sequences

1 Introduction

Approximately 17.5 million people worldwide die of fatal cardiovascular diseases every year [1]. To diagnose a human heart condition, quantitative assessment of the heart is a preliminary and vital task that helps in treatment planning for a patient [2–5]. Numerous modalities are used for imaging of the complete cardiac cycle of the human heart including echocardiography, computed tomography (CT), radionuclide cine angiography, and cine magnetic resonance imaging (CMRI) [6]. Because of its non-invasive nature and high resolution, CMRI is considered to be a gold standard for quantifying human heart functionality [7, 8]. For quantification purposes, the end systolic and end diastolic performances are considered for the calculation of useful clinical parameters such as end systolic volume (ESV), end diastolic volume (EDV), and ejection fraction (EF). For calculation of these clinical parameters, the left ventricle (LV) must be segmented from CMRI sequences. In daily clinical practice, LV segmentation is performed manually. This manual segmentation of LV regions from CMRI sequences is difficult task, and it takes an average of 20–25 min for an expert to quantify the function of a single heart. In the past few decades, research has been carried out to overcome this problem. As a result, some dedicated software packages have been introduced to carry out the desired task [9, 10]; however, such packages are not fully automated and require human intervention at some level. Researchers have also proposed automatic or semi-automatic solutions for tasks such as active appearance models, random walks, graph cuts, multispeed region growing, Gaussian mixture

© Springer International Publishing AG 2017
M. Wagner et al. (Eds.): ACALCI 2017, LNAI 10142, pp. 169–179, 2017.
DOI: 10.1007/978-3-319-51691-2_15

models, and dynamic programing. The existing approaches involve difficulties when segmenting the LV from basal and apical slices. Especially, traces of aorta in the basal slices compromise the performance of an algorithm. The performance of the graph cut method is good for LV segmentation from cine MRI sequences, but this algorithm faces the problem of high computation time. In the current work, an effort is made to segment the LV region properly in basal and apical slices, where segmentation is normally considered to be difficult and results are not satisfactory. This approach takes advantage of the spatiotemporal continuity of CMRI sequences. For experimental purposes, the second annual data science bowl dataset, which is available on the data science community "Kaggle" [14], was used.

2   Literature Review

The short axis (SAX) view is normally considered for the quantification of human heart functionality [11–24]. This is a two-chamber cross-sectional view of the left and right ventricles. As blood is contained within the LV and is pumped out to the rest of the body with each heartbeat, many researchers only focused on the boundary walls of the LV where the blood pool is contained. These boundary walls are known as the endocardial contour. It is very difficult to extract the endocardial contour in basal and apical slices. Several methods have been developed to complete the desired segmentation task so that the quantification process could be made automatic.

2.1   Histogram-Based Methods

In histogram-based methods, a single traverse through all the pixels in an image is used, and then a histogram of all pixels is computed. Peak and valley values of the histogram are noted and are used to divide the pixels of the image into clusters [13–16]. For clustering of an image, either color or intensity values are used as a parameter. In the case of intensity-based clustering, single or multiple threshold values are selected. On the basis of these threshold values, the images are divided into clusters. Bhan et al. [15] have described automatic segmentation of LV from cine MRIs. In their study, local adaptive K-mean clustering was used to group the pixels of an image into clusters on the basis of intensity. This process helped in the differentiation of foreground pixels from background pixels. After K-mean clustering, connected component labeling was carried out to group different regions on the basis of their properties in order to extract the exact LV region from temporal phases in different slices. In another study [16], fuzzy c-mean clustering was used with connected component labeling to extract the LV region from the MRI frames. Fuzzy c-mean is a pixel-based clustering method used to divide an MRI frame into foreground and background images. Using this method, the researchers reduced the computation time of the process. Gupta et al. [17] proposed a multilevel thresholding mechanism for the segmentation of MRI frames. Their work describes an adaptable segmentation mechanism in which techniques of histogram quantization in groups are used as a preprocessing step. Histogram slope percentage and maximum entropy are used to define multiple threshold values for the segmentation process. The algorithm automatically acquires threshold values by inspection of histograms. Tian et al. [18] used the k-mean algorithm based on histogram analysis, which was used to deal with the intrinsic limitations of k-means and to determine the initial centroids for k-mean clustering. In their study, local maxima were computed by analysis of the histogram. After computing local maxima, the global maximum was determined to select the seed point to initiate the clustering process with the k-means algorithm. The problem with histogram based technique is to properly identify the peak and valley vales for the histogram, because if a low resolution image is provided as an input, the histogram obtained is not appropriate.

2.2 Statistical Model-Based Methods

The statistical model-based methods involve development of a human heart model by learning geometric- or intensity-based features of the heart. The model is globally aligned to an image and is then deformed to fit the contents of the image under observation. Statistical models have two variants: an active shape model (ASM) and an active appearance model (AAM) [19]. The left ventricle segmentation model presented by Danilouchkine et al. [20] uses line parameterization for the preprocessing step. With the help of Fuzzy inference for determination of updated steps for edge detection, problems of under- and over-estimation are solved. Statistical model based methods require segmentation of large training sets to cover the inter-patient variance.

2.3 Region-Based Methods

In this class of method, the image is divided into regions on the basis of different properties of the image such as intensity, texture, and pattern. Wang et al. [21] developed an automated algorithm named LV_FAST in which LV segmentation was carried out using spatiotemporal continuity of the LV. In this algorithm, the researchers used an iteratively decreasing threshold region-growing method to segment the LV region in the entire MRI stack. Li et al. [22] proposed a semi-automated method for the segmentation of epicardium and endocardium of LV. Thickness of myocardium was also calculated in their study. The process of segmentation was initialized by selection of the seed point in the LV cavity. Maximum likelihood was used to determine the LV and thickness of myocardium. The main problem with region-based methods is the seed point initialization. Some methods even require more than one seed point for the segmentation task.

2.4 Graph-Based Methods

In the graph cut method, image segmentation is performed by calculating a graph of the entire image. Graph contains the nodes and edges information of entire image. Each pixel in the image serves as a node in the graph. The node with the minimal cut i.e. the edge having minimal weight is used to differentiate the object pixels from background. In this method, a region of interest (ROI) is needed to initialize the segmentation process. This method provides the optimum global solution, and another positive aspect is extension of the results to 3D or even higher applications. In the study of Ray and Goyal [23], medical parameters like ESV, EDV, and EF were calculated. Graph cut labeling was used for segmentation of cardiac cine MRIs without an initializing seed point for the segmentation process. Urshler et al. [24] suggested a live wire mechanism for segmentation of the left ventricle. This task was completed by the combination of an intelligent scissors algorithm and Dijikstra's algorithm. However, a problem with the proposed method is that it needs an expert radiologist for seed initialization. Graph based methods require high computation time for segmentation per frame.

2.5   Deformable Model-Based Methods

In deformable model-based methods, region boundaries are delineated using 2D closed curves or a 3D surface that deforms due to internal or external forces. External forces can be derived from the feature set or by the original picture itself and deform the curve or surface to locate the desired shape in the image including lines, contours, or edges. Zheng et al. [25] defined a shape prior that can be used to detect local variations. In this method, an annotated heart model was used to image objects by optimizing similarity or affine transformation between features of the annotated model and the image under observation. In deformable models the main problem is how to initiate the delineation problem. This area is less explored from the researchers.

2.6   Atlas-Based Methods

In the atlas-based methods, an atlas of different structures in a given image type is created. Using atlas information, an image can be segmented into different objects by mapping. These methods coordinate the space of the given image to that of the atlas through the registration process. In contrast to deformable models, atlas-based segmentation is carried out implicitly based on shape information, and then either labeled areas from different atlases are concatenated [26] or registered atlases are deformed to define an image [27]. In atlas based methods, it's a complicated task to develop an atlas which can cover all the cases encounter in real-time patients data.

3   Methodology

Figure 1 shows the segmentation process adopted in this study. The process is divided into two phases. The first phase includes seed point selection to initiate the segmentation process and the segmentation of all midlevel slices. Seed point selection is carried out using criteria developed in reference [21], in which heart localization was carried out by calculating a difference image using two temporal phases among the slices from the MRI stack of a patient's data. The first temporal phase is the nominal end diastolic frame, and the second is the nominal end systolic frame. The algorithm used for segmenting all phases in middle slices is region growing [28]. Extracting the LV endocardial contour in middle slices is easy because LV region temporal continuity

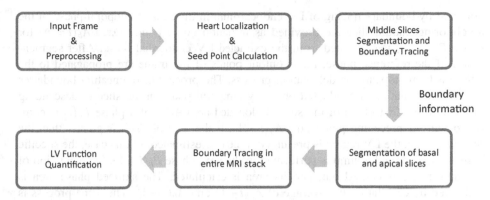

Fig. 1. Work flow of the segmentation process

in each phase in these slices is smooth. The second phase of the process is to obtain the endocardial contour information in the most basal and apical slices of the stack. Cine MRI imaging sequences lack smooth temporal continuity in the most basal and apical slices.

For this reason, segmentation of the left ventricle in such slices is a challenging task, and a simple algorithm fails in such areas. Thus, development of a more sophisticated mechanism is needed for the desired task.

To track the endocardial edge information in basal and apical slices of the MRI stack, a gradient vector flow (GVF)-based active contour method is used [29]. This method needs 2D plane or 3D surface information to initiate the contour delineating process in the temporal frame under observation. GVF based active contour does not need the initialization values close to the boundary, it converges to the boundary. GVF is snake based algorithm, here 2D snake is defined by $v(s) = [x(s), y(s)]$. GVF minimizes the energy function E as:

$$E = \int_0^1 E_{\text{int}}(v(s)) + E_{image}(v(s)) + E_{con}(v(s)) \mathrm{d}s$$

Where, E_{int} is used to show the energy of the contour due to bending, E_{image} is the intensity contained in the image and E_{con} is known as constrained energy. By minimizing the energy function GVF is able to differentiate between foreground and background pixels. So by tracking foreground and background pixels algorithm is able to obtain the edge map of the image. After having edge map the initiated contour converges to the desired nearest contour in the edge map extracted. As GVF needs curve information to initiate the delineation process (snake). For this purpose, the contour information extracted in phase one from middle slices is used to initiate the delineation process of apical and basal slices. To initiate the delineation process in the basal slice, the phase in apical slice which nearest to the last phase of middle slice towards basal direction is selected as a reference point since it shows spatiotemporal continuity to its neighboring slice, i.e. $P_b(i = n)$, where b is the basal slice, and n is the maximum temporal phase in the slice, which is 5 in our case. Final contour points obtained by boundary tracing of LV endocardium in the nearest temporal phase of the neighboring middle slice are provided as initiation curve points. Area $A_b(i = n)$ for phase $P_b(i = n)$ is calculated from the extracted LV endocrdial mask. After segmentation of the reference phase, final contour points of the frame are propagated to the adjacent frame to start the delineation process. The process of delineating boundaries and area calculation is conducted on every temporal phase in the slice in descending order until the first phase of the slice. Calculated area $A_b(i)$ of a phase $P_b(i)$ is compared with its preceding phase area $A_b(i - 1)$. If the area of $P_b(i)$ is greater than the preceding one, the LV region is presumed to be overestimated. In this case, the specific case is skipped, and a jump is performed to the next phase $P_b(i + 1)$. Segmentation of the new phase is carried out, and its area is calculated. The skipped phase area is estimated by calculating the average of $A_b(i + 1)$ and $A_b(i - 1)$. The same process is carried out on the apical slice except that the reference phase in the slice is the first temporal phase and the contour information is propagated from first to last temporal phases in the slice. Extracted masks of the LV region are passed through some morphological operations to fill the holes that arise during the segmentation process. To keep the contour smooth, a membrane and thin plate energy mechanism are used. After calculating the area of each temporal phase in the MRI slices, quantification parameters for the heart such as ESV, EDV, and EF are calculated.

4 Experimental Results

The experiments were carried out on the second annual data science bowl, available online at the data science community "Kaggle." In this data set, MRI sequences from more than 1000 patients are given. Each stack of MRI contain 30 images, which are associated with single cycle of heart. In Figs. 2 and 3, a typical MRI stack of single patient is presented. In Fig. 2, a typical diastolic cycle of from a patient data is presented and in Fig. 3, a typical systolic cycle is given. These two cycles constitutes to single heartbeat. From these two figure, it can be seen that there are 30 frames. These frames are divided into six slices through the vertical axis, and each slice contains five temporal phases (horizontal axis). In this study, we utilize a hybrid approach composed of thresholding-based region growing and a GVF-based active contour method using temporal continuity as a key for the segmentation of cine MRI images.

Using thresholding-based region growing segmentation, it was easy to segment and estimate the area of the LV blood pool in midlevel slices. Results of the segmentation and estimation in middle slices is given in the figure with frames having green LV region. However by using the mentioned method segmentation results for apical and basal slices were not good. Here the algorithm segmented the LV region improperly, which in turn resulting in bad estimate of LV area. To tackle this problem GVF-based active contour segmentation was carried out in these slices. Figure 4, shows the results of the GVF-based active contour model in a single temporal phase of a basal slice. The delineation process of basal and apical slices is complicated compared with middle slices. The results show that application of GVF-based active contour with the help of temporal information from the previous phases in adjacent slices gives satisfactory results.

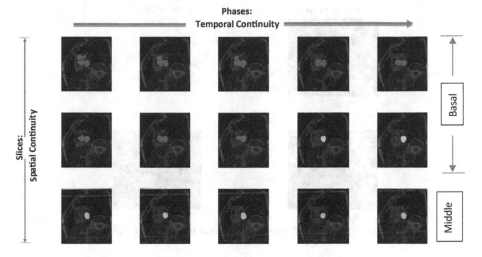

Fig. 2. Diastolic cycle of heart

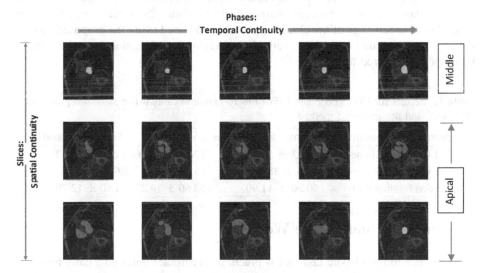

Fig. 3. Systolic cycle of heart

Results of the proposed method are compared with one of the pre implemented automatic LV segmentation technique named LV_FAST [21]. The results are compared in terms of quantification parameters EDV, ESV, and EF, which are listed in Table 1. First column of the table shows the ground truth data provided for EDV, ESV, and EF respectively by the experts using manual segmentation. This ground truth data is available online along with the data set which is used for the current work [14]. Second and third columns of the table show the results for LV-FAST, and the proposed method, respectively. All the readings listed in the table are in the form of mean and

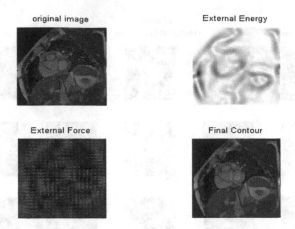

Fig. 4. Delineation of a typical temporal phase from basal slice

standard deviation. For experiment purpose 100 random cases were selected from the data set. Segmentation process was applied to MRI stack of the chosen 100 cases and at the end quantification parameters were calculated. From the table it can be easily noticed that the readings of the clinical parameters obtained using the proposed method is closer to the ground truth data available i.e. having less deviation from the original readings as compared to LV-FAST.

Table 1. Results for EDV, ESV and EF of the 100 random cases using manual segmentation, LV-FAST, and the proposed method

Quantification parameter	Manual segmentation	LV-FAST	Proposed method
End diastolic volume (ml)	174.3 ± 53.11	176.2 ± 31.46	175.4 ± 51.52
End systolic volume (ml)	67.8 ± 38.71	65.73 ± 72	66 ± 38.97
Ejection fraction (%)	60.30 ± 11.90	62.60 ± 14.23	61.60 ± 12.79

5   Conclusion and Future Work

LV quantification is a trivial task that is practiced in cardiac clinics on a daily basis. As manual segmentation of a patient's whole MRI stack is a time consuming task, researchers have introduced automatic mechanisms to speed up segmentation of the stack for the quantification process. Such automatic mechanisms fail when segmenting basal and apical slices because temporal continuity is not as smooth in these slices as in middle slices. Thus, the focus of our research was to introduce an algorithm that can overcome this difficulty. It can be verified from the result section that the thresholding-based region growing segmentation performed well in middle slices but failed in apical and basal slices. By the addition of extra segmentation step to the pipeline the issue is resolved. The results of our algorithm provided satisfactory results when segmenting the basal and apical slices; therefore, this approach can be considered for real-time applications. Future aspects of the work might explore volumetric parameters in the left ventricle in the 3D domain, which would provide better quantification.

Acknowledgments. This work was supported by the Korea Institute of Energy Technology Evaluation and Planning (KETEP) and the Ministry of Trade, Industry & Energy (MOTIE) of the Republic of Korea (No. 20162220100050); in part by The Leading Human Resource Training Program of Regional Neo Industry through the National Research Foundation of Korea (NRF) funded by the Ministry of Science, ICT, and Future Planning (NRF-2016H1D5A1910564); and in part by the Business for Cooperative R&D between Industry, Academy, and Research Institute funding for the Korea Small and Medium Business Administration in 2016 (Grant No. C0395147, S2381631).

References

1. W. H. Orgaization. World Health Orgaization of Cardiovascular Diseases (2016). http://www.who.int/cardiovascular_diseases/en/
2. McManus, D.D., Shah, S.J., Fabi, M.R., Rosen, A., Whooley, M.A., Schiller, N.B.: Prognostic value of left ventricular end-systolic volume index as a predictor of heart failure hospitalization in stable coronary artery disease: data from the heart and soul study. J. Am. Soc. Echocardiogr. **22**(2), 190–197 (2009)
3. van den Bosch, A.E., Robbers-Visser, D., Krenning, B.J., Voormolen, M.M., McGhie, J.S., Helbing, W.A., Roos-Hesselink, J.W., Simoons, M.L., Meijboom, F.J.: Real-time transthoracic three-dimensional echocardiographic assessment of left ventricular volume and ejection fraction in congenital heart disease. J. Am. Soc. Echocardiogr. **19**(1), 1–6 (2006)
4. White, H.D., Norris, R., Brown, M.A., Brandt, P., Whitlock, R., Wild, C.: Left ventricular end-systolic volume as the major determinant of survival after recovery from myocardial infarction. Circulation **76**(1), 44–51 (1987)
5. Hadhoud, M.M., Eladawy, M.I., Farag, A., Montevecchi, F.M., Morbiducci, U.: Left ventricle segmentation in cardiac MRI images. Am. J. Biomed. Eng. **2**(3), 131–135 (2012)
6. Bhan, A.: Parametric models for segmentation of Cardiac MRI database with geometrical interpretation. In: 2014 International Conference on Signal Processing and Integrated Networks (SPIN), pp. 711–715 (2014)
7. Caudron, J., Fares, J., Lefebvre, V., Vivier, P.-H., Petitjean, C., Dacher, J.-N.: Cardiac MRI assessment of right ventricular function in acquired heart disease: factors of variability. Acad. Radiol. **19**(8), 991–1002 (2012)
8. Petitjean, C., Dacher, J.-N.: A review of segmentation methods in short axis cardiac MR images. Med. Image Anal. **15**(2), 169–184 (2011)
9. Van der Geest, R., Jansen, E., Buller, V., Reiber, J.: Automated detection of left ventricular epi-and endocardial contours in short-axis MR images. Comput. Cardiol. **1994**, 33–36 (1994)
10. O'Donnell, T., Funka-Lea, G., Tek, H., Jolly, M.-P., Rasch, M., Setser, R.: Comprehensive cardiovascular image analysis using MR and CT at siemens corporate research. Int. J. Comput. Vis. **70**(2), 165–178 (2006)
11. Frangi, A.F., Niessen, W.J., Viergever, M.A.: Three-dimensional modeling for functional analysis of cardiac images, a review. IEEE Trans. Med. Imaging **20**(1), 2–5 (2001)

12. Frangi, A.F., Rueckert, D., Schnabel, J.A., Niessen, W.J.: Automatic construction of multiple-object three-dimensional statistical shape models: application to cardiac modeling. IEEE Trans. Med. Imaging **21**(9), 1151–1166 (2002)
13. Pham, D.L., Xu, C., Prince, J.L.: Current methods in medical image segmentation 1. Ann. Rev. Biomed. Eng. **2**(1), 315–337 (2000)
14. Kaggle: Second Annual Data Science Bowl. https://www.kaggle.com/c/second-annual-data-science-bowl
15. Bhan, A., Goyal, A., Ray, V.: Fast fully automatic multiframe segmentation of left ventricle in cardiac MRI images using local adaptive k-means clustering and connected component labeling. In: 2015 2nd International Conference on Signal Processing and Integrated Networks (SPIN), pp. 114–119 (2015)
16. Bhan, A., Goyal, A., Dutta, M.K., Riha, K., Omran, Y.: Image-based pixel clustering and connected component labeling in left ventricle segmentation of cardiac MR images. In: 2015 7th International Congress on Ultra Modern Telecommunications and Control Systems and Workshops (ICUMT), pp. 339–342 (2015)
17. Gupta, P., Malik, V., Gandhi, M.: Implementation of multilevel threshold method for digital images used in medical image processing. Int. J. Adv. Res. Comput. Sci. Softw. Eng. **2**(2) (2012)
18. Tian, M., Yang, Q., Maier, A., Schasiepen, I., Maass, N., Elter, M.: Automatic histogram-based initialization of k-means clustering in CT. In: Meinzer, H.-P., Deserno, T.M., Handels, H., Tolxdorff, T. (eds.) Bildverarbeitung für die Medizin 2013, pp. 277–282. Springer, Heidelberg (2013)
19. Ecabert, O., Peters, J., Schramm, H., Lorenz, C., von Berg, J., Walker, M.J., Vembar, M., Olszewski, M.E., Subramanyan, K., Lavi, G.: Automatic model-based segmentation of the heart in CT images. IEEE Trans. Med. Imaging **27**(9), 1189–1201 (2008)
20. Danilouchkine, M., Behloul, F., Lamb, H., Reiber, J.J., Lelieveldt, B.: Cardiac LV segmentation using a 3D active shape model driven by fuzzy inference: application to cardiac CT and MR. IEEE Trans. Inf. Technol. Biomed. **12**(5) (2003)
21. Wang, L., Pei, M., Codella, N.C., Kochar, M., Weinsaft, J.W., Li, J., Prince, M.R., Wang, Y.: Left ventricle: fully automated segmentation based on spatiotemporal continuity and myocardium information in cine cardiac magnetic resonance imaging (LV-FAST). BioMed Res. Int. **2015** (2015)
22. Li, C., Jia, X., Sun, Y.: Improved semi-automated segmentation of cardiac CT and MR images. In: 2009 IEEE International Symposium on Biomedical Imaging: From Nano to Macro, pp. 25–28 (2009)
23. Ray, V., Goyal, A.: Image based sub-second fast fully automatic complete cardiac cycle left ventricle segmentation in multi frame cardiac MRI images using pixel clustering and labelling. In: 2015 Eighth International Conference on Contemporary Computing (IC3), pp. 248–252 (2015)
24. Urschler, M., Mayer, H., Bolter, R., Leberl, F.: The live wire approach for the segmentation of left ventricle electron-beam CT images. In: 26th Workshop of the Austrian Association for Pattern Recognition [AAPR/OEAGM], Graz, Austria (2002)
25. Zheng, Y., Barbu, A., Georgescu, B., Scheuering, M., Comaniciu, D.: Four-chamber heart modeling and automatic segmentation for 3-D cardiac CT volumes using marginal space learning and steerable features. IEEE Trans. Med. Imaging **27**(11), 1668–1681 (2008)
26. van Rikxoort, E.M., Isgum, I., Arzhaeva, Y., Staring, M., Klein, S., Viergever, M.A., Pluim, J.P., van Ginneken, B.: Adaptive local multi-atlas segmentation: application to the heart and the caudate nucleus. Med. Image Anal. **14**(1), 39–49 (2010)

27. Zhuang, X., Rhode, K.S., Razavi, R.S., Hawkes, D.J., Ourselin, S.: A registration-based propagation framework for automatic whole heart segmentation of cardiac MRI. IEEE Trans. Med. Imaging **29**(9), 1612–1625 (2010)
28. Codella, N.C., Weinsaft, J.W., Cham, M.D., Janik, M., Prince, M.R., Wang, Y.: Left ventricle: automated segmentation by using myocardial effusion threshold reduction and intravoxel computation at MR imaging 1. Radiology **248**(3), 1004–1012 (2008)
29. Xu, C., Prince, J.L.: Gradient vector flow: a new external force for snakes, pp. 66–71 (1997)

A Hybrid Feature Selection Scheme Based on Local Compactness and Global Separability for Improving Roller Bearing Diagnostic Performance

M.M. Manjurul Islam, Md. Rashedul Islam, and Jong-Myon Kim[✉]

School of Electrical, Electronics and Computer Engineering,
University of Ulsan, Ulsan, South Korea
m.m.manjurul@gmail.com, rashedcse@gmail.com,
jongmyon.kim@gmail.com

Abstract. This paper proposes a hybrid feature selection scheme for identifying the most discriminant fault signatures using an improved class separability criteria—the local compactness and global separability (LCGS)—of distribution in feature dimension to diagnose bearing faults. The hybrid model consists of filter based selection and wrapper based selection. In the filter phase, a sequential forward floating selection (SFFS) algorithm is employed to yield a series of suboptimal feature subset candidates using LCGS based feature subset evaluation metric. In the wrapper phase, the most discriminant feature subset is then selected from suboptimal feature subsets based on maximum average classification accuracy estimation of support vector machine (SVM) classifier using them. The effectiveness of the proposed hybrid feature selection method is verified with fault diagnosis application for low speed rolling element bearings under various conditions. Experimental results indicate that the proposed method outperforms the state-of-the-art algorithm when selecting the most discriminate fault feature subset, yielding 1.4% to 17.74% diagnostic performance improvement in average classification accuracy.

Keywords: Acoustic emission · Data-driven diagnostics model · Feature selection · Support vector machine · Low speed bearing fault detection and diagnosis

1 Introduction

Bearings are the most crucial component of low-speed machinery because they support heavy loads with stationary rotational speeds and are subject to unexpected failures [1]. If bearing defects remain undetected, they will eventually lead to catastrophic machine failure. Therefore, reliable fault diagnosis of rolling element bearings (REBs) is an urgent issue in the fault diagnosis research community [1, 2].

Data-driven fault detection and diagnosis (FDD) methods are often the best suited in the context of industry applications [3, 4]. The essence of a data-driven FDD scheme is data (or signal) acquisition, feature extraction and analysis, and classification. In data-driven FDD, vibration and current signals are widely utilized to detect faults to

© Springer International Publishing AG 2017
M. Wagner et al. (Eds.): ACALCI 2017, LNAI 10142, pp. 180–192, 2017.
DOI: 10.1007/978-3-319-51691-2_16

minimize the risk of unexpected machine failures and ensure satisfactory performance of high-speed machinery [3, 4]. On the other hand, acoustic emission (AE) techniques are used to detect faults in the very early stage of cracks and spalls even when the machine operates at very low speed [1, 5].

To realize highly reliable data driven FDD methods, it is necessary to deploy different signal processing techniques to extract intrinsic information about bearing defects from the signal of defective bearings [4–6]. Consequently, to develop an effective FDD strategy that works well for a diverse range of different fault conditions, this paper proposes a heterogeneous feature model, comprising statistical features in time domain, frequency domain, and envelope spectrum of an AE signal, to extract as much fault information as possible. In practice, however, a large number of fault features configuring these high-dimensional feature vectors may contain redundant or irrelevant information, which can degrade diagnosis performance.

Recent intelligent FDD techniques have adopted hybrid feature selection technique (HFS) that exploits the advantages of the filter and wrapper methods [7, 8] to ensure best features so that they can improve classification accuracy and reduce computational complexity in the classification process. The wrapper approach selects the feature subset with feature variables showing the highest classification accuracy for a particular classifier, while the filter approach creates a rank of the feature variables or feature subsets using some property values or an evaluation model [8]. This paper explores an HFS scheme that combines both the wrapper and filter approaches [6–9].

The feature subsets can be generated by performing a complete, sequential or heuristic search (e.g. GA [12]) of the feature space. A complete search ensures a high-quality feature subset, but it is very costly in terms of computational time. In contrast, a sequential forward floating search (SFFS) [10, 11], which is a variant of sequential forward search, is comparatively faster and provides a good tradeoff between computational complexity and quality of selected optimal features. Since one of the most significant tasks in the HFS scheme is to accurately evaluate feature subsets, this paper employs improved class separability criteria, *a key contribution of this study,*— the ratio between local compactness and global separability (LCGS)—for evaluating feature subsets by analyzing class samples distribution in a feature space. Several feature evaluation methods have been proposed depending upon classification accuracy or Euclidean distance-based feature distribution criteria [5, 10, 12]. Kang et al. recently proposed a feature subset evaluation method using intra-class compactness and the inter-class distance calculated using average pairwise Euclidian distances [4]. However, they did not consider all possible feature distributions. Moreover, the intra-class compactness value considers dense areas only and ignores samples that are located in less dense areas or on the outskirts of a class, affecting the multiclass distribution. Similarly, a high distance value between two classes can dominate the distance values between other classes, and hence the overall interclass separation value.

To address this limitation of conventional average distance based methods, this paper proposes HFS-LCGS that uses the new feature evaluation metric, LCGS, as an objective function for SFFS while feature subsets are evaluated in the filter phase to select a series of suboptimal feature subsets. In the wrapper phase of the HFS-LCGS, these suboptimal feature subsets are further evaluated, by estimating the classification accuracy of SVM classifier [13] to select the most discriminant features. Finally, the selected discriminant feature vector is tested for a low-speed rolling element bearing fault diagnosis application.

The remaining parts of this paper are designed as follows. Section 2 explains the experiment setup and AE signal acquisition technique. Section 3 describes the proposed fault diagnosis scheme with hybrid feature selection methodology. Experimental results are given in Sect. 4, and concluding remarks are in Sect. 5.

2 Experiment Setup and Acoustic Emission Signal Acquisition

The standard scheme for measuring the AE signal is introduced in Fig. 1. We employ some of the most widely used sensors and equipment in the real industries. To capture intrinsic information about defect-bearing and bearing with no defect (BND) conditions, the study records AE signals at 250 kHz sampling rate using a PCI-2 system that is connected with a wide-band AE sensor (WS α is from Acoustics Corporation of Physical [5]). The effectiveness of experiment setup and datasets can be studied further in [5, 14]. In this study, AE signals are collected for formulating four experimental datasets of different crack sizes (i.e., small crack and big crack) and different operating speed (i.e., 300 rpm, 500 rpm). Table 1 presents the summary of different datasets. Each dataset contains eight types of signal including defect free and seven defective bearing based on crack position: (a) bearing with outer race crack (BCO), (b) bearing with inner crack (BCI), (c) bearing with roller race crack (BCR), and combination of these faults, i.e. (d) bearing with inner and outer cracks (BCIO); (e) bearing with inner and outer cracks (BCOR) (f) bearing with inner and roller cracks (BCIR) and (g) inner, outer, and roller cracks (BCIOR) and (h) normal condition (BND).

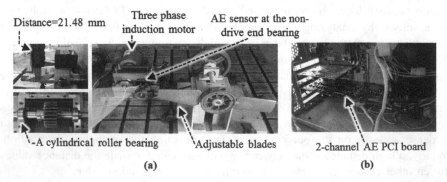

Fig. 1. Screenshot of the self-designed experiment setup, (a) standard equipment setup, (b) PCI based AE system for data acquisition.

Table 1. Summary of acoustic emission (AE) data acquisition conditions, including the use of two different operating conditions and two crack sizes

Dataset	Average rotational speed (RPM)	Sizes of cracks in the bearing's outer and/or inner roller raceways		
		Length	Width	Depth
Dataset 1[a]	300	3 mm	0.35 mm	0.30 mm
Dataset 2[a]	500			
Dataset 3[a]	300	12 mm	0.49 mm	0.50 mm
Dataset 4[a]	500			

[a]90 AE signals for each fault type; sampling frequency f_s = 250 kHz; each signal is 10 s long.

3 Proposed Fault Diagnosis Methodology

Figure 2 depicts an overall flow diagram of the fault diagnosis method used in the study. The method is composed of the two important processes: a discriminatory feature selection process for deciding the most discriminatory fault signature subset and an online performance evaluation process for validating the effectiveness of the proposed hybrid feature selection.

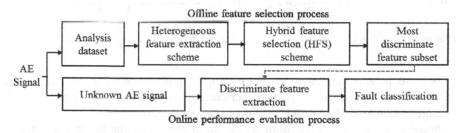

Fig. 2. An overall block diagram of improved bearing fault diagnosis model with HFS scheme

3.1 Heterogeneous Feature Extraction Models

One of the main ideas of this study is that diverse feature extraction paradigms are simultaneously combined to generate a hybrid pool of features, which has the higher discriminative power of accurately detecting each fault. None of the formerly analyzed publications [6, 15] propose a combination of feature models from different single processing techniques, thus prompting us to the representative feature models of this study, i.e., statistical features from time domain and frequency domain of the raw AE signal and envelope power spectrum magnitudes.

The most prevalently used time-domain statistical features are RMS, crest factor (CF), square root of amplitude (SRA), impulse factor (IF), shape factor (SF), kurtosis value (KV), peak-to-peak value (PPV), skewness value (SV), and kurtosis factor

Table 2. Ten time-domain statistical features of an AE signal

Root mean Square $RMS = \left(\frac{1}{N}\sum_{i=1}^{N} x_i^2\right)^{1/2}$	$SRA = \left(\frac{1}{N}\sum_{i=1}^{N} \sqrt{|x_i|}\right)^2$	$CF = \dfrac{\max(|x_i|)}{\left(\frac{1}{N}\sum_{i=1}^{N} x_i^2\right)^{1/2}}$	$IF = \dfrac{\max(|x_i|)}{\frac{1}{N}\sum_{i=1}^{N}|x_i|}$	$SF = \dfrac{\left(\frac{1}{N}\sum_{i=1}^{N} x_i^2\right)^{1/2}}{\frac{1}{N}\sum_{i=1}^{N}|x_i|}$
$KV = \frac{1}{N}\sum_{i=1}^{N}\left(\frac{x_i-\bar{x}}{\sigma}\right)^4$	$SV = \frac{1}{N}\sum_{i=1}^{N}\left(\frac{x_i-\bar{x}}{\sigma}\right)^3$	$PPV = \max(x_i) - \min(x_i)$	$MF = \dfrac{\max(|x_i|)}{\left(\frac{1}{N}\sum_{i=1}^{N}\sqrt{|x_i|}\right)^2}$	$KF = \dfrac{\frac{1}{N}\sum_{i=1}^{N}\left(\frac{x_i-\bar{x}}{\sigma}\right)^4}{\left(\frac{1}{N}\sum_{i=1}^{N} x_i^2\right)^2}$

(KF) margin factor (MF), whereas the frequency-domain statistical features are RMS frequency (RMSF), frequency center (FC), and root variance frequency (RVF). Tables 1 and 2 provide the time- and frequency-domain statistical features, along with the mathematical relations to calculate them. A total number of statistical parameters (i.e. features) is (10 + 3) or 13.

In addition to above features, there are four characteristics, or defects, frequencies: Ball Pass Frequency Inner raceway (BPFI), Ball Spin Frequency (BSF), and Ball Pass Frequency Outer raceway (BPFO) and Fundamental Train Frequency (FTF), at which faulty symptoms must be observable [15]. Therefore, statistical values (e.g. calculated around the harmonics of these defect frequencies in an envelope power spectrum) are useful for bearing fault diagnosis [14]. These four faulty symptoms can be described in Eq. (1) [5, 15]:

$$BPFO = \frac{N_{rollers} \times F_{shaft}}{2}\left(1 - \frac{B_d}{P_d}\cos\alpha_{cangle}\right), BPFI = \frac{N_{rollers} \times F_{shaft}}{2}\left(1 + \frac{B_d}{P_d}\cos\alpha_{cangle}\right),$$

$$BSF = \frac{P_d \times F_{shaft}}{2 \times B_d}\left(1 - \left(\frac{B_d}{P_d}\cos\alpha_{cangle}\right)^2\right), \text{ and, } FTF = \frac{F_{shaft}}{2}\left(1 - \frac{B_d}{P_d}\cos\alpha_{cangle}\right), \tag{1}$$

These frequencies depend on several parameters: number of rollers ($N_{rollers}$), shaft speed (F_{shaft}), pitch diameter (P_d), the roller diameter (B_d), and contact angle (α_{cangle}), which are available in the bearing manufacturer specification.

Though envelope power spectrum is efficient in identifying the bearing defect, it is important to note that a bearing defect symptom is not easily detectible around harmonics of the defect frequency (BPFO, BPFI, 2 × BSF) in the power spectrum since bearing fault signal is inherently nonlinear and stationary [5]. It is, therefore, convenient to find frequency band using band pass filter to identify the defect region. Further, an enveloping power spectrum is highly sensitive to events with very low impacts (e.g. sidebands). Therefore, we construct a rectangular window by carefully analyzing bearing dynamic characteristics that can be seen Fig. 3. These formulations of defect regions are defined in Eqs. (2), (3) and (4) respectively for outer, inner and roller defects, Outer race defect window range:

$$from \left(1 - \frac{AV_{order}}{2}\right) \cdot (BPFO_h), \text{ to } \left(1 + \frac{AV_{order}}{2}\right) \cdot (BPFO_h), \tag{2}$$

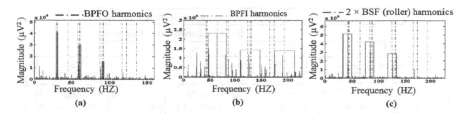

Fig. 3. Defect frequency range in envelope spectrum (a) outer, (b) inner, (c) roller defects

Inner race defect window range:

$$from \left(1 - \frac{AV_{order}}{2}\right) \cdot \left(BPFI_h - 2 \cdot S_{shaft}\right), \quad to \quad \left(1 + \frac{AV_{order}}{2}\right) \cdot \left(BPFI_h + 2 \cdot S_{shaft}\right),$$

(3)

Roller defect window range:

$$from \left(1 - \frac{AV_{order}}{2}\right) \cdot \left(BPFO_h - 2 \cdot FTF\right), \quad to \quad \left(1 + \frac{AV_{order}}{2}\right) \cdot \left(BPFO_h + 2 \cdot FTF\right).$$

(4)

where 'h' is the number the harmonics, and we consider up to 4 harmonics. AV defines the arbitrary variation to fit the window around the defect frequency BPFO, BPFI, and $2 \times$ BSF, where a minimum value of margin is considered to fit the rectangle; in this case, the value is 2% of the defect frequency [16]. Therefore, $3 \times 4 = 12$ envelope features were extracted, i.e. no. characteristic frequencies $\times$ no. harmonics. In summary, the dimensionality of feature model used in HFS-LCGS feature selection process is $N_{feature} \times N_{anal.samples} \times N_{classes}$ where number features, $N_{feature} = 25$, the number of analysis data samples, $N_{anal.samples} = 30$, and the number of fault classes, $N_{classes} = 8$.

3.2 Proposed HFS-LCGS Scheme

Figure 4 describes the overall process of the proposed HFS-LCGS, which consists of a filter-based feature selection part in which the feature subsets are evaluated based on local compactness and global separability (LCGS) criteria, and a wrapper based part that selects the optimal features based on classification accuracy.

It is quite evident that the effectiveness of HFS-LCGS depends on the robustness of the feature evaluation metric, the LCGS when the subsets are assessed with SFFS (Table 3).

As shown in the Fig. 4, this paper first evaluates the feature subset on randomly selected 1/3rd of the analysis dataset and repeat this process for N iterations. More details of this HFS-LCGS approach are given below.

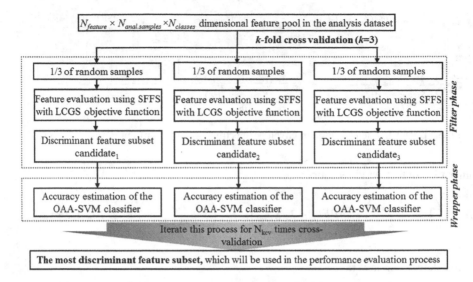

Fig. 4. Overall procedure of the developed hybrid feature selection (HFS) scheme

Table 3. Ten frequency-domain statistical features of an AE signal

$$RMSF = \left(\frac{1}{N} \sum_{i=1}^{N} f_i^2 \right)^{1/2} \quad \Big| \quad FC = \frac{1}{N} \sum_{i=1}^{N} f_i \quad \Big| \quad RVF = \left(\frac{1}{N} \sum_{i=1}^{N} (f_i - FC)^2 \right)^{1/2}$$

(1) *A feature evaluation metric to assess the quality of feature subset in HFS-LCGS.*

SFFS is used to yield discriminate fault signature subset candidates at the filter-based feature selection phase. To find the useful subset candidates, a precise feature evaluation metric is required. As explained in Sect. 1, a recent feature evaluation metric based on average Euclidian distance used to measure within-class distance and between-class distance [4]. In practice, the average distance based feature evaluation metric does not consider the complexity of class and significantly overlooks the overlap in between-class distances. Our study develops an improved evaluation metric as local compactness for within-class distance and global separability for between class distance. To compute local compactness for a specific feature (e.g. f_{nth}), the mean of feature distribution (C_c_M) of each class and the distance of outmost sample (C_c_dist) (instead of average distance) from the class mean is calculated. Finally, local compactness of each feature variable is calculated by averaging all C_c_dist. Figure 5(a) presents the process of local compactness factor calculation and the Eq. (5) depicts the final calculation of local compactness (LC) factor.

$$Local\_compactness(LC) = \frac{1}{N_c} \sum_{c=1}^{N_c} d_c, \tag{5}$$

Where N_c is the total number of classes and d_c is the distance of the outmost sample from the class mean.

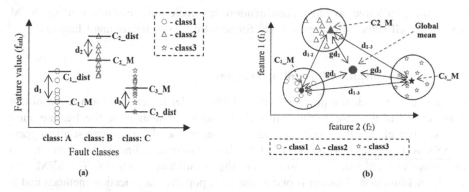

Fig. 5. The conception of proposed evaluation metric—local compactness and global separability (LCGS) calculation, (a) local compactness (e.g. in 1-D feature space) and (b) global separability, where black circles define the local compactness (e.g. in 2-D feature space)

To calculate the global separability, a global mean of all samples of all classes and mean of the individual class are calculated. The class separability distances (i.e. $d_{1,2}$), which represent the distance between the mean of one class to that of another, as well as the global separability distances (i.e. gd_1), which represent the distance between the mean of a class to the global mean, are computed, as can be seen in Fig. 5(b) for an example 3-class. Finally, the global separability (GS) is calculated by Eq. (6), which can be extended for any finite number of multi-class (i.e. 8 classes in this study) separability measure. The overall process is depicted in Fig. 5(b).

$$Global\_separability(GS) = \frac{1}{N_c} \sum_{c=1}^{N_c} \left((gd_c) + \sum_{c \neq j, j=1}^{c} (d_{cj}) \right) \qquad (6)$$

Now that LCGS feature evaluation metric is at hand, we define a function, OBJ, to combine GS and LS, and consider the simplest form in Eq. (7) to maximize the OBJ function (as the ratio of highest value of GS and the lowest value of LC):

$$OBJ = \frac{GS}{LC} \qquad (7)$$

The evaluation metric in Eq. (7) is utilized for any feature subset yield by SFFS to get a series of discriminant feature subset candidates, which are further utilized with classifier in the wrapper approach to obtain the most discriminant features.

(2) Accuracy estimation of the SVM classifier in the wrapper method of HFS-LCGS.

In the wrapper-based feature selection of HFS-LCGS scheme, it is necessary to predict classification accuracy of the SVM classifier using a couple of discriminatory feature subset candidates due to the multiple cross-validations in the proposed hybrid feature selection scheme. As seen in Fig. 4, the execution process for hybrid feature selection is performed using k-fold cross-validation ($k = 3$). After N times ($N = 10$) cross-validations, this study contains $N \times k$ discriminatory feature subset candidates.

Hence, the predictive average classification accuracies are estimated using SVM classifier for all selected feature subsets for selecting most discriminant feature.

3.3 Fault Classification for Online Diagnosis

As depicted in Fig. 3, the proposed HFS-LCGS model selects the most discriminant feature elements that are further utilized for online validation of the bearing fault diagnosis model. In the online process, we also use the one-against-all support (OAASVM) classifier [13] for multi-faults classification with linear kernel function to validate our selected feature sets in terms of the classification accuracy. The SVM with linear kernel function classifier is one of the most popular classification methods and is widely used due to simplicity and computational efficiency.

4 Experiment Results and Discussion

The proposed methodology is tested on four datasets with eight fault types obtained from different operating conditions, as shown in Table 1. The datasets are divided into two categories: one for offline feature analysis for discriminant feature selection and the other for online evaluation. The analysis datasets consist of 30 of the 90 signals for each fault type for a given speed condition. The remaining 60 signals (is kept higher than analysis data to ensure the reliability of diagnosis performance) of each fault class are used as the unknown signals for online evaluation of the proposed fault diagnosis scheme.

The designed objective function in Eq. (7) is highly effective for assessing the features quality by calculating LCGS value. As explained in Sect. 3.2(2), $N \times k$ (or total 30) discriminatory feature subset candidates are created by the proposed HFS-LCGS. Predictive classification accuracy of 30 discriminatory features subject candidates is estimated by OAASVM classifier, as seen in Fig. 6 for dataset 1. In the wrapper based analysis, the final subset is then selected for each dataset (see Table 1) based on not only predictive accuracy but also the frequency of the discriminatory feature subset candidates. To verify the above results of HFS-LCGS, we compare with a state-of-the-art feature evaluation metric using average distance in [4]. Table 4 summarizes the most discriminant features for the proposed HFS-LCGS and [4].

Finally, in online fault diagnosis process, only the most discriminant features (see Table 4) are extracted from the unknown signals of the evaluation dataset, and the OAASVM classifier [13] is applied to calculate the classification accuracy. Additionally, k-fold cross validation (k-cv) [17], an efficient method for estimating generalized classification performance, is deployed to evaluate the diagnosis performance of the developed HFS-LCGS versus the state-of-art algorithm [4], in terms of average classification accuracy (avg.) and sensitivity that are defined as below [17]:

$$avg. = \frac{\sum\limits_{k}^{L} N_{rtp}}{N_{sample}} \times 100(\%), \quad and \quad Sensitivity = \frac{N_{rtp}}{N_{rtp} + N_{tfn}} \times 100\% \qquad (8)$$

Table 4. Final most discriminant feature set of four datasets

Datasets	Methodology	
	The most discriminant feature subset by HFS-LCGS (Proposed)	The most discriminant feature subset by state-of-the-art algorithm [4]
Dataset 1	{2, 10}	{10, 11, 13}
Dataset 2	{2, 9, 11}	{9, 10, 13, 17, 19}
Dataset 3	{1, 13, 14}	{2, 10, 11, 19, 20}
Dataset 4	{2, 13}	{2, 12, 13, 17}

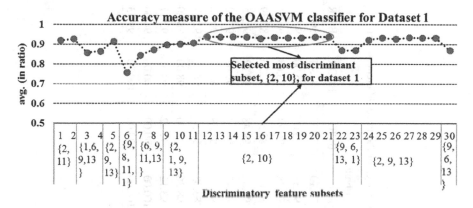

Fig. 6. Estimated classification accuracy of SVM classifier for 30 feature subsets candidates

where sensitivity is the number of positive classes that are correctly identified as positive, L is the number of fault classes or categories (i.e. $L = 8$ in this study), N_{rtp} is the rate of true positives, and the number total samples is N_{sample}.

Experimental results listed in Table 5 clearly demonstrate that the proposed feature selection model outperforms the other approaches under different conditions. In the datasets for small crack size, the weakly generated fault signals are not significantly distinguishable, affecting the classification performance. The proposed feature selection model selects the best subset of features with the best distribution in the high-dimensional feature space to increase the classification performance of the fault diagnosis system. In contrast, the existing average distance based approaches do not consider the distribution of features and render a reduced classification performance.

To further analyze this effectiveness phenomenon, our paper exploits a two-dimensional representation of discriminative feature selected by the developed HFS-LCGS and by the state-of-the-art method. It is evident from Fig. 7 that the proposed algorithm selects feature subset with most separable class distribution compared to its counterpart.

Table 5. Average sensitivities of the three different models

Datasets	Methodologies	Average sensitivity of each fault types								Avg. (%)
		BCO	BCI	BCR	BCIO	BCOR	BCIR	BCIOR	BND	
Dataset 1	All features	87.57	85.84	77.10	78.37	81.44	86.24	83.00	83.11	82.83
	[4]	85.00	93.00	96.33	93.00	95.00	90.55	91.00	90.43	91.79
	Developed HFS-LCGS	96.74	95.68	96.48	96.74	93.68	96.61	96.88	96.06	96.11
Dataset 2	All features	80.66	82.13	82.66	82.53	82.53	82.39	82.26	82.21	82.17
	[4]	89.28	93.08	94.62	89.48	96.22	91.35	90.22	93.97	92.28
	Developed HFS-LCGS	98.13	98.93	97.47	99.33	99.07	99.20	99.07	98.82	**98.75**
Dataset 3	All features	91.69	92.00	93.69	92.49	82.09	90.36	91.96	96.00	91.29
	[4]	91.9	95.1	83.03	93.57	98.3	92.77	93.03	95.43	92.89
	Developed HFS-LCGS	100.00	100.00	98.36	100.00	98.00	98.80	100.00	99.40	99.32
Dataset 4	All features	92.31	93.92	93.12	92.22	93.31	92.17	98.00	93.30	93.54
	[4]	100.00	100.00	100.00	100.00	100.00	96.00	92.59	99.50	98.51
	Developed HFS-LCGS	100.00	100.00	100.00	100.00	100.00	99.33	100.00	99.92	99.91

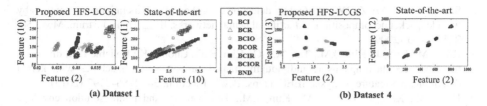

(a) Dataset 1   **(b) Dataset 4**

Fig. 7. 2D visualization of most discriminant feature subset results by developed HFS-LCGS and the state-of-the-art for (a) Dataset 1 and (b) dataset 4

5 Conclusions

The HFS-LCGS method was developed to select discriminant features by calculating local compactness and global separability (LCGS), which is not achievable in traditional Euclidian distance based separability. The key contribution of HFS-LCGS is to assess the quality of feature subsets based on LCGS. This evaluation metric is designed as the ratio of local class compactness and global separability. Using this evaluation metric, SFFS yields discriminant feature subset candidates and the most discriminant feature subsets, which is finally determined via accuracy estimating of the SVM classifier in the wrapper approach. Experimental results indicate that the proposed method is more effective for identifying the most discriminatory feature subset by achieving diagnostic performance improvements from 1.4% to 17.74% in average classification accuracy. Moreover, our study proves that the proposed hybrid feature selection can effectively reduce computational overhead for fault diagnosis since HFS-LCGS selects the most compact features subset from a high-dimensional features vector.

Acknowledgments. This work was supported by the Korea Institute of Energy Technology Evaluation and Planning (KETEP) and the Ministry of Trade, Industry & Energy (MOTIE) of the Republic of Korea (No. 20162220100050), in part by The Leading Human Resource Training Program of Regional Neo industry through the National Research Foundation of Korea (NRF) funded by the Ministry of Science, ICT and future Planning (NRF-2016H1D5A1910564), in part by Business for Cooperative R&D between Industry, Academy, and Research Institute funded Korea Small and Medium Business Administration in 2016 (Grants No. C0395147, Grants S2381631), and in part by Basic Science Research Program through the National Research Foundation of Korea (NRF) funded by the Ministry of Education(2016R1D1A 3B03931927).

References

1. Widodo, A., Kim, E.Y., Son, J.-D., Yang, B.-S., Tan, A.C.C., Gu, D.-S., Choi, B.-K., Mathew, J.: Fault diagnosis of low speed bearing based on relevance vector machine and support vector machine. Expert Syst. Appl. **36**, 7252–7261 (2009)
2. Zhao, M., Jin, X., Zhang, Z., Li, B.: Fault diagnosis of rolling element bearings via discriminative subspace learning: visualization and classification. Expert Syst. Appl. **41**, 3391–3401 (2014)

3. Sadeghian, A., Ye, Z., Wu, B.: Online detection of broken rotor bars in induction motors by wavelet packet decomposition and artificial neural networks. IEEE Trans. Instrum. Meas. **58**, 2253–2263 (2009)

4. Kang, M., Kim, J., Kim, J.M., Tan, A.C.C., Kim, E.Y., Choi, B.K.: Reliable fault diagnosis for low-speed bearings using individually trained support vector machines with kernel discriminative feature analysis. IEEE Trans. Power Electron. **30**, 2786–2797 (2015)

5. Kang, M., Kim, J., Wills, L.M., Kim, J.M.: Time-varying and multiresolution envelope analysis and discriminative feature analysis for bearing fault diagnosis. IEEE Trans. Industr. Electron. **62**, 7749–7761 (2015)

6. Li, Z., Yan, X., Tian, Z., Yuan, C., Peng, Z., Li, L.: Blind vibration component separation and nonlinear feature extraction applied to the nonstationary vibration signals for the gearbox multi-fault diagnosis. Measurement **46**, 259–271 (2013)

7. Liu, C., Jiang, D., Yang, W.: Global geometric similarity scheme for feature selection in fault diagnosis. Expert Syst. Appl. **41**, 3585–3595 (2014)

8. Yang, Y., Liao, Y., Meng, G., Lee, J.: A hybrid feature selection scheme for unsupervised learning and its application in bearing fault diagnosis. Expert Syst. Appl. **38**, 11311–11320 (2011)

9. Zhang, K., Li, Y., Scarf, P., Ball, A.: Feature selection for high-dimensional machinery fault diagnosis data using multiple models and radial basis function networks. Neurocomputing **74**, 2941–2952 (2011)

10. Rauber, T.W., Boldt, F.D.A., Varej, F.M.: Heterogeneous feature models and feature selection applied to bearing fault diagnosis. IEEE Trans. Ind. Electron. **62**, 637–646 (2015)

11. Lu, L., Yan, J., de Silva, C.W.: Dominant feature selection for the fault diagnosis of rotary machines using modified genetic algorithm and empirical mode decomposition. J. Sound Vib. **344**, 464–483 (2015)

12. Kanan, H.R., Faez, K.: GA-based optimal selection of PZMI features for face recognition. Appl. Math. Comput. **205**, 706–715 (2008)

13. Chih-Wei, H., Chih-Jen, L.: A comparison of methods for multiclass support vector machines. IEEE Trans. Neural Netw. **13**, 415–425 (2002)

14. Islam, M.M.Manjurul, Khan, Sheraz, A., Kim, J.-M.: Multi-fault diagnosis of roller bearings using support vector machines with an improved decision strategy. In: Huang, D.-S., Han, K. (eds.) ICIC 2015. LNCS (LNAI), vol. 9227, pp. 538–550. Springer, Heidelberg (2015). doi:10.1007/978-3-319-22053-6_57

15. Kang, M., Kim, J., Choi, B.-K., Kim, J.-M.: Envelope analysis with a genetic algorithm-based adaptive filter bank for bearing fault detection. J. Acoust. Soc. Am. **138**, EL65–EL70 (2015)

16. Randall, R.B., Antoni, J.: Rolling element bearing diagnostics—a tutorial. Mech. Syst. Signal Process. **25**, 485–520 (2011)

17. Rodriguez, J.D., Perez, A., Lozano, J.A.: Sensitivity analysis of k-fold cross validation in prediction error estimation. IEEE Trans. Pattern Anal. Mach. Intell. **32**, 569–575 (2010)

Reliable Fault Diagnosis of Bearings Using Distance and Density Similarity on an Enhanced k-NN

Dileep Kumar Appana, Md. Rashedul Islam, and Jong-Myon Kim[(✉)]

School of Electrical, Electronics and Computer Engineering,
University of Ulsan, Ulsan 44610, South Korea
dk.appana@gmail.com, rashed.cse@gmail.com,
jongmyon.kim@gmail.com

Abstract. The k-nearest neighbor (k-NN) method is a simple and highly effective classifier, but the classification accuracy of k-NN is degraded and becomes highly sensitive to the neighborhood size k in multi-classification problems, where the density of data samples varies across different classes. This is mainly due to the method using only a distance-based measure of similarity between different samples. In this paper, we propose a density-weighted distance similarity metric, which considers the relative densities of samples in addition to the distances between samples to improve the classification accuracy of standard k-NN. The performance of the proposed k-NN approach is not affected by the neighborhood size k. Experimental results show that the proposed approach yields better classification accuracy than traditional k-NN for fault diagnosis of rolling element bearings.

Keywords: K-NN · Fault diagnosis · Bearings · Distance-based similarity · Density-based similarity

1 Introduction

With advancements in technology and increasing global competitiveness, it has become imperative for industries to implement appropriate maintenance strategies to optimize both overall equipment effectiveness and productivity [1]. Rotating machinery is widely used in various industries. Thus, to prevent sudden operational failures, condition monitoring of bearings has become an integral part of maintenance programs, as bearing defects account for a significant proportion of the equipment failure [2]. Accurate and reliable diagnosis of bearing defects is therefore an important research problem.

Many data driven approaches have been proposed to diagnose bearing defects. These methods are generally accomplished in three stages: data acquisition, feature extraction, and fault detection and diagnosis. The first stage involves probing with accelerometers to quantify the vibration levels of machine components, especially the bearing housing [3]. To extract features for fault diagnosis, the feature vector of these vibration signals is extracted through time domain, frequency domain, and time–frequency analysis [4]. For classification, several classifiers have been used, including k-nearest neighbor (k-NN).

© Springer International Publishing AG 2017
M. Wagner et al. (Eds.): ACALCI 2017, LNAI 10142, pp. 193–203, 2017.
DOI: 10.1007/978-3-319-51691-2_17

The k-NN is non-parametric approach and eager learning generates an explicit model at training time. This method classifies a new test sample based on the majority of its k nearest training samples [5]. The k nearest training samples are determined by calculating the distances of the test sample from all the other samples in the training data. However, this traditional implementation is computationally expensive though its speedup classification is feasible for industrial environments [6]. First, determining the appropriate neighborhood size or the value of k can be a problem. There are no general rules, and it has to be done empirically on a case-by-case basis. This limitation affects both the classification accuracy and the computation time of the k-NN classifier. Second, the variation in the relative densities of the training samples belonging to different classes can result in misclassification due to the use of only a distance-based measure of similarity in traditional k-NN [7].

To overcome this drawback inherent in k-NN, many researchers have developed algorithms with both fixed k and varying k for k-NN. Jiang et al. [8] proposed choosing k only for a two-class classifier if the classes are unbalanced. Hand and Vinciotti [9] proposed selective-based neighborhood naïve Bayes, a one-layout-one cross-validation approach, where the k value is dynamically chosen. A weight-adjusted k-NN algorithm was proposed that adds weights when calculating the distances in the training data [10]. Jia et al. [11] employed a distance-weighted k-NN method in which a weighted class probability estimate is added to the class labels in order to make a decision on the class information. Wesam and Murtaja [12] proposed a technique in which the classification can easily be done if there are clusters of different densities, where classification of the bearing faults is done through using a local outlier factor. This method utilizes distance- and density-based information to detect the outliers. Despite these improvements in the accuracy of class information for the test sample, the sensitivity to the k value persists.

Unlike traditional k-NN, which seeks to increase the reliability of the fault diagnosis of the bearing by reducing the method's sensitivity to k, in this paper, we propose a density-weighted distance-based similarity measure to improve the accuracy of k-NN. We apply a distance-based probabilistic k-NN algorithm, and we employ a probability density factor to scale the calculated metric to determine the class information of the test sample.

The remaining parts of this paper are organized as follows. Section 2 describes the proposed algorithm, including a density-weighted distance-based similarity measure for fault diagnosis. Section 3 presents the experimental results, and Sect. 4 provides the conclusions of this paper.

2   Proposed Methodology

When a vibration signal is obtained that has fault signatures, the proposed methodology extracts the feature vector and computes the membership value of each class in the test sample. Based on each of these values, a decision is made regarding which class the sample belongs to. This procedure is shown in Fig. 1.

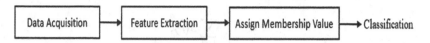

Fig. 1. Proposed methodology for classification using a density-weighted distance-based similarity metric.

2.1 Data Acquisition

For data acquisition, we employed a test bench that uses IMS bearing data repository. Recording were made on four bearing with accelerometers, that were installed on a shaft and kept at a constant speed of 2000 rpm and a radial load of 6000 lbs. These recordings of 1-second duration are made every 10 min at a fixed sampling rate of 20 kHz. With a test-to-failure experiment, failure occurred after exceeding the designed life time of the bearing [13]. In the experiment, we used three data recordings with the following faults: a bearing crack inner fault (BCIF), a bearing crack roller fault (BCRF), and a bearing crack outer fault (BCOF). BCIF, BCRF occurred on bearing 3 and bearing 4 in test set 1, and BCOF occurred on bearing 1 of test set 2. We applied a 3-sigma rule of thumb as a threshold to differentiate the data between normal and faulty bearing information. For applying the threshold value, we calculated the root mean square (RMS) value of each second of recorded data, and we defined an RMS value that fell beyond the threshold as indicating faulty signal information. Thus we have obtained 146 of 2155, 689 of 2155, 282 of 984 data samples as faulty BCIF, BCRF, BCOF samples from all samples of bearing 3 and bearing 4 of set 1, and bearing 1 of set 2 respectively.

2.2 Feature Extraction

According to [14], the mapping process of a measured sensor signal into the feature vector space is considered a significant step for formulating intelligent fault diagnosis schemes, where statistical parameters from the time and frequency domains are employed. The feature extraction process has been validated by many researchers [15–18]. In this study, we consider only the faulty part of the signal after applying a threshold, and we use the same faulty signatures for identification of bearing defects obtained over the given 1-second data recordings, $x(n)$. The statistical parameter in the time domain includes the square root of the amplitude (SRA):

$$SRA = \left(\frac{1}{N} \sum_{n=1}^{N} \sqrt{|x(n)|} \right), \tag{1}$$

where N is the total number of samples in 1 s of data sampled at 20 kHz.

The three parameters in the frequency domain are the frequency center (FC), the root mean square frequency (RMSF), and the root variance frequency (RVF):

$$FC = \frac{1}{N}\sum_{f=1}^{N} S(f),$$
(2)

$$RMSF = \sqrt{\frac{1}{N}\sum_{f=1}^{N} S(f)^2},$$
(3)

$$RVF = \sqrt{\frac{1}{N}\sum_{f=1}^{N} (S(f) - FC)^2},$$
(4)

where $S(f)$ is the magnitude response of the fast Fourier transform of $x(n)$ and N is the number of frequency bins.

2.3 Assign Membership Values to the Test Sample

To assign a set of membership values (MVs) to the test sample, the probabilities of the class information based on distance and density are needed. When a test sample is added to a space distributed with training samples data with different class information, the sample's probability of a class is determined from its nearest neighbor information. In addition, the test sample is grouped with each of the available classes, and the corresponding probabilities based on the densities are calculated. Using these two probabilities, a membership value is computed for each associated class. We consider a finite data sample $\{(t_1, x_1), \ldots (t_N, x_N)\}$, where each $t_n \in \{1, 2.., C\}$ denotes the class label and the D-dimensional feature vector $x_N \in R^D$.

2.3.1 Probability of Class Information Based on the Distance (α)

As shown in Fig. 2, when a new test sample is introduced, its k nearest neighbors are identified based on the Euclidean distances to every sample, and the probability of the test sample class information is calculated by using a measure of likelihood for a particular class [14].

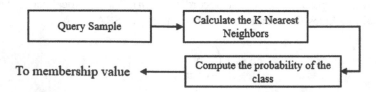

Fig. 2. Calculation of the probability of a class for new test samples.

In one scenario, a new test sample $\hat{y}_1$ in the data-distributed space falls in between three classes, as shown in Fig. 3. The computed nearest neighbors are samples of class 1 and class 3, two from each, and one sample of class 2 ($k = 5$ is taken), so the probabilities of the test samples for classes 1, 2, and 3 are 0.4, 0.2 and 0.4, respectively. In another scenario, for a new test sample $\hat{y}_2$, all computed nearest neighbors are of the same class, class 2. Thus, the probabilities of new samples of classes 1, 2, and 3 are 0, 0, and 1, respectively. These obtained values are used to compute the membership factor for each class.

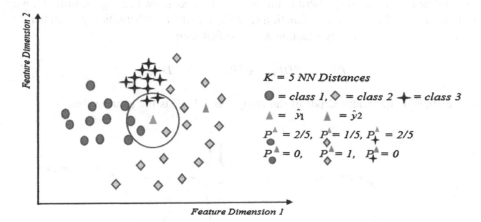

Fig. 3. Probabilities of classes for a test sample, based on distance.

2.3.2   Probability of Class Information Based on the Density (β)

As shown in Fig. 4, when a new test sample $\hat{y}_1$ is added to the data distributed space, we need to group the new sample into a class based on the information from the training data samples.

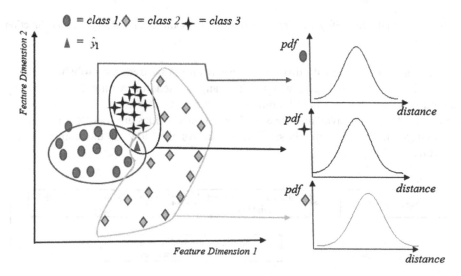

Fig. 4. Probabilities of classes for a sample, based on density.

The k nearest neighbors are determined based on the Euclidean distances between all data samples. The maximum of nearest neighbors distances of every sample in the class are considered for computing the probability density function (*PDF*) for that particular data group. Thus the selected nearest neighbor distance measures PDFs might yield the same probability for different samples both with higher distances and smaller distances, and in order to explicitly avoid confusion in classification, the probabilities of the density distribution are modified, as shown in Fig. 5. Initially, we find the peak of the distribution function (*PDF$_{max}$*), and the probabilities that fall before the maximum of the density function are modified using

$$\overrightarrow{PDF} = PDF_{\max} + (PDF_{\max} - PDF), \tag{5}$$

where $\overrightarrow{PDF}$ is the modified pdf of the sample and *PDF* is the actual value.

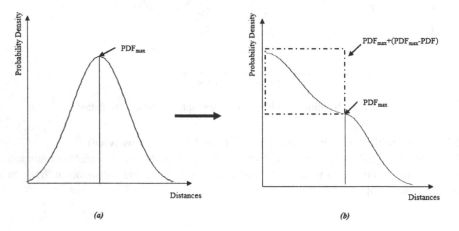

(a)   (b)

Fig. 5. (a) Actual probability density distribution (b) modified probability density function distribution.

Once the modified density distribution has been normalized, the probability of the test sample is considered as a weight that can be used for scaling the probability obtained from the distance-based similarity of that particular class. This entire procedure is repeated for all available classes. The obtained values are used to compute the membership factor for each class. Figure 6 shows the flow of the computational procedure.

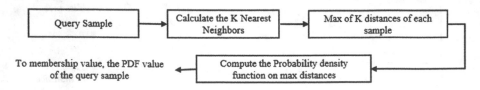

Fig. 6. Computing the probability of class information based on density.

2.3.3   Assigning Membership Values

For N test data samples, we assign the membership value (MV) for C classes by using the following formula:

$$MV_n^t = \alpha^t + (1 - \alpha^t)\beta^t, \; n = 1, 2, 3 \ldots N, \; t = 1, 2, 3 \ldots C \; MV \in (0, 1), \qquad (6)$$

where $\alpha \in (0, 1)$ is the probability of a class of the test sample based on the distance, and $\beta \in (0, 1)$ is the probability of a class based on density similarity.

Let us consider the scenarios, shown in Fig. 3, with two test data samples $\overrightarrow{y_1}$ and $\overrightarrow{y_2}$. The sample $\overrightarrow{y_2}$ is surrounded by the k nearest neighbors of the same class, and the probability of α is 1 for that particular class and 0 for the remaining classes. In this case, the sample belongs to class 2, and the decision is made on distance or density information. Thus, when we compute our formula, the density scaling does not impact the determination of the membership value. In the case of data sample $\overrightarrow{y_1}$, among the k nearest neighbors, the majority rule of the traditional k-NN classifier would be prone to misclassification. In the proposed method, when computing the membership value for a class, our formula includes the probability of density-based information and scales the probability based on the distance information accordingly, therefore providing more reliable information regarding the class information of the test data sample.

2.4   Classification

For each test data sample, we have a set of membership values for each available class. We find the maximum of the membership values to determine the class information of a test sample:

$$C_{\bar{y}} = \max(MV^t), t = 1, 2, 3 \ldots C_n.$$

The calculated class information is then compared to the original class information of the test sample to determine the efficiency of the proposed algorithm.

3   Experimental Results and Analysis

We tested the proposed algorithm on the IMS bearing dataset, considering three types of fault signature class information: BCIF, BCRF, and BCOF. Because typical k-NN does not have a training stage, it does not entail a training time cost. To evaluate the proposed methodology, we divided all the data samples from the dataset into two parts (1:1), randomly assigning them to either a training dataset or a test dataset. Then, we assigned each sample in the test dataset a set of membership values, which were scaled factors based on distance and density similarity measures. The class of a sample was determined based on the maximum value of the set of membership values for all

Table 1. Accuracy of the proposed method compared with traditional k-NN.

k	Algorithm	BCIF	BCOF	BCRF
2	Traditional	99.60	79.30	92.60
	Proposed	99.20	83.20	97.38
3	Traditional	93.54	86.20	79.94
	Proposed	98.10	84.60	96.84
4	Traditional	89.90	79.30	81.87
	Proposed	100.0	85.00	96.16
5	Traditional	80.82	88.32	84.09
	Proposed	96.13	87.89	96.59
6	Traditional	80.82	81.20	80.44
	Proposed	96.34	92.08	93.82
7	Traditional	83.40	74.60	69.97
	Proposed	94.50	92.30	93.82
8	Traditional	91.23	83.40	87.75
	Proposed	93.10	92.64	93.80
9	Traditional	84.60	79.30	62.45
	Proposed	91.75	93.45	93.05
10	Traditional	87.33	86.90	86.53
	Proposed	92.33	91.53	93.85
11	Traditional	89.90	65.00	98.87
	Proposed	100.0	87.10	90.07
12	Traditional	89.05	82.44	80.66
	Proposed	93.40	92.35	93.04
13	Traditional	78.00	70.00	78.80
	Proposed	91.40	92.50	93.61
14	Traditional	88.90	65.00	88.05
	Proposed	92.50	93.01	92.54
15	Traditional	89.00	79.00	83.08
	Proposed	94.90	91.03	90.49
16	Traditional	84.33	84.55	78.42
	Proposed	93.01	92.00	91.95
17	Traditional	85.66	85.66	85.66
	Proposed	94.67	91.33	91.27
18	Traditional	98.00	74.30	78.80
	Proposed	92.10	93.00	93.33
19	Traditional	91.00	79.00	81.10
	Proposed	92.22	92.27	92.89
20	Traditional	91.32	73.00	86.21
	Proposed	94.12	91.35	91.58

available classes, which differentiates our proposed approach from other modified k-NN classification techniques by making it insensitive to the k value.

To determine the classification accuracy, we compared the class information obtained using the proposed method to the original class information of the test sample. In this study, we examined the statistical feature set that is used by many researchers to identify various bearing conditions in performance evaluation processes. In our experiment, we performed a k-fold cross-validation for a k-value set at 5. To evaluate the performance of our algorithm, we compared our proposed method to the traditional k-NN classification technique. The results are provided in Table 1 for different values of k and for the 3 tested fault signature classes. Figure 7 compares the overall efficiencies for the traditional k-NN and for our proposed method. We observe that, when using traditional k-NN, the classification accuracy varies with the neighborhood size k. However, our proposed method is not sensitive to the k value. Especially at higher values of k, the individual classification of classes is more consistent than with traditional k-NN.

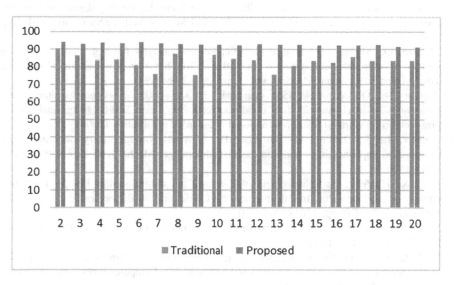

Fig. 7. Comparison of overall experimental accuracies of the proposed versus traditional k-NN.

4 Conclusions

In this study, we have proposed an improved k-NN classifier that uses a density-weighted distance-based similarity measure. The proposed method improves the diagnostic performance by using our fault diagnosis scheme for rolling element bearings, which we tested based on bearing fault data obtained from IMS. The proposed method showed significant improvement in accuracy, compared to traditional k-NN, and its performance was robust to variations in the value of k, unlike traditional

k-NN. These improvements reduce the complexity and increase the reliability of classification, as the empirical calculation of the optimal value of k is no longer required.

Acknowledgements. This work was supported by the Korea Institute of Energy Technology Evaluation and Planning (KETEP) and the Ministry of Trade, Industry & Energy (MOTIE) of the Republic of Korea (No. 20162220100050). It was also supported by The Leading Human Resource Training Program of Regional Neo Industry through the National Research Foundation of Korea (NRF) funded by the Ministry of Science, ICT, and Future Planning (NRF-2016H1D5A1910564), by the Business for Cooperative R&D between Industry, Academy, and Research Institute funded by the Korea Small and Medium Business Administration in 2016 (Grants S2381631, C0395147), and by Basic Science Research Program through the National Research Foundation of Korea (NRF) funded by the Ministry of Education (2016R1D1A 3B03931927).

References

1. Dong, S., Shirong, Y., Baoping, T., Chen, L., Tianhong, L.: Bearing degradation process prediction based on the support vector machine and Markov model. Shock Vib. **2014**, 15 p. (2014)
2. Thorsen, O., Magnus, D.: Failure identification and analysis for high voltage induction motors in petrochemical industry. In: 1998 IEEE Industry Applications Conference, Thirty-Third IAS Annual Meeting, vol. 1, pp. 291–298 (1998)
3. Hansen, D., Olsson, A.H.: ISO standard 13373-2: 2005: condition monitoring and diagnostics of machines–vibration condition monitoring–part 2: processing, analysis and presentation of vibration data. International Standards Organization (2009)
4. Andrew, J.K.S., Daming, L., Banjevic, D.: A review on machinery diagnostics and prognostics implementing condition-based maintenance. Mech. Syst. Signal Process. **7**, 1483–1510 (2006)
5. Xiao, X., Huafeng, D.: Enhancement of K-nearest neighbor algorithm based on weighted entropy of attribute value. In: 5th International Conference on Biomedical Engineering and Informatics (BMEI), pp. 1261–1264 (2012)
6. Wu, Y., Ianakiev, K., Venu, G.: Improved k-nearest neighbor classification. Pattern Recogn. Lett. **35**(10), 2311–2318 (2002)
7. Baoli, L., Yu, S., Lu, Q.: An improved k-nearest neighbor algorithm for text categorization. In: Proceedings of the 20th International Conference on Computer Processing of Oriental Languages, Shenyang, China (2003)
8. Jiang, L., Zhihua, C., Dianhong, W., Siwei, J.: Survey of improving K-nearest-neighbor for classification. In: 4th International Conference on Fuzzy Systems and Knowledge Discovery, pp. 679–683 (2007)
9. Hand, D.J., Vinciotti, V.: Choosing k for two-class nearest neighbor classifiers with unbalanced classes. Pattern Recogn. Lett. **24**(9), 1555–1562 (2003)
10. Shiliang, S., Huang, R.: An adaptive k-nearest neighbor algorithm. In: IEEE 7th International Conference on Fuzzy Systems and Knowledge Discovery, vol. 1, pp. 91–94 (2010)
11. Jia, W., Cai, Z., Gao, Z.: Dynamic K-nearest-neighbor with distance and attribute weighted for classification. In: IEEE International Conference on Electronics and Information Engineering, vol. 1, pp. V1–356 (2010)

12. Wesam, A., Murtaja, M.: Finding within cluster dense regions using distance based technique. Int. J. Intell. Syst. Appl. **2**, 42 (2012)
13. Lee, J., Qiu, H., Yu, G., Lin, J.: Rexnord Technical Services, Bearing Data Set, IMS, University of Cincinnati, NASA Ames Prognostics Data Repository (2007)
14. Kim, C.H., Uddin, S., Islam, R., Kim, J.M.: Many-core accelerated local outlier factor based classifier in bearing fault diagnosis. In: IEEE 18th International Conference on Computer and Information Technology, pp. 445–449 (2015)
15. Xia, Z., Shixiong, X., Wan, L., Cai, S.: Spectral regression based fault feature extraction for bearing accelerometer sensor signals. Sensors **10**, 13694–13719 (2012)
16. Yaqub, M., Iqbal, G., Joarder, K.: Inchoate fault detection framework: adaptive selection of wavelet nodes and cumulant orders. IEEE Trans. Instrum. Meas. **3**, 685–695 (2012)
17. Li, B., Lie, Z.P., Liu, D., Mi, S., Ren, G., Tian, H.: Feature extraction for rolling element bearing fault diagnosis utilizing generalized S transform and two-dimensional non-negative matrix factorization. J. Sound Vib. **10**(330), 2388–2399 (2011)
18. Kang, M., Islam, R., Kim, J., Kim, J.M., Pecht, M.: A hybrid feature selection scheme for reducing diagnostic performance deterioration caused by outliers in data-driven diagnostics. IEEE Trans. Industr. Electron. **63**(5), 3299–3310 (2016)

Towards Solving TSPN with Arbitrary Neighborhoods: A Hybrid Solution

Bo Yuan[1,2(✉)] and Tiantian Zhang[1,2]

[1] Intelligent Computing Lab, Division of Informatics,
Graduate School at Shenzhen, Tsinghua University,
Shenzhen 518055, People's Republic of China
yuanb@sz.tsinghua.edu.cn, 2573546543@qq.com
[2] Shenzhen Engineering Laboratory of Geometry Measurement Technology,
Graduate School at Shenzhen, Tsinghua University,
Shenzhen 518055, People's Republic of China

Abstract. As the generalization of TSP (Travelling Salesman Problem), TSPN (TSP with Neighborhoods) is closely related to several important real-world applications. However, TSPN is significantly more challenging than TSP as it is inherently a mixed optimization task containing both combinatorial and continuous components. Different from previous studies where TSPN is either tackled by approximation algorithms or formulated as a mixed integer problem, we present a hybrid framework in which metaheuristics and classical TSP solvers are combined strategically to produce high quality solutions for TSPN with arbitrary neighborhoods. The most distinctive feature of our solution is that it imposes no explicit restriction on the shape and size of neighborhoods, while many existing TSPN solutions require the neighborhoods to be disks or ellipses. Furthermore, various continuous optimization algorithms and TSP solvers can be conveniently adopted as necessary. Experiment results show that, using two off-the-shelf routines and without any specific performance tuning efforts, our method can efficiently solve TSPN instances with up to 25 regions, which are represented by both convex and concave random polygons.

Keywords: TSP · TSPN · Neighborhood · Hybrid · Metaheuristic

1 Introduction

TSP (Travelling Salesman Problem) is a well-known combinatorial optimization problem, which has been extensively studied in the past decades [1]. Given a set of n cities and their locations, an optimal (shortest) cyclic tour is required that visits each city once and only once. Although it is possible to work out the optimal solution via brute force search for small n values, TSP is an NP-hard problem and the size of the search space (possible permutations of cities) grows quickly as n increases, making exact methods computationally prohibitive. Since TSP has found wide applications in robot motion planning, logistics and manufacturing, there are already a number of techniques that can effectively tackle TSP instances with hundreds of cities using approximation, heuristic or metaheuristic algorithms [2–4]. Furthermore, the classical

© Springer International Publishing AG 2017
M. Wagner et al. (Eds.): ACALCI 2017, LNAI 10142, pp. 204–215, 2017.
DOI: 10.1007/978-3-319-51691-2_18

TSP can be also extended to non-Euclidean spaces as well as a variety of interesting problems, such as Asymmetric TSP and Generalized TSP (One-of-a-Set TSP) [5].

TSPN (TSP with Neighborhoods) is an extension of TSP in which each city is represented by a continuous region called neighborhood and the optimal solution is the shortest path that visits/connects all regions [6]. It is easy to see that when the size of the region reduces to zero, TSPN is identical to TSP. There are several scenarios in practice that can be formulated as TSPN. For example, given a set of geographically distributed wireless sensors, it may be necessary to use a mobile robot to collect the data from each sensor. Since each sensor has an effective communication range, typically represented by a disk, the mobile robot can download the data once it reaches the boundary of the disk, instead of the exact location of the sensor itself. Similarly, a postman delivering parcels to villages does not necessarily need to visit each household in person. Instead, one resident in each village can serve as the agent to distribute parcels to other residents in the same village. In both cases, the objective of route planning is to find the shortest cyclic path that intersects with each region.

A formal definition of TSPN is as follows:

$$\text{minimize: } \sum_{i=1}^{n-1} d\left(p_{\tau(i)}, p_{\tau(i+1)}\right) + d\left(p_{\tau(n)}, p_{\tau(1)}\right) \tag{1}$$

subject to:

$$p_i \in Q_i \subset \mathbb{R}^m, \quad i \in [1, n] \tag{2}$$

$$\tau(i) \in [1, n], \tau(i) \neq \tau(j), \quad \forall i \neq j \tag{3}$$

According to Eq. 1, a TSPN tour contains n path segments, which sequentially connect n regions. Equation 2 requires that each access point p must be within its corresponding region Q. The fundamental property of TSP is ensured in Eq. 3 so that each access point is visited once and only once. In our work, we assume that the distances between any two points are symmetric.

TSPN is significantly more challenging than TSP as it contains both combinatorial and continuous components. In fact, it is necessary to identify a proper access point for each region as well as simultaneously find the optimal permutation of these access points, which is itself a TSP task. These two objectives are also correlated. Given a set of access points, its quality depends on the specific permutation while the quality of a permutation depends on the access points selected. Since the objective function contains different variable types, most optimization techniques cannot be applied in a straightforward manner. After all, due to the presence of the continuous component, the search space of TSPN is infinite, making it impossible to guarantee an optimal solution, unless additional constraints are imposed on the regions.

In the literature, TSPN is largely attempted by approximation algorithms, which aim at finding a PTAS (Polynomial-Time Approximation Scheme) for TSPN [7–10]. The major issue is that strict assumptions on neighborhoods (e.g., disks or *fat* objects of comparable sizes) are essential for producing relatively compact approximation factors, which are still often very large along with high time complexity. Since the implementations of these algorithms can be complicated and very few if any experimental studies have been reported, their practicability remains unclear. TSPN can be also formulated as a non-convex Mixed-Integer Nonlinear Program (MINLP), which has the attractive feature that fixing all the integer variables can yield a convex nonlinear problem [11]. However, although the technique is claimed to be highly efficient, only TSPN instances with up to 16 regions were tested. Furthermore, since each region is specified by a set of inequalities, all regions are effectively restricted to convex polygons. There are also a few studies on using metaheuristics for solving TSPN where the regions are represented by disks of varying sizes [12, 13].

In practice, the shapes of regions can be complex. For example, a large number of wireless sensors can be deployed in several areas that are distant from each other. However, within each area, sensors may be densely distributed (sufficiently close to each other) so that it is possible to transfer data from all sensors to a specific sensor using multi-hop communication. As a result, instead of requiring the mobile robot to visit each sensor, it only needs to visit a single sensor located in each area. Since the communication range of each sensor is a disk, the neighborhood can be viewed as the overlapping of many disks, creating an arbitrarily complex region (Fig. 1).

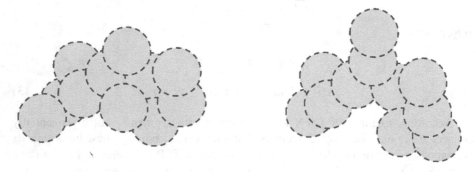

Fig. 1. An example of two clusters of wireless sensors. The effective range of each sensor is shown as a disk and the overall shape of each cluster is very complex.

In this paper, we present a hybrid framework for solving TSPN with arbitrary neighborhoods. The key feature is that there is little if any assumption on the shape of regions, other than being able to sequentially represent each possible access point along the region boundary. Meanwhile, the continuous component (optimization of access points) is handled by a competent metaheuristic while the combinatorial component (optimization of the order of access points) is handled by an efficient TSP solver. Actually, the TSP solver is used as the fitness function in the metaheuristic to evaluate the quality of candidate access points and is otherwise independent from the metaheuristic. By doing so, our method can benefit from state-of-the-art techniques in both communities and is easy to apply by using off-the-shelf implementations.

Section 2 gives the representation of neighborhoods and access points used in our work. It also shows the extra challenge due to non-convex regions. Section 3 presents the details of the proposed hybrid framework while experiment results are shown in Sect. 4 to demonstrate the performance of our method. This paper is concluded in Sect. 5 with some discussions on the direction of future work.

2 Methodology

For the convenience of computing, each region (neighborhood) is specified by a random simple polygon in the 2D Euclidean space. The number of edges can be manually controlled and each polygon can be either convex or concave (Fig. 2), reflecting the most general situation. Note that any neighborhoods can be reasonably approximated by polygons with a large number of edges.

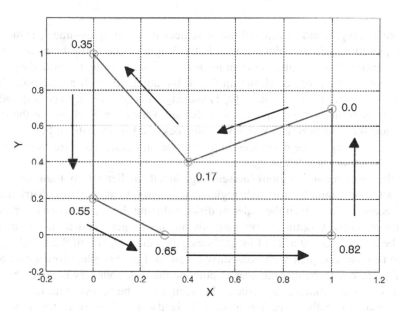

Fig. 2. A concave polygon with 6 vertices. The top-right vertex is assumed to be the starting point. Each vertex is encoded as a continuous value along the anti-clockwise direction.

Meanwhile, creating random simple polygons is not a trivial task. A simple polygon means a polygon without any intersecting sides. In this paper, we use an open source routine based on the Delaunay triangulation of a set of random points [14]. Depending on the desired complexity of polygons, a number of random points are generated within an area and a polygon is then created based on them. Alternatively, given a specific region (e.g., the map of a city), we can sequentially sample data points along the boundary to form the polygon.

Once the parameters (coordinates of vertices) of a polygon are determined, a key factor is how to represent each access point. In the 2D space, each access point can be naïvely represented by its X and Y coordinates. However, it is not convenient as two values are needed (with possibly different ranges) and special constraint handling is required to make sure that the access point is valid (located on the boundary). More specifically, metaheuristics often apply operators such as crossover and mutation on candidate solutions, altering their values randomly. As a result, a simple box-bounded search space is preferred as metaheuristics often do not come with advanced constraint handling strategies.

For regular shapes such disks, it is possible to use the polar coordinate system according to which each access point is encoded as an angle value. Since there is no specific assumption on the shape of neighborhoods, we cannot rely on any parametric representation of the boundary. Instead, we propose to use the following coding scheme, which is applicable to any type of polygons:

$$E(\mathbf{x}) = \frac{\sum_{i=0}^{k-1} d(v_i, v_{i+1}) + d(v_k, \mathbf{x})}{L} \qquad (4)$$

Given a polygon and its ordered list of vertices $v_0, \ldots, v_{n-1}$, assume v_k is the vertex directly preceding access point x and L is the length of the entire boundary. Access point x is encoded as the ratio between its distance from v_0 along the boundary and the perimeter of the polygon, as shown in Eq. 4. By doing so, each access point is represented by a single variable within $[0, 1)$ and any value within $[0, 1)$ corresponds to a unique access point on the boundary. Note that any vertex can by chosen as the starting point v_0 and the direction (clockwise vs. anti-clockwise) is not critical. Figure 2 shows the encoded values of the 6 vertices following the anti-clockwise direction where the top-right vertex is regarded as v_0.

Finally, non-convex regions present significant challenges to traditional TSPN techniques. For example, for disk regions, it is easy to predict the distribution of optimal access points given the order of disks, reducing the search space dramatically. Furthermore, convex optimization methods are no longer valid as the search area cannot be represented by a set of inequalities. Also, the structure of the search space is likely to be more complex with non-convex regions. For example, given a disk and an external point x, assume that the nearest point on the disk boundary is x'. As the access point moves away from x', the distance between x and the access point is expected to increase monotonically, creating a smooth landscape. However, for non-convex regions, this is not necessarily the truth. Instead, the resulting landscape may be highly multimodal with several peaks (local optima), which creates much higher-level difficulty for optimization techniques.

3 Framework

The motivation of proposing a hybrid framework is largely due to the fact that solving TSPN involves two sub-tasks: the optimization of the locations of access points (continuous) and the optimization of the order of access points (combinatorial). The classical optimization community has produced many efficient TSP solvers, which can reliably find high quality tours for problems with hundreds of cities within a fairly small amount of time. Meanwhile, the metaheuristic community has come up with competent stochastic algorithms that can effectively handle multimodal problems with little assumption on their structure (e.g., being convex or differentiable). After all, although metaheuristics can be used to solve TSP, their performance is typically not comparable to state-of-the-art TSP solvers based on well-studied heuristics.

The objective is to introduce a general TSPN solution, which builds upon existing research outcomes and can hide most of the unnecessary details from practitioners. Unlike many existing studies that present specifically tailored methods, which are often sophisticated and difficult to deploy, our framework is easy to implement by incorporating off-the-shelf routines. Although it is possible to formulate TSPN as a mixed optimization problem where the two types of variables are optimized simultaneously, the two sub-tasks can be accomplished separately. In Fig. 3, the metaheuristic is dedicated to optimizing the locations of access points while the quality (fitness) of each set of candidate access points is evaluated by a TSP solver, which returns the length of the TSP tour (expected to be identical or sufficiently close to the optimal tour for small scale problems). By doing so, the two sub-tasks are solved alternately, which reduces the complexity of the original problem and makes different algorithms work on their most suitable problems. In fact, users only need to specify the coding scheme and select the desired optimization routines (Algorithm 1).

Algorithm 1: Hybrid TSPN Solution

```
Input:   Coordinates of vertices of n polygons
Output:  p(access points), τ(permutation)
P ← a population of random n D vectors
Repeat until stopping criteria met
   Repeat evaluate each vector pᵢ in P
         C ← Decode(pᵢ)
         [Lᵢ, τᵢ] ← TSP_Solver(C)
         Return tour length Lᵢ as the fitness
   End
   P ← Metaheuristic(P, L)
End
Return best p* and τ* found
```

Given n regions, the original optimization problem is as follows where x is an n–D real vector (locations) and τ is the permutation of n regions:

$$\min_x \min_\tau f(x, \tau) \qquad (5)$$

In Eq. 5, $f(x, \tau)$ returns the length of the tour defined by x and τ. In the proposed framework, the objective function used by the metaheuristic is:

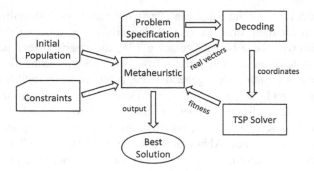

Fig. 3. The proposed hybrid framework for solving TSPN with arbitrary neighborhoods

$$g(x) = f(x, \tau^*) \text{ where } \tau^* : \min_\tau f(x, \tau) \tag{6}$$

According to Eq. 6, $g(x)$ works by finding the optimal τ^* for the given x and returning the corresponding $f(x, \tau^*)$ value as the quality of the candidate solution. It is clear that, if $f(x, \tau)$ takes its minimum value at $[x^g, \tau^g]$, it is always the truth that $g(x^g)$ is also the minimum value of $g(x)$, which proves the correctness of our method.

4   Experiments

The objective of the experiments is to demonstrate the simplicity and effectiveness of the proposed framework. For this purpose, we selected an open source metaheuristic routine CMA-ES [15, 16] due to its featured capability of working with small populations and handling complex dependences among variables and an open source TSP solver [17]. These two methods were not meant to be the optimal choices and no specific performance tuning was conducted.

4.1   Case Studies

Each polygon was created randomly within a 1-by-1 area with up to 6 edges, which can be either convex or concave. The diversity of generated polygons can be observed intuitively in Fig. 4. All polygons were distributed randomly within a 5-by-5 area without overlapping. Most of the parameter settings in CMA-ES were as the default, except the search boundary, which was bounded between 0 and 1 in each dimension, in accordance with the encoding scheme. Note that the dimension of the continuous search space is equal to the number of regions. As to the TSP solver, it works by randomly selecting a starting node and building an initial tour using the nearest neighbor method, which is then gradually improved by the 2-opt algorithm.

Figure 4 shows an example of a TSPN tour among 10 polygons. The access point of each region is shown in circle. For TSPN, it is generally not feasible to have the prior knowledge about the optimal tour. Meanwhile, existing TSPN techniques are often not directly applicable to complex neighborhoods and cannot be used for comparison

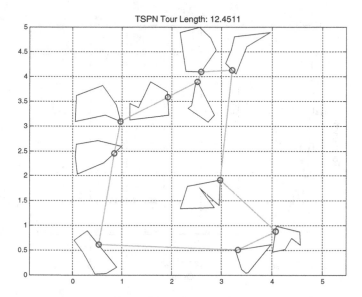

Fig. 4. A 10-region TSPN tour, showing the selected access point of each region

purpose. Nevertheless, it is still possible to verify the effectiveness of our method by examining the performance curve in Fig. 5. At the beginning of iteration, the length of the best tour was around 15.5. In fact, each tour in the initial population was created by randomly selecting a set of access points and applying the TSP solver to find the corresponding shortest path. As a result, these tours were partially optimized TSPN solutions and can be used as the base line. After only 50 iterations, the length of the best tour was already reduced to 12.5 and kept improving slightly till 12.45, which was a common pattern across different trials. After all, for this relatively small scale instance, the quality of the resulting tour can be also inspected visually.

Figure 6 shows an example of a TSPN tour among 25 polygons. It is clear that, for problems at this scale, it is already very difficult to manually work out a near-optimal solution. However, our method constructed a TSPN tour with length under 17 and the quality of the tour can again be observed: there were several cases where a single line segment connected multiple regions, a desirable feature for producing short tours.

The efficiency of our method is also evident. On an entry level desktop computer with Intel i5-3470S at 2.9 GHz CPU, 10-region TSPN instances were typically solved to a reasonable level in less than 5 s while 25-region TSPN instances required less than 15 s. Note that metaheuristics such as CMA-ES often feature good potential of parallelism and one to two orders of magnitude speedup can be expected using advanced parallel computing techniques such as GPU computing [18].

4.2   Problem Analysis

Finally, it is equally important to have some insights into the structure of the problem to understand the challenges confronted by optimization algorithms. We focus on the

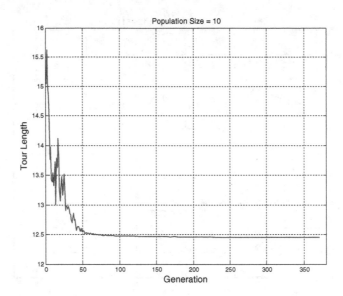

Fig. 5. The current best solution during iteration, showing the fast convergence of CMA-ES

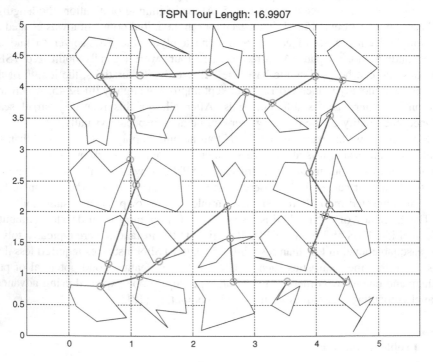

Fig. 6. A 25-region TSPN tour, showing the selected access point of each region

continuous sub-task as the combinatorial part (TSP) has been extensively studied in the literature. Figure 7 (left) shows a TSPN instance with three polygons so that the optimal permutation is trivial. Totally 10,000 random candidates were generated with each one represented by a 3-D vector within the range [0, 1). The fitness of each candidate was evaluated by the length of the corresponding tour (i.e., a triangle). The candidate with the shortest distance was regarded as the optimal solution and its distances to all other candidates were calculated.

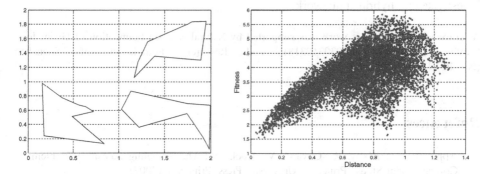

Fig. 7. A TSPN example with three polygons (left) and the fitness-distance plot (right), which shows the relationship between the quality of candidates and their distances to the best solution.

In Fig. 7 (right), each candidate is represented by its Euclidean distance to the best solution (horizontal axis) and its fitness value (vertical axis). This type of plot is often referred to as the fitness-distance plot [19], which can provide intuitive information about the difficulty of problems. It is clear that in the region close to the best solution, there is a positive correlation between fitness and distance: the closer a candidate to the best candidate, the better its quality. This pattern generally indicates optimization friendly problem structure, as it provides an effective guidance on the search direction. However, things are quite different on the far side. Candidates in these regions tend to get worse (longer tours) when moving closer to the best candidate, which may unfortunately create a deceptive search space and mislead the optimization process.

There are a number of factors that can influence the correlation between fitness and distance. For example, the pattern in Fig. 7 (right) may imply that the problem is inherently multimodal and traditional gradient based methods may not work well. Note that the encoding scheme will also have direct impact on the problem structure.

5 Conclusion

As a class of optimization problems with significant practical implications, TSPN with arbitrary neighborhoods presents unprecedented challenges to approximation algorithms and convex optimization techniques and no effective solutions are available in the literature. In our work, we present a novel hybrid framework that combines competent algorithms from both continuous and combinatorial optimization communities to tackle TSPN with complex neighborhoods. Without the need to directly confront a mixed optimization problem, our method features demonstrated simplicity (largely using off-the-shelf routines), flexibility (imposing little assumption on neighborhoods) and efficiency (solving non-trivial TSPN instances in seconds). The current preliminary study can serve as the foundation for more comprehensive research on solving large-scale TSPN instances as well as many interesting related problems such as the safari route problem and the zookeeper route problem. We will also make the source code available online to help researchers and practitioners further extend and investigate this hybrid framework.

Acknowledgement. This work was supported by Natural Science Foundation of Guangdong Province (No. 2014A030310318) and Research Foundation of Shenzhen (No. JCYJ20160301153317415).

References

1. Applegate, D., Bixby, R., Chvátal, V., Cook, W.: The Traveling Salesman Problem: A Computational Study. Princeton University Press, Princeton (2007)
2. Arora, S.: Polynomial time approximation schemes for Euclidean traveling salesman and other geometric problems. J. ACM **45**, 753–782 (1998)
3. Larrañaga, P., Kuijpers, C., Murga, R., Inza, I., Dizdarevic, S.: Genetic algorithms for the travelling salesman problem: a review of representations and operators. Artif. Intell. Rev. **13**, 129–170 (1999)
4. Helsgaun, K.: An effective implementation of the Lin-Kernighan traveling salesman heuristic. Eur. J. Oper. Res. **126**, 106–130 (2000)
5. Alatartsev, S., Stellmacher, S., Ortmeier, F.: Robotic task sequencing problem: a survey. J. Intell. Robot. Syst. **80**, 279–298 (2015)
6. Arkin, E.M., Hassin, R.: Approximation algorithms for the geometric covering salesman problem. Discret. Appl. Math. **55**, 197–218 (1994)
7. Mitchell, J.: A PTAS for TSP with neighborhoods among fat regions in the plane. In: Proceedings of the Eighteenth Annual ACM-SIAM Symposium on Discrete Algorithms, pp. 11–18 (2007)
8. Elbassioni, K., Fishkin, A., Sitters, R.: Approximation algorithms for the Euclidean traveling salesman problem with discrete and continuous neighborhoods. Int. J. Comput. Geom. Appl. **19**, 173–193 (2009)
9. Chan, T., Elbassioni, K.: A QPTAS for TSP with fat weakly disjoint neighborhoods in doubling metrics. Discret. Comput. Geom. **46**, 704–723 (2011)
10. Dumitrescu, A., Tóth, C.: Constant-factor approximation for TSP with disks (2016). arXiv: 1506.07903v3 [cs.CG]
11. Gentilini, I., Margot, F., Shimada, K.: The travelling salesman problem with neighborhoods: MINLP solution. Optim. Methods Softw. **28**, 364–378 (2013)
12. Yuan, B., Orlowska, M., Sadiq, S.: On the optimal robot routing problem in wireless sensor networks. IEEE Trans. Knowl. Data Eng. **19**, 1252–1261 (2007)
13. Chang, W., Zeng, D., Chen, R., Guo, S.: An artificial bee colony algorithm for data collection path planning in sparse wireless sensor networks. Int. J. Mach. Learn. Cybern. **6**, 375–383 (2015)

14. Random 2D Polygon Code. http://stackoverflow.com/questions/8997099/algorithm-to-generate-random-2d-polygon
15. CMA-ES Source Code. https://www.lri.fr/~hansen/cmaes_inmatlab.html
16. Hansen, N., Ostermeier, A.: Completely derandomized self-adaptation in evolution strategies. Evol. Comput. **9**, 159–195 (2001)
17. TSPSEARCH. http://www.mathworks.com/matlabcentral/fileexchange/35178-tspsearch
18. Kirk, D., Hwu, W.: Programming Massively Parallel Processors: A Hands-on Approach. Morgan Kaufmann, San Francisco (2012)
19. Jones, T., Forrest, S.: Fitness distance correlation as a measure of problem difficulty for genetic algorithms. In: Proceedings of 6th International Conference on Genetic Algorithms, pp. 184–192 (1995)

Detectable Genetic Algorithms-Based Techniques for Solving Dynamic Optimisation Problem with Unknown Active Variables

AbdelMonaem F.M. AbdAllah$^{(\boxtimes)}$, Daryl L. Essam, and Ruhul A. Sarker

School of Engineering and Information Technology,
University of New South Wales, (UNSW@ADFA), Canberra 2600, Australia
a.abdallah@student.adfa.edu.au,
{d.essam,r.sarker}@adfa.edu.au

Abstract. A dynamic Optimisation Problem with Unknown Active Variables (DOPUAV) is a dynamic problem in which the activity of the variables changes as time passes, to simulate the dynamicity in the problem's variables. In this paper, several variations of genetic algorithms are proposed to solve DOPUAV. They are called Detectable techniques. These techniques try to detect where the problem changes, before detecting the active variables. These variations are tested, then the best variation is compared with the best previously used algorithms namely Hyper Mutation (HyperM), Random Immigration GA (RIGA), as well as simple GA (SGA). The results and statistical analysis show the superiority of our proposed algorithm.

Keywords: Active · Detectable · Dynamic optimisation problems · Genetic algorithms

1 Introduction

Dynamic optimisation (DO) is one of the most important optimisation circumstances that relates to real-life applications. This is because most of these applications change as time passes e.g. the traffic congestion and conditions in transportation. Therefore, DO has received increasing attention in the optimisation research area. In the literature of DO, most of the research considered dynamicity in functions and constraints. In these types of dynamic optimisation, the objective functions and the problem's constraints change as time passes. However, there are motivations to investigate other types of dynamicity, e.g. variables and their boundaries [1, 2]. In 2014, we proposed a dynamic optimisation problem with changeable effective variables, in which the effective/active variables change as time passes [3]. Additionally, a class of algorithms was proposed to solve such problems. These algorithms tried to detect the active variables at regular intervals of a specific number of generations. They were called periodic genetic algorithms (PerGAs). One of the PerGAs variations was superior when compared with a simple GA (SGA).

© Springer International Publishing AG 2017
M. Wagner et al. (Eds.): ACALCI 2017, LNAI 10142, pp. 216–227, 2017.
DOI: 10.1007/978-3-319-51691-2_19

In this paper, the Dynamic Optimisation Problem with Unknown Active Variables (DOPUAV) is further investigated. DOPUAV is a dynamic problem, in which the activity of its variables changes as time passes, to simulate the dynamicity in the problem's variables. To solve it, we propose a type of algorithms, which tries to detect if a problem changes every specific number of generations. Then, if a change is detected, the algorithm attempts to detect the active variables. These types of algorithms are called the Detectable approaches. Therefore, they consist of two basic processes, i.e. problem change detection and active variables detection. This paper investigates these processes to solve DOPUAV. Then, this type of algorithms is paired with genetic algorithms (DetGAs), additionally some variations of DetGA are compared to determine the best variation of such algorithms. Finally, the best variation is compared with the best previously used algorithm, periodic GA (PerGA) [3], along with state-of-the-art dynamic algorithms, i.e. Hyper Mutation (HyperM), and Random Immigration GA (RIGA), as well as simple GA (SGA).

The rest of this paper is organised as follows. In Sect. 2, the dynamic optimisation problem with unknown active variables (DOPUAV) is defined. In Sect. 3, the detectable Genetic Algorithms-based (DetGA) is proposed and its processes are presented. In Sect. 4, some DetGA variations are coded, tested and compared, and then the best variation is compared with the best previously used algorithm, along with the above stated dynamic algorithms. Furthermore, a discussion of the implications of the results and some suggestions for future work concludes this paper in Sect. 5.

2   Dynamic Optimisation Problem with Unknown Active Variables

The dynamic Optimisation Problem with Unknown Active Variables (DOPUAV) is a dynamic optimisation problem in which the activity of its variables changes as time passes. Therefore, in some time periods a particular set of variables affect the objective function while others do not.

To simulate such a dynamic problem, a mask is used to define which variables should be active and inactive. This mask consists of zeros and ones and has a length equal to the problem's dimensions. These zeros and ones are similar to coefficients for problem variables, where ones are multiplied by the active variables, and zeros are multiplied by the inactive variables. The creation of the problem mask is presented in the next section.

2.1   Mask Creation

To formulate DOPUAV, the activity of the variables is simulated using a mask. A mask is a vector of the same length as the problem's dimensionality, and it consists of binary values of zeros and ones. In this mask, a 'Zero' value indicates that the variable is currently inactive, while a 'One' value represents an active variable.

An example of how the mask would be created as follows. Suppose that a problem has 5 variables as its maximum number of variables, and that 40% of these variables are inactive. Therefore, 2 random indices are generated, for example, 2 and 4, and are given 'Zero' values to simulate the inactivity of these variables, as shown in Fig. 1.

| 1 | 0 | 1 | 0 | 1 |

Fig. 1. Example for a problem mask

To evaluate a solution with this mask, mask values are multiplied by the actual values of the solution's variables, then this multiplication result will be evaluated to get the objective function value of that solution. Figure 2 clarifies this process as follows:

Mask values	1	0	1	0	1
Solution values	3	2	-3	4	5
Actual values to be evaluated	3	0	-3	0	5

Fig. 2. Using the mask for solution evaluation

Suppose that the sphere function ($\sum x^2$) is used as an objective function, so the fitness value of this solution is 43 (9 + 9 + 25), not 63 (9 + 4 + 9 + 16 + 25), as it would be if the solution's variables were used on their own.

2.2   An Illustrative Example for DOPUAV

In this section, an illustrative example is provided to clarify how a DOPUAV would be a challengeable problem for conventional algorithms.

Suppose that the sphere function is used as an objective function, and it has two variables (x_1 and x_2), and there are different problem masks over three time periods. In the 1st time period, a problem mask is [1, 0]. In the 2nd time period, a problem mask is [0, 1]. In the 3rd time period, a problem mask is [1, 1].

Let a simple genetic algorithm (SGA) be used to solve this DOPUAV, to test how it might perform. During this process, the convergence and standard deviations of the three variable are detected over the best 10 solutions in each generation. This GA has a real-coded representation, tournament selection, single-point crossover and uniform mutation. The experimental settings are presented in Table 1. Note that these settings are the same in the remaining part of this paper, unless otherwise stated.

Table 1. Experimental settings

Parameter	Settings
Population size	50
Selection pressure	Two chromosomes
Crossover probability	0.60
Mutation probability	0.10
Elitism probability	0.02

Variables' Convergence

The convergence of the variables represents where variable values converge towards a specific value. The convergence of variable x_1 and x_2 are shown in Figs. 3 and 4 respectively as follows:

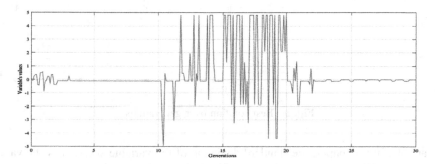

Fig. 3. The convergence of the first variable

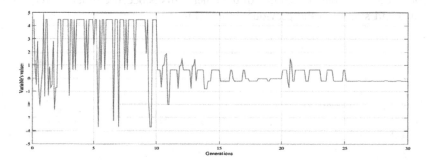

Fig. 4. The convergence of the second variable

From these figures, it is clear that when a variable is active it converges to a specific value that would achieve better fitness function (0 value for the optimal solution). The figures show that x_1 converge from the 1st to the 100th generation; as it is active. When x_1 is switched to be inactive from the 101st to the 200th generation, it randomly diverges to different values, while x_2 converges as it is switched to be active. Also, from the 201st to the 300th generation, both x_1 and x_2 converge as being active. Finally, Fig. 5 shows how the activity of the variables affect the fitness function convergence.

From Figs. 3 and 4, when a variable is active it affects the objective functions and the solving algorithms, so it converges. On the other hand, when inactive it diverges. Finally, in Fig. 5, when the activity of the variable changes the best solution increases at generation 10 and 20. Therefore, DOPUAV might be difficult for conventional algorithms to solve.

Here, we also tried to record and track one of the properties of the variables e.g. the standard deviation of each variable to check how it might be affected by the activity of

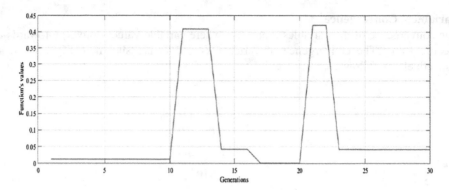

Fig. 5. Best solution over generations

the variable. In this paper, the standard deviation of the variable shows how the values of a variable differ from each other in the best 10 solutions in the current population.

In this figure, it is clear that when a variable is active in a time period, its standard deviation becomes smaller than that of the other. This is because of its convergence, as illustrated and shown in the previous figures (Fig. 6).

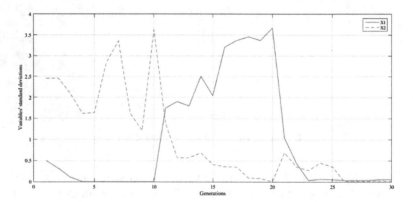

Fig. 6. Variables' standard deviations over generations

3   Detectable Genetic Algorithms-Based Techniques

Detectable Genetic Algorithms-based techniques (DetGAs) are GAs that try to detect whether there is a change in the problem or not. If a change is detected it tries to detect the current mask that affects the problem in the current time period. Therefore, DetGAs try to save fitness evaluations by not periodically detecting the mask every number of generations, in contrast to periodic GAs (PerGAs) [3]. Figure 7 shows the basic structure for a DetGA.

Note that during the mutation process, variables that are detected as inactive are not mutated. This is to prevent them diverging, as shown in the previous section.

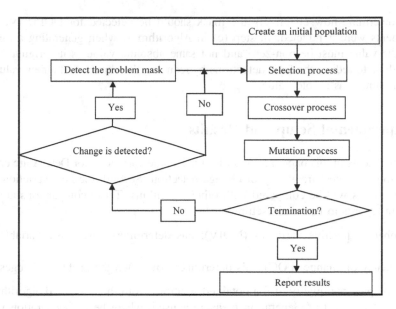

Fig. 7. The basic structure of the DetGA

3.1   Change Detection Process

In the change detection process, a solution is regularly re-evaluated every g genera-tions, where g is a parameter that determines how often the problem change should be detected. If the fitness value of this solution is changed, the problem is detected to be changed, otherwise not. In DOPUAV, the change of the inactive variables affects the problem fitness landscape in contrast to DOP that have changes in the fitness function or constraints [4], where changes might affect only a part of its landscape. Therefore, one solution (detector) is used for change detection of DOPUAV.

3.2   Mask Detection Process

When a change is detected, a mask detection process (Algorithm 1) is used. Hence the efficiency of an algorithm for solving DOPUAV depends on determining and tracking the active dimensions to be optimised. This is because inactive variables do not undergo mutation process.

(a) A random solution is chosen from the current population.

(b) Calculate its actual fitness, let it be F1.

(c) For each dimension, a random value is generated:

  (c.i) The value of the objective function (fitness) is recalculated for the solution with the new random value, let it be F2.

  (c.ii) If $F1$ is equal to $F2$, then this dimension is detected as inactive (its detected mask value is equal to 0), otherwise it is detected as active (its detected mask value is equal to 1).

Algorithm 1: Single-point sample mask detection procedure

To determine how effectively the mask should be detected for DOPUAV, some experiments were conducted. In step (c) in Algorithm 1, when generating a random value, the value must be non-zero and not same absolute value as its original value. This is done to reduce the false detections by reducing the chance that a new value has the same fitness as its old value.

4 Experimental Setup and Results

The experiments in this paper are twofold. First, some variations for DetGA are created to determine the best frequency of change detection. Second, the best variation from these variations will be compared with other algorithms. These comparisons are conducted in regards to two main settings:

- Number of inactive variables (NOIV); this determines how many variables are inactive
- Frequency of change (FOC); this determines how often the problem changes.

To compare the quality of the obtained solutions from the compared algorithms, a variation of the Best-of-Generation measure is used, where best-of-generation values are averaged over all generations [5]. The average of the Best-of-Generation measure (ABOG) is calculated as follows:

$$\bar{F}_{BOG} = \frac{1}{N} \sum_{j=1}^{N} \left(\frac{1}{G} \sum_{i=1}^{G} F_{BOG_{ij}} \right) \tag{1}$$

where $\bar{F}_{BOG}$ is the mean best-of-generation fitness, G is the number of generations, N is the total number of runs and $F_{BOG_{ij}}$ is the best-of-generation fitness of generation i of run j of an algorithm on a problem [6]. As mentioned in the literature, one of the pitfalls of ABOGs is bias, as problems have different scales in different change periods. Furthermore, solved functions have different scales for their objective functions values. The $\bar{F}_{BOG}$ of each change of a function is normalised between 0 and 1, using the best and worst $\bar{F}_{BOG}$ for all compared algorithms at each change. Then, these values are averaged over the total number of changes.

In this paper, eight different objective functions are used. Of these, five are completely separable problems, while the last three functions are non-separable. The five separable problems are Sphere, Ackley, Griewank, Restrigin and Weierstrass [7], while the other three are non-separable functions, namely, Levy, Rosenbrock and Trid [8]. Note that fitness evaluations used in the problem change detection and mask detection processes are calculated from the allowed budget of FOC.

4.1 DetGA Variations

To evaluate the performance of the proposed techniques, first some variations are created for comparison to determine how often the problem change should be effectively detected to solve DOPUAV. These variations are DetGA1, DetGA5, DetGA10 and DetGA20 in which the problem change is detected every 1, 5, 10 and 20 generations respectively. Experimental settings are shown in Table 2.

Table 2. Problems parameters

Parameter	Settings
Number of variables	20
The frequency of change (FOC)	500, 2000, 8000
The severity of change (NOIV)	5 and 10 inactive variables

ABOGs Normalised Scores

First, the DetGA variations are compared using the normalised scores for ABOGs, as previously mentioned. Note that lower values are better and the lowest are shown as bold and shaded entries. Tables 3 and 4 show results of normalised ABOFGs for the compared techniques in regards to the NOIV and the FOC respectively.

Table 3. ABOGs normalised score for DetGAs variations in regards to NOIV

NOIV	DetGA1	DetGA5	DetGA10	DetGA20
5	**0.1248**	0.4685	0.6843	0.7416
10	**0.0910**	0.4130	0.7083	0.7988
Average	**0.1079**	0.4407	0.6963	0.7702

Table 4. ABOGs normalised score for DetGAs variations in regards to FOC

FOC	DetGA1	DetGA5	DetGA10	DetGA20
500	**0.0682**	0.4070	0.5898	0.8592
2000	**0.1474**	0.4414	0.7630	0.7308
8000	**0.1080**	0.4738	0.7362	0.7206
Average	**0.1079**	0.4407	0.6963	0.7702

From the previous tables, it is clearly observed that DetGA1 is the best DetGA compared with others. Also, the performance of the DetGAs degrades when the period of the change detection increases: DetGA1 outperforms DetGA5, DetGA5 outperforms DetGA10, etc.

Freidman Test

A statistical significance test was also used to rank the group of algorithms. That test was the non-parametric Friedman test, which is similar to the parametric repeated measure ANOVA [1, 9]. A non-parametric statistical test was used because the obtained solutions of the compared algorithms are not normally distributed. The Friedman test was performed with a confidence level of 95% ($\alpha = 0.05$) on all the values, with regard to the particular variations of the parameters of DOPUAVs, with the null hypothesis being that there is no significant differences among the performances of the compared algorithms. The computational value of the p-value is a very small value, less than 0.00001. The Friedman average ranks test for the compared DetGAs is shown in Table 5; this table supports the above-mentioned observations.

Table 5. Friedman test ranks test for DetGAs

	DetGA1	DetGA5	DetGA10	DetGA20
Average rank	1.78	2.38	2.88	2.96

4.2 Comparing with State-of-the-Art Algorithms

In this section, to evaluate the performance of the best variation for DetGA (DetGA1), it is compared with some other state-of-the-art algorithms to solve DOPUAVs. These algorithms are:

- Best PerGAs (PerGA5) [3],
- Simple GA (SGA),
- Hypermutation Genetic Algorithm (HyperM) and
- Random Immigration Genetic Algorithm (RIGA)

The first GA is the best variation of Periodic GAs (PerGAs), which periodically detect the mask of the problem every 5 generations. The second GA is a simple GA (SGA), in which its operators work normally without any modifications. In other words, processes of selection, crossover and mutation deal with all variables without any consideration of the activity of variables. The other two algorithms (HyperM and RIGA) are used because these two algorithms have been extensively and intensively studied, so using them facilitates comparing new experimental data with existing results. In both HyperM and RIGA, base mutation equals 0.001 [10, 11]. In HyperM, the hyper rate of the mutation is assigned to 0.5 [10], whereas, in RIGA, the percentage of random immigration is assigned to 0.3 [11]. Note that HyperM switches to hyper-mutation rate when the fitness of the best found solution is increased in minimisation problems, otherwise, it uses the base mutation rate.

ABOGs Normalised Scores

First, these algorithms are compared using the normalised scores for ABOGs. Note that lower values are better and the lowest are shown as bold and shaded entries. Table 6 shows results of normalised ABOFGs for the compared techniques in regards to NOIV, whereas Table 7 shows the comparison in regards to FOC.

Table 6. ABOGs normalised score for the compared algorithms in regards to NOIV

NOIV	DetGA1	PerGA5	SGA	RIGA	HyperM
5	0.0298	0.1543	0.4551	0.6769	0.8100
10	0.0247	0.1418	0.1908	0.5749	0.9439
Average	0.0272	0.1481	0.3229	0.6259	0.8769

Table 7. ABOGs normalised score for the compared algorithms in regards to FOC

FOC	DetGA1	PerGA5	SGA	RIGA	HyperM
500	0.0429	0.1524	0.2302	0.5957	0.9456
2000	0.0259	0.1825	0.3478	0.6088	0.8926
8000	0.0129	0.1092	0.3909	0.6733	0.7926
Average	0.0272	0.1481	0.3229	0.6259	0.8769

From the previous tables, first in regards to NOIV, as NOIV increases, the number of active variables decreases, which simplifies the problem by containing a smaller number of variables that affect the objective function. So the scores are getting less when NOIV increases. However, as HyperM had a very low base mutation rate so its performance degrades as the number of active variables decreases. In contrast, as FOC increases, variables have more time to incorrectly mutate. So, for SGA and RIGA, their scores get worse as FOC increases. However, FOC does not adversely affect HyperM; this is because of its low rate.

Between the state-of-the-art algorithms, HyperM is the worst as its default mutation rate is too low (0.001) and it is triggered to use the hyper mutation rate if and only if the fitness of the current best solution is higher than the new best solution in the current generation. Therefore, this trigger condition might not be applied in DOPUAVs. Finally, algorithms that take into consideration the activity of the variables outperform all other compared algorithms, especially DetGA1. This is because DetGA1 uses the mask detection process when the problem changes; this lets it save more fitness evaluations.

Wilcoxon Signed-Rank Test

A Wilcoxon signed rank test [12] was used to statistically judge the difference between paired scores. As a null hypothesis, it is assumed that there is no significant difference between the obtained values of two samples, whereas the alternative hypothesis is that there is a significant difference at a 5% significance level. Based on the obtained results, one of three signs (+, −, and ≈) is assigned when the first algorithm was significantly better, worse than, or no significant difference with the second algorithm, respectively. Here, DetGA1 is compared with the other algorithms. Tables 8 and 9 show the Wilcoxon signed rank test in regards to NOIV and FOC, respectively.

Table 8. Wilcoxon signed rank test results for compared algorithms in regards to the NOIV

NOIV	Comparison	Better	Worse	Significance
5	DetGA1-to-PerGA5	200	40	+
	DetGA1-to-SGA	192	48	+
	DetGA1-to-RIGA	239	19	+
	DetGA1-to-HyperM	238	2	+
10	DetGA1-to-PerGA5	223	17	+
	DetGA1-to-SGA	187	53	+
	DetGA1-to-RIGA	237	3	+
	DetGA1-to-HyperM	239	1	+

Table 9. Wilcoxon signed rank test results for compared algorithms in regards to the FOC

FOC	Comparison	Better	Worse	Significance
500	DetGA1-to-PerGA5	130	30	+
	DetGA1-to-SGA	126	34	+
	DetGA1-to-RIGA	160	0	+
	DetGA1-to-HyperM	159	1	+
2000	DetGA1-to-PerGA5	145	15	+
	DetGA1-to-SGA	124	36	+
	DetGA1-to-RIGA	154	6	+
	DetGA1-to-HyperM	159	1	+
8000	DetGA1-to-PerGA5	148	12	+
	DetGA1-to-SGA	129	31	+
	DetGA1-to-RIGA	160	0	+
	DetGA1-to-HyperM	159	1	+

From Wilcoxon signed rank test results, it is clearly shown that DetGA1 is significantly the best algorithm for solving DOPUAVs.

Friedman Test

Finally, a Freidman average ranks test is used to rank the algorithms. Its results are shown in Table 10; this table supports the above-mentioned observations.

Table 10. Freidman test mean ranks for the compared algorithms

	DetGA1	PerGA5	SGA	RIGA	HyperM
Mean Rank	1.34	2.29	2.75	4.06	4.56

5   Summary and Future Work

The Dynamic Optimisation Problem with Unknown Active Variables (DOPUAV) is a dynamic problem, in which the activity of the variables changes as time passes, to simulate the dynamicity in a problem's variables. In this paper, Detectable genetic algorithms (DetGAs) are used to solve DOPUAV. DetGAs try to detect as a problem changes, before detecting the active variables. From DetGAs tested variations, DetGA1, which detects the problem every generation, outperforms the others. Furthermore, DetGA1 is compared with state-of-the-art algorithms, and from these comparisons, DetGA1 proved that it was better, based on statistical analysis compared to all the compared algorithms.

There are many directions for future work. The first direction, because Detectable GA consumes fitness evaluations for detecting problem change, might be better to implicitly detect the mask by observing some behaviour of the problem variables, rather than detecting the problem mask. The second direction is attempting to solve the paired DOPUAVs with dynamic constrained optimisation problems (DCOPs) [4].

References

1. Cruz, C., González, J.R., Pelta, D.A.: Optimization in dynamic environments: a survey on problems, methods and measures. Soft. Comput. **15**, 1427–1448 (2011)
2. Nguyen, T.T., Yangb, S., Branke, J.: Evolutionary dynamic optimization: a survey of the state of the art. Swarm Evol. Comput. **6**, 1–24 (2012)
3. AbdAllah, A.F.M., Essam, D.L., Sarker, R.A.: Solving dynamic optimisation problem with variable dimensions. In: Dick, G., et al. (eds.) SEAL 2014. LNCS, vol. 8886, pp. 1–12. Springer, Heidelberg (2014). doi:10.1007/978-3-319-13563-2_1
4. Nguyen, T.T.: Continuous dynamic optimisation using evolutionary algorithms. Ph.D., p. 300. School of Computer Science, The University of Birmingham, Birmingham (2010)
5. Morrison, R.W.: Performance measurement in dynamic environments. In: GECCO Workshop on Evolutionary Algorithms for Dynamic Optimization Problems, pp. 5–8 (2003)
6. Yang, S., Nguyen, T.T., Li, C.: Evolutionary dynamic optimization: test and evaluation environments. In: Yang, S., Yao, X. (eds.) Evolutionary Computation for DOPs. SCI, vol. 490, pp. 3–37. Springer, Heidelberg (2013). doi:10.1007/978-3-642-38416-5_1
7. Li, C., Yang, S., Nguyen, T.T., Yu, E.L., Yao, X., Jin, Y., Beyer, H.-G., Suganthan, P.N.: Benchmark generator for CEC 2009 competition on dynamic optimization (2008)
8. Simon Fraser University. http://www.sfu.ca/~ssurjano
9. García, S., Molina, D., Lozano, M., Herrera, F.: A study on the use of non-parametric tests for analyzing the evolutionary algorithms' behaviour: a case study on the CEC'2005 special session on real parameter optimization. J. Heuristics **15**, 617–644 (2009)
10. Cobb, H.G.: An investigation into the use of hypermutation as an adaptive operator in genetic algorithms having continuous, time-dependent nonstationary environments. Naval Research Laboratory (1990)
11. Grefenstette, J.J.: Genetic algorithms for changing environments. In: Maenner, R., Manderick, B. (eds.) Parallel Problem Solving from Nature, vol. 2, pp. 137–144. North Holland (1992)
12. Corder, G.W., Foreman, D.I.: Nonparametric Statistics for Non-Statisticians: A Step-by-Step Approach. Wiley, New York (2009)

Neighbourhood Analysis: A Case Study on Google Machine Reassignment Problem

Ayad Turky[1]([✉]), Nasser R. Sabar[2], and Andy Song[1]

[1] School of Computer Science and I.T., RMIT University, Melbourne, Australia
{ayad.turky,andy.song}@rmit.edu.au
[2] Queensland University of Technology, Brisbane, Australia
nasser.sabar@qut.edu.au

Abstract. It is known that neighbourhood structures affect search performance. In this study we analyse a series of neighbourhood structures to facilitate the search. The well known steepest descent (SD) local search algorithm is used in this study as it is parameter free. The search problem used is the Google Machine Reassignment Problem (GMRP). GMRP is a recent real world problem proposed at ROADEF/EURO challenge 2012 competition. It consists in reassigning a set of services into a set of machines for which the aim is to improve the machine usage while satisfying numerous constraints. In this paper, the effectiveness of three neighbourhood structures and their combinations are evaluated on GMRP instances, which are very diverse in terms of number of processes, resources and machines. The results show that neighbourhood structure does have impact on search performance. A combined neighbourhood structures with SD can achieve results better than SD with single neighbourhood structure.

Keywords: Google Machine Reassignment Problem · Neighbourhood structures · Cloud computing · Evolutionary algorithms

1 Introduction

Cloud computing is a fast growing area, which is to provide network access to computing resources including storage, processing and network bandwidth [2,4]. Service providers like Google and Amazon need to manage a large-scale data centers of which the computing resources are to be shared by end users with high quality of service. Recently, with the steady growth of cloud services and Internet, the importance of solving such resource management problems becomes one of the most important targets in the optimisation community [4]. Our study aims to investigate better methodology to optimise cloud computing resource allocation. The task can be considered as a combinatorial optimisation problem.

In particular Google Machine Reassignment Problem (GMRP) is used as the benchmark task. GMRP is proposed at ROADEF/EURO challenge 2012 competition [1]. The main goal of this problem is to optimise the usage of cloud computing resources by reassigning a set of processes across a pool of servers subject to a set of hard constraints which can not be violated. A number of

M. Wagner et al. (Eds.): ACALCI 2017, LNAI 10142, pp. 228–237, 2017.
DOI: 10.1007/978-3-319-51691-2_20

algorithms have been proposed to solve GMRP. These include simulated annealing [11,12,15], variable neighbourhood search [5], constraint programming-based
large neighbourhood search [9], large neighbourhood search [3], multi-start iterated local search [8], memetic algorithm [13], late acceptance hill-climbing [14]
and restricted iterated local search [6].

In this work, we study the behaviours of different neighbourhood structures
on GMRP. A well known local search algorithm, steepest descent (SD) [10], is
used as the base method, as it is completely parameter free [7,17]. SD starts with
an initial solution, then generates a neighbourhood solution. SD repeatedly sub-
stitutes the current solution by the best newly generated solution until there is
no more improvement [17]. Three different neighbourhood structures are investigated in this work. They are Shift, Swap and reassigning big process. The effects
of these neighbourhood structures and their combinations on SD algorithm are
evaluated on instances of GMRP from ROADED/EURO 2012 challenge. These
instances are very diverse in size and features.

The remainder of the paper is organised as follow: In Sect. 2, we present the
problem description. Section 3 describes the neighbourhood structures with the
SD algorithm. Section 4 explains the experimental setting including the problem
instances. Section 5 shows the experimental results. Section 6 is for discussion
which mainly covers the comparison with state of the art methods. This study
is concluded at Sect. 7. The future work is discussed in the last section.

2   Problem Description

GMRP is a combinatorial optimisation problem proposed at ROADEF/EURO
Challenge 2012 Competition [1]. The main elements of this problem are a set of
machines M and a set of processes P. The goal of this problem is to find the
optimal way to assign process $p \in P$ to machines $m \in M$ in order to improve the
usage of a given set of machines. One machine consists of a set of resources such
as CPUs and RAM. One process can be moved from one machine to another to
improve overall machine usage. The allocation of processes must not violate the
following hard constraints:

- *Capacity constraints:* the sum of requirements of resource of all processes does
  not exceed the capacity of the allocated machine.
- *Conflict constraints:* processes of the same service must be allocated into different machines.
- *Transient usage constraints:* if a process is moved from one machine to another,
  it requires adequate amount of capacity on both machines.
- *Spread constraints:* the set of machines is partitioned into locations and
  processes of the same service should be allocated to machines in a number
  of distinct locations.
- *Dependency constraints:* the set of machines are partitioned into neighbourhoods. Then, if there is a service depends on another service, then the process
  of first one should be assigned to the neighbouring machine of second one or
  vice versa.

A feasible solution to GMRP is a process-machine assignment which satisfies all hard constraints and minimises the weighted cost function as much as possible which is calculated as follows:

$$f = \sum_{r \in R} weight_{loadCost}(r) \times loadCost(r)$$

$$+ \sum_{b \in B} weight_{balanceCost}(b) \times balanceCost(b)$$

$$+ weight_{processMoveCost} \times processMoveCost$$

$$+ weight_{serviceMoveCost} \times serviceMoveCost$$

$$+ weight_{machineMoveCost} \times machineMoveCost \tag{1}$$

where R is a set of resources, $loadCost$ represents the used capacity by resource r which exceeds the safety capacity, $balanceCost$ represents the use of available machine, $processMoveCost$ is the cost of moving a process from its current machine to a new one, $serviceMoveCost$ represents the maximum number of moved processes over services and $machineMoveCost$ represents the sum of all moves weighted by relevant machine cost. $weight_{loadCost}$, $weight_{balanceCost}$, $weight_{processMoveCost}$, $weight_{serviceMoveCost}$ and $weight_{machineMoveCost}$ define the importance of each individual cost.

For more details about the constraints, the costs and their weights can be found on the challenge documentation [1]. Note that the quality of a solution is evaluated by the given solution checker, which returns fitness measure to the best solution generated by our proposed algorithm. Another important aspect of this challenge is the time limit. All methods have to finish within the 5-minute timeframe to ensure the fairness of the comparison.

3   Methodology

The aim of this paper is to study the behaviours of different neighbourhood structures on the algorithm for GMRP. We use steepest descent (SD) algorithm to facilitate this study. Fundamentally SD is in the family of gradient descent algorithms, which are to find a local minimum for a certain problem. It starts with an initial random solution and uses a step function to move the search process to other possibly better solutions. The solutions of the next steps are usually in negative direction of the gradient. The move of solution is an iterative process which will eventually converge to the best or the local minimum. It is a kind of first-order algorithm as only the first derivative of the function is used for the descent. Formally the process can be described as:

$$X_{s+1} = X_s - \lambda \nabla f(X_s) \tag{2}$$

where X_s is the solution at Step s, $\nabla f()$ is the gradient or the first derivative. In the formula λ is the step size. Based on the choice of this size, variations of descent algorithm can be generated for example Backtracking, Barzilai and

Borwein. SD is also one type of gradient descent variations. In SD, the step size λ is simply the "best" choice which leads to the minimum objective value. SD can be expressed as:

$$\lambda_s = \arg\min_{\lambda} f(X_k - \lambda \nabla f(X_s)) \tag{3}$$

where the step size at Step s is the minimum descent hence called steepest descent algorithm. The descent process is repetitive and will stop when there is no more improvement [7,10,17]. SD converges linearly and is sensitive to the landscape of problems.

The reason why we choice SD algorithm is that SD is completely parameter free. As shown in the above formulae of SD, no parameter tuning is necessary. This feature allows us to compare different neighbourhood structures without bias from parameter settings [7,17].

Note that SD is traditionally used for continuous non-linear optimisation problems. SD can be modified to suit combinatorial optimisation problems. In this study we enumerate all neighbourhoods around the current solution instead of using Eqs. 2 and 3. The modified SD for GMRP is illustrated in Fig. 1.

The initial solution is generated randomly based on the given instance and evaluated using Eq. 1. The search algorithm then looks around the neighbours of the current solution using a neighbourhood structure. In this work, we use three different neighbourhood structures within SD to deal with GMRP. They are:

- **Shift neighbourhood structure:** A neighbour solution is generated by selecting a process in the current solution and shifting it from its current machine to a different machine.
- **Swap neighbourhood structure:** A neighbour solution is generated by selecting two processes in the current solution and swapping them. These two processes are located at different machines.
  Move Big: In this approach a process with large size is selected and moved to a different machine. The size of such a process is equal to the total resources that required by this process. Moving big processes seems more effective in keeping balance in machine loads.

A search process could use one of the three neighbourhood structures to generate the solutions of next iteration. In addition these three structures can be combined as one structure which is denoted as *Combined*. With the "Combined" structure, a neighbour solution is generated by randomly picking one of the three structures during the search process of SD. The aim is to combine the advantages of these three structures so the search can be more effective. The stopping condition is either no improvement can be found or the maximum time limit is reached. Note GMRP challenge does have a 5-minute limit meaning the search process can not be running for longer than that time period. This is to ensure the real-time or near real-time performance of the optimisation algorithms. The solution returned at termination of SD will be considered as the final solution.

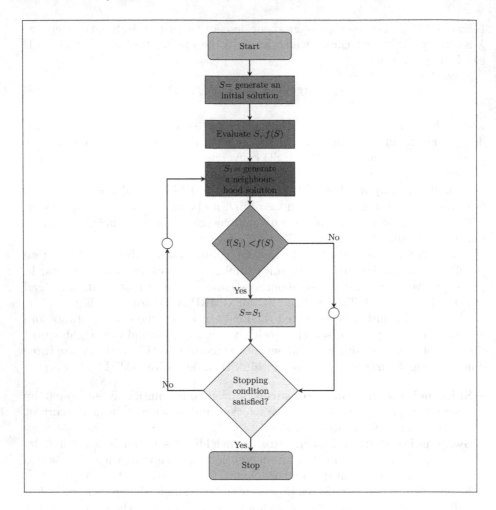

Fig. 1. Flowchart of Steepest Descent (SD) algorithm

4   Experiments

As mentioned early GMRP instances proposed in ROADEF/EURO 2012 challenge are used in this investigation. This is a well-known benchmark for clouding computing optimisation. Five different instances are involved in this study. They have different characteristics in terms of number of machines, number of processes, neighbourhood, and so on. Table 1 shows the main characteristics of the these instances.

These parameters in the table are:

- R is the number of processes;
- TR is the number of resources that need transient usage;
- M is the number of machines;

Table 1. The characteristics of the GMRP instances

Instance	R	TR	M	P	S	L	N	B	SD	Initial cost
a1_1	2	0	4	100	79	4	1	1	0	49,528,750
a1_2	4	1	100	1000	980	4	2	0	40	1,061,649,570
a1_3	3	1	100	1000	216	25	5	0	342	583,662,270
a1_4	3	1	50	1000	142	50	50	1	297	632,499,600
a1_5	4	1	12	1000	981	4	2	1	32	782,189,690

- P is the number of processes;
- S is the number of services;
- L is the number of locations;
- N is the number of neighbourhoods;
- B is number of triples;
- SD is the number of service dependencies;
- $InitialCost$ is the cost assigned with these instances.

As can be seen from Table 1, the number machines in these instances ranges from 4 to 100, and the number of processes ranges from 100 to 1,000. They are quite diverse and could evaluate the impact of neighbourhood structure more effectively. For each experiment we run the search process 30 times on every instance. This is to ensure the results are representative enough and to minimise bias in the comparisons.

5 Results

The experimental results over 30 runs on the four neighbourhood structures are summarised in Table 2. The comparison is based on the best obtained results for each instances. The smaller the number, the lower the cost hence the better the result. In the table, the result in bold is the best result among all neighbourhood structure on one instance, e.g. the best of that row.

Table 2. Comparing four neighbourhood structures: Shift, Swap, Move-Big and Combined

Instance	Shift	Swap	Move-Big	Combined
a1_1	44,306,887	44,306,935	44,306,635	**44,306,501**
a1_2	777,650,528	777,650,817	777,650,474	**777,645,128**
a1_3	583,006,941	583,006,983	583,006,897	**583,006,051**
a1_4	251,015,689	251,015,688	251,015,659	**251,015,654**
a1_5	727,579,589	727,579,586	727,579,582	**727,579,474**

It can be seen that on all instances, the combined neighbourhood structure achieved the best result. All bold results are in the column of "Combined". In fact "Combined" neighbourhood achieved the best on all instances. This result indicates the effectiveness of combined neighbourhood structures compared to other. It can be more adaptive towards the search space by contributing different types of neighbours during a search.

Another observation from the results is that "Move-big" performed considerably better than "Shift" and "Swap". That shows the need of moving a block of processes in generating neighbours. Both "Shift" and "Swap" generate neighbours with single process change. Their performances are quite similar although "Shift" appears slightly better than "Swap".

The results are further analysed by conducting a Wilcoxon statistical test to examine whether a significant difference ($\alpha = 0.05$) exists between the combined neighbourhood structures and other structures (Shift, Swap and Move-Big). Table 3 shows the p-values for all tested instances. From the table, we can see that the p-values on all instances are less than 0.05 which means the combined neighbourhood structures is significantly better than others.

Table 3. The p-values of combined neighbourhood structures against Shift, Swap and Move-Big

Combined VS	Shift	Swap	Move-big
Instance	p-value	p-value	p-value
a1_1	0.00	0.00	0.01
a1_2	0.00	0.00	0.02
a1_3	0.02	0.03	0.00
a1_4	0.00	0.00	0.02
a1_5	0.01	0.00	0.00

6 Discussion

From the above experimental results we can see that the neighbourhood structures do have impact on search performance. Different structure copes with search space differently. With the combined neighbourhood structure, the search can better adapt to the surrounding hence appear more effective.

Although the aim of this study is not to achieve the best possible results for GMRP, but to investigate the impact of neighbourhood structures, we can still compare with the results with that from state of the art algorithms reported in the literature. These leading algorithms include:

1. **MNLS:** Multi-neighborhood local search [16].
2. **VNS:** Variable neighbourhood search [5].
3. **CLNS:** CP-based large neighbourhood search [9].
4. **LNS:** Large neighbourhood search [3].
5. **MILS:** Multi-start iterated local search [8].
6. **SA:** Simulated annealing [11].

Restricted iterated local search [6] is another leading algorithm. However it has no results reported on these GMRP instances hence we excluded it from the comparison. Table 4 lists the results from the aforementioned six leading algorithms for GMRP, plus the results from our SD with combined neighbourhood structure.

Table 4. Comparing with state of the art algorithms on GMRP

	a1_1	a1_2	a1_3	a1_4	a1_5
MNLS	**44,306,501**	777,535,597	**583,005,717**	**248,324,245**	**727,578,309**
VNS	**44,306,501**	777,536,907	583,005,818	251,524,763	727,578,310
CLNS	**44,306,501**	778,654,204	583,005,829	251,189,168	727,578,311
LNS	**44,306,575**	788,074,333	583,006,204	278,114,660	727,578,362
MILS	**44,306,501**	780,499,081	583,006,015	258,024,574	727,578,412
SA	**44,306,935**	**777,533,311**	583,009,439	260,693,258	727,578,311
SD Combined	**44,306,501**	777,645,128	583,006,051	251,015,654	727,579,474

Based on Table 4, we can see that "SD Combined" is at least comparable to these leading algorithms. On instance a1_1, it achieved lowest cost although a few others also achieved equivalent performance. On instance a1_2, "SD Combined" is better than CLNS. It is also better than LNS and SA on a1_3. On a1_4 our method is only second to MNLS and better than the rest including VNS, CLNS, LNS, MILS and SA. On the last instance a1_5, our method is marginally worse than these leading algorithms. It should be noted that MNLS is a multiple neighbourhood algorithm while our study only uses single neighbourhood structure at this stage. Therefore it is easily to see why MNLS has such a good performance.

7   Conclusions

In this paper, we investigated the effect of different neighbourhood structures on the search performance when solving Google Machine Reassignment problem which is a typical combinatorial optimisation task. We investigated three single structures "Shift", "Swap" and "Move Big", and a combined structure. The search itself is based on steepest descent algorithm which is a kind of parameter free local search. Five instances from the Google challenge were used to evaluated the performance of the algorithm. Based on the experimental results, we conclude that neighbourhood structure does have impact on the search performance.

Based on this study we can see that the combined neighbourhood structure is more effective than a single neighbourhood structure. This is possibly due to the ability to choose a structure based on search status. In term of a single structure, generating neighbours based on moving blocks of processes seems more effective than that based on moving single processes.

The comparison between combined neighbourhood structure plus steepest descent with existing state of the art algorithms shows that our method is at least comparable to these leading methods. Although the aim of this study is not to claim top performance, the study shows that with right neighbourhood structures it is possible to achieve top performance.

8 Future Work

This study opens a range of directions for future investigations. One extension is to involve multiple neighbours during the search similar to a population based search. This would lead to high effectiveness and a new method which can outperform other methods. Another immediate future work is involving more instances for evaluation. More neighbourhood structures will be investigated as well such as swapping multiple processes.

References

1. Roadef/euro challenge 2012: Machine reassignment. http://challenge.roadef.org/2012/en/
2. Armbrust, M., Fox, A., Griffith, R., Joseph, A.D., Katz, R., Konwinski, A., Lee, G., Patterson, D., Rabkin, A., Stoica, I., et al.: A view of cloud computing. Commun. ACM 53(4), 50–58 (2010)
3. Brandt, F., Speck, J., Völker, M.: Constraint-based large neighborhood search for machine reassignment. Ann. Oper. Res. 242(1), 63–91 (2016)
4. Calheiros, R.N., Ranjan, R., Beloglazov, A., De Rose, C.A., Buyya, R.: Cloudsim: a toolkit for modeling and simulation of cloud computing environments and evaluation of resource provisioning algorithms. Softw.: Practice Exp. 41(1), 23–50 (2011)
5. Gavranović, H., Buljubašić, M., Demirović, E.: Variable neighborhood search for Google machine reassignment problem. Electron. Discrete Math. 39, 209–216 (2012)
6. Lopes, R., Morais, V.W.C., Noronha, T.F., Souza, V.A.A.: Heuristics and matheuristics for a real-life machine reassignment problem. Int. Trans. Oper. Res. 22(1), 77–95 (2015)
7. Lü, Z., Hao, J.-K., Glover, F.: Neighborhood analysis: a case study on curriculum-based course timetabling. J. Heuristics 17(2), 97–118 (2011)
8. Masson, R., Vidal, T., Michallet, J., Penna, P.H.V., Petrucci, V., Subramanian, A., Dubedout, H.: An iterated local search heuristic for multi-capacity bin packing and machine reassignment problems. Expert Syst. Appl. 40(13), 5266–5275 (2013)
9. Mehta, D., O'Sullivan, B., Simonis, H.: Comparing solution methods for the machine reassignment problem. In: Milano, M. (ed.) CP 2012. LNCS, vol. 7514, pp. 782–797. Springer, Heidelberg (2012). doi:10.1007/978-3-642-33558-7_56
10. Papadimitriou, C.H., Steiglitz, K.: Combinatorial Optimization: Algorithms and Complexity. Courier Corporation, North Chelmsford (1982)
11. Ritt, M.R.P.: An algorithmic study of the machine reassignment problem. Ph.D. thesis, Universidade Federal do Rio Grande do Sul (2012)

12. Sabar, N.R., Song, A.: Grammatical evolution enhancing simulated annealing for the load balancing problem in cloud computing. In: Proceedings of the 2016 on Genetic and Evolutionary Computation Conference, pp. 997–1003. ACM (2016)

13. Sabar, N.R., Song, A., Zhang, M.: A variable local search based memetic algorithm for the load balancing problem in cloud computing. In: Squillero, G., Burelli, P. (eds.) EvoApplications 2016. LNCS, vol. 9597, pp. 267–282. Springer, Heidelberg (2016). doi:10.1007/978-3-319-31204-0_18

14. Turky, A., Sabar, N.R., Sattar, A., Song, A.: Parallel late acceptance hill-climbing algorithm for the Google machine reassignment problem. In: Kang, B.H., Bai, Q. (eds.) AI 2016. LNCS (LNAI), vol. 9992, pp. 163–174. Springer, Heidelberg (2016). doi:10.1007/978-3-319-50127-7_13

15. Turky, A., Sabar, N.R., Song, A.: An evolutionary simulating annealing algorithm for Google machine reassignment problem. In: Leu, G., Singh, H.K., Elsayed, S. (eds.) Intelligent and Evolutionary Systems. PALO, vol. 8, pp. 431–442. Springer, Heidelberg (2017). doi:10.1007/978-3-319-49049-6_31

16. Wang, Z., Lü, Z., Ye, T.: Multi-neighborhood local search optimization for machine reassignment problem. Comput. Oper. Res. **68**, 16–29 (2016)

17. Qinghua, W., Hao, J.-K., Glover, F.: Multi-neighborhood tabu search for the maximum weight clique problem. Ann. Oper. Res. **196**(1), 611–634 (2012)

Optimisation Algorithms and Applications

Multi-objective Optimisation with Multiple Preferred Regions

Md. Shahriar Mahbub[1,2], Markus Wagner[3(✉)], and Luigi Crema[1]

[1] Fondazione Bruno Kessler, Via Sommarive 18, 38123 Povo, Trento, Italy
[2] University of Trento, Via Sommarive 9, 38123 Povo, Trento, Italy
[3] University of Adelaide, Adelaide, SA 5005, Australia
`markus.wagner@adelaide.edu.au`

Abstract. The typical goal in multi-objective optimization is to find a set of good and well-distributed solutions. It has become popular to focus on specific regions of the objective space, e.g., due to market demands or personal preferences.

In the past, a range of different approaches has been proposed to consider preferences for regions, including reference points and weights. While the former technique requires knowledge over the true set of trade-offs (and a notion of "closeness") in order to perform well, it is not trivial to encode a non-standard preference for the latter.

With this article, we contribute to the set of algorithms that consider preferences. In particular, we propose the easy-to-use concept of "preferred regions" that can be used by laypeople, we explain algorithmic modifications of NSGAII and AGE, and we validate their effectiveness on benchmark problems and on a real-world problem.

Keywords: Multi-objective optimization · Preference · Evolutionary algorithm

1 Introduction

For the last two decades, multi-objective evolutionary algorithms (MOEA) have been successfully used to solve multi-objective optimization (MOO) problems. Most real-world problems are MOO problems rather than single objective problems, where it is often found that multiple conflicting objectives exist. Typically, the goal of a MOEA is to find a set of trade-off solutions that are well-distributed over the objective space. Ideally, these solutions are on or at least close to the true set of trade-offs called Pareto front. Sometimes, however, the decision makers/users have little interest in exploring the entire objective space. It may be more interesting to them to explore some preferred regions of a front due to market demands, due to financial pressure, or simply due to curiosity.

Let us consider an energy system optimization problem, where the goal is to minimize CO_2 emission and annual cost [14]. In this case, a reference system is analyzed (generally the current system), optimized systems are identified, and

© Springer International Publishing AG 2017
M. Wagner et al. (Eds.): ACALCI 2017, LNAI 10142, pp. 241–253, 2017.
DOI: 10.1007/978-3-319-51691-2_21

then compared with the reference system. Decision makers are often interested in exploring several regions defined by either CO_2 emission or annual cost. For example, if a reference scenario has x amount of CO_2 emissions, the interesting regions could be 10–20% and 35–40% reduction of x.

There are a few algorithmic advantages in exploring preferred regions over exploring the entire objective space. These include faster convergence speed and better approximation of Pareto front [15]. Based on the idea of incorporating user preference, a wide range of different concepts and algorithms has been proposed (see [1,25] for comprehensive surveys, as it is impossible to list all relevant work here), such as (i) defining reference-point(s) [18,19] and specifying weights in the objective space [9,16]. However, the problem with these approaches typically is that it is difficult to set the corresponding parameters without knowing the shape of the true Pareto front. Therefore, we propose modifications of generic algorithms that require only very intuitive preference encoding in the form of intervals, as outlined above in the energy system example above.

The structure of this article is as follows. First, we introduce basic definitions in Sect. 2 including the idea of preferences for MOEAs. In Sect. 3 we show how we integrate preference information in two algorithms. Lastly, we present and discuss the results of our experimental studies in Sects. 4 and 5.

2   Definitions and Basic Principles

Without loss of generality, a multi-objective problem can be formulated as:

$$min\ F(A) = (f_1(A), f_2(A), ...f_m(A))^T \qquad A \in \mathbb{R}^n \qquad (1)$$

where $A = (a_1, ..., a_n)$ is a vector of n decision variables and m is the number of objectives. In the context of multi-objective optimisation, the optimal solutions are also referred to as non-dominated solutions. In a minimization problem, a solution A is considered non-dominated in comparison to another solution A^* when no objective value of A^* is less than that of A and at least one objective value of A^* is greater than that of A. If necessary, the feasibility of solutions can be considered as well, however, this is not necessary in our study. For a more complete introduction to multi-objective optimization, we refer the interested reader to the overview articles [4,12,24].

There is a fundamental difference between how reference points and weights are defined, and how our preferred regions are defined. A reference point is defined by specifying values for all the dimensions for a point in the objective space. In contrast to this, a preferred region is defined by specifying an upper and lower bound of one particular dimension. For example, if a two-objective problem (objectives are plotted along x and y-axes) is considered, a user can define three preferred regions by setting three upper and lower bounds for intervals along either the x or y axis. Figure 1 illustrates an example of three preferred regions (bounded by three different color vertical lines). In this figure, we also show three reference points (gray crosses) which might have been set by a user. As the user lacks knowledge about the shape of the front, these points are not on the true Pareto front. Consequently, it is left up to the MOEA to follow its own interpretation of "closeness" in order to distribute the solutions around the reference. One outcome is that the solution density is high near the reference point and the density decreases with increasing distance (see Fig. 1 for the outcome of one run by r-NSGAII [7] using the shown reference points). As mentioned before, it is also possible to use weights in the objective space in order to encode preferences. In Fig. 1 we indicate this using a color gradient along the x-axis, where a preference for smaller x-values is encoded. The preference formulation for a single objective using weights is relatively simple, however, the formulation becomes tricky when multiple objectives are preferred, and it becomes very complicated when reference points or preferred regions are to be encoded (using weights). The concept of our interval-based regions, on the other hand, is straightforward to use even for laypeople. To the best of our knowledge, even though there are lots of similar approaches, this is the first time this rather simple concept of intervals along axes is used in the context of MOO.

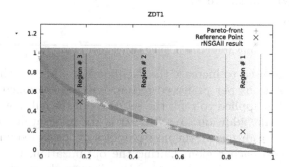

Fig. 1. Reference points, weights in the objective space, and preferred regions. (Color figure online)

3   Preferred Regions for Different MOEAs

In the following, we present the ideas related to preferred regions and the adaptation of the ideas into different MOEAs.

3.1   Ideas Adopted in pNSGAII

We adopt several ideas in NSGAII [6] resulting in pNSGAII. Algorithm 1 presents the main loop of the proposed pNSGAII. There are couple of modifications with respect to the original NSGAII. Firstly, each solution is associated with a particular region (step # 4). Secondly, a parent selection procedure is used (step # 8); thirdly, the individuals of a merged population (containing solutions of the previous generation and the offspring) are associated with nR regions (step # 11) such that for each region, $2*\alpha_i$ individuals are associated. Based on the association, the merged population is divided into nR sub-populations (step # 12).

Algorithm 1. Main loop of pNSGAII

1: nR ▷ Number of given regions
2: α ▷ A set containing user-defined preferred number of solutions for each region; α_i is the number of preferred solutions for i^{th} region
3: Initialize population P with $\sum_{i=1}^{nR} \alpha_i$ random individuals and $O \leftarrow \emptyset$
4: Associate α number of solutions with nR regions
5: **while** Stopping criteria not met **do**
6:     **for** $z \leftarrow 1$ to nR **do**
7:         **for** $j \leftarrow 1$ to $\alpha_z/2$ **do**
8:             Select two parents using modified parent selection procedure
9:             Generate offspring and add to O
10:     $P \leftarrow P \cup O$
11:     Associate $2 * \alpha$ number of solutions with nR regions
12:     Divide P into nR sub-populations ($SP_i; i = 1, \ldots, nR$)
13:     **for** $i \leftarrow 1$ to nR **do**
14:         Rank SP_i and select α_i solutions based on ranking and crowding distance
15:         Add these solutions to SP_i
16:     $P \leftarrow \bigcup_{i=1}^{nR} SP_i$

Sub-populations are used to increase the likelihood of achieving the targeted α_i well-distributed solutions per preferred region. Lastly, a modified ranking procedure (step # 14) is applied to rank the solutions of the sub-populations.[1]

The first important addition to pNSGAII is the association of solutions to regions. Before the optimization, the user provides the preferred number of solutions associated with each region. During the optimization, the solutions are assigned greedily to the regions based on the distance between solutions and regions (see Algorithm 2). The distance from a solution (that is outside of the region) to a region is calculated as $min(|f_i(A) - R_u|, |f_i(A) - R_l|)$, where $f_i(A)$ is the objective value (the objective dimension on which a user specifies the ranges) of a solution. The distance is 0 if a solution is inside a preferred region. Finally, Fig. 2 illustrates an example of Algorithm 2 in step # 11 of Algorithm 1.

In our parent selection procedure, a parent is selected in either one of the following two ways: (i) from the same region that the procedure is currently working on (z^{th} region, step # 6 of Algorithm 1), (ii) from other regions. The selection of parents from other regions depends on a user-defined probability p_{ps}. This approach enables us to prevent an algorithm from getting trapped on a local multi-dimensional front, which we have observed in preliminary experiments.

When a parent is selected from the current working region, a tournament selection based approach is adopted. To select a parent, a given number of tournaments are played between randomly selected associated individuals (associated

---

[1] Consequently, our pNSGAII is somewhat equivalent to an island model approach for multi-objective optimization, with islands being responsible for preferred regions. In contrast to existing island model-MOO approaches (e.g. [2]), we are focussing on user-defined parts of the search space that are defined in an easy-to-use way.

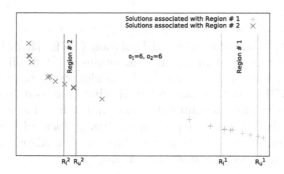

Fig. 2. Association of solutions with regions

Algorithm 2. Associating regions to solutions

1: R_u, R_l ▷ Upper and lower bounds of given regions
2: S ▷ A set containing all the solutions
3: $c\alpha \leftarrow 0$ ▷ Current number of associated solutions with regions
4: **for** $s \in S$ **do**
5:      **for** $i \leftarrow 1$ to nR **do**
6:          **if** s is within R_u^i and R_l^i **And** $c\alpha_i < \alpha_i$ **then**
7:              Associate s with i^{th} region; $c\alpha_i \leftarrow c\alpha_i + 1$ and exit the loop
8:      **if** s is not yet associated **then**
9:          Depending on the status of $c\alpha_j$, associate s with the region j that has minimum distance to s (if $c\alpha_j = \alpha_j$, associate s with the region that has second least distance)
10:         $c\alpha_j \leftarrow c\alpha_j + 1$

---

with the zth region). The winner is decided based on the ordered criteria: (i) distance from a given region, (ii) overall constraints violation [5], (iii) dominance relation. The order of the criteria is strictly followed. Therefore, if a solution is closer than another solution with respect to a given region, then the subsequent two criteria are not considered. The overall constraint violation and dominance relations come into play when two solutions are within the given region.

To rank the individuals, we propose a ranking procedure based on dominance relations and closeness of an individual to the preferred regions (same ordered criteria as in parent selection). However, we do not apply the proposed ranking procedure in all generations, as narrowing down the search to some particular regions from the beginning may be problematic. Therefore, for a particular generation (Step # 14, Algorithm 1), only one of the two ranking procedures (i.e., default NSGAII ranking procedure and proposed ranking procedure) is applied with probability $p_{rk} = \left(\frac{usedBudget}{totalBudget}\right)^n$. The shape of this schedule can be controlled through the exponent n. For $n = 1$, the probability of applying the proposed ranking procedure is increased linearly over time. For larger values of n, the probability increases sharply in later stages of the algorithm's run.

3.2   pAGE

The algorithm Approximation-Guided Evolution (AGE) [3] in its original formulation uses an archive A in which it maintains a list of all non-dominated solutions seen. This archive can grow and thus slow down the algorithm. In its newer version, AGE maintains an archive A^ϵ that is an ϵ-approximation of all non-dominated solutions encountered [21,23] and it uses more efficient parent selection [22]. In the following, we present two straightforward uses of the archive to guide the optimization towards preferred regions (see Algorithm 3). We name the two different uses *pAGEonline* and *pAGEoffline*.

Algorithm 3. $(\mu + \lambda)$-Approximation Guided Evolution with preferences

---

1: Initialize population P with μ random individuals, and set archive $A \leftarrow P$.
2: **for** each generation **do**
3:      Initialize offspring population $O \leftarrow \emptyset$
4:      **for** $j \leftarrow 1$ to λ **do**
5:          Select two random individuals from P, and apply crossover and mutation
6:          Add new individual to O, if it is not dominated by any individual from P
7:      Insert each offspring in the archive A and in the population, i.e., $P \leftarrow P \cup O$
8:      *[pAGEonline]* remove each outlier from P with p_r
9:      **while** $|P| > \mu$ **do**
10:          Remove p from P for which the approximation of A by P is the smallest when p is left away
11: *[pAGEoffline]*   12.1: Remove all outliers from archive A
                    12.2: $P \leftarrow A$
                    12.3: if $|P| > \mu$ then apply steps 9–10 to reduce the P

---

pAGEonline largely corresponds to any of the above-mentioned AGE variants. After the generation of the offspring set O based on the population P, AGE would normally proceed to consider the union $P \cup O$ and then reduce this set greedily to approximate the archive. At this point, we insert one action (step # 8): from the union $P \cup O$ we remove each of the solutions that are outside the preferred regions with probability p_r.

In preliminary experiments we observed that a static choice of $p_r = 1$ can be problematic, as this always removes all outliers. As an alternative to this we decided to increase p_r by reusing the exponential schedule for p_{rk} that we already use in pNSGAII. This way, the pressure remains low for a long time, which allows pAGEonline to find the front, and in the last generations pAGEonline can focus on spreading out the solutions within the preferred regions. Note that this schedule is by no means optimal.

pAGEoffline corresponds to the original AGE with post-processing added. First, pAGEoffline removes all *outliers* (solutions outside the preferred regions) from the archive A, and it assigns a copy of this reduced archive to the population P. Then, as P might be larger than the desired population size, we use AGE's internal reduction mechanism from steps # 9–10 so that P approximates A well.

4   Experimental Study

We conduct a range of experiments to analyze the performance of our proposed algorithms pNSGAII, pAGEonline, and pAGEoffline. The benchmark problems include five two-dimensional benchmark problems from the ZDT family [11] and two three-dimensional problems from the DTLZ family [11]. To the best of our knowledge, no directly comparable algorithms for multiple preferred regions are available from the literature; algorithms that consider reference point(s) have a different goal, which puts them at a disadvantage by definition (see Sect. 2). Therefore, we compare our approaches with their original algorithms, and we vary the evaluation budgets and population sizes to investigate the effectiveness.

4.1   Experimental Setup

We developed all algorithms in the jMetal framework [8], which is a Java-based multi-objective meta-heuristic framework. Initially, each pMOEA variant is tested on the ZDT family with two configurations, based on population size μ and maximum function evaluations (FE). Table 1 presents the different configurations used in the experiments. The configurations are chosen in this way to demonstrate the efficiency of pMOEA in terms of convergence speed.

We consider short and long runs with an evaluation budget of $FE = 12000$ and $FE = 24000$ respectively. On the ZDT[2] family, we conduct only short runs of the pMOEAs, and we compare these with short and long runs of the original MOEAs to investigate the efficiency. For the DTLZ[3] functions, we only use a single configuration of the original algorithm since the solutions with an increased population size, are otherwise the solutions would be very thinly spread out over the three-dimensional front.[4]

In this study, the regions are defined in terms of R_l and R_u along the first objective. The regions are $[0.80, 0.95]$, $[0.40, 0.50]$ and $[0.15, 0.20]$. Moreover, we set $\alpha = [10, 10, 10]$ for pNSGAII so that 10 solutions will be associated with each region - this was chosen arbitrarily, however, it is possible to have different numbers of solutions associated with different regions. Simulated binary crossover, polynomial mutation, and binary tournament selection [6] are used with their default values in the jMetal framework. In addition, $n = 10$ is used for p_{rk} and p_r for pNSGAII and pAGEonline, respectively. $p_{ps} = 0.20$ is used within pNS-GAII's parent selection procedure. In pAGEonline, $\epsilon_{grid} = 0.01$ is used for the approximating archive.

---

[2] The ZDT functions are used as provided by the jMetal framework. The number of decision variables is 30 for ZDT1/2/3 and 10 for ZDT4/6.

[3] Number of decision variables is 12 for DTLZ2/3, as set in the jMetal framework.

[4] If we use $\mu = 30$ for typical MOEA (please see Table 1) then it is less probable to find adequate number of solutions in preferred regions, that makes it difficult to compare with pMOEA. In addition, compared in terms of FE, MOEA uses 50 less function evaluations than pMOEA only because the number is compatible with μ (no extra function evaluations after completing last generation).

Table 1. Configurations in terms of population size μ and evaluation budget FE to test the efficiency of the interval-based preferences.

Problem	Algorithm	μ	FE
ZDT	pMOEA	30	12000
	MOEA	30	12000
		100	12000
		100	24000
DTLZ	pMOEA	30	50000
	MOEA	150	49950

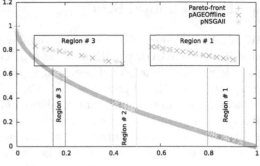

Fig. 3. Pareto fronts obtained by pAGEoffline and pNSGAII on ZDT1 problem.

Over the years, a number of evaluation metrics for multi-objective optimization algorithms have been proposed. We use the popular ones available in the jMetal framework, i.e., the covered hypervolume (HV) [10], and additive ϵ-approximation (EPS) [13] to measure the performance of the MOEAs[5]. We use them with a simple modification, i.e., separately for each preferred region. As the true Pareto front is required for the calculation of EPS values, we use the ones provided by the jMetal framework. From these, we extract the regional fronts from the original ones by discarding all outliers. To calculate HV values, we define the reference point for each region to be based on the extreme values in the preferred region. For example, in the introductory Fig. 1, these reference points are (0.2, 0.62), (0.5, 0.38), and (0.95, 0.1). It is important to note that performance indicators for preference-incorporating algorithms exist (e.g. [10]), however, these are for reference point-based approaches and thus not applicable.

We run each algorithm independently 100 times and report the averaged indicator values in the following.[6]

4.2 Results and Discussion

Firstly, we present in Fig. 3 an example of Pareto fronts obtained. We can observe that the solutions are concentrated in the user-defined regions.

Next, we report the results in terms of mean values and the corresponding standard deviations of HV and EPS for each region. Figure 4 shows a subset of the results. In different colours and by using markers of different shapes, we show how our pMOEAs perform compared to their original variants. The top two rows of plots show the results for the NSGAII variants (colour ●, different shapes indicating the different configurations), and in the third row we show the AGE results (colour ●). In the following, we summarize the results (See footnote 6).

---

[5] We do not report other indicator values, such as inverted generational distance (IGD) [20] or the Hausdorff distance [19] due to space constraints.

[6] We uploaded all code and results to https://github.com/shaikatcse/pMOEAs. This includes pSPEA2 as an algorithm and also IGD indicator values.

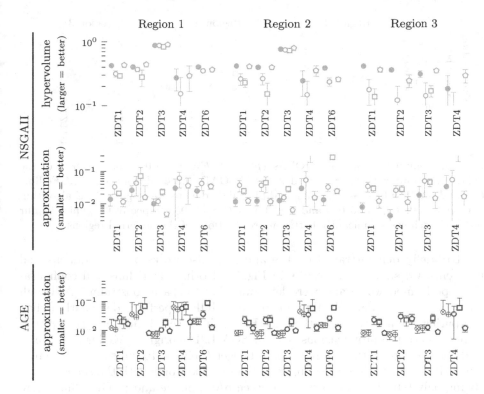

Fig. 4. Comparison of our pMOEAs with their original variants on the ZDT functions with $m = 2$. The Regions 1–3 are defined in Sect. 4.1. Shown are the means and standard deviations of 100 independent runs. From top to bottom, we show the results of NSGAII variants (colour ●), and AGE variants (colour ●). Within each block of four (respectively five) markers, we first show our pMOEA variant with ●, then with ○ and □ the original algorithm with two population sizes ($\mu = 30$ and $\mu = 100$, $FE = 12,000$ each), and then with ○ the original algorithm with twice the evaluation budget ($\mu = 100$, $FE = 24,000$). For pAGE, instead of solid circles, the crossed circles denote our pAGEoffline (×) and pAGEonline (+) variants. In short, the original algorithm with twice the evaluation budget typically performs similar to our pMOEAs. (Color figure online)

Most of the time, pNSGAII outperforms NSGAII with the same evaluation budget ($FE = 12000$) regardless of μ. pNSGAII performs similarly to NSGAII ($FE = 24000$) a number of times, i.e. on all regions for ZDT1/ZDT2 and regions #1/#2 for ZDT6. pNSGAII fails to converge on ZDT4 due to local optima.

The next row in Fig. 4 demonstrates the comparison of pAGE variants (i.e., online and offline) and AGE with different configurations; we limit ourselves to approximation values due to space constraints. pAGEonline and offline perform consistently better in comparison to the generic AGE (with $FE = 12000$ regardless of μ) for almost all the regions and all the problems. When comparing with AGE ($FE = 24000$), sometimes pAGE performs better (ZDT1 and ZDT3), sometimes similar (ZDT2, ZDT6) and sometimes worse (ZDT4).

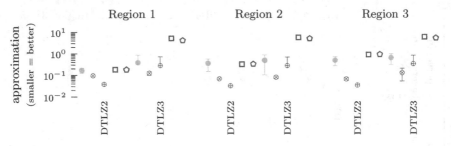

Fig. 5. Comparison of our pMOEAs ($\mu = 30$, $FE = 50,000$) on a subset of the DTLZ functions with $m = 3$. ● denotes pNSGAII and ● denotes our pAGEoffline (×) and pAGEonline (+) variants, and □ and ◇ denote the original AGE algorithm with $\mu = 100$, $FE = 50,000$ and $\mu = 150$, $FE = 49,950$ respectively. Typically, our pMOEAs achieve significantly better approximations of the preferred regions.

To briefly demonstrate that the approach also works on three-dimensional problems, we show a few results in Fig. 5; all other algorithms and configurations performed worse and were left away due to space constraints. Although on the two-dimensional ZDT problems, all pMOEAs performed similarly (when comparing them with each other, see Fig. 4), it is clear from Fig. 5 that pAGE achieves better approximations than pNSGAII. The original AGE is not able to find the front given the computational budget (being 1–10 units away), whereas our pMOEAs achieve good approximations of the fronts with the same budget (being only 0.05–0.5 unit away). Between pAGEonline and pAGEoffline, there is no clear winner.

We conclude from these results that our pMOEAs are efficient and effective for considering user-defined regions.

5   pNSGAII on Energy System Optimization Problem

To investigate the performance of our approach on a real-world problem, we have applied pNSGAII on an energy system optimization problem [14]. We are not considering pAGE here as it does not have any means of dealing with constraints.

The general goal of the problem is to identify multiple optimal systems in order to minimize CO_2 emission and annual cost. Here, we want to identify multiple optimal systems for three specific regions of interest (i.e., 10 solutions for each region) for the Aalborg energy system [17]. The three regions are defined in terms of CO_2 emission (i.e., [0.40, 0.5], [0.0, 0.15] and [−0.40, −0.50]). For example, we are interested in identifying 10 optimal solutions in a region within 0.40 to 0.5 million tons of CO_2 emission. Details of energy system optimization framework and Aalborg energy system can be found in [14].

The result is illustrated in Fig. 6; x-axis presents emission in million tons and y-axis presents annual cost in million Danish Krone. The gray points represent the true Pareto front, which is approximated by considering the outcomes of 240 independent runs of multi-objective algorithms. The red marker show the solutions found by our pNSGAII ($\mu = 30$, $EF = 6000$, problem-specific constraint

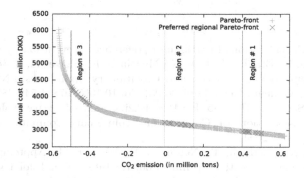

Fig. 6. Result of the energy system optimization. Shown is the final solution set computed by pNSGAII. (Color figure online)

handling was added): 10 solutions per region are found, and they are very close to optimal solutions. As the experiment achieved these set goals, we conclude that our proposed approach can not only be successfully applied to test functions, but also to real-world optimization problems.

6   Conclusions

In this article, we proposed the concept of incorporating multiple user preferences into MOEAs via the use of intervals. The concept was designed with laypeople in mind who might not have detailed knowledge about the objective space.

We presented modifications for two MOEAs to handle multiple preferences, and we demonstrated the resulting capability on two- and three-dimensional test problems. On two-dimensional problems, our pMOEAs typically achieve the same hypervolume and additive approximation values as the original algorithms, where the latter had twice the evaluation budget. On three-dimensional problems, our online and offline variants of AGE with preferences perform best. Finally, the effectiveness of the algorithm is investigated on a real-world problem.

As solutions can be spread too diversely over the objective space for higher dimension problems (having more than 3 objectives), we think that preferences in general can be an interesting option for decision makers.

Our future work will include the adaption of the techniques to the higher dimensional problems. Technically, the extension is straightforward, as the intervals just have to be added to an internal array. Whether the approaches are effective in higher-dimensional objective spaces remains to be seen.

Acknowledgements. This work has been supported by the ARC Discovery Early Career Researcher Award DE160100850.

References

1. Branke, J.: Consideration of partial user preferences in evolutionary multiobjective optimization. In: Branke, J., Deb, K., Miettinen, K., Słowiński, R. (eds.) Multiobjective Optimization: Interactive and Evolutionary Approaches. LNCS, vol. 5252, pp. 157–178. Springer, Heidelberg (2008). doi:10.1007/978-3-540-88908-3_6
2. Branke, J., Schmeck, H., Deb, K.: Parallelizing multi-objective evolutionary algorithms: cone separation. In: Congress on Evolutionary Computation (CEC), vol. 2, pp. 1952–1957 (2004)
3. Bringmann, K., Friedrich, T., Neumann, F., Wagner, M.: Approximation-guided evolutionary multi-objective optimization. In: International Joint Conference on Artificial Intelligence (IJCAI), pp. 1198–1203. AAAI (2011)
4. Chand, S., Wagner, M.: Evolutionary many-objective optimization: a quick-start guide. Surv. Oper. Res. Manag. Sci. $20(2)$, 35–42 (2015)
5. Deb, K.: An efficient constraint handling method for genetic algorithms. Comput. Methods Appl. Mech. Eng. $186(2–4)$, 311–338 (2000)
6. Deb, K., Pratap, A., Agarwal, S., Meyarivan, T.: A fast and elitist multiobjective genetic algorithm: NSGA-II. Trans. Evol. Comp. $6(2)$, 182–197 (2002)
7. Deb, K., Sundar, J., Udaya Bhaskara, R.N., Chaudhuri, S.: Reference point based multi-objective optimization using evolutionary algorithms. Int. J. Comput. Intell. Res. 2, 635–642 (2006)
8. Durillo, J.J., Nebro, A.J.: jMetal: a Java framework for multi-objective optimization. Adv. Eng. Softw. 42, 760–771 (2011)
9. Friedrich, T., Kroeger, T., Neumann, F.: Weighted preferences in evolutionary multi-objective optimization. In: Wang, D., Reynolds, M. (eds.) AI 2011. LNCS (LNAI), vol. 7106, pp. 291–300. Springer, Heidelberg (2011). doi:10.1007/978-3-642-25832-9_30
10. Guo, Y., Zheng, J., Li, X.: An improved performance metric for multiobjective evolutionary algorithms with user preferences. In: Congress on Evolutionary Computation (CEC), pp. 908–915 (2015)
11. Huband, S., Hingston, P., Barone, L., While, L.: A review of multiobjective test problems and a scalable test problem toolkit. Trans. Evol. Comput. $10(5)$, 477–506 (2006)
12. Ishibuchi, H., Tsukamoto, N., Nojima, Y.: Evolutionary many-objective optimization: a short review. In: Congress on Evolutionary Computation (CEC), pp. 2419–2426 (2008)
13. Laumanns, M., Thiele, L., Deb, K., Zitzler, E.: Combining convergence and diversity in evolutionary multiobjective optimization. Evol. Comput. $10(3)$, 263–282 (2002)
14. Mahbub, M.S., Cozzini, M., Østergaard, P.A., Alberti, F.: Combining multi-objective evolutionary algorithms and descriptive analytical modelling in energy scenario design. Appl. Energ. 164, 140–151 (2016)
15. Mohammadi, A., Omidvar, M., Li, X.: A new performance metric for user-preference based multi-objective evolutionary algorithms. In: Congress on Evolutionary Computation (CEC), pp. 2825–2832 (2013)
16. Nguyen, A.Q., Wagner, M., Neumann, F.: User preferences for approximation-guided multi-objective evolution. In: Dick, G., Browne, W.N., Whigham, P., Zhang, M., Bui, L.T., Ishibuchi, H., Jin, Y., Li, X., Shi, Y., Singh, P., Tan, K.C., Tang, K. (eds.) SEAL 2014. LNCS, vol. 8886, pp. 251–262. Springer, Heidelberg (2014). doi:10.1007/978-3-319-13563-2_22

17. Østergaard, P.A., Mathiesen, B.V., Möller, B.: A renewable energy scenario for Aalborg municipality based on low-temperature geothermal heat, wind power and biomass. Energy **35**(12), 4892–4901 (2010)
18. Purshouse, R.C., Deb, K., Mansor, M.M., Mostaghim, S., Wang, R.: A review of hybrid evolutionary multiple criteria decision making methods. In: 2014 IEEE Congress on Evolutionary Computation (CEC), pp. 1147–1154. IEEE (2014)
19. Rudolph, G., Schütze, O., Grimme, C., Trautmann, H.: A multiobjective evolutionary algorithm guided by averaged Hausdorff distance to aspiration sets. In: Tantar, A.-A., et al. (eds.) EVOLVE - A Bridge between Probability, Set Oriented Numerics, and Evolutionary Computation V. AISC, vol. 288, pp. 261–273. Springer, Heidelberg (2014). doi:10.1007/978-3-319-07494-8_18
20. Sato, H., Aguirre, H., Tanaka, K.: Local dominance using polar coordinates to enhance multiobjective evolutionary algorithms. In: Congress on Evolutionary Computation (CEC), pp. 188–195 (2004)
21. Wagner, M., Bringmann, K., Friedrich, T., Neumann, F.: Efficient optimization of many objectives by approximation-guided evolution. Eur. J. Oper. Res. **243**(2), 465–479 (2015)
22. Wagner, M., Friedrich, T.: Efficient parent selection for approximation-guided evolutionary multi-objective optimization. In: Congress on Evolutionary Computation (CEC), pp. 1846–1853 (2013)
23. Wagner, M., Neumann, F.: A fast approximation-guided evolutionary multi-objective algorithm. In: Genetic and Evolutionary Computation Conference (GECCO), pp. 687–694. ACM (2013)
24. Wagner, T., Beume, N., Naujoks, B.: Pareto , aggregation-, and indicator-based methods in many-objective optimization. In: Obayashi, S., Deb, K., Poloni, C., Hiroyasu, T., Murata, T. (eds.) EMO 2007. LNCS, vol. 4403, pp. 742–756. Springer, Heidelberg (2007). doi:10.1007/978-3-540-70928-2_56
25. Wierzbicki, A.P.: Reference point approaches. In: Gal, T., Stewart, T.J., Hanne, T. (eds.) Multicriteria Decision Making, vol. 21, pp. 237–275. Springer, Heidelberg (1999)

An Adaptive Memetic Algorithm for the Architecture Optimisation Problem

Nasser R. Sabar[1] and Aldeida Aleti[2(✉)]

[1] Queensland University of Technology, Brisbane, Australia
nasser.sabar@qut.edu.au
[2] Faculty of Information Technology, Monash University, Melbourne, Australia
aldeida.aleti@monash.edu

Abstract. Architecture design is one of the most important steps in software development, since design decisions affect the quality of the final system (e.g. reliability and performance). Due to the ever-growing complexity and size of software systems, deciding on the best design is a computationally intensive and complex task. This issue has been tackled by using optimisation method, such as local search and genetic algorithms. Genetic algorithms work well in rugged fitness landscapes, whereas local search methods are successful when the search space is smooth. The strengths of these two algorithms have been combined to create memetic algorithms, which have shown to be more efficient than genetic algorithms and local search on their own. A major point of concern with memetic algorithms is the likelihood of loosing the exploration capacity because of the 'exploitative' nature of local search. To address this issue, this work uses an adaptive scheme to control the local search application. The utilised scheme takes into account the diversity of the current population. Based on the diversity indicator, it decides whether to call local search or not. Experiments were conducted on the component deployment problem to evaluates the effectiveness of the proposed algorithm with and without the adaptive local search algorithm.

Keywords: Architecture optimisation · Adaptive memetic algorithm · Component deployment

1 Introduction

The design of software architectures is one of the most creative and difficult stages of software development. The decisions made at this stage affect the quality of the final system. For instance, deciding how to deploy software components into the hardware architecture affects the reliability of the system. When frequently interacting components are deployed into different hardware hosts, the failure rate of the network being used will have an impact on the reliability of the system. Perhaps a better solution is to deploy these frequently interacting components into the same hardware host. This, however, has an impact on safety, due to common cause failures. If one of the components is a redundant replica of

M. Wagner et al. (Eds.): ACALCI 2017, LNAI 10142, pp. 254–265, 2017.
DOI: 10.1007/978-3-319-51691-2_22

the other, the components should be deployed into different hosts. As a result, the failure of the hardware unit that hosts one of the redundant components is not going to affect the working of the other components, and the system may continue without failing.

In small-scale software systems, where quality considerations are limited to one or two non-functional attributes, making design decisions may not be difficult. However, software systems are becoming more complex, with more quality attributes to consider, which usually conflict with each other, such as cost and reliability. The scale of software systems is also growing, which makes software architecture design an increasingly difficult endeavour. In order to assist software architect with design decision, optimisation methods can be used. Many examples of such approaches can be found in the literature, where optimisation methods have been applied to software product line architectures [14], to assist with class design [24] and software architecture design [2,17].

Current approaches in automating the architecture design space exploration focus on search-based methods [4]. This is mainly due to the complexity of the problem, which is usually related to the large set of possible solutions, and the non-linear and non-differentiable quality attributes, such as safety, reliability and performance. The area is broadly known as search-based software engineering (SBSE), and is concerned with finding a near-optimal solution in a reasonable amount of time for problems where exact methods are not feasible. Examples of search-based methods applied to software architecture design are genetic algorithms (GAs) [8] and local search (LS) [11]. GAs are stochastic search methods that mimic the evolutionary process of natural selection in solving optimisation problems. The crossover and mutation operators create new solutions from existing solutions by combining information from parent solutions, or introducing new information. LS examines a set of neighbouring points and moves to the one having the best fitness (smallest in minimisation problems, and highest in maximisation problems). The process is then iterated from the newly chosen solution.

Since LS only considers neighbouring solutions, it is prone to getting stuck in a local optima [1]. This is not an issue for GAs. On the other hand, results from the applications of traditional GAs demonstrate that these methods may experience slow convergence when solving constrained optimisation problems [22]. The strengths of GAs and LS have been combined to create a new optimisation method known as memetic algorithm (MA). MAs incorporates LS with the traditional GA to compensate for its slow convergence as LS possesses an efficient exploitation process. Yet, the application of LS at every iteration has a great effect on the behaviour of the MA and search efficacy. This is mainly due to the fact that calling LS at every iteration is computationally expensive and the search may lose the exploration capacity.

To address this issue, we propose an adaptive memetic algorithm (AMA), which adaptively controls the application of LS based on the diversity of the current population. The adaptation scheme does not only save computational time but can also balance between GA exploration and LS exploitation. The proposed AMA is applied to component deployment optimisation problem [2,6], which is one of the aspects that has to be considered during architecture design of embedded systems. A set of experiments is designed with randomly generated instances, which are used to evaluate the performance of the proposed AMA. A comparison between the results of GA, LS, the standard MA and proposed AMA is conducted.

The findings from this work help in designing better optimisation algorithms for software architecture optimisation problems, and more in general, for software engineering problems. They show that combining the strengths of optimisation methods by hybridising them lead to better optimisation strategies. The adaptation mechanisms is necessary, since different problem instances may have different fitness landscapes, which makes certain search strategies more successful than others. The success of the search method is problem dependent, hence adaptive methods that change the search strategy based on feedback from the optimisation process outperform static search strategies.

2   Related Work

The component deployment problem, and the effect of the deployment architectures on the quality of the final system has been observed by many authors, in both software and embedded systems domain [20,21], focusing on models propagating hardware quality attributes to the software level. A systematic literature review on software architecture optimisation methods provides an overview of the different models used to estimate the quality of a software system [4].

Methods that automate the design space exploration with respect to various quality attributes and constraints use approximate methods. Some approaches consider user requirements as constraints [16], whereas others seek an optimal deployment, or at least solutions that are near-optimal [6], often in combination with constraints [2,6]. Aleti et al. [5] formulated the component deployment problem as a biobjective problem with data transmission reliability and communication overhead as fitness functions. Memory capacity constraints, location and colocation constraints were considered in the formulation. The problem was later re-formulated in terms of reliability optimisation, and solved using a constraint programming technique [26].

In general, approximate algorithms used for the optimisation of software architectures fall into two categories: heuristic [6,12] and meta-heuristics methods, such as genetic algorithms [2,3], tabu search [19] and ant colony optimisation (ACO) [5,26]. The review of the related approaches shows that approximate optimisation methods, and in particular evolutionary algorithms, are widely and successfully used to solve complex problems in the area of software architectures. However, these achievements are the result of careful algorithm design which involves substantial efforts in defining a problem's representation and the selection of the algorithm parameters [2]. These efforts are a reflection of the fact that approximate methods behave differently for different problems and even problem instances [9].

In recent years, there has been an increasing attention on developing variants of adaptive memetic algorithms (AMAs). Most of these works are concerned with either how to adaptively change the parameter settings of employed local search algorithm or how to adaptively select a local search algorithm at each stage of the evolution process [22]. Yet, only a few works focused on how to adaptively decide if the local search should be applied or not. For example, Neri et al. [23] proposed a fast adaptive memetic algorithm that utilises a pool of local search algorithms for continuous optimisation problems. The application of the local search algorithm is controlled by fitness diversity of the current population, improving the performance of the MA.

Krasnogor and Smith [18] proposed MA with self-adaptive local search for the travelling salesman problem. The Monte Carlo like local search is executed in two different ways: when the population is diverse, it tries to exploit the current area of the search space and when the diversification of the population is low, it acts as a exploration method. The proposed MA was found to produce very promising results. Tang et al. [25] introduced a parallel memetic algorithm for solving large scale combinatorial optimisation problems. The method employs two diversity strategies: static adaptive strategy and dynamic adaptive strategy to control the application of the local search algorithm. Both strategies were tested on the large-scale quadratic assignment problems and it was shown that MA with adaptive produce competitive solutions when compared to the traditional MA.

Despite their success in solving difficult optimisation problems, MAs and adaptive MAs have not been applied to the software architecture optimisation problem. Adaptive MAs adjust the search strategy to the problem being optimised using feedback from the optimisation process. The adaptation of the search strategy is motivated by the fact that different problems require different optimisation methods [10]. When new problems arise, it is not possible to know beforehand what optimisation strategy would be successful. Ideally, the optimisation method should be adapted during the run [7], which prompted the application of an adaptive MA to solve the component deployment problem.

3   Component Deployment

One of the most crucial decisions that have to be made during the design of embedded systems is the deployment of software components to the hardware hosts, and the assignment of inter-component communications to network links. The way the components are deployed affects many aspects of the final system, such as the processing speed of the software components, how much hardware is used or the reliability of the execution of different functionalities [5, 21].

Software components are denoted as $\mathcal{C} = \{c_1, c_2, ..., c_n\}$, where $n \in \mathbb{N}$. The software system starts its execution in one software component. During the execution of the system, other components may be activated. Each component is annotated with the following properties: memory size sz expressed in kilobytes (KB), workload wl, which is the computational cost measured in million instructions (MI), initiation probability q_i, denoting the probability that the execution of a system starts from component c_i.

Software components may interact during the execution of the software system. Each interaction from component c_i to c_j is annotated with the following properties: data size ds_{ij} in kilobytes, refers to the amount of data transmitted from software component c_i to c_j during a single communication event, next-step probability p_{ij} the probability that the execution of component c_i ends with a call to component c_j.

The hardware architecture is composed of a distributed set of hardware hosts, denoted as $\mathcal{H} = \{h_1, h_2, ..., h_m\}$, where $m \in \mathbb{N}$ is the number of the hardware units, with different capacities of memory, processing power, access to sensors and other peripherals. The parameters of the hardware architecture are as follows: memory capacity (cp) expressed in kilobytes, processing speed (ps) is the instruction-processing capacity of the hardware unit, expressed in million instructions per second (MIPS), failure rate (fr), which characterises the probability of a single hardware unit failure. The hardware hosts are connected via links denoted as $\mathcal{N} = \{n_1, n_2, ...n_s\}$, with the following properties: data rate (dr_{ij}) is the data transmission rate of the bus, expressed in kilobytes per second (KBPS), failure rate (fr_{ij}) is the exponential distribution characterising the data communication failure of each link.

The component deployment problem is defined as $D = \{d \mid d : \mathcal{C} \to \mathcal{H}\}$, where D is the set of all functions assigning components to hardware resources. Each deployment solution is encoded as $d_i = [d_i(c_1), d_i(c_2), ..., d_i(c_n)]$, where $d_i(c_j)$ represents the hardware host where component c_j is deployed.

3.1 Reliability Estimation

The reliability of a software system is obtained from the mean and variance of the number of executions of components, and the failure parameters of the components [21]. Initially, the reliability of a component c_i is calculated as $R_i = e^{-\text{fr}_{d(c_i)} \cdot \frac{\text{wl}_i}{\text{ps}_{d(c_i)}}}$, where $d(c_i)$ is the deployment function that gives the host where the component c_i has been allocated. The reliability of a communication network is a function of the data rates dr and data sizes ds required for software communication. The reliability of the communication between component c_i and c_j is calculated as $R_{ij} = e^{-\text{fr}_{d(c_i)d(c_j)} \cdot \frac{ds_{ij}}{dr_{d(c_i)d(c_j)}}}$.

The reliability of a software systems depends on the number of times each component is executed. The *expected number of executions* for each component $v : C \to \mathbb{R}_{\geq 0}$ is estimated as $v_i = q_i + \sum_{j \in \mathcal{I}} v_j \cdot p_{ji}$, where $\mathcal{I}$ denotes the index set of all components. The execution transfer probabilities p_{ji} are represented in a matrix form $P_{n \times n}$, where n is the number of components. Similarly, the probabilities q_i of initiating the execution at component c_i are represented by matrix $Q_{n \times 1}$. The matrix of expected number of executions for all components $V_{n \times 1}$ is calculated as $V = Q + P^T \cdot V$.

The reliability of a system is also affected by the failure rate of the network. The higher the network usage, the higher is the probability of producing an incorrect output. Naturally, the execution of a software system cannot start in a network link, and the only predecessor of link l_{ij} is component c_i. Hence, the expected number of using the network links $v : C \times C \rightarrow \mathbb{R}_{\geq 0}$ is calculated as $v_{ij} = v_i \cdot p_{ij}$. Finally, the reliability of a deployment architecture $d \in D$ is

$$R = \prod_{i=1}^{n} R_i^{v_i} \prod_{i,j \text{ (if used)}} R_{ij}^{v_{ij}}. \tag{1}$$

Equation (1) is the objective function used for optimising the deployment of software components to hardware hosts.

Hardware resources have limited memory, which enforces a constraint on the possible components that can be deployed into each hardware host. During the allocation of software components, memory restrictions have to be dealt with, in order to make sure that there is available memory in the hardware units. Formally, the memory constraint is defined as $\sum_{i=1}^{n} sz_i x_{ij} \leq cp_j, \quad \forall j \in \{1, \ldots, m\}$, where x_{ij} is 1 if the software component i is deployed on the hardware unit j, and 0 otherwise.

4   Adaptive Memetic Algorithm

Similar to a traditional GA, the adaptive memetic algorithm (AMA) [22] starts with a population of solutions, which may be randomly generated or obtained through expert knowledge. AMA repeatedly modifies solutions through the application of crossover and mutation operators. The selection operator chooses the next generation of solutions.

Different from GA, AMA employs LS in an adaptive manner to refine the solution quality and to improve the convergence process. However, LS is a computationally expensive process, since at each step, it has to evaluate all neighbouring solutions (worst case). Furthermore, LS is an intensification process which may lead to premature convergence, hence it should be applied with care.

To minimise the computational cost, and carefully tune the balance between exploration by GA and exploitation by LS, AMA employs a population diversity-based metric to decide when to apply LS. Most likely, when population diversity is low, LS-based intensification would not help to improve the quality of the solutions, since the population might have already converged. On the other hand, high diversity in the population means that the exploration process has created a good spread of solutions in the search space, and LS has more space for improvement (intensification). The pseudocode of the proposed AMA is shown in Algorithm 1.

AMA takes as input the population size (PS), crossover rate (CR), mutation rate (MR) and the maximum number of generations (Max_G) (line 1). Next, a population of PS solutions are randomly generated (line 2) and then evaluated (line 3). The main loop of AMA is executed for a fixed number of generations (lines 5–24). At each generation, AMA selects two parents from the given population of solutions (lines 7 and 8) using stochastic universal sampling (SUS). Next, AMA checks the crossover probability condition (line 9), and calls the crossover operator (single-point crossover) to combine the selected parents

---

Algorithm 1. Adaptive memetic algorithm

---

1 **Input**: Population size, PS, crossover rate, CR, mutation rate, MR, and the maximum number of generations, Max_G;

2 $P\_Sol \leftarrow$ RANDOMLYGENERATEPOPULATION(PS);

3 Evaluate P_Sol;

4 $iter \leftarrow 0$;

5 **while** $iter < Max\_G$ **do**

6 | /*Selection procedure*/;

7 | $P_1 \leftarrow$ SUS(P_Sol) ;

8 | $P_2 \leftarrow$ SUS(P_Sol) ;

9 | **if** RAND($[0,1]$)$<CR$ **then**

10 | | /*Apply the crossover operator*/;

11 | | $P'_1, P'_2 \leftarrow$ CROSSOVER(P_1, P_2);

12 | **end**

13 | **if** RAND($[0,1]$) $<MR$ **then**

14 | | /*Apply the mutation operator*/;

15 | | MUTATE(P'_1, P'_2);

16 | **end**

17 | $\mathcal{D} \leftarrow 1 - \left| \frac{f_{avg} - f_{best}}{f_{worst} - f_{best}} \right|$;

18 | **if** $\mathcal{D} > th$ **then**

19 | | /*Call the local search algorithm*/;

20 | | LS(P'_1, P'_2);

21 | **end**

22 | Update the population (P_Sol);

23 | $iter \leftarrow iter + 1$;

24 **end**

25 **Output** Best solution found

(line 11). Based on the mutation probability (line 13), the solutions generated by the crossover operator are modified by the one-flip mutation operator, which changes the mapping of a random component from a given offspring (line 15). Next, AMA calculates the diversity of the population [23] as follows (line 17):

$$\mathcal{D} = 1 - \left| \frac{f_{\text{avg}} - f_{\text{best}}}{f_{\text{worst}} - f_{\text{best}}} \right| \tag{2}$$

where f_{avg}, f_{best} and f_{worst} are the average fitness of the population, the fitness of the best solution, and the fitness of the worst solution, respectively. LS is executed if the diversity metric is greater than the threshold value th (line 20). In this work, we use the simple descent local search algorithm (SDLS). SDLS takes both offsprings (P'_1, P'_2) and iteratively improves their quality by checking their neighbours and substituting them with the first better neighbour. The one-flip procedure is used as the neighbourhood operator.

One-flip neighbourhood operator changes the allocation of a single component, and produces a new solution d'_i from an existing solution d_i by changing the mapping of a single components; for example, for a given

k: $d'_i = [d_i(c_1), d'_i(c_2), ..., d_i(c_k), ..., d_i(c_n)]$, while the original parent solution is equal to $d_i = [d_i(c_1), d_i(c_2), ..., d_i(c_k), ..., d_i(c_n)]$. From one solution d_i, we can generate $2n$ new solutions corresponding to the n positions and 2 values for each position. The local search procedure is applied for a predefined number of function evaluations.

5   Experiments

To evaluate the performance of the adaptive memetic algorithm, we perform a set of experiments on randomly generated instances from the components deployment problem. The problems are generated using realistic ranges for the software and hardware parameters. The tool with the problem generator, optimisation algorithms and results can be downloaded from http://users.monash. edu.au/~aldeidaa/ArcheOpterix.html.

5.1   Experimental Settings

Approximation algorithms and heuristics are not guaranteed to give the optimal solution of an optimisation problem. However, they can provide good solutions in practice under circumstances where complete algorithms are not justifiable, difficult to implement, impractical or simply not needed. Hence, results concerning the performance of approximate algorithms such as memetic algorithms, are usually reported as mean values over repeated trials. For the current comparison, all algorithms were granted 100 000 function evaluations per trial, repeating the trials 30 times for each optimisation scheme and problem instance. The allocation of 100 000 is based on pilot experiments. Although there are indications that all algorithms still make small but steady improvements after this number of evaluations, the improvements are minor.

5.2   Problem Instances

The validity of the presented experiments may be questioned on the grounds that the results may only reflect the performance of the approaches in certain problem instances, and there is a chance that the approaches may perform differently for other problems. In the design of experiment, we aimed at reducing this threat by generating problem instances of different sizes and characteristics. Instead of manually setting specific problem properties, we developed a problem generator integrated in ArcheOpterix [3]. The configuration of the problem instances are:

```
13 hosts 23 components (H13_C23), 18 hosts 28 components (H18_C28),
18 hosts 35 components (H18_C35), 24 hosts 35 components (H24_C35),
24 hosts 41 components (H13_C23), 30 hosts 44 components (H30_C44),
45 hosts 67 components (H45_C67), 45 hosts 87 components (H45_C87).
```

5.3   Benchmark Optimisation Algorithms

The proposed AMA is compared against traditional MA, GA, and LS. LS is computationally expensive, hence it should be used with reservations. In AMA, LS algorithm is used when the diversity of the solutions, measured using Eq. 2 drops. The value of the threshold (th) is set to 0.8. This is a hyper-parameter that may require to be tuned for different optimisation problem instances.

The crossover and mutation rates for the genetic algorithm, MA and AMA are set to 0.9 and 0.1 respectively. The population size is 50. At every iteration, 40 new solutions are created. The population size is preserved through an elitist strategy, which selects the best individuals. The tuning of the hyper-parameter and parameter values was performed using a sequential parameter optimisation technique [13]. To decrease the number of runs required for parameter tuning, we employ a racing technique, which uses a variable number of runs depending on the performance of the parameter configuration. Hyper-parameter and parameter configurations are tested against the best configuration so far, using at least the same number of function evaluations as employed for the best configuration.

6   Results

The experiments were performed on a 64-core 2.26 GHz processor computer. There was little difference in the run-times of the different optimisation schemes for the same problem instances. The main difference in run-time was observed between the different problem instances. Solving the smaller instances was obviously faster, since the evaluation of the quality attributes takes less time.

Results from the experiments in terms of mean and standard deviation for the compared algorithms (AMA, MA, GA and LS) are shown in Table 1. The proposed AMA outperforms the other optimisation schemes in all problem instances in terms of mean performance. This indicates that the adaptive application of LS algorithm is beneficial when used in combination with the GA.

On its own, LS has a really poor performance, and is outperformed by all the other optimisation methods in the majority of the problems used in the experiments. For the largest problem (H45_C87), however, the local search performs better than GA. This is not only the largest instance, but also the most constrained one. Hence the feasible areas of the search space are limited. The LS algorithm performs small steps, hence once a feasible solution is found, LS is efficient in exploiting that region of the search space. The crossover operator of GA, on the other hand, becomes disruptive, and is not able to generate feasible solutions.

The second best-performing algorithm is the traditional MA, which uses LS deterministically. The performance of the LS on its own is overall worse than the other methods. This could be due to the high computational cost associated with evaluating all neighbouring solutions (worse case scenario).

As AMA consistently outperforms the three other optimisation schemes, we use the Kolmogorov-Smirnov (KS) non-parametric test to check for a statistical

Table 1. The mean and standard deviation of results for all problem instances and optimisation schemes.

Problem	AMA		MA		GA		LS	
	mean	std	mean	std	mean	std	mean	std
H13_C23	**0.999887**	0.6e-5	0.999884	0.5e-5	0.999883	0.4e-5	0.999869	0.6e-5
H18_C28	**0.999862**	0.2e-5	0.999860	0.3e-5	0.999849	0.7e-5	0.999847	0.5e-5
H18_C35	**0.999835**	0.2e-5	0.999833	0.2e-5	0.999833	0.2e-5	0.999819	0.5e-5
H24_C35	**0.998633**	2.8e-5	0.998571	2.4e-5	0.998543	1.3e-5	0.998484	2.4e-5
H24_C41	**0.998977**	1.4e-5	0.998937	2.0e-5	0.998968	0.7e-5	0.998792	3.3e-5
H30_C44	**0.999998**	0.0	0.999996	0.0	0.999995	0.0	0.999994	0.0
H45_C67	**0.993284**	4.3e-5	0.993224	4.6e-5	0.993194	4.5e-5	0.993011	6.5e-5
H45_C87	**0.999992**	0.0	**0.999992**	0.0	0.999991	0.0	**0.999992**	0.0

difference. The 30 independent runs of the repeated trials for each of the optimisation scheme and problem instances were submitted to the KS test analysis. AMA was compared to the other three optimisation schemes, with a null hypothesis of no significant difference between the performances (AMA vs. MA, AMA vs. GA, and AMA vs. LS). The significance coefficients (p-values) of the tests are shown in Table 2.

Table 2. KS tests of results from all problem instances and optimisation schemes: adaptive memetic algorithm (AMA) is compared against a memetic algorithm (MA), a genetic algorithm (GA), and a local search (LS) method.

	H13C23	H18C28	H18C35	H24C35	H24C41	H30C44	H45C67	H45C87
AMA-MA	0.05	0.04	0.05	<0.01	<0.01	<0.01	0.01	<0.01
AMA-GA	0.02	<0.01	0.2	<0.01	<0.01	<0.01	0.01	<0.01
AMA-LS	<0.01	<0.01	<0.01	<0.01	<0.01	<0.01	<0.01	<0.01

The results from the KS tests, which were used for checking if there is any significant difference between the datasets under the assumption that they are not normally distributed, result in a rejection of the null hypothesis at a 95% confidence level in the majority of the trials. This indicates that the superior performance of the proposed AMA is statistically significant.

There is only one trial (H18_C35) where the performance of AMA, although better than the performance of the GA, is not statistically significantly better. AMA is a combination of GA and LS. In this trial, the LS performs poorly, which may explain why the AMA is not as successful as in the other cases. The fitness landscape of H18_C35 seems to be rugged and multi-modal, which creates difficult gradients that are an impediment for the LS. An adaptation of the threshold value used for the selection of LS (Eq. 2) may solve this issue. In future work, the adaptation of the threshold value for the LS selection is a priority.

7   Conclusion

This work presented an adaptive memetic algorithm for the architecture optimisation problem. The proposed algorithm uses the simple descent local search algorithm to refine the quality of the solution and to improve the convergence process. To avoid the situation of being more exploitative than explorative as well as reducing the computational time wastage, an adaptive scheme is used to control the simple descent application frequency. Computational experiments were carried out using the component deployment optimisation instances to assess the performance of the proposed adaptive memetic algorithm against genetic algorithm, traditional memetic algorithm and local search algorithm. The proposed adaptive memetic algorithm excelled compared to the benchmark algorithms, which shows that adaptively controlling the local search application frequency during the search process can assist the memetic algorithm to get the best results.

Acknowledgements. This research was supported under Australian Research Council's Discovery Projects funding scheme, project number DE 140100017.

References

1. Aarts, E.H., Lenstra, J.K.: Local Search in Combinatorial Optimization. Princeton University Press, Princeton (2003)
2. Aleti, A.: Designing automotive embedded systems with adaptive genetic algorithms. Autom. Softw. Eng. **22**, 1–42 (2014)
3. Aleti, A., Björnander, S., Grunske, L., Meedeniya, I.: ArcheOpterix: an extendable tool for architecture optimization of AADL models. In: Model-Based Methodologies for Pervasive and Embedded Software (MOMPES), pp. 61–71. ACM and IEEE Digital Libraries (2009)
4. Aleti, A., Buhnova, B., Grunske, L., Koziolek, A., Meedeniya, I.: Software architecture optimization methods: a systematic literature review. IEEE Trans. Softw. Eng. **39**(5), 658–683 (2013)
5. Aleti, A., Grunske, L., Meedeniya, I., Moser, I.: Let the ants deploy your software - an ACO based deployment optimisation strategy. In: ASE, pp. 505–509. IEEE Computer Society (2009)
6. Aleti, A., Meedeniya, I.: Component deployment optimisation with Bayesian learning. In: Proceedings of the 14th International ACM Sigsoft Symposium on Component Based Software Engineering, pp. 11–20. ACM (2011)
7. Aleti, A., Moser, I.: Predictive parameter control. In: Genetic and Evolutionary Computation Conference, pp. 561–568 (2011)
8. Aleti, A., Moser, I.: Entropy-based adaptive range parameter control for evolutionary algorithms. In: Conference on Genetic and Evolutionary Computation Conference, pp. 1501–1508. ACM (2013)

9. Aleti, A., Moser, I., Meedeniya, I., Grunske, L.: Choosing the appropriate forecasting model for predictive parameter control. Evol. Comput. **22**(2), 319–349 (2014)
10. Aleti, A., Moser, I., Mostaghim, S.: Adaptive range parameter control. In: IEEE Congress on Evolutionary Computation, pp. 2405–2412 (2012)
11. Arafeh, B.R., Day, K., Touzene, A.: A multilevel partitioning approach for efficient tasks allocation in heterogeneous distributed systems. J. Syst. Archit. - Embed. Syst. Des. **54**(5), 530–548 (2008)
12. Assayad, I., Girault, A., Kalla, H.: A bi-criteria scheduling heuristic for distributed embedded systems under reliability and real-time constraints. In: Dependable Systems and Networks, pp. 347–356. IEEE Computer Society (2004)
13. Bartz-Beielstein, T., Lasarczyk, C., Preuss, M.: Sequential parameter optimization. In: IEEE Congress on Evolutionary Computation, pp. 773–780. IEEE (2005)
14. Colanzi, T.E., Vergilio, S.R.: Applying search based optimization to software product line architectures: lessons learned. In: Fraser, G., de Souza, J.T. (eds.) SSBSE 2012. LNCS, vol. 7515, pp. 259–266. Springer, Heidelberg (2012). doi:10.1007/978-3-642-33119-0_19
15. da Silva Maximiano, M., Vega-Rodríguez, M.A., Gómez-Pulido, J.A., Sanchez-Perez, J.M.: A hybrid differential evolution algorithm to solve a real-world frequency assignment problem. In: Computer Science and Information Technology, pp. 201–205. IEEE (2008)
16. Kichkaylo, T., Karamcheti, V.: Optimal resource-aware deployment planning for component-based distributed applications. In: HPDC: High Performance Distributed Computing, pp. 150–159. IEEE Computer Society (2004)
17. Koziolek, A., Koziolek, H., Reussner, R.: Peropteryx: automated application of tactics in multi-objective software architecture optimization. In: Quality of Software Architectures, pp. 33–42. ACM (2011)
18. Krasnogor, N., Smith, J.: A memetic algorithm with self-adaptive local search: TSP as a case study. In: GECCO, pp. 987–994 (2000)
19. Kulturel-Konak, S., Coit, D.W., Baheranwala, F.: Pruned pareto-optimal sets for the system redundancy allocation problem based on multiple prioritized objectives. J. Heuristics **14**(4), 335–357 (2008)
20. Meedeniya, I., Buhnova, B., Aleti, A., Grunske, L.: Architecture-driven reliability and energy optimization for complex embedded systems. In: Heineman, G.T., Kofron, J., Plasil, F. (eds.) QoSA 2010. LNCS, vol. 6093, pp. 52–67. Springer, Heidelberg (2010). doi:10.1007/978-3-642-13821-8_6
21. Meedeniya, I., Buhnova, B., Aleti, A., Grunske, L.: Reliability-driven deployment optimization for embedded systems. J. Syst. Softw. **84**, 835–846 (2011)
22. Neri, F., Cotta, C.: Memetic algorithms and memetic computing optimization: a literature review. Swarm Evol. Comput. **2**, 1–14 (2012)
23. Neri, F., Tirronen, V., Karkkainen, T., Rossi, T.: Fitness diversity based adaptation in multimeme algorithms: a comparative study. In: IEEE Congress on Evolutionary Computation, CEC 2007, pp. 2374–2381. IEEE (2007)
24. Simons, C.L., Parmee, I.C., Gwynllyw, R.: Interactive, evolutionary search in upstream object-oriented class design. IEEE Trans. Softw. Eng. **36**(6), 798–816 (2010)
25. Tang, J., Lim, M.H., Ong, Y.S.: Diversity-adaptive parallel memetic algorithm for solving large scale combinatorial optimization problems. Soft Comput. **11**(9), 873–888 (2007)
26. Thiruvady, D., Moser, I., Aleti, A., Nazari, A.: Constraint programming and ant colony system for the component deployment problem. Procedia Comput. Sci. **29**, 1937–1947 (2014)

Resource Constrained Job Scheduling with Parallel Constraint-Based ACO

Dror Cohen[1], Antonio Gómez-Iglesias[2], Dhananjay Thiruvady[3,4(✉)],
and Andreas T. Ernst[3]

[1] Faculty of Information Technology, Monash University, Clayton, VIC, Australia
[2] Texas Advanced Computing Center, University of Texas at Austin,
Austin, TX, USA
[3] School of Mathematical Sciences, Monash University, Clayton, VIC, Australia
dhananjay.thiruvady@gmail.com
[4] Bayesian Intelligence Pty Ltd, Clayton, VIC, Australia

Abstract. Hybrid methods are highly effective means of solving combinatorial optimization problems and have become increasingly popular. In particular, integrations of exact and incomplete methods have proved to be effective where the hybrid takes advantage of the relative performance of each individual method. However, these methods often require significant run-times to determine good feasible solutions. One way of reducing run-times is to parallelize these algorithms. For large NP-hard problems, parallelization must be done with care, since changes to the algorithm can affect its performance in unpredictable ways. In this paper we develop two parallel variants of constraint-based ACO and test them on a problem arising in the Australian mining industry. We demonstrate that parallelization significantly reduces run times with each parallel variant providing advantages with respect to feasibility and solution quality.

1 Introduction

Combinatorial optimization problems (COPs) that are NP-hard are of significant interest in Operations Research. Metaheuristics can be effective at solving these problems [4] but often breakdown when the COPs involve non-trivial hard constraints. Thus, combining Metaheuristics with exact methods designed to deal with constraints, such as constraint programming (CP) [11] provides a way of identifying good feasible solutions.

Thiruvady and colleagues [20] considered a Resource Constrained Job Scheduling (RCJS) problem which typically arises in mining supply chains. Here, every mine (machine) requires a number of jobs to be completed to meet demand at the ports. Production restrictions and maintenance requirements at the mine mean that the jobs possibly start after a delay (release times). Additionally, there are precedences between jobs which are enforced by the arrival of ships at the ports requiring different minerals. While the jobs execute, they use a resource (e.g. electricity) of which there is limited capacity (a renewable resource [5]). The ships must be loaded at ports at pre-specified preferred times (soft due

© Springer International Publishing AG 2017
M. Wagner et al. (Eds.): ACALCI 2017, LNAI 10142, pp. 266–278, 2017.
DOI: 10.1007/978-3-319-51691-2_23

times) which leads to minimizing tardiness as the objective. Moreover, in order to meet contractual obligations the ships must be loaded within a short window following the preferred time (hard due times). While hybrid methods have been shown to be effective on this problem, the run-time requirements are often large. For example, [20] ran their algorithms for 30 min and were still unable to find feasible solutions for some large instances.

Parallel implementations of ACO have been shown to effectively reduce run-times [7,8,13,16]. Randall and Lewis [13] (parallel ants or solutions) and Ling et al. [9] (parallel colonies) use MPI to investigate a parallel implementation of ACO on the travelling salesman problem. The study by Ellabib et al. [8] also shows that local search can be incorporated in a straight-forward manner.

To the authors' knowledge, few studies consider ACO with multi-core shared memory programming [7,18]. Delisle et al. [7] consider a scheduling problem in an aluminium casting centre and show that ACO can be effectively parallelized for this problem. Thiruvady et al. [18] conducted a study of parallel ACO on the RCJS problem without the hard deadline. While their parallel implementation is effective, in the presence of the hard deadline line, ACO itself is not effective. Thus, a straightforward extension to the problem considered here is not possible. Studies with parallel Beam search are even scarcer. During the search candidate partial solutions are compared together and only the most promising ones kept for the next iteration. This introduces dependency between solutions during construction, potentially making parallel implementation less efficient. One example is the study by Ravishanker [14], who proposed a parallel implementation of Beam search for speech recognition on multiple cores with a shared memory architecture.

In this study, we develop two parallel variants of CP-Beam-ACO [17], a hybrid combining Beam-ACO [3] and CP. We investigate their performance on the RCJS problem described earlier [20]. While parallelization is conceptually straight-forward, there are several difficulties in practice. Firstly, the methods have to lend themselves to a parallel framework and it is not obvious how to do so in the context of Beam search and CP. Secondly, while CP-Beam-ACO can be theoretically parallelized, the efficiency of parallelization depends on implementation details where minor changes can lead to significantly different results. We find that effective parallelization can indeed be obtained, however, the two different schemes are better suited to finding feasibility or improving solution quality.

The paper is organized as follows. The details of the problem are presented in Sect. 2. Section 3 presents the CP-Beam-ACO hybrid and Sect. 4 presents the parallelized variants. Section 5 provides details of the experiments conducted and the results. A critical discussion is provided in Sect. 6 and Sect. 7 concludes the paper.

2   Problem Specification

We are given a number of machines $\mathcal{M} = \{1, \ldots, l\}$ where a number of jobs $\mathcal{J} = \{1, \ldots, n\}$ must be executed. A job i is associated with a release time

(r_i), processing time (p_i), soft due time (d_i), hard deadline $(\bar{d}_i)$, a weight (w_i), resource usage (g_i) and the machine on which the job must execute (m_i). Each machine may only execute one job at a time and once a job commences, it must complete. Jobs on a machine may have precedences between them, i.e., $i \rightarrow j$ forces i to complete before j commences. We represent a solution to the problem by sequence of jobs $\pi = \{\pi_1, \ldots, \pi_n\}$. This sequence can be used to generate a resource feasible schedule $(x(\pi))$ where start times for all jobs can be assigned $(\mathcal{S} = \{s_1, \ldots, s_n\})$. Note that it may not be possible to find a scheduling scheme $x(\cdot)$ such that all hard deadlines are met. Denote the set of jobs executing at time t by P_t. Then

$$P_t = \{j \mid s_j \leq t < s_j + p_j, j \in \mathcal{J}\} \tag{1}$$

$x(\pi)$ is *resource feasible* if

$$\sum_{k \in P_t} g_k \leq \mathcal{G} \qquad \forall t \tag{2}$$

where g_k is the resource requirement of job k which uses some proportion of the maximum resource available $\mathcal{G}$. Thus, the resource consumption of all jobs executing at the same time must not exceed the available resource. If it is not possible to meet the hard deadline for all tasks, the next obvious objective is to finish each task as early as possible, known as minimizing tardiness, as explored in [2,15,20]. In line with these studies, we seek to minimize the total weighted-tardiness $x(\pi)$

$$f(x(\pi)) = \sum_{i=0}^{n} w_{\pi_i} \times T(x(\pi_i)) \tag{3}$$

where $T(x(\pi_i)) = max(s_{\pi_i} + p_{\pi_i} - d_{\pi_i}, 0)$ is the tardiness of the job π_i.

3   CP-Beam-ACO

Here we briefly review the CP-Beam-ACO algorithm described in [20]. Further details can be found in the original work. The high-level ACO algorithm is presented in Algorithm 1.

After initialization of the pheromones ($\mathcal{T}$, line 3), the main algorithm (lines 4–10) for each of n_a ants proceeds as follows:

ConstructJobSequence(): A random number $q \in (0, 1]$ is drawn and compared with a pre-defined parameter $q_0 = 0.5$. If $q < q_0$, job k is selected as the ith job $(\pi_i = k)$ according to

$$k = \max_{j \in \mathcal{J} \setminus \{\pi_1, \ldots, \pi_{i-1}\}} \tau_{ij} \times \eta_j \tag{4}$$

otherwise, k is selected probabilistically according to

$$\mathbf{p}(\pi_i = k) = \frac{\tau_{ik} \times \eta_k}{\sum_{j \in \mathcal{J} \setminus \{\pi_1, \ldots, \pi_{i-1}\}} (\tau_{ij} \times \eta_j)} \tag{5}$$

where η_k is a heuristic value defined as w_k/d_k which favors selecting jobs with large weights and early due times. Every selection of a job k at position i has the following update

$$\tau_{ik} = \tau_{ik} \times \rho + \tau_{min} \tag{6}$$

which ensures diversification. ρ is the learning rate (to apply evaporation) and $\tau_{min} = 0.001$ ensures that there is always a non-zero probability for selecting any job at any position.

PlaceJobs(): A schedule $\sigma(\pi)$ is obtained from a sequence via the placement scheme discussed in [20]. Starting at the first time point a feasible schedule can be ensured that satisfies the precedence and resource constraints. Note that, the sequence of jobs may violate the constraints. However, to account for precedences, jobs are only placed once their preceding jobs have been completed. The resulting solution is added to the set of solutions for that iteration S_{iter}.

Algorithm 1. ACS for the RCJS problem

1: INPUT: An RCJS instance
2: $\pi^{bs} :=$ NULL (global best)
3: initialize $\mathcal{T}$
4: **while** termination conditions not satisfied **do**
5:    $S_{iter} := \emptyset$
6:    **for** $j = 1$ to n_a **do**
7:       $\pi_j :=$ ConstructJobSequence()
8:       PlaceJobs(π_j)
9:       $S_{iter} := S_{iter} \cup \{\pi_j\}$
10:    **end for**
11:    $\pi^{ib} := \text{argmin}\{f(\pi)|\pi \in S_{iter}\}$
12:    $\pi^{ib} :=$ LocalSearch()
13:    Update(π^{ih},π^{bs})
14:    PheromoneUpdate($\mathcal{T},\pi^{hs}$)
15:    $cf :=$ ComputeConvergence(π^{ib})
16:    **if** $cf = true$ **then** initialize $\mathcal{T}$ **end if**
17: **end while**
18: OUTPUT: π^{bs}

After the main loop concludes, the best solution from that iteration is chosen π^{ib} (line 11). LocalSearch(): The iteration best solution π^{ib} is potentially improved by (a) randomly swapping pairs of jobs a fixed number of times (b) by selecting an index l randomly, selecting a m jobs from l and moving them to the end of the sequence. All jobs at $l + m$ to the end of the sequence are moved up to m (known as β-sampling [21]). If either of these leads to an improvement π^{ib} is updated. Update(π^{ib}, π^{bs}): π^{bs} is set to π^{ib} if $f(\sigma(\pi^{ib})) < f(\sigma(\pi^{bs}))$ where $f(\sigma(\pi^{ib}))$ is the total weighted tardiness of the solution. PheromoneUpdate($\mathcal{T}, \pi^{bs}$): The global best solution is used to update the pheromones. For job i appearing at position j, τ_{ij} is updated according to

$$\tau_{ij} = \tau_{ij} \times \rho + \delta_{\pi^{bs}} \tag{7}$$

where $\delta_{\pi^{bs}} = Q/f(\sigma(\pi^{bs}))$ and Q is a scaling factor chosen so that $0.01 \leq \delta_{\pi^{bs}} \leq 0.1$. $\rho = 0.01$ is the learning rate discussed earlier. If a global best solution is unavailable, there is no reward (a negative reward may be investigated in the future). ComputeConvergence(π^{ib}): If π^{ib} does not change for 10 iterations, we assume convergence and the pheromone matrix is re-initialized: $\tau_{ij} = 0.5\ \forall i, j$.

In the CP-Beam-ACO, the ConstructJobSequence() routine is implemented as a probabilistic Beam search with CP. This procedure is presented in Algorithm 2. A solution consists of two sequences $(\bar{\pi}, \hat{\pi})$, the first being the partial sequence and the second being a list of waiting jobs. In selectJob($D, \mathcal{T}$), a job is selected using the pheromones. It is tested with the CP solver[1] if all its preceding jobs (PR_j) have been scheduled (updateJobs($\bar{\pi}$, $\hat{\pi}$, j), where j is the selected job). Once j is added to $\bar{\pi}$, $\hat{\pi}$ is examined to determine which jobs may be scheduled next, and these jobs are scheduled as soon as possible considering the release times. The job is placed in the waiting list if its predecessors have not been completed (line 13). The current partial solution is now placed in the Beam if it has passed the CP test or if the new job is waiting (line 15). The final step is to determine promising solutions (Reduce(B_{t+1}, θ)) via an estimate and θ best of these are selected.

Algorithm 2. ConstructJobSequence (Probabilistic Beam Search with CP)

1: INPUT: $(\theta, \mu, \mathcal{T})$
2: $B_0 = \{\pi_1 = (), \ldots, \pi_\theta = ()\}$
3: $t = 0$
4: **while** $t < n$ **and** $|B_t| > 0$ **do**
5:     **for** $i \in B_t$ **do**
6:         $k \leftarrow 0$, $D = \text{domain}(\pi_{t+1}^i)$
7:         **while** $k < \mu \wedge D \neq \emptyset$ **do**
8:             $(\bar{\pi}, \hat{\pi}) \leftarrow \pi^i$, $feasible = true$
9:             $j = \text{selectJob}(D, \mathcal{T})$
10:            **if** PR_j in $\sigma(\bar{\pi})$ **then**
11:                $feasible = \text{updateJobs}(\bar{\pi}, \hat{\pi}, j)$
12:            **else**
13:                $\hat{\pi} \leftarrow \text{append}(\hat{\pi}, j)$
14:            **end if**
15:            **if** $feasible$ **then** $B_{t+1} = B_{t+1} \cup (\bar{\pi}, \hat{\pi})$
16:            $k \leftarrow k + 1$, $D = D \setminus j$
17:        **end while**
18:    **end for**
19:    $B_{t+1} = \text{Reduce}(B_{t+1}, \theta)$
20:    $t \leftarrow t + 1$
21: **end while**
22: OUTPUT: $\text{argmax}\{f(\pi) \mid \pi \in B_{n-1}\}$

The estimate is an important step that can significantly improve the search. Here we follow other studies [10,17,19,20] and use *stochastic sampling* as a generic way of obtaining estimates.

4   Parallel CP-Beam-ACO

In the previous section we introduced the CP-Beam-ACO algorithm. In what follows we described how the execution of this algorithm can be parallelized.

---

[1] The CP solver maintains all the constraints in the system. A job j is posted to the solver and either success or failure is returned.

4.1 Parallelized Stochastic Sampling

We profiled a typical execution of the algorithm and found that the sampling loop (in $\mathsf{Reduce}(B_{t+1}, \theta)$) was the most CPU-intensive component. Thus, parallelization of the sampling loop is a reasonable approach to reducing the run-time of this algorithm. Parallelizing the sampling loop means that all cores would attempt to access the pheromone matrix. To avoid simultaneous access, we restricted the pheromone matrix in two ways. In the first, termed *full lock*, the entire pheromone matrix is locked each time it is accessed by a core. The drawback of this method is that a core may need to wait until a previous core has updated the matrix before accessing it, reducing performance. In the second method, we locked each row of the matrix. This method reduces the time a core may need to wait for another core (we measured this at $52\,\mu s$), but incurs additional overheads due to the multiple locks. This method also has the advantage of limiting the impact of false sharing on ccNUMA (cache coherent Non Uniform Memory Access) architectures [6], a well-known effect of shared memory approaches on this architecture. If two cores modify the same cache line, then this line needs to be reloaded decreasing performance. By locking the entire row of the matrix, we are reducing the probability of more than one processor accessing the same cache line. We profiled a typical serial execution of the algorithm on one instance and determined the maximal theoretical speedup, as described by Amdahl's law [1].

$$S(n) = \frac{1}{B + \frac{1}{n}(1 - B)} \tag{8}$$

Here S is the maximal speedup available, B is the percentage of the algorithm that must be run in parallel, and n is the number of cores available. We tested the speedup achieved as a function of the number of cores for different number of samples. All tests were run on an Intel Xeon Processor E5-2650 with 8 physical cores (no Hyper-Threading). This machine has two processors on each node, so that up to 16 cores could be used. However, we have chosen to run only on 8 cores to avoid the impact of inter-socket communication.

4.2 Full Parallelization

This parallelization variant considers multiple Beam-ACO instances running in parallel while sharing the same pheromone matrix. We employed a similar strategy to the sampling parallelization by locking the rows of the matrix. In this method, the algorithm is run nearly entirely in parallel and so the theoretical maximal speedup is roughly equal to the number of cores. However, this method constitutes a change in algorithm so that direct comparison in terms of speedup with the original algorithm would be misleading, as the algorithm's performance must also be taken into account, as we demonstrate in Sect. 5. We thus consider as serial implementation the modified version with the parallelization deactivated and running on a single core. When evaluating this method we fixed the number of samples at 32. We emphasize that this way of parallelizing the algorithm effectively generates 8 times (for 8 cores) as many solutions (ants) as the parallel stochastic sampling approach. The pheromone matrix is shared across all these solutions, and modified during subsequent calls to the PheromoneUpdate() routine.

5 Experiments and Results

CP-Beam-ACO was implemented in C++ and compiled using Intel Compiler 14.1. OpenMP was used [6] for the parallel implementations. All experiments were run on a computer with 2 Intel Xeon E5-2650 processors running at 2.00 GHz and a 20 Mb cache on each node. This amounts to a total of 16 cores but as previously mentioned we use up to 8 cores to keep all the communication intra-socket. Each algorithm was run 19 times per instance (the 20th run timed-out on a subset of the instances) and allowed one hour of wall clock time.

We conducted experiments on the problem instances from the study by [20] and also used the same hard due times. For a complete comparison of the two parallelized variants we examined available speedup as well as the ability to find feasible solutions and the resulting solution qualities.

5.1 Comparing Speedup

Figure 1 shows the available speedup (time taken for serial version/time taken for parallel version) for 1–8 cores for the two parallel variants. The best possible improvement (dashed black line) and the maximal theoretical speedup (96 samples, dashed blue line) are shown for comparison. The figure shows that the Full parallel variant (solid black line) achieves excellent speedup. Parallelizing the stochastic sampling loop is also effective, but this is only maintained for 8 cores and when using 64 or more samples. Thus, when speedup is the only consideration, the best results are obtained for the Full parallel variant followed by parallel sampling with 64 or more samples.

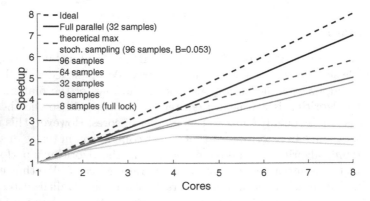

Fig. 1. Speedup as a function of the number of cores for the Full parallel and parallel stochastic sampling variants. See legend for details. (Color figure online)

The figure also demonstrates the relative weakness of the *full lock* method (solid green line). When using 4 cores, the speedups of this version and the 8 samples implementation are similar, but the performance of the *full lock* version decreases when the number of cores increases due to the deadlocks in the critical section. For this reason we focused on the version in which the rows of the pheromone matrix are locked, which we simply refer to as parallel sampling.

5.2 Comparing Feasibility

We first compared the feasibility results obtained with all implementations. We focus on instances where feasibility is difficult to find and do not report results for instances in which all implementations always or never find feasibility. Figure 2 shows the probability of finding a feasible solution for five instances in which finding feasibility was difficult. Our results show that using fewer than 16 or more than 96 samples tends to decrease the chance of finding feasibility. For the full parallel version, 32 samples were used but this particular variant was comparatively ineffective at finding feasibility irrespective of the number of samples selected. A potential reason for this is that the multiple beam-searches share the same pheromone matrix, effectively reducing the learning rate. For the serial implementation we chose the optimal number of samples separately for each instance. In other words, we compare the parallel implementations against the best performing serial version. Thus, Fig. 2 demonstrates that there is always a parallel solution that is an improvement over its serial counterpart.

Overall, these results show that parallelizing provides a net benefit for the algorithm performance and that stochastic sampling is a useful guide towards

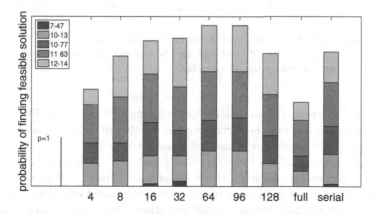

Fig. 2. Probability of finding feasible solutions for all implementations. A scale corresponding to 100% is shown on the left (black line). The results are shown for five instance in which finding feasibility was difficult. The x axis specifies the implementation. The numbers 4, 8, 16, 32, 64, 96 and 128 are the number of samples used. Full is the Full parallel implementation with 32 samples and serial is the Full parallel implementation running on one core.

finding feasibility. There is a trade-off point at 96 samples after which the excess stochastic sampling is not useful. This may be because the extra time spent on stochastic sampling results in fewer iterations and less time spent on the CP component, which may not be useful.

5.3   Comparing Solution Quality

Next we compared the solution quality of the parallelized variants. We chose instances in which feasibility is found at least once, discarding instances in which some of the implementations always fail. Figure 3 shows the % difference to the best solution. Interestingly, the solution qualities worsen with increasing samples. The full parallel implementation is by far the best performing algorithm, followed by the parallelized sampling variant with only four samples. Thus, if feasibility is found, the full parallel implementation is the algorithm of choice.

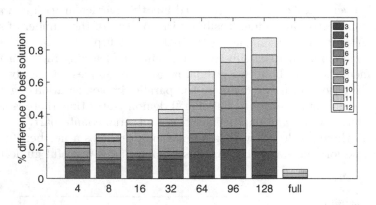

Fig. 3. Solution quality for all parallel implementations averaged over machine size. The numbers 4, 8, 16, 32, 64, 96 and 128 are the number of samples used. Full is the full parallel implementation with 32 samples.

When we focus on solution quality for problems in which feasibility is difficult to find we see a similar trend - increasing the number of samples results in worse solution quality. Figure 4 shows the % difference to the best solution for the four most difficult problems. We have removed problem 7–47 from this comparison since only implementations with 16 or 32 samples found feasible solutions. For these difficult problems using only four samples is the most effective implementation, followed by the full parallel implementation. Comparing against the serial version (with optimal number of samples chosen) we see that there is always a superior parallel implementation.

These results show that stochastic sampling is well suited for finding feasibility. However, once feasibility is found, a larger number of samples does not result in improved solution quality. One indicator of solution quality is the number of iterations performed by the algorithm - more iterations improve the solutions.

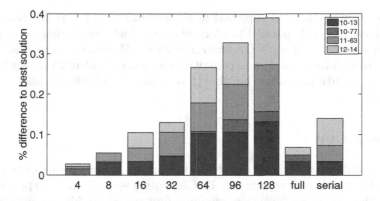

Fig. 4. Solution quality results for all implementations for four difficult instances. The numbers 4, 8, 16, 32, 64, 96 and 128 are the number of samples used. Full is the full parallel implementation with 32 samples and serial is the Full parallel implementation running on one core.

We examined the relationship between the number of iterations and solution quality to see if this can explain our results. Figure 5 shows the % difference to maximum number of iterations performed (pink bars) as well as the % difference to best solution (blue bars).

The figure clearly shows that increasing the number of samples results in fewer overall iterations and reduced solution quality. This implies that once feasibility is found, higher quality solutions are obtained by iterating more, not by increasing the number of samples. This contrasts with the previous finding

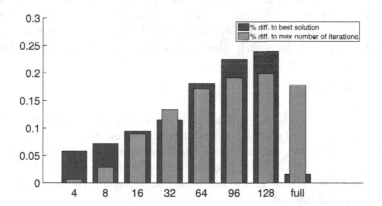

Fig. 5. Superimposing % difference to maximum number of iterations performed (pink bars) on % difference to best solution (blue bars), averaged across all instances. Both quantities have been normalized to sum to one in order to fit on the same scale. The numbers 4, 8, 16, 32, 64, 96 and 128 are the number of samples used. Full is the full parallel implementation with 32 samples. (Color figure online)

that more samples lead to improved feasibility finding (Fig. 2). The comparison also includes the Full parallel implementation which shows that good quality solutions are obtained with far fewer iterations. However, we emphasize that the Full parallel implementation constitutes a change in algorithm for which the number of iterations cannot be directly compared with the parallel sampling algorithm.

6   Discussion

The two parallelized variants showed significant improvements in speedup compared to the serial counterpart (Fig. 1). Comparing each algorithm's performance revealed that each parallelization scheme is best suited for different criteria. Parallelizing the sampling loop allowed significant run-time improvement when using 64 or more samples (Fig. 1). The combined improvement in run-time and larger number of samples was best suited for finding feasible solutions (Fig. 2). In contrast, the second parallelized variant, in which multiple Beam-ACO instances ran in parallel, was comparatively poor at finding feasible solutions but far superior at finding better solutions if feasibility was found (Fig. 3).

Since the two parallelized variants constitute two different algorithms, it is not trivial to reduce the relative strengths of these parallelized variants to a single source. However, two key factors deserve further consideration. First, due to the nature of parallelization, the Full parallel variant achieved excellent improvement in run-time. Put differently, the Full parallel method made better use of the available computing resources in a given time frame compared to the parallelllized stochastic sampling loop. Secondly, our results are consistent with a trade-off between finding feasible and good quality solutions. Parallelizing the stochastic sampling loop and using more samples means that more of the search space is sampled, and this clearly aids in finding feasibility. However, on instances where obtaining feasibility is easier, beam search is more effective at honing in on promising areas of the search space, resulting in better quality solutions.

7   Conclusion

In this study, we considered parallel variants of a constraint-based ACO algorithm for resource constraint job scheduling. We show that parallel variants of the CP-Beam-ACO are more effective than their serial counterparts. We found that the choice of implementation depends on the criteria of evaluation - whether feasibility (parallelized stochastic sampling) or quality of the solution (full parallelization) are of interest.

Previously, CP-Beam-ACO has been shown to be effective on similar problems to the one considered here [17, 19]. One possible future direction is to investigate whether or not the parallel implementations considered here are also useful on those problems. We would expect that as the relative importance of the CP solver and stochastic sampling is different for these problems, some modifications may be necessary to obtain optimal performance. Understanding which parallel variant is best suited for a given problem requires further investigation. A second possibility is to consider parallel implementations via MPI [12]. There are likely to be significant advantages with a full parallel version especially if we are able to make use of several hundred nodes. There may not be a similar advantage with stochastic sampling, because increasing the number of samples beyond a critical point does not result in further gains.

References

1. Amdahl, G.M.: Validity of the single processor approach to achieving large scale computing capabilities. In: Proceedings of the April 18–20, 1967, Spring Joint Computer Conference, AFIPS 1967 (Spring), pp. 483–485. ACM, New York (1967)
2. Ballestín, F., Trautmann, N.: An iterated-local-search heuristic for the resource-constrained weighted earliness-tardiness project scheduling problem. Int. J. Prod. Res. **46**, 6231–6249 (2008)
3. Blum, C.: Beam-ACO: hybridizing ant colony optimization with beam search: an application to open shop scheduling. Comput. Oper. Res. **32**, 1565–1591 (2005)
4. Blum, C., Roli, A.: Metaheuristics in combinatorial optimization: overview and conceptual comparison. ACM Comput. Surv. **35**, 268–308 (2003)
5. Brucker, P., Drexl, A., Mohring, R., Neumann, K., Pesch, E.: Resource-constrained project scheduling: notation, classification, models, and methods. Eur. J. Oper. Res. **112**, 3–41 (1999)
6. Chapman, B., Jost, G., van der Pas, R.: Using OpenMP: Portable Shared Memory Parallel Programming (Scientific and Engineering Computation). The MIT Press, Cambridge (2007)
7. Delisle, P., Krajecki, M., Gravel, M., Gagné, C.: Parallel implementation of an ant colony optimization metaheuristic with OpenMP. In: Proceedings of the 3rd European Workshop on OpenMP of International Conference on Parallel Architectures and Compilation Techniques (EWOMP 2001) (2001)
8. Ellabib, I., Calamai, P., Basir, O.: Exchange strategies for multiple ant colony system. Inf. Sci. **177**(5), 1248–1264 (2007)
9. Ling, C., Hai-Ying, S., Shu, W.: A parallel ant colony algorithm on massively parallel processors and its convergence analysis for the travelling salesman problem. Inf. Sci. **199**, 31–42 (2012). WOS: 000304221600003
10. López-Ibáñez, M., Blum, C., Thiruvady, D., Ernst, A.T., Meyer, B.: Beam-ACO based on stochastic sampling for makespan optimization concerning the TSP with time windows. In: Cotta, C., Cowling, P. (eds.) EvoCOP 2009. LNCS, vol. 5482, pp. 97–108. Springer, Heidelberg (2009). doi:10.1007/978-3-642-01009-5_9
11. Marriott, K., Stuckey, P.: Programming with Constraints. MIT Press, Cambridge (1998)
12. Pedemonte, M., Nesmachnow, S., Cancela, H.: A survey on parallel ant colony optimization. Appl. Soft Comput. **11**(8), 5181–5197 (2011)
13. Randall, M., Lewis, A.: A parallel implementation of ant colony optimization. J. Parallel Distrib. Comput. **62**(9), 1421–1432 (2002)
14. Ravishankar, M.K.: Parallel implementation of fast beam search for speaker-independent continuous speech recognition (1993)
15. Singh, G., Ernst, A.T.: Resource constraint scheduling with a fractional shared resource. Oper. Res. Lett. **39**(5), 363–368 (2011)

16. Stützle, T., López-Ibáñez, M., Dorigo, M.: A Concise Overview of Applications of Ant Colony Optimization. Wiley, New York (2010)
17. Thiruvady, D., Blum, C., Meyer, B., Ernst, A.: Hybridizing beam-ACO with constraint programming for single machine job scheduling. In: Blesa, M.J., Blum, C., Gaspero, L., Roli, A., Sampels, M., Schaerf, A. (eds.) HM 2009. LNCS, vol. 5818, pp. 30–44. Springer, Heidelberg (2009). doi:10.1007/978-3-642-04918-7_3
18. Thiruvady, D., Ernst, A.T., Singh, G.: Parallel ant colony optimization for resource constrained job scheduling. Ann. Oper. Res. **242**, 1–18 (2014)
19. Thiruvady, D., Meyer, B., Ernst, A.T.: Car sequencing with constraint-based ACO. In: Proceedings of the 13th Annual Conference on Genetic and Evolutionary Computation, GECCO 2011, pp. 163–170. ACM, New York (2011)
20. Thiruvady, D., Singh, G., Ernst, A.T., Meyer, B.: Constraint-based ACO for a shared resource constrained scheduling problem. Int. J. Prod. Econ. **141**(1), 230–242 (2013). Meta-heuristics for manufacturing scheduling and logistics problems
21. Valls, V., Quintanilla, S., Ballestín, F.: Resource-constrained project scheduling: a critical activity reordering heuristic. Eur. J. Oper. Res. **149**, 282–301 (2003)

An Iterated Local Search with Guided Perturbation for the Heterogeneous Fleet Vehicle Routing Problem with Time Windows and Three-Dimensional Loading Constraints

Ayad Turky[1,2,3], I. Moser[1,2,3]([✉]), and Aldeida Aleti[1,2,3]

[1] School of Computer Science and Information Technology,
RMIT University, Melbourne, Australia
ayad.turky@rmit.edu.au, aldeida.aleti@monash.edu
[2] Department of Computer Science and Software Engineering,
Swinburne University of Technology, Melbourne, Australia
imoser@swin.edu.au
[3] Faculty of Information Technology, Monash University, Melbourne, Australia

Abstract. An Australian company is faced with the logistics problem of distributing small quantities of fibre boards to hundreds of customers every day. The resulting Heterogeneous Fleet Vehicle Routing Problem with Time Windows and Three-Dimensional Loading Constraints has to be solved within a single hour, hence the use of a heuristic instead of an exact method. In previous work, the loading was performed after optimising the routes, which in some cases generated infeasible solutions in need of a repair mechanism. In this work, the feasibility of the loading constraints is maintained during the route optimisation. Iterated Local Search has proved very effective at solving vehicle routing problems. Its success is mainly due to its biased sampling of locl optima. However, its performance heavily depends on the perturbation procedure. We trialled different perturbation procedures where the first one perturbs the given solution by moving deliveries that incur the highest cost on the objective function, whilst the second one moves deliveries that have been shifted less frequently by the local search in previous iterations. Our industry partner provided six sets of daily orders which have varied characteristics in terms of the number of customers, customer distribution, number of fibre boards and fibre boards' sizes. Our investigations show that an instance becomes more constrained when the customer order contains many different board sizes, which makes it harder to find feasible solutions. The results show that the proposed perturbation procedures significantly enhances the performance of iterated local search specifically on such constrained problems.

Keywords: Iterated local search · Perturbation operator · Vehicle routing problem · Time windows · 3-Dimensional loading constraints

© Springer International Publishing AG 2017
M. Wagner et al. (Eds.): ACALCI 2017, LNAI 10142, pp. 279–290, 2017.
DOI: 10.1007/978-3-319-51691-2_24

1   Introduction

The vehicle routing problem (VRP) describes the problem of finding an optimal distributing schedule between depot and customers using a fleet of vehicles [11]. Due to its practical application in supply chain management, transportation and logistics, several variants have been proposed over the last 40 years, most prominently the Capacitated VRP (CVRP), VRP with Time Windows (VRPTW), Multiple Depot VRP (MDVRP) and the Periodic VRP (PVRP). The Three-Dimensional Loading Capacitated VRP (3L-CVRP) was formulated only 2006 as the combination of the VRP and Three-Dimensional Loading, where the objective is not only to find a set of routes but also to satisfy the given constraints imposed by the 3-dimensional nature of the goods and vehicle [11]. Consequently, due to its practical importance, a number of studies have addressed this problem with the inclusion of various constrains such as heterogeneous fleet and time windows [18].

The distribution problem faced by our industry partner combines three-dimensional loading of fibre boards with a heterogeneous fleet and time windows (3L-HFCVRPTW). Both VRP and loading have been proved tp be $\mathcal{NP}$-hard problems and our 3L-HFCVRPTW is combination of VRP and loading. It is highly unlikely that an exact algorithm exists which can solve a 3L-HFCVRPTW of practical complexity to optimality within the time frame prescribed by the processes of our industry partner.

In previous work it was observed that calling the loading module after route optimisation often generates infeasible solutions [17]. In this work, we apply an Iterated Local Search (ILS) algorithm to the 3L-HFCVRPTW that calls the loading module during the optimisation process. ILS improves on an initial solution by locally optimising it and has proved successful with VRP problems before [1,7,20]. Importantly, ILS can easily be hybridised with other optimisation heuristics [3]. Its success has been shown to be highly dependent on the perturbation procedure employed [3]. Lourenço et al. [15] expressed this notion as "A good perturbation transforms one excellent solution into an excellent starting point for a local search". In this work, we propose two perturbation procedures for the ILS. The first perturbs the current solution by moving deliveries which incur the highest cost on the objective function, while the second one moves deliveries that have been moved the least frequently. The performance of the proposed algorithm is assessed using six real-world instances provided by our industrial partner, which are very diverse in size and features. An extensive experimental comparison was conducted to evaluate the value added by the perturbation procedures.

2   Related Work

The Vehicle Routing Problem (VRP) was first introduced by Dantzig and Ramser [8]. Over the years, VRP and it variants have been widely researched in the optimisation literature. A comprehensive review on the VRP and it variants is available in [4,5,13,22].

The 3L-CVRP is based on the integration of CVRP and three-dimensional loading. A large number of methods have been successfully applied to this problem. A review of the integration of VRP and loading is available in [24]. Gendreau et al. [11] applied a taboo search to the 3L-CVRP that treats the loading problem as a subproblem which takes into account additional constraints such as the sequence, fragility and stability.

Tarantilis et al. [21] devised six heuristics for placing rectangular items within a vehicle. After each placement, the coordinates for the next possible placements are calculated. While minimising the length of the load, the heuristics place the next item prioritising the width or height axis, maximising the touching surface along the width or height axis and maximising the touching surfaces excluding the walls of the item. The heuristics are employed in the order of complexity until a feasible solution has been found. The algorithm creates feasible initial solutions by ordering customers in descending order by item volume and assigning them to a minimal number of routes subject to successful packing. If no feasible solution is found, a vehicle is added to form a new route. A guided local search employs one of three search moves with equal probability: relocation of customer within route, swap of customers, relocating a customer to another route. In each case, the entire neighbourhood (all possible placements of the chosen customer according to the move) is considered, while preserving feasibility. A tabu list is used for the reversal of moves.

Duhamel et al. [9] applied a GRASP and Evolutionary Local Search (ELS) to the 3L-CVRP, which develops initial solutions by combining the tours and splitting them again. Before splitting, a perturbation is introduced, and a local search consisting of 2-opt transpositions are applied within and between routes. The load construction algorithm considers 90° rotations but and treats the height dimension as a cost. It includes a look-ahead step for pre-empting placements that prohibit new additions of items. The route building is completed before the resulting sequence of orders is submitted to the load building procedure. The method is compared to Gendreau et al. [11] and Fuellerer et al. [10] and appears to achieve better solutions in most trial runs.

Fuellerer et al. [10] devised an ant colony optimisation (ACO) approach to the 3L-CVRP which employs the bottom left [2] and touching perimeter algorithms [14] for the ensuing loading phase. The ACO implementation is an adaptation of the savings algorithm [6] by Reimann et al. [19]. It assigns each customer to a separate route, then calculates the possible savings from combining the routes and probabilistically chooses one of the combinations based on both pheromone and savings heuristic. The pheromone values are updated based on the F best solutions; each solution contributes pheromone according to its rank. To accommodate the packing task, a second heuristic is added which describes the packing density achieved by including each item in a route. The ACO construction phase, which is followed by a local search, allows infeasible solutions and includes a penalty value in the objective function. The results are compared with the tabu search approach by Gendreau et al. [11].

Moura and Oliveira [16] considered a VRP with time windows integrated with the container loading problem (CLP) where the objective is to minimise the number of vehicles used with a subgoal of minimising the total travel time. In addition to enforcing vehicle capacity, a stable load must be formed. The algorithms applied are random search, 2-opt local search and GRASP with a local search component.

Wei et al. [25] describe a 3L-HFVRP formulation which includes a heterogeneous fleet and three-dimensional loading. Route optimisation takes place first, the result is then checked for feasibility using the loading algorithm. The route optimisation comprises multiple stages which start from an initial solution built according to Clarke and Wright's algorithm [6]. The subsequent local and global search phases alternate adaptively depending on the improvements made. Two global search strategies, a ruin-reconstruct approach which removes large-volume orders and reinserts them, and a concat-split method, which combines all routes and subdivides them again, are applied according to their relative success rates. The shake procedure, which randomly picks two or three orders from the same route and inserts them optimally into a second route (also used by Tricoire et al. [23]) can be seen as a semi-global move intended to escape from possible local optima in between local search moves.

Recently, Junqueira and Morabito [12] applied simulated annealing and record-to-record travel algorithms to generate the routing paths. The performances of the proposed algorithms were evaluated using the vehicle routing benchmark instances and real world instances provided by Brazilian company. The proposed algorithms produce relatively good solutions for real instances.

3   Problem Description

The Melbourne distribution centre (MDC) of our industry partner plans the next-day deliveries during one hour after the cut-off time for orders. The MDC is equipped with three types of custom-made delivery trucks with flat platforms and spaces for dividers which keep the stacks of fibre boards in place.

Customers can order boards of different sizes, each in different quantities. The quantities are typically small - larger orders are delivered separately. Boards are packed into 'packs' and stacked on the truck platforms. If a customer orders several sizes, it may be meaningful to subdivide the delivery for this customer into several packs and place them onto different stacks on the trucks, while strictly maintaining LIFO order. The number of trucks needed for the deliveries depends on the capacity of the truck and the volume of the orders.

The problem at hand can formally be described as a complete graph G (V, E) where V represents a set of customers $V = \{0, ..., n\}$, 0 denotes the MDC and $\{1, ..., n\}$ represent customers. The vertices are connected by edges $E = \{e_{ij} : i \neq j \ and \ i, j \in V\}$.

Objective Function: Each edge is associate with a travel distance c_{ij} expressed in minutes. Melbourne traffic is heavy on certain roads and fluctuates greatly during the day, hence distances do not reflect the problem accurately. The assumption $c_{ij} = c_{ji}$ is a simplification made for this first formulation. Equation 1 expresses the summation of the cost; e_{ij} takes the value 0 if the edge between customers i and j is not used, 1 otherwise. Position 0 denotes the MDC and connects to twice as many customers as there are routes. Waiting times δ_i only apply when the truck arrives before the start of the time window of customer i.

$$f(x) = \sum_{i=0}^{n} \sum_{j=0, j \neq i}^{n} e_{ij} c_{ij} + \sum_{i=1}^{n} \delta_i \qquad (1)$$

Depending on the availability of a forklift on site, and the number of packs to be delivered, customer drop-offs may take between 5 and 25 min, considered as the service time s_i.

Most customers are happy to receive their delivery any time during the day, but a subset of 10–20% of all customers can only receive their deliveries. The time window constraint is expressed in Eq. 2, which expresses that all travel $c_{i,i+1}$ and service times s_i of the customers $\{0...k-1\}$ in route r_x combined have to be greater than or equal to the start time of customer k's time windows start time t_k^s and smaller than the end time t_k^e reduced by the service time s_k of customer k. It is assumed that the load has to be unloaded before the end of the time window, and that an early arrival incurs a waiting time δ which adds to the objective value of the solution.

$$t_k^s - \delta \leq \sum_{i=0, i \in r_x}^{k-1} c_{i,i+1} + s_i \geq t_k^e - s_k \qquad (2)$$

The problem is described in more detail in [17].

4   Proposed Methodology

The ILS application proposed here relies on an initial feasible solution. While constructing the initial solution, the algorithm calls loading module to enforce the loading constraints. At each iteration of the local search procedure, the algorithm calls the loading module to check the modified solution for a predefined number of iterations. The locally optimised solution is accepted only if it is feasible.

4.1   Initial Solution

The initial solution is created using the Nearest Neighbour (NN) heuristic. NN starts at the depot and adds the closest customer, then the customer closest to the last added subject to the loading constraints. When no further customer can be added, a new route is created.

4.2   Routing Module

The route optimisation is effected by ILS in combination with two alternative permutation procedures.

ILS is a generic heuristic framework that can cover any optimisation strategy that works on a single solution. The optimisation process alternates between a global diversification move and a local search which makes small improving steps, often, but not necessarily, taking the solution to a local optimum. In most cases, the local search procedure is defined as a process that makes small improving moves until no improvement is possible, such as stochastic local search or steepest descent. The ILS algorithm as defined by Lourenço et al. [15], however, does not prescribe the local search to be greedy. It only has to define reasonably small moves that form a neighbourhood around the current solution. A listing of the generic ILS is shown in Algorithm 1.

Algorithm 1: Generic Iterated Local Search

---
1 $s \leftarrow GenerateInitialSolution()$;
2 **while** *termination criterion not met* **do**
3     $s' \leftarrow$ Local search (s);
4     $s'' \leftarrow$ Acceptance criterion $(s', s, history)$;
5     $s \leftarrow$ Perturbation $(s'', history)$;
6 **end**

The algorithm locally optimises the current solution, then verifies whether the resulting solution is accepted for perturbation. If not, the perturbation procedure, which is a global move aimed at diversification, perturbs the previous solution again. Within this framework, we define the perturbation and local search procedures as well as the acceptance criterion to suit the fibre board delivery problem as follows.

1. *Local search*: We adopted a stochastic local search which accepts only moves that improve the quality. The choice of local search move can affect the performance of the algorithm significantly. In this work we consider combinations of the following choices of local search move for the 3L-HFCVRPTW:

   - **swap** chooses two deliveries randomly within a route and transposes them.
   - **displacement** selects a delivery from a route and moves it to a different location in the same route.
   - **routeshift** selects a random customer delivery to move to a different route.

   A local search which does not permit shifting deliveries between routes is too restrictive to achieve good optima. Therefore, routeshift is always combined with either swap or displacement or both in our algorithm.

2. *Perturbation procedure*: The perturbation procedure plays an important part in the performance of ILS, helping the search diversify and escape from local optima. In the simplest case, the perturbation procedure re-randomises a locally optimised solution by randomly moving some deliveries from their

current positions in a route and inserting them in a different position in the same or different route. However, this can lead to very poor decisions which position some deliveries so suboptimally that the ensuing local search is likely to reverse the change and revert to the same local optimum. Using domain information in the perturbation can be expected to lead to better starting solutions for the local search. Naturally, the changes have to lead to a diversification rather than attempting to further optimise a locally optimal solution. In this work, we experimented with the following perturbation moves:

(a) **Frequency-based perturbation (F-ILS)**: This procedure perturbs the current solution by prioritising less frequently displaced deliveries. A delivery is always moved to the position that minimises the delivery's contribution to the objective function. Note that the position depends on the remainder of the solution, as the delivery has to be moved between two deliveries that immediately follow each other in the current solution.

(b) **Cost-based perturbation (C-ILS)**: This procedure chooses the customers that are currently the most expensive to visit in terms of the objective function. They are relocated at the cheapest position as in the frequency-based procedure.

3. *Acceptance criterion*: The acceptance criterion decides whether to accept or reject the solution generated by the local search procedure for the next iteration. In this work, we only accept a solution when it is better than the previously known best.

4.3   Loading Module

The loading module optimises the placement of customer deliveries in the customised vehicles. It receives a permutation of customer orders prescribed by the outcome of the routing module. The boards of a delivery have to be packed into one or more packs to be placed in stacks that are laid out on the platform of the truck.

Once all sizes have been determined, a preliminary layout on the bottom of the truck including the number of 'rows' of stacks is decided. Because all parts of a customer delivery have to be accessible from either side of the truck, a row can have one or two stacks abreast.

Given the preliminary layout, the loading module uses a depth-first search algorithm to place each pack on a stack. If a pack placement leads to an invalid solution given the constraints and the heights of the stacks, it is removed and possibly re-packed before another placement on stacks is attempted. If none of the possible placements succeeds, the algorithm backtracks to remove further customer layers before rebuilding the layers again. The recursive backtracking procedure is exhaustive and only viable due to the relative homogeneity of the board sizes and the fact that the choices of alternative packs are limited by the number of stacks.

5   Experimental Setup

In this section, we introduce the benchmark instances that were used in our experimental studies and the parameter settings of the algorithms.

5.1   Benchmark Instances

We use six different 3L-HFCVRPTW instances provided by our industrial partner. Theses instances have various characteristics in terms of number of customers, customer distribution, number of items and items size. Table 1 shows the main characteristics of the 3L-HFCVRPTW instances.

Table 1. Features of the instances

Instance	Number of customers	Total number of items	Total demands
LM-20JAN-1	158	3711	178100KG
LM-14MAR-2	130	2922	155214KG
LM-11MAR-3	120	2458	108786KG
LM-13DEC-4	95	2528	153445KG
LM-17MAR-5	106	2175	148221KG
LM-21MAR-6	110	2797	117475KG

Because each customer's delivery has to be bundled into packs and placed on one or more stacks in a LIFO order and a board can be no larger than 1.5 times the width and depth of the board underneath, customer orders with large numbers of different sizes are more challenging to place than deliveries with boards of a single size. Figure 1 shows the distribution of combinations of item

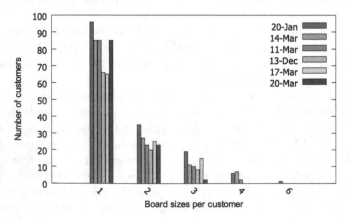

Fig. 1. Histogram of the number of different board sizes a delivery contains (1 means all boards in the delivery are of the same size), while the y-axis refers to the number of deliveries that have these numbers of different sizes.

sizes in all instances. The loading problem becomes more complex the more diverse the boards in a delivery are in size. If a customer orders 3 different sizes, this delivery likely has to be split up to be allocated to several stacks. This, in turn, leads to more stacks that accommodate the different sizes without violating the rule of a maximum overhang of 1/3 of a board.

5.2   Comparison of Algorithms

In addition to the F-ILS and C-ILS algorithms that perturb solutions based on frequency of displacement and cost of access respectively, we also included a random displacement procedure for comparison (R-ILS). Each perturbation strategy was paired with one of the local search strategies - routeshift with either displacement (d-rs) or swap (s-rs) or both (d-s-rs) as described in Sect. 1.

5.3   ILS Parameter Settings

To tune the three parameters required for ILS, we have conducted preliminary trials using 30 independent trials with different parameters combinations. Based on the results, the stopping criterion was set to 100 non-improving evaluations of the acceptance criterion (line 4 of Algorithm 1), the perturbation size is set to 10% of the total number of customers in each instance, and the local search termination criterion is set to 10 non-improving fitness evaluations.

6   Results and Discussion

The computational results over 30 runs of the nine ILS algorithms for the six 3L-HFCVRPTW instances are summarised in Table 2. The results are compared in terms of best, worst and average (Avg) total delivery time (makespan) as well as the number of fitness evaluations (FE) spent. In the table, we indicate in bold font the best results obtained across algorithms. In all cases, C-ILS performs best, but requires the largest number of function evaluations.

The results in Table 2 show that C-ILS with both displacement and swap move performs better than the competing ILS algorithms in terms of both best and average results. Permutations which shift the most costly customers to visit seems the best strategy by a large margin. The results also confirm that a relatively greedy perturbation procedure helps maintain better solutions to locally optimise. Displacing the deliveries that have the longest access path is almost in itself a local search move, and we would suspect that this might not help diversification. Strong perturbations do not seem to benefit the solution. Even the frequency-based choice of delivery to move performs significantly better than the random choice.

All local search strategies include routeshift to ensure the algorithm is able to reassign deliveries to different routes. Combining both swap and displacement with routeshift clearly provides superior results with all instances. Almost all algorithms provide their best result using all three operators (with the exception

Table 2. Comparison of the R-ILS, C-ILS and F-ILS perturbation strategies combined with local search moves displacement (d), swap (s) and routeshift (rs).

Dataset	#	Initial solution	R-ILS d-rs	s-rs	d-s-rs	F-ILS d-rs	s-rs	d-s-rs	C-ILS d-rs	s-rs	d-s-rs
LM-20JAN-1	Best	4475	4426	4423	4392	4364	4351	4292	4252	4276	**4147**
	Worst	-	4474	4474	4472	4470	4472	4392	4296	4292	**4199**
	Avg	-	4453.4	4452.66	4441.63	4435.4	4435.33	4344.06	4269.93	4284.3	**4169.46**
	FE	-	391,503	**387,701**	397,012	486,991	471,131	461,498	506,707	503,014	512,108
LM-14MAR-2	Best	5872	5783	5805	5784	5560	5525	5562	4631	4641	**4521**
	Worst	-	5871	5872	5872	5798	5772	5784	4796	4796	**4596**
	Avg	-	5844.73	5838.26	5839.03	5735.93	5730.06	5734.2	4741.93	4734.13	**4561.6**
	FE	-	**477,098**	496,810	477,109	534,393	551,608	572,751	681,201	685,617	688,653
LM-11MAR-3	Best	3962	3792	3749	3737	3574	3498	3469	3188	3171	**2932**
	Worst	-	3954	3946	3896	3954	3946	3896	3305	3298	**2999**
	Avg	-	3873.76	3840.53	3841.7	3865.53	3827.86	3832.76	3246.5	3250.73	**2962.9**
	FE	-	487,688	**481,667**	483,647	518,172	525,087	542,012	581,391	587,607	587,989
LM-13DEC-4	Best	2433	2425	2423	2420	2276	2236	2201	1964	1893	**1821**
	Worst	-	2433	2431	2433	2433	2431	2433	1998	1999	**1898**
	Avg	-	2430.4	2427	2426.9	2425.33	2420.6	2419.33	1979.63	1945.96	**1858**
	FE	-	892,971	892,931	892,950	892,901	**891,547**	897,851	911,586	919,763	905,712
LM-17MAR-5	Best	4322	3964	3853	3810	3724	3713	3701	3476	3456	**2997**
	Worst	-	3997	3997	3996	3997	3995	3948	3764	3494	**3094**
	Avg	-	3978.66	3904.11	3934.8	3970.66	3894.63	3833.73	3558.63	3472.1	**3045.9**
	FE	-	**873,640**	873,864	873,989	878,074	879,112	879,182	881,007	881,543	885,177
LM-21MAR-6	Best	4213	3875	3897	3841	3765	3763	3621	3338	3216	**3140**
	Worst	-	3998	3999	3993	3984	3979	3979	3494	3375	**3296**
	Avg	-	3950.06	3946.26	3947.06	3939.2	3937.5	3934.06	3442.23	3311.6	**3247.93**
	FE	-	715,310	723,218	**711,167**	784,911	781,813	787,952	857,671	861,855	893,360

of R-ILS and F-ILS on the LM-14MAR-2 instance, where the differences are negligible). To achieve the superior quality, C-ILS(displacement-swap-routeshift) uses the most function evaluations across the algorithms.

To answer the question whether the diversity of the delivered goods influence the solution, we calculated the percentage of improvement the best solution made compared to the initial solution. LM-20JAN is by far the most diverse data set, the only one with up to 6 different boards in some deliveries. Its improvement over the initial solution is only 7% compared to 23% for all others. The LM-17MAR-5 dataset has a maximum of 3 different board sizes per customer, and its improvement over the initial solution is 30%. It appears the number of different boards has a significant influence on the optimisability of the data sets.

Table 3. The p-values of the results of C-ILS(displacement-swap-routeshift) versus all other algorithms

Dataset	R-ILS(d-rs)	R-ILS(s-rs)	R-ILS(d-s-rs)	F-ILS(d-rs)	F-ILS(s-rs)	F-ILS(d-s-rs)	C-ILS(d-rs)	C-ILS(s-rs)
LM-20JAN-1	2.18E-56	1.63E-56	3.84E-51	1.83E-41	4.05E-42	2.36E-39	2.67E-31	9.21E-43
LM-14MAR-2	6.65E-75	3.40E-84	3.29E-82	1.93E-66	9.85E-68	4.35E-69	7.65E-81	4.49E-82
LM-11MAR-3	4.49E-66	1.61E-68	1.65E-72	1.97E-56	9.41E-55	5.59E-55	3.87E-44	6.01E-46
LM-13DEC-4	2.44E-72	3.19E-72	3.69E-72	7.99E-62	2.17E-58	2.09E-55	3.85E-32	1.10E-18
LM-17MAR-5	3.88E-76	1.31E-60	5.99E-62	3.64E-63	1.27E-57	4.15E-56	1.24E-43	1.61E-56
LM-21MAR-6	4.14E-60	1.28E-61	2.01E-60	2.05E-55	2.24E-56	8.03E-49	3.49E-30	4.72E-09

To verify the significance of the differences, we carried out a statistical comparisons using Wilcoxon test with 0.05 confidence level. Table 3 shows the p-values of C-ILS(displacement-swap-routeshift), which confirm that the differences are significant across algorithms and instances.

7 Conclusion

ILS has been shown to be a successful approach to VRP problems before. Our experiments show that the permutation strategy as well as the local search neighbourhood have a decisive influence on solution quality. Applying a perturbation that chooses the deliveries to move according to the magnitude of their current cost contributions leads to clearly superior results. Similarly, using both a swap and a displacement move in combination with an inter-route shift move in the local search procedure has shown to benefit the results greatly.

References

1. Avci, M., Topaloglu, S.: An adaptive local search algorithm for vehicle routing problem with simultaneous and mixed pickups and deliveries. Comput. Ind. Eng. **83**, 15–29 (2015)
2. Baker, B., Coffman Jr., E., Rivest, R.: Orthogonal packings in two dimensions. SIAM J. Comput. **9**(4), 846–855 (1980)
3. Blum, C., Roli, A.: Metaheuristics in combinatorial optimization: overview and conceptual comparison. ACM Comput. Surv. (CSUR) **35**(3), 268–308 (2003)
4. Bräysy, O., Gendreau, M.: Vehicle routing problem with time windows, part i: route construction and local search algorithms. Transp. Sci. **39**(1), 104–118 (2005)
5. Bräysy, O., Gendreau, M.: Vehicle routing problem with time windows, part ii: metaheuristics. Transp. Sci. **39**(1), 119–139 (2005)
6. Clarke, G., Wright, J.W.: Scheduling of vehicles from a central depot to a number of delivery points. Oper. Res. **12**(4), 568–581 (1964)
7. Cuervo, D.P., Goos, P., Sörensen, K., Arráiz, E.: An iterated local search algorithm for the vehicle routing problem with backhauls. Eur. J. Oper. Res. **237**(2), 454–464 (2014)
8. Dantzig, G.B., Ramser, J.H.: The truck dispatching problem. Manag. Sci. **6**(1), 80–91 (1959)
9. Duhamel, C., Lacomme, P., Quilliot, A., Toussaint, H.: A multi-start evolutionary local search for the two-dimensional loading capacitated vehicle routing problem. Comput. Oper. Res. **38**(3), 617–640 (2011)
10. Fuellerer, G., Doerner, K.F., Hartl, R.F., Iori, M.: Metaheuristics for vehicle routing problems with three-dimensional loading constraints. Eur. J. Oper. Res. **201**(3), 751–759 (2010)
11. Gendreau, M., Iori, M., Laporte, G., Martello, S.: A tabu search algorithm for a routing and container loading problem. Transp. Sci. **40**(3), 342–350 (2006)
12. Junqueira, L., Morabito, R.: Heuristic algorithms for a three-dimensional loading capacitated vehicle routing problem in a carrier. Comput. Ind. Eng. **88**, 110–130 (2015)
13. Laporte, G.: The vehicle routing problem: an overview of exact and approximate algorithms. Eur. J. Oper. Res. **59**(3), 345–358 (1992)

14. Lodi, A., Martello, S., Vigo, D.: Heuristic and metaheuristic approaches for a class of two-dimensional bin packing problems. INFORMS J. Comput. **11**(4), 345–357 (1999)
15. Lourenço, H.R., Martin, O.C., Stützle, T.: Iterated local search. In: Glover, F., Kochenberger, G.A. (eds.) Handbook of Metaheuristics, vol. 57, pp. 320–353. Springer, Boston (2003)
16. Moura, A., Oliveira, J.F.: An integrated approach to the vehicle routing and container loading problems. OR Spectr. **31**(4), 775–800 (2009)
17. Pace, S., Turky, A., Moser, I., Aleti, A.: Distributing fibre boards: a practical application of the heterogeneous fleet vehicle routing problem with time windows and three-dimensional loading constraints. Procedia Comput. Sci. **51**, 2257–2266 (2015)
18. Pollaris, H., Braekers, K., Caris, A., Janssens, G.K., Limbourg, S.: Vehicle routing problems with loading constraints: state-of-the-art and future directions. OR Spectr. **37**(2), 297–330 (2015)
19. Reimann, M., Doerner, K., Hartl, R.F.: D-ants: savings based ants divide and conquer the vehicle routing problem. Comput. Oper. Res. **31**(4), 563–591 (2004)
20. Silva, M.M., Subramanian, A., Ochi, L.S.: An iterated local search heuristic for the split delivery vehicle routing problem. Comput. Oper. Res. **53**, 234–249 (2015)
21. Tarantilis, C., Zachariadis, E., Kiranoudis, C.: A hybrid metaheuristic algorithm for the integrated vehicle routing and three-dimensional container-loading problem. IEEE Trans. Intell. Transp. Syst. **10**(2), 255–271 (2009)
22. Toth, P., Vigo, D.: The Vehicle Routing Problem. Society for Industrial and Applied Mathematics (2002)
23. Tricoire, F., Doerner, K., Hartl, R., Iori, M.: Heuristic and exact algorithms for the multi-pile vehicle routing problem. OR Spectr. **33**(4), 931–959 (2011)
24. Wang, F., Tao, Y., Shi, N.: A survey on vehicle routing problem with loading constraints. In: International Joint Conference on Computational Sciences and Optimization, CSO 2009, vol. 2, pp. 602–606. IEEE (2009)
25. Wei, L., Zhang, Z., Lim, A.: An adaptive variable neighborhood search for a heterogeneous fleet vehicle routing problem with three-dimensional loading constraints. IEEE Comput. Intell. Mag. **9**(4), 18–30 (2014)

A Memetic Cooperative Co-evolution Model for Large Scale Continuous Optimization

Yuan Sun[1(✉)], Michael Kirley[2], and Saman K. Halgamuge[3]

[1] Department of Mechanical Engineering, The University of Melbourne,
Parkville, VIC 3010, Australia
yuans2@student.unimelb.edu.au
[2] Department of Computing and Information Systems, The University of Melbourne,
Parkville, VIC 3010, Australia
mkirley@unimelb.edu.au
[3] Research School of Engineering, The Australian National University,
Canberra, ACT 2601, Australia
saman.halgamuge@anu.edu.au

Abstract. Cooperative co-evolution (CC) is a framework that can be used to 'scale up' EAs to solve high dimensional optimization problems. This approach employs a divide and conquer strategy, which decomposes a high dimensional problem into sub-components that are optimized separately. However, the traditional CC framework typically employs only one EA to solve all the sub components, which may be ineffective. In this paper, we propose a new memetic cooperative co-evolution (MCC) framework which divides a high dimensional problem into several separable and non-separable sub-components based on the underlying structure of variable interactions. Then, different local search methods are employed to enhance the search of an EA to solve the separable and non-separable sub-components. The proposed MCC model was evaluated on two benchmark sets with 35 benchmark problems. The experimental results confirmed the effectiveness of our proposed model, when compared against two traditional CC algorithms and a state-of-the-art memetic algorithm.

Keywords: Cooperative co-evolution · Memetic algorithm · Large scale global optimization · Continuous optimization problem

1 Introduction

Large scale optimization problems are very challenging for evolutionary algorithms (EAs) to solve. This in part may be attributed to the fact that (a) the search space of an optimization problem grows exponentially as the dimensionality increases [1]; (b) the complexity of an optimization problem usually grows as the dimensionality increases [2]; and (c) the computational cost of using some EAs (e.g., estimation of distribution algorithms) when solving very high-dimensional problems is extremely high [3].

© Springer International Publishing AG 2017
M. Wagner et al. (Eds.): ACALCI 2017, LNAI 10142, pp. 291–300, 2017.
DOI: 10.1007/978-3-319-51691-2_25

Cooperative co-evolution (CC) [4] has been used with some success to 'scale up' EAs to solve high dimensional problems [5–7]. This approach employs a divide and conquer strategy, which decomposes a high dimensional problem into several sub-components that are optimized cooperatively. When optimizing each sub-component, representatives (typically the best sub-solutions found) from other sub-components are combined with individuals in the optimized sub-component, to form complete candidate solutions that can be evaluated. However, the traditional CC framework typically employs only one EA to solve all the sub-components, which may be ineffective.

In this paper, we propose a new memetic cooperative co-evolution (MCC) framework, which employs local search methods to enhance the search of an EA. The proposed MCC framework decomposes a large scale optimization problem into several sub-components based on the variable interaction structures. Then, an EA can be used to solve each sub-component cooperatively. Different local search methods (S operator [8] and R operator [9]) are selected to improve the best solution found by the EA for the separable and non-separable sub-components respectively. The S operator perturbs one decision variable at a time, therefore it is sufficient to solve separable sub-components. The R operator perturbs all the decision variables together to adapt to the local gradient of the fitness landscape, therefore, it is more appropriate to use when attempting to solve non-separable sub-components. The step sizes of the local search methods are updated using the diversity of the current population in the EA.

We have evaluated the efficacy of the proposed MCC framework using benchmark problems from the special sessions on large scale global optimization at CEC'2010 [10] and CEC'2013 [11]. Comprehensive numerical simulations showed that the proposed MCC framework achieved significantly better solution quality than the traditional CC framework. When compared against a state-of-the-art memetic algorithm, it achieved comparable or better solution quality.

The remainder of this paper is organized as follows. Section 2 describes the traditional CC framework. Section 3 describes the proposed MCC framework in detail. Section 4 describes the experiments to evaluate the proposed MCC framework, and analyzes the experimental results. Section 5 concludes the paper.

2   Cooperative Co-evolution

The standard cooperative co-evolution (CC) [4] framework consists of two stages: *decomposition* and *optimization*.

In the decomposition stage, an optimization problem is decomposed into several sub-components. The existing decomposition methods can be classified into two different categories: *predetermined decomposition* and *automatic decomposition*. The predetermined decomposition methods determine the number of sub-components and the size of each sub-component before the decomposition stage starts, e.g., uni-variable grouping [4], S_k grouping [12], random grouping [13], delta grouping [14] and k-means grouping [15]. These methods work well when combined with EAs to solve fully separable problems. However, the performance deteriorates quickly when used to solve partially separable problems

---

Algorithm 1. Memetic Cooperative Co-evolution

1: Automatically decompose a large scale problem into several sub-components
2: **while** Cycle < CycleMax **do**
3:   **for** each sub-component s_j **do**
4:     Apply an EA on the sub-component s_j
5:     **if** s_j is a separable sub-component **then**
6:       Apply S operator on the best solution found by the EA
7:     **else**
8:       Apply R operator on the best solution found by the EA
9:     **end if**
10:   **end for**
11: **end while**
12: **return** the best solution ever found

---

or fully non-separable problems. The main reason is that such approaches do not take the underlying variable interaction structure into consideration.

The automatic decomposition methods automatically identify and place the interacting decision variables into the same sub-component. It is important to note that automatic decomposition caters to the underlying variable interaction structure encapsulated within the search landscape. Representative automatic decomposition methods include differential grouping [5], extended differential grouping [16], global differential grouping [17], cooperative co-evolution with variable interaction learning [18], statistical variable interdependence learning [19], and the fast variable interdependence searching [20].

In the optimization stage, an evolutionary algorithm can be used to optimize each sub-component based on a context vector. The context vector is a complete candidate solution, typically consisting of the best sub-solutions from each sub-component. When optimizing the i_{th} sub-component, the context vector (excluding the i_{th} sub-solution) is used to combine with the individuals in the i_{th} sub-component, to form complete candidate solutions that can be evaluated. It has been recently found that using only one context vector may be too greedy [21]. Therefore, the adaptive multi-context CC [21] framework is proposed, which employs more than one context vector to co-evolve sub-components.

3   Memetic Cooperative Co-evolution

In this section, the proposed memetic cooperative co-evolution (MCC) model is described in detail (Algorithm 1).

In the decomposition stage, any automatic decomposition method can be used to divide a large scale optimization problem into several sub-components. An automatic method decomposes an optimization problem based on the underlying structure of variable interactions. Taking the following objective function as an example

$$f(\boldsymbol{x}) := x_1^2 + x_2^2 + (x_3 - x_4)^2 + (x_4 - x_5)^2 + (x_6 - x_7)^2, \boldsymbol{x} \in [-1, 1]^7, \qquad (1)$$

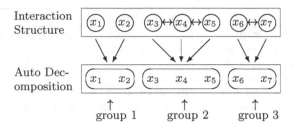

Fig. 1. The variable interaction structure and the automatic decomposition of the objective function given in Eq. (1). The notation $x_i \leftrightarrow x_j$ denotes that decision variable x_i directly interacts with x_j.

decision variables $\{x_3, x_4, x_5\}$ interact, as well as $\{x_6, x_7\}$. Therefore, the decision variables should be divided into three sub-components $\{x_1, x_2\}$, $\{x_3, x_4, x_5\}$ and $\{x_6, x_7\}$, as shown in Fig. 1.

It is important to note that the level of interaction between given decision variables may be different. For example, in Eq. (1), both (x_3, x_4) and (x_3, x_5) interact with each other. However, x_3 and x_4 interact directly; x_3 and x_5 are linked by x_4. The former is called *direct interaction* and the latter is called *indirect interaction*. The formal definitions of direct interaction and indirect interaction are described in [16,22].

In the optimization stage, an EA can be used to solve each sub-component cooperatively. If the sub-component consists of a group of separable decision variables, a local search method – S operator [8] is used to further improve the best solution found by the EA. The S operator perturbs one decision variable at a time, therefore it is sufficient to solve separable problems. If the sub-component consists of a group of non-separable decision variables, the R operator [9] is used to further improve the best solution found by the EA. The R operator perturbs all the decision variables together to adapt to the local gradient of the fitness landscape, therefore, it is more appropriate to use when attempting to solve non-separable problems. The differences between the S and R operators are illustrated in Fig. 2.

The step sizes of the S and R operators are updated using the diversity of the current population in the EA:

$$Step\_S = \min\big(r, 0.1(\boldsymbol{ub} - \boldsymbol{lb})\big), \; Step\_R = \min\big(r, 0.04(\boldsymbol{ub} - \boldsymbol{lb})\big), \tag{2}$$

where $\boldsymbol{ub}$ and $\boldsymbol{lb}$ are the upper bounds and lower bounds of the search space, and r is the diversity of the current population, which is estimated as follows:

$$r = \frac{1}{N} \sum_{i=1}^{N} ||\boldsymbol{x}_{best}, pop(i, :)||_2, \tag{3}$$

where pop is the current population, $\boldsymbol{x}_{best}$ is the best solution in the current population, and N is the population size. Please note that the initial step size for S operator is larger than the initial step size for R operator. The reason for

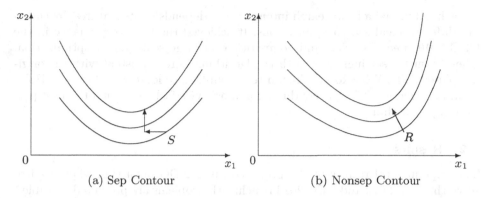

(a) Sep Contour   (b) Nonsep Contour

Fig. 2. The search approaches of the S and R operators. Figure (a) and (b) are the contours of a separable and non-separable fitness landscapes respectively. The S operator searches in the direction of each decision variable. The R operator searches in the direction of the local derivative.

this is that S operator always decreases the step size during the search, while the R operator can increase or decrease the step size later on.

4 Experiments

4.1 Methodology

The decomposition method – extended differential grouping (XDG) [16] and the EA – Self-adaptive Differential Evolution with Neighborhood Search (SaNSDE) [23] were embedded into the proposed memetic cooperative co-evolution (MCC) model to evaluate its efficacy. The XDG method was used, as it can identify both direct and indirect variable interactions. The SaNSDE algorithm was selected for its good performance and wide usage to solve large scale optimization problems. We denote the proposed memetic algorithm as MCC-XDG.

The proposed MCC-XDG algorithm was used to solve the CEC'2010 [10] and CEC'2013 [11] large scale benchmark problems. The maximum number of function evaluations was set to 3×10^6, divided between the decomposition stage and optimization stage. The threshold value for XDG was set to 0.1, and the population size for SaNSDE was set to 50. In each cycle, the maximal number of iterations for SaNSDE was set to 200, and the maximal number of function evaluations for local search methods was set to $10d$, where d is the dimensionality. For each benchmark problem, the median, mean and standard deviation of the best solutions found by the MCC-XDG algorithm based on 30 independent runs were recorded.

The performance of the MCC-XDG algorithm was compared with the performance of two traditional CC algorithms: DECC-XDG (SaNSDE with XDG) and DECC-G (SaNSDE with random grouping [13]), as well as a state-of-the-art memetic algorithm: MA-SW-Chains [24]. The MA-SW-Chains algorithm assigns to each individual a local search intensity that depends on its features, by chaining different local search applications. It achieved the best performance in the CEC 2010 special session and competition on large scale global optimization. The parameter settings for the three algorithms were consistent with the original papers. The Wilcoxon rank-sum test (significance level $\alpha = 0.05$) with Holm p-value correction [25] was conducted in a pairwise fashion to find the best performing algorithm.

4.2 Results

The experimental results of the proposed MCC-XDG algorithm when used to solve the CEC'2010 and CEC'2013 benchmark problems are presented in Table 1 and Table 2 respectively. It achieved the best solution quality on 17 out of 20 CEC'2010 benchmark problems and 8 out of 15 CEC'2013 benchmark problems when compared against three other algorithms. The experimental results showed that the MCC-XDG algorithm can solve some of the benchmark problems to great accuracy (median), e.g., CEC'2010 f_1, f_3, f_6 to f_8, f_{11}, f_{12}, f_{16} and f_{17}.

Comparison with DECC-XDG. The proposed MCC-XDG algorithm achieved equal or better results across all the CEC'2010 and CEC'2013 benchmark problems compared against the DECC-XDG algorithm. In some cases, the median of the best solution found by the MCC-XDG is much better than that found by the DECC-XDG algorithm. Taking CEC'2010 f_7 as an example, the median of the best solution found by MCC-XDG is 5.86×10^{-21}, which is much smaller (better) than the median of the best solution found by DECC-XDG (2.34×10^2). It is important to note that the only difference between the MCC-XDG and DECC-XDG algorithms is that MCC-XDG uses local search methods to enhance the search of the EA – SaNSDE, while DECC-XDG only uses SaNSDE to solve each sub-component. Therefore, the experimental results confirmed the effectiveness of the MCC model and the local search methods.

Comparison with DECC-G. The proposed MCC-XDG algorithm achieved equal or better results than the DECC-G algorithm across all the benchmark problems except for CEC'2010 f_2 and CEC'2013 f_2. The DECC-G algorithm uses a predetermined decomposition method – random grouping. On CEC'2010 f_2 and CEC'2013 f_2, the DECC-G achieved the best solution quality when compared against the other three algorithms. However, on other benchmark problems especially partially non-separable problems (CEC'2010 f_4 to f_{18} and CEC'2013 f_4 to f_{11}), the DECC-G algorithm was outperformed by the other three algorithms. The reason for this is that the DECC-G algorithm (random grouping) decomposes an optimization problem without considering any variable interaction.

Comparison with MA-SW-Chains. The proposed MCC-XDG algorithm achieved comparable or better results than a state-of-the-art memetic algorithm

Table 1. The results of the proposed MCC-XDG algorithm when used to solve the CEC'2010 benchmark problems. The MCC-XDG algorithm is compared with DECC-XDG, DECC-G and MA-SW-Chains. The best performances are highlighted in bold (Wilcoxon rank-sum tests ($\alpha = 0.05$) with Holm p-value correction).

Func	Stats	MCC-XDG	DECC-XDG	DECC-G	MA-SW-Chains
f_1	Median	**0.00e+00**	5.57e+02	6.06e-14	2.67e-14
	Mean	**6.08e-29**	1.37e+04	9.14e-14	3.80e-14
	Std	**2.21e-28**	4.11e+04	7.87e-14	4.91e-14
f_2	Median	2.96e+03	4.42e+03	**1.16e+02**	8.47e+02
	Mean	3.04e+03	4.43e+03	**1.13e+02**	8.40e+02
	Std	2.51e+02	1.56e+02	**2.64e+01**	4.88e+01
f_3	Median	**1.42e-14**	1.68e+01	1.79e+00	5.16e-13
	Mean	**7.55e-01**	1.67e+01	1.77e+00	5.76e-13
	Std	**3.77e+00**	3.53e-01	3.14e-01	2.73e-13
f_4	Median	3.55e+11	7.38e+11	1.17e+13	**3.10e+11**
	Mean	3.73e+11	7.37e+11	1.09e+13	**2.97e+11**
	Std	1.41e+11	1.44e+11	2.83e+12	**6.19e+10**
f_5	Median	**8.15e+07**	1.54e+08	2.25e+08	2.30e+08
	Mean	**8.64e+07**	1.53e+08	2.46e+08	2.18e+08
	Std	**2.55e+07**	2.27e+07	5.40e+07	5.75e+07
f_6	Median	**3.55e-09**	1.64e+01	4.94e+06	2.45e+00
	Mean	4.10e+04	1.63e+01	5.03e+06	1.42e+05
	Std	2.05e+05	3.60e-01	8.77e+05	3.96e+05
f_7	Median	**5.86e-21**	2.34e+02	4.40e+06	7.94e-03
	Mean	**6.21e-21**	7.50e+02	5.13e+06	1.17e+02
	Std	**2.02e-21**	1.62e+03	3.69e+06	2.37e+02
f_8	Median	**8.18e-19**	6.55e+00	8.71e+07	2.70e+06
	Mean	1.43e+06	4.78e+05	7.34e+07	6.90e+06
	Std	1.95e+06	1.32e+06	3.16e+07	1.90e+07
f_9	Median	1.41e+06	1.12e+08	2.43e+08	1.48e+07
	Mean	1.59e+06	1.15e+08	2.41e+08	1.49e+07
	Std	8.42e+05	1.33e+07	2.67e+07	1.61e+06
f_{10}	Median	2.32e+03	5.23e+03	9.47e+03	**2.02e+03**
	Mean	2.33e+03	5.23e+03	9.98e+00	**2.01e+03**
	Std	1.14e+02	1.40e+02	1.29e+03	1.59e+02
f_{11}	Median	**1.62e-05**	1.07e+01	2.53e+01	3.77e+01
	Mean	**3.07e-01**	1.08e+01	2.51e+01	3.86e+01
	Std	**7.17e-01**	8.89e-01	1.45e+00	8.06e+00
f_{12}	Median	**2.83e-06**	1.21e+04	4.49e+04	3.09e-06
	Mean	**4.40e-06**	1.23e+04	4.47e+04	3.24e-06
	Std	6.20e-06	2.50e+03	5.11e+03	**5.78e-07**
f_{13}	Median	**8.83e+00**	3.83e+03	3.12e+03	8.61e+02
	Mean	**1.86e+01**	3.76e+03	3.99e+03	9.83e+02
	Std	**3.12e+01**	1.34e+03	2.52e+03	5.66e+02
f_{14}	Median	**1.05e+07**	6.01e+08	5.88e+08	3.23e+07
	Mean	**1.07e+07**	5.97e+08	5.85e+08	3.25e+07
	Std	3.08e+06	3.42e+07	4.44e+07	2.46e+06
f_{15}	Median	**2.48e+03**	6.35e+03	6.63e+03	2.67e+03
	Mean	**2.46e+03**	6.34e+03	8.60e+03	2.68e+03
	Std	9.87e+01	9.01e+01	3.22e+03	9.95e+01
f_{16}	Median	**2.23e-12**	**1.78e-08**	7.89e+01	9.32e+01
	Mean	5.59e-01	**1.77e-08**	7.76e+01	9.95e+01
	Std	8.66e-01	**1.83e-09**	1.46e+01	1.53e+01
f_{17}	Median	**5.54e-01**	1.25e+05	1.78e+05	1.28e+00
	Mean	**8.51e-01**	1.26e+05	1.76e+05	1.27e+00
	Std	9.23e-01	5.34e+03	1.02e+04	**1.24e-01**
f_{18}	Median	**3.11e+02**	1.36e+03	2.57e+04	1.41e+03
	Mean	**3.77e+02**	1.38e+03	2.44e+04	1.57e+03
	Std	2.61e+02	1.39e+02	1.24e+04	6.73e+02
f_{19}	Median	**2.64e+05**	1.72e+06	7.87e+05	3.75e+05
	Mean	**2.67e+05**	1.73e+06	7.74e+05	3.80e+05
	Std	2.56e+04	1.14e+05	3.94e+04	2.34e+04
f_{20}	Median	6.80e+02	3.49e+04	3.36e+03	1.04e+03
	Mean	6.88e+02	2.01e+05	3.39e+03	1.06e+03
	Std	1.66e+02	8.09e+05	3.04e+02	9.38e+01

Table 2. The results of the proposed MCC-XDG algorithm when used to solve the CEC'2013 benchmark problems. The MCC-XDG algorithm is compared with DECC-XDG, DECC-G and MA-SW-Chains. The best performances are highlighted in bold (Wilcoxon rank-sum tests ($\alpha = 0.05$) with Holm p-value correction).

Func	Stats	MCC-XDG	DECC-XDG	DECC-G	MA-SW-Chains
f_1	Median	**0.00e+00**	5.32e-01	1.31e-11	7.12e-13
	Mean	**3.16e-29**	3.73e+01	2.58e-11	1.34e-12
	Std	**9.51e-29**	1.24e+02	3.83e-11	2.45e-12
f_2	Median	5.50e+03	1.29e+04	**8.24e+01**	1.24e+03
	Mean	5.81e+03	1.27e+04	**8.53e+01**	1.25e+03
	Std	1.29e+03	6.40e+02	**2.71e+01**	1.05e+02
f_3	Median	2.01e+01	2.13e+01	2.01e+01	**6.83e-13**
	Mean	2.01e+01	2.13e+01	2.01e+01	**6.85e-13**
	Std	1.27e-02	1.64e-02	3.10e-03	**2.12e-13**
f_4	Median	**3.28e+09**	7.87e+09	8.48e+10	**2.75e+09**
	Mean	**3.43e+09**	8.07e+09	9.00e+10	**3.81e+09**
	Std	**1.03e+09**	2.02e+09	3.63e+10	**2.73e+09**
f_5	Median	4.22e+06	4.00e+06	8.61e+06	**2.03e+06**
	Mean	4.21e+06	4.21e+06	8.27e+06	**2.25e+06**
	Std	9.80e+05	6.86e+05	1.32e+06	**1.30e+06**
f_6	Median	1.00e+06	1.06e+06	1.05e+06	**6.33e+02**
	Mean	1.00e+06	1.06e+06	1.05e+06	**1.86e+04**
	Std	1.28e+04	1.32e+03	1.44e+03	**2.54e+04**
f_7	Median	**1.27e+04**	1.40e+07	2.82e+08	4.03e+06
	Mean	**1.47e+04**	1.40e+07	3.53e+08	3.85e+06
	Std	**1.03e+04**	5.88e+06	2.35e+08	6.34e+05
f_8	Median	6.30e+13	2.77e+14	2.50e+15	**4.60e+13**
	Mean	7.72e+13	3.16e+14	2.90e+15	**4.62e+13**
	Std	4.10e+13	1.89e+14	1.31e+15	**9.02e+12**
f_9	Median	2.60e+08	4.92e+08	5.68e+08	**1.36e+08**
	Mean	2.55e+08	4.90e+08	5.94e+08	**1.44e+08**
	Std	4.69e+07	2.83e+07	1.36e+08	**2.55e+07**
f_{10}	Median	9.12e+07	9.42e+07	9.28e+07	**3.34e+02**
	Mean	9.14e+07	9.43e+07	9.29e+07	**3.72e+04**
	Std	8.53e+05	3.20e+05	5.88e+05	**6.25e+04**
f_{11}	Median	**7.09e+06**	6.08e+08	5.19e+10	2.10e+08
	Mean	**1.27e+07**	6.27e+08	5.93e+10	2.10e+08
	Std	**1.20e+07**	2.84e+08	4.23e+10	2.35e+07
f_{12}	Median	**6.63e+02**	3.82e+03	3.35e+03	1.25e+03
	Mean	**7.03e+02**	4.40e+03	3.41e+03	1.24e+03
	Std	**1.84e+02**	2.02e+03	2.85e+02	8.33e+01
f_{13}	Median	**1.99e+06**	1.01e+09	5.56e+09	1.91e+07
	Mean	**3.14e+06**	1.22e+09	5.74e+09	1.98e+07
	Std	**2.25e+06**	5.13e+08	2.37e+09	2.30e+06
f_{14}	Median	**1.20e+07**	2.34e+09	6.35e+10	1.43e+08
	Mean	**1.25e+07**	3.44e+09	7.68e+10	1.45e+08
	Std	**3.18e+06**	2.94e+09	4.96e+10	1.60e+07
f_{15}	Median	**6.63e+05**	9.65e+06	5.03e+06	5.80e+06
	Mean	**6.67e+05**	1.00e+07	5.13e+06	5.98e+06
	Std	**1.59e+05**	1.51e+06	4.36e+05	1.42e+06

– MA-SW-Chains across the CEC'2010 benchmark problems. The main difference between the MCC-XDG and MA-SW-Chains algorithms is that MCC-XDG solves an optimization problem by a divide and conquer strategy, while MA-SW-Chains solves an optimization problem as a whole. Therefore, the experimental results confirmed the effectiveness of the divide and conquer strategy – cooperative co-evolution. It is important to note that on CEC'2010 f_3, the proposed MCC-XDG algorithm was reported to outperform the MA-SW-Chains algorithm, in spite of the fact that the mean of the best solution found by MCC-XDG is worse than the mean of the best solution found by MA-SW-Chains. The reason for this is that the Wilcoxon rank sum test examines whether two samples are from continuous distributions with equal medians instead of means. On the CEC'2013 benchmark problems, the proposed MCC-XDG algorithm performed equally well with the MA-SW-Chains algorithm.

5 Conclusion

In this paper, we have investigated the effectiveness of the cooperative co-evolution framework when used to 'scale up' EAs to solve large scale optimization problems. A new memetic cooperative co-evolution framework was proposed, which employs local search methods (S and R operators) to enhance the search of an EA to solve separable and non-separable sub-components. Comprehensive experimental results showed that the proposed memetic cooperative co-evolution framework improved the performance of the traditional cooperative co-evolution framework. When compared against a state-of-the-art memetic algorithm, it achieved comparable or better solution quality.

References

1. Omidvar, M.N., Li, X., Tang, K.: Designing benchmark problems for large-scale continuous optimization. Inf. Sci. **316**, 419–436 (2015)
2. Weise, T., Chiong, R., Tang, K.: Evolutionary optimization: pitfalls and booby traps. J. Comput. Sci. Technol. **27**(5), 907–936 (2012)
3. Dong, W., Chen, T., Tino, P., Yao, X.: Scaling up estimation of distribution algorithms for continuous optimization. IEEE Trans. Evol. Comput. **17**(6), 797–822 (2013)
4. Potter, M.A., Jong, K.A.: A cooperative coevolutionary approach to function optimization. In: Davidor, Y., Schwefel, H.-P., Männer, R. (eds.) PPSN 1994. LNCS, vol. 866, pp. 249–257. Springer, Heidelberg (1994). doi:10.1007/3-540-58484-6_269
5. Omidvar, M.N., Li, X., Mei, Y., Yao, X.: Cooperative co-evolution with differential grouping for large scale optimization. IEEE Trans. Evol. Comput. **18**(3), 378–393 (2014)
6. Mei, Y., Li, X., Yao, X.: Cooperative coevolution with route distance grouping for large-scale capacitated arc routing problems. IEEE Trans. Evol. Comput. **18**(3), 435–449 (2014)
7. Tan, K.C., Yang, Y., Goh, C.K.: A distributed cooperative coevolutionary algorithm for multiobjective optimization. IEEE Trans. Evol. Comput. **10**(5), 527–549 (2006)

8. Tseng, L., Chen, C.: Multiple trajectory search for large scale global optimization. In: IEEE Congress on Evolutionary Computation, CEC 2008, IEEE World Congress on Computational Intelligence, pp. 3052–3059. IEEE (2008)
9. Rosenbrock, H.: An automatic method for finding the greatest or least value of a function. Comput. J. **3**(3), 175–184 (1960)
10. Tang, K., Yao, X., Suganthan, P.: Benchmark functions for the CEC 2010 special session and competition on large scale global optimization. Technique report, USTC, Natrue Inspired Computation and Applications Laboratory, no. 1, pp. 1–23 (2010)
11. Li, X., Tang, K., Omidvar, M.N., Yang, Z., Qin, K.: Benchmark functions for the CEC 2013 special session and competition on large-scale global optimization. Gene **7**(33), 8 (2013)
12. Van den Bergh, F., Engelbrecht, A.P.: A cooperative approach to particle swarm optimization. IEEE Trans. Evol. Comput. **8**(3), 225–239 (2004)
13. Yang, Z., Tang, K., Yao, X.: Large scale evolutionary optimization using cooperative coevolution. Inf. Sci. **178**(15), 2985–2999 (2008)
14. Omidvar, M.N., Li, X., Yao, X.: Cooperative co-evolution with delta grouping for large scale non-separable function optimization. In: 2010 IEEE Congress on Evolutionary Computation (CEC), pp. 1–8. IEEE (2010)
15. Mahdavi, S., Rahnamayan, S., Shiri, M.E.: Multilevel framework for large-scale global optimization. Soft Comput. 1–30 (2016)
16. Sun, Y., Kirley, M., Halgamuge, S.K.: Extended differential grouping for large scale global optimization with direct and indirect variable interactions. In: Proceedings of the 2015 on Genetic and Evolutionary Computation Conference, pp. 313–320. ACM (2015)
17. Mei, Y., Omidvar, M.N., Li, X., Yao, X.: A competitive divide-and-conquer algorithm for unconstrained large-scale black-box optimization. ACM Trans. Math. Softw. (TOMS) **42**(2), 13 (2016)
18. Chen, W., Weise, T., Yang, Z., Tang, K.: Large-scale global optimization using cooperative coevolution with variable interaction learning. In: Schaefer, R., Cotta, C., Kołodziej, J., Rudolph, G. (eds.) PPSN 2010. LNCS, vol. 6239, pp. 300–309. Springer, Berlin (2010). doi:10.1007/978-3-642-15871-1_31
19. Sun, L., Yoshida, S., Cheng, X., Liang, Y.: A cooperative particle swarm optimizer with statistical variable interdependence learning. Inf. Sci. **186**(1), 20–39 (2012)
20. Ge, H., Sun, L., Yang, X., Yoshida, S., Liang, Y.: Cooperative differential evolution with fast variable interdependence learning and cross-cluster mutation. Appl. Soft Comput. **36**, 300–314 (2015)
21. Tang, R., Wu, Z., Fang, Y.: Adaptive multi-context cooperatively coevolving particle swarm optimization for large-scale problems. Soft Comput. 1–20 (2016)
22. Sun, Y., Kirley, M., Halgamuge, S.K.: Quantifying variable interactions in continuous optimization problems. IEEE Trans. Evol. Comput. (in press)
23. Yang, Z., Tang, K., Yao, X.: Self-adaptive differential evolution with neighborhood search. In: IEEE Congress on Evolutionary Computation, CEC 2008, IEEE World Congress on Computational Intelligence, pp. 1110–1116. IEEE (2008)
24. Molina, D., Lozano, M., Herrera, F.: MA-SW-chains: memetic algorithm based on local search chains for large scale continuous global optimization. In: 2010 IEEE Congress on Evolutionary Computation (CEC), pp. 1–8. IEEE (2010)
25. Sheskin, D.J.: Handbook of Parametric and Nonparametric Statistical Procedures. CRC Press, Boca Raton (2003)

Investigating the Generality of Genetic Programming Based Hyper-heuristic Approach to Dynamic Job Shop Scheduling with Machine Breakdown

John Park[1(✉)], Yi Mei[1], Su Nguyen[1,2], Gang Chen[1], and Mengjie Zhang[1(✉)]

[1] Evolutionary Computation Research Group, Victoria University of Wellington,
P.O. Box 600, Wellington, New Zealand
{John.Park,Yi.Mei,Su.Nguyen,Aaron.Chen,Mengjie.Zhang}@ecs.vuw.ac.nz
[2] Hoa Sen University, Ho Chi Minh City, Vietnam

Abstract. Dynamic job shop scheduling (DJSS) problems are combinatorial optimisation problems that have been extensively studied in the literature due to their difficulty and their applicability to real-world manufacturing systems, e.g., car manufacturing systems. In a DJSS problem instance, jobs arrive on the shop floor to be processed on specific sequences of machines on the shop floor and unforeseen events such as dynamic job arrivals and machine breakdown occur that affect the properties of the shop floor. Many researchers have proposed genetic programming based hyper-heuristic (GP-HH) approaches to evolve high quality dispatching rules for DJSS problems with dynamic job arrivals, outperforming good man-made rules for the problems. However, no GP-HH approaches have been proposed for DJSS problems with dynamic job arrivals and machine breakdowns, and it is not known how well GP generalises over both DJSS problem instances with no machine breakdown to problem instances with machine breakdown. Therefore, this paper investigates the generality of GP for DJSS problem with dynamic job arrivals and machine breakdowns. To do this, a machine breakdown specific DJSS dataset is proposed, and an analysis procedure is used to observe the differences in the structures of the GP rules when evolved under different machine breakdown scenarios. The results show that performance and the distributions of the terminals for the evolved rules is sensitive to the frequency of machine breakdowns in the training instances used to evolve the rules.

1 Introduction

In the field of operations research, job shop scheduling (JSS) and other scheduling problems have been extensively researched for the past 50 years [1]. In a JSS problem, there is a *shop floor* that usually contains a fixed number of *machines* and the machines are used to process incoming *jobs* [1]. A job needs to be processed on a sequence of specific machines and machines on the shop floor can only process one job at a time. The goal in a JSS problem is to find a *schedule*,

© Springer International Publishing AG 2017
M. Wagner et al. (Eds.): ACALCI 2017, LNAI 10142, pp. 301–313, 2017.
DOI: 10.1007/978-3-319-51691-2_26

a solution that gives the sequences of times that the jobs are processed at the machines, that is the optimal given an *objective function* [1]. For example, in a JSS problem with makespan as the objective, the goal is to find a schedule which completes all jobs as early as possible [1].

In a real-world scenario, it is likely that unforeseen events such as dynamic job arrivals and machine breakdowns affect the properties of the shop floor in a JSS problem instance [2]. A JSS problem instances with dynamic job arrivals is called a *dynamic* JSS (DJSS) problem instance [2]. In a DJSS problem instance with dynamic job arrivals, the properties of the arriving jobs are unknown (until they arrive on the shop floor) and the number of jobs that arrive on the shop floor is unknown. To handle DJSS problems with dynamic job arrivals, researchers have proposed various dispatching rule approaches. Dispatching rules [1] are iterative heuristics that determine the job that is selected to be processed by the machine when it is available. This decision process for determining the job that is selected by the available machine is called a *decision situation* [3]. Dispatching rules are effective for DJSS problems with dynamic job arrivals because they can react quickly to the arrival of new jobs and can cope with the dynamic environment [4]. In addition, because they are easy to interpret by operators on the shop floor [4], they are used extensively in real-world manufacturing environments, e.g., semi-conductor manufacturing [5]. However, a limitation of dispatching rule approaches is that they are tailored to a specific JSS problem. Although humans are very good at identifying good building blocks for heuristics [6], constructing effective heuristics from the building blocks require extensive trial-and-error testing [4,5]. Therefore, genetic programming based hyper-heuristic (GP-HH) approaches have been proposed in the literature to automatically evolve dispatching rules for DJSS problems [7]. GP-HH is provided heuristic building blocks, DJSS problem instances for training and searches in the heuristic space to find high quality solutions for the DJSS problem [6]. It has been shown in the literature that GP evolved rules generally perform better than man-made rules for different DJSS problems [7].

There are several factors that need to be considered to develop an effective GP-HH approach to DJSS problems. One of the factors is that evolved rules need to *generalise* well [6,7]. In other words, the evolved rules trained over a specific problem domain needs to perform well on unseen problem instances both within and outside the problem domain. Generality has been covered in the literature for DJSS problems with dynamic job arrivals [7]. However, although generality of GP for DJSS with dynamic job arrivals have been investigated [4,5,7], it is not known how well GP can generalise for over DJSS problem instances with no machine breakdowns and with machine breakdowns. When a machine breakdown occurs, any job that is being processed on the machine is interrupted and the machine needs to be repaired for a specific amount of time before it is back "online" again. Machine breakdowns can severely disrupt the processing that occurs on the shop floor.

1.1   Goal

The goal of this paper is to investigate the *generality* of GP for DJSS problems with dynamic job arrivals and machine breakdowns, and to analyse the terminals that are effective for DJSS problem instances with machine breakdowns. By analysing the generalisation ability of the evolved rules, it may be possible to determine whether the standard GP-HH approach is suitable for the DJSS problem with machine breakdowns. Otherwise, if the standard GP-HH approach cannot generalise well over the DJSS problems with machine breakdowns, then the analysis of the terminals may provide insight for developing new extensions to the standard GP-HH approach that are more effective for the DJSS problem. To achieve the goal, this paper carries out the following objectives:

(a) Develop a new DJSS dataset for generating problem instances with dynamic job arrivals and machine breakdown.
(b) Investigate the generality of an existing GP-HH [4,8] by evolving and evaluating the rules over different combinations of machine breakdown scenarios.
(c) Analyse the structure of the GP rules to extract information on the distributions of the terminals for the evolved rules.

1.2   Organisation

First, we cover the background to DJSS in Sect. 2, which provides the problem definitions and outlines sample GP-HH approaches to DJSS problems. Afterwards, Sect. 3 describes the testing framework that is used to test the generality of GP-HH approach for the DJSS problem. Section 4 describes the benchmark GP-HH approach that is used to evolve the rules, the fitness function and the GP parameters. Finally, Sect. 5 gives the results and an analysis of the findings, and Sect. 6 gives the concluding remarks and future works.

2   Background

This section covers the problem definition, including the notations used and the description of the DJSS problem with dynamic job arrivals and machine breakdowns. It then discusses the related work to DJSS problems in the literature.

2.1   Problem Definition

We use the following notation for the DJSS problem handled by the GP-HH approach. There are M machines on the shop floor, and a job j arrives on the shop floor with the sequence of operations $\sigma_{1j}, \ldots, \sigma_{(N_j)j}$. The processing time for the operation σ_{ij} is denoted as p_{ij}, and the operation's ready time is denoted as r_{ij}. In addition, the time when a job arrives on the shop floor is abbreviated to r_j. A job j also has a due date d_j and a weight w_j. If the completion time C_j is greater than the job's due date d_j, then the job is tardy and has tardiness $T_j = C_j - d_j$. From this, the mean weighted tardiness (MWT) for a schedule is defined as $\frac{1}{N} \sum_j^N w_j T_j$ [1]. MWT and other tardiness objectives have commonly been used in the literature to evaluate the effectiveness of heuristics for DJSS problems [4,5,8].

The two dynamic components for the DJSS problem are dynamic job arrivals and machine breakdowns. In a DJSS problem instance with dynamic job arrival, a job j's attributes are unknown until job j arrives on the shop floor at time r_j. On the other hand, machine breakdowns are unforeseen events where a machine m is shut down at time $b_t{}^m$, and requires $t_r{}^m$ time to repair the machine. During the repair time, the machine is unable to process any new operations. If a job's operation is being processed on the machine at the moment of the machine breakdown, then the operation is suspended and resumed after the machine is repaired and is available. In other words, if a job j's operation σ_{ij} was started at s_{ij} at machine m before the machine breaks down at time $b_t{}^m$ and requires $t_r{}^m$ time to repair. Then the job j's operation is resumed at time $b_t{}^m + t_r{}^m$, and the operation completes at $s_{ij} + p_{ij} + t_r{}^m$. This definition of machine breakdown was proposed by Holthaus [9].

2.2   Related Work

Many researchers have developed priority-based dispatching rule approaches to handling different DJSS problems. Examples of priority-based dispatching rule are cost over time (COVERT) rule and apparent tardiness cost (ATC) rule [10] for JSS problems with tardiness objectives. Additionally, other effective man-made dispatching rule approaches have been proposed and investigated in the literature for JSS problems [1]. In particular, Holthaus [9] investigates the performances of man-made dispatching rules that DJSS problems with dynamic job arrivals and machine breakdowns for different objective functions. He showed that for due date related objectives, including MWT, the rules have different performances for the different configurations associated with two attributes: the average time it takes for the machine to be repaired and the approximate amount time the machines are broken down for over the duration of the job processing.

In addition to manually designing dispatching rules, there have been many GP-HH approaches that evolve dispatching rules to DJSS problems in the literature [3–5,7,8]. In addition, several of the GP-HH approaches to JSS also investigate the generality of GP evolved rules by applying them to different problem domains [4,5]. Nguyen et al. [4] showed that GP rules evolved using static JSS problem instances do not perform as well as some man-made dispatching rules (such as the ATC rule) in a DJSS problem with dynamic job arrivals. Therefore, if problem instances are encountered outside of the problem domain that the rules were trained on, new rules may need to be evolved to be competitive with existing approaches to the problem instances. On the other hand, Burke et al. [6] proposed a method improving the generality of rules evolved by GP for a 2-D bin packing problem. They generate both "best-fit" GP rules by applying the GP over training sets consisting of problem instances with specific properties and "generalist" GP rules by evolving the rules over problem instances with different properties. They showed that GP can evolve good reusable rules, and general rules can sometimes outperform best-fit rules. Finally, Branke et al. [7] provides a survey of various evolutionary computation approaches to scheduling problems in the literature that also addresses the generality of GP evolved rules.

JSS problems with machine breakdowns have also been covered extensively in the literature. Many research have proposed predictive-reactive [2] approaches to DJSS problems with machine breakdowns. Predictive-reactive algorithms first generate an initial schedule for the DJSS problem instance, and then generates a new schedule, i.e., reschedules, when a machine breaks downs during processing. They have been effectively applied to JSS problems where the job properties are known *a priori*, but are not suitable for DJSS problems with dynamic job arrivals, as the schedule needs to constantly be updated with the arrival of new jobs. Therefore, for DJSS problems with dynamic job arrivals and machine breakdowns, completely-reactive approaches [2,9], where the schedule is generated during processing, have been proposed. This includes dispatching rule approaches. Ouelhadj and Petrovic [2] provides a survey for various approaches to DJSS problems with machine breakdowns.

3   Framework for Investigating the Generality of GP

This section describes the framework that is used to investigate the generality of GP-HH for DJSS problems with dynamic job arrivals and machine breakdowns. This covers the DJSS dataset containing the problem instances with machine breakdowns, how the rules are evolved from problem instances with different machine breakdown scenarios from the dataset, and the procedure for analysing the structures of the GP evolved rules.

3.1   Generating DJSS Problem Instances Using Simulations

The standard approach in the literature to generate DJSS problem instances is to use discrete-event simulations [3,5,8,9]. This means that the job arrivals, the machine breakdown events and the repair times for the breakdowns are generated stochastically. For this paper, the dataset Δ used to evaluate the generality of GP is modified from the dataset proposed by Holthaus [9], which has been used effectively to evaluate and analyse man-made dispatching rules in DJSS problems with dynamic job arrivals and machine breakdowns. The following parameters are kept consistent as the ones originally used by Holthaus. The problem instances have $M = 10$ machines on the shop floor. The processing times for an operation for a job is generated from a uniform distribution between $[1, 49]$. In other words, the mean processing time of the operations is $\mu = 25$. For generating an arriving job, the arrival times of the jobs are generated according to a Poisson process with mean λ. The utilisation rate is a standard parameter used in DJSS discrete-event simulations that defines the expected proportion of time that the machines are occupied processing the jobs against the total duration of simulation [5,9]. Because of this, the mean arrival time is often defined by the utilisation rate of the problem instances, and is given in Eq. (1)

[5,9]. In the equation, ρ is the utilisation rate and p_M is the expected number of operations per job divided by the number of machines. The utilisation rate is set to $\rho = 0.9$, which is consistent with Holthaus's dataset. For our paper, there is no re-entry, i.e., a job cannot have at least two separate operations on the same machine [1]. This means that a job can have at most 10 operations, and the number of operations per job is modified to be random between 2 to 10 operations, i.e., $p_M = (2 + 10)/2 = 6$.

$$\lambda = \frac{\rho \times p_M}{(1/\mu)} \tag{1}$$

The due date of arriving job j $d_j = r_j + h\sum_{i=1}^{N_j} p_{ij}$, where h multiplied to the sum processing times of the job is the due date tightness factor. Tightness of $h = 3$ and $h = 5$ are used, where $h = 3$ represents tight due dates and $h = 5$ loose due dates. This is adjusted from the original tightness values of $h = 4, 8$ used by Holthaus [9], as preliminary experiments found that due date tightness $h = 8$ resulted in GP evolved rules generating schedules for problem instances where the MWT values are zero. The weight of a job is either 1, 2, or 4 with probabilities 0.2, 0.6 and 0.2 respectively, which is a standard method of generating weights for jobs in due-date related DJSS problems [4,8]. For each problem instance, there is a "warm-up" period of 500 jobs which do not contribute towards the objective value, and jobs continue arriving until the 2500th job has been completed. However, all jobs that have arrived on the shop floor need to be completed before the problem instance is completed. From Holthaus's dataset [9], the machine repair times and the times between machine breakdowns (excluding the repair times) are exponentially distributed. The mean repair time (RTM) and the mean time between machine breakdowns (BTM) are the same for all machines on the floor. In addition, for the configuration used to generate a problem instance, RTM depends on the mean processing times of the operations μ and the machine breakdown level parameter (BL). The machine breakdown level can be considered as the proportion of time the machine is being repaired during processing, e.g., if BL = 0.025 and the all jobs took 2500 time units to process, then the total repair time for all machines is approximately $0.025 \times 2500 = 62.5$ time units. In other words, the machine breakdown level is given by BL = RTM/(BTM+RTM), which means that BTM = RTM/BL−RTM [9]. The dataset has variable configurations for the following parameters: due date tightness (h), mean repair times of machines (RTM) and breakdown level (BL). The configurations can have RTM $\in \{\mu, 5\mu, 10\mu\}$ and BL $\in \{0, 0.025, 0.05\}$. Overall, the two due date tightness configurations and the configurations for the machine breakdowns results in a total of 18 different configurations.

3.2   GP-HH Training Procedure

To evolve and evaluate the GP rules, different subsets of DJSS problem instances in the dataset are used to evolve different sets of GP rules. Figure 1 shows an overview of how the dataset Δ is used to evolve different sets of GP rules that are

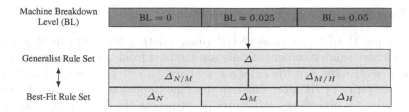

Fig. 1. Overview of how the dataset used for the DJSS problem is partitioned to train GP rules specialised for different machine breakdown configurations.

either "generalists" or "best-fit" over the machine breakdown level (BL). The generalist rules are designed to be effective for the different machine breakdown scenarios, whereas the best-fit rules [6] are designed to be effective for specific machine breakdown scenarios. For the scope of this paper, the machine breakdown level parameter allows us to analyse the generality of GP rules in DJSS problems with dynamic job arrivals and machine breakdowns. First, the dataset Δ containing 18 different configurations for generating problem instances is partitioned into three subsets based on the machine breakdown level. In the subsets, machine breakdown level BL = 0 means that the generated problem instances do not have machine breakdowns, BL = 0.025 and BL = 0.05 means that the generated problem instances have "medium" and "high" levels of machine breakdowns respectively. The subsets are denoted as Δ_N, Δ_M and Δ_H respectively and contain six different configurations. The best-fit rules are evolved from Δ_N, Δ_M and Δ_H and are designed to cope with the specific level of machine breakdown. Additionally, $\Delta_{N/M}$ and $\Delta_{M/H}$ combine two smaller subsets together (e.g. Δ_N and Δ_M for $\Delta_{N/M}$, and are used to evolve "intermediate" sets of rules. If the intermediate rules are competitive by the best-fit rules, e.g., rule evolved from Δ_H does not perform significantly worse than $\Delta_{M/H}$ for problem instances with BL = 0.05, then it is likely that GP can generalise well over different machine breakdown scenarios even without incorporating information about machine breakdowns. Finally, all possible configurations in the dataset Δ, i.e., configurations from Δ_N, Δ_M and Δ_H combined, are used to evolve the final set of general rules. Overall, this results in a total of 6 sets of GP rules that range from generalists to best-fit over the DJSS problem. This procedure was first covered by Burke et al. [6] for improving the generality of the GP-HH approach for a bin packing problem.

The set of rules evolved from a specific training set is denoted as 'DR-' with the suffix as the training set. For example, DR-N denotes the set of GP evolved rules which have been evolved from subset Δ_N, i.e., problem instances with no machine breakdowns. In addition, at each generation, the seeds used to stochastically generate the jobs and the machine breakdowns are rotated for the training procedure of the GP-HH. This means that the problem instances used in one generation will be different to the problem instances used for the next generation. This has shown to improve the generalisation ability of the evolved rules for DJSS problems [5].

3.3 Rule Terminal Analysis Procedure

For analysing the effectiveness of GP rules, existing literature have proposed methods where small numbers of rules are sampled from the sets of evolved rules and the tree structures of the rules are analysed [4,5,8]. However, for investigating the generality of GP over different machine breakdown scenarios, it may be more effective to analyse the structures of entire sets of rules instead of sampling specific rules from the sets, as GP needs to be able to evolve good rules consistently. However, it is too cumbersome to directly analyse the tree structures of the sets of rules directly. Therefore, the distributions of the terminals that make up the GP rule is analysed. For example, if the due date terminal occurs more frequently for the rules in DR-H than the rules in DR-N, then it means that processing urgent job is more important for problem instances with high level of machine breakdowns than problem instances with no machine breakdowns. To calculate the distribution, the proportion of the terminals that make up an evolved rule is first calculated. For example, suppose that an evolved rule has 23 PT terminals out of 150 terminals that make up the rule. Then the 23/150 is the proportion of PT terminals that make up the rule. Afterwards, the proportions are normalised over the set of evolved rules.

4 Experimental Design

This section covers the benchmark GP-HH approach that is investigated for this paper, which is based off existing GP-HH approaches. This includes the GP representation, terminal set, function set and fitness measure used for the individuals. Afterwards, the parameters used for the GP-HH is detailed.

4.1 GP Representation, Terminals and Function Sets

The most prominent method of evolving priority-based dispatching rule using GP is to use a tree-based GP, where the individuals represent arithmetic function trees [7]. For this paper, we modify the arithmetic representation proposed by Nguyen et al. [4] to evolve priority-based dispatching rules. In addition, a look-ahead terminal set proposed by Hunt et al. [8] that have effectively been applied to a DJSS problem with unforeseen job arrivals will be incorporated into the terminal set. The list of terminals used for the GP-HH process are shown in Table 1 for a job j waiting at machine m^*.

The function set includes of the arithmetic operators $+$, $-$, $\times$, and protected $/$, where protected $/$ returns one if the denominator is zero. The rest of the operators for the function set are if, which returns the value of the second branch if the value of the first branch is greater than or equal to zero or returns the value of the third branch otherwise, max and min operators.

Table 1. Terminal set for GP

Standard	RJ	Operation ready time of job j
	PT	Operation processing time of job j
	RO	Remaining number of operations of job j
	RT	Remaining total processing times of job j
	RM	Machine m^*'s ready time
	DD	Due date d_j
	W	Job's weight w_j
	#	Random number from 0 to 1
Look-ahead	NPT	Next operation processing time of job j
	NNQ	Number of idle jobs waiting at the next machine
	NQW	Average waiting time of last 5 jobs at the next machine
	AQW	Average waiting time of last 5 jobs at all machines

4.2   Calculating a GP Individual's Fitness

For the evaluation procedure, the individuals are applied to the DJSS training instances as *non-delay* dispatching rules [1]. A non-delay dispatching rule greedily attempts to minimise the idle time from when a machine is available to when it starts processing the next job [1]. From this, the MWT over the training instances is normalised using the ATC rule, where a standard $k = 3$ value is used for the ATC parameter [10]. The normalisation procedure have been used in the literatures [5] to reduce the bias towards specific problem instances that are more likely to have a higher optimal MWT values than other problem instances in the training set. Given that $\text{MWT}_{\omega,\gamma}$ and $\text{MWT}_{ref,\gamma}$ are the MWT of the schedule generated by individual ω and the reference rule for training instance γ respectively, the fitness f_ω of an individual ω is given in Eq. (2).

$$f_\omega = \frac{1}{|\Delta_{train}|} \sum_{\gamma \in \Delta_{train}}^{T_{train}} \frac{\text{MWT}_{\omega,\gamma}}{\text{MWT}_{ref,\gamma}} \tag{2}$$

4.3   GP Parameter Settings

The parameters used for GP are modified from the parameters used by GP-HH approaches to DJSS problems in the literature [4,8] after carrying out parameter tuning on the population size and the crossover, mutation and reproduction rates. After the parameter tuning, the population size is set to 256 to reduce the computational cost, and the number of generations is set to 51. The crossover, mutation and reproduction rates are 80 %, 10 % and 10 % respectively. The maximum depth of an individual is 8, and the maximum depth of an individual that can be initialised is 2. Tournament selection of size 7 is used during the selection process. Finally, the parameter value used for the ATC reference rule is set to $k = 3.0$ [10].

5   Experimental Results

This section covers the evaluation of the GP-HH approach over the DJSS problem with dynamic job arrivals and machine breakdowns. First, 30 independent runs of the GP processes are carried out over the training sets, resulting in DR-N, DR-M, DR-H, DR-N/M, DR-M/H and DR-All each consisting of 30 rules. The sets of GP evolved rules are applied to the problem instances in the test set, and the qualities of the schedules are compared against each other as part of the general evaluation procedure. Afterwards, an analysis on the structures of the evolved rules is carried out.

5.1   Evolved Rule Performance Evaluation

Each configuration in the test set is used to generate 30 different problem instances as part of the test set. In total, this results in a total of $18 \times 30 = 540$ test instances using the 18 different configurations. The sets of GP evolved rules are then applied to the test instances to generate schedules for the problem instances, and the MWT of the schedules are compared against each other as part of the general evaluation procedure. A set of GP evolved rules is *significantly* better than another rule set if the difference in the MWT values satisfies the two sided Student's t-test at $p = 0.05$. The performances of the rule sets over the different problem instances are shown in Fig. 2. Each box plot shows the results over

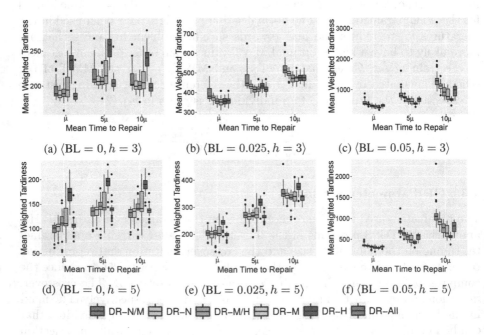

(a) $\langle BL = 0, h = 3 \rangle$ (b) $\langle BL = 0.025, h = 3 \rangle$ (c) $\langle BL = 0.05, h = 3 \rangle$

(d) $\langle BL = 0, h = 5 \rangle$ (e) $\langle BL = 0.025, h = 5 \rangle$ (f) $\langle BL = 0.05, h = 5 \rangle$

DR–N/M   DR–N   DR–M/H   DR–M   DR–H   DR–All

Fig. 2. The comparisons of the mean weighted tardiness performances of the GP rules evolved over different training sets over the problem instances in the test set.

problem instances in a configuration, and the configurations are categorised by the breakdown level and due date tightness, where $\langle BL = 0.025, h = 3 \rangle$ denotes that breakdown level is 2.5 % and due date tightness is 3.

From the results, we can see that for the problem instances generated with $BL = 0$ and $BL = 0.05$ DR-N and DR-H generally perform well over the respective problem domain they are trained on, but perform poorly on problem instances with high level of machine breakdowns (for DR-N) and problem instances with no machine breakdowns (for DR-H). Under the statistical test, the difference in the performance is significant between DR-N and DR-H. When the best-fit rules DR-N and DR-H are compared to the intermediate rules DR-N/M and DR-M/H, the two best-fit rules perform slightly better than the intermediate rules over their respective machine breakdown levels the specialise rules are evolved on. The difference in the performances are significant between DR-H and DR-M/H, but not between DR-N and DR-N/M. However, on machine breakdown level $BL = 0.025$, it is observed that most sets of rules with the exception of DR-H have a similar performance to each other, where the slight differences in the performances are not significant. Finally, the generalist rule DR-All perform well over problem instances with no machine breakdowns and problem instances with machine breakdown level $BL = 0.025$, but performs significantly worse than DR-H and DR-M/H for problem instances with $BL = 0.05$. Overall, it may be likely that standard GP-HH approach may not be able to generalise well when it comes to DJSS problems with dynamic job arrivals with machine breakdowns, and the quality of the rules evolved by a standard GP-HH approach is likely to sensitive to the proportion of time that the machine is broken down during the simulation.

5.2   GP Terminal Distribution Analysis

After evaluating the performances of the GP evolved rules, the terminals that are used by the GP rules are compared against each other to analyse the make up of the rules. For the sets of GP rules, the proportion of the rule structure made up of the terminals are shown in Fig. 3.

From Fig. 3, the most prominent terminals that are used by all sets of rules is the processing time of current operation (PT), followed by the due date of the job (DD) and the number of jobs waiting at the next machine (NNQ). On the other hand, DR-H have a higher proportion of due date terminal compared to the other sets of evolved rules. This is likely due to the fact that in problem instances with high machine breakdown level (e.g. $BL = 0.05$) processing time becomes unreliable in determining on predicting the expected duration of time that a job requires on the machine for the operation to complete. Compared to problem instances with lower machine breakdown levels (e.g. $BL = 0$ and $BL = 0.025$), it is more likely in the problem instances with high machine breakdown levels that the machine breaks down during processing of a job. This results in the job getting stuck on the machine while it is being repaired and taking longer than expected to finish processing. Instead, processing urgent jobs may be more reliable method of generating good schedules for problem instances

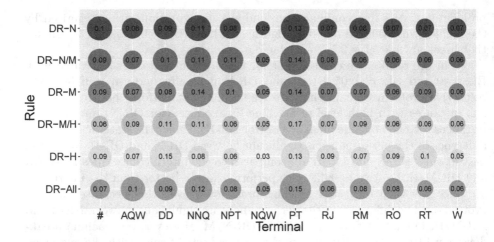

Fig. 3. The proportion of terminals used by the sets of rules evolved by the GP-HH approaches.

with high level of machine breakdowns. Therefore, this may potentially result in individuals that use high proportion of the processing time terminal, that prioritise processing shorter job processing times, generating worse schedules for the problem instances than individuals that use high proportion of the due date terminal, that prioritise processing urgent jobs. In addition, DR-H has a lower proportion of terminals that take the attributes for when the job reaches the next machine (NNQ, NPT and NQW), as the additional uncertainty introduced by the high level of machine breakdown may make the terminals less effective at reducing the myopic nature of dispatching rules [8].

6   Conclusions

This paper investigates the generality of a standard GP-HH approach to a DJSS problem subject to dynamic job arrivals and machine breakdowns. This is done by first developing a DJSS dataset for evaluating GP-HH approaches. Afterwards, a standard GP-HH approach that evolves priority-based dispatching rules is applied to a new dataset for generating DJSS problem instances. Finally, the distributions of the terminals in the GP rules evolved from different machine breakdown scenarios are analysed. From the performance results and the results of analysing the terminal distributions, this paper makes the following findings:

(a) GP-HH approaches in the literature have been shown to be generalise well over different problem domains (including JSS) [6,7]. However, for the DJSS problem with dynamic job arrivals and machine breakdowns, the results show that a standard GP-HH approach is sensitive to the level of machine breakdowns. In addition, a generalist set of rules evolved by a standard GP-HH approach is unable to cover for high level of machine breakdowns.

(b) Analysis of the distribution of the terminals for the evolved rules show that there are higher proportions of DD terminal and lower proportion of NNQ, NPT, NQW and PT terminals in rules evolved on training instances with high levels of machine breakdowns compared to the other evolved rules. This is likely due to the added uncertainty associated with the duration of time required to process a job.

For future work, a GP-HH approach that incorporates terminals that use machine breakdown specific attributes could potentially evolve rules that can outperform rules evolved by a standard GP-HH approach and improve the generality of GP rules over different machine breakdown scenarios. For example, it is likely that incorporating terminals such as the next time the machine is expected to break down and the expected true processing time may generate rules which perform well over both DJSS problem instances with and without machine breakdowns.

References

1. Pinedo, M.L.: Scheduling: Theory, Algorithms, and Systems, 4th edn. Springer, Heidelberg (2012)
2. Ouelhadj, D., Petrovic, S.: A survey of dynamic scheduling in manufacturing systems. J. Sched. **12**(4), 417–431 (2009)
3. Hildebrandt, T., Branke, J.: On using surrogates with genetic programming. Evol. Comput. J. (ECJ) **23**(3), 1–25 (2015)
4. Nguyen, S., Zhang, M., Johnston, M., Tan, K.C.: A computational study of representations in genetic programming to evolve dispatching rules for the job shop scheduling problem. IEEE Trans. Evol. Comput. **17**(5), 621–639 (2013)
5. Hildebrandt, T., Heger, J., Scholz-Reiter, B.: Towards improved dispatching rules for complex shop floor scenarios: a genetic programming approach. In: Proceedings of the 12th Annual Conference on Genetic and Evolutionary Computation, pp. 257–264 (2010)
6. Burke, E.K., Hyde, M., Kendall, G., Woodward, J.: A genetic programming hyper-heuristic approach for evolving 2-D strip packing heuristics. IEEE Trans. Evol. Comput. **14**(6), 942–958 (2010)
7. Branke, J., Nguyen, S., Pickardt, C.W., Zhang, M.: Automated design of production scheduling heuristics: a review. IEEE Trans. Evol. Comput. **20**(1), 110–124 (2016)
8. Hunt, R., Johnston, M., Zhang, M.: Evolving "less-myopic" scheduling rules for dynamic job shop scheduling with genetic programming. In: Proceedings of the 2014 Conference on Genetic and Evolutionary Computation, pp. 927–934 (2014)
9. Holthaus, O.: Scheduling in job shops with machine breakdowns: an experimental study. Comput. Ind. Eng. **36**(1), 137–162 (1999)
10. Vepsalainen, A.P.J., Morton, T.E.: Priority rules for job shops with weighted tardiness costs. Manag. Sci. **33**(8), 1035–1047 (1987)

Exploratory Analysis of Clustering Problems Using a Comparison of Particle Swarm Optimization and Differential Evolution

Sobia Saleem[✉] and Marcus Gallagher

School of Information Technology and Electrical Engineering,
University of Queensland, Q. 4702 Queensland, Australia
s.saleem@uq.edu.au, marcusg@uq.edu.au

Abstract. The size, scope and variety of the experimental analyses of metaheuristics has increased in recent years, aiming to develop new procedures and techniques to improve our understanding of optimization algorithms and problems. In this paper, we compare particle swarm optimization and differential evolution on a set of real-world clustering problems. Generally, experimental comparisons focus on presenting a statistical summary of algorithm performance, however this hides valuable information about the algorithm behaviour on the problems in question. Instead, we take an exploratory approach, focussing on extracting deeper insights and understanding from the experimental results data. We make progress on understanding the fitness landscapes of the set of clustering problems, as well as analysing current and previous experimental results for algorithms applied to these problems. Consequently, the paper makes two contributions: (a) Advancing our understanding of what factors make this set of problem instances easy or hard for given algorithms; (b) Demonstrating the need to be careful in experimental evaluations and that better insights can be obtained with exploratory analysis.

1 Introduction

A large number of algorithms, including evolutionary algorithms and metaheuristics have been developed for solving black-box optimization problems. An important current research direction is to better understand the relationship between different classes and instances of black-box optimization problems and algorithms. For example, what types of problems does some Algorithm, A perform well on, and what is it about those problems and Algorithm A that makes this so?

In this paper, we use a set of real-world data clustering problems that has recently been explored and used to evaluate several algorithms. We apply instantiations of two of the most well known and widely used nature-inspired metaheuristics: Particle Swarm Optimization (PSO) and Differential Evolution (DE). We take an interactive, exploratory approach, focussed on understanding more about the problem instances and building on previous experimental results.

M. Wagner et al. (Eds.): ACALCI 2017, LNAI 10142, pp. 314–325, 2017.
DOI: 10.1007/978-3-319-51691-2_27

An outline of the paper is as follows. In Sect. 2, we review relevant literature on clustering using PSO and DE, and the clustering benchmark problem set to be used. Sect. 3 gives details of our experiments, as well as presenting a typical summary of the performance results and a comparison with previous results on the same problem set. Section 4 presents the main analysis of the results. A summary of the paper and conclusions are given in Sect. 5.

2   Background

2.1   Experimental Algorithmics and Exploratory Landscape Analysis in Continuous Black-Box Optimization

The field of experimental algorithmics has developed over many years across computer science [18,24]. More recently it has received growing attention in evolutionary computation and metaheuristics. Bartz-Beielstein discusses the application of experimental methodologies to the design and analysis of metaheuristics including techniques from experimental design and statistics [4]. This includes Sequential Parameter Optimization (SPO): an iterative methodology for improving the performance of algorithms via exploratory data analysis and computational statistics. As implied by the No Free Lunch Theorems, meaningful performance differences between algorithms are possible with respect to a given class or type of problems. Consequently, there has been growing interest in Exploratory Landscape Analysis (ELA) techniques to study features of problems that can be used to discriminate, categorize and compare algorithm behaviour [19,21]. In this paper, we adopt these methodologies. Rather than focussing on tuning algorithms for peak performance, we focus on deepening our understanding of a specific set of problem instances, via the application of algorithm instances and analysis of the results data.

In recent years a number of benchmark problem sets have been developed, including the BBOB problem sets and the CEC benchmarks [13,16]. Problem generators have also been proposed as a source of benchmark problems [11,25]. While these benchmarks are useful for evaluating and comparing algorithms, they are for the most part artificial test functions. In this paper we utilize a real-world representative set of data clustering problems.

2.2   Clustering, PSO and DE

In this paper we are concerned with continuous black-box optimization. Specifically, we focus on partitional data clustering, an important class of problems in machine learning and data analysis [2]. Given a set $X = \{x_1, x_2, ..., x_n\} \subseteq \mathbb{R}^d$ of n data points, the sum of squares clustering problem is to find a set of k cluster centers $C = \{c_1, c_2, ..., c_k\} \in \mathbb{R}^d$ to minimize:

$$f(C|X) = \sum_{i=1}^{n} \sum_{j=1}^{k} b_{i,j} \left\| x_i - c_j \right\|^2$$

where

$$b_{i,j} = \begin{cases} 1 \ \text{if} \|x_i - c_j\| = min_j \|x_i - c_j\| \\ 0 \qquad otherwise \end{cases}$$

Note that this defines an optimization problem of dimensionality $k \times d$.

Clustering has been the focus of a large amount of literature from different fields, including operations research, optimization and metaheuristics. The focus of our work is to try and improve our understanding of a set of clustering problems, to identify problem features and properties that can subsequently be used to develop more powerful comparisons of algorithms and to gain insights into the mapping between problems and algorithms. In this paper, we select two of the most well-known and widely used algorithms in continuous evolutionary optimization: PSO and DE. Even when we restrict our attention to these two algorithms, the clustering literature is still substantial. Literature reviews on PSO-based clustering are given by [1,23]. Unfortunately (as discussed in [12]), it is difficult to compare and extract insights from the large amount of experimental results presented in much of the literature. Researchers have used many different datasets and k values to create test problems. Different evaluation criteria (e.g. inter-cluter distance, quantization error) have also been used.

A Genetic Algorithm variant was proposed for clustering in [7], using the Iris and other real world datasets. Evaluation was based on the rand index, SSE and the validity index. A hybrid of DE and PSO is proposed in [26] which used the Caliński and Harabasz (CH) index and Silhouette statistic (SIL) index as evaluation criteria for several real world data sets. Three different criteria including Marriott's Criteria, Trace Within Criteria and Variance Ratio Criteria were used in [15]. [10,20] have used inter clustering and intra clustering distance as a performance metric for clustering on Iris and other data sets. One of the papers using DE for clustering claims that the Iris dataset, (i.e. with $k = 3$), does not pose much difficulty towards algorithms [22]. The experiments below agree with this, but also show that the Iris dataset can pose a significant challenge for algorithms when different values of k are used. Another paper [8] has clustered the Ruspini data set using particle swarms i.e. PSO and included plots of Ruspini dataset with different number of cluster centres used. The results are interesting but there is no further analysis to try and understand why the difficulty level of problem changes with the value of k.

2.3   A Benchmark Set of Clustering Problem Instances

Recently, a set of clustering problem instances was proposed for the evaluation and comparison of continuous black-box optimization algorithms [12]. These problem instances have been previously used in the literature, but without a standard problem definitions and some unawareness of existing work, it is difficult to compare these results or extract useful insights from them. For each problem instance, an initial feasible solution space is specified based on the data. The global optima are now reported for these problems to high precision [9] (see http://realopt.uqcloud.net/ for more details). This problem set is scalable, easy to understand, representative of a class of real-world problems, and appears to be challenging for many algorithms.

Experimental results on these problems show that Covariance Matrix Adaptation Evolutionary Strategies(CMA-ES) are able to find higher quality solutions (sometimes the global optimum) than the widely-used (non-black-box) k-means clustering algorithm. In fact, the performance of k-means strongly deteriorates on larger problem instances, as does the Nelder-Mead simplex algorithm. Nevertheless, finding the global optimum for some of the larger problem instances was unsuccessful even for CMA-ES. The problem set was also used in [5] who applied two versions of Differential Evolution (DE). The results improved on the performance of CMA-ES. However, some of the problems instances appear to be very challenging, with very low success rates reported to date.

2.4 Correcting the Global Optimum of the German Towns (k=9) Problem

We have recently become aware that, unfortunately, one of the global optimum values originally reported in [9] appears to be incorrect. For the German Towns ($k = 9$) problem, the value was reported as 7.80442e9. However, subsequent papers [3,14] use the value 8.42374e9 and declare it to be the global optimum, however this error does not appear to be explicitly stated in any paper. This means that it is possible (though perhaps unlikely) that the success rates reported in [5] and in [12] (i.e. whether the global optimum was found on any trial) are incorrect. In this paper we use the revised value.

3 Experimental Details and Performance Results

3.1 Experimental Details

We used Matlab implementations of both algorithms from the Yarpiz website (http://yarpiz.com/category/metaheuristics). We make no attempt to tune the parameters of the algorithms, using common/default values. Each algorithm was given a population size of 100. The parameters used for DE are: CR = 0.1, f1 = 0.2 and f2 = 0.8. For PSO we used the following parameters: Inertia Weight(w) = 1.0, Damping Ratio (wdamp) = 0.99, Personal Learning Coefficient(c1) = 1.5, Global Learning Coefficient(c2) = 2.0. The mean and standard deviation values of the best found objective function values over one hundred uniform random restarts are reported in Table 1. Success Rate (SR) counts how many times the algorithm could actually reach the global optimum value (to at least six significant figures) out of the one hundred trials. We started with a large number of function evaluations but we noticed that both of the algorithm instances converged after at most 2000 evaluations on these problems. Hence, each restart is given a fixed budget of 2000 function evaluations.

Table 1. Experimental results for DE and PSO on German Towns, Iris and Ruspini. The best results for each problem are highlighted in bold.

D	k	f*	DE	SR	PSO	SR
G	2	6.02547e+11	6.0255e+11 (1.4e+07)	85/100	**6.0255e+11 (0)**	**100/100**
	3	2.94506e+11	2.9451e+11 (7.1e+06)	57/100	**2.9451e+11 (0)**	**100/100**
	4	1.04474e+11	**1.0448e+11 (8.1e+06)**	54/100	1.2158e+11 (5.4e+10)	**91/100**
	5	5.97615e+10	**6.0660e+10 (6.2e+09)**	32/100	8.6410e+10 (2.0e+10)	**34/100**
	6	3.59085e+10	**4.0340e+10 (1.1e+10)**	9/100	6.5306e+10 (2.3e+10)	**23/100**
	7	2.19832e+10	**2.5219e+10 (5.7e+09)**	**9/100**	5.1067e+10 (2.3e+10)	5/100
	8	1.33854e+10	**1.8831e+10 (6.5e+09)**	0/100	4.3374e+10 (2.2e+10)	**3/100**
	9	8.42374e+09	**1.5839e+10 (7.3e+09)**	0/100	3.6884e+10 (1.7e+10)	0/100
	10	6.44648e+09	**1.3871e+10 (5.1e+09)**	0/100	3.1273e+10 (1.8e+10)	0/100
I	2	152.3478	**1.5234e+02 (2.8e-14)**	**100/100**	1.5234e+02 (2.8e-14)	100/100
	3	78.85144	**7.8854e+01 (1.0e-02)**	41/100	8.6937e+01 (2.3e+01)	**55/100**
	4	57.22847	**5.9921e+01 (2.2e+00)**	1/100	6.5611e+01 (1.3e+01)	**39/100**
	5	46.4461	5.9888e+01 (5.3e+00)	1/100	**5.5976e+01 (8.7e+00)**	**10/100**
	6	39.0399	6.3657e+01 (5.3e+00)	0/100	**4.8645e+01 (6.5e+00)**	**6/100**
	7	34.2982	6.7888e+01 (5.8e+00)	0/100	**4.6121e+01 (7.7e+00)**	0/100
	8	29.9889	7.0228e+01 (4.8e+00)	0/100	**4.1810e+01 (6.2e+00)**	0/100
	9	27.7860	7.2046e+01 (5.3e+00)	0/100	**3.9792e+01 (7.1e+00)**	0/100
	10	25.8340	7.3952e+01 (5.8e+00)	0/100	**3.8060e+01 (5.5e+00)**	0/100
R	2	89337.8321	**8.9338e+04 (0)**	**100/100**	8.9338e+04 (0)	100/100
	3	51063.4750	**5.1085e+04 (3.9e+01)**	**76/100**	5.1103e+04 (4.5e+01)	57/100
	4	12881.0512	**1.2881e+04 (1.0e-11)**	**100/100**	1.2881e+04 (1.0e-11)	100/100
	5	10126.7197	**1.0138e+04 (1.2e+02)**	**98/100**	1.0396e+04 (5.2e+02)	73/100
	6	8575.4068	**8.6645e+03 (1.7e+02)**	**42/100**	8.7862e+03 (3.4e+02)	31/100
	7	7126.1985	7.6699e+03 (8.3e+02)	**21/100**	**7.5064e+03 (4.0e+02)**	17/100
	8	6149.6390	7.4918e+03 (1.3e+03)	**9/100**	**6.5029e+03 (3.8e+02)**	7/100
	9	5181.6518	7.2541e+03 (1.5e+03)	7/100	**5.6709e+03 (3.9e+02)**	**11/100**
	10	4446.2821	7.5048e+03 (1.4e+03)	2/100	**4.8793e+03 (3.6e+02)**	**15/100**

3.2 Results Summary

For the smallest problem sizes (e.g. $k = 2, 3$), both algorithms performed very well, locating the global optimum with a high success rate. On the German Towns problems, DE has a better average performance than PSO but (with the exception of $k = 7$), the success rate of PSO is higher than DE. On the Iris problems, DE is best for small problems but for $k \geq 5$ PSO performs better in terms of average fitness value. PSO has a higher success rate for $k = 3 - 6$, particularly for $k = 4$ ($\frac{39}{100}$ compared to $\frac{1}{100}$). Both algorithms have very poor or no success in finding the global optimum for larger problems. On the Ruspini problems DE performs better for lower dimensions and, in contrast to the German Towns and Iris problems, DE has a higher success rate than

PSO ($k = 2 - 8$). For $k = 7 - 10$, PSO has a better average performance. but for higher values of k ($k > 7$) PSO has a higher Success Rate and better mean objective function value. We focus mainly on the Ruspini dataset as it is two dimensional and its results are easily visualizable. Our results are generally similar to those in [5]. They are typically a little worse, however we have used only 2000 fitness function evaluations compared to (up to) 20000. Our success rates are estimated from 100 runs compared to 50. Large differences between our results and Berthier's [5] occur for the success rates of algorithms on two of the Ruspini problems. We obtained 100% for $k = 4$ and 98% for $k = 5$, whereas Berthier reported 0–2% success for CMA-ES, DE and PDE ([5], Table 3).

4 Exploratory Results Analysis

4.1 Fitness Distributions and Attractors of Experimental Trials

Significant insights can be gained by looking at the results of the individual trials in our experiments. The scale of fitness values differs across the problem instances and datasets: therefore we divide by the global optimum fitness values for each problem and obtain performance ratio values. Figure 1 shows the distribution of these values for each trial. It is evident from the figure that even when the number of attraction points is large, their distribution tends to be non-Gaussian, with many results clustered around certain fitness values. Over the problem set DE typically finds more attractors than PSO. It is also clear that the "performance profiles" of each algorithm are significantly different across the different datasets. In the case of German Towns, solutions found by DE are closer to the global optimum but in case of Ruspini and Iris, solutions found by PSO are more close to global optimum. The mean and standard deviation values in Table 1 are the perfect summary of data that follows a Gaussian distribution, however our fitness results are far from Gaussian.

Table 2 shows counts of the number of different fitness values (i.e. convergence points) found for each problem, which gives an empirical estimate (and at least a lower bound) of the number of attractors for PSO and DE. For some problems (Iris with $k = 2$, Ruspini with $k = 2$ and 4), one or both algorithms had only one attractor (the global optimum). In this case, the mean performance trivially equals the attractor fitness value and the standard deviation is zero (Table 1). When the number of attractors is small, the mean and standard deviation are often a misleading summary of the results. For example, the Ruspini $k = 3$ problem has two attractors (Table 2) which are both found with reasonable probability (Table 1; DE finds the global optimum 76 times and the other attractor 24 times while PSO finds the global optimum 57 times and the other attractor 43 times). For these results, the mean lies between the two values (weighted by the attraction frequencies). In other words, the algorithms never find a solution with fitness value close to the mean! This effect is likely when any algorithm converges to a relatively small number of attractors, though this is something rarely reported in papers presenting experimental results. For the Iris problem instances, Table 1 shows that both algorithms have a high success rate

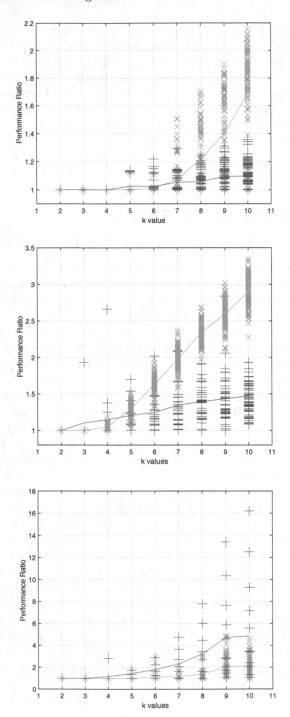

Fig. 1. Fitness values found by DE (red×) and PSO (blue+) for the Ruspini (Top), Iris (middle) and German Towns (bottom) problem instances. The average of the results for each algorithm is also shown with a line. (Color figure online)

Table 2. The number of unique solutions found for DE and PSO on the problem set, from 100 trials.

k		2	3	4	5	6	7	8	9	10
German	DE	3	8	20	39	76	89	97	100	100
German	PSO	1	1	2	3	6	8	10	14	14
Iris	DE	1	47	100	100	100	100	100	100	100
Iris	PSO	1	3	12	24	34	41	51	58	70
Ruspini	DE	1	2	1	3	13	49	77	92	99
Ruspini	PSO	1	2	1	7	16	30	44	60	60

for $k = 3$ which is the natural number of clusters in the data. The performance degrades quickly after k = 5. Surprisingly, DE always gets stuck in a diferent solution for $k \geq 4$. Even for $k = 3$ it finds the global optimum only 47 times. PSO is attracted towards fewer different solutions. But overall its success rate is not much larger. For $k = 4$ we also observe that the mean fitness function value for DE is better than PSO however the success rate for PSO is higher than DE. This is an indication that relying on mean performance values can be misleading.

4.2 Natural Clusterings: Examining Results Around the Ruspini $k = 4$ Instance

In the results for DE and PSO, the average performance for the Ruspini $k = 3$ problem is worse compared with $k = 4$ and 5. This is interesting because the performance of algorithms generally degrades with increasing dimensions (with the notable exception of the Griewank function [17]). This behaviour was also observed for k-means, CMA-ES and DE in [5,12]. To understand this behaviour we focused on the solution that each algorithm finds. For $k = 3$ both algorithms find only two different solutions that have very similar fitness values. But the solutions (Fig. 2) are very different (roughly symmetrical: one cluster center at the top and two at the bottom, or vice-versa). We hypothesize that the fitness landscape contains two major basins of attraction (at least for DE and PSO). That is why we see a performance degradation with $k = 3$. For the $k = 4$ problem, both algorithms perform very well, always finding the global optimum. Figure 2 shows that the Ruspini dataset is naturally arranged such that it visually forms four major clusters. It is argued [6] that cluster center solutions become stable when we cluster data according to the natural clustering of the dataset. For DE and PSO, the fitness landscape has a single major basin of attraction. For the $k = 5$ problem, the average fitness for DE is better than PSO. This is because PSO is attracted to seven different solutions. On the other hand, DE only finds three attractors. These different solutions are shown in Fig. 3.

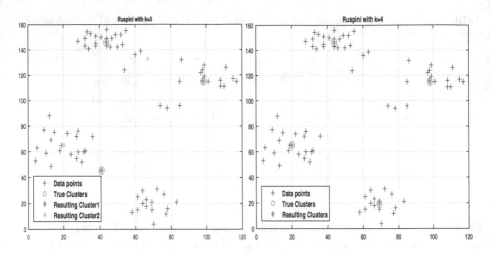

Fig. 2. Solutions found for Ruspini instances with $k = 3$ and $k = 4$ plotted on each other.

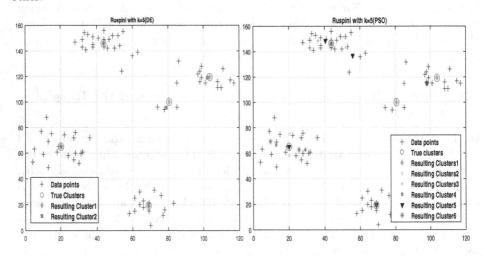

Fig. 3. Solutions found for Ruspini instances with $k = 5$. DE has three attractors while PSO has seven. "True clusters" indicate the global optimum with other attractors shown as resulting cluster1,2...)

4.3 Neutrality in the Standard Problem Formulation

Visualization of the solutions found by the algorithms on larger problem sizes reveals that the problem formulation causes a significant effect on the fitness landscapes. We have seen that on larger Ruspini problem instances, DE converges to a larger number of poorer solutions compared to PSO, resulting in a large standard deviation in the results. Figure 4 compares example solutions for the algorithms for $k = 9$ and 10. We can see that the solutions found by DE often have a cluster centre which is not located close to any of the data points. Such a cluster centre makes no contribution to the fitness function since it is not the closest centre for any data point. It follows that the fitness landscape is neutral with respect to this cluster centre (i.e. two of the variables in the solution vector). The landscape is perfectly flat in response to changes to these variables as long as the cluster center accounts for no data points. The problem is commonly formulated in this way (e.g. [2]) though sometimes a constraint is added, requiring that every cluster center account for at least one data point (e.g. [3]).

The above insight could be used to improve the performance of algorithms (e.g. with a restart strategy). Berthier's Progressive Differential Evolution (PDE) works by optimizing with respect to a single cluster centre and then iteratively adding new centres (e.g. every 100th generation in his experiments). Intuitively, this seems less vulnerable to end up in a neutral region of the landscape, which may explain the performance improvement reported for PDE [5] Alternatively, the problem could be formulated to incorporate the constraint (e.g. using a penalty term). One the other hand, neutrality might be a feature that occurs in other real-world problems (e.g. in machine learning where sparse models are widely used). In that case, it is of interest to see how algorithms perform when faced with problems that have some degree of neutrality.

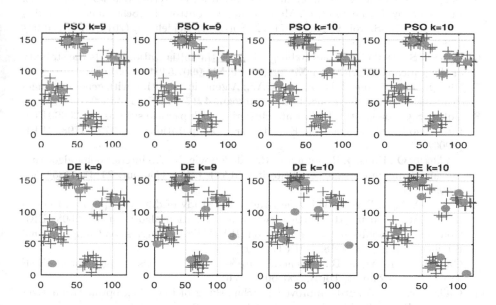

Fig. 4. Example solutions for Ruspini problems with $k = 9$ and $k = 10$.

5 Summary

This paper has presented an exploratory experimental study of clustering benchmark problems, using instances of DE and PSO. The results reveal important problem features, notably the natural clustering in the data and the existence of flat regions on the fitness landscape. This leads to a better understanding of the performance of algorithms on these problems. More generally, the paper advocates an exploratory, problem-centric approach to the experimental analysis of algorithms.

References

1. Alam, S., Dobbie, G., Koh, Y.S., Riddle, P., Rehman, S.U.: Research on particle swarm optimization based clustering: a systematic review of literature and techniques. Swarm Evol. Comput. **17**, 1–13 (2014)
2. Alpaydin, E.: Introduction to machine learning. MIT press, Cambridge (2014)
3. Bagirov, A.M.: Modified global k-means algorithm for minimum sum-of-squares clustering problems. Pattern Recogn. **41**(10), 3192–3199 (2008)
4. Bartz-Beielstein, T.: Experimental Research in Evolutionary Computation: The New Experimentalism. Springer-Verlag New York Inc., New York (2006)
5. Berthier, V.: Progressive differential evolution on clustering real world problems. In: Bonnevay, S., Legrand, P., Monmarché, N., Lutton, E., Schoenauer, M. (eds.) EA 2015. LNCS, vol. 9554, pp. 71–82. Springer, Heidelberg (2016). doi:10.1007/978-3-319-31471-6_6
6. Bubeck, S., Meila, M., von Luxburg, U.: How the initialization affects the stability of the k-means algorithm. arXiv preprint arXiv:0907.5494 (2009)
7. Chang, D.X., Zhang, X.D., Zheng, C.W.: A genetic algorithm with gene rearrangement for k-means clustering. Pattern Recogn. **42**(7), 1210–1222 (2009)
8. Cohen, S.C., de Castro, L.N.: Data clustering with particle swarms. In: 2006 IEEE International Conference on Evolutionary Computation, pp. 1792–1798. IEEE (2006)
9. Du Merle, O., Hansen, P., Jaumard, B., Mladenovic, N.: An interior point algorithm for minimum sum-of-squares clustering. SIAM J. Sci. Comput. **21**(4), 1485–1505 (1999)
10. Esmin, A.A.A., Pereira, D.L., De Araujo, F.: Study of different approach to clustering data by using the particle swarm optimization algorithm. In: 2008 IEEE Congress on Evolutionary Computation (IEEE World Congress on Computational Intelligence), pp. 1817–1822. IEEE (2008)
11. Gallagher, M., Yuan, B.: A general-purpose, tunable landscape generator. IEEE Trans. Evol. Comput. **10**(5), 590–603 (2006)
12. Gallagher, M.: Towards improved benchmarking of black-box optimization algorithms using clustering problems. Soft Comput. **20**, 1–15 (2016)
13. Hansen, N., Finck, S., Ros, R., Auger, A.: Real-parameter black-box optimization benchmarking 2009: noiseless functions definitions. Research report RR-6829, INRIA (2009)
14. Hansen, P., Mladenović, N.: J-means: a new local search heuristic for minimum sum of squares clustering. Pattern Recogn. **34**(2), 405–413 (2001)

15. Karthi, R., Arumugam, S., Rameshkumar, K.: Comparative evaluation of particle swarm optimization algorithms for data clustering using real world data sets. IJCSNS Int. J. Comput. Sci. Netw. Secur. **8**(1), 203–212 (2008)

16. Liang, J., Qu, B., Suganthan, P.: Problem definitions and evaluation criteria for the cec 2014 special session and competition on single objective real-parameter numerical optimization. Technical report 201311, Nanyang Technological University, Singapore (2013)

17. Locatelli, M.: A note on the Griewank test function. J. Global Optim. **25**(2), 169–174 (2003)

18. McGeoch, C.: Experimental algorithmics. Commun. ACM **50**(11), 27–31 (2007)

19. Mersmann, O., Preuss, M., Trautmann, H.: Benchmarking evolutionary algorithms: towards exploratory landscape analysis. In: Schaefer, R., Cotta, C., Kołodziej, J., Rudolph, G. (eds.) PPSN 2010. LNCS, vol. 6238, pp. 73–82. Springer, Berlin (2010). doi:10.1007/978-3-642-15844-5_8

20. Van der Merwe, D., Engelbrecht, A.P.: Data clustering using particle swarm optimization. In: The 2003 Congress on Evolutionary Computation, CEC 2003, vol. 1, pp. 215–220. IEEE (2003)

21. Munoz, M.A., Kirley, M., Halgamuge, S.K.: Exploratory landscape analysis of continuous space optimization problems using information content. IEEE Trans. Evol. Comput. **19**(1), 74–87 (2015)

22. Paterlini, S., Krink, T.: High performance clustering with differential evolution. In: Congress on Evolutionary Computation, CEC 2004, vol. 2. IEEE (2004)

23. Rana, S., Jasola, S., Kumar, R.: A review on particle swarm optimization algorithms and their applications to data clustering. Artif. Intell. Rev. **35**(3), 211–222 (2011)

24. Rardin, R.L., Uzsoy, R.: Experimental evaluation of heuristic optimization algorithms: a tutorial. J. Heuristics **7**, 261–304 (2001)

25. Rönkkönen, J., Li, X., Kyrki, V., Lampinen, J.: A framework for generating tunable test functions for multimodal optimization. Soft Comput. **15**(9), 1689–1706 (2011)

26. Xu, R., Xu, J., Wunsch, D.C.: Clustering with differential evolution particle swarm optimization. In: IEEE Congress on Evolutionary Computation, pp. 1–8. IEEE (2010)

A PSO-Based Reference Point Adaption Method for Genetic Programming Hyper-Heuristic in Many-Objective Job Shop Scheduling

Atiya Masood[✉], Yi Mei, Gang Chen, and Mengjie Zhang

Victoria University of Wellington, Wellington, New Zealand
{masood.atiy,yi.mei,aaron.chen,mengjie.zhang}@ecs.vuw.ac.nz

Abstract. Job Shop Scheduling is an important combinatorial optimisation problem in practice. It usually contains many (four or more) potentially conflicting objectives such as makespan and mean weighted tardiness. On the other hand, evolving dispatching rules using genetic programming has demonstrated to be a promising approach to solving job shop scheduling due to its flexibility and scalability. In this paper, we aim to solve many-objective job shop scheduling with genetic programming and NSGA-III. However, NSGA-III is originally designed to work with uniformly distributed reference points which do not match well with the discrete and non-uniform Pareto front in job shop scheduling problems, resulting in many useless points during evolution. These useless points can significantly affect the performance of NSGA-III and genetic programming. To address this issue and inspired by particle swarm optimisation, a new reference point adaptation mechanism has been proposed in this paper. Experiment results on many-objective benchmark job shop scheduling instances clearly show that prominent improvement in performance can be achieved upon using our reference point adaptation mechanism in NSGA-III and genetic programming.

Keywords: Job shop scheduling · Many-objective optimisation · Genetic programming · Reference points

1 Introduction

Job Shop Scheduling (JSS) [12] is one of the most important combinatorial optimisation problems in practice and has a wide range of applications in many industries such as manufacturing and cloud computing. In a JSS problem, a group of jobs with predetermined routes are assigned to a fixed set of machines. The problem requires us to design a schedule that dictates job processing in an optimal way so that some pre-defined objectives (e.g. makespan, tardiness and total revenue) can be achieved successfully without violating any domain-specific constraints.

JSS problems are known to be *NP-hard* [1]. As a matter of fact, no exact methods exist in practice to obtain optimal schedules within a reasonable amount

© Springer International Publishing AG 2017
M. Wagner et al. (Eds.): ACALCI 2017, LNAI 10142, pp. 326–338, 2017.
DOI: 10.1007/978-3-319-51691-2_28

of time when the number of jobs and machines becomes large. Hence heuristic and meta-heuristic methods play a more dominating role for solving many practical JSS problems. Among these methods, *dispatching rules* are frequently exploited due to their flexibility, scalability and efficiency, especially when a job shop exhibits high levels of dynamics.

Conceptually, dispatching rules can be treated as priority functions that assign priorities to every job waiting to be processed by a machine. Whenever the machine becomes idle, the job with the highest priority value according to a dispatching rule will be selected for processing. Such a dispatching rule will therefore incrementally determine the complete schedule for any JSS problems. In this paper we will focus mainly on *non-delay* dispatching rules since they avoid any unnecessary delay on idle machines whenever there are incomplete jobs pending on them.

Despite of prominent success, designing useful dispatching rules remains to be a challenging research problem. Particularly dispatching rules designed manually based on one JSS problem instance or one scheduling objective (e.g. minimizing the mean flow time) often perform poorly when the scheduling conditions change (e.g. minimizing the maximal tardiness). To tackle this challenge, many researchers have successfully developed *Genetic Programming Hyper-Heuristic* (GP-HH) techniques for automatic design of dispatching rules under various scheduling objectives. A comprehensive survey on related GP-HH research works can be found in [2,3].

It is widely evidenced in the literature that JSS by nature presents several potentially conflicting objectives, including for example the makespan, mean flowtime, maximum tardiness, maximum lateness, total workload and proportion of tardy jobs. A very recent work also suggests that it is important to consider *many objectives* (i.e. more than three objectives) concurrently while solving a wide range of JSS problems [8]. Driven by this understanding, a new algorithm called GP-NSGA-III that seamlessly combines GP-HH with NSGA-III [5] was proposed, which is one of the state-of-the-art evolutionary many-objective optimisation algorithm [8]. In comparison to other approaches that combine GP-HH with multi-objective optimisation algorithms including NSGA-II [4] and SPEA2 [15], GP-NSGA-III can achieve significantly better performance on 4-objective and 5-objective JSS problems [8].

Despite the promising results with GP-NSGA-III, it was found that many references points are *useless*, i.e. they are never associated with any dispatching rules on the evolved Pareto front. Similar observations have also been witnessed in [7] while applying NSGA-III to other optimisation problems. There is a close relationship between the number of useless points and the performance of the algorithm. Therefore, to evolve high-quality dispatching rules, it is essential to match the distribution of the reference points with the distribution of the Pareto front, which is often irregular (e.g. discrete and non-uniform).

To address this key issue in GP-NSGA-III, the main goal of this study is to develop an effective reference point adaptation mechanism to enhance the match between reference points and the Pareto-front evolved by GP-HH. Guided by this goal, we have developed a new adaptation mechanism inspired by *Particle Swarm Optimisation* (PSO) which has been proven to be highly effective for approximating arbitrary distributions such as the fitness landscape [6,10]. In this paper, to prevent all reference points from converging to a small area in the objective space, we have modified the standard particle dynamics in PSO so that every reference point (i.e. a separate particle in PSO) can be optionally attracted towards one of multiple *global best* locations. We have also removed the influence of *personal best* locations since they may not promise good matches with the evolved Pareto-front in future generations.

Driven by the aim of reducing the number of useless reference points and enhancing the matches between the reference points and the evolved Pareto-front, we organize the rest of paper as follows. Section 2 covers the research background, including the JSS problem description, the reference point adaptation problem and the related works. Section 3 introduces GP-A-NSGA-III in detail. Section 4 reports the experimental design. Section 5 covers results and discussions. Finally, Sect. 6 concludes this paper and highlights possible future research.

2   Research Background

In this section, the JSS problem will be described first. Then we will discuss some related works.

2.1   Description of JSS Problems

In a JSS problem, N jobs are initially assigned to M machines. Each job $j_i, 1 \leq i \leq N$ has a sequence of m operations to be performed, i.e. $\{o_i^1, \ldots, o_i^m\}$. Each operation o_i^k should be processed on one machine $m_i^k, 1 \leq i \leq M$ with the processing time p_i^k. Let r_i^k be the time for operation o_i^k to be ready for processing. R_i is the *ready time* of the first operation of job j_i, which is also known as the *release time*. Any solution to such a JSS problems has to comply with three common constraints, as described below.

1. An operation is performed on a machine without interruption. This means that all operations are non-preemptive.
2. The operation cannot start until its previous operation has been completed. In the other words, the operations follow precedence constraints.
3. Each machine is persistently available and should process only one operation of any job at any given time.

Similar to [8], we consider JSS problems with four objectives, i.e. the mean flowtime, maximal flowtime, mean weighted tardiness and maximal weighted tardiness. Clearly, each objective is expected to be minimised.

2.2   Problem for Using Uniformly Distributed Reference Points

As mentioned in the introduction, NSGA-III is originally designed to work with a fixed set of uniformly distributed reference points. However, for many combinatorial optimisation problems such as the JSS problems, the true Pareto-front is usually irregular and discontinuous. Therefore direct application of NSGA-III will lead to many *useless points*.

In essence, reference points are adopted in NSGA-III to replace the crowding distance mechanism introduced in NSGA-II for high-dimensional objective space and hence to promote *solution diversity* [5]. Clearly, if only a few reference points are truly associated with the Pareto-optimal dispatching rules evolved by GP-HH at the current generation, it is not easy to distinguish and select these rules to improve diversity for future generations. In other words, a majority of useful reference points will be associated with many candidate dispatching rules. Some rules can be far from the corresponding reference point. Such a dispatching rule should enjoy higher selection opportunity but may not be selected during evolution simply because it is associated with a popular reference point. Due to the above reason, we found that better matches between reference points and the evolved Pareto-front can help enhance solution diversity and therefore the performance of GP-NSGA-III. As a consequence, developing a reference point adaptation mechanism becomes a key research issue to be tackled in this paper.

2.3   Related Work

A study of the literature shows that many past research works focused primarily on solving single-objective JSS problems [11]. Recently, huge efforts have been made in the *evolutionary computation* (EC) community to develop multi-objective algorithms for JSS. Among these algorithms, Pareto-optimal methods have clearly attracted substantial research attention [9]. Inspired by their success, a few efforts have also been made towards addressing many-objective JSS problems [8]. Particularly, the GP-NSGA-III algorithm proposed in [8] is amongst the first in the literature to try to cope with exponentially increasing objective space by using NSGA-III. However, the use of uniformly distributed reference points in NSGA-III presents a new research challenge.

Jain and Deb have already proposed an interesting mechanism for adjusting reference points in NSGA-III [7]. However, their mechanism requires the number of reference points to be changed dynamically and is difficult to implement in high-dimensional objective space. When the number of reference points becomes large, the efficiency of their mechanism may also be affected. Nevertheless, their mechanism is very effective for addressing constrained general-purpose optimisation problems. Without considering constraints, we prefer to adopt a much simpler approach for reference point adaptation. Specifically our approach does not change the total number of reference points during evolution and is easy to implement regardless of the number of objectives under consideration. It is particularly suitable for the JSS problems described in Subsect. 2.1.

3   Adaptive Reference Points for Many-Objective JSS

The framework of the proposed GP-A-NSGA-III is described in Algorithm 1. The framework is similar to that of the GP-NSGA-III [8], and the differences (for adaptive reference points) are highlighted. Particularly, when initialising the reference points (line 2), a velocity vector V is initialised along with the position vector X for each reference point. Then, the PSO parameters are specified (line 3). In each generation, the reference points are updated (line 10) after each population update.

Algorithm 1. The framework of GP-A-NSGA-III.

    Input   : A training set I_{train} and rules P
    Output: A set of non-dominated rules P^*
1   Initialise and evaluate the population P_0 of rules by the ramped-half-and-half method;
2   Initialise the position X and velocity V of reference points Z ;
3   Set parameter w_{min}, w_{max}, c_2 ;
4   Calculate the reference points Z Set $g \leftarrow 0$;
5   **while** $g < g_{max}$ **do**
6   Generate the offspring population Q_g using the crossover, mutation and reproduction of GP;
7   **foreach** $Q \in Q_g$ **do** Evaluate rule Q;
8      $R_g \leftarrow P_g \cup Q_g$;
9   Form the new population P_{g+1} from R_g by the NSGA-III selection;
10   Update(Z) ;
11     $g \leftarrow g + 1$;
12 **end**
13 **return** *The non-dominated individuals* $P^* \subseteq P_{g_{max}}$;

3.1   Reference Point Update

The PSO-based reference point update scheme Update(Z) is described in Algorithm 2. In the algorithm, each reference point is seen as a particle. The fitness of a particle is defined as the number of individuals in the population associated to it, which is to be maximised. That is, the global best particle is the one with the most individuals associated to it. Note that when updating the velocity (line 6), the term for the local best position is ignored. It can be seen that the fitness of particles (reference points) depends on the distribution of the whole swarm, and the positions of other particles. Thus, it may not be meaningful to move towards the local best, which can become worse upon movements of other particles. Furthermore, there is no elitism for the global best (line 3). This way, the reference points can have sufficient diversity.

Algorithm 2. Update of the reference points.

Input : Reference points $Z = (X, V)$
Output: Updated reference points Z^g
1 Calculate fitness $fit(Z_i)$= number of individuals associated for each $Z_i \in Z$;
2 Calculate $w = w_{max} - g \cdot (w_{max} - w_{min})/g_{max}$;
3 Calculate the global best $Z^* = \arg\max\{fit(Z)\}$;
4 **for** $i = 1 \to NumParticles$ **do**
5   **for** $j = 1 \to NumObjs$ **do**
6          $V^g_{i,j} = w * V^{g-1}_{i,j} + c_2 * rand() * (Z^* - X^{g-1}_{i,j})$;
7          $X^g_{i,j} = X^{g-1}_{i,j} + V^g_{i,j}$;
8   **end**
9 **end**
10 **return** $Z^g = (X^g, V^g)$;

Algorithm 3. The fitness evaluation.

Input : A training set I_{train} and an individual (rule) P
Output: The fitness $f(P)$ of the rule P
1 **foreach** I in I_{train} **do**
2   Construct a schedule $\Delta(P, I)$ by applying the rule P to the JSS instance I;
     Calculate the objective values $f(\Delta(P, I))$;
3 **end**
4 $f(P) \leftarrow \frac{1}{|I_{train}|} \sum_{I \in I_{train}} f(\Delta(P, I))$; ;
5 **return** $f(P)$;

3.2 Fitness Evaluation

For evaluating each GP individual (lines 1 and 7 of Algorithm 1), it is applied to a set of JSS training instances I_{train} as a dispatching rule, and the normalised objective values of the resultant schedules are set to its fitness values. The pseudo code of the fitness evaluation is given in Algorithm 3.

4 Experimental Design

To verify the effectiveness of the proposed adaptive reference point scheme, we compared the performance of GP-A-NSGA-III with the baseline GP-NSGA-III in the experimental studies. We selected the Taillard (TA) static JSS benchmark instances [13] as the testbed. The TA set has been widely used as the test JSS instances in literature. It consists of 80 instances (ID from 1 to 80) divided into 8 groups, each having 10 instances. The number of jobs varies from 15 to 100 and the number of machines ranges from 15 to 20. The instances belonging to the same group have the same numbers of jobs and machines. In the experiments, the 80 TA instances were split in half, each with 40 instances. Then, one subset was used as the training set and the other was the test set. Since the instances are static, all the jobs are available from time zero. The due date $dd(j_i)$ of each job j_i is calculated as $dd(j_i) = \lambda \times \sum_{k=1}^{m} p_i^k$, where the due date factor λ is set to 1.3. In the experiments, we considered four potentially conflicting objectives: *mean flowtime (MF), maximal weighted tardiness (MaxWT), maximal flowtime (MaxF) and mean weighted tardiness (MWT)*. For both GP-A-NSGA-III and GP-NSGA-III, 40 independent runs were conducted.

4.1   Parameter Settings

Both GP-A-NSGA-III and GP-NSGA-III adopt the GP representation (tree-based) and evolutionary operators (e.g. initialisation, crossover and mutation) along with the fitness evaluation scheme of NSGA-III. For both compared algorithms, the population size is set to 1024. The crossover, mutation and reproduction rates are set to 85%, 10% and 5% respectively. The maximal depth is set to 8. The population is initialised by the ramp-half-and-half method. In each generation, the parents are selected by the tournament selection with size of 7. The maximal number of generations is set to 51. The terminal set is described in Table 1. The function set includes the basic arithmetic operators (the protected division operator returns 1 if the denominator is zero), the 2-argument "min" and "max" operators and the 3-argument "If" operator that returns the second argument if the first argument is positive, and the third argument otherwise.

For the PSO parameters, we set $c_2 = 2$, $w_{min} = 0.4$ and $w_{max} = 0.9$, which are standard settings used by many existing works.

Table 1. Terminal set of GP for JSS.

Attribute	Notation
Processing time of the operation	PT
Inverse processing time of the operation	IPT
Processing time of the next operation	NOPT
Ready time of the operation	ORT
Ready time of the next machine	NMRT
Work remaining	WKR
Number of operation remaining	NOR
Work in the next queue	WINQ
Number of operations in the next queue	NOINQ
Flow due date	FDD
Due date	DD
Weight	W
Number of operations in the queue	NOIQ
Work in the queue	WIQ
Ready time of the machine	MRT

In the experiments, the two commonly used measures in multi-objective optimisation, i.e. *Inverted Generational Distance* (IGD) [14] and *Hyper-Volume* (HV)

[16] are used to compare the algorithms. To calculate IGD and HV, we first normalised the objectives into the range [0,1] by linear normalisation. The maximal and minimal values for each objective were obtained from the results of all the runs of both compared algorithms. After the normalisation, the nadir point was set to $(1,1)$ for calculating HV. Note that IGD needs a set of uniformly distributed points in the true Pareto front, which cannot be known in multi-objective JSS problems. Therefore, we approximate the true Pareto front by selecting the non-dominated solutions among the final solutions from all the runs of the two compared algorithms.

5   Results and Discussions

During the GP search process, a rule is evaluated on the 40 training instances, and the fitness function for each objective is defined as the average normalised objective value of the schedule obtained by applying that rule to each of the 40 training instances. For each algorithm, 40 GP runs obtained 40 final dispatching rules. Then, the rules were tested on the 40 test instances.

5.1   Overall Results

Table 2 shows the mean and standard deviation of the test performance (HV and IGD) of the rules obtained by GP-NSGA-III and GP-A-NSGA-III. In addition, for each test instance, the *Wilcoxon rank sum* test with the significance level of 0.05 was conducted separately on both the HV and IGD of the rules obtained by the two compared algorithms. That is, if p-value is smaller than 0.05, then the best algorithm is considered significantly better than the other algorithm. The significantly better results was marked in bold. The table reveals that GP-A-NSGA-III performs significantly better than GP-NSGA-III in most of the test instances. In the case of HV, GP-A-NSGA-III performed significantly better on 24 out of 40 test instances. On the other hand, GP-NSGA-III performed significantly better only on 6 instances. For the remaining 10 instances, the two compared algorithms performed statistically the same. In regard to IGD, Table 2 exhibits the same pattern. GP-A-NSGA-III achieved significantly better performance on 21 out of the 40 test instances. In contrast, GP-NSGA-III performed significantly better on 13 instances.

When taking a closer look at the Table 2, it can be found that GP-A-NSGA-III not only performed better on smaller instances but also is more effective on more challenging and larger instances. For some test instances (e.g. instances 1, 10, 24), GP-A-NSGA-III achieved a huge improvement. This demonstrates the usefulness of the proposed adaptive reference point scheme, which can find better association with population members and thus obtained well distributed reference points.

Table 2. The mean and standard deviation over the HV and IGD values of the 40 independent runs of the compared algorithms in the 4-obj experiment. The significantly better results are shown in bold.

Problem instances		HV		IGD	
ID	#J_#M	GP-NSGA-III	GP-A-NSGA-III	GP-NSGA-III	GP-A-NSGA-III
1	15_15	.0096 (.0145)	**.2414 (.0368)**	.0265 (.0008)	**.0088 (.0113)**
2	15_15	.1600 (.0182)	**.1666 (.0110)**	.0254 (.0005)	**.0218 (.0004)**
3	15_15	.0806 (.0125)	**.0906 (.0127)**	.0205 (.0008)	.0292 (.0006)
4	15_15	**.1263 (.0183)**	.0692 (.0091)	**.01765 (.0007)**	.0218 (.0006)
5	15_15	.1661 (.0202)	.1752 (.0192)	**.0190 (.0005)**	.0237 (.0007)
6	20_15	.1271 (.0176)	**.1421 (.0139)**	**.0154 (.0004)**	.0211 (.0004)
7	20_15	.2488 (.0683)	**.2538 (.0695)**	.0079 (.0013)	.0077 (.0014)
8	20_15	.1115 (.0201)	**.2015 (.0253)**	.0186 (.0006)	.01819 (.0026)
9	20_15	.1700 (.0148)	**.1839 (.0219)**	.0170 (.0005)	**.0149 (.0005)**
10	20_15	.1086 (.0151)	**.3580 (.0366)**	**.0156 (.0002)**	.0160 (.0003)
11	20_20	.0114 (.0038)	**.1087 (.0118)**	.0299 (.0006)	**.0240 (.0008)**
12	20_20	.0852 (.0133)	**.1206 (.0134)**	**.0173 (.0004)**	.0222 (.0006)
13	20_20	.1540 (.0151)	.1569 (.0326)	.0188 (.0003)	**.0137 (.0002)**
14	20_20	.0504 (.01103)	**.0704 (.0118)**	.0328 (.0008)	**.0272 (.0007)**
15	20_20	**.3985 (.0225)**	.2454 (.0199)	**.0109 (.0004)**	.0150 (.0002)
16	30_15	.2465 (.030)	.2375 (.0234)	**.0144 (.0006)**	.0140 (.0002)
17	30_15	.1813 (.0096)	**.2278 (.0229)**	.0138 (.0003)	**.0097 (.0004)**
18	30_15	**.3198 (.0233)**	.1957 (.0132)	**.0131 (.0004)**	.0152 (.0003)
19	30_15	.2789 (.0126)	**.3004 (.0197)**	.0150 (.0004)	**.0114 (.0004)**
20	30_15	**.2575 (.0312)**	.2124 (.0312)	**.0144 (.0005)**	.0195 (.0003)
21	30_20	.1347 (.0657)	**.2325 (.0792)**	.0135 (.0022)	**.0098 (.0014)**
22	30_20	.2365 (.0472)	**.3027 (.0470)**	.0065 (.0010)	**.0052 (.0006)**
23	30_20	.2944 (.0398)	.2984 (.0410)	.0046 (.00004)	.0045 (.0005)
24	30_20	.3812 (.0503)	**.6161 (.0174)**	.0070 (.0009)	**.0018 (.0004)**
25	30_20	.5199 (.0477)	.5290 (.0396)	.0059 (.0012)	**.0046 (.0005)**
26	50_15	.4563 (.0417)	**.4872 (.0270)**	.0051 (.0009)	**.0039 (.0004)**
27	50_15	.5710 (.0361)	.5685 (.0304)	.0040 (.0009)	**.0032 (.0003)**
28	50_15	.4598 (.0398)	**.4966 (.0250)**	.0049 (.0010)	**.0036 (.0003)**
29	50_15	.4862 (.0372)	**.5125 (.0251)**	.0045 (.0007)	**.0037 (.0003)**
30	50_15	.4510 (.0406)	**.4732 (.0240)**	.0033 (.0005)	**.0026 (.0002)**
31	50_20	.5085 (.0424)	**.5147 (.0295)**	.0053 (.0008)	**.0042 (.0004)**
32	50_20	.4378 (.0476)	.4266 (.0375)	.0046 (.0006)	.0041 (.0004)
33	50_20	.3422 (.0266)	**.4383 (.0838)**	.0125 (.0006)	**.0069 (.0051)**
34	50_20	.3828 (.0384)	.4089 (.0262)	.0036 (.00005)	**.0030 (.00029)**
35	50_20	.5558 (.0349)	**.5763 (.0165)**	.0025 (.0005)	**.0020 (.0001)**
36	100_20	**.3648 (.0179)**	.2972 (.0093)	**.010 (.0003)**	.0130 (.0006)
37	100_20	**.3442 (.0142)**	.2844 (.0101)	**.0086 (.0003)**	.0107 (.0003)
38	100_20	.3006 (.0196)	.3025 (.0136)	.0067 (.0009)	.0066 (.0002)
39	100_20	.6495 (.0185)	.6515 (.0191)	.0010 (.0001)	.0010 (.0001)
40	100_20	.3658 (.0158)	**.3828 (.0100)**	**.0085 (. (.0003)**	.0088 (.0002)

5.2   Further Analysis

To further investigate how the adaptive reference point scheme affect the GP search process, we plot (a) the average number of useless references points (those associated with no individual in the population); (b) the average HV of the non-dominated solutions obtained so far and (c) the average IGD of the non-dominated solutions obtained so far for each generation during the 40 independent runs of the two compared algorithms, as given in Fig. 1.

From Fig. 1, it is obvious that the adaptive reference point scheme can significantly reduce the number of useless points during the GP search process. Without adaptive points, the number of useless references points in GP-NSGA-III kept increasing from 910 to about 980. On the contrary, in GP-A-NSGA-III, the number of useless reference points first increased and then decreased to almost the same level as the beginning. This indicates that especially at the later stage of the search, the adaptive reference point scheme led to less useless reference points, and thus a better refinement of the regions around the population.

Figure 1 show that GP-A-NSGA-III obtained better convergence curves in terms of both HV and IGD. This shows that the reduction of useless reference points can lead to better non-dominated sets.

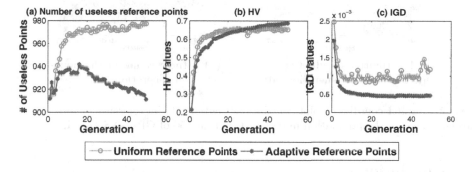

Fig. 1. The curves of the average number of useless reference points, HV and IGD values of the non-dominated solutions on the training set during the 40 independent GP runs.

Figure 2 shows the distribution of the reference points and the fitness values of the population in generations 1 and 50 of GP-A-NSGA-III. It can be seen that in generation 1, the reference points are close to the initial uniform distribution, and the fitness distribution of the population is relatively uniform as well. In generation 50, on the other hand, the distributions of the reference points and the fitness values of the population become very similar to each other. This is consistent with our expectation, which is to use a similar distribution of reference points as that of the population to fine tune the promising area around the population.

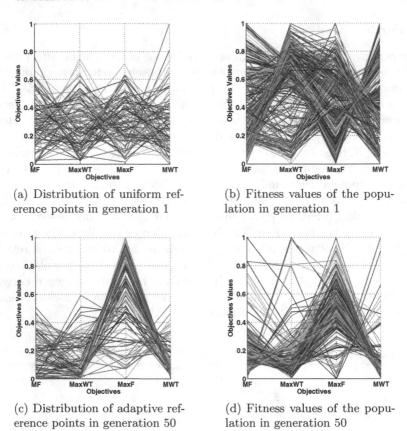

(a) Distribution of uniform reference points in generation 1

(b) Fitness values of the population in generation 1

(c) Distribution of adaptive reference points in generation 50

(d) Fitness values of the population in generation 50

Fig. 2. Parallel coordinate plot for the distribution of the reference points and the fitness values of the population in generations 1 and 50 of GP-A-NSGA-III.

6   Conclusion

The goal of this study was to identify a key research issue involved in using NSGA-III effectively, i.e. the simple adoption of uniformly distributed reference points failed to promote solution diversity during evolution and affected the performance of GP-HH. This goal has been successfully achieved by proposing a new reference point adaptation mechanism inspired by PSO. Important changes to particle dynamics in PSO have also been introduced in our mechanism to prevent majority of reference points from converging to small areas in the objective space. In the subsequent experimental evaluations based on the Taillard benchmark set, we successfully showed that the proposed reference point adaptation mechanism can significantly improve the performance of GP-HH and NSGA-III in terms of both HV and IGD.

In the future, we plan to study the potential usefulness of Gaussian Processing modelling techniques for more accurate approximation of the Pareto front.

The use of local search and niching techniques could also significantly improve solution diversity and boost performance of GP-NSGA-III. Their use with our reference point adaptation mechanism deserves further investigation.

References

1. Błażewicz, J., Domschke, W., Pesch, E.: The job shop scheduling problem: conventional and new solution techniques. Eur. J. Oper. Res. **93**(1), 1–33 (1996)
2. Branke, J., Nguyen, S., Pickardt, C., Zhang, M.: Automated design of production scheduling heuristics: a review. IEEE Trans. Evol. Comput. **20**(1), 110–124 (2016)
3. Burke, E.K., Hyde, M.R., Kendall, G., Ochoa, G., Ozcan, E., Woodward, J.R.: Exploring hyper-heuristic methodologies with genetic programming. In: Mumford, C.L., Jain, L.C. (eds.) Computational Intelligence: Collaboration, Fusion and Emergence. ISRL, vol. 1, pp. 177–201. Springer, Heidelberg (2009). doi:10.1007/978-3-642-01799-5_6
4. Deb, K., Pratap, A., Agarwal, S., Meyarivan, T.: A fast and elitist multiobjective genetic algorithm: NSGA-II. IEEE Trans. Evol. Comput. **6**, 182–197 (2002)
5. Deb, K., Jain, H.: An evolutionary many-objective optimization algorithm using reference-point-based nondominated sorting approach, part I: solving problems with box constraints. IEEE Trans. Evol. Comput. **18**(4), 577–601 (2014)
6. Eberhart, R., Kennedy, J.: A new optimizer using particle swarm theory. In: Proceedings of 6th International Symposium on Micro Machine and Human Science, MHS 1995, pp. 39–43. IEEE (1995)
7. Jain, H., Deb, K.: An evolutionary many-objective optimization algorithm using reference-point based nondominated sorting approach, part II: handling constraints and extending to an adaptive approach. IEEE Trans. Evol. Comput. **18**(4), 602–622 (2014)
8. Masood, A., Mei, Y., Chen, G., Zhang, M.: Many-objective genetic programming for job-shop scheduling. In: IEEE WCCI 2016 Conference Proceedings. IEEE (2016)
9. Nguyen, S., Zhang, M., Johnston, M., Tan, K.C.: Dynamic multi-objective job shop scheduling: a genetic programming approach. In: Uyar, A.S., Ozcan, E., Urquhart, N. (eds.) Automated Scheduling and Planning. SCI, vol. 505, pp. 251–282. Springer, Heidelberg (2013). doi:10.1007/978-3-642-39304-4_10
10. Owen, A., Harvey, I.: Adapting particle swarm optimisation for fitness landscapes with neutrality. In: IEEE Swarm Intelligence Symposium. IEEE (2007)
11. Park, J., Nguyen, S., Zhang, M., Johnston, M.: Evolving ensembles of dispatching rules using genetic programming for job shop scheduling. In: Machado, P., Heywood, M.I., McDermott, J., Castelli, M., García-Sánchez, P., Burelli, P., Risi, S., Sim, K. (eds.) EuroGP 2015. LNCS, vol. 9025, pp. 92–104. Springer, Heidelberg (2015). doi:10.1007/978-3-319-16501-1_8
12. Pinedo, M.L.: Scheduling: Theory, Algorithms, and Systems. Springer Science & Business Media, New York (2012)
13. Taillard, E.: Benchmarks for basic scheduling problems. Eur. J. Oper. Res. **64**(2), 278–285 (1993)
14. Zhang, Q., Zhou, A., Zhao, S., Suganthan, P.N., Liu, W., Tiwari, S.: Multiobjective optimization test instances for the CEC 2009 special session and competition. University of Essex, Colchester, UK and Nanyang Technological University, Singapore, special session on performance assessment of multi-objective optimization algorithms, Technical report pp. 1–30 (2008)

15. Zitzler, E., Laumanns, M., Thiele, L.: SPEA2: Improving the strength Pareto evolutionary algorithm. In: EUROGEN 2001. Evolutionary Methods for Design, Optimization and Control with Applications to Industrial Problems, pp. 95–100 (2002)
16. Zitzler, E., Thiele, L., Laumanns, M., Fonseca, C.M., Da Fonseca, V.G.: Performance assessment of multiobjective optimizers: an analysis and review. IEEE Trans. Evol. Comput. $7(2)$, 117–132 (2003)

Optimal Power Allocation of Wireless Sensor Networks with Multi-operator Based Constrained Differential Evolution

Yanan Li, Wenyin Gong[✉], and Zhihua Cai

School of Computer Science, China University of Geosciences,
Wuhan 430074, People's Republic of China
wygong@cug.edu.cn

Abstract. Optimal power allocation (OPA) is considered to be one of the key issues in designing a wireless sensor network (WSN). Generally, the OPA in WSN can be formulated as a numerical optimization problem with constraints. Differential evolution (DE) is a powerful evolutionary algorithm for numerical, however, the success of DE in solving a specific problem crucially depends on appropriately choosing suitable mutation strategy and its associated control parameter values. Meanwhile, there is no single parameter setting and strategy that is able to consistently obtain the best results for the OPA with different number of sensor nodes. Based on the above considerations, in this paper, a multi-operator based constrained differential evolution is proposed, where *probability matching* and *constrained credit assignment* techniques are used so as to adaptively select the most suitable strategy in different phase of the search process for the OPA. Additionally, the parameter adaptation technique is used to avoid the fine-tuning of DE parameters for different problems. The proposed algorithm has been evaluated in several OPA with different number of sensor nodes, and its performance is compared with single-strategy based DE variants and other methods. Experimental results indicate that the proposed algorithm is able to provide better results than the compared methods.

1 Introduction

A wireless sensor network (WSN) is a network of distributed autonomous devices that can sense or monitor physical or environmental conditions cooperatively. In WSNs, there exists a large number of small, inexpensive, spatially distributed sensor nodes that are deployed in an ad hoc manner in vast geographical areas for remote operations and these nodes can acquire, process, and transmit data over wireless medium. WSNs also are used in numerous applications such as security detection, traffic tracking, environmental monitoring, because of characteristics of the low cost and ease of operation [1]. In addition, battery supply, storage resources and commutation bandwidth tremendously restrict the communication and computational capabilities of sensor nodes [2]. Therefore, there has been significant research concentrate that revolves around reaping and minimizing

© Springer International Publishing AG 2017
M. Wagner et al. (Eds.): ACALCI 2017, LNAI 10142, pp. 339–352, 2017.
DOI: 10.1007/978-3-319-51691-2_29

energy. But above all, it may be impossible to replace or change the batteries of the sensor nodes because of cost and operating environment considerations [3]. Therefore, the optimal power allocation can be considered as one of the crucial issues for designing a WSN.

Differential evolution (DE), which was firstly proposed by Storn and Price [4], is one of the most powerful EAs for global numerical optimization. The advantages of DE are its simple structure, ease of use, speed, and robustness, which leads it on many applications, such as data mining, neural network training, pattern recognition, digital filter design, engineering design, etc. [5]. More applications of DE can be found in the literature [6].

The OPA in WSN can be seen as a constrained numerical optimization problem [3]. In addition, the optimal power allocation in WSNs have attained considerable attention. Recently, there are several algorithms are proposed for OPA, such as particle swarm optimization (PSO) [3,7,8], hybrid DE with biogeography-based optimization [9]. Both the two algorithms achieved good performance for independent and identically distributed (i.i.d.) and correlated data fusion in WSNs. In addition, due to the advantages of DE in the numerical optimization, recently, DE has been successfully used for the constrained optimization problems (COPs) by means of employing the constraint-handling techniques [10]. Meanwhile there is no single parameter setting and strategy that is able to consistently obtain the best results for the OPA with different number of sensor nodes [11]. Therefore, it is worth exploring more effective algorithm for OPA.

Differential mutation is the crucial operator in DE which is operated based on the distribution of solutions in the current population. New offsprings are created by combining the parent individual and the mutant individual. Only if the offspring has better fitness value, it can replace its parent. However, it is a difficult and crucial task to choose which mutation strategy for the performance of the DE [12,13]. Based on the above consideration, in this paper, we proposed a multi-operator differential evolution based on *Probability Matching* and *constrained credit assignment* for solving the OPA. The proposed method is referred to as PM-MDE, in short.

2 Preliminaries

In this section, we first briefly describe the optimal power allocation in WSNs, followed by the description of the classical DE algorithm. Then, the constraint-handling technique used in this work is introduced. Finally, adaptive strategy selection is presented.

2.1 Optimal Power Allocation in WSNs

Generally, the power allocation problem can be considered as a constrained numerical optimization problem and it also can be formulated as follows [3]:

$$\min_{G_k \geq 0} \sum_{k=1}^{L} G_k^2 \tag{1}$$

subject to

$$P(E) = Q(\tfrac{1}{2}\sqrt{m^2 e^T A \textstyle\sum_L^{-1} A e}) \le \varepsilon,$$
$$G_k \ge 0,$$
$$K = 1, \dots, L. \tag{2}$$

where ε is the required fusion error probability threshold, L indicates the number of sensor nodes, m represents the deterministic signal and G_K is the amplifier gain at node k. e is the L-length vector with all ones. The covariance matrix is $\sum_L = A^T \sum_v A + \sum_w$, where $A = diag(H_1 G_1, \dots, H_L G_L)$, $\sum_v$ is the observation and $\sum_w$ is receiver noise covariances. Specially, when the local observations and the receiver noise are both i.i.d., the probability of fusion error can be simplified to:

$$P(E) = Q\left(\frac{m}{2}\sqrt{\sum_{k=1}^{L}\frac{H_K^2 G_K^2}{\delta_v^2 H_K^2 G_K^2 + \delta_\omega^2}}\right) \le \varepsilon. \tag{3}$$

The inequality in (3) can be expressed as follows:

$$\beta \le \sqrt{\sum_{k=1}^{L}\frac{H_K^2 G_K^2}{\delta_v^2 H_K^2 G_K^2 + \delta_\omega^2}} \tag{4}$$

where $\beta = \frac{2}{m}Q^{-1}(\varepsilon)$ and $Q(\cdot)$ is the complementary Gaussian cumulative distribution function. δ_v means the variances of the observation noise and δ_w represents the receiver noise. H_k indicates the channel fading coefficient. It is needed to point that H_k follows an exponential distribution (i.e., Rayleigh fading) with unit mean [9].

Besides the above situation, when the sensor observations are spatially correlated, the observation noise covariance matrix $\sum_v$ can be formulated as follows [14]:

$$\sum_v = \delta_v^2 \begin{pmatrix} 1 & \rho^d & \cdots & \rho^{d(L-2)} & \rho^{d(L-1)} \\ \rho^d & 1 & \cdots & \rho^{d(L-3)} & \rho^{d(L-2)} \\ \vdots & \vdots & \ddots & \vdots & \vdots \\ \rho^{d(L-1)} & \rho^{d(L-2)} & \cdots & \rho^d & 1 \end{pmatrix} \tag{5}$$

The inequality in (3) can be expressed as follows:

$$\beta \le \sqrt{e^T A \textstyle\sum_n^{-1} A e} \tag{6}$$

where $d_j = d(j-1), j = 1, \dots L$, which means the sensor nodes are equally spaced along a straight line. Because $\sum_v$ is not diagonal, it is difficult to evaluate $\sum_n^{-1}$ in closed form. Therefore, it is necessary to introduce a specific sensor network model which derives an upper bound for $P(E)$ and is proposed by Wimalajeewa and Jayaweera [3]. Finally, DE algorithm becomes suitable to use for OPA under arbitrary correlated observation.

2.2   Differential Evolution

DE is a simple yet efficient evolutionary algorithm (EA) for global numerical optimization [4]. For the population initialization, a uniform distribution is usually used in the literature within the search space. After initialization, DE generates offsprings based on combining the parent individual and several other individuals of the same population which means that offsprings are generated according to mutation operation and crossover operation. An offspring is evaluated by a fitness function and then replaces the parent individual only if it has an equal or better fitness value. DE repeats this procedure that generates offsprings and replaces parent individual until a predefined termination criterion is satisfied. Generally, the terminal conditions can be fixed either the maximum number of fitness function evaluations (Max_NFFEs) or define a desired solution value to be reached (VTR).

3   Multi-operator Based Differential Evolution (PM-MDE)

In this section, we will introduce our proposed PM-MDE algorithm in detail. It is previously mentioned that there are many mutation strategies in DE and it is hard to choose the most suitable strategy for different problem in the different stage of evolution. Therefore, it is significant to autonomously select appropriate mutation strategy for OPA. To achieve this performance, in this work, we propose the multi-operator differential evolution for OPA based on *Probability Matching* (PM) technique and *credit assignment* method [15]. The PM technique and the credit assignment method are integrated into DE to implement the adaptive strategy selection and the relative fitness improvement calculation. Moreover, the parameter adaptation method of CR and F proposed in [16] is adopted in this work.

3.1   Strategy Selection and Probability Matching

Following [17], in this subsection the adaptive strategy selection will be introduced. Firstly, it can be supposed that we have $K(K > 1)$ strategies in the pool $A = \{a_1, \ldots, a_k\}$ and a probability vector can be described like $P(t) = \{p_1(t), \ldots, p_K(t)\} (\forall t : p_{\min} \leq p_i(t) \leq 1; \sum_{i=1}^{K} p_i(t) = 1)$. The $r_a(t)$ presents reward which be achieved by a strategy a after its application at time t. The PM method is used to adaptively update the probability $P_a(t)$ of each strategy a based on its reward. $q_a(t)$ is the known quality (or empirical estimate) of a strategy a, that is updated as follows [18]:

$$q_a(t+1) = q_a(t) + \alpha \cdot [r_a(t) - q_a(t)], \tag{7}$$

where $\alpha \in (0, 1]$ is the adaptation rate. The PM method updates the probability $P_a(t)$ as follows [15, 18]:

$$p_a(t+1) = p_{\min} + (1 - K \cdot P_{\min}) \frac{q_a(t+1)}{\sum_{i=1}^{K} q_i(t+1)}. \tag{8}$$

where $p_{\min} \in (0, 1]$ represents the minimum probability value of each strategy, the objective of this is to ensure no operator gets lost. It is indicated by Eq. (8) that when only one strategy achieves a reward during a long period of time and all other strategies receive no reward, then its selection probability $P_a(t)$ converges to $p_{\max} = p_{\min} + (1 - K \cdot p_{\min})$. It also can be seen that $\sum_{a=1}^{K} p_a(t) = 1$ and $0 < P_{\min} < \frac{1}{K}$.

3.2 Constrained Credit Assignment

As mentioned above, the OPA problem is a constrained optimization problem. Therefore, to assign the credit for each search operator, we need to design the constrained credit assignment technique. In this work, the constraint-handling technique named improved adaptive trade-off model [19] is employed, which was proposed by Wang and Cai and is the improved version of ATM [20]. In IATM, the population can be divided into three situations such as infeasible situation, semi-feasible situation and feasible situation.

In the infeasible situation, the solutions are measured based on their constraint violation. In the semi-feasible situation, the population includes both feasible and infeasible solutions and it can be divided into the feasible group (Z_1) and the infeasible group (Z_2) based on the feasibility of each solution. The infeasible individuals in the semi-feasible situation should be handled and evaluated based on their constraint violation. Then, the objective function can be seen as $f(\mathbf{x})$ and $\mathbf{x}$ is the vector of the solution. The objective function value $f(\mathbf{x}_i)$ of the solution $\mathbf{x}_i$ is converted into

$$f'(\mathbf{x}_i) = \begin{cases} f(\mathbf{x}_i), & i \in Z_1 \\ \max\{\varphi \cdot f(\mathbf{x}_{best}) + (1 - \varphi) \cdot f(\mathbf{x}_{worst}), f(\mathbf{x}_i)\}, & i \in Z_2 \end{cases} \quad (9)$$

where φ represents the feasibility ratio of the last population, and $\mathbf{x}_{best}$ and $\mathbf{x}_{worst}$ are the best and worst individual in the feasible group Z_1, respectively. After achieving the changed objective function value of each individual, then it should be normalized as

$$f_{\mathrm{nor}}(\mathbf{x}_i) = \frac{f'(\mathbf{x}_i) - \min\limits_{j \in Z_1 \cup Z_2} f'(\mathbf{x}_j)}{\max\limits_{j \in Z_1 \cup Z_2} f'(\mathbf{x}_j) - \min\limits_{j \in Z_1 \cup Z_2} f'(\mathbf{x}_j)}. \quad (10)$$

In addition, the normalized constraint violation can be evaluated as

$$C_{\mathrm{nor}}(\mathbf{x}_i) = \begin{cases} 0, & i \in Z_1 \\ \dfrac{C(\mathbf{x}_i) - \min\limits_{j \in Z_2} C(\mathbf{x}_j)}{\max\limits_{j \in Z_2} C(\mathbf{x}_j) - \min\limits_{j \in Z_2} C(\mathbf{x}_j)}, & i \in Z_2 \end{cases} \quad (11)$$

where $C(\mathbf{x})$ represents the distance of the solution $\mathbf{x}$ from the boundaries of the feasible set, which also reflects the degree of its constraint violation.

Then, the final fitness function is obtained as follows:

$$f_{\mathrm{final}}(\mathbf{x}_i) = f_{\mathrm{nor}}(\mathbf{x}_i) + C_{\mathrm{nor}}(\mathbf{x}_i). \quad (12)$$

In the feasible situation, it is to say that all solutions are feasible in the population, the performance of the situation can be evaluated by the objective function value.

Based on the above fitness transformation technique, similar to the method in [21], the relative fitness improvement η_i can be calculated by

$$\eta_i = \begin{cases} \frac{\delta_1}{f(\mathbf{u}_i)} \cdot (f(\mathbf{x}_i) - f(\mathbf{u}_i)), & \text{feasible situation} \\ \frac{\delta_2}{C(\mathbf{u}_i)} \cdot (C(\mathbf{x}_i) - C(\mathbf{u}_i)), & \text{infeasible situation} \\ \frac{\delta_3}{f_{\text{final}}(\mathbf{u}_i)} \cdot (f_{\text{final}}(\mathbf{x}_i) - f_{\text{final}}(\mathbf{u}_i)), & \text{semi-feasible situation} \end{cases} \quad (13)$$

where $i = 1, \ldots, \mu$. δ is the objective fitness of the best-so-far solution in the population. $\mathbf{x}_i$ and $\mathbf{v}_i$ are the parent and its offspring, respectively.

In [17], four different credit assignment methods are presented, and the averaged normalization reward is able to provide highly-competitive results through benchmark functions. Based on this consideration, the averaged normalization reward is selected for the credit assignment in this work and is listed as follows:

$$r_a(t) = \frac{r'_a(t)}{\max\limits_{a=1,\ldots,K} r'_a(t)} \quad (14)$$

where $r'_a(t)$ is calculated as

$$r'_a(t) = \frac{\sum_{i=1}^{|S_a|} |S_a|}{|S_a|} \quad (15)$$

and S_a is the set of all relative fitness improvement η_i of a strategy a ($a = 1, \cdots, K$) at generation t.

3.3 Strategy Pool

DE has realized using different mutation strategies to achieve different performance for solving different problems. Instead of employing the computationally enormous trial-and-error search for the most suitable mutation strategy, we maintain a strategy candidate pool including four mutation strategies. In this work, we choose several effective mutation strategies commonly referred to in DE literatures and choose some of them to construct the strategy candidate pool which are listed as follows:

(1) "DE/rand/1":

$$\mathbf{v}_i = \mathbf{x}_{r1} + F \cdot (\mathbf{x}_{r2} - \mathbf{x}_{r3}) \quad (16)$$

(2) "DE/current-to-best/1":

$$\mathbf{v}_i = \mathbf{x}_i + F \cdot (\mathbf{x}_{best} - \mathbf{x}_i) + F \cdot (\mathbf{x}_{r_2} - \mathbf{x}_{r_3}) \quad (17)$$

(3) "DE/rand-to-best/1":

$$\mathbf{v}_i = \mathbf{x}_{r1} + F \cdot (\mathbf{x}_{best} - \mathbf{x}_{r1}) + F \cdot (\mathbf{x}_{r_2} - \mathbf{x}_{r_3}) \quad (18)$$

Algorithm 1. The pseudo-code of PM-MDE

1: Set $\mu_F = 0.5; \mu_{CR} = 0.5$
2: Generate the initial population randomly
3: Evaluate the fitness for each individual
4: Set $K = 4, p_{min} = 0.05, \alpha = 0.3$, and $\beta = 0.8$
5: For each strategy a, set $q_a(t) = 0$ and $p_a(t) = 1/K$
6: **while** The halting criterion is not satisfied **do**
7:     Set $S_{CR} = \emptyset; S_F = \emptyset$
8:     **for** $i = 1$ to NP **do**
9:         $CR_i = rndn_i(\mu_{CR}, 0.1)$ $F_i = rndc_i(\mu_F, 0.1)$
10:         Select the strategy SI_i based on its probability
11:         Select uniform randomly $r_1 \neq r_2 \neq r_3 \neq r_4 \neq r_5 \neq i$
12:         $j_{rand} = rndint(1, D)$
13:         **for** $j = 1$ to D **do**
14:             **if** rndreal$_j[0,1) < CR$ **or** $j == j_{rand}$ **then**
15:                 **if** $SI_i == 1$ **then**
16:                     $u_{i,j}$ is generated by strategy (16)
17:                 **else if** $SI_i == 2$ **then**
18:                     $u_{i,j}$ is generated by strategy (17)
19:                 **else if** $SI_i == 3$ **then**
20:                     $u_{i,j}$ is generated by strategy (18)
21:                 **else if** $SI_i == 4$ **then**
22:                     $u_{i,j}$ is generated by strategy (19)
23:                 **end if**
24:             **else**
25:                 $u_{i,j} = x_{i,j}$
26:             **end if**
27.   **end for**
28:     **end for**
29:     **for** $i = 1$ to NP **do**
30:         Evaluate the offspring $\mathbf{u}_i$ based on constraint-handling technique
31:         **if** $f(\mathbf{u}_i)$ is better than **or** equal to $f(\mathbf{x}_i)$ **then**
32:             $CR_i \rightarrow S_{CR}; F_i \rightarrow S_F$
33:             Replace $\mathbf{x}_i$ with $\mathbf{u}_i$
34:         **end if**
35:     **end for**
36:     Update the value of μ_{CR} and μ_F
37:     Calculate the reward $r_a(t)$ for each strategy
38:     Update the probability $p_a(t)$ for each strategy
39: **end while**

(4) "DE/current-to-rand/1 ":

$$\mathbf{v}_i = \mathbf{x}_i + F \cdot \left(\mathbf{x}_{r1} - \mathbf{x}_i\right) + F \cdot \left(\mathbf{x}_{r_2} - \mathbf{x}_{r_3}\right) \tag{19}$$

where $\mathbf{x}_{best}$ is the best individual in the current generation, $r_1, r_2, r_3, r_4, r_5 \in \{1, \ldots, NP\}$ and $r_1 \neq r_2 \neq r_3 \neq r_4 \neq r_5 \neq i$.

It is noteworthy that there are many other strategies could also be incorporated in the pool; the above strategies are just used as an example for the evaluation of the proposed method. It must also be pointed out that the size of the strategy pool and the selection of the strategies used in the pool is not sure and there are no theoretical studies as of today on the choice of the optimal number of available strategies and on the selection of strategies to form the strategy pool [12]. Therefore, by combining the above-mentioned two aspects with the DE algorithm, the PM-MDE method is developed. The pseudo-code of PM-MDE is illustrated in Algorithm 1. During evolution, at each generation t, there is only one strategy SI_i been selected based on the choice probability of the strategy for each target parent i. Then the offspring is generated by employing the selected strategy. The relative fitness improvement η_i based on constraint handling technique is calculated and stored in the set S_{SI_i} after evaluating the offspring. Finally, parameters value of PM-MDE algorithm such as the reward, quality and probability of each strategy are updated. In addition, to remedy the parameter fine-tuning, in this work, the parameter adaptation technique proposed in [16] is used in PM-MDE.

4   Experimental Results and Analysis

In this section, we perform comprehensive experiments to evaluate the performance of PM-MDE and compare the results of our methods with a algorithm named CBBO-DE, which is a hybridization of BBO algorithm and DE algorithm for OPA.

4.1   Experimental Settings

Without loss of generality, for all experiments, we use the following parameters unless a change is mentioned:

- Population size: $NP = 100$;
- $\mu_{CR} = 0.5$ and $\mu_F = 0.5$ [4];
- Number of strategies: $K = 4$; minimal probability: $p_{min} = 0.05$; adaptation rate: $\alpha = 0.3$;
- Maximum Number of Fitness Function Evaluations (Max_NFFEs): $30,000$.

Moreover, all experiments were run 30 times. Simulations have been carried out for various values of parameters: fusion error threshold ε, correlation degree ρ, and number of sensors (L), and the performances of the different algorithms are shown for different combinations: $\rho = \{0, 0.01, 0.1, 0.5\}$. $\rho = 0$ represents the uncorrelated case. The fusion error threshold ε takes its values in $\{0.1, 0.05, 0.01, 0.001\}$. The observation signal-to-noise ratio (SNR) r_0 was set at $10\,\mathrm{dB}$.

4.2   Numerical Results

In this section, in order to compare the performance of the adaptive strategy selection for OPA, the DE with fixed strategy and recently proposed algorithm for OPA are considered. For fair comparison, the adaptive parameters control keeps the same in all simulation. The statistical features (mean, and standard deviation values) of the best feasible solutions obtained after 30 independent runs for each case study are used to evaluate the performance of the competing algorithms. Numerical results of competing algorithms for OPA problems in WSNs are shown in Tables 1, 2, 3, 4 and 5 when the observations are i.i.d and

Table 1. Numerical results of DE with fixed strategy and PM-MDE to optimal power allocation in WSNs when the observation are i.i.d. with $\rho = 0, \varepsilon = 0.1$ and different number of sensors.

L	PM-MDE	DE^1	DE^2	DE^3	DE^4
	Mean±(Std)	Mean±(Std)	Mean±(Std)	Mean±(Std)	Mean±(Std)
10	**3.17E+00 ± (3.43E-11)**	3.17E+00 ± (3.38E-06)	3.17E+00 ± (8.65E-09)	3.17E+00± (8.53E-10)	3.17E+00± (1.99E-03)
20	**1.93E+00 ± (3.71E-07)**	1.93E+00 ± (1.10E-06)	1.93E+00 ± (8.52E-06)	1.93E+00 ± (1.69E-04)	1.97E+00 ± (1.43E-02)
50	8.67E-01 ± (4.23E-03)	8.68E-01± (1.24E-03)	**8.66E-01 ± (2.45E-04)**	8.75E-01 ±(3.69E-03)	1.24E+00 ± (9.33E-02)
100	**8.52E-01 ± (2.35E-02)**	5.78E+01 ± (3.77E+01)	6.54E+03 ± (9.84E+02)	1.53E+03 ± (1.35E+02)	4.07E+00 ± (9.53E-01)
150	**9.59E-01 ± (7.99E-02)**	1.31E+00 ± (8.52E-02)	2.44E+00 ± (2.75E-01)	8.74E+03 ± (3.85E+03)	2.45E+02 ± (7.61E+01)
200	**1.08E+00 ± (3.78E-01)**	1.28E+01 ± (5.12E+01)	3.49E+02 ± (7.76E+01)	8.88E+04 ± (2.87E+04)	2.00E+03 ± (5.06E+02)

1, 2, 3, 4 respectively represent DE algorithm with DE/rand/1, DE/best/1, DE/current-to-best/1, DE/rand-to-best/1 strategy.

Table 2. Numerical results of PM-MDE with CBBO-DE to optimal power allocation in WSNs when the observation are i.i.d. with $\rho = 0, \varepsilon = \{0.1, 0.05, 0.01, 0.001\}$ and different number of sensors.

ε	PM-MDE	CBBO-DE
	Mean ± (Std)	Mean ± (Std)
$L = 10$		
0.1	3.1727E+00 ± (9.2849E-05)	**3.1725E+00 ± (1.1803E-06)**
0.05	**5.9254E+00 ± (5.5930E-08)**	5.9723E+00 ± (4.4272E-05)
0.01	1.5130E+01 ± (3.5448E-08)	1.1530E+01 ± (8.0724E-10)
0.001	4.0317E+01 ± (3.9498E-04)	**4.0245E+01 ± (5.5876E-06)**
$L = 20$		
0.1	1.9343E+00 ± (1.3791E-03)	**1.9333E+00 ± (1.4882E-03)**
0.05	**3.6141E+00 ± (1.7754E-03)**	3.6413E+00 ± (1.0540E-03)
0.01	9.1009E+00 ± (4.0275E-03)	**9.0985E+00 ± (6.7927E-04)**
0.001	2.1601E+01 ± (4.2999E-03)	**2.1598E+01 ± (6.4187E-04)**
$L = 50$		
0.1	**1.1192E+00 ± (6.2244E-02)**	2.7516E+00 ± (3.9133E-01)
0.05	**1.9591E+00 ± (9.7700E-02)**	4.5611E+00 ± (6.5277E-01)
0.01	**4.7101E+00 ± (8.9643E-02)**	6.2178E+00 ± (5.0805E-01)
0.001	**1.0306E+01 ± (1.2003E-01)**	1.1093E+01 ± (6.0068E-01)

Table 3. Numerical results of PM-MDE with CBBO-DE to optimal power allocation in WSNs when the observation are correlated with $\rho = \{0.01, 0.1, 0.5\}$, $L = 10$, $\varepsilon = \{0.1, 0.05, 0.01, 0.001\}$.

ε	PM-MDE	CBBO-DE
	Mean ± (Std)	Mean ± (Std)
$\rho = 0.01$		
0.1	3.1834E+00 ± (1.6035E-04)	**3.1833E+00 ± (3.8557E-04)**
0.05	**5.9502E+00 ± (4.3685E-07)**	5.9975E+00 ± (4.0340E-05)
0.01	1.5255E+01 ± (3.3372E-08)	1.5255E+01 ± (1.8879E-09)
0.001	**4.0980E+01 ± (3.4452E-04)**	4.1046E+01 ± (4.6323E-04)
$\rho = 0.1$		
0.1	**3.2792E+00 ± (9.9562E-05)**	3.2834E+00 ± (1.1153E-04)
0.05	**6.1755E+00 ± (5.6832E-09)**	6.2391E+00 ± (3.8481E-05)
0.01	**1.6489E+01 ± (4.6071E-06)**	1.6562E+01 ± (3.5623E-09)
0.001	**4.8644E+01 ± (1.1203E-10)**	4.9077E+01 ± (7.8106E-04)
$\rho = 0.5$		
0.1	**3.5839E+00 ± (8.5642E-04)**	3.8583E+00 ± (2.3158E-04)
0.05	**6.9964E+00 ± (3.6859E-04)**	8.1361E+00 ± (8.0422E-05)
0.01	**2.2803E+01 ± (8.8792E-04)**	3.4349E+01 ± (8.0846E-07)
0.001	**1.0778E+02 ± (6.7852E+00)**	7.3514E+02 ± (6.6360E-02)

correlated. In addition, the best result among competing algorithms in Tables 1, 2, 3, 4 and 5 are shown in **boldface**.

Firstly, we choose four strategies which are frequently used in DE literature as the competing algorithm in Table 1. From results in the Table 1 we can see that PM-MDE algorithm we proposed is significantly better than DE with fixed strategies on most of the value of L (sensors) when the observations are i.i.d with $\rho = 0$ and $\varepsilon = 0.1$. Second, in $L = 50$, DE algorithm with DE/best/1 obtains best results and better results were found by PM-MDE among all competing algorithms. Important observations about the convergence rate and stability of different algorithms can be made from the results presented in Table 1 and these results suggest that the overall convergence rate of PM-MDE is the best or second best for OPA in the competing algorithms.

Table 2 shows a comparison of the performances of PM-MDE algorithm and CBBO-DE algorithm, for the different values of ε and L, in the uncorrelated case ($\rho = 0$). Firstly, various simulations of PM-MDE with ε chosen from $\{0.1, 0.05, 0.01, 0.001\}$ shown that PM-MDE algorithm emerged the best candidate result for $L = 10$ and $L = 50$ sensors in terms of the best mean results. For the $L = 20$ sensors case, the CBBO-DE produces the best mean results. Secondly, simulation results also indicate that PM-MDE does function efficiently within the large number of sensors.

Table 4. Numerical results of PM-MDE with CBBO-DE to optimal power allocation in WSNs when the observation are correlated with $\rho = \{0.01, 0.1, 0.5\}$, $L = 20$, $\varepsilon = \{0.1, 0.05, 0.01, 0.001\}$.

ε	PM-MDE	CBBO-DE
	Mean $\pm$ (Std)	Mean $\pm$ (Std)
$\rho = 0.01$		
0.1	**1.9394E+00 $\pm$ (1.7861E-03)**	1.9396E+00 $\pm$ (2.1426E-03)
0.05	**3.6292E+00 $\pm$ (2.6169E-03)**	3.6559E+00 $\pm$ (9.7422E-04)
0.01	9.1634E+01 $\pm$ (3.7387E-03)	**9.1607E+00 $\pm$ (8.9830E-04)**
0.001	2.1842E+01 $\pm$ (3.1386E-03)	2.1842E+01 $\pm$ (3.9883E-03)
$\rho = 0.1$		
0.1	1.9908E+00 $\pm$ (3.5774E-03)	**1.9905E+00 $\pm$ (1.3193E-03)**
0.05	**3.7594E+00 $\pm$ (3.6727E-03)**	3.7958E+00 $\pm$ (1.8885E-03)
0.01	**9.7554E+01 $\pm$ (5.4935E-03)**	9.7894E+01 $\pm$ (9.1896E-04)
0.001	**2.4182E+01 $\pm$ (3.4839E-03)**	2.4324E+01 $\pm$ (1.9630E-03)
$\rho = 0.5$		
0.1	**2.1879E+00 $\pm$ (7.4038E-03)**	2.3026E+00 $\pm$ (2.1919E-03)
0.05	**4.3232E+00 $\pm$ (2.1397E-02)**	4.8357E+00 $\pm$ (2.7079E-03)
0.01	**1.2547E+01 $\pm$ (8.5490E-02)**	1.5865E+01 $\pm$ (3.2673E-03)
0.001	**3.6247E+01 $\pm$ (9.1529E-02)**	6.0685E+01 $\pm$ (6.5080E-02)

Tables 3, 4 and 5 show the results of the comparison with CBBO-DE when the observations are correlated in the case of $L = 10, 20, 50$ sensors for different values of the fusion error probability ε and the degree of correlation ρ, respectively. In the experiments reported above, the results are shown for $\rho = \{0, 0.01, 0.1, 0.5\}$ and $\varepsilon = \{0.1, 0.05, 0.01, 0.001\}$. It can be seen that in each case, PM-MDE respectively outperforms other competing algorithm in 10, 8, and 12. From Table 5, specifically, we can see that PM-MDE has emerged as the best performer since it obtained the best mean results in the all cases. It is similar to the observation from above experiments, where PM-MDE algorithm does show obvious performance improvement for OPA, especially in the large number of sensors PM-MDE algorithm obtains better performance.

Overall, according to the results shown in Tables 1, 2, 3, 4 and 5 and the above analysis, we can conclude that when the observations are i.i.d and correlated (Tables 3, 4 and 5), the performance improvement for PM-MDE, compared to the other competing algorithm, was better for $L = 10, 20$, and 50 sensors. Meanwhile, PM-MDE obtains better results for the larger sensors.

Table 5. Numerical results of PM-MDE with CBBO-DE to optimal power allocation in WSNs when the observation are correlated with $\rho = \{0.01, 0.1, 0.5\}$, $L = 50$ senors, $\varepsilon = \{0.1, 0.05, 0.01, 0.001\}$ and different number of sensors.

ε	PM-MDE	CBBO-DE
	Mean $\pm$ (Std)	Mean $\pm$ (Std)
$\rho = 0.01$		
0.1	**1.2346E+00 $\pm$ (1.1103E-01)**	2.7742E+00 $\pm$ (5.6072E-01)
0.05	**2.0543E+00 $\pm$ (8.4439E-02)**	4.1691E+00 $\pm$ (3.8860E-01)
0.01	4.8249E+00 $\pm$ (1.3068E-01)	6.0532E+00 $\pm$ 7.9833E-01
0.001	**1.0521E+01 $\pm$ (7.3975E-02)**	1.0746E+01 $\pm$ (3.3081E-01)
$\rho = 0.1$		
0.1	**1.2406E+00 $\pm$ (9.4525E-02)**	3.0813E+00 $\pm$ (4.3000E-01)
0.05	**2.1356E+00 $\pm$ (8.8744E-02)**	4.3770E+00 $\pm$ (6.2806E-01)
0.01	5.1088E+00 $\pm$ (8.1419E-02)	6.6532E+00 $\pm$ (1.0134E+00)
0.001	**1.1284E+01 $\pm$ (1.2038E-01)**	1.1669E+01 $\pm$ (5.8073E-01)
$\rho = 0.5$		
0.1	**1.3432E+00 $\pm$ (8.8691E-02)**	2.9672E+00 $\pm$ (4.6985E-01)
0.05	**2.4334E+00 $\pm$ (5.5883E-02)**	4.6214E+00 $\pm$ (5.7670E-01)
0.01	6.2096E+00 $\pm$ (1.1285E-01)	7.4210E+00 $\pm$ (3.2418E-01)
0.001	**1.4824E+01 $\pm$ (1.5434E-01)**	1.8449E+01 $\pm$ (3.6772E-02)

5 Conclusions

Optimal power allocation (OPA) is considered to be one of the key issues in designing a wireless sensor network (WSN). In this paper, multi-operator differential evolution is proposed for the optimal power allocation in WSNs. Combining with the constraint-handling technique, DE can be used to deal with OPA. However, the DE performance mainly depends on mutation and crossover operators. This new algorithm adaptively chooses the suitable strategy for a specific problem, meanwhile the *probability matching* technique and *credit assignment* method are integrated into DE algorithm. In addition, PM-MDE is compared with DE algorithm using fixed strategy and CBBO-DE algorithm proposed in [11] for OPA. The numerical results indicate that PM-MDE has outperformed the other competing algorithms for several types of simulation case studies, including both independent local observation cases and correlated observation cases. It has also been observed that, PM-MDE algorithm function efficiently within the large number of sensors.

Acknowledgments. The work was supported in part by the National Natural Science Foundation of China under Grant Nos. 61573324, 61375066, and 61203307.

References

1. Yick, J., Mukherjee, B., Ghosal, D.: Wireless sensor network survey. Comput. Netw. **52**(12), 2292–2330 (2008)
2. Kulkarni, R., Forster, A., Venayagamoorthy, G.: Computational intelligence in wireless sensor networks: a survey. IEEE Commun. Surv. Tutor. **13**(1), 68–96 (2011)
3. Wimalajeewa, T., Jayaweera, S.: Optimal power scheduling for correlated data fusion in wireless sensor networks via constrained PSO. IEEE Trans. Wirel. Commun. **7**(9), 3608–3618 (2008)
4. Storn, R., Price, K.: Differential evolution–a simple and efficient heuristic for global optimization over continuous spaces. J. Glob. Optim. **11**(4), 341–359 (1997)
5. Das, S., Abraham, A., Konar, A.: Automatic clustering using an improved differential evolution algorithm. IEEE Trans. Syst. Man Cybern. A, Syst. Hum. **38**(1), 218–237 (2008)
6. Das, S., Suganthan, P.N.: Differential evolution: a survey of the state-of-the-art. IEEE Trans. Evol. Comput. **15**(1), 4–31 (2011)
7. Wimalajeewa, T., Jayaweera, S.K.: PSO for constrained optimization: optimal power scheduling for correlated data fusion in wireless sensor networks. In: IEEE 18th International Symposium on Personal, Indoor and Mobile Radio Communications, PIMRC 2007, pp. 1–5 (2007)
8. Kulkarni, R., Venayagamoorthy, G.: Particle swarm optimization in wireless-sensor networks: a brief survey. IEEE Trans. Syst. Man Cybern. Part C: Appl. Rev. **41**(2), 262–267 (2011)
9. Boussaïd, I., Chatterjee, A., Siarry, P., Ahmed-Nacer, M.: Hybridizing biogeography-based optimization with differential evolution for optimal power allocation in wireless sensor networks. IEEE Trans. Veh. Technol. **60**(5), 2347–2353 (2011)
10. Coello, C.A.C.: Theoretical, numerical constraint-handling techniques used with evolutionary algorithms: a survey of the state of the art. Comput. Methods Appl. Mech. Eng. **191**(11–12), 1245–1287 (2002)
11. Gong, W., Cai, Z.: An empirical study on differential evolution for optimal power allocation in WSNs. In: International Conference on Natural Computation, pp. 635–639 (2012)
12. Qin, A.K., Huang, V.L., Suganthan, P.N.: Differential evolution algorithm with strategy adaptation for global numerical optimization. IEEE Trans. Evol. Comput. **13**(2), 398–417 (2009)
13. Qin, A.K., Suganthan, P.N.: Self-adaptive differential evolution algorithm for numerical optimization. In: IEEE congress on evolutionary computation (CEC 2005), pp. 1785–1791. IEEE (2005)
14. Dow, M.: Explicit inverses of Toeplitz and associated matrices. ANZIAM J. **44**(E), 185–215 (2003)
15. Goldberg, D.E.: Probability matching, the magnitude of reinforcement, and classifier system bidding. Mach. Learn. **5**(4), 407–425 (1990)
16. Zhang, J., Sanderson, A.C.: JADE: adaptive differential evolution with optional external archive. IEEE Trans. Evol. Comput. **13**(5), 945–958 (2009)
17. Gong, W., Fialho, A., Cai, Z.: Adaptive strategy selection in differential evolution. In: Branke, J. (Ed.) Genetic and Evolutionary Computation Conference (GECCO 2010), pp. 409–416. ACM Press (2010)

18. Thierens, D.: An adaptive pursuit strategy for allocating operator probabilities. In: Proceedings of Genetic and Evolutionary Computation Conference GECCO 2005, New York, NY, USA, pp. 1539–1546. ACM (2005)
19. Wang, Y., Cai, Z., Zhou, Y., Zeng, W.: An adaptive tradeoff model for constrained evolutionary optimization. IEEE Trans. Evol. Comput. **12**(1), 80–92 (2008)
20. Brest, J., Greiner, S., Boškovic, B., Mernik, M., Zumer, V.: Self-adapting control parameters in differential evolution: a comparative study on numerical benchmark problems. IEEE Trans. Evol. Comput. **10**(6), 646–657 (2006)
21. Ong, Y.-S., Keane, A.J.: Meta-Lamarckian learning in memetic algorithms. IEEE Trans. Evol. Comput. **8**(2), 99–110 (2004)

CEMAB: A Cross-Entropy-based Method for Large-Scale Multi-Armed Bandits

Erli Wang[1]([✉]), Hanna Kurniawati[2], and Dirk P. Kroese[1]

[1] School of Mathematics and Physics, The University of Queensland,
Brisbane, QLD 4072, Australia
e.wang2@uq.edu.au, kroese@maths.uq.edu.au
[2] School of Information Technology and Electrical Engineering,
The University of Queensland, Brisbane, QLD 4072, Australia
hannakur@uq.edu.au

Abstract. The multi-armed bandit (MAB) problem is an important model for studying the exploration-exploitation tradeoff in sequential decision making. In this problem, a gambler has to repeatedly choose between a number of slot machine arms to maximize the total payout, where the total number of plays is fixed. Although many methods have been proposed to solve the MAB problem, most have been designed for problems with a small number of arms. To ensure convergence to the optimal arm, many of these methods, including state-of-the-art methods such as UCB [2], require sweeping over the entire set of arms. As a result, such methods perform poorly in problems with a large number of arms. This paper proposes a new method for solving such large-scale MAB problems. The method, called Cross-Entropy-based Multi Armed Bandit (CEMAB), uses the Cross-Entropy method as a noisy optimizer to find the optimal arm with as little cost as possible. Experimental results indicate that CEMAB outperforms state-of-the-art methods for solving MABs with a large number of arms.

Keywords: Cross-Entropy method · Sequential decision making · Multi-armed bandit

1 Introduction

A fundamental question in sequential decision making is how to select the best action sequence even if the consequence of each action may not be exactly known. In its simplest form, this question can be studied as a Multi-Armed Bandit (MAB) [9] problem. Under this framework, selecting an action is akin to selecting which slot machine to play from a number of such machines. The question becomes how to balance between playing machines that have been giving good rewards in the past (often called exploitation) and machines that have not been tried before (often called exploration), such that the total reward received is as close as possible to the total reward that would have been received if the player had always played the highest-paying machine.

© Springer International Publishing AG 2017
M. Wagner et al. (Eds.): ACALCI 2017, LNAI 10142, pp. 353–365, 2017.
DOI: 10.1007/978-3-319-51691-2_30

Many methods, such as ε-greedy [13], softmax [11], and UCB [2], have been proposed to solve the above problem of balancing exploration and exploitation. In fact, many of such methods have become the foundation of today's Reinforcement Learning [11]. However, except for a few [4,6], most methods [5] try and estimate the reward of each and every action, to ensure that the best action is not missed. Therefore, their effectiveness is limited to problems with a relatively small number of arms (e.g., fewer than 20). Unfortunately, this assumption is quickly becoming unrealistic in a growing number of applications. For instance, one can now choose from hundreds of drug cocktails – combinations of various types of drugs at various dosages – in personalized medicine, choose one of hundreds of different combinations of investment portfolios, and select a subset of tens of millions of possible combinations of data and sensors that can be used to analyze consumer preferences. As a result, most of today's methods for solving MABs [5] are no longer effective for solving the more recent large-scale problems.

To alleviate the difficulty of solving MABs with a large number of discrete actions, we propose a novel method called Cross-Entropy-based Multi-Armed Bandit (CEMAB). Key to CEMAB is the use of the Cross-Entropy (CE) method [10] as a stochastic optimization method to identify the best action. By doing so, CEMAB can significantly reduce the number of actions to test before identifying the best action, assuming that the reward for pulling an arm is retrieved from an unknown fixed distribution. Preliminary results on standard test cases for MAB indicate that the number of arms to pull before CEMAB identifies the (close to) optimal arms is not directly dependent on the number of arms in the problem, which indicates that CEMAB is able to scale up well. This observation is supported by our simulation results, where tests on various MAB problems with up to 10,000 arms indicate that CEMAB outperforms state-of-the-art MAB solvers on large problems.

2   Background and Related Work

2.1   Multi-Armed Bandit Problem

The MAB problem was first described in [9]. In this problem, a gambler has to decide which of several slot machines (often called arms) to play, where each machine gives a different reward according to some unknown distribution. The goal is to maximize the total reward of all the plays. Ideally, the player should only pull the machine that yields, on average, the highest reward.

More formally, let the set of arms be denoted by $\mathcal{K} = \{1, \ldots, |\mathcal{K}|\}$. Each arm $k \in \mathcal{K}$ corresponds to an unknown reward distribution D_k with support $[0, 1]$ and expectation μ_k. In this paper, we assume that the reward distributions are fixed (that is, they do not change over time) and independent of each other. At each time step t, an arm $k_t \in \mathcal{K}$ is pulled and a reward r_{k_t}, drawn from D_{k_t}, is received. Many objective functions have been proposed for MAB [5]. In this paper, we use the simple objective [9] to maximize the expected total reward received within a fixed number T of plays, i.e.,

$$\max_{(k_1,k_2,\ldots,k_T)\in\mathcal{K}^T} \mathbb{E}\left[\sum_{t=1}^{T} r_{k_t}\right] = \max_{(k_1,k_2,\ldots,k_T)\in\mathcal{K}^T} \sum_{t=1}^{T} \mu_{k_t}. \tag{1}$$

An equivalent goal is to minimize the total regret [2], which is:

$$\min_{(k_1,k_2,\ldots,k_T)\in\mathcal{K}^T} \left(T\max_{k\in\mathcal{K}}\mu_k - \sum_{t=1}^{T}\mu_{k_t}\right). \tag{2}$$

Various methods for solving MAB have been proposed. The rest of this subsection provides a brief overview of the most commonly-used methods, which we will use for comparison later on.

ε-greedy [13]. The ε-greedy method is the simplest and most widespread way to solve the MAB problem. At each time step, the algorithm has a probability ε to select an arm uniformly at random (exploration) and a probability $1-\varepsilon$ to choose the arm with the highest estimated reward so far (exploitation). In general, this strategy does not converge to the optimal arm.

Softmax [11]. Softmax picks each arm with a probability according to its empirical performance. The probability of each arm in Softmax can be based on the Boltzmann distribution $p_k = e^{\hat{\mu}_k/\mathcal{T}} / \sum_{k=1}^{|\mathcal{K}|} e^{\hat{\mu}_k/\mathcal{T}}$, where $\hat{\mu}_k$ is an estimate of the expected reward μ_k and $\mathcal{T}$ is the temperature. If $\mathcal{T}$ is very small, the arm with the highest estimated reward will have a large probability of being chosen (exploitation). In contrast, when $\mathcal{T}$ is very large, all $\{p_k\}$ are approximately equal, so that in this case Softmax is purely exploring.

Exp3 [3]. Exp3 (exponential weight algorithm for exploration and exploitation) is a famous variant of Softmax. The probability of choosing arm k is defined by $p_k = (1-\gamma)w_k/\sum_{j=1}^{|\mathcal{K}|} w_j + \gamma/|\mathcal{K}|$. The weights $\{w_j\}$ are updated after each step. In particular, after arm k is chosen (yielding reward r_k), the weight w_k is updated as $w_k \leftarrow w_k \exp^{\gamma r_k/p_k|\mathcal{K}|}$. It can be shown that the "weak regret", defined as $\left(T\max_{k\in\mathcal{K}}\mu_k - \sum_{t=1}^{T} r_t\right)$, is bounded under Exp3.

UCB [2]. The UCB is a family of algorithms for which optimal logarithmic regret can be achieved uniformly over time, assuming that all reward distributions have bounded support [2]. The simplest member of this family is UCB1. It records the number of times that each arm has been played, visits(k), and after each choice k updates its current estimate of μ_k via $\hat{\mu}_k \leftarrow \hat{\mu}_k + (r_k - \hat{\mu}_k)/\text{visits}(k)$. At the beginning, each arm is played once (full sweep). Subsequently, at each time t arm k is chosen that satisfies $k = \text{argmax}_{k=1,\ldots,|\mathcal{K}|}\hat{\mu}_k + \sqrt{C\log t/\text{visits}(k)}$.

Thompson Sampling (TS) [1]. Thompson sampling is a Bayesian sampling algorithm based on [12]. For each arm k, the knowledge of the expected reward μ_k is described by a Beta(α_k, β_k) distribution. At time t, random variables $\theta_k, k = 1,\ldots,|\mathcal{K}|$ are generated from each of these distributions. The index k^* corresponding to the largest of the $\{\theta_k\}$ is the arm to play. If r is the corresponding reward, then a Bernoulli trial B with probability r is generated. If $B = 1$, then α_{k^*} is increased by 1, otherwise β_{k^*} is increased by 1.

All of the above methods have been designed for various types of reward function, e.g., stochastic and deterministic, and have various ways to commit to arms that have performed well so far. However, they have not been designed for problems with a large number of arms. In fact, the state-of-the art method, UCB, explicitly requires a sweep of the entire set of arms, which will be problematic when the MAB problem has hundreds or thousands of arms. This problem is exactly the focus of our paper.

2.2   Cross-Entropy (CE) Method for Noisy Optimization

The CE method [10] is a randomized optimization method that has proved to be very useful for solving noisy optimization problems; i.e., optimization problems in which the objective function is contaminated by noise. As the MAB problem can be viewed as a type of noisy optimization problem, the CE can be viable.

To introduce the CE idea, suppose the goal is to find the optimum of a function $S(x)$ on a set $\mathcal{X}$, where $S(x)$ is not known, but estimates $\hat{S}(x)$ can be obtained, e.g., by simulation. The CE method consists of the following steps:

1. Generate independent samples $X_1, \ldots, X_N$ from some probability distribution on $\mathcal{X}$, parameterized by a vector $\mathbf{v}$. For every $x \in \mathcal{X}$, the corresponding family of distributions should contain the "degenerate distribution" at x, which assigns all its probability mass to the point x.
2. Obtain estimates of the corresponding function values $\hat{S}(X_1), \ldots, \hat{S}(X_N)$, and identify the worst of the best $N_e = \rho N$ samples — the so-called *elite* samples. Typically, $\rho \in (0.01, 0.1)$.
3. Update the parameter $\mathbf{v}$ based on the elite samples. This involves the minimization of the Kullback-Leibler divergence (cross-entropy distance). In practice this often means that the parameters are updated according to their maximum likelihood estimates, using only the elite samples.

The method thus produces a sequence of parameters $\mathbf{v}_1, \mathbf{v}_2, \ldots$ that converges to (approximately) the parameter value that corresponds to the degenerate distribution at the maximizer x^*.

3   Cross-Entropy-based Multi-Armed Bandit (CEMAB)

3.1   The Method

The key idea of CEMAB is to transform the MAB problem into a simpler stochastic optimization problem, and then solve this simpler problem using CE. To this end, notice that, under the assumption that the reward distributions of the arms do not change over time, the maximum reward of MAB (i.e., (1)) can be simplified as follows:

$$\max_{(k_1, k_2, \ldots, k_T) \in \mathcal{K}^T} \sum_{t=1}^{T} \mu_{k_t} = T \cdot \max_{k \in \mathcal{K}} \mu_k. \tag{3}$$

Solving the right hand side of (3) is in general simpler than solving the original MAB problem (left hand side of (3)) because, the solutions of the simplified problem lies in a space of size $|\mathcal{K}|$, while the solution of the original problem lies in a space of size $|\mathcal{K}|^T$. This difference in computational complexity becomes more pronounced as the number of arms increases. Therefore, to be effective in solving MABs with a large number of arms, CEMAB finds the best sequence of arms by searching the optimal arm to play.

Despite this simplification, the stochastic nature of MAB remains, as the expected reward μ_k of any arm $k \in \mathcal{K}$ is not known a priori and can only be estimated by playing the arm. Therefore, to keep the total reward high, CEMAB strives to avoid using arms with low rewards as much as possible when searching for the best arm. To this end, CEMAB adopts CE for noisy optimization and modifies it to suit the nature of the MAB problem. It uses the quantile statistics in CE and carefully adapts it to degrade the probability of selecting the bad arms gracefully, such that it can find the best arm quickly, while avoiding pulling arms with low reward as much as possible but without starving the arms that might be optimal. The CEMAB algorithm is presented in Algorithm 1, which is followed by a discussion of the algorithm.

Algorithm 1. CEMAB Method

Input: The number of arms $|\mathcal{K}|$, a (black box) function `reward()` to sample random rewards. CE parameters: sample size N, elite sample size $N_e = \rho N$ and learning rate $\alpha \in (0, 1)$. Maximum number of plays T (for simplicity, we assume $T = MN$).

Output: Total reward G.

1 Set $\mu \leftarrow 0_{1 \times |\mathcal{K}|}$, visits $\leftarrow 0_{1 \times |\mathcal{K}|}$ and $p \leftarrow (1/|\mathcal{K}|)_{1 \times |\mathcal{K}|}$.

2 for $\tau \leftarrow 1$ to M do

3     $A \leftarrow [\,]$.   // empty matrix

4   for $i \leftarrow 1$ to N do

5   Draw an arm k from the discrete distribution parameterized by p.

6         $r \leftarrow$ `reward`(k).   // Draw an immediate reward

7         $G \leftarrow G + r$.

8   visits$(k) \leftarrow$ visits$(k) + 1$.

9         $\mu(k) \leftarrow \mu(k) + (r - \mu(k))/$visits$(k)$.

10        $A \leftarrow [X; [k, \mu(k)]]$.   // Append row $[k, \mu(k)]$ to A

11     $\tilde{p} \leftarrow$ update$(|\mathcal{K}|, N_e, A)$.

12   Using the learning rate α, update p as

$$p \leftarrow (1 - \alpha)\,p + \alpha\,\tilde{p}. \qquad (4)$$

13 return G

To find the optimal arm k^* (i.e., the arm that solves the right-hand-side of (3)), CE starts by initializing the probability p of pulling a particular arm uniformly (Line 1). It iteratively chooses an arm (say $k \in \mathcal{K}$) to play, based on the probability p, receives a reward r, which is drawn randomly from the unknown distribution D_k, and updates the estimated expected reward μ_k (Line 9). This

---

Algorithm 2. update($|\mathcal{K}|, N_e, A$) for CEMAB-truncated

---

1 **for** $k \leftarrow 1$ **to** $|\mathcal{K}|$ **do**

2   Rearrange A by sorting its rows according to the second column, from largest to smallest.

3      $\tilde{p}(k) = \frac{1}{N_e} \sum_{j=1}^{N_e} I_{\{A(j,1)=k\}}$

4 **return** $\tilde{p}$

Algorithm 3. update($|\mathcal{K}|, -, A$) for CEMAB-proportional

---

1 **for** $k \leftarrow 1$ **to** $|\mathcal{K}|$ **do**

2   For each arm k sampled in A, get the latest estimate $\mu(k)$.

3      $\tilde{p}(k) = \frac{p_k \mu(k)}{\sum_{j=1}^{K} p_j \mu(j)}$.

4 **return** $\tilde{p}$

---

sampling and estimation process repeats until one is confident that updating the selection probability p will benefit the optimization procedure. Once the probability is updated, the iterative sampling and estimation procedure repeats using the new selection probability.

Key to the performance of CE is how it updates its selection probability (Lines 11–12). A straightforward application of CE for noisy optimization would estimate the expected reward of all of the arms, and only after all estimates are improved, the probability p is updated. However, in the MAB problem, an estimate of the expected reward of any arm can only be improved by playing an arm, and each play incurs a reward. Therefore, CEMAB updates the probability p in an asynchronous manner: It clusters a sequence of N samples of the arm into a single batch and updates the probability p after each batch ends. Note that at the end of each batch the estimated expected reward of some of the arms may not have improved at all. Therefore, a smoothing mechanism (Line 12) is needed, to avoid being overcommitted to the new estimate of the different arms and also to guarantee that each arm has a non-zero probability of being visited.

Similar to most CE-based algorithms, CEMAB updates the probability p on the basis of the estimate $\hat{S}$ of the samples. The question is how the probability p should be updated based on the set of samples (Line 11). To this end, we propose two strategies: CEMAB-truncated and CEMAB-proportional. In CEMAB-truncated, we use the traditional CE updating formula, ignoring any arm that does not make it to the elite sample set. Specifically, the probability update rule for CEMAB-truncated is in Algorithm 2. In CEMAB-proportional, we assign the probability based on the estimated values $\hat{S}$ of each arm after the batch ends, and never set the probability of selecting an arm to be zero. The description of this update strategy is given in Algorithm 3.

3.2 Time Complexity and Convergence Properties

Similar to many state-of-the-art methods for solving MABs, such as Exp3 [3] and UCB [2], the most time-consuming part of CEMAB is its update step, i.e., Line 11 of Algorithm 1. For CEMAB-truncated, each update will take $O(N \log(N) + \max(|\mathcal{K}|, N_e))$, where the first component is due to sorting the samples within a batch (Line 2 of Algorithm 2). For CEMAB-proportional, each update will take $O(|\mathcal{K}|)$. Although Thompson sampling, Exp3 and UCB (current state-of-the-art methods) require $O(|\mathcal{K}|)$ for each update too, the number of updates for CEMAB is much less than for these two methods. Exp3 and UCB update their probability for selecting an arm at each step, but CEMAB updates its probability for selecting the arms only once per batch, i.e., $M = T/N$ times for a total of T plays.

CEMAB-proportional is guaranteed to converge to the optimal expected reward, assuming that the cumulative distribution function of the reward of the optimal arm is strictly increasing. The proof is a straightforward application of the proof of the CE-proportional algorithm for noisy optimization [7]. We do not have a theoretical proof that CEMAB-truncated will converge to the optimal expected reward. However, under the aforementioned assumption on the cumulative distribution function, CEMAB-truncated converges to the quantile of the total reward function. This proof is a straightforward application of the proof of the commonly used CE algorithm for noisy optimization in [8]. CEMAB-truncated is more aggressive in its distribution update compared to CEMAB-proportional, and therefore we can expect that CEMAB-truncated tends to converge to a particular arm faster than CEMAB-proportional, which is good if the quantile function of the total reward is equivalent to the expected total reward.

4 Experimental Results

The goal of our experiments are two-fold: First is to test the proposed methods against existing MAB methods on well-known benchmarks and understand the properties of the proposed methods better (Sect. 4.1), so as to also help us in setting the parameters for tests on large MAB problems. The second and ultimate goal is to test the performance of our proposed methods on large MAB problems (Sect. 4.2).

We compare the empirical performance of ε-greedy (with 0 initialization), ε-greedy (play once), Softmax, Exp3, and UCB1, with our proposed CE-based methods on discrete (Bernoulli) and continuous (truncated Gaussian) reward distributions. Note that we use two types of ε-greedy: One initializes the estimate of the expected reward to zero (denoted as E1), while the other initializes the estimate of the expected reward based on the reward received when playing the arm once (denoted as E2). The reason for these two versions is that we found significant performance differences between ε-greedy with these two different initializations, as will be seen later on.

4.1   Small-Scale MABs

Experimental Setup

We test our methods and comparators on 10 small-scale MAB problems, with up to 10 arms. Table 1 details the reward distributions of these problems.

The first 6 problems (i.e., B1–B6) are MABs with discrete reward distributions, which is the benchmark used in [2]. The reward of each arm in each of these problems is sampled from a Bernoulli distribution, where the success probability corresponds to the probability of generating a reward of 1 and the failure probability corresponds to the probability of generating a reward of 0. For example, B1 defines an MAB with 2 arms, where the reward of arm 1 follows a Bernoulli distribution with success probability 0.9, while the reward of arm 2 follows a Bernoulli distribution with success probability 0.6. B1–B3 specify MABs with 2 arms and B4–B6 define MABs with 10 arms, where the reward of each arm is Bernoulli distributed. Note that B3 and B6 are relatively "difficult", because the reward of the optimal arm has a higher variance and the gaps $\mu^* - \mu_k$, $k = 1, \ldots, 10$ are small.

The last 4 problems (i.e., G1–G4) are MABs with continuous reward distributions, in particular truncated normal distributions with support $[0, 1]$. Table 1 specifies the mean and standard deviation of the Gaussian distribution of each arm in each MAB problem. In this set of problems, G2 and G4 are quite challenging. The standard deviations of the reward distributions in these two problems

Table 1. Bx refers to Bernoulli distributions and Gx to truncated Gaussian distributions.

	1	2	3	4	5	6	7	8	9	10
Mean of B1	0.9	0.6								
Mean of B2	0.9	0.8								
Mean of B3	0.55	0.45								
Mean of B4	0.9	0.6	0.6	0.6	0.6	0.6	0.6	0.6	0.6	0.6
Mean of B5	0.9	0.8	0.8	0.8	0.7	0.7	0.7	0.6	0.6	0.6
Mean of B6	0.55	0.45	0.45	0.45	0.45	0.45	0.45	0.45	0.45	0.45
Mean of G1	0.3	0.6								
Std of G1	0.2	0.2								
Mean of G2	0.3	0.6								
Std of G2	0.6	0.2								
Mean of G3	0.5	0.2	0.4	0.3	0.8	0.1	0.7	0.8	0.3	0.9
Std of G3	0.3	0.2	0.3	0.1	0.1	0.2	0.5	0.4	0.2	0.1
Mean of G4	0.5	0.2	0.4	0.3	0.8	0.1	0.7	0.8	0.3	0.9
Std of G4	0.5	0.5	0.5	0.5	0.5	0.5	0.5	0.5	0.5	0.5

are large and the support of these distributions also overlap significantly, which makes it difficult to distinguish between the best arm and bad arms.

To set the parameters for testing, we first run a set of preliminary tests for each algorithm on each problem in Table 1 with a wide range of parameters. The parameters are summarized in Table 2. For each algorithm, the best parameters are those that maximize the most problems across the 10 MAB problems described above.

Table 2. Parameter range

Method	Parameters tested	Best parameter
CEMAB-truncated	$N \in [50, 100], \rho \in [0.1, 0.5], \alpha \in [0.6, 1]$	$N = 50, \rho = 0.5, \alpha = 0.8$
CEMAB-proportional	$N \in [50, 100], \alpha \in [0.7, 1]$	$N = 50, \alpha = 0.7$
ε-greedy (E1 and E2)	$\varepsilon \in [0.01, 0.4]$	$\varepsilon = 0.1$ (E1), $\varepsilon = 0.05$ (E2)
Softmax	$t \in [0.01, 0.5]$	$t = 0.1$
Exp3	$\gamma \in [0.1, 0.7]$	$\gamma = 0.2$
UCB	$C \in [0.05, 3]$	$C = 0.1$

Results

Figure 1 presents the performance of CEMAB and the comparator methods in B5, B6, G3, and G4, which are the more difficult problems among the 10 small problems defined in Table 1. The trend for the performance of the other MAB problems is similar, and hence we do not present them due to space constraints.

In this set of problems, TS achieves the lowest total regret in B5 and B6, followed by UCB and both CEMABs. In G3 and G4, UCB takes first place, while one of the CEMABs is second. The reason is that in B6 the best arm (i.e., arm 1) does not show significant performance difference at the beginning, and it is quite easy for CE-truncated to underestimate this arm and set a probability zero during updating step. Once this happens, CEMAB-truncated fails to identify the best arm, and as time progresses the difference in the total regret will become more apparent. However, by avoiding this aggressive update, CEMAB-proportional perform well and is similar to UCB in G4. It is important to note that the best empirical parameter here is $C = 0.1$, rather than the default value $C = 2$.

Softmax and Exp3, have the worst performance. In Softmax, the use of the Boltzmann distribution is likely to exaggerate an arm with a "good" estimate. For Exp3, it is important to note that this method is designed for non-stochastic MAB problems. A particular arm is highly influenced by only the current reward rather than the current estimate of the reward for each arm, which is a downside for stochastic problems, which we address in this paper.

It is also interesting to note that the performance of the simplest algorithm, ε-greedy, differs significantly when applying different initializations. Variant E1 initializes the reward estimate of each arm with 0, while variant E2 initializes

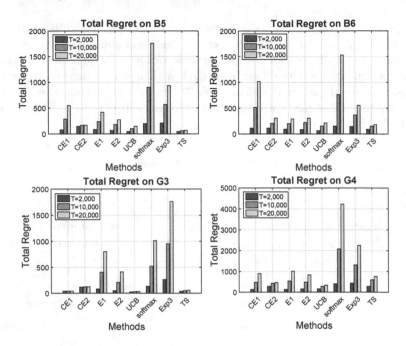

Fig. 1. The average total regret on 4 problem sets, B5, B6, G3 and G4. All algorithms use the best parameters and all experiments are repeated 50 times.

the reward estimate based on the reward received when playing the arm once. The performance of E2 is better in this set of small-scale problems. However, in the next section we will see that E1 is better for large-scale problems.

4.2 Large-Scale MABs

To assess CEMAB's performance for large problems, we test the algorithms on problems with an increasing number of arms. For each number of arms, we test the algorithms on four different MAB problems, as shown in Table 3, which consists of two LB (Large Bernoulli) that represent MABs whose reward distributions are Bernoulli distributed and two LG (Large Gaussian) that represent MABs whose reward distributions are truncated Gaussian with support $[0, 1]$.

Table 3. Large-scale MAB settings

LB1	$\mu_k \sim \mathsf{U}(0, 1)$
LB2	10% of $\mu_k \sim \mathsf{U}(0.75, 1)$ and the rest of $\mu_k \sim \mathsf{U}(0, 0.25)$
LG1	$\mu_k \sim \mathsf{U}(0, 1), \sigma_k \sim \mathsf{U}(0, 0.25)$
LG2	10% of $\mu_k \sim \mathsf{U}(0.75, 1)$ and the rest of $\mu_k \sim \mathsf{U}(0, 0.25), \sigma_k \sim \mathsf{U}(0, 0.25)$

Table 4. The average total reward for large MABs. All algorithms use the best parameters (as per Table 2) and all experiments are repeated 200 times. The best method is highlighted in boldface. If the difference between the best and second best method is not statistically significant (meaning that one method lies in the 95% confidence interval of the other), we highlight both of them.

$\|\mathcal{K}\|$	Method	LB1				LB2			
		The number of plays T				The number of plays T			
		1,000	5,000	10,000	20,000	1,000	5,000	10,000	20,000
100	CE1	**893**	**4749**	**9569**	19207	718	4106	8342	16817
	CE2	806	4612	9463	19184	741	4192	8571	17341
	E1	864	4572	9230	18547	**820**	4139	8288	16597
	E2	868	4686	9460	19010	767	4167	8437	17022
	UCB	833	4674	9538	19225	787	**4311**	**8788**	**17796**
	softmax	859	4407	8866	17798	801	4127	8305	16686
	Exp3	580	3564	7702	16285	241	2610	6202	13550
	TS	856	4695	9557	**19323**	678	4168	8634	17615
1,000	CE1	**896**	**4788**	**9651**	**19380**	784	4493	9130	18402
	CE2	810	4655	9559	**19409**	792	**4538**	**9207**	18850
	E1	868	4510	9131	18496	771	4352	8885	18019
	E2	500	4129	8802	18532	197	3852	8635	18217
	UCB	499	3812	8358	17906	197	3730	8568	18361
	softmax	875	4470	8989	18043	**853**	4445	8976	18074
	Exp3	507	2666	5643	12378	202	1122	2601	7114
	TS	530	4027	8957	18556	305	3949	8925	**18897**
10,000	CE1	**895**	**4784**	**9644**	19367	795	4554	9251	18649
	CE2	809	4655	9554	**19393**	**800**	**4574**	**9358**	18969
	E1	863	4479	9025	18158	761	4322	8812	17818
	E2	515	2492	5013	14126	181	1004	2007	11022
	UCB	515	2486	5007	12135	182	1004	2007	9880
	softmax	832	4341	8786	17734	776	4264	8725	17734
	Exp3	500	2510	5040	10154	201	1006	2026	4109
	TS	511	2707	5811	13091	207	1191	3081	10433

$\|\mathcal{K}\|$	Method	LG1				LG2			
		The number of plays T				The number of plays T			
		1,000	5,000	10,000	20,000	1,000	5,000	10,000	20,000
100	CE1	**885**	**4624**	**9297**	**18644**	772	4378	8884	17897
	CE2	800	4484	9150	18512	767	4435	9068	18341
	E1	868	4463	8973	17995	783	4411	8977	18109
	E2	877	4562	9177	18415	**879**	4685	9443	18956
	UCB	804	4450	9110	18506	863	**4777**	**9705**	**19578**
	softmax	833	4242	8513	17067	813	4282	8682	17551
	Exp3	559	3449	7457	15737	281	2752	6678	14878
	TS	785	4406	9071	18477	851	**4779**	**9706**	**19580**
1,000	CE1	**876**	**4599**	**9254**	18564	778	**4405**	8937	18004
	CE2	782	4441	9109	18499	763	4381	**8990**	18236
	E1	865	4532	9180	18542	768	4340	**8895**	18043
	E2	499	4358	9183	**18835**	238	4051	8818	**18351**
	UCB	500	3560	7750	16852	238	3440	8071	17711
	softmax	811	4125	8281	16609	**816**	4235	8535	17165
	Exp3	504	2624	5493	11865	242	1287	2831	7095
	TS	563	3713	8186	17729	312	3670	8378	18004
10,000	CE1	**877**	**4612**	**9281**	18618	**779**	**4394**	8913	17951
	CE2	788	4470	9153	18572	770	4369	**8934**	**18113**
	E1	876	4568	**9247**	**18656**	774	4313	8815	17894
	E2	488	2475	4997	14736	241	1207	2394	11942
	UCB	488	2477	4997	12390	240	1207	2393	9131
	softmax	794	4102	8275	16648	740	4030	8227	16690
	Exp3	501	2506	5027	10108	239	1200	2412	4865
	TS	507	2661	5637	12469	244	1339	3164	9783

For LB1, the success probability (i.e., the probability of sampling a reward of 1) of each reward distribution is uniformly sampled from $(0, 1)$. For LB2, 10% of the arms have rewards drawn from a Bernoulli distribution whose success probability is sampled from $(0.75, 1)$ and 90% have rewards drawn from a Bernoulli distribution whose success probability is sampled from $(0, 0.25)$. For LG1, the means are uniformly sampled from interval $(0, 1)$, while for LG2, 10% of the means are sampled from $(0.75, 1)$ uniformly at random and 90% are sampled from $(0, 0.25)$ uniformly at random. The standard deviations for both LG1 and LG2 are sampled uniformly at random from $(0, 0.25)$ for each arm. All of these parameters for the reward distributions are sampled independently for each arm. It is not hard to see that LB2 and LG2 is harder than LB1 and LG1, since it requires a strategy that has a good capability of exploring, rather than keep playing the best arm so far.

For these tests, each algorithm uses the best parameters as found in Table 2. The results of these tests for $|\mathcal{K}| = 100$, 1000, and 10000 are summarized in Table 4. The results indicate that, as the number of arms increases, CEMAB outperforms all other methods, including UCB. The reason for the significantly decreasing performance of UCB is that it must play each arm at least once to estimate the performance of each arm, so that it can converge to the optimal solution. However, exactly because of this, its performance becomes impractical as the number of arms increases. On the other hand, CEMAB incrementally improves its estimate on the performance of the arms based on sampling, without ever requiring to play the entire set of arms at first. This causes the convergence property of CEMAB to be weaker than UCB, but its empirical performance to be significantly better in large problems.

It is also interesting to note that the simple ε-greedy with zero initial estimate (E1) is a relatively strong competitor. In fact, for problems with a large number of arms, this simple methods is a stronger competitor than the state-of-the-art UCB. Note that for the Gaussian reward case, the gap between rewards is much less than for the Bernoulli case. As a result, even if an arm that is played is not very good, the reward obtained by playing a better arm will not be much higher. This could be a reason why the performance of E1 is comparable to CEMAB's in the Gaussian, while it loses in the Bernoulli case.

5   Conclusion

We proposed a new approach, CEMAB, for solving MABs with a large number of discrete arms. It uses the Cross-Entropy method as a noisy optimization method to search for the best arm with as little regret as possible. We presented and evaluated the CEMAB algorithm with two variants for the updating procedure. Using results on CE for noisy optimization, one of the variants is guaranteed to converge to the optimal arm, under certain conditions on the reward function. Empirical results on a number of MAB problems with an increasing number of arms indicate that CEMAB outperforms state-of-the-art methods.

Acknowledgments. This work was supported by the Australian Research Council Centre of Excellence for Mathematical and Statistical Frontiers (ACEMS) under grant number CE140100049. Erli Wang would also like to acknowledge the support from the University of Queensland through the UQ International Scholarships scheme.

References

1. Agrawal, S., Goyal, N.: Analysis of Thompson sampling for the multi-armed bandit problem. In: COLT, p. 39.1 (2012)
2. Auer, P., Cesa-Bianchi, N., Fischer, P.: Finite-time analysis of the multiarmed bandit problem. Mach. Learn. **47**(2–3), 235–256 (2002)
3. Auer, P., Cesa-Bianchi, N., Freund, Y., Schapire, R.E.: The non-stochastic multi-armed bandit problem. SIAM J. Comput. **32**(1), 48–77 (2002)
4. Bubeck, S., Munos, R., Stoltz, G., Szepesvari, C.: X-armed bandits. J. Mach. Learn. Res. **12**(May), 1655–1695 (2011)
5. Burtini, G., Loeppky, J., Lawrence, R.: A survey of online experiment design with the stochastic multi-armed bandit (2015). arXiv preprint: arXiv:1510.00757
6. Coquelin, P.A., Munos, R.: Bandit algorithms for tree search. In: UAI, pp. 67–74 (2007)
7. Goschin, S., Littman, M.L., Ackley, D.H.: The effects of selection on noisy fitness optimization. In: Proceedings of the 13th Annual Conference on Genetic and Evolutionary Computation, pp. 2059–2066. ACM (2011)
8. Goschin, S., Weinstein, A., Littman, M.L.: The cross-entropy method optimizes for quantiles. In: ICML (3), pp. 1193–1201 (2013)
9. Robbins, H.: Some aspects of the sequential design of experiments. Bull. Am. Math. Soc. **58**(5), 527–535 (1952)
10. Rubinstein, R.Y., Kroese, D.P.: The Cross-Entropy Method: A Unified Approach to Combinatorial Optimization, Monte-Carlo Simulation and Machine Learning. Springer, New York (2004)
11. Sutton, R.S., Barto, A.G.: Reinforcement Learning: An Introduction. MIT Press, Cambridge (1998)
12. Thompson, W.R.: On the likelihood that one unknown probability exceeds another in view of the evidence of two samples. Biometrika **25**(3/4), 285–294 (1933)
13. Watkins, C.: Learning from delayed rewards. Ph.D. thesis, University of Cambridge, England (1989)

Binary PSO for Web Service Location-Allocation

Boxiong Tan[✉], Hai Huang, Hui Ma, and Mengjie Zhang

Victoria University of Wellington, Wellington, New Zealand
{Boxiong.Tan,hui.ma,mengjie.zhang}@ecs.vuw.ac.nz, simonhuang211@gmail.com

Abstract. Web services are independently programmable application components which scatter over the Internet. Network latency is one of the major concerns of web service application. Thus, physical locations of web services and users should be taken into account for web service composition. In this paper, we propose a new solution based on the modified binary PSO-based (MBPSO) approach which employs an adaptive inertia technique to allocating web service locations. Although several heuristic approaches have been proposed for web service location-allocation, to our best knowledge, this is the first time applying PSO to solve the problem. A simulated experiment is done using the WS-DREAM dataset with five different complexities. To compare with genetic algorithm and original binary PSO approaches, the proposed MBPSO approach has advantages in most situations.

1   Introduction

The advent of Service Oriented Architecture (SOA) has significantly reformed the software industry. From 2006, many industry leaders, such as IBM, eBay, and HP, adopt SOA and "They are all reported seeing benefits from it." [20]. The reason for SOA becoming increasingly popular is that SOA meets two significant industrial requirements: scalability and reusability.

These two requirements can not be achieved without the help of web services. A web service, also called an atomic web service, is a self-describing, self-contained software which can be published on the Internet and invoked by other web services [7]. This characteristic allows integration among inter-organizational and heterogeneous services on the Web at runtime. Because each service runs separately, computation and storage resource can be dynamically added to it. Hence, there is no resource bottleneck that limits the performance; The scalability is achieved. In addition, an atomic service can be composited in a variety of service compositions. The great reusability and scalability are the most important features and advantages of SOA [23].

Currently, most enterprise level of SOA applications is SOAP-based [4]. The SOAP-based web service technology has been developed since 1999; its development environment and tools are well established. However, a fundamental problem, which limits the performance of the SOAP-based application, is that they communicate with HTTP verb "post", which does not have an idempotent semantic [8]. Therefore, SOAP-based applications do not support web cache.

© Springer International Publishing AG 2017
M. Wagner et al. (Eds.): ACALCI 2017, LNAI 10142, pp. 366–377, 2017.
DOI: 10.1007/978-3-319-51691-2_31

Hence, without the support of multiple levels of Web caches, network latency has become a neglected issue in a SOA application design. One intuitive solution is to deploy web services to the locations that close to user concentrated area so that the network latency is minimized. Currently, many researchers are aware of the location-allocation problem [18,25] and included location-awareness into their research. Most of these research deal with web service composition developers' perspective on the selection of web services with location-awareness. While our research is intended to look for a near-optimal web service allocation plan for web service providers so that their profit can be maximized.

Some conventional optimization techniques are proposed in [1,25] to address the location-allocation problem. Integer programming and greedy algorithm are applied in their approaches. Due to the nature of integer programming, it is extremely slow when applying on a large amount of data. In [12], we proposed a formulation and a single-objective Memory Filtering Genetic Algorithm (MFGA) to solve the problem and the experiment shows that our approach performs well. However, as the web service location-allocation is a multi-objective problem in nature. A multi-objective optimization approach is more appropriate to address the problem.

In this paper, we propose a multi-objective approach for web service location-allocation problem with an aggregation method. Two decisive Quality of Service (QoS) aspects: cost and response time, are established as optimization objectives. In addition, another powerful heuristic algorithm, Particle Swarm Optimization (PSO) is used to solve the problem.

PSO, introduced by Kennedy and Eberhart in 1995 [14], is one significant branch of swarm intelligence paradigms. In recent decades, a considerable amount of research applied PSO in solving real-world optimization problems [27]. The idea of PSO originates from the swarm behavior of birds flocking and fish schooling. In PSO, a collective intelligence is used to guide individuals to search for global optimal solutions [5].

There are continuous, discrete [22], and binary [16] variants of PSO. The nature of web service location-allocation problem is binary (explained in Sect. 3.1). Therefore, in this paper, we propose a modified binary PSO-based (MBPSO) approach which applied dynamic inertia weight for solving the web service location-allocation. More precisely, three main objectives shown in below will be investigated.

- To propose a multi-objective formulation for service location-allocation problem.
- To propose a MBPSO approach can be used to solve the service location-allocation problem.
- To evaluate the proposed MBPSO approach in terms of its effectiveness and efficiency in solving the service location-allocation problem, comparing with other existing approaches.

The remainder of this paper is organized as follows. Section 2 is a review of recent research on web service location-allocation and the binary PSO. Section 3 is a description of web service location-allocation and our proposed problem model. Section 4 presents MBPSO approach to the web service location-allocation. Sections 5 and 6 present experimental evaluation results of our proposed MBPSO approach to service location-allocation problem. Finally, we draw our conclusions and future prospects in Sect. 7.

2 Related Work and Background

2.1 Related Work

The majority of recent studies on web service quality can be sorted into two categories, service selection [26] and service composition [9]. In general, service selection is to seek the better service instances while service composition is to build better service workflow. The objective of these research is similar, to improve the service quality in several dimensions, e.g. response time, service execution cost, service availability, and service reliability. However, these studies are from the perspective of service consumers and ignoring service providers have more privileges to improve the service qualities.

Comparing with service selection and service composition, web service location-related research is a newborn in this domain. In study [19], Liu and Lu, have proved that location and time have a big impact on service quality and propose a location-related service composition framework. However, this study does not contain any comparison with other existing approaches. In study [25], authors proposed using integer programming techniques to solve the web service location-allocation problem. However, the results show integer programming can not obtain satisfactory performance in a large-scale dataset.

Although web service location-allocation still in its infant stage. Traditional location-allocation problem has been extensively investigated. Using PSO-based approaches to solve the traditional location-allocation problem also appear in recently years. Studies [10;11] have proposed using discrete particle swarm to solve the location-allocation problem, the results show PSO-based approaches can achieve a better performance than many meta-heuristic approaches, such as genetic algorithm (GA) and simulated annealing (SA). However, the nature of web service location-allocation problem is quite different. Traditional location-allocation problem usually is based on one kind of facility, such as fire station and hospital. Hence, the location optimization just considers the distance from a service consumer to the nearest facility. However, for web service location-allocation we need to consider the distance from multiple users to multiple services. In [12], a genetic algorithm based approach was used as a heuristic method to optimized the service allocation matrix. In this paper, a MBPSO was used as a heuristic method to optimize the proposed problem.

2.2 Review of Binary PSO

The originated purpose of PSO is to solve the continuous problems. It has also been proven that PSO has advancement than other meta-heuristic approaches in solving the continuous problem [6]. To solve binary problems, Kenndy and Eberhart [15] introduce binary PSO (BPSO). Service location-allocation problem is a binary problem. Therefore, we present a brief review of PSO and BPSO in this section. Suppose that our search space is d-dimensional, a particle i is a potential solution in this d-dimensional space. A d-dimensional vector is used to represent the particle position, say $X_i = (x_{i1}, x_{i2}, \ldots, x_{id})$. A swarm is a set of potential solutions in current optimization problem search space. The velocity vector represents the next movement and direction of a particle, which is defined as $V_i = (v_{i1}, v_{i2}, \ldots, v_{id})$. $P_{i,best}$ and $P_{g,best}$ respectively represent the personal best and global best position. Hence, they are also represented as a d-dimensional position vector. The position and velocity of each particle is updated by iteration according to $P_{i,best}$ and $P_{g,best}$. Due to the evolutionary nature, the position and velocity of each particle is updated by iteration according to $P_{i,best}$ and $P_{g,best}$. The position and velocity of particles are updated by the following formulae:

$$V_i^{t+1} = w \cdot V_i^t + c_1 \varphi_1 (P_{i,best} - X_i) + c_2 \varphi_2 (P_{g,best} - X_i) \tag{1}$$

$$X_i^{t+1} = X_i^t + V_i^{t+1} \tag{2}$$

where c_1 and c_2 are positive constants, whereas φ_1 and φ_2 arc two random variables with range between 0 and 1. w is the inertia weight which represents the impact of current velocity on the new velocity. The feature that drives PSO is social interaction. The behaviour of particles within the swarm is affected by each other.

A velocity clamp was introduced to avoid the phenomenon of "swarm exploration" [16]. In order to keep the swarm from moving far beyond the search space, velocity is limited within the range $[-v_{max}, v_{max}]$. v_{max} is normally defined as $v_{max} = k \times x_{max}$ [2], where k is a clamping factor. In a case where the search space is bounded by $[-x_{min}, x_{max}]$, $v_{max} = k \times (x_{max} - x_{min})/2$.

In BPSO, the main change is that the velocity does not reprcsents the next movement and direction for particles. Velocity is a probability that effects a bit (position) of particle to takes on 1 or 0. In the BPSO, for updating velocities will be the samc as Eq. 1. For updating particle the vector position is restricted to only 1 and 0. The updating equation in Eq. 2 is reformulate in Eq. 3.

$$X_i^{t+1} = \begin{cases} 0 & \text{if } Rand \geq S(V_i^{t+1}) \\ 1 & \text{if } Rand < S(V_i^{t+1}) \end{cases} \tag{3}$$

where S is the sigmoid function that transform the particle velocity to the probability as the following Eq. 4. $Rand$ is the random number which range from 0 to 1.

$$S(V_i^{t+1}) = \frac{1}{1 + e^{-V_i^{t+1}}} \tag{4}$$

3   Problem Modelling

3.1   Problem Description

The aim of service location-allocation problem is to find appropriate physical locations for web service composition so that both overall response time and cost are reduced.

The overall response time is largely depend on the communication of atomic web services. That is, an atomic service could communicate with end-user or other web services depend on their functionalities. Considering all sources of invocations of web services is infeasible and cumbersome. One solution is to only take into account the invocation from end-users. Consequently, we are trying to deploy all atomic services to the locations that close to end-users. This solution not only reduces the overall network latency but also hugely reduces the computational complexity. To ensure that a service composition is complete, we define a constraint that force every service to be deployed at least at one location.

The other objective is to reduce the establish cost of atomic services. Apparently, deploying all atomic services to every end-user's location could ensure the best quality. But it is also unnecessary to guarantee high quality for every end-user. A web service provider always desires a solution that minimize the cost as well as maximize the quality. Therefore, the second objective is to deploy services to locations that produces minimum cost.

In order to accomplish these two objectives, three types of input data are used in the formulation - network latency, service demand, and service establish cost. They are expressed in matrix forms.

network latency matrix T_{ij} denotes the network latency between an user concentrated location i and a candidate location j. A user concentrated location is the location that has a large number of end-users of a web service composition. A candidate location is a location at where we consider deploying web services. *service demand matrix* F_s denotes the popularity of an atomic service s. Each entry is a percentile that indicates the importance of an atomic service among the service composition. In order to obtain this data, a data preprocessing procedure is described in Sect. 5.1 which is first introduced in [12]. *establish cost matrix* C_{sj} denotes the establish cost of an atomic service s in a candidate location j.

A web service is either deploy or not deploy in a location. Thus, the nature of web service location-allocation problem is binary. We define a binary matrix *web service allocation matrix* A_{sj} as the representation of a solution which denotes deployment of an atomic service s at a candidate location j. An entry is either 1 or 0 which denotes deployment or not. In the next section, we would apply the above data to establish two objective functions and the fitness function.

3.2   Problem Objectives

As we mentioned in the previous section, the web service location-allocation problem can be seen as a multi-objective problem. The first objective intends to reduce the overall latency of a service composition. This objective function can be explained in two intuitive purposes. Firstly, popular atomic web services are encouraged to be deployed at multiple locations so that it reduces the overall latency. Secondly, the location with lower latency is always preferred.

$$TotalTime = \sum_{s=1} \sum_{i=1} r_{is} f_s \qquad (5)$$

Where r_{is} is the response time between a user location i and a service s. r_{is} can be obtained using the network latency matrix T_{ij} and the web service allocation matrix A_{sj}:

$$r_{is} = MIN\{t_{ij} | j \in \{1, \ldots, n\} \text{ and } a_{sj} = 1\} \qquad (6)$$

r_{is} denotes the minimum response time from an atomic web service s to a user location i. When there are multiple deployments of a service, a candidate location with smaller latency value is always chosen. Although the choice of minimum latency might not be true in a real-life scenario, it encourages the optimization process to minimize the response time.

One of the objectives is to minimize the overall cost, which is the sum of all deployed services.

$$TotalCost = \sum_{j=1} \sum_{s=1} c_{sj} a_{sj} \qquad (7)$$

Finally, we apply an aggregation method that combines two objectives into a fitness function (Eq. 8). Parameters w_1 and w_2 are the constant weights for the response time objective and cost objective respectively.

$$FitnessFunction = MIN((w_1 \sum_{i=1} \sum_{s=1} r_{is} f_i + w_2 \sum_{j=1} \sum_{s=1} c_{sj} a_{sj}) * P) \qquad (8)$$

P is a penalty function for punishing a solution that violates the service constraint. When all services have been deployed, the fitness value remains unchanged. Otherwise, its fitness value is punished by multiplying a large number N. This technique is called death penalty [17].

$$P = \begin{cases} 1 & \text{if } \sum_j a_{sj} \geq 1 \\ N & \text{otherwise} \end{cases} \qquad (9)$$

4 Modified BPSO for Web Service Location-Allocation

4.1 Encoding Scheme

In BPSO, a particle is a potential solution which is represented by a fix-length binary vector. However, a potential service allocation solution is often represented by a binary matrix. In order to use BPSO, we need to transfer service location-allocation design represented in a binary matrix into PSO particle representation. As seen in Fig. 1, a matrix used for represent service allocation and relevant calculation are transferred into a vector which can then be used for the BPSO evolutionary progress. In a binary service location allocation matrix, an element A_{sj} denote whether service s is allocated at location j.

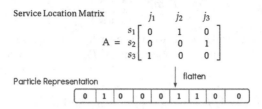

Fig. 1. Encoding scheme example

4.2 Algorithm

As shown in Algorithm 1, the particles are generated in random position with corresponding velocity randomly. Then, the swarm will get into the evolutionary process. First, calculating the fitness value for each particle and replace the personal best if current fitness value is better. After this step, searching the global best individual in the whole population. Last, updating the velocity and particle position according to Eqs. 1, 3 and 4. Repeat the evolutionary process until the termination condition is met.

Algorithm 1. BPSO for Web Service Location-allocation

Initialize particles(swarm)P
Initialize velocity V_i^0 For each particle X_i
while Termination Condition is not met **do**
　for Each particle X_i **do**
　　Calculate the fitness value
　　if New fitness value is better than personal best $P_{i,best}$ **then**
　　　Set new fitness value as $P_{i,best}$
　　end if
　end for
　Select the best particle as global best $P_{g,best}$
　for Each particle X_i **do**
　　Update V_i^t according to Eq. 1
　　Do Velocity Clamping
　　Update X_i according to Eq. 3 and Eq. 4
　end for
end while

4.3   Parameters

As we discussed in Sect. 2.2, choosing parameters are difficulties for BPSO because their underlying effects are different than the original one. In BPSO,the parameters includes c_1, c_2 and w. Both c_1 and c_2 are acceleration coefficients, which determine the influences of personal best and global best solution on particle's current velocity. As we can see in velocity update Eq. 1, term $c_1\varphi_1(P_{i,best} - X_i)$ represents the influence of the personal best position vector. Term $c_2\varphi_2(P_{g,best} - X_i)$ represents the influence of global best position to current particle position. If term $c_1\varphi_1(P_{i,best} - X_i)$ has a relatively large value, the flight of a particle will be driven to its personal best position, otherwise particle will be driven more to the global best position. Existing studies proposed many method to optimized these parameters.

While w is the inertia weight which controls the influence of previous velocity. We employ an adaptive inertia weight parameter that proposed by Yi et al. [21]. The adapative inertia makes the search start with exploration gradually move towards exploitation. During the evolution process, inertia weight linear increasing according to Eq. 10, where π and $\overline{\pi}$ stand for the number of iteratioins elaspsed and the maximal number of iterations respectively. $\underline{w}$ and $\overline{w}$ denote the lower and upper bounds of w. $0 \leq \rho \leq 1$ is the parameter to control the number of iterations to make w increase from $\underline{w}$ to $\overline{w}$. If $\rho = 0$, there is no adapation in inertia. If $\rho = 1$, w linearly increases throughout the search process.

$$w = \begin{cases} \underline{w} + \frac{\pi \cdot (\overline{w} - \underline{w})}{\rho \cdot \overline{\pi}} & \text{, if } \pi \leq \rho \cdot \overline{\pi} \\ \overline{w} & \text{, if } \rho \cdot \overline{\pi} < \pi \leq \overline{\pi} \end{cases} \tag{10}$$

5   Design of Experiments

In this section, experiments are designed for comparing the performance of MBPSO, MFGA and BPSO. Two measurements are taken into account, execution time and fitness value. Execution time is the searching time which excluded the file IO operations. Fitness values are the calculation results based on the fitness function Eq. 8.

5.1   Dataset

The datasets used for the experiments were generated from the WS-DREAM dataset [28]. The WS-DREAM dataset is a collection of historical data from 339 users and 5824 web services located in different locations. It records several non-functional attributes about the web services, including latency, throughput, availability, etc. We generate the *network latency matrix* by selecting a subset of 339 by 5824 matrix of latency. For example, in Table 1, in order to generate the first problem, which contains 20 user locations and 15 candidate locations. We randomly select 20 rows which denote 20 user locations, then we select 15 columns which are the candidate locations. Next step is to replace the columns that contain "null" by other columns to ensure the dataset is complete. The *Service establish cost matrix* were randomly generated from a normal distribution with $\mu = 100$ and $\sigma = 20$. The *service demand matrix* is generated follow several steps that described in Algorithm 2 with Problem 2 as an example. We assign each atomic service a weight k to represent the *atomic service demand*. k is randomly selected from Pareto distribution because according to the popular 20-80-rule, 20% of service requests count for 80% of overall service requests [13]. We randomly select r services as a stimulation of a web service composition. Hence, the term $1/r_s$ denotes the *service position weight*.

Algorithm 2. Generate service demand matrix

Generate a set of symbolic atomic services $W = \{w_1, w_2, \ldots, w_{30}\}$
for 1 to 10 **do**
    Randomly generate a number $r \in [1, 30]$
    Randomly select r atomic services
    Assign each atomic services a weight $k \in [0, 1]$ generate from a Pareto distribution
    with $scale = 100$ and $shape = 1$.
end for
calculate the demand of each atomic web service according to $f_s = \sum_{s=1}^{10} k_s * 1/r_s$

Furthermore, all the input data involved in this experiments were normalized into interval $[0, 1]$. Five problems of different complexity levels of data were extracted from WS-DREAM. Table 1 outlines the extracted data and it corresponding attributes.

Table 1. Hypothetical web service location-allocation problems

Problem ID	User location	Candidate location	Composite services	Atomic services
1	10	5	1	5
2	20	15	5	20
3	40	25	10	50
4	40	25	20	100
5	80	40	40	200

5.2   Environment and Parameters

The experiments were conducted on a personal laptop with 2.3 GHz CPU and 4.0 GB RAM. For each approach, 30 independent runs are performed for each problem with constant population size 100. The maximum number of iteration is 250, but it will termination earlier if some condition is met, such as objective value is not changed during 10 iterations. The weight of response time and establish cost were set to 0.5 and 0.5, which means the importance of response time and establish cost were equivalent in this model. It is also can be adjusted when service providers have different preferences. For MFGA, the initial crossover and mutation possibility are 0.6 and 0.2, which is the configuration in our previous study [12]. We apply tournament selection with tournament size of 10 and elitism which carry over the top 20 individuals into the next generation without modification. For PSO-based approaches, We set c_1 and c_2 equal 1.427 according to study [3]. In MBPSO, We set $\rho = 0.9$, $\underline{w} = 0.4$, and $\overline{w} = 1.0$ in adaptive inertia according to [21]; in standard BPSO we set $w = 0.689$ according to study [3]. Velocity clamping is one crucial issue in BPSO. Since the parameters cause opposite behavior between continuous PSO and BPSO. In continuous PSO, a large velocity encourages exploration; while in BPSO, a larger velocity limits the possibility of changing the bit. Therefore, the velocity should be clamped in a small range. We set the clamping factor to 8 in order to obtain $V_{max} = 4$ in these experiments, because it is always allow a possibility of $s(V_{max}) = 0.0018$ for a bit to flip [24].

6   Results and Analysis

This section shows the experimental results of MBPSO, BPSO and MFGA approaches in solving the service location-allocation problems with our predefined complexity levels. Table 2 demonstrates the fitness value and execution time comparison of three algorithms; the fitness is smaller the better as we are minimizing the fitness function. Each row represents the values and standard deviation among three methods on a predefined problem. We apply Wilcoxon signed rank test on the fitness values and mark the statistical significant values.

Table 2. Fitness value and execution time (second) comparison among BPSO, MBPSO, and MFGA

Problems	Fitness			Execution time		
	Methods					
	BPSO	MBPSO	MFGA	BPSO	MBPSO	MFGA
1	0.034 ± 0.003	0.033 ± 0.003	**0.028** ± 0.0002	0.22 ± 0.03	0.21 ± 0.02	0.18 + 0.04
2	0.168 ± 0.005	0.146 ± 0.009	00.15 ± 0.004	6.54 ± 0.67	6.18 ± 0.1	5.40 ± 0.09
3	0.202 ± 0.002	**0.186** ± 0.006	0.192 ± 0.002	60.6 ± 1.92	60.4 + 1.57	57.01 ± 1.67
4	0.218 ± 0.001	**0.207** ± 0.004	0.21 ± 0.002	116.9 ± 1.05	117.2 ± 1.89	112.81 ± 1.84
5	0.231 ± 0.0007	**0.225** ± 0.0008	0.227 ± 0.0006	957.2 ± 10.3	962.0 ± 12.9	954.1 ± 11.1

As illustrated in Table 2, overall, the performance of MBPSO has an advantage in solving larger problems. MFGA is significantly better than PSO approaches for the first problem and there is no significant difference for the second problem. As the complexity increases, MBPSO shows a stronger search ability. In comparison between BPSO and MBPSO, clearly, MBPSO is better than original approach in every problem. Due to the adaptive inertia weights, MBPSO would first move fast in the search space and gradually focuses on local area. It proves that the adapative inertia not only good at solving well-defined test functions, but also performance well in real-world problem.

In terms of execution time, MFGA has a clear advantage, because MFGA uses a memory pool to store the top 10 percent of chromosomes. This technique can reduce the repeated evaluation time. There is no significant difference between BPSO and MBPSO as their only difference is the adaptive inertia.

In summary, our proposed MBPSO can effectively and effeciently solve the web service location-allocation problem in most cases.

7 Conclusion and Future Work

In this paper, we propose a multi-objective with an aggregation method to formulate the web service location-allocation problem. We also apply a MBPSO to search for a near-optimal solution. We have shown that the MBPSO can be used to solve service location-allocation problem in a relatively efficient and effective way, similar to our previous proposed MFGA based approach.

Future work probably includes more constraints into the problem model (i.e. throughput, availability, and reliability). We will also investigate the settings of the parameters used in the MBPSO approaches.

References

1. Aboolian, R., Sun, Y., Koehler, G.J.: A location allocation problem for a web services provider in a competitive market. Eur. J. Oper. Res. 194(1), 64–77 (2009)
2. Blondin, J.: Particle Swarm Optimization: A Tutorial (2009)
3. Clerc, M., Kennedy, J.: The particle swarm-explosion, stability, and convergence in a multidimensional complex space. IEEE Trans. Evol. Comput. 6(1), 58–73 (2002)
4. Curbera, F., Duftler, M., Khalaf, R., Nagy, W., Mukhi, N., Weerawarana, S.: Unraveling the web services web: an introduction to SOAP, WSDL, and UDDI. IEEE Internet Comput. 6(2), 86 (2002)
5. Curbera, F., Khalaf, R., Mukhi, N., Tai, S., Weerawarana, S.: The next step in web services. Commun. ACM 46(10), 29–34 (2003)
6. Eberhart, R.C., Shi, Y.: Particle swarm optimization: developments, applications and resources. In: Proceedings of the 2001 Congress on Evolutionary Computation, vol. 1, pp. 81–86. IEEE (2001)
7. Erl, T.: SOA: Principles of Service Design, vol. 1. Prentice Hall, Upper Saddle River (2008)
8. Fielding, R., Gettys, J., Mogul, J., Frystyk, H., Masinter, L., Leach, P., Berners-Lee, T.: Hypertext transfer protocol-HTTP/1.1, Rfc 2616, (1999, 2009)
9. Garriga, M., Flores, A., Cechich, A., Zunino, A.: Web services composition mechanisms: a review. IETE Tech. Rev. 32(5), 376–383 (2015)
10. Ghaderi, A., Jabalameli, M., Barzinpour, F., Rahmaniani, R.: An efficient hybrid particle swarm optimization algorithm for solving the uncapacitated continuous location-allocation problem. Netw. Spat. Econ. 12(3), 421–439 (2012)
11. Guner, A.R., Sevkli, M.: A discrete particle swarm optimization algorithm for uncapacitated facility location problem. J. Artif. Evol. Appl. (2008)
12. Huang, H., Ma, H., Zhang, M.: An enhanced genetic algorithm for web service location-allocation. In: Decker, H., Lhotská, L., Link, S., Spies, M., Wagner, R.R. (eds.) DEXA 2014. LNCS, vol. 8645, pp. 223–230. Springer, Heidelberg (2014). doi:10.1007/978-3-319-10085-2_20

13. Huang, L., Nie, J.: Using pareto principle to improve efficiency for selection of QoS web services. In: 2010 7th IEEE Consumer Communications and Networking Conference, pp. 1–2. IEEE (2010)
14. Kennedy, J., Eberhart, R., et al.: Particle swarm optimization. In: Proceedings of IEEE International Conference on Neural Networks, Perth, Australia, vol. 4, pp. 1942–1948 (1995)
15. Kennedy, J., Eberhart, R.C.: A discrete binary version of the particle swarm algorithm. In: 1997 IEEE International Conference on Systems, Man, and Cybernetics, Computational Cybernetics and Simulation, vol. 5, pp. 4104–4108. IEEE (1997)
16. Khanesar, M.A., Teshnehlab, M., Shoorehdeli, M.A.: A novel binary particle swarm optimization. In: Mediterranean Conference on Control and Automation, MED 2007, pp. 1–6. IEEE (2007)
17. Kramer, O.: A review of constraint-handling techniques for evolution strategies. Appl. Comput. Intell. Soft Comput. (2010)
18. Liu, J., Tang, M., Zheng, Z., Liu, X., Lyu, S.: Location-aware and personalized collaborative filtering for web service recommendation. IEEE Trans. Serv. Comput. **9**(5), 686–699 (2016)
19. Liu, Z., Lu, T.: A location & time related web service distributed selection approach for composition. In: 2010 9th International Conference on Grid and Cooperative Computing (GCC), pp. 296–301. IEEE (2010)
20. McKendrick, J.: Ten companies where SOA made a difference in 2006 (2006)
21. Mei, Y., Li, X., et al.: An Analysis of the Inertia Weight Parameter for Binary Particle Swarm Optimization (2012)
22. Moraglio, A., Di Chio, C., Togelius, J., Poli, R.: Geometric particle swarm optimization. J. Artif. Evol. Appl. **2008**, 11 (2008)
23. Rao, J., Su, X.: A survey of automated web service composition methods. In: Cardoso, J., Sheth, A. (eds.) SWSWPC 2004. LNCS, vol. 3387, pp. 43–54. Springer, Heidelberg (2005). doi:10.1007/978-3-540-30581-1_5
24. Jordchi, A.R., Jasni, J.: Particle swarm optimisation for discrete optimisation problems: a review. Artif. Intell. Rev. **43**(2), 243–258 (2015)
25. Sun, Y., Koehler, G.J.: A location model for a web service intermediary. Decis. Support Syst. **42**(1), 221–236 (2006)
26. Wahab, O.A., Bentahar, J., Otrok, H., Mourad, A.: A survey on trust and reputation models for web services: single, composite, and communities. Decis. Support Syst. **74**, 121–134 (2015)
27. Zhang, Y., Wang, S., Ji, G.: A comprehensive survey on particle swarm optimization algorithm and its applications. Math. Prob. Eng. (2015)
28. Zhang, Y., Zheng, Z., Lyu, M.R.: WSExpress: a QoS-aware search engine for web services. In: Proceedings of the IEEE International Conference on Web Services (ICWS 2010), pp. 83–90 (2010)

A MOEA/D with Non-uniform Weight Vector Distribution Strategy for Solving the Unit Commitment Problem in Uncertain Environment

Anupam Trivedi[1]([✉]), Dipti Srinivasan[1], Kunal Pal[1], and Thomas Reindl[2]

[1] National University of Singapore, Singapore, Singapore
`eleatr@nus.edu.sg`
[2] Solar Energy Research Institute of Singapore, Singapore, Singapore

Abstract. In this paper, a multiobjective evolutionary algorithm based on decomposition (MOEA/D) based is proposed to solve the unit commitment (UC) problem in uncertain environment as a multi-objective optimization problem considering cost, emission, and reliability as the multiple objectives. The uncertainties occurring due to thermal generator outage and load forecast error are incorporated using expected energy not served (EENS) reliability index and EENS cost is used to reflect the reliability objective. Since, UC is a mixed-integer optimization problem, a hybrid strategy is integrated within the framework of decomposition-based MOEA such that genetic algorithm (GA) evolves the binary variables while differential evolution (DE) evolves the continuous variables. To enhance the performance of the presented algorithm, novel non-uniform weight vector distribution strategies are proposed. The effectiveness of the non-uniform weight vector distribution strategy is verified through stringent simulated results on different test systems.

1 Introduction

The unit commitment (UC) problem is one of the most important problems in power system operation. The UC is a day-ahead scheduling problem and comprises of two tasks: one is determining the on/off status of the thermal units; the other is the power dispatch which requires distributing the system load demand to the committed thermal units. The classical UC problem requires effectively performing the above two tasks to meet the forecasted load demand over a particular time horizon, satisfying a large set of units and system constraints and meeting the (only) objective of minimizing the system operation cost [1]. The UC is a nonlinear, mixed-integer, combinatorial, high-dimensional, and highly constrained optimization problem, and belongs to the set of NP-hard problems [1]. Due to its economic importance, the UC has for long been a problem of significant interest for power system companies.

This work was supported by the Ministry of Education under Grant R-263-000-B49-112 and Energy Market Authority of Singapore under Grant R-263-000-B14-279.

© Springer International Publishing AG 2017
M. Wagner et al. (Eds.): ACALCI 2017, LNAI 10142, pp. 378–390, 2017.
DOI: 10.1007/978-3-319-51691-2_32

In the literature, several stochastic search based techniques such as genetic algorithm (GA) [2,3], particle swarm optimization (PSO) [4], differential evolution [5], hybrid of GA and DE [6,7] etc., have been proposed for solving the classical UC problem. These stochastic search based techniques have attracted wide recognition due to their ease of implementation, capability of accommodating complex problem characteristics, and attaining optimal/near-optimal solution.

The UC problem is generally solved in the literature with system operation cost as the single (economic) objective function while the objectives related to emission and the reliability are generally neglected. Nevertheless, for realistic decision making, the system operators would prefer to consider various uncertainties in the problem, and include emission and reliability as additional objectives along with system operation cost, and obtain trade-off optimal solutions [8]. However, UC considering system operation cost, emission, and reliability as the multiple objectives is a nonlinear, mixed-integer, combinatorial, high-dimensional, highly constrained multiobjective optimization problem. Hence, it is a challenge to efficiently incorporate the various uncertainties and solve UC as a multi-objective optimization problem to obtain different trade-off optimal solutions [8].

1.1   Brief Review of Methods Proposed for Multiobjective UC Problem

Recently, several studies have solved the UC problem as a MOP considering objectives such as system operation cost, emission, reliability, transmission losses. In [9], an algorithm based on integration of NSGA-II (non-dominated sorting genetic algorithm-II) [10] with problem specific genetic operators, priority list (PL) based heuristic initialization, and repair operation, is presented for the multi-objective economic/emission (MOEE-UC) problem. In [11], a multi-objective memetic evolutionary algorithm (EA) based on combination of NSGA-II and problem specific local search operators is proposed to solve the MOEE-UC problem. In [12], an enhanced hybrid multi-objective evolutionary algorithm based on decomposition (MOEA/D) is proposed to solve the MOEE-UC problem.

In [8], the NSGA-II based algorithm presented in [9] is extended, and the multi-objective economic/emission/reliability UC (MOEER-UC) problem is solved in which reliability is included as an additional objective along with economic and emission objectives. A fuzzy assisted hybrid of (a) binary and real-coded artificial bee colony (ABC) algorithm [13] and (b) binary and real-coded cuckoo search algorithm (CSA) [14] have been proposed to solve the UC problem considering system operation cost, emission, and reliability objectives.

1.2   Proposed Work

In this paper, the MOEER-UC problem i.e., multi-objective UC problem considering system operation cost, emission, and reliability as the multiple conflicting objectives is addressed. The uncertainties occurring due to thermal unit outage and load forecast error are taken into account. These uncertainties are incorporated using expected energy not served (EENS) reliability index while EENS cost is used to reflect the reliability objective.

To solve the MOEER-UC problem, the framework of multi-objective evolutionary algorithm based on decomposition (MOEA/D) [15] is selected. MOEA/D is an evolutionary multi-objective optimization framework proposed by Zhang and Li in 2007 [15]. MOEA/D decomposes a multiobjective optimization problem into a number of scalar optimization subproblems and optimizes them in a collaborative manner using an evolutionary algorithm. Each subproblem is optimized by utilizing the information from its several neighboring subproblems only. An improved version of MOEA/D, termed MOEA/D-DE, in which the SBX crossover operator is replaced by the DE operator is suggested by Li and Zhang in 2009 [16]. Since the proposition of the original MOEA/D framework, several studies have been conducted in the literature either to overcome the limitations in design components of the original MOEA/D, or to improve the performance of MOEA/D. Interested readers are referred to a recent survey on decomposition-based MOEAs [17].

Inspired from the performance of MOEA/D and MOEA/D-DE in the literature, in this paper, the framework of MOEA/D-DE [16] is chosen. In their original study, MOEA/D as well as MOEA/D-DE are mainly investigated on continuous MOPs. However, as mentioned earlier, the UC is a mixed-integer optimization problem and thus the algorithm employed should be able to efficiently explore both the binary search space as well as the continuous search space. Therefore, to efficiently solve the mixed-integer UC problem, in this paper, a hybrid methodology is incorporated within the MOEA/D framework. In the proposed algorithm, GA and DE are synergized such that GA evolves the binary component of the solution (i.e., chromosome) while DE evolves the continuous component of the solution. Such a hybrid algorithm of GA and DE has been found to be promising on the single-objective UC problem [6,7] as well as on the bi-objective UC problem [12].

In the original study of MOEA/D [15] and most of its subsequent variants, the weight vectors corresponding to different scalar optimization subproblems are uniformly distributed. However, in this paper, MOEA/D with uniform weight vector distribution is not found to obtain well distributed set of trade-off solutions. Thus, in this paper, two non-uniform weight vector distribution strategies are developed and investigated to enhance the performance of MOEA/D-DE on the MOEER-UC problem.

The rest of the paper is organized as follows. Section 2 presents the problem formulation. Section 3 presents the framework of the hybrid MOEA/D-DE. Section 4 presents the proposed non-uniform weight vector distribution strategies and the experimental study. Section 5 presents the conclusions and the future work.

2 Problem Formulation

In this section, the multi-objective UC problem formulation is presented. It is noted that the nomenclature is presented in Table 1.

Table 1. Nomenclature

Indices	
i	Generating unit index
t	Hourly time index
Variables	
E_i^t	Pollutants produced by unit i at hour t in lb
f_i^t	Fuel cost of unit i at hour t in \$/h
P_i^t	Power generated by unit i at time t
$T_{ON,i^t}/T_{OFF,i^t}$	Continuously on/off time of unit i up to hour t
u_i^t	Unit commitment status of unit i at time t $(1 = ON, 0 = OFF)$
Constants	
a_i, b_i, c_i	Fuel cost coefficients of unit i
a_{1i}, b_{1i}, c_{1i}	Emission coefficients of unit i
CR	Crossover rate of Differential Evolution
CSC_i	Cold start-up cost of unit i
F	Scaling factor of Differential Evolution
HSC_i	Hot start-up cost of unit i
L^t	Load demand at hour t
max_gen	Maximum generations/iterations
MUT_i/MDT_i	Minimum up/down time of unit i
N	Number of generating units
$P_{min,i}$	Rated lower limit generation of unit i
$P_{max,i}$	Rated upper limit generation of unit i
SD_i^t	Shut-down cost of unit i at hour t
SU_i^t	Start-up cost of unit i at hour t
SR^t	System spinning reserve requirement at hour t
$T_{cold,i}$	Cold start hour of unit i
T_{max}	Number of hours considered (scheduling horizon)

2.1 Objective Functions

1. System Operation Cost: The first objective function (F_1) is to minimize the system operation cost (SOC), where SOC includes the fuel cost and the transition cost of all the generating units over the entire scheduling horizon [11]. The fuel cost f_i^t of unit i is considered to be quadratic function of its power output during hour t [11].

$$f_i^t = a_i P_i^{t^2} + b_i P_i^t + c_i \tag{1}$$

The transition cost is the sum of the start-up costs and the shut-down costs. In this paper, the shut-down costs have not been taken into consideration in accordance with the literature [11] while the start-up cost is modeled as follows:

$$SU_i^t = \begin{cases} HSC_i, & \text{if } MDT_i \le T_{OFF,i}^t \le MDT_i + T_{cold,i} \\ CSC_i, & \text{if } T_{OFF,i}^t > MDT_i + T_{cold,i} \end{cases} \tag{2}$$

Subsequently, the first objective function is given by minimization of the following cost function [11].

$$F_1 = \sum_{t=1}^{T_{max}} \sum_{i=1}^{N} \left(f_i^t . u_i^t + SU_i^t (1 - u_i^{t-1}) u_i^t \right) \tag{3}$$

2. *Emission:* The second objective function (F_2) is the reduction of emission of air-pollutants into the atmosphere [11].

$$F_2 = \sum_{t=1}^{T_{max}} \sum_{i=1}^{N} \left(E_i^t . u_i^t \right) \tag{4}$$

where E_i^t (lb) represents the quantity of pollutants produced by unit i at time t and is defined in accordance with the literature [11] as:

$$E_i^{\;t} = a_{1i} P_i^{t^2} + b_{1i} P_i^t + c_{1i} \tag{5}$$

3. *Expected Energy Not Served (EENS) Cost:* The third objective function (F_3) is to maximize the reliability of the system. The function used to represent the reliability of the system is the expected energy not served (EENS) cost [18] which is defined as the product of the expected energy not served (EENS) and value of lost load (VOLL) determined using survey [18]. It is noted that VOLL represents the average value (in \$/MWh) that consumers place on the accidental loss of 1 MWh of electricity [18]. Since, predicting the generation outages and deviation of load demand from the forecasted demand during the actual implementation of a particular generation schedule is impossible, only an EENS cost (also called outage cost) can be computed. The EENS cost is given by:

$$F_3 = VOLL \times EENS_{tot} \tag{6}$$

where $EENS_{tot}$ is total expected unserved energy for the entire scheduling horizon.

It is noted that the lower the EENS cost, the higher is the reliability of the system and vice-versa.

2.2   Constraints

1. System power balance: the total power generation at hour t must be equal to the load demand for that hour.

$$\sum_{i=1}^{N} (P_i^t \cdot u_i^t) = L^t, t = 1, 2, \ldots T_{max} \tag{7}$$

2. Unit minimum up/down time: if a unit i is turned on/off, it must remain on/off for at least its minimum up/down time (MUT_i/MDT_i) duration.

$$\begin{aligned} T_{ON,i}^t &\geq MUT_i \\ T_{OFF,i}^t &\geq MDT_i \end{aligned} \tag{8}$$

3. Unit generation limits: for stable operation, the power output of each generator is restricted within its limits.

$$P_{min,i} \leq P_i^t \leq P_{max,i} \tag{9}$$

4. Maximum system operation cost: this constraint is incorporated as:

$$F_1 \leq SOC_{max} \tag{10}$$

where F_1 represents the objective function system operation cost and SOC_{max} is the user-defined upper limit for solution's SOC.
5. Maximum Emission: this constraint is incorporated as:

$$F_2 \leq Emis_{max} \tag{11}$$

where F_2 represents the objective function emission and $Emis_{max}$ is the user-defined upper limit for solution's emission.
6. Maximum EENS cost: this constraint is incorporated as:

$$F_3 \leq EENSC_{max} \tag{12}$$

where F_3 represents the objective function EENS cost and $EENSC_{max}$ is the user-defined upper limit for solution's EENS cost.

3   Proposed Algorithm

In this section, the proposed algorithm MOEA/D-DE is vividly presented in the context of the MOEER-UC problem.

3.1   Chromosome Representation

For every chromosome, a $N \times T_{max}$ binary unit commitment matrix (UCM) represents the thermal generator on/off status and a $N \times T_{max}$ real power matrix (RPM) represents the corresponding power dispatch. It is noted that a chromosome's actual generation schedule is represented by its resultant power matrix (Res.PM) which is obtained by multiplying the corresponding elements of UCM and RPM.

3.2   Generation of Initial Population

The initial population (i.e., UCM and RPM of the chromosomes) is randomly generated.

3.3   Fitness Evaluation

Since, UC is a highly constrained optimization problem, the performance of the algorithm depends upon how the algorithm handles the constraints.

Boundary Constraint Handling
The generator limit constraints given by (9) are handled according to the bound handling approach known as set on boundary.

Load Demand Equality Constraint Repair Operator
In the proposed algorithm, a repair operator based on priority list (PL) of the thermal units is applied to repair chromosomes that violate the load demand equality constraint [8].

Constraint Violation Evaluation
At first, all the constraints are normalized because different constraints may take different orders of magnitude. Thereafter, all normalized constraint violations are added to calculate the overall constraint violation of a chromosome.

Objective Function Evaluation
The system operation cost and emission objectives are calculated for each chromosome using its Res.PM (which is obtained by multiplying the corresponding elements of UCM and RPM as mentioned earlier) while the EENS cost objective is evaluated using the procedure detailed in Sect. 4.

3.4   Variation Operation: Hybrid of GA with DE

The variation operation is the step where GA and DE are synergized at every generation. In the variation operation, the binary UC variables are evolved using GA operators while the continuous power dispatch variables are evolved using DE operators [6]. The GA operators are window crossover, swap window mutation, and window mutation while the DE operators are DE/rand/1 mutation and binomial crossover. Interested readers are referred to the study [12] for further details.

3.5   Replacement

At every generation, once corresponding to an index i the variation operation is completed i.e., the child's (say $x_{child's}$) UCM and RPM are created using GA and DE, respectively; the UCM and RPM are combined to evaluate the fitness of the x_{child}. Thereafter, x_{child} is compared with a randomly picked solution in the neighborhood (say y) of index i and the replacement/update of neighborhood takes place according to the rules based on superiority of feasibility [12].

3.6 Stopping Criterion

The algorithm stops if the maximum number of generations (set as input) is reached. Once the algorithm stops, the solutions in the final population of MOEA/D-DE represent the trade-off optimal solutions obtained for the problem.

4 Experimental Study

In this section, the proposed non-uniform weight vector distribution strategies are presented and the performance of the proposed algorithm is investigated on the MOEER-UC problem. The proposed algorithm is developed on C platform and executed on PC with Intel 3.10 GHz processor. To investigate the scalability, the proposed algorithm is tested on the MOEER-UC problem for power systems with 10, 20, and 60 units in a 24 h scheduling horizon [11]. The standard deviation (σ_{load}^{t}) of the load forecast error is assumed to be 5% of the hourly load demand [19] and VOLL is assumed to be 5000\$/MWh [18]. For each experiment, 15 independent simulation trials are conducted to investigate the robustness of the proposed algorithm. To investigate the performance of the proposed algorithm, three separate performance indicators have been used - Generational Distance (GD) [20] for convergence, Generalized Spread [20] for diversity and Hypervolume (HV) [20] for combined assessment of convergence and diversity.

4.1 Case Study - MOEA/D-DE with Non-uniform Weight Vector Distribution

At first, MOEA/D-DE with uniform weight vector distribution is implemented on 10, 20 and 60 unit systems. Figure 1a, b, and c depict the distribution of the final non-dominated solutions found by MOEA/D-DE in a single run (with best HV metric) on 10, 20, and 60 unit systems. These results show that there is a limitation in the performance of MOEA/D-DE as many solutions are clustered at the boundary.

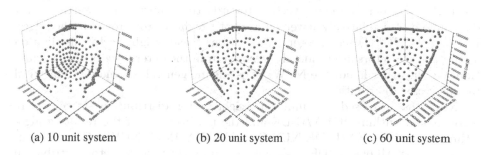

    (a) 10 unit system   (b) 20 unit system   (c) 60 unit system

Fig. 1. The distribution of the final non-dominated solutions found by MOEA/D-DE with uniform weight vector distribution scheme on different test systems.

It is well known that the performance of decomposition-based MOEAs is highly dependent on the weight vector generation method. The original MOEA/D and MOEA/D-DE employ evenly distributed weight vectors generated using the simplex-lattice design method. However, the assumption that an evenly [9] or uniformly [19] distributed weight vectors can provide uniformly distributed P-O solutions has been comprehensively refuted in some recent studies [21].

Thus, in this paper, two novel weight-vector distribution strategies are investigated within the framework of MOEA/D-DE. The target of the proposed strategies is to help MOEA/D-DE achieve a better distribution in the middle of the P-O front while maintaining the performance in terms of convergence throughout the P-O front. The proposed weight-vector distribution strategies are as follows:

1. In the first non-uniform weight-vector distribution scheme, named NUWD, an increased number of weight vectors are first generated using the simplex-lattice design method. Thereafter, the weight vectors are randomly removed from the outer layers of the distribution to help the algorithm focus its search more towards the center of the PF. Figure 2a shows the uniform weight-vector distribution employed for a three-objective optimization problem in the original MOEA/D-DE [16]. The weight vectors generated using the proposed NUWD strategy is depicted in Fig. 2b. Thus, in the NUWD scheme, more number of subproblems are allocated to find increased number of solutions towards the center of the PF while relatively fewer subproblems are allocated towards the edges of the PF.
2. In the second non-uniform weight-vector distribution scheme, named NUWD-Cos, the following sinusoidal function is selected to generate the weight vector distribution:

$$\lambda_i^{k'} = g(\lambda_i^k) = (acos(2\lambda_i^k - 1)/\pi) \quad i = 1, 2, \ldots, NP; k = 1, 2. \quad (13)$$

where $\lambda_i^{k'}$ replaces λ_i^k as input in the algorithm MOEA/D-DE. The weight vectors generated using the proposed NUWD-Cos strategy is depicted in Fig. 2c.

It is observed from Figs. 2b and c that both the NUWD strategies generate higher number of weight vectors towards the center of the weight vector distribution and relatively fewer number of weight vectors towards the edges. Further, the NUWD scheme generates asymmetrical weight vector distribution as the weight vectors are randomly removed from the outer layer of the distribution. On the other hand, the NUWD-Cos scheme generates a more symmetrical weight vector distribution.

Next, the proposed non-uniform weight-vector distribution strategies are incorporated within MOEA/D-DE and the performance of the resulting algorithms, named MOEA/D-DE-NUWD and MOEA/D-DE-NUWD-Cos, are compared against MOEA/D-DE (i.e., with the uniform weight vector distribution (UWD) strategy). Figures 3, 4, and 5 illustrate the comparison of the UWD and the NUWD variants for 10, 20, and 60 unit systems on the basis of GD,

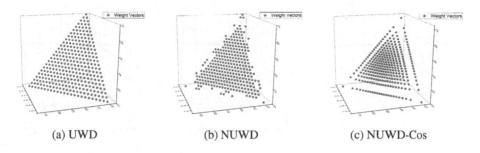

(a) UWD   (b) NUWD   (c) NUWD-Cos

Fig. 2. (a) Uniform weight vector distribution (UWD) in the original MOEA/D-DE, (b) proposed NUWD scheme, and (c) proposed NUWD-Cos scheme for 3-objective optimization problem.

Spread, and HV metric, respectively. Following are the observations from the above figures:

– The performance of the UWD and the NUWD variants is comparable in terms of GD metric (refer Fig. 3).
– In terms of spread metric, the NUWD-Cos variant significantly outperforms the UWD and the NUWD variant on 20 and 60 unit systems (refer Fig. 4).
– In terms of HV metric, the NUWD-Cos variant is significantly superior to the UWD and the NUWD variant on all the test systems (refer Fig. 5).

To further analyze the performance in the objective space, the distribution of the final non-dominated solutions with the highest HV values found on 10, 20, and 60 unit systems by the NUWD-Cos variant is plotted in Fig. 6, respectively. It is visually evident from the figures that the NUWD-Cos variant attracts more solutions towards the center and provides significantly better distribution of solutions than the UWD variant (refer Fig. 1), particularly on the 20 and 60 unit systems.

This case study demonstrated that the non-uniform weight vector distribution strategy (NUWD-Cos) significantly improves the performance of MOEA/D-DE on the MOEER-UC problem. However, Fig. 6 shows that even with the

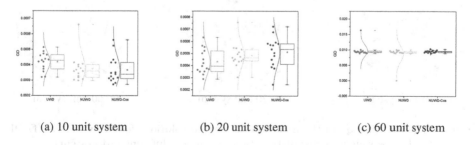

(a) 10 unit system   (b) 20 unit system   (c) 60 unit system

Fig. 3. GD metric comparison among MOEA/D-DE with UWD, NUWD, and NUWD-Cos weight vector distributions on different test systems

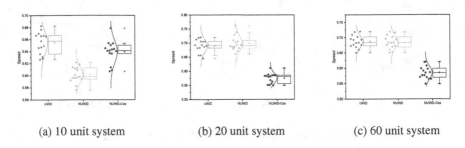

(a) 10 unit system   (b) 20 unit system   (c) 60 unit system

Fig. 4. Spread metric comparison among MOEA/D-DE with UWD, NUWD, and NUWD-Cos weight vector distributions on different test systems

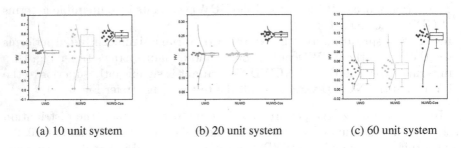

(a) 10 unit system   (b) 20 unit system   (c) 60 unit system

Fig. 5. HV metric comparison among MOEA/D-DE with UWD, NUWD, and NUWD-Cos weight vector distributions on different test systems.

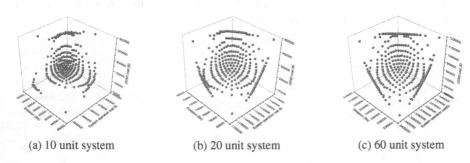

(a) 10 unit system   (b) 20 unit system   (c) 60 unit system

Fig. 6. The distribution of the final non-dominated solutions found by MOEA/D-DE with NUWD-Cos weight vector distribution scheme on different test systems.

NUWD-Cos weight vector distribution strategy, there is clustering of solutions towards the edges of the PF but the severity is less. This indicates that in the future, there is scope for further improvement in the performance of the proposed MOEA/D-DE on the MOEER-UC problem.

5   Conclusions and Future Work

In this paper, a MOEA/D based on hybrid of GA and DE was applied to solve the UC problem considering system operation cost, emission, and reliability as the multiple conflicting objectives in uncertain environment.

However, a limitation was observed in the performance of hybrid MOEA/D-DE as several solutions were found to be clustered at the boundary of the objective space. Therefore, two non-uniform weight vector distribution (NUWD) strategies were proposed to bias the search direction of MOEA/D-DE in the three-objective space and reduce the clustering of solutions. The comparative analysis of MOEA/D-DE and MOEA/D-DE with the proposed NUWD strategies i.e., MOEA/D-DE-NUWD and MOEA/D-DE-NUWD-Cos, revealed that MOEA/D-DE-NUWD-Cos significantly outperforms the other two variants, and provides much better distribution of solutions. However, it was observed that with MOEA/D-DE-NUWD-Cos as well, there is clustering towards the edges of the trade-off surface but the severity is less. Hence, in future, more sophisticated weight vector distribution strategies can be designed to improve the performance of the proposed algorithm on MOEER-UC problem.

Further, it is noted that the NUWD strategies proposed in this paper are problem specific. In other words, the NUWD strategies were developed to specifically tackle the limitation of UWD strategy with respect to the performance of algorithm on MOEER-UC problem. Thus, the proposed NUWD strategies are not generic and cannot be adopted to obtain uniform distribution of solutions on other problems. However, this paper shows that NUWD strategies may lead to improved performance of decomposition-based MOEAs. An interesting future work can be investigation of the performance of MOEA/D-AWA [22] on MOEER-UC problem, in which weight vector adaptation strategy is incorporated. Moreover, novel weight vector adaptation strategies can be developed.

References

1. Wood, A.J., Woolenberg, B.: Power Generation Operation and Control. Wiley, New York (1996)
2. Kazarlis, S.A., Bakirtzis, A.G., Petridis, V.: A genetic algorithm solution to the unit commitment problem. IEEE Trans. Power Syst. 11(1), 83–92 (1996)
3. Datta, D.: Unit commitment problem with ramp rate constraint using a binary-real-coded genetic algorithm. Appl. Soft Comput. 13(9), 3873–3883 (2013)
4. Yuan, X., Su, A., Nie, H., Yuan, Y., Wang, L.: Unit commitment problem using enhanced particle swarm optimization algorithm. Soft Comput. 15(1), 139–148 (2011)

5. Datta, D., Dutta, S.: A binary-real-coded differential evolution for unit commitment problem. Int. J. Electr. Power Energy Syst. **42**(1), 517–524 (2012)
6. Trivedi, A., Srinivasan, D., Biswas, S., Reindl, T.: Hybridizing genetic algorithm with differential evolution for solving the unit commitment scheduling problem. Swarm Evol. Comput. **23**, 50–64 (2015)
7. Trivedi, A., Srinivasan, D., Biswas, S., Reindl, T.: A genetic algorithm differential evolution based hybrid framework: case study on unit commitment scheduling problem. Inf. Sci. **354**, 275–300 (2016)
8. Trivedi, A., Srinivasan, D., Sharma, D., Singh, C.: Evolutionary multi-objective day-ahead thermal generation scheduling in uncertain environment. IEEE Trans. Power Syst. **28**(2), 1345–1354 (2013)
9. Trivedi, A., Pindoriya, N.M., Srinivasan, D., Sharma, D.: Improved multi-objective evolutionary algorithm for day-ahead thermal generation scheduling. In: 2011 IEEE Congress of Evolutionary Computation (CEC), pp. 2170–2177, June 2011
10. Deb, K., Pratap, A., Agarwal, S., Meyarivan, T.: A fast and elitist multiobjective genetic algorithm: NSGA-II. IEEE Trans. Evol. Comput. **6**(2), 182–197 (2002)
11. Li, Y.F., Pedroni, N., Zio, E.: A memetic evolutionary multi-objective optimization method for environmental power unit commitment. IEEE Trans. Power Syst. **28**(3), 2660–2669 (2013)
12. Trivedi, A., Srinivasan, D., Pal, K., Saha, C., Reindl, T.: Enhanced multiobjective evolutionary algorithm based on decomposition for solving the unit commitment problem. IEEE Trans. Ind. Inform. **11**(6), 1346–1357 (2015)
13. Chandrasekaran, K., Hemamalini, S., Simon, S.P., Padhy, N.P.: Thermal unit commitment using binary/real coded artificial bee colony algorithm. Electr. Power Syst. Res. **84**(1), 109–119 (2012)
14. Chandrasekaran, K., Simon, S.P.: Multi-objective scheduling problem: hybrid approach using fuzzy assisted cuckoo search algorithm. Swarm Evol. Comput. **5**, 1–16 (2012)
15. Zhang, Q., Li, H.: MOEA/D: a multiobjective evolutionary algorithm based on decomposition. IEEE Trans. Evol. Comput. **11**(6), 712–731 (2007)
16. Li, H., Zhang, Q.: Multiobjective optimization problems with complicated Pareto sets, MOEA/D and NSGA-II. IEEE Trans. Evol. Comput. **13**(2), 284–302 (2009)
17. Trivedi, A., Srinivasan, D., Sanyal, K., Ghosh, A.: A survey of multi-objective evolutionary algorithms based on decomposition. IEEE Trans. Evol. Comput. **PP**(99), 1 (2016)
18. Ortega-Vazquez, M.A., Kirschen, D.S.: Optimizing the spinning reserve requirements using a cost/benefit analysis. IEEE Trans. Power Syst. **22**(1), 24–33 (2007)
19. Billinton, R., Allan, R.N.: Reliability Evaluation of Power Systems. Plenum, London (1996)
20. Jiang, S., Ong, Y.S., Zhang, J., Feng, L.: Consistencies and contradictions of performance metrics in multiobjective optimization. IEEE Trans. Cybern. **44**(12), 2391–2404 (2014)
21. Giagkiozis, I., Purshouse, R., Fleming, P.: Generalized decomposition and cross entropy methods for many-objective optimization. Inf. Sci. **282**, 363–387 (2014)
22. Qi, Y., Ma, X., Liu, F., Jiao, L., Sun, J., Wu, J.: MOEA/D with adaptive weight adjustment. Evol. Comput. **22**(2), 231–264 (2014)

Author Index

Printed in the United States
By Bookmasters